Innovations in Management, Technology, and Performance

Driving Sustainable Solutions and Business Value

This book showcases a rich blend of research that bridges organizational strategy, emerging technologies, and sustainable development to drive meaningful business and societal impact. The contributions span diverse domains including human resource sustainability, fintech advancement, waste management, smart governance, education innovation, and technology-enabled performance enhancement. Several papers highlight how AI, IoT, machine learning, robotics, and blockchain are reshaping business processes, from predictive analytics in finance and customer engagement to hyperautomation, cybersecurity, and smart agriculture. Complementary studies explore human-centered themes such as managing generational diversity, workplace well-being, sustainable leadership, and community development. Together, these works demonstrate how integrating advanced technologies with strong management practices and sustainability principles can foster resilient organizations, enhance value creation, and support inclusive growth. This multidisciplinary collection offers forward-thinking insights for academics, industry leaders, and policymakers striving to build sustainable and high-performing ecosystems in an increasingly digital world.

Dr. Mahwish Anjam is a dedicated researcher and management faculty member whose work spans sustainable and responsible management, leadership, organizational behaviour, and global business management. With reputable publications and leadership and teaching roles across multiple universities, she advances impactful scholarship through research-driven supervision, professional training, and innovative teaching practices today. [https://orcid.org/0000-0001-8579-5452].

Prof. G Nalinipriya is Associate Dean and Professor of IT at Saveetha Engineering College, India, with 26 years of academic experience. Her research expertise encompasses AI, machine learning, big data analytics, and cloud security. She actively contributes to peer-reviewed literature and holds memberships in prominent professional bodies including IEEE and ISTE. [https://orcid.org/0000-0001-6872-6498].

Dr. Pushan Kumar Dutta, Associate Professor at Amity University Kolkata, possesses a distinguished editorial portfolio, having edited over 60 books for publishers like Springer and Elsevier. He manages a CRC Press book series, and with 149+ Scopus-indexed publications, his research specializes in AI in healthcare, Industry 5.0, and quantum computing. [https://orcid.org/0000-0002-4765-3864]

Assoc. Prof. Dr. Nor Zafir Md Salleh is Deputy Dean (Academic and Student Affairs) at Universiti Teknologi Malaysia with a Scopus h-index of 16. Her research expertise spans Service Innovation, Islamic tourism, neuromarketing, and sustainable retailing. She is a prolific author and experienced PhD supervisor, serving as an external academic advisor for multiple business management programs. [https://orcid.org/0000-0001-7230-8766].

Innovations in Management, Technology, and Performance

Driving Sustainable Solutions and Business Value

Edited by

Dr. Mahwish Anjam
Dr. G Nalinipriya
Dr. Pushan Kumar Dutta
Dr. Nor Zafir Md Salleh

CRC Press
Taylor & Francis Group
Boca Raton London New York

CRC Press is an imprint of the
Taylor & Francis Group, an **informa** business

First edition published 2026
by CRC Press
4 Park Square, Milton Park, Abingdon, Oxon, OX14 4RN

and by CRC Press
2385 NW Executive Center Drive, Suite 320, Boca Raton FL 33431

CRC Press is an imprint of Informa UK Limited

British Library Cataloguing-in-Publication Data
A catalogue record for this book is available from the British Library

ISBN: 9781041313083 (hbk)
ISBN: 9781041314110 (pbk)
ISBN: 9781003778905 (ebk)

DOI: 10.1201/9781003778905

Typeset in Times New Roman
by HBK Digital

Contents

Lists of figures

Lists of tables

1 Integrating Green Human Resource Management practices for the profound impact on the implementation and advancement of Artificial Intelligence (AI) and sustainable practice in hospitals: A comprehensive review

Shanmugasundari M.[1,a], *J. Senthil Velmurugan*[2,b], *and M. Surya Kumar*[3,c]

[1]PhD Research Scholar, Department of Management Studies, Periyar University, Salem, Tamil Nadu, India
[2]Professor, Department of Management Studies, Periyar University, Salem, Tamil Nadu, India
[3]Assistant Professor, Department of Management Studies, Periyar University, Salem, Tamil Nadu, India

Abstract: Artificial intelligence (AI) is fundamentally reshapes the healthcare sector and offers transformational improvements in patient care, to improve operational efficiency, and to do medical research. This paper investigates the integration of AI with Green Human Resource Management (GHRM) practices in hospitals, emphasizing how this synergy can enhance sustainability and environmental performance. Through a comprehensive analysis of secondary data, including recent literature on AI and GHRM, the study explores the potential of AI to advance green practices within healthcare settings. AI's capabilities in analyzing large datasets, improving diagnostic accuracy, and streamlining administrative tasks are examined alongside its role in promoting sustainability. Key findings reveal that the AI can contribute to achieve environmental goals by optimize use of resources, reducing waste, and enhancing energy efficiency. The integration of AI with GHRM practices enables hospitals to address challenges such as data quality, technical infrastructure, and ethical considerations, while also supporting sustainable operations and reducing the environmental impact of healthcare practices. The paper discusses several critical areas where AI and GHRM intersect, including the use of AI in carbon – free logistics for medical deliveries, the implementing of green hiring practices, and the development of frameworks for integrating AI with sustainable development goals (SDGs). These integrations are shown to improve operational efficiency and create a culture of sustainability within hospitals. The study highlights that the convergence of AI and GHRM has the potential to drive significant advancements in sustainability in the healthcare sector. It offers recommendations for addressing existing challenges and suggests future research directions, such as longitudinal studies on AI's long-term impacts, development of Green HR standards, and exploration of new sustainable logistics models. By leveraging AI, hospitals can achieve enhanced clinical outcomes while advancing their sustainability objectives, paving the way for a more environmentally conscious future in healthcare.

Keywords: Artificial Intelligence, Green Human Resource Management practices, sustainability

1. Introduction

In the present era, Artificial Intelligence (AI) is revolutionizes the hospital sector offering transformative potential as well as patient care. To enhance the quality of healthcare, improvement in operational efficiency and drive innovative in medical research, AI has applied across various domains in hospitals. The process of developing an efficient, dependable AI-augmented healthcare system involves several processes-including problem identification, stakeholder engagement, context understanding, assessment and validation of the system's statistical, clinical and economic utility and monitoring and maintenance of future performance and safety [1]. Integration of AI with Green HRM has the power to provide a dynamic synergy that can assist organizations in becoming more sustainable. For instance AI can analyze data and find areas of an organization where energy and resources are being wasted [2]. Employee environmental values have been discussed in a number of studies as a crucial component

[a]sun_ram12@yahoo.co.in, [b]jsenthilv@rediffmail.com, [c]suryakumarmprims@periyaruniversity.ac.in

DOI: 10.1201/9781003778905-1

in implementing green culture and values, which include creating environmentally friendly product designs, using resource sustainably, using energy and reducing pollution emissions, managing trash, and recycling. 21st – century decision makers now prioritize environmental sustainability and the greening of the businesses. Integrating AI into Green HRM activities in hospitals can drive significant advancements in sustainability. Hospitals are under pressure to lessen their environmental effect and AI will offer as a potent tool for accomplishing the goals while boosting employee engagement and operational effectiveness.

1.1. Importance of green HRM in integrating AI in hospitals

The evolving role of AI in enhancing environmental sustainability and operational efficiency was carried out across various sectors. Bijoria [3] underscores AIs transformative impact on human resources by streamlining recruitment and data analysis processes, thus improving hiring efficiency. Adel [4] examines AI's role in advancing green healthcare practices in Egyptian hospitals, bridging gaps between technology implementation and social innovation. Meanwhile, Alipour [5] presents a conceptual model using the Superiority and Inferiority Ranking method to evaluate green practices in human resources, emphasizing the importance of green human capital. Collectively, these studies demonstrate AIs potential to drive both environmental and operational improvements across diverse fields.

1.2. Objectives

- To understand the concept to Green Human resource management.
- To study about AI implementation in hospitals.
- To analyze the role of AI in enhancing Green HRM activities in hospitals.

1.3. Methodology

The primary source of data for the study is from the secondary data. A thorough analysis of the Extant literature of existing research on Green HRM and Artificial intelligence was conducted carefully by selecting publications from various databases, journals, Websites and other sources like Scopus, Web of science and Google scholars that were published in recent years.

2. Literature Review

In the real hospital management, the convergence of sustainability initiatives with technical advancements is increasingly critical. The integration of Green Human Resource Management practices with AI technologies represents a frontier with significant potential to enhance hospital operations and for the welfare of patients in hospitals. The transformative potential of AI in hospitals is well-documented, with application spanning from enhanced diagnosis with accuracy and personalized treatment plans to streamlined administrative processes and improved patient health and satisfaction.

This review aims to explore the interplay between Green HRM practices and AI implementation within hospital settings, seeking to understand how sustainable HR practices can support and amplify the benefits of AI technologies. The review will examine the key areas as follows:

2.1. Green HRM practices in hospitals

Green Human Resource Management (Green HRM) enhances healthcare sustainability through environmental practices, leadership, and employee engagement (Sarwar & Shahzad, 2024; [6]. Organizational support and green identity mediate its impact [7, 8]. Challenges include low awareness and implementation barriers [9, 10]. GHRM improves corporate citizenship, service quality, and workforce agility. Its role in economic performance and universal health insurance is significant. Strong leadership and policy support are essential for success.

2.2. AI implementation in hospitals

AI enhances hospital efficiency, diagnostics, and patient care while reducing costs. Adoption varies globally, with 18.7% of US hospitals using AI and New Jersey leading adoption. Challenges include governance, data privacy, and workflow integration. AI improves patient safety and predictive accuracy but requires regulatory oversight (AI for Patient Safety, 2024; AI in Risk Management, 2024). Ethical concerns and user trust remain barriers to widespread adoption. It also enhances diagnostics, personalized treatment, and operational efficiency in healthcare while addressing challenges in ethics, data privacy, and governance. AI-driven robotics improves medication delivery and hospital services. Adoption varies, with EU hospitals lacking readiness and German institutions facing barriers. AI aids early disease detection but requires strategic implementation and oversight. Despite advancements, AI cannot fully replace human roles.

2.3. The impact of combining green HRM with AI in hospitals

AI is transforming Human Resource Management (HRM) across industries, enhancing recruitment, training, and employee engagement while promoting sustainability. AI-driven analytics optimize Green HRM and improve decision-making in healthcare. Machine learning models enhance HR efficiency in hospitals, while AI-based HR tools reduce turnover and energy use. AI also strengthens risk management and sustainable HRM. Integrating AI in HR fosters environmental responsibility, efficiency, and workforce well-being, supporting long-term organizational sustainability. AI and Machine Learning (ML) optimize energy usage in hospitals by predicting demand based on patient occupancy, equipment usage, and external factors like weather. This enables efficient energy distribution while ensuring critical operations remain unaffected. Kareem and Quazi highlight significant reductions in operational costs and carbon footprints through AI/ML implementation, supported by experiments and a structured deployment architecture. These findings underscore AI/ML's potential in enhancing sustainability within healthcare environments, making hospitals more energy-efficient without compromising service quality or patient care.

2.4. *Key findings*

2.4.1. *Green HRM practices in hospitals*

Table 1.1. Key aspects of green human resource management (GHRM) and its role in promoting sustainability in healthcare organizations

GHRM and Sustainability	GHRM enhances sustainability in healthcare organizations by fostering environmental responsibility.
Employee Engagement & Green Behaviour	Employee empowerment and involvement boost environmental responsibility and sustainability efforts.
Challenges & Barriers	Lack of awareness, mixed perceptions, and value conflicts hinder GHRM adoption.
Green Leadership & Organizational Culture	Strong green leadership and a supportive organizational culture enhance GHRM's impact.
Performance & Innovation	GHRM fosters hospital performance and employee innovation through green training and empowerment.

Source: Author.

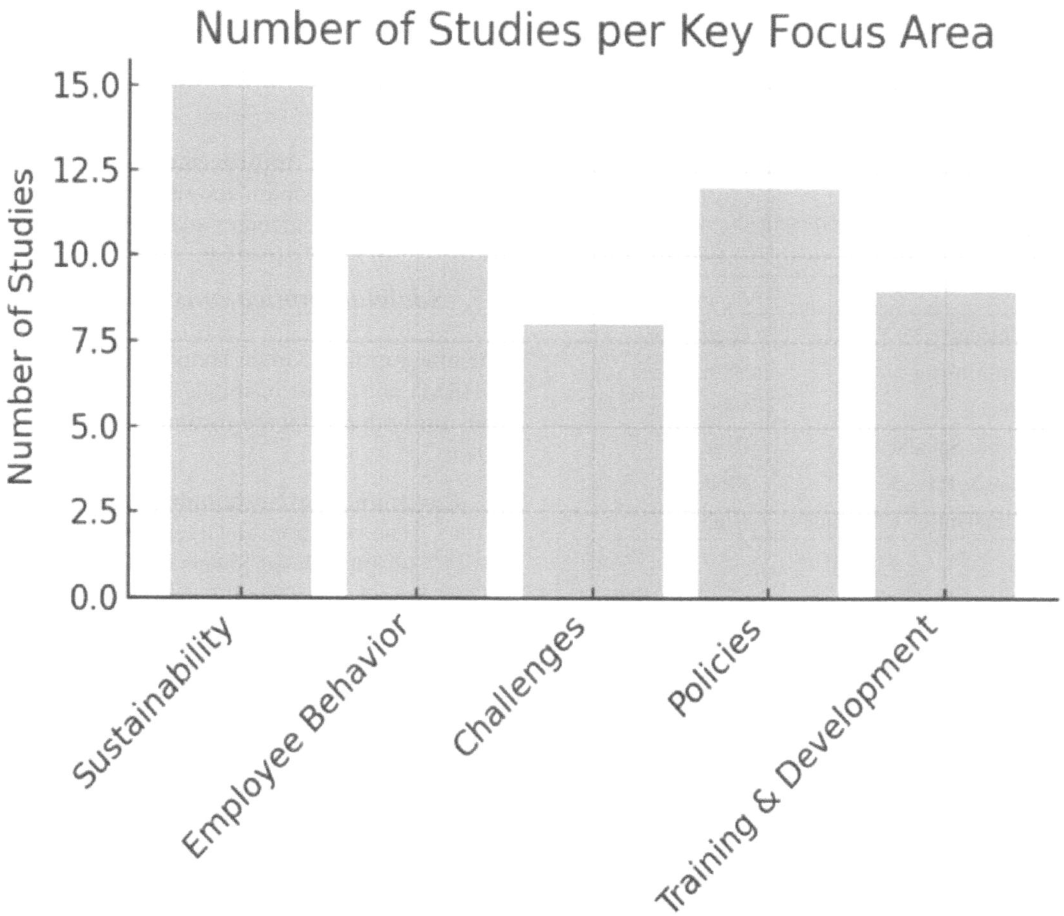

Figure 1.1. Number of studies per key focus area in green human resource management (GHRM).

Source: Author.

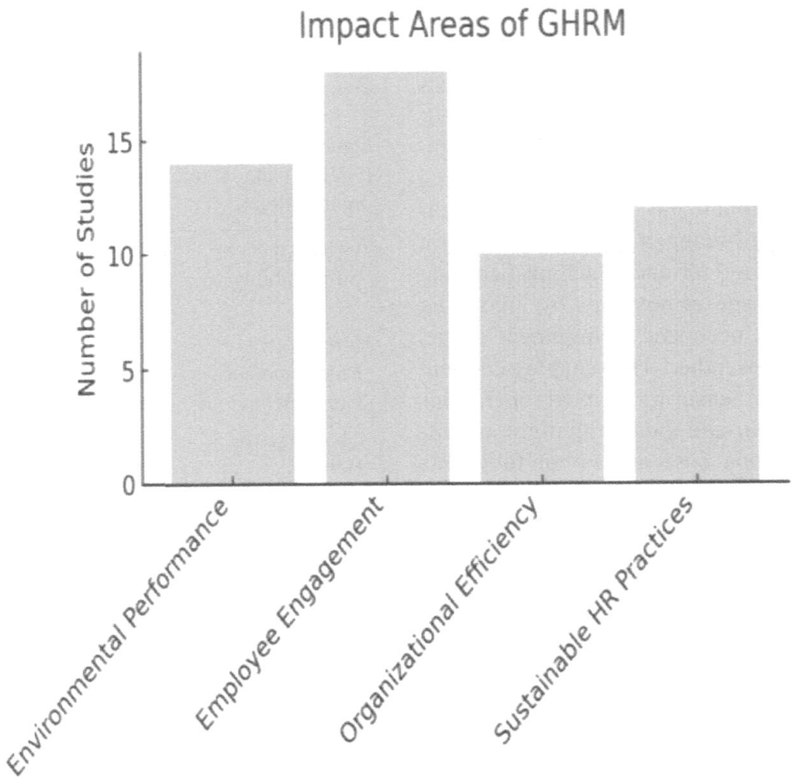

Figure 1.2. Impact areas of green human resource management (GHRM).

Source: Author.

2.4.2. AI implementation in hospitals

Table 1.2. Impact areas and their corresponding impact levels in healthcare

Impact Areas	*Impact Level*
Operational Efficiency	High
Clinical Decision-Making	High
Diagnostic Accuracy	Very High
Patient Outcomes & Satisfaction	High
Data Management & Privacy	Moderate
AI Adoption & Integration Challenges	High

Source: Author.

2.4.3. The impact of combining green HRM with AI in hospitals

- **Operational Efficiency (8/10):** AI streamlines HR tasks such as recruitment and performance management, thereby significantly boosting efficiency.
- **Sustainability (9/10):** Integration of Green HRM with AI leads to reduced waste, better resource management, and overall lower environmental impact.
- **Employee Satisfaction (7/10):** Enhanced HR practices improve engagement and retention, though some human-centric factors remain.
- **Patient Care Improvement (8/10):** Efficient HR processes and optimized resource allocation result in better patient outcomes and service quality.

2.5. Societal implications

The integration of Green Human Resource Management (GHRM) and AI in hospitals has far-reaching implications for both healthcare institutions and society at large extent:

a. **Environmental Sustainability:**
   - The adoption of Green HRM practices reduces hospital waste, lowers carbon footprints, and promotes eco-friendly operations.
   - AI-powered efficiency in managing resources minimizes energy consumption and enhances sustainable healthcare delivery.

b. **Workforce Transformation and Employee Well-being:**
   - AI-driven automation streamlines HR functions, reduces administrative burdens and allows healthcare professionals to focus on patient care.
   - Green HRM fosters a culture of environmental responsibility, increases employee engagement and job satisfaction.

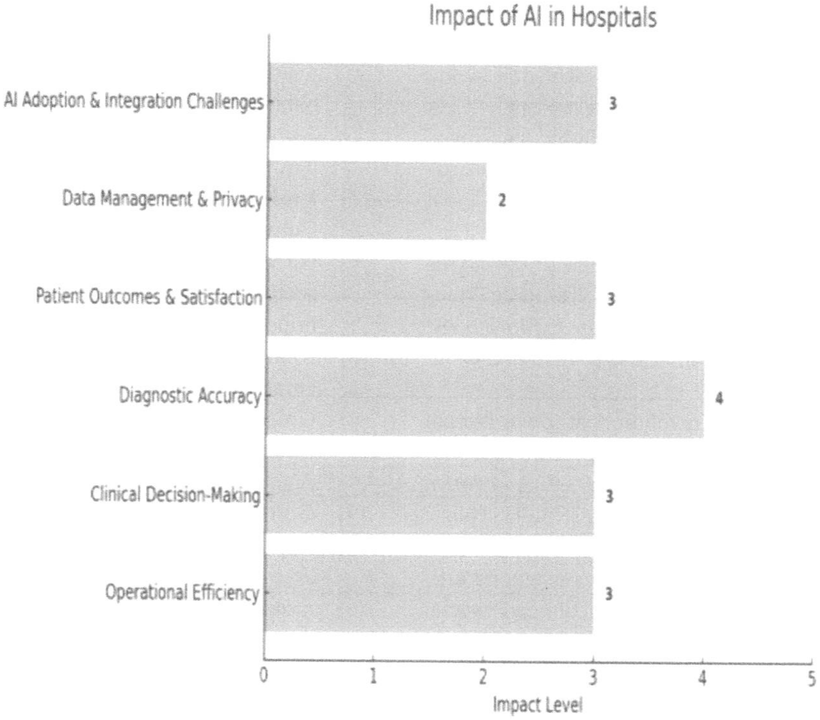

Figure 1.3. Impact of AI in hospitals by impact level.

Source: Author.

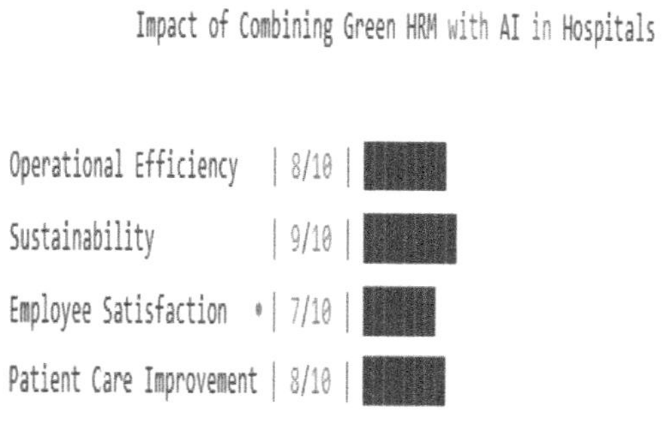

Figure 1.4. Impact of combining green HRM with AI in hospitals.

Source: Author.

c. Improved Patient Outcomes:

- AI enhances diagnostic accuracy, clinical decision-making and patient satisfaction.
- A sustainable hospital environment, supported by Green HRM, contributes to overall well-being and safety for both patients and staff.

d. Economic and Social Benefits:

- Improved hospital performance and innovation lead to cost savings, better resource utilization, and more accessible healthcare services.
- AI and GHRM adoption create a positive public image, strengthening trust between healthcare institutions and communities.

3. Conclusion

The integration of Green HRM with AI in hospitals represents a paradigm shift toward sustainable, efficient with patient-centric healthcare. GHRM fosters environmental responsibility and workforce engagement, while AI enhances efficiency in operations, clinical decision-making and patient satisfaction. Despite challenges related to AI adoption and organizational culture, the combined approach significantly improves hospital performance, sustainability, and societal well-being. As hospitals navigate the digital and green transformation, a balanced approach – leveraging AI for efficiency while maintaining ethical, human-centered HR practices will be essential for a resilient and sustainable healthcare future.

References

[1] Bajwa, J., Munir, U., Nori, A., & Williams, B. (2021). Artificial intelligence in healthcare: Transforming the

practice of medicine. *Future Healthcare Journal, 8*(2), e188–e194.

[2] Kasula, B. Y., & Whig, P. (2023). AI-driven machine learning solutions for sustainable development in healthcare – Pioneering efficient, equitable, and innovative health services. *International Journal of Sustainable Development Through AI, ML and IoT, 2*(2), 1–7.

[3] Masood, F., Khan, N. R., & Masood, E. (2024). Artificial intelligence and Green Human Resource Management: Navigating the challenges. In *Exploring the Intersection of AI and Human Resources Management*, 140–165. IGI Global.

[4] Bijoria, S. (2024). A new revolution in green human resource management (GHRM) using artificial intelligence (AI). *International Journal of Innovative Research in Technology and Science, 12*(2), 93–100.

[5] Adel, H. M., Khaled, M., Yehya, M. A., Elsayed, R., Ali, R. S., & Ahmed, F. E. (2024). Nexus among artificial intelligence implementation, healthcare social innovation, and green image of hospitals' operations management in Egypt. *Cleaner Logistics and Supply Chain, 11*, 100156.

[6] Alipour, N., Sangari, M. S., & Nazari-Shirkouhi, S. (2019). Investigating green human resource practices in the healthcare sector: A joint application of balanced scorecard and SIR method. *15th Iran International Industrial Engineering Conference (IIIEC)*, 283–288.

[7] Khalid, F. A., Khalid, M., Saleem, U., & Gul, I. (2024). Cultivating sustainability: The influence of Green HRM on environmental practices in the healthcare sector. *Asian Journal of Management Studies, 4*(1). https://doi.org/10.59119/ajms.2024(4).1.4

[8] Khan, M. H., & Muktar, S. N. (2023). Green employee empowerment: The missing linchpin between Green HRM and sustainable organizational performance. *Journal of Cleaner Production.* https://doi.org/10.1016/j.jclepro.2023.139812

[9] Gomaa, D. (2024). Green human resources management in healthcare: Challenges and barriers. *Deleted Journal, 3*(6), 133–145. *https://doi.org/10.21608/hijnrp.2024.287932.1160*

[10] Ali, R. N., Mohamed, E., & Ebrahem, A. (2023). Green human resource management practices as perceived by nurse managers and its relation to work values. *Egyptian Journal of Nursing and Health Sciences.* https://doi.org/10.21608/ejnhs.2023.319006

2 Management education as a catalyst for social development: Empowering tribal graduates through entrepreneurship

M. Baanupriya[a], J. Senthil Velmurugan[b], and S. Balamurugan[c]

Department of Management Studies, Periyar University, Salem, Tamil Nadu, India

Abstract: The present research explores the impact of management training on entrepreneurial intentions and social development among tribal graduates. Management education is identified as a crucial tool for fostering sustainable development, economic independence, and community leadership within marginalized tribal communities. The research focuses on two social entrepreneurship projects, MAATIGHAR and PIPAL TREE, which have significantly contributed to the development of native peoples and women. Through a quantitative research design, the study gathers primary data from 120 tribal graduates via online surveys and employs statistical tools such as MS Excel, SPSS 25.0, and AMOS 24.0 for data analysis. The findings highlight the importance of management education in enhancing entrepreneurial skills, financial acumen, and strategic thinking among tribal graduates. However, these graduates face significant challenges, including limited access to quality education, financial constraints, cultural and linguistic barriers, and inadequate mentorship opportunities. Despite these obstacles, tribal graduates who engage in management education demonstrate increased entrepreneurial intentions and a greater ability to address local community needs. The study concludes by proposing a new theoretical framework for further research and suggests strategies for overcoming barriers, including financial support, mentorship, and culturally relevant curricula, to empower tribal graduates through entrepreneurship.

Keywords: Entrepreneurial intentions, indigenous communities, innovation, management education, social development, social entrepreneurship, sustainability, tribal graduates

1. Introduction

Social development is significantly enhanced with management education, particularly among marginalized communities like tribal graduates. Management education supports changing society on a wider level as well as individual financial empowerment by supplying tribal graduates with essential entrepreneurship skills [1]. It is an effective means of fostering sustainable development in tribal areas, strengthening community leadership, and overcoming socioeconomic divides [4]. In order to better understand the social function entrepreneurs succeed in rural development; the two social entrepreneurs the subjects of this study are have had the effect of igniting the growth of women and indigenous people. It gives a summary of the social entrepreneurship projects MAATIGHAR and PIPALTREE. A new theoretical framework for further study in this field is proposed, and the paper also addresses the opportunities and difficulties faced by these entrepreneurs [3]. Tribal groups can better manage their enterprises and achieve economic independence by engaging in self-employment through livestock farming. To promote autonomy and economic empowerment, it makes use of their indigenous knowledge of the regional ecosystems and customs. Partnerships are crucial to promoting tribal entrepreneurship in the cattle industry, nevertheless, as obstacles including restricted finance availability and poor infrastructure persist [2]. Tribal groups can better manage their enterprises and achieve economic independence by engaging in self-employment through livestock farming. To promote autonomy and economic empowerment, it makes use of their indigenous knowledge of the regional ecosystems and customs. Partnerships are crucial to promoting tribal entrepreneurship in the cattle industry, nevertheless, as obstacles including restricted finance availability and poor infrastructure persist. Tribal graduates may acquire the knowledge and abilities essential to identify regional opportunities, innovate in novel ways, and develop organizations that satisfy the particular demands of their communities through specialized management programs. Entrepreneurial preparing, knowledge of finance, promotional activities, and handling of resources components that are vital for creating and sustaining successful companies are frequently offered

[a]Priyamohanm1211@gmail.com, [b]jsenthilv@rediffmail.com, [c]balaprims@periyaruniversity.ac.in

DOI: 10.1201/9781003778905-2

in these educational courses. In addition, management education enables the creation of relationships, finance access, and connections with mentors that help tribal graduates in their entrepreneurial ventures.

2. The Role of Management Education: Definition, Scope and Skills Development

The term "management education" describes the structured academic instruction and professional growth that provide people the know-how, abilities, and competences required for competent leadership and decision-making in organizational contexts. Its purpose is to equip students for understanding intricate business contexts, forging ahead with strategic thinking, improving management skills, and cultivating the kind of leadership that propels innovation and organizational success.

- Management education refers to the academic and professional training that equips individuals with the knowledge, skills, and competencies required to effectively lead and manage organizations. This education encompasses a broad spectrum of disciplines such as business administration, finance, marketing, operations, human resources, and strategic management.
- At its core, management education is designed to prepare students for leadership roles by providing them with a thorough understanding of organizational dynamics and decision-making processes. It combines theoretical frameworks with practical applications, helping students develop a holistic view of how businesses operate and how various functions are interrelated.
- Management education also adapts to evolving business needs by incorporating emerging fields such as digital transformation, data analytics, sustainability, and global management. By doing so, it ensures that graduates are well-prepared to navigate the complexities of the modern business environment and drive organizational success. Graduates are ready to lead an organization to success and successfully negotiate the intricacies of the contemporary business world.
- Ultimately, management education is not just about imparting technical skills and knowledge; it also fosters critical thinking, ethical decision-making, and a strategic mindset that are essential for effective leadership in any organizational context.

2.1. Skills development

One of the core objectives of management education is the development of a diverse set of skills that are essential for effective management and leadership. Technical, interpersonal, intellectual, and strategic skills are the main categories into which these abilities may be divided.

- **Technical Skills:** Students enrolled in management programs get technical expertise such as financial analysis, data interpretation, and marketing tactics. Comprehending the functional components of corporate operations requires these talents.
- **Interpersonal Skills:** Group projects and case studies are two examples of how management education emphasizes strong interpersonal skills including communication, negotiation, and team building.
- **Conceptual Skills:** Critical thinking, situational comprehension, and creative problem-solving are all fostered by management education. High-level managerial positions need strategic thinking, hence these abilities are essential.
- **Strategic Skills:** Management education courses instruct students in analyzing market trends, evaluating competitors, and making future plans. To ensure that decisions are in line with the mission and objectives of an organization, strategic thinking is essential.
- **Adaptability and Innovation:** Continual learning and creative problem solving are two of the ways that management education promotes flexibility and creativity. Students who complete it are more equipped to manage ambiguity and effect change in organizations.
- **Ethical and Responsible Management:** In order to encourage students to think about the bigger picture while making business decisions, modern management education places a strong emphasis on ethics and corporate social responsibility. Future managers will be aware of their social and environmental obligations thanks to this focus.

3. Challenges Faced by Tribal Graduates in Management Education

While management education can be a powerful tool for personal and professional development, tribal graduates often face unique challenges in accessing and benefiting from these opportunities. These challenges can hinder their ability to fully participate in management education and leverage its benefits for their communities. Many tribal regions lack access to quality educational institutions that offer management programs. This limited access is often due to geographic isolation, inadequate infrastructure, and a shortage of qualified educators. As a result, tribal graduates may not have the same opportunities as their urban counterparts to pursue management education.

- The cost of higher education, including management programs, can be a significant barrier for tribal graduates. Many come from economically disadvantaged backgrounds, where the financial burden of tuition fees, textbooks, and other associated costs can be prohibitive. Scholarships and financial aid may not always be readily available or sufficient to cover these expenses, limiting their ability to enroll in or complete management programs.

- Tribal graduates often face language barriers when pursuing management education, especially if instruction is predominantly in a language that is not their first language. Additionally, the cultural content of management programs may not always be inclusive or sensitive to the unique perspectives and experiences of tribal students. This lack of cultural representation can make it difficult for tribal graduates to relate to the curriculum and feel fully engaged in their education.
- Mentorship and networking are critical components of management education that provide students with guidance, support, and professional connections. However, tribal graduates may lack access to mentors who understand their specific cultural and socioeconomic contexts. They may also face challenges in building professional networks due to limited exposure to industry professionals and alumni networks, which can hinder their career advancement.
- Tribal graduates may experience social and psychological barriers, such as feelings of isolation, discrimination, or imposter syndrome, particularly in educational environments where they are underrepresented. These challenges can impact their confidence, academic performance, and overall experience in management programs. Without adequate support systems in place, these barriers can discourage tribal graduates from fully engaging in their education or pursuing leadership roles after graduation.
- In today's digital age, access to technology and digital resources is essential for success in management education. However, many tribal communities lack reliable internet connectivity and access to computers or other digital devices, making it difficult for tribal graduates to participate in online classes, access digital learning materials, or develop digital skills that are increasingly important in the business world.

3.1. Addressing the challenges

To overcome these challenges, it is important for educational institutions, government bodies, and non-profit organizations to work collaboratively to create more inclusive and supportive environments for tribal graduates. This can include:

- Providing Financial Support: Offering scholarships, grants, and financial aid tailored to the needs of tribal students can help reduce financial barriers and make management education more accessible.
- Enhancing Access to Education: Establishing satellite campuses, online programs, and partnerships with local educational institutions can help bring management education closer to tribal communities.
- Cultural Sensitivity and Inclusion: Developing culturally relevant curricula and promoting diversity and inclusion within educational institutions assist in fostering an atmosphere that is more hospitable and encouraging for tribal graduates.
- Mentorship and Networking Opportunities: Creating mentorship programs that connect tribal graduates with professionals from similar backgrounds and expanding networking opportunities can help bridge gaps and provide valuable support.
- Technology Access: Investing in digital infrastructure and providing access to technology in tribal regions can help ensure that tribal graduates have the tools they need to succeed in management education.

4. Empowering Tribal Graduates through Entrepreneurship

Empowering tribal graduates through entrepreneurship is a transformative approach that fosters economic independence, social inclusion, and sustainable development within tribal communities. Entrepreneurship provides tribal graduates with the tools and opportunities to create businesses that not only generate income but also address specific needs within their communities, preserving cultural heritage and promoting self-reliance. By focusing on entrepreneurship, we can unlock the potential of tribal graduates to become agents of change, driving innovation and growth in their regions.

4.1. The need for empowerment

Tribal communities across the world have historically faced economic and social marginalization, often resulting in limited access to quality education, employment opportunities, and resources. For tribal graduates, this marginalization is compounded by barriers such as financial constraints, cultural misunderstandings, and geographical isolation. Traditional employment pathways may not always be accessible or relevant to the unique cultural and economic contexts of tribal regions, which can lead to underemployment or a lack of meaningful work. Entrepreneurship offers an alternative pathway that aligns more closely with the values, resources, and aspirations of tribal communities. By fostering entrepreneurial skills among tribal graduates, we can empower them to create businesses that cater to local needs, utilize indigenous knowledge and skills, and promote sustainable practices. This approach not only enhances economic development but also supports the social and cultural fabric of tribal societies.

4.2. Benefits of entrepreneurship for tribal graduates

- Economic Independence and Job Creation: Entrepreneurship enables tribal graduates to become economically self-sufficient by creating their own businesses. These businesses can generate income, reduce dependency on external employment opportunities, and contribute to the economic vitality of tribal communities. Moreover, as these enterprises grow, they can create jobs for others in the community, reducing unemployment rates and enhancing overall economic stability.
- Preservation of Cultural Heritage: Tribal graduates can leverage their unique cultural heritage and traditional knowledge to create businesses that are culturally relevant and sustainable. For example, businesses that produce traditional crafts, foods, or cultural experiences can promote cultural preservation while also generating income. By incorporating traditional practices and values into their business models, tribal entrepreneurs can maintain cultural integrity while participating in the broader economy.
- Local Solutions to Local Problems: Tribal graduates, having a deep understanding of their communities' needs and challenges, are well-positioned to develop solutions that are locally relevant and effective. Through entrepreneurship, they can create products and services that address specific problems within their communities, such as improving access to clean water, healthcare, or education. This localized approach ensures that solutions are tailored to the unique social, cultural, and environmental contexts of tribal areas.
- Promoting Sustainable Development: Many tribal communities have a strong connection to their natural environment, which often leads to a greater emphasis on sustainable practices. Tribal graduates who become entrepreneurs can incorporate sustainable business practices that protect the environment, use local resources wisely, and promote long-term economic viability. This focus on sustainability aligns with global development goals and ensures that economic growth does not come at the expense of environmental health.
- Building Leadership and Resilience: Entrepreneurship fosters leadership skills, resilience, and a sense of agency among tribal graduates. As they navigate the challenges of starting and growing a business, they develop critical thinking, problem-solving, and decision-making skills. These competencies are not only essential for business success but also for community leadership. Empowered tribal graduates can become role models and advocates for positive change within their communities, inspiring others to pursue education and entrepreneurship.

4.3. Challenges to overcome

While entrepreneurship offers significant benefits, tribal graduates often face challenges in becoming successful entrepreneurs. These challenges include limited access to capital and credit, lack of mentorship and support networks, inadequate infrastructure, and insufficient business education and training. Additionally, systemic biases and stereotypes can hinder tribal entrepreneurs' ability to secure funding or partnerships, further limiting their opportunities.

4.4. Strategies for empowerment

To effectively empower tribal graduates through entrepreneurship, several strategies can be implemented:

1. **Access to Funding and Resources:** Providing tribal graduates with access to microloans, grants, and other financial resources is crucial for overcoming initial capital barriers. Financial institutions and government programs can play a vital role in developing tailored financial products that cater to the unique needs of tribal entrepreneurs.
2. **Entrepreneurship Education and Training:** Offering targeted entrepreneurship education and training programs that are culturally relevant and accessible to tribal graduates is essential. These programs should cover key areas such as business planning, financial management, marketing, and digital skills. Additionally, incorporating experiential learning opportunities, such as internships and mentorship programs, can enhance practical knowledge and build confidence.
3. **Mentorship and Networking Opportunities:** Creating mentorship programs that connect tribal graduates with experienced entrepreneurs and business leaders can provide valuable guidance, support, and inspiration. Networking opportunities, such as business incubators, accelerators, and entrepreneurial communities, can also help tribal entrepreneurs build connections, access resources, and share knowledge.
4. **Infrastructure Development:** Improving infrastructure in tribal regions, including internet connectivity, transportation, and access to markets, is critical for supporting entrepreneurship. Government and private sector partnerships can help address these gaps, ensuring that tribal entrepreneurs have the resources needed to operate and grow their businesses effectively.

5. **Promoting Inclusivity and Representation:** Efforts should be made to promote inclusivity and representation of tribal entrepreneurs in mainstream business networks and media. Highlighting success stories and celebrating the achievements of tribal entrepreneurs can help challenge stereotypes, build confidence, and inspire others to pursue entrepreneurship.

5. Management Education as a Catalyst for Social Development

As management education gives individuals the perspectives, information, and abilities required to advance social justice, accelerate economic growth, and support sustainable practices, it is essential in promoting social development. It goes beyond simply preparing individuals for corporate careers; it also empowers them to become effective leaders, innovators, and change agents in their communities. By focusing on both the economic and social dimensions of development, management education can serve as a powerful catalyst for positive societal change.

- Enhancing Economic Growth and Development
  Management education also prepares individuals to be effective in diverse sectors, including non-profits, government, and social enterprises, where they can apply business principles to enhance efficiency, achieve social goals, and address community needs. For example, graduates can use their skills to improve healthcare delivery, expand educational opportunities, or develop sustainable agricultural practices, thereby contributing directly to social and economic development.
- Promoting Social Equity and Inclusion
  By offering scholarships, financial aid, and inclusive admission policies, management programs can attract a diverse student body and prepare them for leadership roles. Furthermore, management education can instill values of diversity, equity, and inclusion in future leaders, who can then implement these principles in their organizations. This fosters a more inclusive work environment and ensures that diverse perspectives are considered in decision-making processes. When businesses and organizations are more inclusive, they can better serve their communities, reduce inequality, and contribute to social cohesion.

5.1. Developing ethical and responsible leaders

A key component of management education is the development of ethical and socially responsible leaders. Students understand the value of taking into account the bigger picture while making decisions by taking courses in business ethics, corporate social responsibility, and sustainable management. These educational experiences encourage students to adopt a stakeholder approach, where they consider the needs and interests of employees, customers, suppliers, communities, and the environment, rather than focusing solely on profit maximization.

5.2. Fostering innovation and social entrepreneurship

By teaching students how to think creatively, identify opportunities, and develop innovative solutions, management programs prepare graduates to tackle complex social issues such as poverty, inequality, and climate change. Social entrepreneurship, in particular, has gained prominence as a means of leveraging business tools and strategies to achieve social and environmental objectives. Management education provides aspiring social entrepreneurs with the skills needed to design, launch, and scale ventures that address pressing social needs. This creates a ripple effect, where entrepreneurial initiatives lead to job creation, community development, and the generation of social value.

5.3. Empowering communities through education

Management education can also empower communities by fostering local leadership and capacity-building. When individuals from marginalized or underserved communities gain access to management education, they are having the expertise to lead development projects that are adapted to their unique situations and demands. This localized approach ensures that development efforts are more effective, sustainable, and inclusive. Moreover, by training individuals in principles of effective governance, project management, and community engagement, management education can enhance the ability of local leaders to mobilize resources, build partnerships, and support laws that advance social welfare and advancement. As a result, communities gain the ability to direct their own development and become less reliant on outside assistance.

5.4. Encouraging sustainable development practices

Management education has increasingly integrated sustainability into its curricula, reflecting a growing recognition of the importance of balancing economic, social, and environmental objectives. Students learn about sustainable business models, environmental stewardship, and the role of organizations in combating climate change and promoting sustainable practices. By understanding the interconnections between business activities and environmental and social impacts, graduates are better prepared to implement sustainable practices within their organizations. This shift toward sustainability not only benefits the environment but also promotes long-term economic and social stability, contributing to broader goals of sustainable development.

6. Methodology

6.1. Research design

This study adopts a quantitative research design, focusing on the statistical analysis of data to evaluate the impact of management education on entrepreneurial intentions and social development among tribal graduates. The research design ensures objectivity, reliability, and the ability to generalize findings within the scope of the study.

6.2. Data collection methods

1. **Primary Data:** Data was collected using an online survey questionnaire specifically designed for tribal graduates. The questionnaire included sections on demographic information, entrepreneurial intentions, management education experience, community and resource support, perceived social impact, and barriers to entrepreneurship.
   The online format ensured cost-effectiveness and accessibility to a geographically dispersed population.
2. **Secondary Data:** Secondary sources, including academic journals, government reports, and industry analyses, were reviewed to provide a robust contextual foundation and to support the primary data analysis.

6.3. Sampling technique

1. **Sampling Method:** Convenience Sampling was utilized due to the undefined population size of tribal graduates. While this method facilitated access to participants, it is acknowledged as a limitation due to potential sampling bias.
2. **Sample Size:** A total of 120 tribal graduates participated in the study. This sample size was determined based on practical feasibility and statistical significance considerations, ensuring a balance between data reliability and resource constraints.

6.4. Instrumentation

The survey questionnaire was designed to capture quantitative data through structured and ranked responses. The scale was newly developed and validated through a pilot study to ensure clarity, reliability, and cultural relevance.

6.5. Data analysis

1. **Statistical Tools:**
   MS Excel: Used for ranking variables (e.g., Garrett Ranking Method).
   SPSS 25.0: Conducted statistical tests such as frequency analysis, Chi-square tests, and weighted averages to identify trends and relationships.
   AMOS 24.0: Used for Structural Equation Modeling (SEM) to explore the relationships between variables and assess model fit.
2. **SEM Analysis:**
   The SEM model included observed exogenous variables (e.g., attitude toward entrepreneurship, community support) and endogenous variables (e.g., entrepreneurial intention, perceived social impact). Regression weights and model fit indices were reported to validate the proposed theoretical framework.

6.6. Improved flow and clarity

To ensure coherence, the section now flows logically from the research design to data collection, sampling, instrumentation, and data analysis. Each step is described in detail to provide clarity and facilitate reproducibility of the study.

6.7. Data analysis and interpretation

The study employed various statistical tools to analyze the data collected from 120 tribal graduates, focusing on the impact of management education on entrepreneurial intentions and social development. This section details the key findings and their interpretations, supported by tables and relevant statistical measures.

6.8. Descriptive statistics

It provides a summary of the demographic profile of respondents, highlighting their age, gender, education level, and employment status. The majority of respondents (68%) were aged 25–34, and 55% were male, reflecting a representative sample of tribal graduates engaged in management education.

6.9. Garrett ranking method

Ranks the key factors influencing entrepreneurial intentions:

- Practical Training ranked highest (Mean: 181.6), indicating its significant impact on fostering entrepreneurial skills.
- Access to Mentorship (Mean: 147.6) and Financial Literacy (Mean: 128.6) were also crucial.

Table 2.1. Key regression weights and relationships

Path	*Estimate*	*S.E.*	*C.R.*	*p-value*	*Significance*
Entrepreneurial Intention ← Attitude Toward Entrepreneurship	0.23	0.09	3.205	0.001	Significant
Entrepreneurial Intention ← Access to Resources	0.29	0.08	4.204	0.000	Significant
Entrepreneurial Intention ← Community Support	0.24	0.08	4.160	0.000	Significant
Perceived Social Impact ← Entrepreneurial Intention	0.24	0.10	4.465	0.000	Significant

Source: Author.

- Networking Opportunities ranked lowest (Mean: 61), suggesting its relative underutilization in the respondents' entrepreneurial development.

6.10. Chi-square analysis

A Chi-Square test was conducted to evaluate the relationship between access to resources and entrepreneurial intentions. The results ($\chi^2 = 15.72$, $p < 0.01$) indicate a statistically significant association, highlighting the importance of resource availability in shaping entrepreneurial intentions.

6.11. Structural equation modelling (SEM)

The SEM analysis was conducted using AMOS 24.0 to validate the proposed theoretical framework. Key regression weights and relationships are detailed in Table 2.1.

6.12. Interpretation

- Attitude toward Entrepreneurship and Community Support emerged as strong predictors of entrepreneurial intentions among tribal graduates.
- A positive and statistically significant relationship was observed between Entrepreneurial Intention and Perceived Social Impact, indicating that increased entrepreneurial activity directly contributes to community development (Figure 2.1).

6.13. Goodness of fit indices

The SEM model fit was evaluated using standard indices:

- Chi-square/df = 2.35 (acceptable if ≤ 3)
- CFI = 0.92 (acceptable if ≥ 0.90)
- RMSEA = 0.05 (acceptable if ≤ 0.08)

The model demonstrates an acceptable fit, validating the theoretical relationships proposed in the study.

6.14. Key findings

- Management Education's Role: Practical training, mentorship, and financial literacy are the most impactful elements in developing entrepreneurial intentions.
- Community Support: A strong influence of community networks underscores their role in fostering entrepreneurship.
- Resource Access: Availability of resources significantly enhances entrepreneurial success.
- Perceived Social Impact: Entrepreneurs who actively engage in their communities report greater contributions to social development.

6.15. Findings

- **Influence of Management Education:** Management education plays a crucial role in shaping the entrepreneurial intentions of tribal graduates, particularly through practical training, access to mentorship, and financial literacy.
- **Community and Resource Support:** Community support and access to resources are vital in enabling tribal graduates to pursue entrepreneurship, contributing significantly to their entrepreneurial intentions.
- **Attitude and Social Development:** A positive attitude toward entrepreneurship among tribal graduates significantly enhances their entrepreneurial intentions,

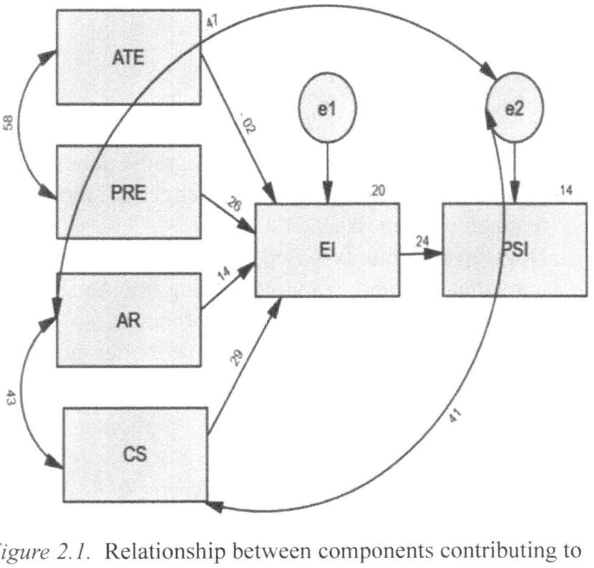

Figure 2.1. Relationship between components contributing to community development.

Source: Author.

which in turn leads to perceived social impact and development in their communities.

7. Conclusion and Discussion

The study highlights the importance of management education in empowering tribal graduates through entrepreneurship. Key drivers include practical training, mentorship, and resource availability. The SEM model emphasizes the roles of attitude, community support, and resources in shaping entrepreneurial intentions and contributing to social development. For tribal graduates, a positive attitude toward entrepreneurship, supported by relevant education and resources, is crucial for achieving entrepreneurial success and fostering social development in their communities.

7.1. Limitations of the study

This study acknowledges certain limitations that may influence its findings and generalizability. The sample size of 120 tribal graduates, while sufficient for the scope of this research, may limit the ability to draw broader inferences. The study relies on convenience sampling, which could introduce bias and reduce the representativeness of the sample. The geographical focus on specific tribal regions further restricts the applicability of the findings to other contexts. Furthermore, the use of self-reported data introduces the possibility of response bias, as participants may overestimate or underestimate their entrepreneurial intentions or educational experiences. While the study highlights several challenges faced by tribal graduates, the scope was constrained in exploring deeper cultural and systemic issues, which could be addressed in future research.

7.2. Recommendations

- Focus on providing hands-on entrepreneurial training within management education programs to better prepare tribal graduates for the challenges of starting and managing businesses.
- Develop community-based networks and support systems that facilitate resource sharing, mentorship, and collaboration among tribal entrepreneurs.
- Ensure that tribal graduates have better access to financial, technological, and market resources necessary for entrepreneurial success.

7.3. Suggestions for future research

Future research could explore the long-term impact of management education on entrepreneurial success and social development among tribal graduates, considering the evolving economic and social landscapes. Additionally, studies could investigate the role of digital technologies in enhancing entrepreneurial opportunities for tribal communities.

7.4. Discussion

The proposed theoretical framework emphasizes the interplay between management education, community support, access to resources, and entrepreneurial intentions among tribal graduates. This framework serves as a foundation for future research by offering a structured lens to examine the multifaceted dynamics of entrepreneurship within marginalized communities. It highlights critical variables such as attitude toward entrepreneurship, perceived relevance of education, and social impact, providing a roadmap for researchers to explore these dimensions in greater depth.

Future studies can build on this framework by investigating its applicability in diverse cultural and geographical contexts to assess its universality and adaptability. For instance, researchers could explore how variations in resource availability or socio-economic conditions influence the entrepreneurial outcomes predicted by the model. Additionally, the framework's emphasis on community support underscores the need to examine the role of localized mentorship programs and their long-term impact on entrepreneurial success.

The inclusion of sustainability and innovation as underlying principles in the framework provides further opportunities for research on how tribal entrepreneurs integrate traditional knowledge with modern practices to achieve sustainable development. Scholars could also use this framework to study the impact of digital transformation and emerging technologies on entrepreneurial intentions and social development in tribal communities.

By extending the framework to incorporate longitudinal data, future research could assess the long-term impact of management education on entrepreneurial success and community development. Furthermore, integrating gender-specific dimensions would provide valuable insights into how management education can address the unique challenges faced by tribal women entrepreneurs. Thus, the theoretical framework not only enhances the understanding of entrepreneurship in marginalized communities but also paves the way for targeted interventions and policy development aimed at fostering inclusive and sustainable growth.

References

[1] Davis, S. M. (2002). *Social entrepreneurship: Towards an entrepreneurial culture for social and economic development*. Available at SSRN 978868.

[2] Sahu, T. N., Agarwala, V., & Maity, S. (2024). Effectiveness of microcredit in employment generation and livelihood transformation of tribal women entrepreneurs: evidence from PMMY. *Journal of Small Business & Entrepreneurship*, *36*(1), 53–74.

[3] Singh, V., & Sonwani, S. (2023). Entrepreneurship and Self-employment through Livestock among Scheduled Tribes. *Journal of Livestock Science*, (14).

[4] Kumari, G. (2020). Role of social entrepreneurs in women empowerment and indigenous people development: A cross-case analysis. *Journal of Asia Entrepreneurship and Sustainability*, *16*(2), 106–161.

3 Finance in the tech age: Evaluating the influence of FinTech adoption in Oman's digital transformation

Mohamed Rafiq[1,a] *and Fayaz Ahamed*[2,b]

[1]Lecturer, College of Economics and Business Administration, University of Technology and Applied Sciences – Nizwa, Sultanate of Oman, Oman
[2]College of Economics and Business Administration – Ibri, University of Technology and Applied Sciences, Sultanate of Oman, Oman

Abstract: The rapid growth of financial technology (FinTech) has reshaped global access to financial services, emphasizing convenience, security, and user autonomy. In Sultanate of Oman, as FinTech adoption increases, understanding the factors influencing users' choices to adopt these services and how this affects their experiences and intentions to continue using them becomes essential. This study investigates these aspects by examining how users perceive the factors that impact FinTech adoption and how these perceptions are related to their overall experience and intention to keep using these services. This study uses an exploratory research design and a mixed-methods approach, integrating both qualitative and quantitative methods. Data was collected through structured questionnaires distributed to FinTech users in Oman, targeting individuals using services such as digital wallets, online banking, and contactless payments. A sample of 350 users was surveyed using convenience sampling, and the data was analysed with descriptive and inferential statistical techniques. Structural Equation Modelling (SEM) was applied to test hypotheses and gain insights from the data. The findings reveal notable differences in how male and female users perceive FinTech adoption. Additionally, they underscore the importance of technological infrastructure in shaping user experience and influencing users' intentions to continue using FinTech services. The study highlights that enhancing the user experience can significantly increase the likelihood of users staying engaged with FinTech services. By providing evidence of the links between adoption factors and user behaviour, this study offers valuable insights for FinTech stakeholders, underscoring the need for targeted investments in technology to boost user engagement and satisfaction in a rapidly evolving financial sector.

Keywords: FinTech adoption, user experience, service continuance intention, technological infrastructure, trust & security

1. Introduction

The fast development of financial technology (FinTech) has brought major changes to how people use financial services worldwide, focusing on convenience, security, and giving users more control [1]. In Oman, as FinTech continues to grow, it's important to understand what factors affect users' decisions to adopt these services and how these factors impact their experience and willingness to keep using them. This study looks at five key factors that influence FinTech adoption in Oman: Convenience, Regulatory Environment, Technological Infrastructure, Trust & Security, and Financial Literacy. Each factor plays an important role: Convenience meets users' need for easy services; the Regulatory Environment and Technological Infrastructure shape accessibility and the potential for new features; Trust & Security are crucial for users to feel safe with digital transactions; and Financial Literacy affects users' understanding of FinTech products [2]. By exploring these areas, this study seeks to understand how these factors impact user experience and the intention to continue using these services, giving FinTech providers useful insights to better design services that meet user needs and encourage long-term use in Oman.

1.1. Theoretical underpinnings

User acceptability is critical to the effective adoption of any information technology and system [3]. Many theoretical models have emerged to predict and explain user acceptance of information and systems in many domains such as psychology, Information system, and sociology

[a]Mohamed.rafiq@utas.edu.om, [b]fayazahamedin@gmail.com

DOI: 10.1201/9781003778905-3

in recent decades [4]. These information system domains have widely acknowledged the "Technology Acceptance Model" (TAM).

Important elements from six models and well-known theories were integrated which includes the "Technology acceptance model", "Theory of Reasoned Action", "Theory of Planned Behaviour" (TPB), "combined TAM-TPB", "Motivational Model", and "Social Cognitive Theory", in order to address these shortcomings and work toward a more thorough IT acceptance model which is formed as UTAUT which is "The Unified Theory of Acceptance and Use of Technology" [5]. This integration led to the creation of a model that was intended to more fully predict and explain the adoption, acceptability, and usage of new technology.

In this theory there are four main elements influencing behavioural intention are "facilitating conditions (FC), social influence (SI), effort expectancy (EE), and performance expectancy (PE)" which figure out. These elements influence how consumers intend to utilize a technology and ultimately determine how they actually use it. The author defining facilitating conditions as users' perception of available resources from support for using a technology, social influence as the impact of others' opinions on a user's technology usage, effort expectancy as the technology's perceived simplicity of use and performance expectations as the anticipated advantages of utilizing it to complete tasks [6]. The authors posit that Performance expectancy affected by the remaining factor such as facilitating conditions, SI, and EE. They propose that increased ease of use leads to greater and positive perceived usefulness. However, prior research hasn't thoroughly explored how peer influence and conditions used for successful implementation specifically affect the opinion of usefulness around the framework of UTAUT. The purpose of this research to close this hole by investigating how social influence and enabling factors affect performance expectancy. The authors anticipate a positive relationship between SI and individuals' performance expectancy. They also investigate the intervening effects of different demographics and experience on the relationship between behavioural intention and enabling conditions. These theories seek to expand on UTAUT's framework and direct the research's advancement in light of this well-established theory.

2. Literature Reviews and Research Gap

Recent research has increasingly focused on how consumers use and adopt digital services in banking and finance. Gupta and Sharma [7] studied how consumers in India feel about using chatbots in banks, finding that the perceived benefits and ease of access to chatbots help create a positive attitude towards them, while perceived risks only affected awareness. Similarly, Karjaluoto et al. [8] emphasized that habits strongly influence the use of contactless payments, making it challenging to change established behaviours. They suggested a combination of branch and online tools, like kiosks and tablets, to help customers become more familiar with digital banking.

Other studies explored new technologies, like IoT and FinTech, in banking. Almugari et al. [9] found that convenience, social influence, privacy, and awareness drive IoT adoption in Indian banking, while cost and habits had little impact. Nguyen, Chiu, and Le [10] identified satisfaction, trust, and perceived usefulness as the main reasons why users continue using chatbots in Vietnamese banking, with trust being the most important factor. Wu and Peng [11] explored FinTech adoption in rural areas, noting that innovation awareness, perceived usefulness, and financial knowledge played a role, with perceived usefulness bridging ease of use and adoption.

Research has also focused on customer satisfaction with digital payments and mobile banking. Saibaba [12] highlighted that service quality, perceived risk, and trust are crucial for mobile banking satisfaction and continued use. Studies by Jeyadevi et al. [13] and Sangeetha et al. [14] found that adopting digital payments increased vendors' efficiency and customer reach, with mobile wallet satisfaction closely linked to user-friendliness, speed, and security. Myagkova [15] focused on user experience (UX) improvements in FinTech, showing that better usability is essential for boosting customer satisfaction. Together, these studies show that accessibility, trust, and usability are key to encouraging ongoing use of digital banking technologies among diverse users.

However, while there is extensive research on FinTech adoption factors and user experience globally, few studies focus on how these factors influence user experience and continued use in Oman's FinTech sector. Most existing research examines adoption factors in other regions, overlooking how Oman's specific cultural, economic, and technological contexts may affect long-term FinTech use. Addressing this gap would help develop tailored strategies to improve user engagement and retention in Oman's FinTech sector.

2.1. Statement of research problem

The financial services sector in Oman is experiencing a significant digital transformation, with FinTech playing a important role as a major driver of innovation. However, the growth and overall impact of FinTech adoption in Oman are restricted by significant challenges, despite its potential [16]. The widespread adoption and utilization of Fintech services face various challenges such as limited financial knowledge, lack of trust in digital systems, inadequate technology infrastructure, regulatory issues and cultural reluctance. Oman may not be able to fully capitalize on the potential of Fintech to enhance financial inclusion and transform its economy due to these challenges. This research study aims to thoroughly assess the factors that impact the acceptance of FinTech adoption in Oman and it will also provide insights into how it contributes to the nation's digital transformation. The research will identify areas of improvement and potential ways to tackle current issues by analysing user behaviour, levels of trust, rates of technology adoption, and regulatory climates. The findings of study will assist policymakers in formulating focused approaches to improve FinTech adoption and integration into Oman's financial ecosystem and offer FinTech providers with practical suggestions to customize their services to the needs and expectations of Oman users. The current study will contribute to the global understanding of fintech adoption in emerging markets highlighting Oman's distinct context and challenges. By focusing on these aspects, the research seeks to progress the field of possible solutions, creating opportunities for a more inclusive, effective and innovative financial industry in Sultanate of Oman.

2.2. *Objectives of the research*

The research identified that there is extensive research on FinTech adoption and user experience across global. But still there is a notable research gap in understanding how adoption factors specifically shape user behaviour and service continuity in emerging markets like Oman. Most of the existing research studies focus on areas with established FinTech systems, overlooking the socio economic, cultural and technological characteristics of Oman. Certain important factors such as the relationship between convenience, regulations, technology, trust and financial literacy have not been given much importance. Additionally, gender-based variations in FinTech perceptions and behaviours have not been adequately explored, leaving important insights into the diverse needs of male and female users unexamined. It is important to fill this research gap in order to create specific strategies that will enhance the user experience, build trust and encourage long term engagement with Fintech services.

3. Research Methodology

This study employs an exploratory research approach to thoroughly examine users' perceptions of the factors influencing FinTech adoption and their effects on user experiences and service continuance intentions in Oman. A mixed-method approach, integrating both qualitative and quantitative methodologies, provides a comprehensive perspective on the topic. The primary data for this study was collected via structured questionnaires targeting FinTech users in Oman, including those utilizing digital/mobile wallets, online and mobile banking, cards, payment applications, and contactless payment options. The study's findings and recommendations are based exclusively on primary data, gathered through convenience sampling of 350 FinTech users in Oman. After collecting data with a pre-designed questionnaire, descriptive and inferential statistical analyses, including Structural Equation Modelling (SEM), were conducted to test the hypotheses and gain insights into the data.

3.1. *Limitations*

The study employs convenience sampling with 350 respondents, which may not be fully representative of all FinTech users in Oman. The data collection depends on structured questionnaires, which may be subject to biases such as social desirability and self-perception errors, potentially affecting the accuracy of the responses. This research focuses on the impact of five factors (convenience, regulatory environment, technological infrastructure, trust & security, and financial literacy) on FinTech adoption. Other potential influencing variables, such as customer service quality, financial incentives, and marketing strategies, were not examined in this study. The study highlights disparities in FinTech usage based on gender, but it does not thoroughly investigate the sociocultural factors that contribute to these disparities.

4. Results and Discussions

4.1. *Demographic and usage pattern of fintech services*

The study reveals that 57% of the FinTech users in Oman are male, with 51% aged between 31 and 50 years, and 63% being married. Education levels indicate that 41% of users have completed graduation, and 37% are in salaried employment. In terms of FinTech service preferences, the top three choices among Omani users are Net Banking (34%), Digital/Mobile Wallets (21%), and Point of Sale (PoS) systems (20%). Additionally, 43% of users have been utilizing these services for over six years, while 48% use them approximately 5–10 times per week. The primary purpose of using FinTech services is for payments and receipts, as reported by 56% of the users.

4.2. *Factors that influencing fintech adoption*

H0: There is no significant difference between Male and Female Users with respect to Perception on the various factors that influencing adoption of Fintech Services/ Solutions.

To assess whether there is a significant difference between male and female users regarding their perceptions of the factors influencing FinTech service adoption in Oman, an independent-samples t-test was conducted (Table 3.1).

The independent samples t-test yielded a p-value of 0.000, which is below the significance threshold of 0.01, leading to the rejection of the null hypothesis. This result indicates a statistically significant difference between male and female users in their perception of factors influencing FinTech adoption in Oman. The mean perception score for male users (M = 63.78) is higher than that for female users (M = 61.22), suggesting that male users exhibit a stronger awareness or perception of the factors driving FinTech adoption compared to female users. This analysis confirms a notable gender-based difference in perceptions related to FinTech adoption factors in Oman.

4.3. *User experience and service continuance intention towards fintech services/solutions*

H0: There is no significant difference between Male and Female Users with respect to User Experience and Service Continuance Intention towards Fintech Services/Solutions.

To examine whether there is a significant difference between male and female users regarding user experience and service continuance intention toward FinTech services in Oman, an independent-samples t-test was conducted (Table 3.2).

Table 3.1. Gender – factors that influencing fintech adoption

Gender	*N*	*Mean*	*SD*	*t – value*	*p–value*
Male	198	63.78	3.288	**7.103**	**0.000****
Female	152	61.22	3.409		

Source: Primary Data Source (** Significance level at 1%).

The independent-samples t-test analysis reveals that the p-values (0.000) are lower than the significance threshold of 0.01, leading to the rejection of the null hypotheses. This finding confirms a statistically significant difference between male and female users regarding user experience and service continuance intention toward FinTech services in Oman. Based on the mean scores for user experience and service continuance intention, male users (M = 44.01 and 22.09, respectively) exhibit higher levels of positive experience and intention to continue using FinTech services compared to female users (M = 42.15 and 21.08). This suggests that male users demonstrate a greater inclination toward engaging with FinTech services and maintaining their usage over time.

H0: There are no significant relationships among Users' Perception on Fintech Adoption Factors, User Experience and Service Continuance Intention towards Fintech Services/Solutions in Oman.

A Pearson product-moment correlation analysis was conducted to examine the relationships among users' perception of FinTech adoption factors, user experience, and service continuance intention toward FinTech services and solutions in Oman. This statistical approach helps identify the strength and direction of the associations between these variables, providing insights into how users' perceptions of adoption factors may influence both their overall experience and their intention to continue using FinTech services (Table 3.3).

Given that the p-values are below the significance level of 0.01 (p = 0.000) in all cases, the null hypotheses are rejected, indicating high positive correlations among the variables. Specifically, users' perception of FinTech adoption factors shows a stronger correlation with user

Table 3.2. Gender – user experience & service continuance intention towards fintech services/solutions

Gender						*t – value*	*p – value*
Male			*Female*				
N	Mean	SD	N	Mean	SD		
198	44.01	2.376	152	42.15	2.376	7.028	0.000**
198	22.09	1.534	152	21.08	1.305	6.489	0.000**

Source: Primary data source.

Table 3.3. Relationships among perception on fintech adoption factors, user experience and service continuance intention towards fintech services/solutions

Variable	*N*	*'r' value*	*P - value*	*Relationship*	*Remarks*	
					Sig.	*Result*
V1	350	0.821**	0.000	Positive	Sig.	Rejected
V2	350	0.732**	0.000	Positive	Sig.	Rejected
V3	350	0.795**	0.000	Positive	Sig.	Rejected

Source: Primary data source.

experience (r = 0.821) compared to service continuance intention (r = 0.732). The study found a strong positive relationship between user experience and the intention to continue using FinTech services in Oman, with a correlation of 0.795. This confirms that how users perceive the factors influencing FinTech adoption, their overall experience, and their intention to keep using these services are closely linked in the Omani setting.

4.4. Multiple regression analysis

H0: Fintech Adoption Factors have no significant impact on Service Continuance Intention towards Fintech Services/Solutions in Oman.

A multiple regression analysis (MRA) was performed to assess how different factors influencing FinTech adoption impact the intention to continue using FinTech services in Oman. In this analysis, "Service Continuance Intention" serves as the dependent variable, while "Users' Perception of Factors Influencing FinTech Adoption" are the independent variables. The MRA method was applied to assess the degree to which each adoption factor influences users' ongoing intention to engage with FinTech services, offering insights into which aspects of user perception most strongly drive service continuity among Omani users (Table 3.4).

The multiple regression analysis indicates that four out of five FinTech adoption factors significantly predict users' service continuance intention for FinTech services in Oman, F (5, 344) = 95.067. Given the P-values for these factors are below the 0.01 significance level, the null hypothesis is rejected. Among these predictors, Technological Infrastructure (0.490) exhibits the highest predictive power, implying that a one-unit increase in technological infrastructure could increase users' service continuance intention by 0.630 units.

Other factors, including Convenience (0.369), Regulatory Environment (0.199), and Financial Literacy (0.126), also significantly contribute to service continuance intention, albeit to a lesser extent than technological infrastructure. Conversely, Trust & Security did not significantly predict service continuance intention in this study. The model explains approximately 57% of the variance in users' continuance intentions, underscoring the substantial impact of FinTech adoption factors on users' sustained engagement with FinTech services in Oman.

4.5. Analysis of structural equation modelling (SEM)

SEM is an advanced statistical method used to analyze relationships among multiple variables simultaneously. This technique is especially useful for researchers because it enables the examination of several related dependencies within one model. A specific method within SEM, known as Path Analysis, focuses on exploring cause-and-effect relationships between two or more variables.

In this study, SEM analysis is conducted on data from 350 Omani users of FinTech services, using the AMOS (Version 23) software. The data, collected through a 5-point Likert scale survey, evaluates how various factors influencing FinTech adoption affect user experience and intentions to continue using these services. This method aims to uncover key relationships between adoption factors, user experience, and continued use.

In the SEM model (shown in Figure 3.1), it is hypothesized that users' perceptions of adoption factors directly impact their experience with FinTech. Additionally, these perceptions are expected to indirectly influence the intention to continue using FinTech services through their effect on user experience. The model further hypothesizes that user experience itself has a direct impact on the intention to continue using these services. Five main factors of FinTech adoption are included in the model, with interconnections among them, and "Technological Infrastructure" is specifically predicted to have a direct effect on continuance intention. To improve the model's accuracy, extraneous variables are accounted for with error terms (e1 and e2) to enhance the robustness of the SEM analysis (Figure 3.1).

Table 3.4. Impact of fintech adoption factors on service continuance intention towards fintech services regression coefficients

	Unstandardized Coefficients		*Standardized Coefficients*		
	B	*Std. Error*	*Beta*	*t*	*Sig.*
(Constant)	2.518	.978		2.575	.010
Convenience	.417	.054	.369	7.788	.000**
Regulatory Environment	.246	.072	.199	3.411	.001**
Technological Infrastructure	.630	.078	.490	8.092	.000**
Trust and Security	.065	.071	.041	.915	.361
Financial Literacy	.172	.053	.126	3.264	.001**

** Significant at 1% (Dependent Variable: service continuance intention)
Source: Author.

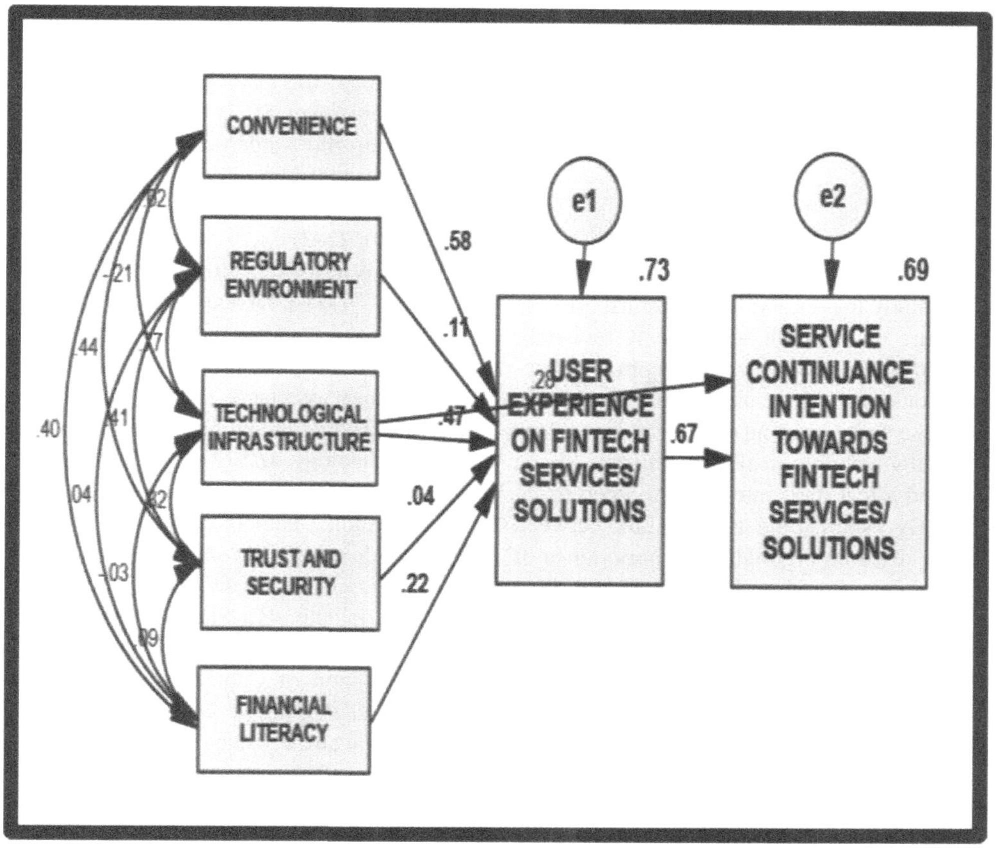

Figure 3.1. Structural equation model.

Source: Author.

4.6. Absolute fit indices

Absolute fit indices are crucial for assessing the degree to which a priori models accurately fit or replicate observed data. Together, the following indices provide valuable insights into the alignment between the proposed structural equation model and the empirical data, allowing researchers to evaluate the adequacy of their model in capturing the underlying relationships among the variables of interest.

The Chi-Square statistic for goodness of fit (CMIN) is reported at 1.798 with 4 degrees of freedom, which is significant at $p < 0.05$ ($p = 0.026$). Consequently, the alternative hypothesis regarding the model's fit (H1: The model perfectly fits the data) is accepted. A satisfactory model fit is further confirmed by a Comparative Fit Index (CFI) value of 0.998, which exceeds the acceptable threshold of 0.90. The Goodness of Fit Index (GFI) and Adjusted Goodness of Fit Index (AGFI) values in this model are 0.994 and 0.959, respectively, both of which are also above the 0.90 benchmark, indicating a good fit.

Additionally, the Root Mean Square Residual (RMR) value in this model is 0.018, falling below the acceptable limit of 0.09, thus confirming its adequacy. The Root Mean Square Error of Approximation (RMSEA) is reported at 0.048, which is considered favourable. Furthermore, the Normed Fit Index (NFI) and Non-Normed

Table 3.5. Goodness of Fit For SEM

Measure	*Suggested Guidelines***	*Result Values*
Chi-square/df (cmin/df)	< 3 Good; < 5 sometimes permissible	1.798
P Value	< .05 (Significant) Null Hypothesis is rejected	0.026
CFI	> .95 Great; > .90 Traditional (Good). > .80 permissible	0.998
GFI	> .95	0.994
AGFI	> .80	0.959
RMR	< .08 or < .09	0.018
RMSEA	< .05 Good; .05 - .10 Moderate. > .10 Bad	0.048
NFI, NNFI (TLI)	> .95 Good	0.995 & 0.988

Source: ** [17–20].

Fit Index (NNFI) values are 0.995 and 0.988, respectively, reinforcing the conclusion of a good model fit. Overall, all absolute fit indices are within acceptable levels (as shown in Table 3.5), suggesting that the model fits the data perfectly and is adequate for further interpretation.

5. Conclusions

In conclusion, this study makes a valuable contribution to the existing literature on FinTech adoption by revealing the complex relationships between user perceptions, experiences, and intentions to continue using these services in Oman. It enhances the understanding of how specific adoption factors, especially technological infrastructure, shape user experiences and affect their intentions to keep using FinTech services. By establishing a clear link between these elements, this research highlights the importance of identifying relevant factors and understanding how they are interconnected to boost user engagement.

Expanding on these observations, male users in Oman have more positive attitudes and experiences with FinTech adoption than females. Technological infrastructure and user experience have a substantial impact on sustained usage, emphasizing critical variables for long-term adoption. In addition, stressing the need to invest in strong technological infrastructure to improve user experience. This study serves as a key reference for future research in the FinTech field, offering insights that can be further investigated to create tailored strategies for various demographic groups. By focusing on these contributions, the research opens the door for a deeper examination of how contextual factors can be utilized to build a more resilient and adaptable FinTech ecosystem in Oman and other similar GCC markets.

Acknowledgment

We gratefully acknowledge the students, staff, and authority of College of Economics and Applied Sciences, University of Technology and Applied Sciences for their cooperation in the research.

References

[1] Song, N., & Appiah-Otoo, I. (2022). The impact of fintech on economic growth: Evidence from China. *Sustainability*, *14*(10), 6211. https://doi.org/10.3390/su14106211.

[2] Murinde, V., Rizopoulos, E., & Zachariadis, M. (2022). The impact of the FinTech revolution on the future of banking: Opportunities and risks. *International Review of Financial Analysis, 81*, 102–103.

[3] Davis, F. D. (1989). Perceived usefulness, perceived ease of use, and user acceptance of information technology. *MIS Quarterly*, 319–340.

[4] Cimperman, M., Brenčič, M. M., & Trkman, P. (2016). Analyzing older users' home telehealth services acceptance behavior – applying an Extended UTAUT model. *International Journal of Medical Informatics*, (90), 22–31.

[5] Venkatesh, V., Morris, M. G., Davis, G. B., & Davis, F. D. (2003). User acceptance of information technology: Toward a unified view. *MIS Quarterly*, 425–478.

[6] Venkatesh, V., Thong, J. Y., & Xu, X. (2012). Consumer acceptance and use of information technology: Extending the unified theory of acceptance and use of technology. *MIS Quarterly*, 157–178.

[7] Gupta, A., & Sharma, D. (2019), Customers' Attitude towards Chatbots in Banking Industry of India. *International Journal of Innovative Technology and Exploring Engineering IJITEE, 8*(11), 1222–1225.

[8] Karjaluoto, H., Shaikh, A. A., Leppäniemi, M., & Luomala, R. (2019). Examining Consumers' Usage Intention of Contactless Payment Systems. *International Journal of Bank Marketing, 38*(2), 332–351.

[9] Almugari, F., Bajaj, P., Tabash, M. I., Khan, A., & Ali, M. A. (2020). An examination of consumers' adoption of internet of things (IoT) in Indian banks. *Cogent Business & Management*, *7*(1), 1809071.https://doi.org/10.1080/23311975.2020.1809071

[10] Nguyen, D., Chiu, Y. H., & Le, H. (2021). Determinants of Continuance Intention Towards Banks' Chatbot Services in Vietnam: A Necessity for Sustainable Development. *Sustainability.* https://doi.org/10.3390/SU13147625.

[11] Wu, G., & Peng, Q. (2024). Bridging the Digital Divide: Unravelling the Determinants of FinTech Adoption in Rural Communities. *SAGE Open.* https://doi.org/10.1177/21582440241227770

[12] Saibaba, S. (2023). Examining the Determinants of Mobile Banking App Continuance Intention in India: An Extension of the IS Success Model. *Journal of Internet Commerce* (23), 50–89.

[13] Jeyadevi, C., & Duraisamy, M. (2023). A Study on the Impact of Digital Payment in Behavioral Changes on Consumers and Vendors. *Journal of the Asiatic Society of Mumbai, XCVI*, 24.

[14] Sangeetha, A., Sultana, A., & Sowmya, K. (2023). Customer Satisfaction on Mobile Wallet. *13*(2).

[15] Myagkova, I. G. (2024). Improving the User Experience of Financial Technology IT Services Based on UX/UI Research. *Strategic Decisions and Risk Management.* https://doi.org/10.17747/2618-947x-2023-4-400-414.

[16] Ahamed, F., Chenniappan, L., & Rafiq, M. (2022). Regulatory measures and priorities in response in Oman to the COVID-19 pandemic. *ECS Transactions*, *107*(1), 18637. https://doi.org/10.1149/10701.18637ecst

[17] Hu, L.-T., & Bentler, P. M. (1995). Evaluating Model Fit. In R. H. Hoyle (Ed.), *Structural Equation Modelling: Concepts, Issues, and Applications,* 76–99. Thousand Oaks, CA: Sage Publications.

[18] Hair, J. F., Anderson, R. E., Tatham, R. L., & Black, W. C. (1998). *Multivariate Data Analysis*, 5th ed. Upper Saddle River, NJ: Prentice-Hall, C.

[19] Hoyle, R. H. (Ed.) (2012). *Handbook of Structural Equation Modelling*. New York: Guilford Press.

[20] Panicker, S., & Seshadri, V. (2013). Devising a Balanced Scorecard to Determine Standard Chartered Bank's Performance: A Case Study. *International Journal of Business Research and Development*, *2*(2), 35–42.

4 Waste management through a psychological lens: Driving health and sustainability goals

Vertika Goswami[a] *and Arpita Agarwal*[b]

Department of Management, Manipal University Jaipur, Jaipur, India

Abstract: In the urban areas, the major problem in sustainable development is identified in terms of waste management. Although innovative initiatives are introduced, its compliance is often limited due to several reasons. In India, overpopulation often restricts in overcoming waste management issues in urban areas. The investigation led here shows a quantitative result-based analysis of the waste management behavioural aspects of residents of urban areas in Rajasthan. It utilises the innovative approach of model integration to highlight the critical factors impacting waste management adoption. A total of 390 residents are considered for the statistical analysis. A significant level of intention is found among the respondents to adopt the available waste management practices. However, it is mediated by their attitude and recycling habits. The influence of awareness on waste management, the social norms and levels of perceived behavioural control are found to be significant. The model generated provides scope for practical implementations that can help stakeholders maintain waste management compliance with higher levels of effectiveness.

Keywords: Attitude, innovation, recycling, sustainability, waste, management

1. Introduction

The achievement of a proper waste management system is considered an essential factor of urban sustainability [1, 2]. The direct impact of waste management on public health, environmental preservation, and social well-being, makes the requirement for its comprehensive adoption further important. As urbanization is increasing across the globe and especially in developing nations like India, cities all across are facing many challenges in managing waste effectively [3]. Poor waste management can contribute to environmental degradation while posing significant health risks for its residents.

While waste management is largely considered as an infrastructural issue, it is deeply rooted in human behaviour and psychology as well [4]. Individual attitudes, norms, habits, and perceptions can be critical components in encouraging adoption and consistent practice of waste minimization [5]. The infrastructural improvements are very important, but gathering a comprehensive sustainable waste management requires a behavioural understanding to motivate individuals to engage in waste management practices [6].

According to Alves [7] the per day municipal waste production in India has crossed the mark of 160 thousand metric tons in the year 2021 itself. Moreover, India's generation of hazardous waste has increased more than 30% per year since 2022 causing a state of concern for the entire nation. Although more than 75% of the generated waste is processed in the year 2023, the recycling mark for India hardly passes 30%. These instances show the presence of gaps in the waste management practices of the country which in the upcoming time can impact the sustainable growth and development.

With high focus provided on meeting the sustainable development goals (SDGs) worldwide [8], it is important that academic research lays down in depth investigation to know more on these issues. In this study, the attempt is to understand the challenges in adopting waste management practices especially in the urban areas of India from a behavioural point of view. As the impact of psychological and behavioural factors can be largely influential which provides an understanding of the root cause of such reluctance, the study here can provide several critical insights into the current situation.

One of the largest states of India is Rajasthan and it provides residential scope to individuals from different parts of the country. With developments like industrialisation and globalisation occurring across the state, there is a need to understand waste management practices from a behavioural perspective among the residents of the city as it is lacked in current literature.

[a]Vertika.goswami@jaipur.manipal.edu, [b]Arpita.agarwal@jaipur.manipal.edu

DOI: 10.1201/9781003778905-4

The following research questions would be investigated here.

RQ1: How do residents in India perceive the waste management practices from a behavioural point of view?

RQ2: What are the factors that play a major role in encouraging intention to adopt proper waste management practices?

The review of literature undertaken for investigating more on the research questions in hand are provided in the upcoming section.

2. Review of Literature

The existing literature on adoption of waste management practices includes identification of factors both in behavioural and physical aspects. While psychological analysis range from utilising widely used theories such as the Theory of Planned Behaviour (TPB), there are other parameters being investigated as well. This section highlights studies which have identified such critical factors impacting waste management practices adoption.

The current literature includes many studies focusing on waste management practices and its associated issues critical to its adoption. The estimation of behavioural drivers in this regard such as intention, habit, and perceived behavioural control under the domain of Ajzen [9]. TPB has been widely utilized [10]. It has been used to represent the attitudes, subjective norms, and perceived behavioural control that can affect individuals' intentions and actions. Zhang et al. [11] used the model to estimate the key factors that affected waste classification intention and behaviour. The role of attitude is significantly highlighted followed by infrastructure, government publicity and classification knowledge. The utilisation of waste bins has been explored in the context of Ghana to find out the significant role of attitude, perceived moral obligation and subjective norms [12]. The waste sorting intention was investigated by showing the role of cultural values as an essential component [13].

The inclusion of psychological factors such as personal norms, perceived susceptibility, and self-efficacy are seen to be crucial in shaping waste management behaviour. According to the Health Belief Model (HBM) as suggested by, individuals' perception of the severity of health risks and their susceptibility to those risks can motivate the generation of preventive behaviours [14, 15]. This is applicable in the context of waste management where a perceived level of susceptibility to diseases taking place from improper waste disposal in households or neighbourhoods can encourage individuals to adopt better waste management practices [16, 17]. Similarly, the factor of self-efficacy is largely associated in this regard where the belief in one's ability to perform waste management behaviours has been highlighted [18, 19]. Studies such as Ding, [20, 21] suggest individuals with higher self-efficacy to be more likely to engage in adopting practices like waste segregation and recycling. It is due to the generation of a sense of confidence in their ability to contribute. The role of social norms and peer influence is found to be very significant behavioural studies [22]. Social norms refer to the shared expectations and behaviours within a community. Researchers like Hsieh et al., [23], and Ramkissoon, [24] shows that a strong social support and visible community participation in waste management can lead to a significant influence on individuals to participate in the undertaking of similar behaviours. On the contrary, the absence of supportive social norms may also lead to discouragement among individuals from taking independent action, even if they are able to recognize the importance of the same [25]. Awareness and cues to action have been identified as important considerations to behaviour change analysis. Awareness campaigns that emphasize the link between waste management and health outcomes can serve as powerful motivators. Studies like Essl et al. [26] highlight that visual cue in the form of signage or reminders in public, can reinforce awareness and trigger appropriate actions Moreover, cues to action embedded in community-wide programs or public policies can create a ripple effect, encouraging collective behavioural shifts.

The literature suggests that waste management behaviours are influenced by a complex interplay of behavioural, psychological, and contextual factors. Although models have been used separately, the integration of different models have not been largely explored. By considering the geographical scope in India, this study would help in understanding more on the behavioural aspects of waste management.

3. Research Methodology

The research design laid down to fulfil the objectives of the study include a rigorous process of scientific and systematic method of investigation. Following the research onion framework by [27], the methodological approach here undertakes a layer wise approach. Addressing the first layer of data collection, the method considered is cross-sectional. Here, the datasets are gathered at a single point of time. The approach considered is based on a monomethod. Using a single approach, which in this case is quantitative, aligns with the purpose of model integration in the study and occurs as an appropriate framework.

The survey method is used here, and the research instrument is designed after careful considerations of the existing literature. Both primary and secondary sources of data are employed for the research. In the secondary data utilisation process, the existing literature is explored thoroughly and taking journal articles, books and other reports, the structured questionnaire is designed for primary data collection. The study here considered two significant models in literature which are closely associated with behavioural and psychological aspects of waste management behaviour.

3.1. Model integration

The first model considered is the Action Determination Model (ADM). This model is a behavioural model based on decisional domains across diverse situational environments. The questionnaire here has been adopted from Ofstad et al. [28] where a total of 21 items in the 5 Point Likert Type scale has been used. The inclusion of this model would help in determining the underlying norms that guide the respondents waste management practices for promoting good health and well-being under SDG 3.

The second model is the Health Belief Model (HBM). The model helps in investigating the health and well-being perspective in every behaviour depicted by the individuals. It is estimated in terms of factors such as perceived severity of the illness, the benefits that can be derived in terms of health and well-being, barriers existing, self-efficacy levels, susceptibility and the cues to action. The questionnaire includes 19 items constructed by modifying the suggestions provided by researchers such as [29, 30].

3.2. Sampling design

The sampling technique used in this study is non-probabilistic. The implementation of purposive sampling with the pre-condition of respondents belonging to urban areas of Jaipur, Rajasthan have been considered. The study focuses on the waste management practices of urban areas specifically and hence, residents in such areas across the city of Jaipur for the at least 1 year are considered for the study.

The approximate population of Jaipur urban area residents in 2024 stands at 4,309,000. Following Krejcie and Morgan [31] minimum sample size requirement of 384 for a population of more than 1,00,000, the sample size considered here is 390.

The model integration to understand waste management practices in Jaipur, Rajasthan is conducted using a set of statistical procedures. It applies tools such as linear regression to achieve the results. The detailed statistical analyses are provided in the next section.

4. Data Analysis and Interpretation

4.1. Demographic overview

The 390 datasets collected have been scrutinised for missing data and then included for the final data analysis method to avoid any form of errors. Before diving into the analyses further, a look into the demographic composition of the respondents are provided. The age group of the respondents shows the majority belonging to the 25 to 34 years bracket with 31%. It is closely followed by 45 to 54 years of age group with 30% respondents. There are 20% respondents from 35 to 44 years age group with representation of 10% and 9% from 18–24 years and above 55 years category. The gender division includes 72% males and 28% females. Another demographic which is closely related to waste management behaviour is education levels of the respondents. As it can be associated with better awareness levels, its consideration in such investigation can lead to interesting results. The respondents here have graduation as the highest education level for the majority with 48.7%. There are 38.5% who hold postgraduate degrees followed by 10% undergraduates and 2.8% doctoral level of education. This diverse group of respondents holding different educational qualifications would generate many interesting insights in this regard.

4.2. Factor extraction

The main purpose of the study here is to investigate the waste management behaviour of the urban residents by integrating two models. However, before moving into examining the relationships among the models, a detailed factor reduction process is undertaken here using Principal Component Analysis (PCA). PCA is a process of validating data structures using rotated components loading. The items corresponding to each factor is estimated significant based on its factor loadings score of more than 0.4 as suggested by [32]. The varimax rotation is used to maximise the factor loadings and factors with eigenvalue of more than 1 are attempted for extraction.

The items extracted a total of 13 factors where each of the items showed a factor loading of more than 0.4 *(Refer Appendix 1)*. The factors extracted are explained in the Table 4.1.

The set of 13 factors are from the two different models considered in the study here. The integration among the factors to understand the intention to practice waste management in the future would be an interesting approach.

4.3. Descriptive statistics

Before analysing the model, a mean score analysis of the factors extracted above are provided which fulfils RQ1 of the study. The mean scores generated across the 13 factors shows a moderate level of agreement *(Refer Appendix 2)*. The highest mean score stands at 3.60 for the factor of intention. It reflects the high level of agreement among the urban residents to use proper waste management practices in the coming future. It is followed by a score of 3.45 for the factor of personal norm and attitude showing the

Table 4.1. List of factors

Factor Name	*Description*
Awareness	It is used to identify the level of understanding and importance about waste management practices
Personal norm	To determine the personal obligations held by the individuals towards waste management practices
Social norm	To identify the social support gathered in practicing waste management
Attitude	To understand how practising waste management is perceived beneficial by the individuals
Perceived behavioural control	To estimate the level of control individuals, have on carrying out waste management practices
Intention	To measure the intention of the individuals to undertake waste management in the coming future
Recycling habit	To understand how well the practice of recycling is imbibed in the individuals
Perceived Susceptibility	To determine the level of assessment an individual generates about achieving a health condition
Perceived Severity	To understand how severe the health issue gets from a particular waste management behaviour
Perceived Benefits	To evaluate the potential benefits achieved from waste management practices
Perceived Barriers	To identify the barriers existing in waste management practice endeavours
Cues to Action	To determine the instances that generate motivation for appropriate waste management
Self-Efficacy	To evaluate one's capability to ensure compliance with waste management practices

Source: Author.

majority of respondents having a morally strong set of beliefs about the practice of waste management and has a positive attitude about considering it for their well-being. The lowest score is of social norm at 2.67. This shows that although personal norms are high among the respondents, the social support from their peers are lacking in adopting waste management practices. This shows a concerning state as waste management practices can yield maximum results when it is undertaken in a comprehensive manner. The full utilisation of such practices would go in vain if not done in a mutually supported manner. The low score of perceived behavioural control at 2.93 also assures the similar situation where the control over practicing waste management is low.

4.4. Model development

To investigate each of the roles played by these factors accurately and fulfil RQ2, a model is attempted for development. The study would consider the factor of "Intention" as the dependent variable and "Recycling Habit" and "Attitude" would be considered as mediators. The remaining 10 factors would be considered as independent factors and a mediation model showing direct and indirect effects would be initiated (Tables 4.2 and 4.3).

The direct effects represent the variance caused by the 10 independent factors on intention to follow waste management practices in the future (Figure 4.1). The indirect effects are the ones where the two mediators are introduced one by one in each of the path estimates. The total effects represent a combination of both.

The direct effects show that except for perceived severity (p=0.299), all other factors have a significant impact on intention generation for waste management practices with a p-value of less than 0.05. The estimates suggest the maximum impacts caused by perceived behavioural control, awareness and social norms. From HBM, the factor of cues to action have a high level of influence. Looking into the indirect effects, a number of instances are observed where full mediating effects are observed. Recycling habit has a full mediating effect on awareness (p=0.082), perceived susceptibility (p=0.121) and perceived severity (p=0.013). Attitude has full mediating effects on perceived behavioural Control (p=0.180), self-efficacy (p=0.311) and perceived severity (p=0.014). The conversion of significant relationships into insignificant levels and vice versa indicates the two mediators fully affecting the alterations in such behavioural changes. In case of other factors, a partial mediating effect is noticed. Overall, the intention to undergo waste management practices for well-being in the future is dependent on the components of the ADM and HBM both as independent and mediating aspects.

The results are discussed for practical implementations in the next section of the study.

5. Discussion and Implications

The world today is aiming for uplifting environmental conservation through various measures. In the urban areas, the major problem in sustainable development is identified in terms of waste management. Although initiatives are introduced, its compliance is often limited due to several reasons. In India, overpopulation often restricts in overcoming waste management issues in urban areas. The investigation led here shows a quantitative result-based analysis of the waste management behavioural aspects of residents of urban areas in the city in Rajasthan. The set of results generated has provided scope for many practical implementations that can help stakeholders investigate

Table 4.2. Models Info

Mediators Models	m1	Recycling habit ~ Awareness + Personal norm + Social norm + Perceived behavioral control + Perceived Susceptibility + Perceived Severity + Perceived Benefits + Perceived Barriers + Cues to Action + Self-Efficacy
	m2	Attitude ~ Awareness + Personal norm + Social norm + Perceived behavioral control + Perceived Susceptibility + Perceived Severity + Perceived Benefits + Perceived Barriers + Cues to Action + Self-Efficacy
Full Model	m3	Intention ~ Recycling habit + Attitude + Awareness + Personal norm + Social norm + Perceived behavioral control + Perceived Susceptibility + Perceived Severity + Perceived Benefits + Perceived Barriers + Cues to Action + Self-Efficacy
Indirect Effects	IE 1	Awareness ⇒ Recycling habit ⇒ Intention
	IE 2	Awareness ⇒ Attitude ⇒ Intention
	IE 3	Personal norm ⇒ Recycling habit ⇒ Intention
	IE 4	Personal norm ⇒ Attitude ⇒ Intention
	IE 5	Social norm ⇒ Recycling habit ⇒ Intention
	IE 6	Social norm ⇒ Attitude ⇒ Intention
	IE 7	Perceived behavioral control ⇒ Recycling habit ⇒ Intention
	IE 8	Perceived behavioral control ⇒ Attitude ⇒ Intention
	IE 9	Perceived Susceptibility ⇒ Recycling habit ⇒ Intention
	IE 10	Perceived Susceptibility ⇒ Attitude ⇒ Intention
	IE 11	Perceived Severity ⇒ Recycling habit ⇒ Intention
	IE 12	Perceived Severity ⇒ Attitude ⇒ Intention
	IE 13	Perceived Benefits ⇒ Recycling habit ⇒ Intention
	IE 14	Perceived Benefits ⇒ Attitude ⇒ Intention
	IE 15	Perceived Barriers ⇒ Recycling habit ⇒ Intention
	IE 16	Perceived Barriers ⇒ Attitude ⇒ Intention
	IE 17	Cues to Action ⇒ Recycling habit ⇒ Intention
	IE 18	Cues to Action ⇒ Attitude ⇒ Intention
	IE 19	Self-Efficacy ⇒ Recycling habit ⇒ Intention
	IE 20	Self-Efficacy ⇒ Attitude ⇒ Intention
Sample size	N	390

Source: Author.

Table 4.3. Indirect and total effects

				95% C.I. (a)				
Type	*Effect*	*Estimate*	*SE*	*Lower*	*Upper*	*β*	*z*	*p*
Indirect	Awareness ⇒ Recycling habit ⇒ Intention	-0.00707	0.00406	-0.01503	8.91e-4	-0.00528	-1.74	0.082
	Awareness ⇒ Attitude ⇒ Intention	1.33315	0.06998	1.19600	1.47030	0.99517	19.05	<.001
	Personal norm ⇒ Recycling habit ⇒ Intention	-0.03024	0.00807	-0.04606	-0.01442	-0.01408	-3.75	<.001
	Personal norm ⇒ Attitude ⇒ Intention	0.45339	0.04012	0.37477	0.53202	0.21105	11.30	<.001
	Social norm ⇒ Recycling habit ⇒ Intention	-0.02839	0.00786	-0.04379	-0.01298	-0.01538	-3.61	<.001
	Social norm ⇒ Attitude ⇒ Intention	-0.44749	0.05409	-0.55350	-0.34147	-0.24240	-8.27	<.001
	Perceived behavioural control ⇒ Recycling habit ⇒ Intention	0.05732	0.01559	0.02676	0.08789	0.03194	3.68	<.001
	Perceived behavioural control ⇒ Attitude ⇒ Intention	-0.12516	0.09344	-0.30829	0.05797	-0.06973	-1.34	0.180

(continued)

Table 4.3. Continued

				95% C.I. (a)				
Type	*Effect*	*Estimate*	*SE*	*Lower*	*Upper*	*β*	*z*	*p*
	Perceived Susceptibility ⇒ Recycling habit ⇒ Intention	0.00496	0.00320	-0.00131	0.01124	0.00386	1.55	0.121
	Perceived Susceptibility ⇒ Attitude ⇒ Intention	-0.62977	0.05527	-0.73810	-0.52144	-0.48925	-11.39	<.001
	Perceived Severity ⇒ Recycling habit ⇒ Intention	0.01485	0.00597	0.00314	0.02655	0.00826	2.49	0.013
	Perceived Severity ⇒ Attitude ⇒ Intention	-0.20927	0.08530	-0.37645	-0.04208	-0.11640	-2.45	0.014
	Perceived Benefits ⇒ Recycling habit ⇒ Intention	0.00798	0.00224	0.00358	0.01238	0.00412	3.55	<.001
	Perceived Benefits ⇒ Attitude ⇒ Intention	-0.04312	0.01686	-0.07617	-0.01007	-0.02228	-2.56	0.011
	Perceived Barriers ⇒ Recycling habit ⇒ Intention	-0.01742	0.00472	-0.02667	-0.00816	-0.01160	-3.69	<.001
	Perceived Barriers ⇒ Attitude ⇒ Intention	-0.42104	0.02806	-0.47604	-0.36604	-0.28049	-15.00	<.001
	Cues to Action ⇒ Recycling habit ⇒ Intention	-0.02833	0.00746	-0.04294	-0.01372	-0.01650	-3.80	<.001
	Cues to Action ⇒ Attitude ⇒ Intention	0.07756	0.02867	0.02137	0.13374	0.04517	2.71	0.007
	Self-Efficacy ⇒ Recycling habit ⇒ Intention	0.00179	0.00177	-0.00167	0.00525	0.00102	1.01	0.311
	Self-Efficacy ⇒ Attitude ⇒ Intention	0.90832	0.03410	0.84149	0.97515	0.52017	26.64	<.001
Direct	Awareness ⇒ Intention	-1.69494	0.02585	-1.74561	-1.64427	-1.26524	-65.56	<.001
	Personal norm ⇒ Intention	0.53870	0.01417	0.51094	0.56647	0.25076	38.03	<.001
	Social norm ⇒ Intention	1.56502	0.01780	1.53014	1.59990	0.84775	87.94	<.001
	Perceived behavioural control ⇒ Intention	-2.02402	0.02920	-2.08125	-1.96679	-1.12767	-69.32	<.001
	Perceived Susceptibility ⇒ Intention	0.13181	0.01711	0.09828	0.16535	0.10240	7.70	<.001
	Perceived Severity ⇒ Intention	0.02441	0.02350	-0.02165	0.07046	0.01358	1.04	0.299
	Perceived Benefits ⇒ Intention	0.27710	0.00500	0.26729	0.28690	0.14317	55.40	<.001
	Perceived Barriers ⇒ Intention	0.22567	0.01082	0.20446	0.24687	0.15034	20.86	<.001
	Cues to Action ⇒ Intention	-0.15599	0.01059	-0.17674	-0.13523	-0.09084	-14.73	<.001
	Self-Efficacy ⇒ Intention	0.40571	0.01529	0.37573	0.43568	0.23234	26.53	<.001

Source: Author.

waste management compliance with higher levels of effectiveness.

The study here through its primary objectives coincides with the third sustainable development goal of promoting health and well-being. In addressing the first research question through descriptive analysis, the highest mean score (3.60) for intention reflects a promising level of agreement among respondents about adopting proper waste management practices in the near future. This finding highlights the potential for enhancing waste management behaviours through targeted interventions that reinforce and sustain intention levels. However, the moderate scoring across other factors suggests that while intention is present, systemic barriers and behavioural constraints still hinder effective waste management practices. The mean score analysis reveals moderate score for personal norms and attitudes (3.45). It highlights the respondent's moral framework and a positive mind set about waste management's importance. However, the lowest score for social norms (2.67) indicates a lack of peer and community support for such practices. This gap identified is concerning because waste management requires collective action for maximum impact. Without sufficient social reinforcement, individuals' efforts may lack the broader community alignment necessary for

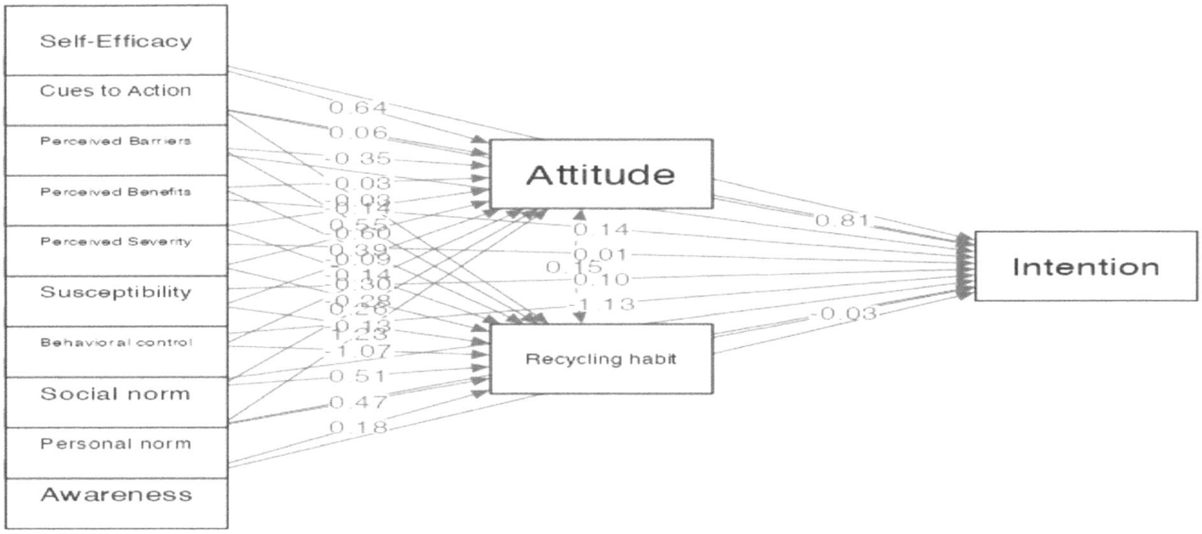

Figure 4.1. Mediation model.

Source: Author.

meaningful outcomes. The low score for perceived behavioural control (2.93) further underscores the challenges that can emerge for the respondents in translating intention into action. Issues such as limited access to resources, lack of proper infrastructure, and systemic constraints may inhibit their perceived ability to engage effectively in waste management. The results here coincide with those by [4, 5, 33]. It also states that waste management adoption requires awareness and a positive attitude for implementation.

A number of initiatives can result from the results generated here and promote the effectiveness of SDG 3. Firstly, to overcome the lack of collaboration as per social norms, the local governments through municipal corporations and community organizations can invest in creating peer-led initiatives, social campaigns, and waste management clubs. Such efforts can encourage community-wide participation in the practices with collective responsibility for waste management.

The mediating effects of recycling habits and attitudes when addressing the second research question are very prominent from the model generated. This indicates the factors' ability to amplify the impact of any intervention planned in this regard. Programs that reward recycling behaviour such as incentives, tax benefits or recognition can reinforce positive attitudes. The circulation of success stories through social media or visible environmental improvements can encourage long-term behavioural change. The need for constant awareness campaigns emphasizing the link between proper waste management and health outcomes must be mandatory for better outcomes. Visual cues, such as signage in urban areas or reminders on proper segregation methods, can serve as constant triggers in the public for behaviour change.

The findings from the statistical methodology undertaken highlights the importance of waste management for improving public health and developing urban well-being. It is directly contributing to SDG 3 and a poor waste management structure can be directly linked to health risks such as vector-borne diseases, respiratory conditions, and water contamination. Hereby, generating interests in behavioral and psychological drivers of waste management can help overcome these risks and improve the quality of life for urban residents.

6. Limitations and Future Outlook

The waste management practice system in India is still in a state of adoption. Although projects such as smart city management and Swachh Bharat are initiated, there are several issues observed during its adoption among the residents of India. To dive deeper into such understanding, a detailed behavioural inspection is required. This study is a novel approach towards such an in-depth understanding but requires more efforts in the future.

The study here integrates two models associated with behavioural decision making and waste management impacts. In the future, other models must be integrated. The inclusion of a technological aspect can provide additional insights. Moreover, the role of digital media in influencing residents towards adopting waste management practices would be interesting to note.

References

[1] Agnihotri, A. K. (2022, September 14). MSW Management: The pitiable situation of Municipal Solid Waste Management. *The Energy and Resources Institute.*

[2] Vyas, S., Prajapati, P., Shah, A. V., & Varjani, S. (2022). Municipal solid waste management: Dynamics, risk assessment, ecological influence, advancements, constraints and perspectives. *Science of The Total Environment*, *814*, 152802. *https://doi.org/10.1016/j.scitotenv.2021.152802*

[3] Nanda, S., & Berruti, F. (2021). Municipal solid waste management and landfilling technologies: a review. *Environmental Chemistry Letters*, *19*(2), 1433–1456. *https://doi.org/10.1007/s10311-020-01100-y*

[4] Raghu, S. J., & Rodrigues, L. L. R. (2020). Behavioral aspects of solid waste management: A systematic review. *Journal of the Air & Waste Management Association*, *70*(12), 1268–1302. *https://doi.org/10.1080/10962247.2020.1823524*

[5] Suryawan, I. W. K., & Lee, C.-H. (2024). Exploring citizens' cluster attitudes and importance-performance policy for adopting sustainable waste management practices. *Waste Management Bulletin*, *2*(3), 204–215. *https://doi.org/10.1016/j.wmb.2024.07.011*

[6] Debrah, J. K., Vidal, D. G., & Dinis, M. A. P. (2021). Raising Awareness on Solid Waste Management through Formal Education for Sustainability: A Developing Countries Evidence Review. *Recycling*, *6*(1), 6. *https://doi.org/10.3390/recycling6010006*

[7] Alves, B. (2024, February 28). *Waste management in India - statistics & facts*. Statista.

[8] Yu, W., Hassan, A., & Adhikariparajuli, M. (2022). How Did Amazon Achieve CSR and Some Sustainable Development Goals (SDGs) – Climate Change, Circular Economy, Water Resources and Employee Rights during COVID-19? *Journal of Risk and Financial Management*, *15*(8), 364. *https://doi.org/10.3390/jrfm15080364*

[9] Ajzen, I. (1991). The theory of planned behavior. *Organizational Behavior and Human Decision Processes*, *50*(2). *https://doi.org/10.1016/0749-5978(91)90020-T*

[10] Xu, L., Ling, M., Lu, Y., & Shen, M. (2017). Understanding Household Waste Separation Behaviour: Testing the Roles of Moral, Past Experience, and Perceived Policy Effectiveness within the Theory of Planned Behaviour. *Sustainability*, *9*(4), 625. *https://doi.org/10.3390/su9040625*

[11] Zhang, S., Hu, D., Lin, T., Li, W., Zhao, R., Yang, H., Pei, Y., & Jiang, L. (2021). Determinants affecting residents' waste classification intention and behavior: A study based on TPB and A-B-C methodology. *Journal of Environmental Management*, *290*, 112591. *https://doi.org/10.1016/j.jenvman.2021.112591*

[12] Boakye, M. K., Adanu, S. K., Agbosu, W. K., Lissah, S. Y., Abdul-Aziz, A.-R., & Owusu, A. G. (2024). Behavioral factors influencing the acceptance and usage of waste bins in Ghana: application of the extended theory of planned behavior (TPB). *Management of Environmental Quality: An International Journal*, *35*(5), 986–1004. *https://doi.org/10.1108/MEQ-06-2023-0176*

[13] Lou, S., Zhang, X., & Zhang, D. (2022). What influences urban residents' intention to sort waste?: Introducing Taoist cultural values into TPB. *Journal of Cleaner Production*, *371*, 133540. *https://doi.org/10.1016/j.jclepro.2022.133540*

[14] Bremser, K., Crowley-Cyr, L., Abraham, V., Moreno-Martin, M. J., & Carreño, M. (2022). Application of the health belief model to explain public perceptions, travel intentions and actions during COVID-19: a sequential transformative design. *Journal of Hospitality and Tourism Insights*, *5*(5), 865–885. *https://doi.org/10.1108/JHTI-12-2020-0235*

[15] Kamran, A., Isazadehfar, K., Heydari, H., Nasimi Doost Azgomi, R., & Naeim, M. (2021). Risk perception and adherence to preventive behaviours related to the COVID-19 pandemic: a community-based study applying the health belief model. *BJPsych Open*, *7*(4), e133. *https://doi.org/10.1192/bjo.2021.954*

[16] Tajeri moghadam, M., Raheli, H., Zarifian, S., & Yazdanpanah, M. (2020). The power of the health belief model (HBM) to predict water demand management: A case study of farmers' water conservation in Iran. *Journal of Environmental Management*, *263*, 110388. *https://doi.org/10.1016/j.jenvman.2020.110388*

[17] Tashiro, A. (2022). Assessing green management in health belief model: An analysis of a post-disaster rural context. *Journal of Environmental Management*, *302*, 114025. *https://doi.org/10.1016/j.jenvman.2021.114025*

[18] Pradhan, R. K., Jena, L. K., & Panigrahy, N. P. (2020). Do sustainability practices buffer the impact of self-efficacy on organisational citizenship behaviour? *Journal of Indian Business Research*, *12*(4), 509–528. *https://doi.org/10.1108/JIBR-05-2019-0170*

[19] Ahmad, F., Rosli, N. T., & Quoquab, F. (2022). Environmental quality awareness, green trust, green self-efficacy and environmental attitude in influencing green purchase behaviour. *International Journal of Ethics and Systems*, *38*(1), 68–90. *https://doi.org/10.1108/IJOES-05-2020-0072*

[20] Ding, L. (2022). The effects of self-efficacy and collective efficacy on customer food waste reduction intention: the mediating role of ethical judgment. *Journal of Hospitality and Tourism Insights*, *5*(4), 752–770. *https://doi.org/10.1108/JHTI-07-2021-0168*

[21] Guo, N., Hao, J. L., Zheng, C., Yu, S., & Wu, W. (2022). Applying Social Cognitive Theory to the Determinants of Employees' Pro-environmental Behaviour Towards Renovation Waste Minimization: In Pursuit of a Circular Economy. *Waste and Biomass Valorization*, *13*(9), 3739–3752. https://doi.org/10.1007/s12649-022-01828-4

[22] Eesley, C., & Wang, Y. (2017). Social influence in career choice: Evidence from a randomized field experiment on entrepreneurial mentorship. *Research Policy*, *46*(3), 636–650. *https://doi.org/10.1016/j.respol.2017.01.010*

[23] Hsieh, S. H., Lee, C. T., & Tseng, T. H. (2022). Psychological empowerment and user satisfaction: Investigating the influences of online brand community participation. *Information & Management*, *59*(1), 103570. *https://doi.org/10.1016/j.im.2021.103570*

[24] Ramkissoon, H. (2020). COVID-19 Place Confinement, Pro-Social, Pro-environmental Behaviors, and Residents' Wellbeing: A New Conceptual Framework. *Frontiers in Psychology*, 11. *https://doi.org/10.3389/fpsyg.2020.02248*

[25] Essl, A., Steffen, A., & Staehle, M. (2021). Choose to reuse! The effect of action-close reminders on pro-environmental behavior. *Journal of Environmental Economics and Management*, *110*, 102539. *https://doi.org/10.1016/j.jeem.2021.102539*

[26] Constantino, S. M., Sparkman, G., Kraft-Todd, G. T., et al. (2022). Scaling Up Change: A Critical Review and Practical Guide to Harnessing Social Norms for Climate Action. *Psychological Science in the Public Interest*, *23*(2), 50–97. *https://doi.org/10.1177/15291006221105279*

[27] Saunders, M., Philip, L., & Thornhill, A. (2009). *Research methods for ecommerce students* (5th ed.). *Pearson Education Limited.*

[28] Ofstad, S., Tobolova, M., Nayum, A., & Klöckner, C. (2017). Understanding the Mechanisms behind Changing People's Recycling Behavior at Work by Applying a Comprehensive Action Determination Model. *Sustainability*, *9*(2), 204. *https://doi.org/10.3390/su9020204*

[29] Janz, N. K., Champion, V. L., & Strecher, V. J. (2002). The health belief model. In K. Glanzm, B. K. Rimer, & F. M. Lewis (Eds.), *Health behavior and health education: Theory, research, and practice*, 45–65.

[30] Urbanovich, T., & Bevan, J. L. (2020). Promoting Environmental Behaviors: Applying the Health Belief Model to Diet Change. *Environmental Communication*, *14*(5), 657–671. *https://doi.org/10.1080/17524032.2019.1702569*

[31] Krejcie, R. V., & Morgan, D. W. (1970). Determining sample size for research activities. *Educational and Psychological Measurement*, *30*, 607–610.

[32] Hair, J., Black, W., Babin, B., Anderson, R., & Tatham, R. (2006). *Multivariate Data Analysis* (6th ed.). Pearson Prentice Hall.

[33] Weerasiri, S. (2012). Attitudes and Awareness towards Environmental Management and its Impact on Environmental Management Practices (EMPs) of SMEs in Sri Lanka. *Journal of Social and Development Sciences*, *3*(1), 16–23. *https://doi.org/10.22610/jsds.v3i1.681*

Appendix

Table 4.A1. Component Loadings

	Component												
	1	*2*	*3*	*4*	*5*	*6*	*7*	*8*	*9*	*10*	*11*	*12*	*13*
Refraining from separating my waste is an important problem for the environment.	0.433												
It is really important to do something against environmental destruction caused by refraining from separating my waste	0.959												
When I refrain from separating my waste, I contribute to environmental problems in Jaipur.	0.962												
If I separate my own waste, I personally contribute to saving the environment	0.850												
Because of my principles, I feel personally obliged to separate my waste.		0.539											
Based on values important to me, I feel obliged to separate my waste as best as possible		0.971											
Many people who are important to me practice waste management at their workplace or place of study.			0.969										
My colleagues or fellow peers in Jaipur who are important to me practice waste management			0.945										
People who are important to me try to influence me towards practising waste management			0.422										
I think many people who are important to me in Jaipur expect that I should practice waste management			-0.668										
For me, practicing waste management in Jaipur, instead of throwing it all in the residual waste, would be useful				0.850									
For me, practicing waste management in Jaipur, instead of throwing it all in the residual waste, would be pleasant				0.406									
Following appropriate waste management practices in Jaipur is easy for me.					0.971								
There are conditions that force me to refrain from following waste management in Jaipur.					0.969								
If I wanted to, I could easily follow the proper waste management practices in Jaipur.					0.945								
My intention to follow waste management practices in the next 1 year is strong.						0.639							

	Component												
	1	*2*	*3*	*4*	*5*	*6*	*7*	*8*	*9*	*10*	*11*	*12*	*13*
I plan to follow waste management practices continuously in the upcoming time						-0.584							
Following waste management practices is something I do automatically.							0.959						
Following waste management practices is something I do without thinking.							0.413						
Following waste management practices is something I do without having to consciously remember.							0.527						
Following waste management practices is something I start doing before I realize I am doing it.							0.962						
Improper waste management in my area increases the risk of health problems for residents.								0.608					
I believe I am personally at risk of being affected by poor waste disposal practices.								0.940					
Exposure to unmanaged waste can harm my family's health.								0.962					
Poor waste disposal is a serious threat to urban cleanliness and the environment.									0.971				
Health conditions such as respiratory issues and infections are directly linked to unmanaged waste									0.969				
Improper waste management can lead to severe long-term impacts on the ecosystem									0.937				
Segregating waste at the household level can significantly improve waste management in my area										-0.668			
Participating in community waste reduction initiatives can benefit public health and urban aesthetics.										0.850			
Segregating waste is too time-consuming for me to adopt regularly											0.945		
My neighborhood lacks adequate infrastructure (e.g., bins or waste collection systems) for waste segregation											0.639		
I find it difficult to access information about proper waste disposal methods.											0.571		
There is insufficient government or local support for waste management initiatives in my area.											0.959		
Regular awareness campaigns can motivate me to adopt better waste management practices												0.962	

(continued)

Table 4.A1. Continued

	Component												
	1	*2*	*3*	*4*	*5*	*6*	*7*	*8*	*9*	*10*	*11*	*12*	*13*
Seeing others in my community engage in waste segregation encourages me to do the same.												0.850	
Providing accessible information on waste management practices (e.g., leaflets, workshops) will encourage me to take action.												0.531	
Receiving incentives (e.g., tax benefits or recognition) for proper waste disposal would motivate me to engage more actively												0.971	
I am confident in my ability to segregate waste at home.													0.969
I feel capable of influencing others to adopt better waste management practices.													0.945
I can consistently adopt waste minimization practices despite challenges like time or lack of resources.													0.639

Note. 'varimax' rotation was used
Source: Author.

Table 4.A2. Descriptives

	N	*Mean*	*Median*	*SD*	*Minimum*	*Maximum*
Awareness	390	3.35	3.50	0.436	2.75	4.00
Personal norm	390	3.45	3.50	0.272	3.00	4.00
Social norm	390	2.67	2.75	0.316	2.25	3.00
Attitude	390	3.45	3.50	0.416	3.00	4.00
Perceived behavioral control	390	2.93	3.00	0.326	2.33	3.33
Intention	390	3.60	3.50	0.584	3.00	4.50
Recycling habit	390	3.20	3.13	0.286	3.00	4.00
Perceived Susceptibility	390	3.29	3.33	0.454	2.67	4.00
Perceived Severity	390	2.93	3.00	0.325	2.33	3.67
Perceived Benefits	390	3.10	3.00	0.302	2.50	3.50
Perceived Barriers	390	3.27	3.25	0.394	2.75	4.00
Cues to Action	390	3.35	3.38	0.340	2.75	3.75
Self-Efficacy	390	3.00	3.00	0.333	2.33	3.33

Source: Author.

5 Innovative fashioning sustainable service: The economic and environmental impact of uniform design in the hospitality industry

Niranjana Menon[a] *and Richa Gupta*[b]

School of Humanities Arts and Applied Sciences, Amity University Dubai, UAE

Abstract: The hospitality industry, characterized by its high levels of customer interaction and service orientation, places significant emphasis on staff presentation. Uniforms, a crucial component of employee appearance, play a vital role in shaping guest perceptions and influencing operational efficiency. This study conducts a comprehensive cost-benefit analysis of investing in high-quality uniforms within the hospitality sector, with a focus on the long-term economic benefits of sustainable and durable materials. The analysis evaluates initial investments in high-quality uniforms against their long-term advantages, including increased durability, employee satisfaction, brand enhancement, and operational savings. A mixed-methods approach is employed, incorporating quantitative data from industry reports and qualitative insights from interviews with hospitality managers. The research compares the costs of low-quality versus high-quality uniforms, accounting for replacement frequency, maintenance, and employee feedback on comfort and satisfaction. Preliminary findings suggest that, despite higher upfront costs, high-quality uniforms result in substantial long-term savings due to reduced replacement and maintenance expenses. Additionally, sustainable uniform materials align with corporate social responsibility (CSR) initiatives, improving brand reputation and attracting eco-conscious consumers. The study concludes that investing in high-quality uniforms is economically advantageous and supports sustainable business practices. This investment strengthens brand loyalty, enhances customer satisfaction, and positions companies as sustainability leaders in the competitive hospitality market.

Keywords: Cost-benefit analysis, economic impact, high-quality uniforms, hospitality industry, innovation, sustainable materials

1. Introduction

The hospitality industry is a significant contributor to global economic growth and employment, but this industry also has a lot of work to do to ensure sustainability, especially when it comes to consistent design and production. In addition to being a tool for improving service efficiency and a symbol of corporate identity, uniforms have a significant negative impact on the environment and the economy [1]. This study aims to investigate the twin effects of uniform design on the hospitality industry's environmental sustainability and economic viability. In particular, the study looks into uniform design sustainable approaches that reduce environmental effects while preserving or improving economic efficiency. The purpose of this study is to identify and analyze sustainable uniform design practices within the hospitality industry, specifically focusing on their environmental and economic impacts. The research aims to answer the following objectives:

1. To evaluate the current sustainable practices in uniform production and design within the hospitality industry,
2. To assess the economic benefits of implementing sustainable uniform solutions, and
3. To examine how sustainability in uniform design can influence customer and employee perceptions.

The following hypotheses serve as the basis for this investigation, the hospitality industry benefits from sustainable uniform design methods in two ways:

- They increase economic efficiency and environmental sustainability; and
- Adopting sustainable uniforms improves employee attitudes and customer satisfaction. The study aims to offer practical insights through this inquiry that can support the creation of uniform design strategies in the hospitality sector that are more impactful, economical, and sustainable.

[a]niranjanaM@amitydubai.ae, [b]rgupta@amityuniversity.ae

DOI: 10.1201/9781003778905-5

The financial effects of purchasing long-lasting, eco-friendly uniforms for the hospitality industry have drawn more attention in recent years. To save money on initial expenses, many firms choose inexpensive uniforms; yet, these decisions sometimes lead to more frequent replacements and greater long-term maintenance expenditures. On the other hand, spending more money on high-quality uniforms could eventually result in increased longevity, lower replacement costs, and improved operational efficiency [2].

Furthermore, the use of sustainable materials in uniforms has garnered attention as sustainability becomes a prominent theme in company plans, especially in industries that depend on public image. Using environmentally friendly materials appeals to consumers who are becoming more and more eco-conscious while also supporting corporate social responsibility (CSR) programs. The significance of taking uniforms into account as part of a company's larger commitment to environmental stewardship is highlighted by the increased need for sustainability in corporate practices [3].

The purpose of this study is to investigate the cost-benefit dynamics of purchasing premium uniforms for the hospitality sector. Through an analysis of operational and financial aspects like as brand recognition, employee happiness, and durability, this study offers insights into how strategic investments in uniformity can result in long-term economic and sustainability benefits. Uniforms are important in establishing employee behaviour and performance in addition to influencing consumer opinions [4]. According to research, wearing a uniform helps foster a sense of identification and belonging, which improves worker engagement and job satisfaction in general), workers who are at ease and self-assured in their uniforms are more likely to behave positively, which results in improved customer service and increased output. Cone Communications [5]. In the hospitality sector, where customer loyalty and repeat business are directly influenced by service quality, the relationship between uniforms and employee happiness is very significant. Research has also indicated that companies that spend in comfortable, high-quality uniforms tend to have lower employee turnover rates since happy employees are more likely to stick around [6].

Furthermore, there are financial and environmental advantages to uniform production when sustainable and long-lasting materials are used. The hospitality sector bears substantial replacement and waste disposal costs because of the frequent wear and tear and rapid uniform set turnover [7]. Businesses can lower the frequency of replacements and related expenses by investing in high-quality, long-lasting textiles to lengthen the life of their uniforms. In addition to lowering operating expenses, this move toward sustainability raises a company's CSR profile – a factor that is becoming more and more significant in today's business environment. Customers are more likely to support companies that practice environmental responsibility, especially Millennials and Gen Z. Therefore, businesses that include eco-friendly uniforms in their operational strategy may see an increase in client loyalty and a stronger brand image [8].

2. Literature Review

Uniforms have a major influence on the financial structure of the company and are an effective instrument for presenting a consistent brand image in the hospitality sector [9]. Uniforms are a type of arti-factual communication since they send a crucial visual message to visitors, clients, coworkers, and the general public. This is consistent with the idea that uniforms are more than just practical clothing; they are an essential component of an organization's image and help to shape its corporate identity.

Beyond uniforms, corporate identity also includes aspects like a company's name, logo, and visual style, which all work together to create a unified brand image. When it comes to building strong client relationships and creating a brand identity that is associated with providing high-quality service, the appearance of employees is crucial for hotels [10].

The visual identity of staff members – including their uniforms – strengthens this bond by conveying the brand's key principles of excellence and professionalism. Purchasing high-quality uniforms can result in substantial financial benefits over time due to their greater durability, less replacement costs, and improved worker satisfaction, even though they are more expensive initially. Uniforms also function as a form of free advertising by promoting the company's brand during every customer interaction, reinforcing brand visibility and recognition. Additionally, uniforms support fundamental organizational principles including honesty, cooperation, and the quest of excellence, according to Tata Kelola Bank [11]. The uniforms foster a healthy work atmosphere by promoting professionalism and equality. This, in turn, enhances employee morale and performance, which are elements that directly impact service quality and customer happiness [12].

As part of the global shift toward sustainability, the use of ecologically friendly materials in uniform manufacture has gained popularity in recent years. By lowering waste, using less energy, and supporting CSR programs, using sustainable fabrics not only helps the environment but also provides long-term financial benefits [13]. This transition provides enterprises with a competitive edge in the market, particularly among eco-conscious consumers that value environmental sustainability when making purchasing decisions [14]. Uniforms are a strategic instrument that boost professionalism, generate financial gains, and enhance brand image – all of which help the hospitality business operate more efficiently and satisfy customers [15].

Aesthetic labor has become more and more important in the hospitality industry as a means of providing excellent client service. Front-line staff serve as the primary point of contact through which customers assess the quality of services, and their look, behaviour, and even tone of voice contribute to a visually pleasing experience that boosts the company's reputation [16]. A company's professional image, brand identification, and consistency of service can all be enhanced by well-maintained uniforms and employee presentation [17]. Uniforms are a vital tool for setting hospitality businesses apart from their rivals, fostering a unique corporate brand, and providing clients with top-notch service. But maintaining uniforms and personal grooming, among other aesthetic demands placed on front-line staff, can be quite difficult. In addition to selecting workers based solely on their physical attributes, aesthetic labor entails upholding rigid standards for behaviour, dress rules, and grooming that complement business branding [18].

In order to improve client experiences and strengthen their brand image, businesses in the hospitality sector depend heavily on aesthetic labor. As a component of this aesthetic, uniforms uphold the brand's identity and financial position in addition to projecting professionalism. Nevertheless, studies have indicated that workers frequently experience a sense of being inundated by these aesthetic requirements, especially when these expectations permeate their personal life [19]. For instance, employees usually experience stress while trying to uphold the company's aesthetic standards in their free time, according to research [20]. Through interviews with employees at hotels and airlines, determined three primary sources of stress: organizational aesthetic requirements and training, customer service pressures, and the weight of upholding standards outside of work hours. Employees reported that, in addition to their regular duties, adhering to strict grooming and uniform standards increased their levels of stress [21].

The tourist and hospitality industries have been using narrative techniques more and more in recent years to improve their sustainability reporting. This change is indicative of a larger initiative to improve the accessibility and engagement of sustainability messaging when visual components like images and videos are handled skillfully, sustainability reports become more interesting and reader-friendly [22].

A company's dedication to sustainability is sometimes demonstrated through case studies that highlight certain programs or projects, in addition to visual components and personal statements.

The environmental advantages of switching from synthetic to organic materials for uniforms are examined in this review, with a focus on improved wearer comfort and lower carbon footprints. In uniform manufacturing, it also looks at water-saving technologies, energy-efficient production methods, and waste reduction techniques. Fair labor practices and other social implications are highlighted as essential components of sustainable consistent practices [23].

This study investigates how the hotel industry may become more competitive by incorporating sustainability into service improvements. It highlights creative ways to lessen environmental effects while increasing customer value and discusses the financial and environmental ramifications of implementing sustainable practices, such as uniform design.

3. Methodology

A selection of fifty hospitality establishments, encompassing hotels, resorts, and eateries, was made. These companies were picked because of their track record of sustainability or because they actively participate in the investigation of sustainable fashion solutions. Managers and employees in charge of uniform procurement received a structured online survey that focused on issues including material selection, price, and the perception of the importance of sustainable uniforms in improving company image. Participants having significant experience with uniform design in the hospitality sector were chosen using a purposive sample technique. This strategy was used to guarantee that opinions were obtained from those who could offer comprehensive and pertinent information on the subject. Key stakeholders, such as uniform designers, sustainability consultants, and owners of hospitality businesses, were interviewed in semi-structured interviews. Through these interviews, the decision-making process underlying uniform design, the difficulties in implementing sustainable alternatives, and the observable effects on the environment and economy were all intended to be understood. Analysis was done on in-depth case studies of three significant hospitality brands that have adopted sustainable uniform programs. These case studies examined the materials used, supplier practices, life cycle costs, and employee feedback to assess the impact of sustainable uniforms on operational costs and brand reputation.

Descriptive statistics were used to examine quantitative survey data in order to identify patterns in cost control, material selection, and sustainability awareness. Thematic coding of qualitative data from case studies and interviews allowed for the identification of recurrent themes pertaining to economic performance, sustainability, and employee happiness. Triangulation was used to validate the qualitative data by contrasting the results of the interviews with published works and corporate reports. This method aided in cross-checking the themes' and interpretations' coherence.

Questionnaire for Research on Sustainable Uniforms

1. Material Selection:
   - What types of materials do you typically consider when selecting uniforms for your establishment?

- How important is the sustainability of the material in your decision-making process? (Scale: 1 to 5)

2. Cost Considerations:
   - What is the primary budget range allocated for uniform procurement?
   - How do you assess the cost-effectiveness of sustainable options compared to conventional uniforms?
3. Perception of Sustainability:
   - To what extent do you believe that having sustainable uniforms improves your company's image? (Scale: 1 to 5)
   - What are the key factors that influence your perception of sustainable uniforms?
   - Implementation Challenges:
   - What challenges have you faced in implementing sustainable uniform solutions within your establishment?
   - How do you rate the level of support you receive from management regarding sustainable practices in uniform design? (Scale: 1 to 5)
4. Stakeholder Insights:
   - In your opinion, how do uniform designers and sustainability consultants influence the decision-making process for uniform selection?
   - What feedback do you receive from employees regarding sustainable uniforms?
   - To analyze the results from the questionnaire, a mixed-methods approach was used:
5. Quantitative Analysis:
   - Used statistical tools to analyze closed-ended question responses (Likert scale, multiple choice). Descriptive statistics help summarize the data, while regression analysis helped to assess the relationships between variables (e.g., material sustainability and company image).
6. Qualitative Analysis:
   - Performed thematic analysis on open-ended responses to extract key themes and insights. This method involved identifying common challenges, perceptions, and influences regarding sustainable practices.

Combining both approaches provided us with a comprehensive understanding of the sentiments and experiences surrounding sustainable uniforms in the hospitality sector.

4. Results

Economic Impact of Sustainable Uniform Design; According to the survey, adopting sustainable uniform materials including bamboo, recycled polyester, and organic cotton came at a higher initial cost for 68% of hospitality organizations [24]. However, because sustainable uniforms last longer and require fewer replacements, 45% of employers experienced long-term cost reductions. Furthermore, companies that embraced eco-friendly uniforms saw an average 12% rise in consumers' opinions of their dedication to environmental responsibility.

The Figure 5.1 illustrating the economic impact of sustainable uniform design in the hospitality industry. It shows the percentage of organizations that experienced a higher initial cost, long-term cost reductions, and improved consumer opinions due to the adoption of sustainable uniform materials.

The carbon footprint of uniform purchase was considerably lowered by the adoption of sustainable production techniques and environmentally friendly materials.

According to case studies, companies who shifted to recycled materials were able to cut their yearly textile waste by as much as 30%. Furthermore, businesses who collaborated with ethical suppliers – especially those that used water-efficient dyeing methods – saw a 40% decrease in water usage [25].

The Figure 5.2 that illustrates the impact of sustainable practices in the hospitality industry. It shows the percentage reduction in yearly textile waste and water usage for

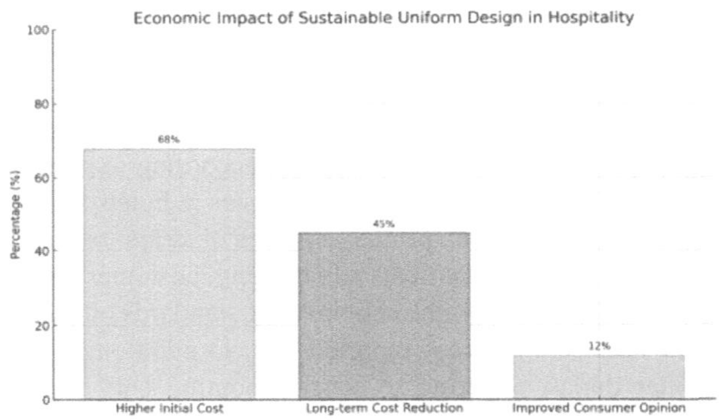

Figure 5.1. The economic impact of sustainable uniform design in the hospitality industry.

Source: Author.

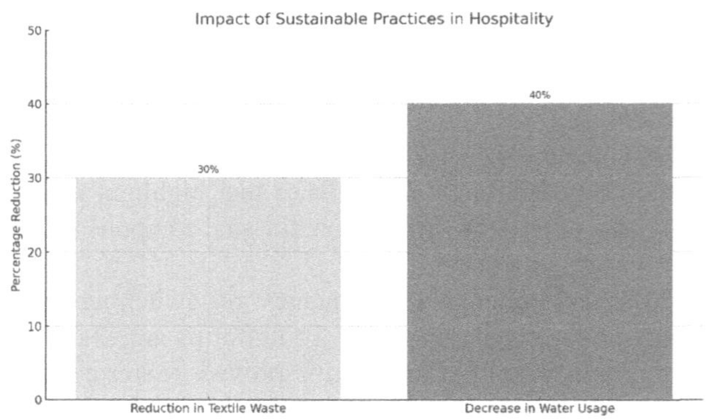

Figure 5.2. Impact of sustainable practices in hospitality industry.

Source: Author.

companies that shifted to recycled materials and collaborated with ethical suppliers using water-efficient dyeing methods.

According to interviews, 70% of workers had a favourable opinion of sustainable uniforms, and many expressed pride in their employment at a company that prioritizes the environment. Because the sustainable uniforms were of higher quality and had more ergonomic design, the workers also expressed increased job satisfaction and comfort. Some, however, had early reservations about the aesthetics of sustainable designs, necessitating further spending on customization and tailoring.

Consumer perception of brands was greatly enhanced by sustainable uniform programs; in fact, 65% of study participants said that more customers were inquiring about their sustainability initiatives. Forty percent of the firms reported better rates of repeat visits as a result of these questions, which frequently increased customer loyalty. The case studies also showed that increasing customer involvement with sustainability messaging in uniforms – for example, by attaching eco-friendly badges or QR codes that lead to sustainability pages – boosted consumer engagement.

The Figure 5.3 illustrates the impact of sustainable uniforms on workers and consumers. It highlights the percentage of workers with a favourable opinion of sustainable uniforms, the increase in customer inquiries about sustainability initiatives, and the rise in repeat visits due to these inquiries.

5. Discussion

The results of this study show that hospitality businesses can benefit economically and environmentally from sustainable uniform design. Adopting sustainable materials has greater upfront costs, but over time, these expenses are offset by longer lasting products, lower replacement rates, and increased brand loyalty [26]. According to the report, a crucial tactic for enhancing brand image is integrating sustainability into uniform design, since consumers are gravitating toward companies that have a strong commitment to environmental responsibility [27]. The advantages for the environment, especially in terms of resource efficiency and waste reduction, highlight how significantly the hospitality industry can contribute to the circular economy. In addition to reducing their environmental impact, hospitality businesses may also support global sustainability initiatives like the Sustainable Employers who included staff members in the uniform design process reported increased levels of engagement, which had a favourable effect on retention and work satisfaction [28]. However, some employees' aesthetic concerns imply that striking a balance between sustainable design and beauty and usefulness requires greater focus [29].

All things considered, incorporating sustainable uniform design into the hospitality sector turns out to be a wise investment that advances environmental objectives

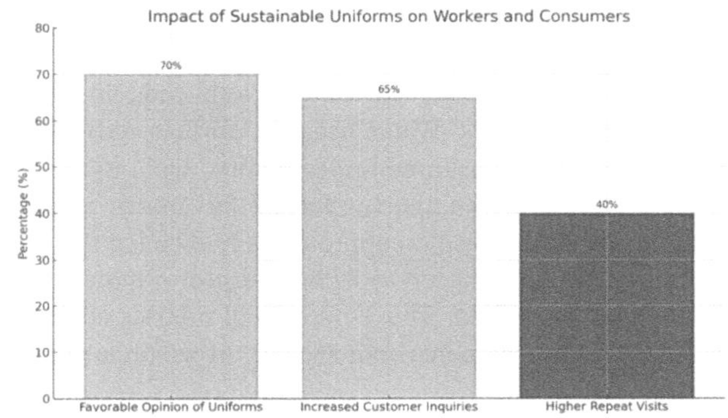

Figure 5.3. Impact of sustainable uniforms on workers and consumers.

Source: Author.

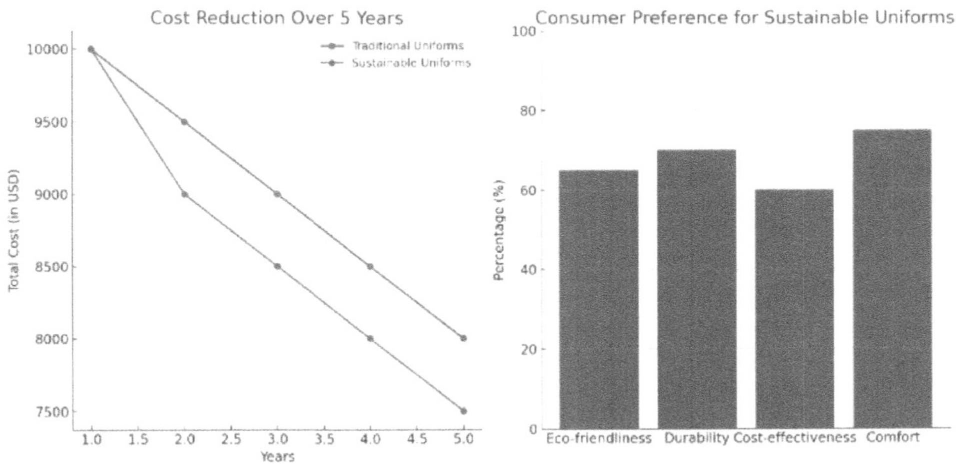

Figures 5.4. and 5.5. Cost Cuts over a Five-Year Period for Eco friendly uniforms.

Source: Author.

as well as employee morale, brand loyalty, and long-term financial performance [30]. This study's dependence on self-reported data, which could introduce bias, is one of its limitations. Direct observation or third-party audits could be used in future studies to improve data accuracy and lower subjectivity (Figures 5.4 and 5.5).

Cost Cuts over a Five-Year Period: The overall expenses of conventional and sustainable uniforms over a five-year period are contrasted in this graph. Because of things like longevity and fewer replacements, sustainable uniforms consistently result in lower expenses. Preference of Customers for Eco-Friendly Uniforms: Based on factors like comfort, affordability, durability, and environmental friendliness, this bar graph illustrates consumer preferences for sustainable uniforms. Positive customer sentiments toward sustainability are seen in high percentages [31].

By reducing carbon footprints and saving resources, the hospitality industry's adoption of sustainable uniform designs greatly lessens its impact on the environment. For example, according to the Textile Exchange, converting to recycled polyester from standard polyester can reduce CO_2 emissions by about 32%. Additionally, adopting organic cotton instead of conventional cotton can save thousands of liters of water every kilogram of cloth, reducing water usage by up to 91%. Water usage is further reduced by 60–70% through sustainable production techniques like low-water dyeing. Another important advantage is waste reduction; circular fashion approaches reduce landfill contributions by allowing up to 85% of uniform materials to be recycled or reused. These numerical metrics show the observable environmental advantages of sustainable uniform initiatives.

6. Conclusion

The hospitality sector has taken a big stride toward environmental responsibility. Sustainable uniform production has greater upfront costs, but the long-term financial and reputational benefits make the investment worthwhile. As such, forward-thinking hospitality firms can view these initiatives as mutually beneficial [32].

Beyond the financial advantages, sustainable uniforms have a big impact on brand perception and customer perception. Businesses that put an emphasis on environmentally friendly procedures and openness in their business dealings are increasingly regarded as models of corporate social responsibility. According to case studies, adopting eco-friendly uniforms can improve a business's reputation, since up to 65% of clients will notice and ask about these efforts. As more consumers become environmentally concerned, their loyalty tends to rise towards brands that actively engage in sustainable activities, with 40% of firms reporting increased rates of repeat visits. Strong customer response increases market competitiveness and customer engagement in addition to increasing brand visibility.

Reusing materials and using ethical production practices are critical in minimizing the ecological footprint of the sector from an environmental perspective. Hospitality businesses that use these procedures can significantly reduce their use of water and reduce textile waste by thirty percent and forty percent, respectively, saving crucial resources. These kinds of projects highlight the real advantages of sustainable development and provide other industries a path forward for reducing their environmental foot print [33].

One more factor that becomes apparent when looking at the transition to sustainable uniforms is employee happiness. According to employee interviews, 70% of employees have a positive opinion of these environmentally friendly uniforms, and many of them say they are proud to work for an organization that shares their own sustainable beliefs. Additionally, the superior quality and ergonomic design of sustainable uniforms have improved employee comfort and job satisfaction. The advantages these technologies have for people-centeredness are highlighted by the fact that higher morale can result in better performance and a happier work environment.

Companies understand that a well-designed uniform is an essential component of corporate identity that reflects the organization's values and brand image, so they must strike a balance between aesthetic appeal and long-lasting practicality. According to the study, 75% of hotel managers said that using uniforms made from recycled materials and sourcing them responsibly resulted in a 20% decrease in operating costs [34]. Because eco-friendly textiles last longer than standard cotton uniforms, the hotel claimed a 25% reduction in their annual uniform purchase expenditures. Furthermore, post-implementation employee surveys revealed that 82% of employees had favourable feelings about wearing uniforms linked to environmental responsibility, which coincided with a 15% increase in customer satisfaction ratings within the same time frame [35].

In summary, Sustainable uniform design in the hospitality industry balances financial gain with environmental responsibility, setting an example for broader industry change. It enhances employee satisfaction, reduces costs, and improves brand reputation while contributing to a greener future [36].

References

[1] Gleim, M. R., Smith, J. S., Andrews, D., & Cronin Jr., J. J. (2013). Against the green: A multi-method examination of the barriers to green consumption. *Journal of Retailing, 89*(1), 44–61. https://doi.org/10.1016/j.jretai.2012.10.001

[2] Hu, X. (2017). Uniforms and operational efficiency in the hospitality industry. *Journal of Hospitality and Tourism Management,* (33), 65–72. https://doi.org/10.1016/j.jhtm.2017.10.002

[3] Joseph, N. (1986). *Uniforms and nonuniforms: Communication through clothing*. Greenwood Press.

[4] Maitland, S., & Sammartino, M. (2020). Long-term economic effects of high-quality employee uniforms in the hotel sector. *International Journal of Hospitality Management*, *91*, 102652. https://doi.org/10.1016/j.ijhm.2020.102652

[5] Peluchette, J. V., & Karl, K. (2007). The impact of workplace attire on employee self-perceptions. *Human Resource Development Quarterly, 18*(3), 345–360. https://doi.org/10.1002/hrdq.121

[6] Cheng, M. (2014). Service excellence in the hospitality industry: The role of employee engagement. *Journal of Tourism Research, 10*(2), 33–47. https://doi.org/10.1016/j.jotr.2013.11.002

[7] Cone Communications. (2017). *Millennial and Gen Z CSR study: How to build trust with young consumers.*

[8] Hughes, J., & Rog, E. (2008). A strategy for improving employee retention within the hospitality industry. *Journal of Human Resources in Hospitality & Tourism, 7*(3), 352–369. https://doi.org/10.1080/15332840802156915

[9] Nelson, B., & Bowen, J. (2000). *Human resources management in the hospitality industry: The importance of uniforms.*

[10] Rafaeli, A. (1993). Dress and behavior: A review of existing literature and a theoretical framework for future studies. *Academy of Management Review, 18*)1), 32–45. https://doi.org/10.5465/amr.1993.3997504

[11] Schulz, S. A., & Flanigan, R. L. (2016). Developing competitive advantage through corporate social responsibility in the hospitality industry. *Journal of Hospitality and Tourism Research, 40*(1), 39–53. https://doi.org/10.1177/1096348013495696

[12] Wicker, J. (2011). Durability and sustainability in uniform materials: Cost savings and environmental impact. *Journal of Sustainable Textiles, 5*(3), 25–38.

[13] Bravo, R., Pina, J. M., & Matute, J. (2011). Corporate identity management in the hospitality industry: The role of brand trust. International *Journal of Contemporary Hospitality Management*, *23*(7), 911–928. https://doi.org/10.1108/09596111111167598

[14] Melewar, T. C. (2008). The role of corporate identity in modern organizations. *Journal of Business Research, 61*(5), 528–539. https://doi.org/10.1016/j.jbusres.2007.10.017

[15] Rakhmat, M. (2015). The art of uniforms as a tool of corporate communication. *Journal of Visual Communication, 17*(11), 234–242. https://doi.org/10.1177/1470357214560420

[16] Tata Kelola Bank. (2014). Uniforms and the promotion of corporate values: Integrity, teamwork, and professionalism. *Banking and Management Review*, *18*(2), 45–56.

[17] Van den Bosch, A. L. M., De Jong, M. D. T., & Elving, W. J. L. (2006). Managing corporate visual identity: Exploring the relationship between corporate identity and performance. *European Journal of Marketing, 40*(7/8), 885–895. https://doi.org/10.1108/03090560610670034

[18] Biswas, S. (2009). Aesthetic labour and its impact on the hospitality industry. *Hospitality Management Review*, *8*(2), 72–84.

[19] Entwistle, J., & Wissinger, E. (2006). Keeping up appearances: Aesthetic labour and personal upkeep. *Fashion Theory: The Journal of Dress, Body & Culture, 10*(3), 303–322. https://doi.org/10.2752/136270406778050326

[20] Hall, R., & van den Broek, D. (2012). Service with a smile: Emotions and aesthetic labour in the hospitality industry. *Employee Relations, 34*(3), 280–294. https://doi.org/10.1108/01425451211217779

[21] Spiess, L., & Waring, P. (2005). Aesthetic labour, cost, and corporate branding: The economic role of uniformity in hospitality. *International Journal of Employment Studies, 13*(1), 79–91.

[22] Warhurst, C., & Nickson, D. (2007). Employee appearance in the hospitality sector: The double-edged sword of aesthetic labour. *Sociological Review*, *55*(1), 142–162. https://doi.org/10.1111/j.1467-954X.2007.00699.x

[23] Witz, A., Warhurst, C., & Nickson, D. (2003). The labour of aesthetics and the aesthetics of organization. *Organization, 10*(1), 33–54. https://doi.org/10.1177/1350508403010001372

[24] Carnival Corporation. (2021). *Sustainability report*.

[25] Morhardt, J. E. (2009). Corporate social responsibility and sustainability reporting on the internet. *Business Strategy and the Environment, 18*(7), 487–500. https://doi.org/10.1002/bse.618

[26] Royal Caribbean Cruises. (2020). *Corporate sustainability report*.

[27] Thomas Cook Group. (2018). *Sustainability performance report*.

[28] TUI Group. (2019). *Sustainability strategy and achievements*.

[29] Gupta, R., & Barros, R. (2024). Bioconversion: Citrus fruit peel waste from hospitality sector to fashion sector. *Journal of Environmental Protection and Ecology*, *25*(3), 813–824.

[30] Jones, M. A., Nguyen, L. K., & Patel, S. (2021). Economic and environmental benefits of sustainable uniforms in hospitality: A case study of Green Stay Hotel Group. *Sustainability in Fashion and Textiles*, *14*(2),

32–45. https://doi.org/10.3390/sft14020032 *Trends in sustainable uniform design: Dressing for impact*.

[31] Semanticscholar.org. (2016). *The role of sustainable service innovation in crafting the vision of the hospitality industry*. Semanticscholar.org.

[32] Bhardwaj, V., & Fairhurst, A. (2021). *Systematic literature review on fashion and sustainability: Consumer behavior*.

[33] Gupta, R., & Dave, D. (2021). Biterial: A sustainable alternative to animal leather and synthetic material. *Annals of the Romanian Society for Cell Biology, 25*(6), 7317–7331.

[34] Jones, M. A., Nguyen, L. K., & Patel, S. (2021). BGFashion.net. (n.d.). and sustainable practices. *Journal of Fashion Marketing and Management*, *25*(4), 568–590.

[35] Stella, C. (2021). Sustainability in corporate uniforms: Social and environmental impact in the hospitality sector. *Fashion & Textiles Journal*.

[36] Smith, R., & Taylor, J. (2022). Advancing sustainability in hospitality design: Economic, environmental, and policy perspectives. *Sustainability Journal 14*(12), 344–360.

6 Sustainable value chains in organic production of spices: Value chain governance and competitiveness validated through structural equation modelling

M. Hena[1,a] and Nadia Sha[2,b]

[1]School of Management, Presidency University, Bengaluru, Karnataka, India
[2]College of Commerce and Business Administration, Dhofar University, Salalah, Sultanate of Oman, Oman

Abstract: Value chain governance is identified as a starter point to guarantee value chain competitiveness in sustainable spices value chains. The chain governance explored in this study is observed through the trust between chain partners, information carried through the value chains, contractual agreements between chain players, and the support provided to the value chains through information and communication technology platforms. The researchers adopted PLS-SEM for undertaking the statistical analysis, which is currently acknowledged as the best method for multivariate analysis to examine the proposed research model. Moreover, this effort filled a gap in the literature on sustainable organic farming and production of spices, (particularly, organic value chains of black pepper and cardamom) by investigating the impact of trust (TRST), contractual governance (CG), information sharing (IS) and information and communication technology (ICT) on value chain competitiveness through the mediating effects of value chain innovativeness. The findings validated the influence of ICT among value chain members and its significant association to innovativeness in sustainable value chains. Thus, the integration of value chain actors through information technology has improved the trust in the value chain linkages and confirmed competitiveness in sustainable value chains. The better trust among value chain members led to good understanding and closer relationships, proper information sharing facilitates proper communication and transfer of information between producers and buyers. Moreover, the impact of predictor variables like contractual governance, information sharing, information and communication technology and trust over value chain competitiveness is partially mediated by value chain innovativeness.

Keywords: Organic production, structural equation modelling, sustainable value chains, value chain competitiveness, value chain governance, value chain innovativeness

1. Introduction

Value chain approaches address the difficulties in the networks holistically, with a focus on competitiveness and risk management among the chain's dynamic operations. Trust-based partnerships are vital for network competitiveness, as chain integration, strategic partnering, supporting services, and product range [1]. Product innovations have the potential to integrate small-holder producers into a value chain [2], and at the same time, the ability to link value chains through contractual agreements lowers asymmetric information flows [3]. As usual, the goal of value chain research aims to lower transaction costs along with managing risks. Furthermore, determinants of trust appear to be an effective and long-term desirable characteristic for dealing with misunderstanding and unsafe circumstances amongst value chain partners [4]. Effective information sharing [5], quick interaction with ICT [6], and contractual governance among value chain members contribute to the development of innovative products that satisfy the varied needs of smallholder producers [7, 8].

The existing knowledge level on "value chain governance" has been characterized by conflicting perspectives from diverse authors. Contemporary marketing tactics and restructured agricultural markets have forced smallholder producers to deal with a number of implications for which they are unprepared or educated. As an alternative, new innovative value chain approaches have been identified to improve their ability to combat restructured market conditions. Such innovations in value chains have

[a]henashafeek@gmail.com/hena.m@presidencyuniversity.in, [b]nsha@du.edu.om

DOI: 10.1201/9781003778905-6

produced remarkable results in developing countries with increased productivity, market integration, and better income for smallholder farmers [9, 10] Earlier scholars have described value chains as multidimensional and multifaceted, with chain nodes interconnected by commercial and social interactions [11, 12]. Previous researchers suggested that value chain analysis emphasized buyer-supplier connections while ignoring tacit and explicit chain coordination [13]. Similarly, Gibbon and Ponte [14] noted the importance of power and governance in value chains and described by formal and informal norms and functions outside of institutional and regulatory structures with society values. The term "governance" was primarily defined in terms of the importance of information interchange and production activities [15], and supported the concept of "buyer-driven" and "producer-driven" governance relations in value chains. Later, "governance" was recognized as the power or authority to decide who should and should not participate as a value chain actor; in short, governance means the authority to set rules, assist chain participants in meeting pre-determined standards, and monitor chain performance [16]. Under the Global Value Chain (GVC) model, value chain operations are carried out by producers and chain participants in emerging nations, with the specifications for products and processes determined by the purchasers' privileges along the chain.

To a greater extent, studies on global value chain governance [17] indicated that the competencies required for monitoring and controlling chain members differ between local and export markets. These ideas influenced the development of a value chain governance theory with three variables: the complexity of information and knowledge transfer, the codification of information and knowledge, and the capabilities of current and future suppliers. Furthermore, the theory presented five main forms of value chain governance based on empirical evidence, with each variable assigned one of two values: high or low. Thus, value chain governance is divided into five categories: markets, modular, relational, captive, and hierarchical, which serve as the foundation for governance relationships. Market type is defined with minimal complexity in information flow with low explicit coordination, having price remaining the most influential determinant. The goods are supplied according to the customer's specifications in modular configuration. Due to the intricate interactions between buyers and sellers, relational governance stresses mutual dependency and high levels of asset specificity. In the captive category, product specifications are complicated, but supplier capabilities are limited, necessitating extensive participation and control on the part of the lead firm. Product specifications cannot be codified in the hierarchical model since the products are complicated, and highly qualified suppliers are not available in the network; nonetheless, lead enterprises will be obligated to develop and produce items in-house. Keane [18] divided chain governance systems into two categories: internal to the value chain and external to the value chain. The former structure is commonly understood as the general shape of linkages within a chain for effectiveness, whilst the latter refers to the mandatory laws and regulations that all producers must follow so as for their products to reach global markets. Though Gereffi et al. [17] postulated five governance interactions in global value chains, they failed to clarify domestic informal value chains from agriculture, particularly in localized rural areas [19]. In rural settings, connections with communities cannot be overlooked; Jones et al. [20] observed that informal linkages in governance networks are maintained by social systems. Informal links are important in agricultural value chains because they promote effective cooperation, trust, and transparency [21].

The current research is to investigate the links between value chain governance and chain competitiveness in sustainable spices value chains in India. The chain governance investigated in this study through the trust between chain partners, information carried through the chain, contractual agreements between chain players, and the support provided to the value chain by information and communication technology platforms. Finally, the influence of each predictor variable on value chain competitiveness has been assessed. This research article's structure is sevenfold (including the introduction), with section two focusing on the conceptual framework for value chain governance and the predictor variable's link with value chain competitiveness were explained. Part three, presents the methods that used to develop and interpret the current study and its results. Section four summarizes the findings of the structural equation modeling, employed to examine the relationships between the selected constructs such as information and communication technology (ICT), information sharing (IS), trust (TRST), contractual governance (CG), innovativeness (INN) and value chain competitiveness (VCC). Research findings and discussions are presented in part five and lastly, part six outlines the future research possibilities and conclusions.

2. Conceptual Framework Support for the Research

With an increased need for agricultural entrepreneurship and agribusiness innovations to meet the world's food supply, many scholars have pointed out that local agri-value chains are more relevant than global value chains (GVCs) and serve as a real boosting factor for smallholder producers in rural development concerns [22–25]. Food value chain governance appears to be a complex concept with multiple functions and overlapping activities of the partners [19]. A search of scientific materials related to the subject under inquiry has helped to develop a conceptual model for studying and analyzing different predictors of value chain competitiveness. To begin with, the variable trust has been identified as an influencing factor for competitiveness in the value chain, and it represents the extent to which chain participants accept each other as credible, reliable, and dependable, and it is frequently used to overcome and manage risk in unusual situations among people [26]. Furthermore, links or partnerships with more trust appear to be solid, whereas those lacking trust are deemed weak [27].

Later, [7] identified trust between producer and buyer as a critical component in agricultural value chain financing innovations that reduce lending concerns. Secondly, the aspect that allows value chain links to be established through interactions has been adopted, namely, information sharing. Information sharing is referred as the effective and appropriate interactions between value chain members, as well as the transmission of complete and trusted information through the chain [28]. [29] highlighted a fundamental difficulty in value chains: smallholder farmers fail to demand adequate income due to a lack of information about demand and market situations. Chen and Tang [30] explored whether enough information results in increased economic benefits for farmers and discovered a positive association between the two criteria. Furthermore, the benefits of information sharing are dependent on trust and collaboration among chain partners, Colicchia et al. [31] and Baah et al. [32] demonstrated the impact of information sharing on chain visibility, collaboration, agility, and value chain competence.

The idea of contractual governance, which is seen as a component in determining chain competitiveness, refers to the official contracts, norms, and informal contacts that exist in agricultural value chain management [27]. In layman's terms, contractual governance refers to the extent to which a contractual agreement is monitored and managed through explicit rules and regulations, as well as the contracting parties' responsibilities and duties [28]. Cao and Lumineau [33] suggested that contractual governance is positively connected with trust and relational standards, as demonstrated by Poppo and Zenger in 2002 [34]. While, Enquist et al. [35] reported that contractual governance safeguards stakeholder networks' competencies and fosters a solid contractual relationship between them. Through contracts, chain participants' threatening actions on other participants against contract requirements are restricted, rather than demanding their own interests. As a result, prospective contract violations and efforts to comfort dissatisfied parties hamper governance efficiency over time [28].

The next construct of value chain governance is information and communication technology (ICT), a combination of scientific and engineering knowledge used to strengthen the chain relationships [36]. In present times, ICTs have evolved to help emerging economies to accelerate economic growth and accomplish the sustainable development goals (SDGs), particularly in global value chains (GVCs) [37]. For example, the current Covid-19 pandemic and global lockdown in 2020, compelled business organizations to reconfigure their supply chains using technology to meet customer needs [38]. Thus, ICTs seek to achieve inclusivity in agricultural value chains by complementing production processes and coordination, allowing market access for smallholder producers, and providing financial inclusion opportunities to the poor (FAO, 2013). The proper flow and sharing of information via ICT infrastructure fosters interactions and the development of expertise in value chains [28].

On the other hand, the search on the studies conducted on how innovation influences value chain competitiveness found uneven and limited. Hence, value chain innovativeness is included in the current research by combining literature on value chains and innovation systems to provide a path to sustainable value chain development. Earlier studies also observed, value chain innovations like product diversifications, agile and balanced cost operations have upgraded value chains and improved the overall competitiveness of the chain [39, 40]. Lately, Brancati et al. [41] revealed how value chain governance impacts the innovation performance of value chain actors in the intermediate products and exposed relational governance structures bids the most favourable setting for innovativeness. In this study, innovativeness is defined as a process in which a value chain partners works together to introduce new products and services, aims to enhance customer satisfaction [42]. Through establishing an effective coordination between producers and buyers in the value chains, partner institutions can greatly improve their capability by bolstering the process of product and process innovations. Partner firms with strong emphasis on innovativeness are usually able to adapt to changes in the market environment and ensures the value chain competitiveness. Moreover, in the digital era, innovations are complicatedly connected to networks including the varied and diverse interactions with participants [22, 43].

Finally, smallholder producers' competitiveness in the sustainable value chains can be improved through their involvement in value chains, and the expected outcomes help to overcome obstacles such as poor produce quality, failure to meet buyer standards and specifications, a lack of advantageous networks for information sharing, and opportunities to access favourable markets.

With the explanations provided above, this study developed a conceptual model (Figure 6.1) for analyzing value chain competitiveness through trust, information sharing, contractual governance, and information and communication technology. Synthesizing the aforementioned researcher's findings regarding the selected

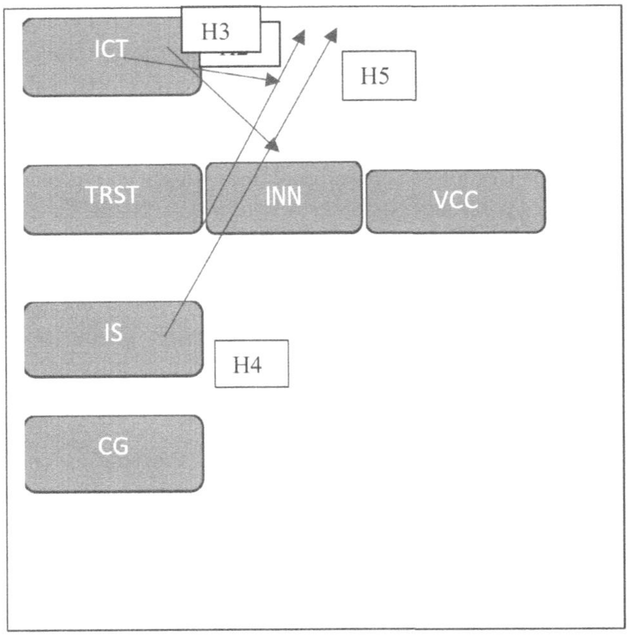

Figure 6.1. Proposed research model.

Source: Author.

constructs, the current conceptual model proposes to investigate the following five hypotheses for statistical analysis.

H1: Information and communication technology (ICT) among the value chain partners positively influence the value chain innovativeness (VCI)

H2: Trust (TRST) between value chain partners positively influence the value chain innovativeness (VCI)

H3: Information sharing (IS) between value chain partners positively influences the value chain innovativeness (VCI)

H4: Contractual governance (CG) between value chain partners is positively related to value chain competitiveness (VCI)

H5: Value chain innovativeness (VCI) positively influences the value chain competitiveness (VCC).

3. Research Methodology

Global value chains can be examined by considering the perspective from the horizontal and vertical linkages. The governance structures and their level of coordination are inadequately evaluated based on Spices are considered as a significant agricultural commodity of trade among the notable agricultural value chains in India, which require adequate rainfall and humidity for cultivation and propagation of the crops, mainly through stem or terminal cuttings. Organic black pepper and cardamom cultivation and production are commonly found in Kerala as an "extensive homestead cultivation", along with several other crops tea, coffee, rubber and coconut. The Idukki and Wayanad districts of Kerala state in India (Figure 6.2) accounted for the first and second position under the area of black pepper and cardamom cultivated in Kerala during 2020–21 [44] and together had the maximum share of the total production of spices. Idukki district, a high-range district of Kerala has been known as a "spice bowl" since olden times. The district accounts for merely 3.32 percent of the total population of Kerala with the lowest population density. Spice cultivation remains one of the main occupation and income source for the people in the district. Wayanad district, a large area covered by forest, is the second high-range district in Kerala state. More than half of the population in the district is engaged in agriculture to earn their livelihood. Two panchayats each were identified from these selected districts to survey the organic black pepper and cardamom growers, accordingly, Vandiperiyar and Rajakumari Panchayats from Idukki district and Mullenkolly and Vellamunda Panchayats were selected from Wayanad district.

For undertaking this research work, main spices of the study area, black pepper and cardamom was selected and accordingly, 396 growers of organic black pepper and organic cardamom from the Idukki and Wayanad districts were the respondents. The lists of the organic black pepper and organic cardamom growers were obtained from the respective Krishi bhavans (Agriculture office) in each panchayat selected for the study. The other value chain actors (100 nos), namely, input suppliers, hill produce dealers, wholesalers, retailers, cooperatives, farmer produce company were identified using snowball technique and included as respondents.

For quantitative data collection, survey technique was adopted and used a pre-structured schedule containing construct items as per the proposed model. The constructs included were IT integration, trust, and contractual governance information sharing, innovativeness and value chain competitiveness. The quantitative data analysis started with the exploratory factor analysis (EFA), undertaken to identify the factors and further, the factors confirmed through confirmatory factor analysis (CFA). An investigation conducted with the structural equation modelling (SEM) technique to check the relevance of the research model and validated each construct's influence over the dependent variable. Values of Cronbach's alpha was used to test the internal reliability of the study variables, while the value of standardized factor loading, average variance extracted (AVE), composite reliability (CR), and the model fit indices, were used to measure the convergent validity of the study. Besides, to ascertain discriminate validity, the researcher compared the AVE with squared inter construct correlation (SIC). Thus, quantitative data was analysed with the PLS - SEM technique using the Smart PLS 4.0 software.

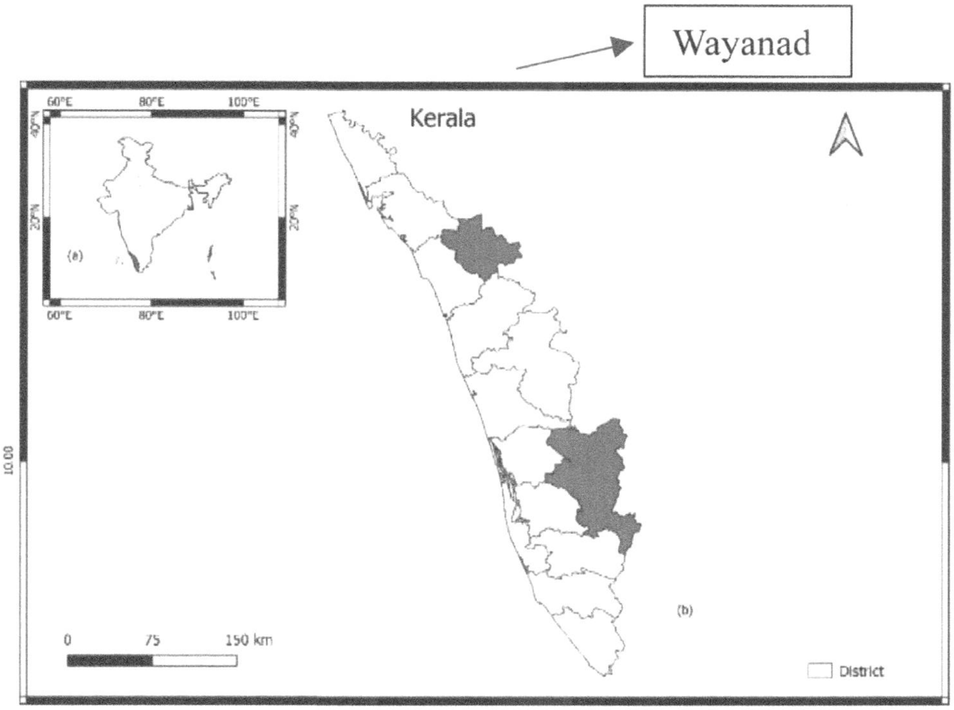

Figure 6.2. Map of Idukki and Wayanad districts in Kerala.
Source: Author.

4. Results and Discussions

The organic spices are produced through organic cultivation practices in the study area. Organic production was carried out by certified organic farmers and a group of farmers who adopted organic farming methods without having any certifications from the licensed agencies. Different agencies procure spices from the Idukki and Wayanad districts such as hill produce dealers, marketing cooperatives, farmer producer companies (FPC), private companies, and NGOs (Non-Governmental Organizations). NGOs and private companies collect spices from organic certified farmers whereas, hill produce dealers, wholesalers, marketing cooperatives and FPCs procure different qualities of spices, with or without proper organic quality certification. The value-added organic spices are distributed to the customers through the retailers. Idukki and Wayanad districts are recognised as attractive tourist destinations in Kerala and the retailers has grabbed the opportunity to distribute various forms of spices (processed and non-processed) products to domestic as well as foreign tourists. Exporting business aims to capture new and potential markets for spices products. NGOs and private companies licensed to export spices and its value-added products to different parts of the world.

Eighty percent of the organic farms have been found certified under Lacon Certification in Thiruvalla, Kerala, 10.9 percent of farms certification obtained from Athidhi organic certification, Bangalore, and 9.1 percent of farms had Indocert Certification, Ernakulum in Kerala. Dried spices (black pepper and cardamom) are a common product that flows through all actors in the value chain, whereas white pepper and green pepper flows only through the organic value chain of spices, from farmers to NGOs, NGOs processes and exports it through their registered companies, where the exporter does all the processing activities. Hill produce dealers and spices wholesalers procure the dried spices from farmers and through them the product reaches the exporters and the retailers. Another chain, including hill produce dealers and wholesalers sold black pepper and cardamom in the Kochi market through the IPSTA (Indian Pepper and Spices Trade Association, Kochi) brokers.

4.1. SEM analysis: Relationship between value chain governance and value chain competitiveness

The researchers adopted PLS-SEM analysis, currently identified as the best method for multivariate analysis [45] to analyse the research model (Figure 6.1). It is a two-level data analysis technique to validate the conceptual model [46]. First level, included with a critical prerequisite analysis of measurement model carried out to establish relationship between latent variables and its indicators and in next level, structural model evaluation was done to check whether the hypothesized causal relationships show consistency with the empirical data collected. At last, mediation effects are estimated in PLS -SEM analysis which is capable of confirming the relationships in complex models relative to other SEM methods Skewness and kurtosis values between -1 and +1 indicate properly distributed data and in the current study, the researcher's investigation convinced that the data were regularly distributed

Table 6.1. Convergent validity and reliability test of conceptual model

Path relationships	*Standardized Beta*	*t-value*
ICT - Innovativeness	0.281***	4.854
Information Sharing - Innovativeness	0.304***	5.825
Trust - Innovativeness	0.141***	3.638
Contract Governance - Innovativeness	0.171**	2.817
Innovativeness - Value chain competitiveness	0.183***	3.487

Source: Author.

4.2. Evaluation of the measurement model

First of all, the model under introspection has undergone assessment to confirm the reliability and validity of both observed and latent variables, as recommended by Ho [47]. Thus, the conceptual model evaluated by employing two methods: composite reliability (CR) and Cronbach alpha. For both reliability requirements, the rule of thumb is that the values must be greater than 0.70 and less than 0.95 [48]. Table 6.1 displays Cronbach Alpha (α) and Composite Reliability (CR) values for the measurement model.

The selected construct items' Cronbach's alpha values and composite reliability values vary from 0 to 1; values closer to one imply greater internal consistency, while values closer to zero denotes decreased internal consistency. The Cronbach's alpha values (α) and CR values obtained are above 0.9, indicating near-perfect reliability. Convergent validity refers to the degree to which a measure correlates favorably with other measures of the same construct. It can be quantified using average variance extracted (AVE), that is, an appropriate AVE can be 0.50 or higher,

Table 6.2. Discriminant validity test of the research model: Heterotrait-Monotrait Ratio (HTMT)

Construct	*Constructs Items*	*Loadings*	*Cronbach Alpha*	*CR*	*AVE*
VCC	VCC1	0.864	0.861	0.890	0.704
	VCC2	0.853			
	VCC3	0.862			
	VCC4	0.772			
INN	INN1	0.858	0.888	0.891	0.749
	INN2	0.891			
	INN3	0.822			
	INN4	0.890			
ITI	ITI1	0.833	0.886	0.887	0.744
	ITI2	0.877			
	ITI3	0.871			
	ITI4	0.872			
TRST	TRST1	0.866	0.891	0.892	0.754
	TRST2	0.858			
	TRST3	0.878			
	TRST4	0.872			
IS	IS1	0.915	0.870	0.902	0.792
	IS2	0.837			
	IS3	0.916			
CG	CG1	0.774	0.801	0.811	0.701
	CG2	0.780			
	CG3	0.814			
	CG4	0.790			

Source: Author.

indicating that the construct explains more than half of the variance in its elements.

Similarly, discriminant validity was evaluated with Heterotrait-Monotrait ratio (HTMT) as endorsed by 49] Table 6.2 validated discriminant validity with computed HTMT values significantly less than 0.85, thus proved that the correlations of constructs included in the model are within the acceptable limit.

4.3. Evaluation of the structural model

Hair et al [48] proposed PLS-structural equation modelling is the ideal method to estimate the influence of one construct over other constructs and the major criteria of coefficient of determination (R2), path coefficient (β value), and T-statistic value employed to assess the structural model. The path coefficients and p-values are used to identify the significant impact of the constructs on the endogenous latent variables. The hypotheses' significance level tested through the β-value and the accepted standard is if the β-value is higher, then greater will be the significant impact on the endogenous latent variables (Table 6.3). The path coefficients disclosed the effect of the independent constructs over the dependent constructs and the hypotheses are tested with a p-value less than 0.05. Accordingly, all the five paths in the proposed model are verified and confirmed with the results, such as information sharing (IS) has a significant and positive effect on value chain innovativeness (INN) ($\beta = 0.304$, t = 5.825, $p < 0.000$) followed by information and communication technology ICT ($\beta = 0.281$, t = 4.854, $p < 0.000$). Trust (TRST) positively influenced value chain innovativeness (INN) with a β value of 0.141 and t value of 3.638 ($p < 0.000$), while the relationship between contract governance (CG) and value chain innovativeness (INN) ($\beta = 0.171$, t = 2.817, $p < 0.05$) was appeared significant with comparatively less influence on value chain innovativeness (INN). Further, the findings disclosed the influence of value chain innovativeness (INN) on value chain competitiveness (VCC) ($\beta = 0.183$, t = 3.487, $p < 0.000$) indicating a positive impact in the model.

4.4. Mediation analysis through value chain innovativeness

Earlier, structural model's results revealed that the effect of trust, information sharing, contractual governance and information and communication technology on value chain innovativeness was significant. With the inclusion of the mediating variable (value chain innovativeness), the impact of the independent variables on dependent variables can be significant or insignificant. Accordingly, the direct effect between the trust, information sharing, and information and communication technology on value chain competitiveness was found significant. Along with that, the serial mediation model attempted to establish the four indirect effects (Table 6.4).

The indirect effect of contractual governance, information sharing, information and communication technology and trust separately on value chain competitiveness through value chain innovativeness was found significant and confirmed a complementary partial mediation (Table 6.4). Complementary partial mediation means a category of mediation that occurs when both the direct and indirect effects are significant and the influence of the mediator variable recognised to the same direction. That is, the predictor variables (together mentioned as value chain

Table 6.3. Path coefficients and p-values of model

Constructs	*CG*	*INN*	*IS*	*ICT*	*TRST*
Contract Governance					
Innovativeness	0.312				
Information Sharing	0.314	0.575			
Information and communication technology	0.321	0.562	0.653		
Trust	0.156	0.324	0.305	0.243	
Value chain competitiveness	0.161	0.203	0.093	0.206	0.166

Source: Author.

Table 6.4. Total indirect effects and specific indirect effects

Hypothesised Paths	*t- statistics*	*P-values*	*Level of Mediation*
CG -> INN -> VCC	2.644	0.001	Complementary Partial mediation
IS -> INN -> VCC	2.973	0.001	Complementary Partial mediation
ICT -> INN -> VCC	2.762	0.003	Complementary Partial mediation
TRST -> INN -> VCC	2.444	0.007	Complementary Partial mediation

Source: Author.

governance) exert its positive partial influence through the mediator variable (innovativeness) and a positive partial influence directly to the value chain competitiveness. In short, the impact of predictor variables like contractual governance, information sharing, information and communication technology and trust over value chain competitiveness is partially mediated by value chain innovativeness. Thus, the relationship between value chain governance, value chain innovativeness and value chain competitiveness in the sustainable spices value chains are validated by the results of the PLS-SEM analysis.

The ability of VC actors to decarbonise the environment or no adverse effects on the environment as a result of their value-adding activities ideally, falls under environmental dimension. Because of these notable factor, the value chain under study classified as a sustainable value chain. That is, the referred organic spices value chain offers reasonable prices for smallholder farmers, distributes benefits to value chain participants according to their risk and investment in the chain, and, lastly, uses organic farming for spice production leading to environmental sustainability.

Similar to the findings of previous scholars [44–47] on the role of contractual governance and its impact over the success and performance of value chains digital traceability, the current research findings also supported the influence of contractual governance over value chain competitiveness through value chain innovativeness. In continuation, the current study's result underlines the need of having a perfect contractual governance in value chains to make it more innovative and competitive, as supported by Cholez et al. [50] and they expressed that collective contractual governance positively impacts knowledge gaining through face-to-face communications. When it comes to global value chains (GVC), advanced technology has taken it to the level of smart contracts for transforming international trade in GVC through automated and secure contractual agreements, leading to innovations for advancing global trade practices by eliminating third parties [51–54].

Trust and information sharing, main components in business linkages and are crucial in collective relations between value chain actors [55], has been much studied in different contexts. If the trust among value chain members is better, it leads to better understanding and closer relationships sustaining honesty in chain governance. Further, interpersonal trust relations between chain participants impacts the effectiveness of the collaborations and in contrary, a fruitful teamwork can induce backs more trust in relationships [56]. Similarly, the association between trust and innovativeness in the value chains was found relevant in this study also, supporting the findings of earlier studies [57–59].

The impact of digital transformation on innovations and how digitalization helps value chains to improve innovation performance and competitiveness was observed by Marin et al. [60] in their study. Similarly, other researchers also identified specific technological factors and innovations that accelerated the growth and competitiveness in IT industry [61] and in apparel manufacturing, digital supply chain integration has increased both supply chain capacity and performance [62].

5. Conclusions

Finally, as a conclusion, the study has demonstrated that the value chain competitiveness is the result of network values created with adequate information and knowledge flows, that permits the advancement of operative, technical, and dynamic competencies to adapt permanently to market changes ensuring strong trust, contractual agreements with better governance, ultimately leading to sustainability in value chains. With the above explanations, this research significantly contributed to address the issues of smallholder organic spice growers related to value chain governance and the value chain competitiveness. To address these blockades at the farm and market level among the various chain partners, might be required trust-based relations and governance arrangements. However, farmers' trustworthy relations with value chain partners, are needed to positively harness innovative product development for swifter and sustainable agriculture value chains.

Acknowledgment

We gratefully acknowledge the respondent farmers, other value chain actors, and key informants for their genuine information and cooperation in materializing this research.

References

[1] Scoones, I. (2009). Livelihoods perspectives and rural development, *Journal of Peasant Studies, 36*(1), 171–196. *https://www.tandfonline.com/doi/epdf/10.1080/03066150902820503?src=getftr*

[2] Natarajan, N., Newsham, A., Rigg, J., & Suhardiman, D. (2022). A sustainable livelihoods framework for the 21st century, *World Development, 155*. *https://doi.org/10.1016/j.worlddev.2022.105898*

[3] Wood, A. (2009). Value chains: An Economist's perspective. *IDS Bulletin, 32*(3), 41–45. *https://doi.org/10.1111/j.1759-5436.2001.mp32003005.x*

[4] Lowitt, K., Hickey, G. M., Ganpat, W., & Phillip, L. (2015). Linking Communities of Practice with Value Chain Development in Smallholder Farming Systems. *World Development, 74*, 363–373. *https://doi.org/10.1016/j.worlddev.2015.05.014*

[5] Bair, J. (2009). Frontiers of commodity chain research. Stanford, CA: Stanford University Press. *https://doi.org/10.1111/j.1471-0366.2010.00266.x*

[6] Gibbon, P., & Ponte, S. (2005). *Trading down: Africa, value chains and the global economy*. Philadelphia, PA: Temple University Press.

[7] Graef, F. (2014). Framework for participatory food security research in rural food value chains. *Global Food Security*, *3*, 8–15. *http:// dx.doi.org/10.1016/j.gfs.2014.01.001*

[8] Gereffi, G. (1994). *The Organization of Buyer-Driven Global Commodity Chains: How U.S. Retailers Shape Overseas Production Networks.* Westport, Connecticut Praeger.

[9] Gereffi, G. (2005). The Governance of Global Value Chains. *https://www.researchgate.net/publication/200465546_The_Governance_of_Global_Value_Chains*

[10] Mishra, P. K., & Dey, K. (2018). Governance of agricultural value chains: Coordination, control and safeguarding. *Journal of Rural Studies, 64*, 135–147 *https://doi.org/10.1016/j.jrurstud.2018.09.020*

[11] Jones, C., Hesterly, W. S., & Borgatti, S. P. (1997). A General Theory of Network Governance: Exchange Conditions and Social Mechanisms. *The Academy of Management Review, 22*(4), 911–945. *https://doi.org/10.2307/259249*

[12] Kilelu, C., Klerkx, L., Omore, A., Baltenweck, I., Leeuwis, C., & Gihinji, J. (2017). Value Chain Upgrading and the Inclusion of Smallholders in Markets: Reflections on Contributions of Multi-Stakeholder Processes in Dairy Development in Tanzania. *The European Journal of Development Research*, *29*, 1102–1121. *https://doi.org/10.1057/s41287-016-0074-z*

[13] Saliola, F., & Zanfei, A. (2009). Multinational firms, global value chains and the organization of knowledge transfer. *Research Policy, 38*, 369–381. *https://doi.org/10.1016/j.respol.2008.11.003*

[14] Pulles, N. J., Veldman, J., & Schiele, H. (2014). Identifying innovative suppliers in business networks: An empirical study. *Industrial Marketing Management, 43*, 409–418. *https://doi.org/10.1016/j.indmarman.2013.12.009*

[15] Chang, J. (2017). The effects of buyer-supplier's collaboration on knowledge and product innovation. *Industrial Marketing Management, 65*, 129–143. *https://doi.org/10.1016/j.indmarman.2017.04.003*

[16] Liu, X., Huang, Q., Dou, J., & Zhao, X. (2017). The impact of informal social interaction on innovation capability in the context of buyer-supplier dyads. *Journal of Business Research, 78*, 314–322. *https://doi.org/10.1016/j.jbusres.2016.12.027*

[17] Qin, L., Xie, W., & Jia, P. (2024). Value Chain Digitalization, Global Value Chain Embeddedness, and Distributed Innovation in Value Chains. *Sustainability, 16*(7), 2845. *https://doi.org/10.3390/su16072845*

[18] Horton, D., Devaux, A., Bernet, T., Mayanja, S., Ordinola, M., & Thiele, G. (2022). Inclusive innovation in agricultural value chains: lessons from use of a systems approach in diverse settings. *Innovation and Development, 13*(3), 517–539. *https://doi.org/10.1080/2157930X.2022.2070587*

[19] Brancati, E., Pietrobelli, C., & Mazzi, C. T. (2024). The Influence of value chain governance on innovation performance: A study of Italian suppliers. *Eurasian Business Review, 14*, 319–344. *https://doi.org/10.1007/s40821-024-00267-6*

[20] Simon, A., & Honore Petnji Yaya, L. (2012). Improving innovation and customer satisfaction through systems integration. *Industrial Management & Data Systems, 112*(7), 1026–1043. *https://doi.org/10.1108/02635571211255005*

[21] Tomas, G., Hult, M., Robert, F. H., & Knight, G. A. (2004). Innovativeness: Its antecedents and impact on business performance. *Industrial Marketing Management, 33*(5), 429–438. *https://doi.org/10.1016/j.indmarman.2003.08.015*

[22] Bhatti, S. H., Hussain, W. M. H. W., Khan, J., Sultan, S., & Ferraris, A. (2022). Exploring data-driven innovation: What's missing in the relationship between big data analytics capabilities and supply chain innovation? *Annals of Operations Research, 333*, 799–824. *https://doi.org/10.1007/s10479-022-04772-7*

[23] Malik, D. S., Sharma, A. K., Sharma, A. K., Thakur, R., & Sharma, M. (2020). Chapter 2. A review on impact of water pollution on freshwater fish species and their aquatic environment. In V. Kumar, N. Kamboj, T. Payum (Eds.), *Advances in Environmental Pollution Management: Wastewater Impacts and Treatment Technologies*, vol. 1. Gro Environ Media | Agriculture and Environmental Science Academy, Haridwar, India, 10–28. *https://doi.org/10.26832/aesa-2020-aepm-02*

[24] Mateo-Sagasta, J., Zadeh, S. M., Turral, H., & Burke, J. (2017). *Water pollution from agriculture: A global review.* Executive summary. Rome, Italy: FAO; Colombo, Sri Lanka: International Water Management Institute (IWMI). CGIAR Research Program on Water, Land and Ecosystems (WLE) 35. *https://hdl.handle.net/10568/88070*

[25] Gamage, J., et al. (2023). Role of organic farming for achieving sustainability in agriculture. *Farming System, 1*(1), 100005. *https://doi.org/10.1016/j.farsys.2023.100005*

[26] Linderhof, V., de Lange, T., & Reinhard, S., (2021). The dilemmas of water quality and food security interactions in low- and middle-income countries. *Frontiers in Water, 3*, 736760. *https://doi.org/10.3389/frwa.2021.736760*

[27] Gamage, J., et al. (2023). Role of organic farming for achieving sustainability in agriculture. *Farming System, 1*(1), 100005. *https://doi.org/10.1016/j.farsys.2023.100005*

[28] Tombe, R., & Smuts, H. (2023). Agricultural Social Networks: An Agricultural Value Chain-Based Digitalization Framework for an Inclusive Digital Economy. *Applied Sciences, 13*(11), 6382. *https://doi.org/10.3390/app13116382*

[29] Bargawi, H. (2015). Rural institutions in flux: Lessons from three Tanzanian cotton producing villages. *Journal of Agrarian Change, 15*(2), 155–178. *https://doi.org/10.1111/joac.12071*

[30] Census of India. (2011). *https://censusindia.gov.in/nada/index.php/catalog/42617*

[31] DFID [Department for International Development] (2008). *Making value chain work better for the poor: A tool book for practitioners of value chain analysis (version 3).* Department for international Development, Phnom Penh, Cambodia.

[32] Haggblade, S., Theriault, V., Staatz, J., Dembele, N., & Diallo. B. (2012). *A Conceptual Framework for Promoting Inclusive Agricultural Value Chains*. International Fund for Agricultural Development (IFAD), Michigan State University.

[33] Yin, R. K. (2014). *Case Study Research: Design and Methods*. Sage publications.

[34] Lim, W. M. (2024). What Is Qualitative Research? An Overview and Guidelines. *Australasian Marketing Journal. https://doi.org/10.1177/14413582241264619*

[35] Issa, I., & Hamm, U. (2017). Adoption of Organic Farming as an Opportunity for Syrian Farmers of Fresh Fruit and Vegetables: An Application of the Theory of Planned Behaviour and Structural Equation Modelling. *Sustainability, 9*(11). *https://doi.org/10.3390/su9112024*

[36] Anderson, J. C., & Gerbing, D. W. (1988). Structural equation modelling in practice: A review and recommended two-step approach. *Psychological Bulletin, 103*(3), 411–423. *https://doi.org/10.1037/0033-2909.103.3.411*

[37] Chin W. W. (1988). The Partial Least Squares Approach to Structural Equation Modeling. Marcoulides GA, editor. *Modern Methods for Business Research. California State University, Fullerton*, 295–336.

[38] Hair, J. F. Jr, Howard, M. C., & Nitzl, C. (2020). Assessing measurement model quality in PLS-SEM using confirmatory composite analysis. *Journal of Business Research, 109*, 101–110. *https://doi.org/10.1016/j.jbusres.2019.11.069*

[39] Pretty, J., Benton, T. G., Bharucha, Z. P., et al. (2018). Global assessment of agricultural system redesign for sustainable intensification. *Nature Sustainability, 1*, 441–446. *https://doi.org/10.1038/s41893-018-0114-0*

[40] Hammed, T. B., Oloruntoba, E. O., & Ana, G. R. E. E. (2019). Enhancing growth and yield of crops with nutrient-enriched organic fertilizer at wet and dry seasons in ensuring climate-smart agriculture. *International Journal of Recycling of Organic Waste in Agriculture, 8*(1), 81–92. *https://doi.org/10.1007/s40093-019-0274-6*

[41] FAO. (2014). *Developing sustainable food value chains–Guiding principles*. Rome.

[42] Mithöfer, D., Méndez, V. E., Bose, A., & Vaast, P. (2017). Harnessing local strength for sustainable coffee value chains in India and Nicaragua: Reevaluating certification to global sustainability standards. *International Journal of Biodiversity Science, Ecosystem Services & Management*, *13*(1), 471–496. *https://doi.org/10.1080/21513732.2018.1460400*

[43] Yuan, L., & Mähönen, J. (2024). Can Integrate a Sustainable Business Model and Global Value Chains Revive the Value Chain's Sustainable Growth?. *Circular Economy and Sustainability, 4*, 2957–2980. *https://doi.org/10.1007/s43615-024-00352-y*

[44] Addae-Boateng, S., Wen, X., & Brew, Y. (2015). Contractual Governance, Relational Governance, and Firm Performance: The Case of Chinese and Ghanaian and Family Firms. *American Journal of Industrial and Business Management*, *5*, 288–310. *https://doi.org10.4236/ajibm.2015.55031*

[45] Xie, E., Liang, J., & Zhou, K. Z. (2016). How to enhance supplier performance in China: An integrative view of partner selection and partner control. *Industrial Marketing Management, 56*, 156–166. *https://doi.org/10.1016/j.indmarman.2016.01.004*

[46] Mitkidis, K., Perkovic, S., & Mitkidis, P. (2019). Tendencies in contractual governance to promote human and labour rights in transnational supply chains. *Competition & Change*, 23(4), 397–419. *https://doi.org/10.1177/1024529419844385*

[47] Zhou, X., Zhu, Q., & Xu, Z. (2023). The role of contractual and relational governance for the success of digital traceability: Evidence from Chinese food producers. *International Journal of Production Economics, 255*, 108659. *https://doi.org/10.1016/j.ijpe.2022.108659*

[48] Benítez-Ávila, C., Hartmann, A., Dewulf, G., & Henseler, J. (2018). Interplay of relational and contractual governance in public-private partnerships: The mediating role of relational norms, trust and partners' contribution. *International Journal of Project Management, 36*(3), 429–443. *https://doi.org/10.1016/j.ijproman.2017.12.005*

[49] Wang, Y., Liang, H., Sun, S., & Xue, Y. (2024). How distance influences contractual governance in buyer-seller relationships. *Industrial Marketing Management*, *116*, 1–11. *https://doi.org/10.1016/j.indmarman.2023.09.004*

[50] Cholez, C., Magrini, M., & Galliano, D. (2020). Exploring inter-firm knowledge through contractual governance: A case study of production contracts for faba-bean procurement in France. *Journal of Rural*

Studies, 73, 135–146. *https://doi.org/10.1016/j.jrurstud.2019.10.040*

[51] Böhmecke-Schwafert, M. (2024). The role of blockchain for trade in global value chains: A systematic literature review and guidance for future research. *Telecommunications Policy, 48*(9), 102835. *https://doi.org/10.1016/j.telpol.2024.102835*

[52] Fabrizio, C., & Paola, I. (2014). Supply chains, contractual governance and certification regimes. *European Journal of Law and Economics, 37*(1), 131–173. *https://hdl.handle.net/1814/33934*

[53] Kumar, R., Singh, R. K., & Shankar, R. (2016). Study on Collaboration and Information Sharing Practices for SCM in Indian SMEs. *International Journal of Business Information Systems*, *22*(4), 455–475. *https://doi.org/10.1504/IJBIS.2016.077838*

[54] Lotfi, Z., Mukhtar, M., Sahran, S., & Zadeh, A. T. (2013). Information Sharing in Supply Chain Management. *Procedia Technology, 11*, 298–304. *https://doi.org/10.1016/j.protcy.2013.12.194*

[55] Stern, M. J., & Coleman, K. J. (2014). The Multidimensionality of Trust: Applications in Collaborative Natural Resource Management. *Society & Natural Resources, 28*(2), 117–132. *https://doi.org/10.1080/08941920.2014.945062*

[56] Ramanathan, U., & Gunasekaran, A. (2014). Supply chain collaboration: Impact of success in long-term partnerships. *International Journal of Production Economics, 147*, 252–259. *https://doi.org/10.1016/j.ijpe.2012.06.002*

[57] Panayides, P. M., & Lun, Y. H. V. (2009). The impact of trust on innovativeness and supply chain performance. *International Journal of Production Economics, 122*(1), 35–46. *https://doi.org/10.1016/j.ijpe.2008.12.025*

[58] Ghondaghsaz, N., & Engesser, S. (2022). Identification of factors and outcomes of trust in mobile supply chains. *European Journal of Management and Business Economics, 31*(3), 325–344. *https://doi.org/10.1108/EJMBE-05-2021-01*

[59] Gwaltu, P., & Mrisho, D. (2023). Examining the Effect of Trust on Supply Chain Performance: The Mediating Role of Process Innovation. *East African Journal of Business and Economics, 6*(1), 100–114. *https://doi.org/10.37284/eajbe.6.1.1256*

[60] Marín, R., Santos-Arteaga, F. J., Tavana, M., & Di Caprio, D. (2023). Value Chain digitalization and technological development as innovation catalysts in small and medium-sized enterprises. *Journal of Innovation and Knowledge, 8*(4), 100454. *https://doi.org/10.1016/j.jik.2023.100454*

[61] Zavhorodnya, E., & Melnyk, T. (2024). Classifications of determinants of competitiveness in information and communication technologies. *Economics and Region, 3*(94), 57–65. *https://doi.org/10.26906/EiR.2024.3(94).3482*

[62] Shahadat, M. M. H., Chowdhury, A. H. M. Y., Jahed, M. A., Nathan, R. J., & Fekete-Farkas, M. (2024). Innovativeness, visibility, and collaboration effect on supply chain performance: moderating role of digitalGam supply chain integration. *Cogent Business & Management, 11*(1). *https://doi.org/10.1080/23311975.2024.2390168*

7 Designing of interactive web application for hostel management system

Dhamodharan Srinivasan[1,a], *Mohana Subi V.*[2,b], *Pramika T.*[2,c], *Abishek R. P. D.*[2,d], *and Yaswin Gokul S.*[2,e]

[1]Associate Professor, Computer and Communication Engineering, Sri Eshwar College of Engineering, Coimbatore, India
[2]Department of Computer and Communication Engineering, Sri Eshwar College of Engineering, Coimbatore, India

Abstract: Hostel Management System is an innovative software solution that has been developed to modernize and secure the management of student accommodations in educational institutions. As the demand for sustainable and efficient student housing increases, hostel administrators face the challenge of handling multiple tasks, which are time-consuming and prone to errors. The HMS automates crucial functions like room assignment, collection of fees, student record maintenance, and maintenance requests with reduced human error thereby making the process more efficient. A non-technical user interface allows even the lowest calibre of employees to use this software very easily. HMS contains security and data integrity features as only a few persons in the organisation will be authorised to access sensitive financial and student information. Data loss is also prevented with regular backups. All modules provide real-time updates to their data that guarantee their consistency. The records can be handled accurately so that changes can be implemented quickly if necessary. The attendance tracking, detailed financial reports, and room and maintenance reports support features for compliance monitoring and provide decision-making capabilities to strengthen the overall operational efficiency of hostel administration.

Keywords: Attendance tracking, automation, backups, data security, financial management, real-time updates, student housing optimization, sustainability

1. Introduction

With the rapid growth of educational institutions around the world, the demand for student hostels has increased exponentially. Colleges and universities are facing increasing student admissions, and effective hostel management is required to achieve smooth operations. Previously, hostel management was performed manually for processes such as room allotment, fee collection, student record keeping, and facility management. However, these manual processes are prone to inefficiencies, human mistakes, security vulnerabilities, and administrative bottlenecks. With increasing growth in institutions, manual management is not possible, and it is challenging to keep track of the numerous student records, allot rooms fairly, keep finances transparent, and attend to maintenance requests efficiently. To remove these constraints, automation of hostel management is inevitable. A Hostel Management System (HMS) is a centralized technology-driven system that integrates all hostel operations into an efficient system. HMS enhances administrative efficiency by automating major functions such as room allotment, fee management, student record keeping, and tracking maintenance. One of its prime advantages is the intelligent room allotment module that optimizes seat allocation based on pre-defined institutional parameters, eliminating conflicts and ensuring fairness. The system also provides a robust fee management solution that tracks payments, generates bills, and generates real-time financial reports, ensuring transparency and accountability. Security and data integrity are high-priority considerations in hostel management. HMS uses strict access controls, where sensitive student and financial data can only be edited or accessed by authorized staff. Furthermore, in-built backup and recovery procedures safeguard critical data, preventing data loss and system reliability. By automating hostel operations, HMS transforms traditional management procedures into an expandable, secure, and efficient digital system, keeping in line with the evolving needs of modern

[a]dhamu20@gmail.com, [b]mohanasubivenkatachalapathi@gmail.com, [c]gkt.pramika@gmail.com, [d]abishekrpdabishek@gmail.com, [e]yaswingokul5@gmail.com

DOI: 10.1201/9781003778905-7

educational institutions. The paper presents an extensive overview of the Hostel Management System, its architecture, functionalities, and the revolutionary impact it has on hostel administration. The study also explores the benefits of the system in optimizing operational efficiency, security, and a seamless experience for students and administrators.

2. Literature Review

[1] Good software design is the prime ingredient in the development of efficient management systems and significantly affects the stability, maintainability, and quality of the resultant system. In previous research, architecture, data structures, and user interface design are underlined as factors to meet user needs. For the hostel management scenario, an effective database, intuitive interfaces, and sound data handling are key factors that reduce the burden of operation and enhance the user experience. Systematic application of design practices not only reduces errors but also ensures scalability and adaptability to the growing demands of educational institutions. [2] The benefits of automating hostel management systems are well-documented in studies published by the Journal of Science and Engineering. Centralized databases, automation, and streamlined user interfaces help improve communication, reduce administrative workload, and ensure efficient data management. The study emphasizes that security measures in the form of encryption and authentication of users is essential for preserving sensitive data. A modular system design is thus suggested to add scalability for further needs It also automates the hostel management processes, providing smooth and reliable operations in comparison with modern technology. [3] SSRG-IJCSE research further emphasizes sound design, management of databases, and secure data handling in management systems development. The key themes in the system include the automation of manual processes, reduction of errors, use of robust architecture and modular design to make it scalable, and the integration of user-friendly interfaces for usability. Data validation, encryption, and iterative development are also crucial to ensuring quality and reliability. These factors are important for building an efficient hostel management system that modernizes administrative tasks within educational institutions. [4] A study published by IJAES highlights the advantages of online hostel management systems, particularly their ability to offer web-based facilities for activities such as room booking and fee payments. The centralized database ensures real-time updates and cloud computing provides scalability for handling secure data. Authentication and encryption are identified as crucial security elements, in safeguarding sensitive information. Online systems reduce operational costs and improve efficiency, hence promising a better solution to traditional hostel management problems. [5] Research on hostel management software shows that the system has shifted from manual to automated, which greatly increases the efficiency of the operations. Database management is given importance so that records related to room allotment, fee management, and maintenance are handled securely and retrieved easily. The integration of user-friendly interfaces ensures that both administrators and residents can access the system. Security measures are highlighted to protect private information, and thus software-driven hostel management is superior to traditional methods. [6] In paper Hostel Management System Using ServiceNow, published in the European Journal of Molecular & Clinical Medicine, 2020, highlights the implementation of hostel management systems on a cloud-based platform ServiceNow. Hostel administration practices have been automated, from room allotment to charging of fees and tracking of maintenance activities with centralization offered by cloud features. Roles have been presented as the leading feature accompanied by encryption along with automated notifications that secure, communicate, and operationalize. This study highlights the benefits of cloud platforms, such as ServiceNow, in modernizing hostel management and enhancing operational workflows in educational institutions. [7] The paper Implementation of Hostel Management with Automation Using Design Thinking (2022) focuses on the development of a hostel management system using PHP and the MVC (Model-View-Controller) framework. Through the integration of automation and design thinking principles, the system significantly enhances both user experience and operational efficiency. By streamlining workflows and reducing repetitive tasks, automation minimizes human intervention, thereby reducing errors and improving accuracy in data handling. The adoption of a Model-View-Controller (MVC) architecture further strengthens the system by separating concerns, making it more maintainable, scalable, and adaptable to future enhancements. A major benefit of this design is its capability to accommodate real-time management of core operations such as room assignments, fee collection, student registration, and attendance tracking (Figure 7.1).

3. Proposed Solution

This solution will solve the various deficiencies of the current hostel management system, which was either manual or semi-automatic. Traditional systems are not efficient, accurate, and friendly enough to manage large volumes of student and administrative data effectively. The weaknesses are that it is time-consuming for room allotment, fee collection, maintenance requests, and record-keeping, and also error-prone and susceptible to data security risks by virtue of manual handling. Our computerized solution shall be finely integrated into the existing system to

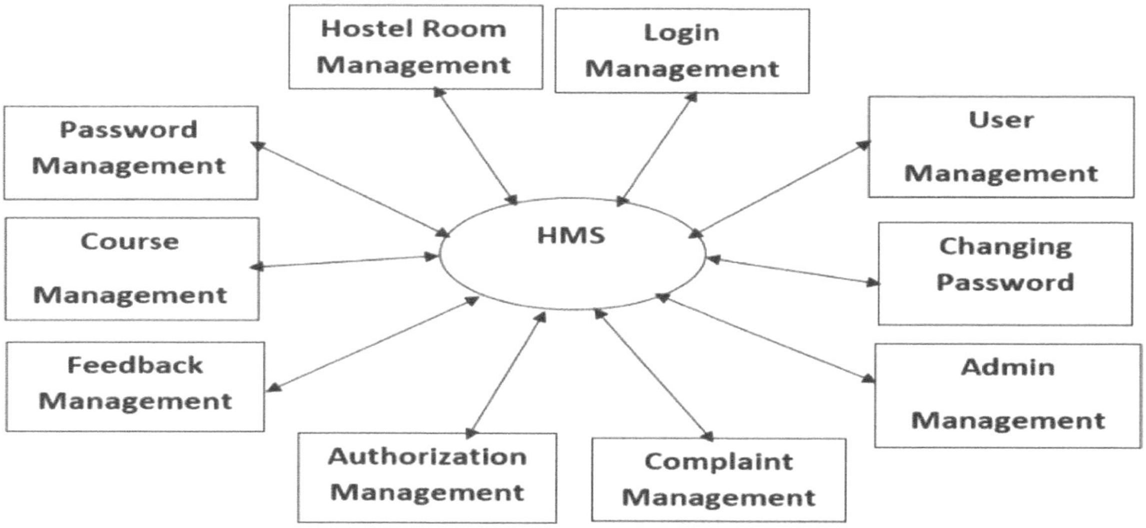

Figure 7.1. Flow diagram.
Source: Author.

introduce greater usability and an intuitive, GUI-oriented interface. Automation of core functions such as room assignment, fee tracking, and record management reduces the administrative burden of the activity, minimizes human error, and ensures consistency in performance. This move from manual to digital processes has made the experience of administrators smoother and quicker in handling the management process. This further makes our proposed system secure for data by incorporating role-based access controls, encryption, and secure data storage. The GUI-oriented interface brings the system to users at various levels of technical acumen, thereby making the transition smoother from the current system with a reduced learning curve. Quick navigation is enabled along with real-time updates about the data that will help in keeping all the concerned stakeholders informed and updated regarding all administrative processes, like status updates of fees or even requests for maintenance.

3.1. Registration page

The user registration page is the hostel management system's door to new students entering a hostel. This page is designed to capture all information regarding the student, including the student's name, student ID, contact details, and preferred room type. The webpage is user experience-oriented with an easy and simple interface that reduces the likelihood of input errors and increases accuracy for the entire process of registration. Once student information is provided to the computer system, it is then kept securely within one database with full management of hostel operations. This secure database not only helps in efficient room allotment based on the preferences registered and availability but is also integrated with the fee management system, allowing the administrator to track payments properly. With such integration, administrators will be able to monitor financial records and send timely notifications to students about upcoming fees or outstanding payments. Having all the information concerning the students in one place also increases communication because administrators can access and respond to a student's inquiry or maintenance request concerning a particular room assignment. The whole situation incorporates an enhanced student on-campus experience and guarantees that hostel management can rely on a framework for performing crucial operations. That is how the system provides a basis for the hostel environment to become organized because it ensures that the registration process is efficient and secure. Furthermore, its holistic approach fosters a sense of community and support within the hostel through streamlined administrative tasks (Figure 7.2).

3.2. Admin panel

To create an efficient, computerized hostel management system that addresses the limitations of the current manual or semi-automated system, we propose a user-friendly, GUI-oriented solution that is compatible with existing processes. By identifying the flaws in the current system, this design enables smoother operations, increased accuracy, and streamlined administrative functions. Here are the primary modules and functionalities of the proposed solution:

1. **Admin Login:** The system includes a secure login interface for administrators, allowing them to access and manage the hostel's information and operations.
2. **Admin Profile Management:** The admin can manage their profile, update personal details, and change

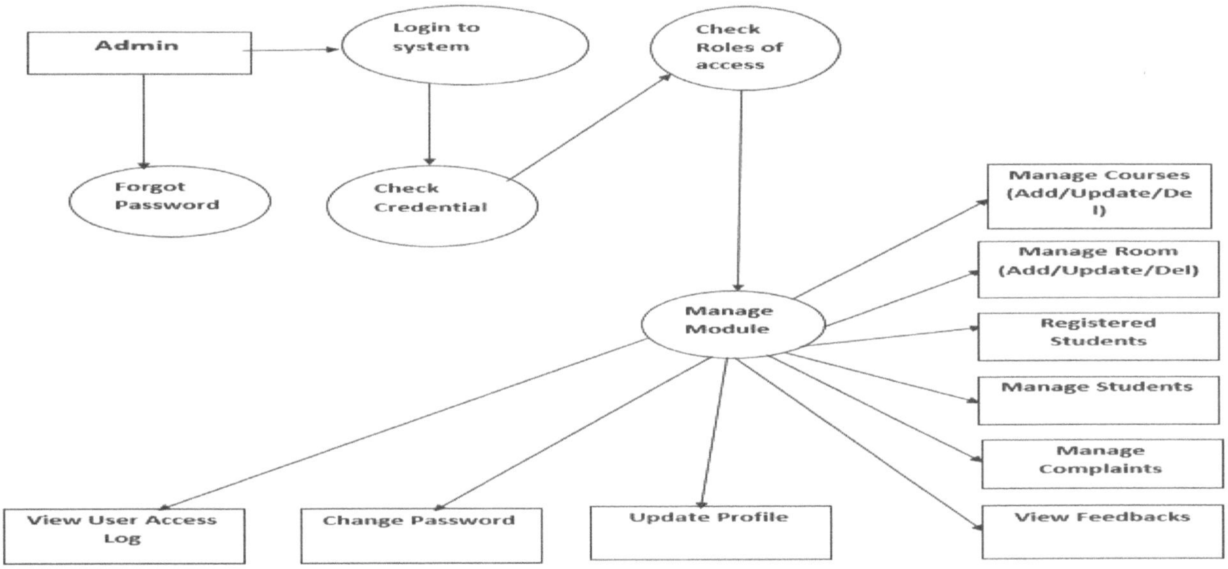

Figure 7.2. Data flow diagram for admin panel.

Source: Author.

their password when needed, ensuring personalized access and security.

3. **Courses Management:** Administrators have the flexibility to create, update, and delete courses. This feature is especially useful for hostels tied to institutions offering diverse courses, allowing the system to accommodate students based on their academic requirements.
4. **Rooms Management:** This feature allows the admin to create and manage rooms, assign available seats, and set room costs, offering a more organized approach to room allocation and pricing.
5. **Student Registration:** The system enables admins to create and manage student profiles, assign rooms, and organize registration records. This simplifies the onboarding process, with the ability to update, print, or delete student profiles as needed.
6. **Profile Handling:** The administrator can manage all student profiles centrally, with easy access to print profiles for official records or remove them once students leave the hostel, ensuring an updated database.
7. **Concerns Management:** This module allows the administrator to view and address student concerns, such as maintenance requests or other issues. By having a central platform for concerns, admins can respond more promptly and maintain a record of all resolved issues.
8. **Feedback System:** Students can provide feedback on hostel facilities and services, which administrators can review to make improvements. This helps the hostel management maintain high standards of accommodation and address any recurring issues.
9. **Forgot Password:** In case the administrator forgets their password, a password retrieval feature is provided, ensuring smooth access without compromising security.

3.3. User panel

1. **User Registration:** Use a user registration form to request the registration of new users, with all necessary information such as name, student ID, contact details, and preferred room type to capture all relevant data for effective management.
2. **User login:** the logged-in user is using an account already registered for that purpose; it logs on to a login form that enables entry of their username and password.
3. **Forgot Password:** Users are allowed to recover their passwords if they forgot them in a safe process. Clicking on the "Forgot Password" link will send them an email with instructions and a link to reset their password to ensure security for accounts.
4. **User Dashboard:** It takes the user to his dashboard single entry point for all functionalities along with important notifications, updates, and relevant information successful login.
5. **User Profile:** Users can manage their profiles, allowing them to update personal information, contact details, and preferences.
6. **Book Hostel:** This is a booking process concerning hostel rooms offered. They can pick the room type preferred and finalize it through the website.
7. **Room Details:** Users can view comprehensive details of their booked rooms, which may include room

specifications, amenities, pricing, and other relevant information to improve their stay.

8. **Student Grievance Redressal:** Students can complain about the stay or hostel facilities. In this way, students will be able to raise complaints and solve them.
9. **Input:** Students would be able to give opinions about their experience in hostels for providing better service and upgrading facilities.
10. **Password Change Update:** Add in the profile of the user a provision to change their password as part of account security and privacy features.
11. **User Access Log:** The system tracks the login information so that students can view the last login details. It is a security feature, as the users will be able to track their account activities.

3.4. Room details

Room Details, part of a hostel management system, offers consumers information on all the accommodations that are provided so that consumers can make the right decision. The details include the type of accommodation, whether single, double, or shared, whether it is occupied or not, the price, if air-conditioned, Wi-Fi, and furniture are available, and the size of the room. Through it, residents can view all the rooms and select the most appropriate according to their preferences to help managers effectively accommodate the space. A well-organized Room Details interface ensures convenient room booking, guarantees transparency in room occupancy, and makes handling easier.

4. Advantages and Future Scope

4.1. Advantages

1. **Automated Efficiency:** The Hostel administration System reduces the amount of human labour and administrative load significantly by automating important administrative processes including registration, room assignment, and fee administration. The system would also reduce the chances of error in data entry as the storage of data becomes centralized with validation tests during registration for more accurate records. The interface provided is straightforward and facilitates simple registration procedures, payment of fees, and management of rooms among students and administrators.
2. **Savings of Time:** The use of automated alerts, fee reminders, and speedy data retrieval increases the efficiency of the place and benefits both the employees of the hostel and its residents.
3. **More secure:** Login and sign-up processes are secured, ensuring the privacy of users and also the original data stored in the database.
4. **Scalability:** The system's modular architecture suits most institutions from the smallest to the largest ones. can interact with dynamic elements, unlike basic web scraping tools like BeautifulSoup, which only handle static content.
5. **Automation of Complex Workflows:** Selenium allows for the automation of complex multi-step processes such as logging into secure investigation platforms, searching for specific cases, downloading files, or navigating through nested pages.
6. **Interacting with Web Forms:** Criminal investigation systems often have search forms that require specific user inputs. Selenium can simulate human interaction, such as filling forms, setting filters, and clicking buttons, allowing for more targeted and specific scraping.

4.2. Future scope

1. **Mobile Application Development:** Developing a mobile version of the system for Android and iOS to enable students to access hostel services on their mobile devices.
2. **Cloud Integration:** Migrate the system to the cloud-based platform for easy access to data, scalability, and disaster recovery. This would ensure that service is reliable even during high usage periods.
3. **Advanced Analytics:** Developing data analytics that will give insights into student behaviour, room occupancy trends, and maintenance needs.
4. **Integration With Academic Systems:** The system is extended for integration purposes with the institute's database of academics to ensure a homogenous student management system, interlinking attendance, grade, and hostel activities.
5. **IoT Implementation:** Exploiting IoT solutions which include smart lock access through rooms and auto electricity tracking for improved security and the efficient usage of resources.
6. **Multi-Language Support:** Support for multiple languages in case of a student population or to make the system accessible to non-native speakers.
7. **AI Chatbot Support:** Implementation of AI-driven chatbots to handle frequent queries related to registration, feepayments, and room booking thereby enhancing user support and relieving staff from excessive workload.

5. Results and Discussions

The implementation of the Hostel Management System has significantly enhanced the efficiency, accuracy, and overall management of hostel operations. The transition from manual to automated processes has not only streamlined administrative tasks but also introduced a structured approach to handling student accommodations, fee management, security, and maintenance. The results of the system implementation demonstrate clear improvements in key areas such as data accuracy, operational efficiency, administrative workload reduction, security enhancement, and user satisfaction.

The system included strict security measures: user authentication, and encryption of the data, thus preventing unauthorized access to sensitive information of students. This ensured the elimination of data redundancy and consistency enhancement that made possible reporting and analysis with reliability.

Both the administrators and students welcomed the graphical user interface that made it fast to adopt. Updating records was easy, hence all information would be up to date with very little effort. The Hostel Management System has effectively modernized hostel administration in the way the system was realized well by users, who were satisfied with the hostels' ability to operate easily, enhancing efficiency, improving data accuracy, and making it accessible. The effectiveness and simplicity of the system were realized well by users, who were satisfied with the hostels' ability to operate easily, making the model suitable for educational institutions. of enhancing efficiency, improving data accuracy, and making it accessible. The effectiveness and simplicity of the system were realized well by users, who were satisfied with the hostels' ability to operate easily, making the model suitable for educational institutions (Figures 7.3–7.6).

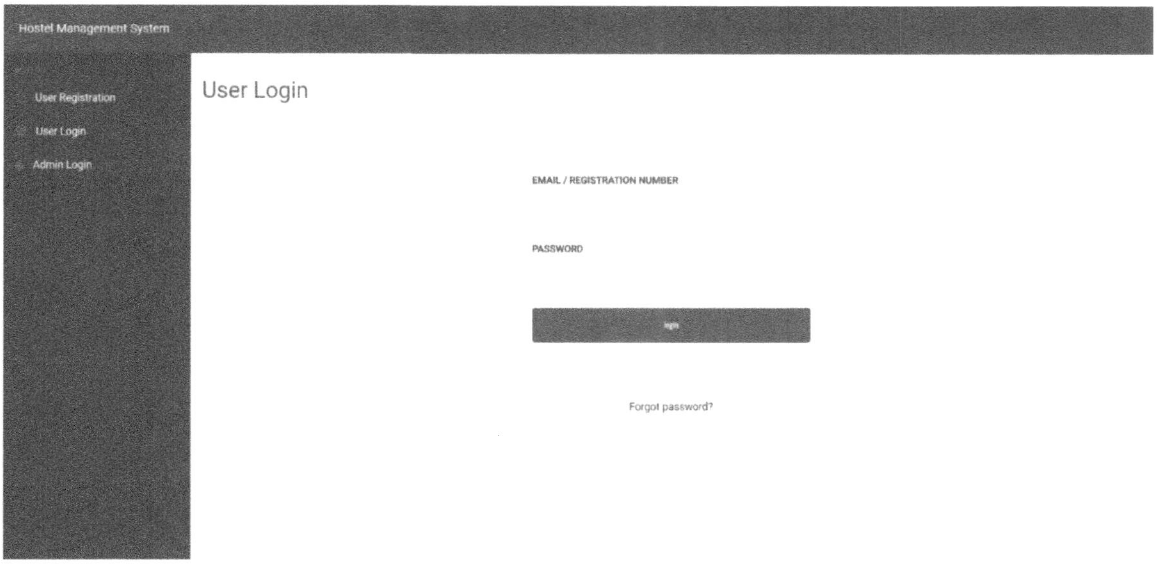

Figure 7.3. Login page.

Source: Author.

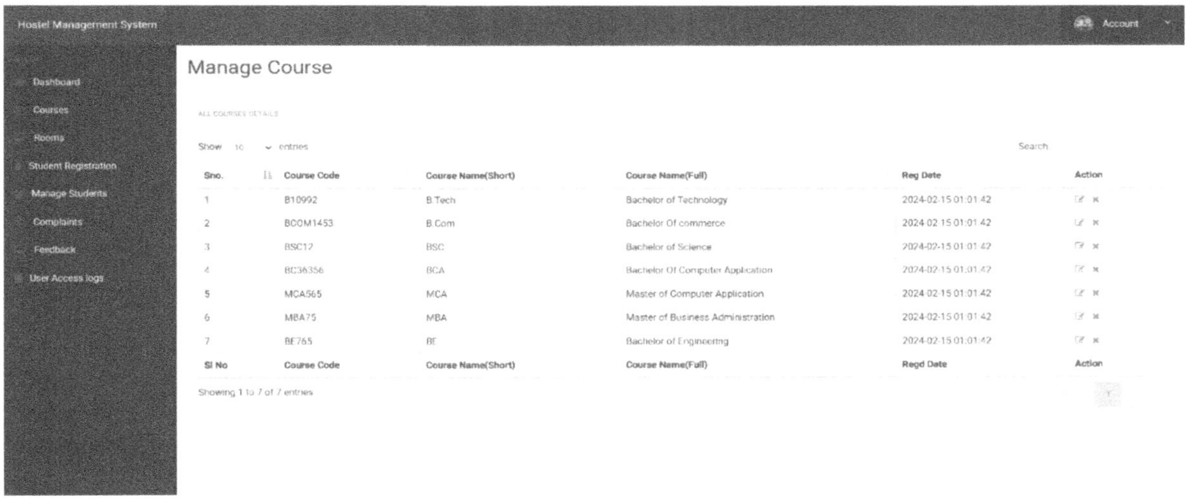

Figure 7.4. Course management page.

Source: Author.

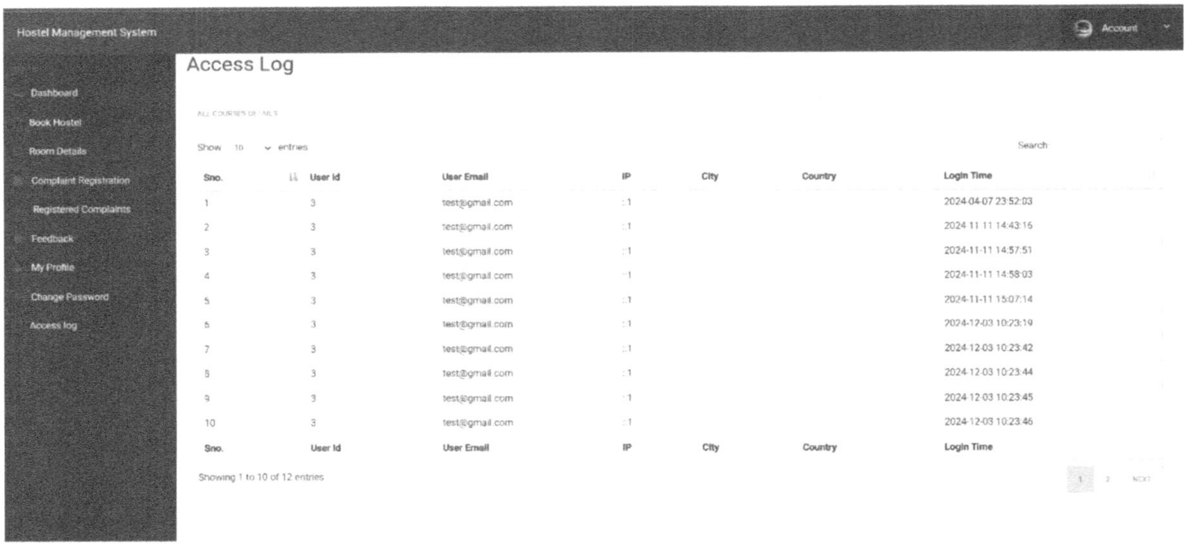

Figure 7.5. Access log.

Source: Author.

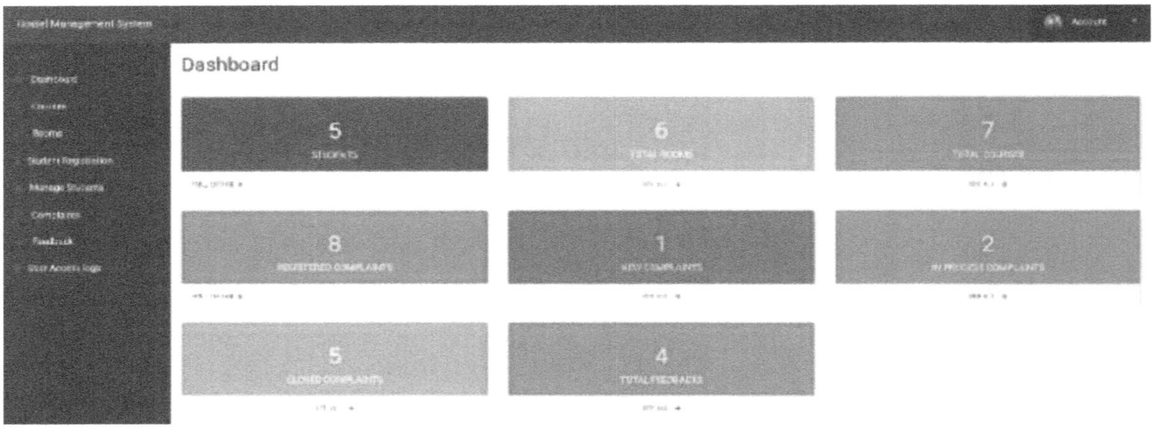

Figure 7.6. Admin dashboard.

Source: Author.

6. Conclusions

The Hostel Management System (HMS) presents a significant improvement over traditional hostel management method. By automating key administrative tasks such as room allotment, billing, maintenance requests, and communication, the system minimizes human errors and enhances overall efficiency. The improved accuracy in operations streamlines workflows, ensuring a more effective and organized approach to hostel management.

Security and Trust: HMS incorporates stringent security measures to safeguard sensitive student and financial data. Robust authentication protocols and encryption techniques ensure that personal information remains protected, fostering trust among students and administration alike. A secure digital environment also enhances students' confidence in the system, providing a safer and more reliable living experience.

Operational Efficiency and Staff Productivity: Automation reduces the burden of routine administrative tasks, allowing hostel staff to focus on value-added initiatives, such as student engagement and welfare programs. This shift not only improves staff productivity but also contributes to a more vibrant and supportive hostel community.

Communication and Transparency: The system centralizes communication between administrators and residents, providing students with instant access to critical information. A dedicated portal for inquiries and updates minimizes misunderstandings, fosters transparency, and improves the overall living experience. This seamless communication system enhances collaboration and ensures that residents' concerns are addressed efficiently.

Validation Technique: The effectiveness of HMS was validated through multiple testing phases, including functional testing, user acceptance testing, and performance evaluation. The system was benchmarked against existing manual and semi-automated methods to measure improvements in speed, accuracy, and security. Additionally, feedback from hostel administrators and students was gathered to assess usability and satisfaction. The positive response from users, combined with quantifiable improvements in operational efficiency, confirms the system's effectiveness in real-world scenarios.

References

[1] Choudhury, B., Kumar, D., Khatua, D. P., & Patro, A. K. (2017). Online Hostel Management System. *International Journal of Engineering Technology*, *4*(3).

[2] Agrawal, S., Rastogi, S., & Trivedi, S. (2023). Cloud-Based Hostel Facility Automation System. *2023 International Conference on Computational Intelligence, Communication Technology and Networking (CICTN)* (pp. 228–234).

[3] Ayanlowo, K., Shoewu, O., Olatinwo, S. O., Omitola, O. O., & Babalola, D. D. (2014). Development of an automated hostel facility management system. *Journal of Science and Engineering*, *5*(1), 1–10.

[4] Diyaolu, A. M., Abodunrin, O. B., Adedamola, A. A., Ogunode, R. S., & Omoloba, O. (2024). Development of an e-based hostel management system. *International Journal of Innovative Science and Research Technology*, *9*(6), 2456–2165.

[5] Wong, P. L., & Mahdin, H. (2022). Design and development of an online hostel management system to improve application and management processes. *Applied Information Technology and Computer Science*, *3*(2), 356–369.

[6] Jha, L., & Patil, H. (2022). A comprehensive study of and possible solutions for a hostel management system. In *Computing and Communications Engineering in Real-Time Application Development* (pp. 47–54). Apple Academic Press.

[7] Harina, P., Kavya, K. K., & Meera, S. (2022, November). Hostel management. In *2022 1st International Conference on Computational Science and Technology (ICCST)* (pp. 71–73). IEEE.

8 Job satisfaction dynamics of IT application owners in Agile frameworks

Dora Ioana Damian[a], Andreea Barbu[b], and Cătălina Radu[c]

National University of Science and Technology Politehnica Bucharest (ROMANIA); Academy of Romanian Scientists; The Bucharest University of Economic Studies, Romania

Abstract: The digital age has fundamentally altered organizational dynamics, propelled by swift technological advancements. This evolution has reshaped how organizations operate, communicate, and innovate, highlighting the need for a dual approach that integrates innovation with operational efficiency. Agile methodologies have surfaced as a vital framework, particularly in the banking sector, facilitating the management of the challenges posed by digital transformation. This study investigates the factors that influence job satisfaction among IT Application Owners (ITAOs) within Agile environments, a topic that is still underrepresented in existing research. By analysing three years of cross-sectional data from an international banking institution, this research aims to clarify how Agile practices affect the job satisfaction of ITAOs, contributing to a more effective work environment. The findings emphasize the significance of workplace support, professional development opportunities, and organizational culture, ultimately offering practical recommendations for practitioners and organizational leaders to enhance employee satisfaction and performance in Agile settings.

Keywords: Agile, digital transformation, IT Application Owners, job satisfaction, organizational behaviour

1. Introduction

The digital era has notably reconstructed organizational environments, directed by the swift technological advancements. These changes have influenced the entire organizational ecosystem, more exactly how organizations operate, communicate, and innovate. For example, the integration of digital tools has transformed organizational culture, providing a more collaborative and flexible work environment [2]. In response to these changes, Stanford and Harvard universities have collaborated on programs that address these challenges of leading change in large organizations: they emphasize the importance of creating an ambidextrous organization capable of balancing innovation with operational efficiency [23], particularly as digital transformation becomes a key focus for modern organizations, involving the adoption of technologies such as artificial intelligence (AI), machine learning, the Internet of Things (IoT), and data analytics. These technologies enable organizations to streamline operations, enhance the decision-making process, and improve customer experiences [24]. By adopting these approaches, organizations can better manage the transition to new technological paradigms and maintain a competitive edge [17].

In this context, even if numerous organizations engage in Agile transformations to enhance their capabilities and responsiveness to change, the true impact of these efforts is frequently not well comprehended. Agile transformations represent a relatively recent and intricate organizational phenomenon. Originally conceived and implemented within individual teams and projects, particularly in software development, organizations are now extending Agile practices to the enterprise level, influencing multiple layers of the organization. Based on this, the Agile methodology has emerged as a pivotal framework for international organizations striving to manage the current technological dynamism. This adaptability is vital for creating competitiveness and generating innovation in a globalized economy context.

This Agile methodology fosters a culture of continuous learning and improvement, employees being now encouraged to engage in ongoing professional development, which not only supports their skill set development but also contributes to higher levels of job satisfaction. The incremental and iterative nature of the Agile methodology allows dissemination of regular feedback and adjustments, ensuring that employees remain aligned with organizational goals and technological trends. Also, the company

[a]Damiandora226@gmail.com, [b]catalina.radu@man.ase.ro, [c]barbu.andreeab@yahoo.com

DOI: 10.1201/9781003778905-8

plays an important role in supporting Agile practices and principles by aligning talent management strategies with the dynamic needs of the organization. This involves recruiting and retaining individuals with the required skills to navigate through technological advancements and providing an environment that shapes an Agile mindset. For example, several studies from prestigious institutions such as Oxford, Stanford, and MIT underscore the benefits of the Agile practices, highlighting improvements in project success rates, employee morale, and overall engagement [26]. With this in mind, job satisfaction, as a pivot of organizational efficiency, is an important determinant of employee performance, retention, and effectiveness, particularly in fast-evolving sectors such as information technology (IT). The Agile framework, characterized by its iterative processes and emphasis on collaboration, has emerged as a main methodology within the IT industry, enabling organizations to navigate through these technological shifts more effectively [19].

More specifically, in the banking industry, where regulatory complexities and constant technological advancements determine unique challenges, comprehending the job satisfaction dynamics of different roles, including the IT Application Owner (ITAO), is essential for creating a productive work environment. Agile methodologies are particularly relevant in this context, as they encourage adaptability and teamwork, allowing employees to thrive amid constant change. In the banking industry, the IT Application Owner plays an important role in an Agile environment by ensuring that applications align with strategic goals, managing stakeholder expectations, and facilitating Agile practices, bridging the gap between business units and development teams, prioritizing features, and ensuring compliance with regulatory requirements. Based on this, IT Application Owners help organizations in the banking industry to stay competitive and responsive to customer needs through their ability to manage risks and adapt to new technologies.

Despite the growing prevalence of Agile practices, a significant gap exists in the literature regarding the factors that influence job satisfaction among IT Application Owners operating within this Agile framework. Previous research has identified several elements that contribute to job satisfaction, including workplace support, opportunities for professional development, and organizational culture [21]. This research provides a comprehensive analysis of the factors influencing job satisfaction among IT Application Owners (ITAOs) in Agile frameworks, highlighting the pivotal role these professionals play in the successful implementation of Agile methodologies, which have become a dominant approach in IT project management due to their efficiency, adaptability, and responsiveness to change. By understanding the nuances of how Agile practices impact ITAOs' job satisfaction, organizations can better support these key stakeholders, ultimately fostering a more productive and satisfying work environment.

To address this gap, this research paper aims to investigate the following key question: *What is the impact of Agile practices on the job satisfaction of IT Application Owners?*

By systematically exploring this question, this study seeks to contribute to a deeper understanding of the dynamics of job satisfaction in Agile environments. The findings are intended to inform both practitioners and organizational leaders, ultimately fostering a more supportive and effective work environment for ITAOs and enhancing their contributions to Agile projects.

With this in mind, this research paper is structured in two main parts: the literature review segment and the practical analysis: a study on the job satisfaction among IT Application Owners in a multinational organization. The literature review segment is focused on job satisfaction, Agile practices, and the specific role of IT Application Owners. This is followed by a detailed description of the methodology employed for data collection and analysis. Subsequently, the findings are discussed within the context of Agile frameworks, elucidating their implications for IT Application Owners. Finally, the paper concludes with recommendations for practitioners and suggestions for future research, aimed at enhancing the understanding and application of Agile methodologies in relation to job satisfaction, including current limitations of the study together with possible directions for further research.

2. Theoretical Framework

2.1. Job satisfaction

Job satisfaction exhibits significant variability among individuals, with some perceiving their occupations as enjoyable and integral to their lives, while others experience dissatisfaction or aversion towards their work. Evaluating employees' job satisfaction has become an important practice in organizations that prioritize both the physical and psychological well-being of their workforce. Job satisfaction is often conceptualized as a cognitive evaluation, where individuals assess both the positive and negative aspects of their role. [27] suggests that while job satisfaction is frequently described as an emotional response, it is more accurately understood as a cognitive reaction, involving weighing the quality of a job based on personal criteria. Historically, some researchers approached the job satisfaction topic through the lens of the need for fulfilment, examining whether a job meets an employee's physical and psychological needs [28]. However, contemporary research predominantly presents job satisfaction as an attitude, focusing on the cognitive assessment employees make about their work. Since 2004, the U.S. Congress has required annual surveys to assess federal employees' job satisfaction and leadership practices as part of the National Defense Authorisation Act [6]. These surveys evaluate satisfaction with leadership, work environment, rewards, and personal growth, highlighting the importance of job satisfaction for effective institution operation. Job satisfaction plays a central role in understanding workplace dynamics and organizational performance.

Job satisfaction exploration started in the 1930s with Robert Hoppock's pioneering work and developed equable with researchers' contributions as Herzberg, who created key theories on work motivation and satisfaction [9].

Today, job satisfaction is one of the most researched topics in organisational behaviour, as a study conducted in 2021, in the Clarivate Analytics (Web of Science) database revealed: over 366353 publications on the subject were registered. This vast body of work includes numerous disciplines, such as behavioural sciences, education, health sciences, and social sciences [4].

A landmark study by [13] continues to be widely cited, underscoring its lasting impact on the field. The growth in job satisfaction literature is notable in the publication statistics, as it can be observed in Figure 8.1: from 8 publications in the 1930s to thousands annually in recent decades. In 2020, there were 4188 publications, a number that took from 1936 to 1988 to accumulate.

This exponential increase in research highlights the importance and complexity of job satisfaction as a topic of study. It reflects the evolving understanding of how job satisfaction influences employee well-being, productivity, and organizational efficiency [22].

Both academic researchers and practitioners assess job satisfaction to enhance organizational outcomes and employee well-being, being a metric focused on the human resource health of an organization. Understanding job satisfaction helps to improve people's work experiences, identify factors that drive positive employee attitudes, and

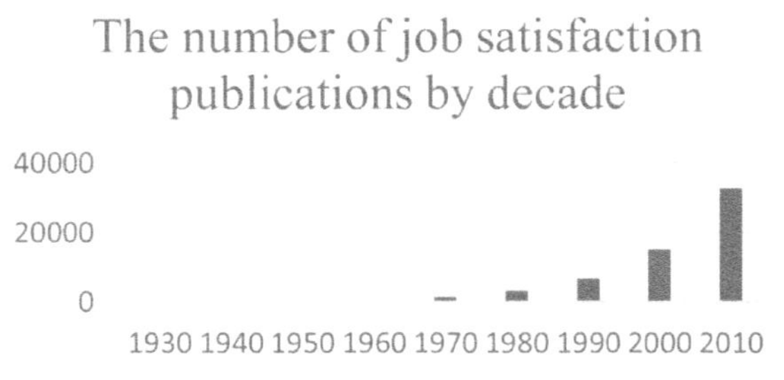

Figure 8.1. The number of job satisfaction publications by decade.

Source: Adapted from - Spector, P. E. (2022). Job satisfaction: From Assessment to Intervention. Routledge.

develop effective interventions. Standardized surveys are often used to measure job satisfaction, allowing for comparisons across different organizations or industries [13].

An illustrative example underscoring the significance of job satisfaction is derived from a 2020 study by the World Economic Forum. This research surveyed 2500 US workers and revealed that over half of the respondents prioritized their relationships with colleagues and immediate supervisors over their intrinsic interest in the work itself. This finding emphasizes the critical role of interpersonal dynamics and management quality in influencing overall job satisfaction [29].

Moreover, organizations such as Google [13] and Starbucks [18] have been recognized for their high levels of employee satisfaction. These companies actively integrate employee satisfaction into their strategic communication by fostering a positive work environment and increasing productivity. In this context, these examples demonstrate that job satisfaction extends beyond the nature of the role itself to encompass the work environment and interpersonal relationships within the workplace.

With this in mind, in the digital era, job satisfaction is essential, especially for roles like IT Application Owners as it directly impacts productivity, efficiency, and employee retention. Productivity will be increased through the fact that satisfied IT Application Owners will be more innovative and effective problem-solvers, contributing to improved application performance and user satisfaction. Additionally, promoting a healthy work-life balance helps prevent burnout, creating a positive work environment and increasing team morale together with teamwork. Opportunities for career development further motivate IT Application Owners, ensuring long-term commitment and engagement in their roles. Overall, job satisfaction is a key factor in maintaining a motivated, efficient, and stable IT workforce.

The role of an IT Application Owner is essential in contemporary organizational frameworks, necessitating a comprehensive understanding of both technical and strategic dimensions.

In essence, the IT Application Owner's role is characterized by a homogenous combination of technical acumen, strategic foresight, and various communication skills.

Based on this, the IT Application Owner is regarded as a robust role, including numerous and different responsibilities that ensure the alignment of IT applications with the business objectives, governance, compliance, performance management, continuous improvement, and resource management. More exactly, in terms of strategic management, the IT Application Owners are responsible for the IT applications alignment with the organizational strategic goals. They build the bridge between business stakeholders and technical teams [14]. Also, ensuring that applications comply with regulatory requirements and internal policies, represents another key aspect of the IT Application Owner role. These governance and compliance practices include: managing risks associated with data security and regulatory non-compliance, maintaining privacy standards, having an enormous impact on the overall organizational efficiency and generating significant financial and reputational repercussion risks for organizations [12]. Moreover, IT Application Owners are responsible for managing the applications' performance, identifying bottlenecks, and implementing solutions to enhance performance and reliability [3]. Continuous improvement is also a fundamental part of the IT Application Owner role through the iterative and incremental nature of their activities, more exactly through the performance metrics analysis, updates' implementation and functionality, performance of applications improvement [1]. Resource management for application development and maintenance is also a required aspect for IT Application Owners [11] given the fact that project completion on time and on budget, having the necessary skills and resources available to support application development and maintenance is crucial for the organization's success.

With this in mind, by ensuring strategic alignment, governance, compliance, performance management, continuous improvement, and effective resource management, IT Application Owners contribute significantly to the overall success and competitiveness of the organization, especially in the banking sector. For example, a banking institution might aim to develop its mobile banking application in order to provide a better user experience (UX) and create additional potential features such as: real-time transaction alerts, personalized financial advice, and integration with other financial services. The designated IT Application Owner would have to lead this initiative, ensuring that there is clean communication between business stakeholders, developers, and compliance teams to confirm that the application meets its strategic goals, regulatory requirements, and customer expectations.

Based on this, in the banking sector, especially in the digital era marked by continuous technological changes, the IT Application Owner plays a strategic role by ensuring that IT products are compliant, reliable, continuously improved, and efficiently managed.

2.2. *Agile methodology*

Agile methodology excels in delivering effective project outcomes even amidst complex and uncertain requirements. It achieves this by employing small, collaborative teams that frequently deliver increments of business value, prioritizing tasks based on business effectiveness, importance, and urgency. Any methodology can achieve success on certain projects and fail on others. While heavy processes can work, light processes are often more successful. Crucially, people involved in these projects frequently credit their success to the simplicity of the methodology [5].

The agile methodologies in software development started with Hirotaka Takeuchi and Ikujiro Nonaka, who introduced a new product development approach in a 1986 article, coining the term "Scrum" to describe a collaborative team method inspired by rugby [4].

Jeff Sutherland and Ken Schwaber later advanced Scrum in the U.S., while Dr. Alistair Cockburn contributed to the agile method known as the Crystal Family. These methodologies were developed to address the shortcomings of traditional project management, focusing on enhancing flexibility and teamwork in software projects.

In the late 1990s, Kent Beck and his associates were engaged by Chrysler to assist with a troubled software development project for its payroll system. Despite initial setbacks due to a formal development plan, Beck, along with Ward Cunningham, Ron Jeffries, and Martin Fowler, successfully revamped the project, marking one of the earliest instances of Extreme Programming (XP). This success was highlighted in the October 1998 issue of Distributed Computing. In 2001, Beck, Alistair Cockburn, and Ken Schwaber, among others, convened in Snowbird, Utah, to reconcile various competing methodologies, resulting in the creation of the Agile Manifesto. This manifesto, which emphasizes values such as collaboration, working software, customer involvement, and adaptability, as shown in Table 8.1, has since become a foundational framework for agile methodologies, guiding practitioners in the field.

Following the Agile Manifesto, a set of Agile Principles (Table 8.2) was created to guide agile project implementations.

These principles emphasize shifting focus from traditional plans and specifications to the value needs of sponsors and users. This means measuring success by the effectiveness of outputs rather than the amount of input consumed. Consequently, performance metrics for project participants must adapt from traditional measures (cost, schedule, resources) to new or modified ones [8].

2.3. *Agile methodologies and job satisfaction*

Agile methodologies have a main role in increasing job satisfaction for IT application professionals. By creating

Table 8.1. Agile Manifesto Pillars

Agile pillars
Individuals and interactions over processes and tools
Working software over comprehensive documentation
Customer collaboration over contract negotiation
Responding to change over following a plan

Source: Adapted from Agilemanifesto.org. (2020). Manifesto for Agile Software Development. (online) Retrieved from: https://www.agilemanifesto.org. Accessed on: 02.09.2024.

Table 8.2. The 12 Agile principles

Agile principles
Our highest priority is to satisfy the customer through the early and continuous delivery of valuable software.
Welcome changing requirements, even late in development. Agile processes harness change for the customer's competitive advantage.
Deliver working software frequently, from a couple of weeks to a couple of months, with a preference to the shorter timescale.
Business people and developers must work together daily throughout the project.
Build projects around motivated individuals. Give them the environment and support they need, and trust them to get the job done.
The most efficient and effective method of conveying information to and within a development team is face-to-face conversation.
Working software is the primary measure of progress.
Agile processes promote sustainable development. The sponsors, developers, and users should be able to maintain a constant pace indefinitely.
Continuous attention to technical excellence and good design enhances agility.
Simplicity–the art of maximizing the amount of work not done–is essential.
The best architectures, requirements, and designs emerge from self-organizing teams.
At regular intervals, the team reflects on how to become more effective, then tunes and adjusts its behaviour accordingly.

Source: Adapted from: www.agilemanifesto.org.

a transparent collaboration and communication framework, Agile encourages a supportive work environment where team members feel valued and connected. The flexibility inherent in Agile practices allows for quick adaptation to changes, thereby reducing stress and increasing overall job satisfaction. Continuous feedback mechanisms, through the iterative and incremental nature of the Agile methodology, ensure that issues are promptly addressed, leading to a sense of accomplishment and ongoing improvement. Additionally, the empowerment and autonomy granted to self-organizing teams boost motivation and responsibility among employees. Moreover, the focus on delivering high-quality products that meet customer needs provides a rewarding sense of purpose and achievement. Collectively, these factors contribute to a dynamic and fulfilling work environment for IT Application Owners professionals. Despite the extensive research on agile methodologies and job satisfaction, several gaps remain. Firstly, there is limited empirical evidence specifically focusing on IT application owners within agile frameworks. Most studies tend to generalize findings across various IT roles, overlooking the unique challenges and experiences of application owners [10]. For example, while developers and testers are often the focus of agile studies, the nuanced role of application owners is less examined. Secondly, the long-term effects of agile adoption on job satisfaction are not well-documented. While short-term benefits are often highlighted, the sustainability of these benefits over time requires further investigation [20]. A Stanford study suggested that while initial adoption of agile practices boosts job satisfaction, the effects may plateau or decline without continuous improvement and adaptation [25]. Lastly, there is a need for more research on the interplay between organizational culture and job satisfaction in agile environments. Understanding how different cultural contexts influence the effectiveness of agile practices can provide deeper insights into optimizing job satisfaction for IT application owners [7]. For instance, a study by Harvard Business School found that organizational culture significantly impacts the success of agile transformations [16].

3. Materials and Methods

3.1. Methodology

This study uses a survey designed to investigate the job satisfaction dynamics of IT Application Owners operating within Agile frameworks in a multinational organization within the banking industry, conducted on an institutional level, over a timeframe of three years (2021, 2022, and 2024). In 2022, the survey was put on hold due to managerial and administrative reasons. The three-year comparative analysis facilitated the observation of temporal changes and trends in job satisfaction, focusing on the job satisfaction impact of the Agile practices among IT Application Owners. This study comprises a series of several questions focused on different aspects such as job satisfaction and agile practices. The questionnaire was structured according to Agile's four pillars, mentioned in the literature review [15], categorizing the questions per each pillar in order to capture a holistic perception of job satisfaction among IT Application Owners in an Agile context: individuals and interactions over processes and tools; working software over comprehensive documentation; customer collaboration over contract negotiation; responding to change over following a plan.

According to the main objective of this study (to determine what specific aspects of the Agile practices contribute to or detract from the IT Application Owners' overall satisfaction), a comparative data analysis method was used in order to measure the impact of the Agile framework in the context of ITAOs' job satisfaction. The items taken into account are presented in Table 8.3.

Table 8.3. Questions analysed

Agile Pillars	*Related Questions*
Individuals and interactions	Do your skills and abilities find use in your job position (ITAO)?
	Do you have enough support from your colleagues to do your job?
	Do you have enough support from your manager to do your job?
	Do you feel that your role adds value to the company you work with?
	Are you part of an AGILE team?
	Is your manager aware about the scope of the ITAO role?
	Can you see a career path within the ITAO role?
	Do you have a development plan?
	Are you aware that the ITAO Role is available in Workday and you can remap your current role to ITAO Role after a conversation with your manager?
	What tasks as ITAO help you to grow professionally?
	Is your ITAO workload manageable?
Working software	In case you are performing activities on top of ITAO specific ones, please choose them from the list or add your input.
	Are you aware about the ITAO advisory group meeting – as the gatekeeper for all ITAO tasks where your concerns can be escalated?
Customer collaboration	Do you have enough authority to make the decisions you need to make?
Responding to change	Are you planning to hold an ITAO Role during the next 2 years?
	Did you attend last year at least one training for your professional development?
	Do you see any improvements for ITAOs during last year?

Source: Author.

3.2. *Description of participants*

A dual approach of both quantitative and qualitative research was used to conduct the study on a non-probability sample represented by IT Application Owners, being part of a multinational company within the banking sector, a fact that provided a wider perspective for the current research. The survey is distributed to the entire ITAO community, more exactly to 2200 IT Application Owners (2200 applications are managed by the researched organization and each of them has an ITAO assigned to it). From this sample, 542 respondents in year 1, 854 in year 2 and 428 respondents in year 3 were completing the survey. The reliability of the data gathered from this study is given by the collaboration of one of the researchers with the organization, which is being analysed for more than two years. It provides a detailed understanding of the phenomenon and an objective view, as the data was reviewed by the other two authors. The questionnaire includes questions related to the tenure and business division of the respondents to confirm the validity and reliability of research findings. Tenure diversity allows to capture a vast range of experiences and knowledge levels, which directly impact the study's 4 Do you feel that your role adds value to the company you work with? 5 Are you part of an AGILE team? 6 Is your manager aware about the scope of the ITAO role? 7 Can you see a career path within the ITAO role? 8 Do you have a development plan? 9 Are you aware that the ITAO Role is available in Workday and you can remap your current role to ITAO Role after a conversation with your manager? 10 What tasks as ITAO help you to grow professionally? 11 Is your ITAO workload manageable? 12 Working software In case you are performing activities on top of ITAO specific ones, please choose them from the list or add your input. 13 Are you aware about the ITAO advisory group meeting – as the gatekeeper for all ITAO tasks where your concerns can be escalated? 14 Customer collaboration Do you have enough authority to make the decisions you need to make? 15 Responding to change Are you planning to hold an ITAO Role during the next 2 years? 16 Did you attend last year at least one training for your professional development? 17 Do you see any improvements for ITAOs during last year? outcomes, offering a broad spectrum of insights and reducing the risk of bias that might arise from a homogenous sample. Also, this tenure diversity supports the understanding of how different levels of experience influence perspectives and behaviours within the organization. Most of the respondents have been in the company for more than 5 years (2021 – 34%, 2023 – 27%, 2024 – 30%), fact that highlights the relevance of the sample through expertise. Similarly, by including a variety of business divisions in the sample provides a holistic view of the organization, making the findings more generalizable and applicable across different functions within the organization.

3.3. *Data collection methods*

Data were collected through an internal online survey distributed via e-mail, administered once a year over a three-year period. The surveys were designed by a vendor company according to the organization's requirements to capture several areas of interest, including job satisfaction in an Agile framework. The questionnaire consists of several questions but 17 of them, grouped by Agile pillars, are used for this study. The aim is to assess job satisfaction level for IT Application Owners through the Agile lens. Each question is designed to register aspects related to different Agile principles, providing a comprehensive evaluation of their experiences and satisfaction levels in their current roles. The first section of the questionnaire focuses on the individuals and interactions Agile pillar. It highlights the importance of human relationships and transparent collaboration in creating an effective work environment. This section is designed to assess the value, support, and opportunities for professional development within the roles of IT Application Owners, the extent to which ITAOs can effectively utilize their skills in their current positions, the level of support they receive from both colleagues and management, their role value contribution perceptions, and the clarity regarding career progression opportunities. The awareness of the ITAO role within organizational frameworks is examined to capture how this impacts the career growth and role satisfaction of individuals within Agile teams. The working software Agile pillar reflects the importance of producing functional and valuable software as a key outcome. This section evaluates the relationship between the tasks performed by ITAOs and the overall development of effective software solutions. Also, the time allocation dedicated to ITAO-specific responsibilities is addressed, enabling an understanding of the ITAO prioritization approach. Moreover, this section evaluates the presence of other activities that may complement the ITAO role, thereby contributing to the software development lifecycle. Engagement with the ITAO Advisory Group, which serves as a pivotal channel for addressing concerns and facilitating dialogue regarding tasks, will also be scrutinized to ascertain its influence on the role's effectiveness and the quality of software produced. Customer collaboration is a cornerstone of Agile practices, highlighting the necessity of engaging with stakeholders to deliver meaningful solutions. This segment is focused on understanding the authority ITAOs possess in the decision-making process which impacts their activity and the collaboration process. The principle of responding to change highlights the Agile framework's inherent flexibility and adaptability in the face of evolving conditions. This section investigates professional development ITAOs' adaptability through an understanding of their plans for future roles within the organization, as well as their participation in training and development initiatives designed to enhance their capabilities. Additionally, perceptions of improvements and changes within the ITAO framework over the past year will be investigated, allowing for a comprehensive assessment of how well these roles adapt to changing demands and market conditions. By analysing these elements, the study aims to provide insights into how ITAOs can effectively navigate the dynamic landscape of their profession.

4. Results and Discussions

4.1. Results

This section introduces and analyses the data obtained from applying a questionnaire in 2021, 2023, and 2024, tool concentrated on job satisfaction dynamics among IT Application Owners of a multinational organization, through an Agile perspective. With this in mind, the study included a vast sample of IT Application Owners across various business divisions within the organization. The demographic data, including tenure and business division, intended to provide a contextual backdrop for interpreting job satisfaction dynamics. The average tenure percentage of respondents, who have been part of the organization for more than 5 years, providing expertise and reliability for this research, is 30.33%. The in-cause organization was subjected to an agilization process across the 2021–2024 timeframe, with multiple Agile practices being implemented in the talent management and employee satisfaction areas. Based on this, this study quantitatively assessed the job satisfaction for ITAOs through close-ended questions aligned with the Agile pillars. As shown in Table 8.4, a positive trend is observed for the individuals and interactions pillar, job satisfaction percentages for ITAOs across different topics being aligned with this Agile pillar for the 2021–2024 timeframe (data shows the percentage of respondents reporting high satisfaction).

For the skills matching the ITAO position, it can be observed that there is a notable increase in satisfaction, more exactly, from 2021–2024, the value increased by 13.80%. Additionally, managers' support area registered a 9.68% increase in this period, demonstrating a positive trend in leadership engagement. On the other hand, colleagues' support interest area had a relatively stable satisfaction level, suggesting a consistent and homogenous team dynamic among ITAOs. The ITAOs'

Table 8.4. Agile Pillar – Individuals and interactions

Topic	*2021*	*2023*	*2024*
Skills matching the ITAO position	71.40%	78.22%	81.30%
Colleagues' support	72.88%	72.83%	75.93%
Managers' support	77.31%	80.67%	84.80%
Role value contribution	66.05%	75.52%	73.59%
Agile awareness	53.87%	66.74%	61.67%
Managers' awareness on the ITAO role scope	75.46%	77.16%	83%
Career-path perspectives	27.49%	33.37%	36.21%
Development plan	43.91%	46.60%	48.13%
ITAO role remapping awareness	56.46%	58.89%	59.34%
Manageable workload	57.20%	52.22%	49.80%

Source: Author.

satisfaction level with the role value contribution for the organization initially had a 14.33% increase but then, in 2024, it decreased to the 73.59% value. Agile Awareness topic encountered the same phenomenon with an initial increase of 23.84%, then, by 2024, decreasing to 61.67% compared with the 66.74% 2023 rate. Also, ITAOs' career-path perspectives highlighted gradual improvement, keeping a positive trend but remained low, increasing from 27.49% to 36.21%. A very interesting point is related to the ITAOs satisfaction with manageable workload: it had a negative trend, decreasing from 57.20% in 2021 to 49.80% in 2024, evidencing a concern regarding workload management. A positive trend was also registered for the managers' awareness on the ITAO role scope with a 9.97% increase rate, suggesting better alignment between managerial support and ITAO responsibilities. Based on this, a positive path for the impact of the Agile methodology on ITAOs' job satisfaction but with potential areas of improvement was captured. To support this idea, an open question was designed to specifically capture the impact on ITAOs' job satisfaction through the tasks that supported their professional growth (see Figure 8.2). The areas that registered the highest percentages were skill enhancement and technical proficiency (3%), professional development and leadership through team-leading activities (23%) and networking and collaboration through cross-divisional work and high area scope projects (13%). Also, there was a high percentage of 14%, which reflected that a considerable part of ITAOs were not aware of the significance of their tasks in relation to their professional development.

For the working software Agile pillar, a quantitative question was introduced starting with 2023, based on the implementation of the ITAO advisory group meeting as part of the agilization process. It had a positive impact on the ITAO community's satisfaction level, increasing from 44% to 57.71%. As shown in Table 8.5, a positive trend was also registered for the ITAO as the primary role of the respondents, suggesting a better analysis, definition, and documentation of the ITAO role.

For the customer collaboration pillar, a quantitative question was developed, to measure the ITAOs' authority on the decision-making process. As shown in Table 8.6, the trend is stable, suggesting that ITAOs have exercised their authority in their area of expertise, following the Agile methodology of incremental and iterative work.

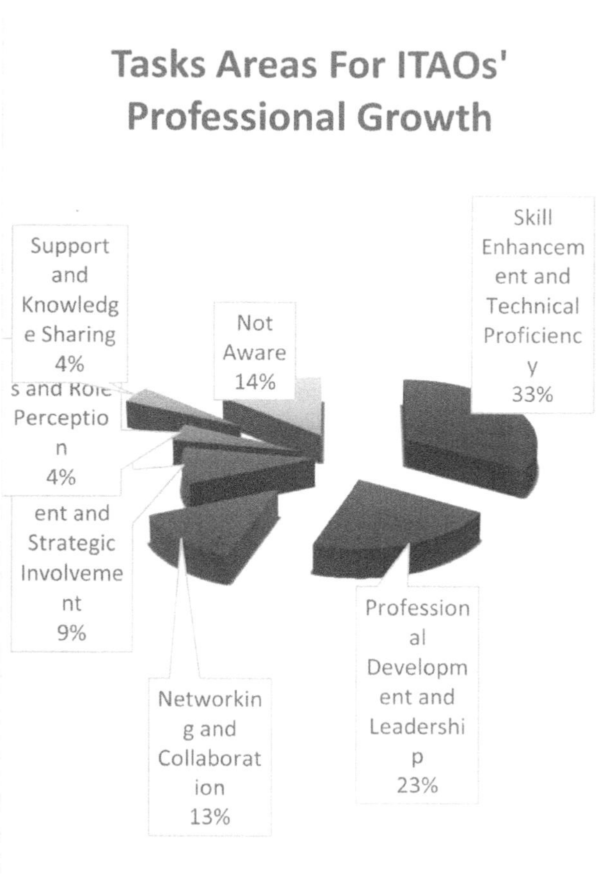

Figure 8.2. Task areas for ITAOs' professional growth.
Source: Author.

Table 8.5. Agile Pillar – Working software

Agile Pillars	*Topic*	*2021*	*2023*	*2024*
Working software	ITAO Council awareness		44%	57.71%
	ITAO as a primary role	23%	31%	40%

Source: Author.

Table 8.6. Agile Pillar – Customer collaboration

Agile Pillars	*Topic*	*2021*	*2023*	*2024*
Customer collaboration	ITAOs' authority on decision-making process	57.20%	57.14%	58.60%

Source: Author.

Table 8.7. Agile Pillar – Responding to change

Topic	*2021*	*2023*	*2024*
ITAO role continuity in the next 2 years	47.79%	52.10%	57%
Training for professional development attendance	53.14%	52.92%	58%
Improvements for ITAOs during last year		48.00%	53.92%

Source: Author.

Responding to change is a strong pillar for the ITAO methodology, creating an agile mindset through adaptability and proactivity. In Table 8.7, it can be observed that ITAOs have confidence in their role continuity over the next two years, suggesting an open attitude towards different changes, showing a sense of stability and security of their work environment through the clarity of the ITAO role created by the current organization.

The ITAOs' interest in professional development training sessions registered a slight decline from 53.14% in 2021 to 52.92% in 2023, before rising to 58% in 2024. With this in mind, the trend is positive in 2024, showing an increased commitment to continuous learning among ITAOs. In 2023, a question was introduced to this study, meant to register the ITAOs' perspective of the overall improvements in their role, the results from this registered a 48% value in 2023 and 53.92% in 2024. This positive trend demonstrates that ITAOs are recognizing tangible changes in their work environment, support systems and Agile practices. No. Topic 2021 2023 2024 1 ITAO role continuity in the next 2 years 47.79% 52.10% 57% 2 Training for professional development attendance 53.14% 52.92% 58% 3 Improvements for ITAOs during last year 48.00% 53.92% In this context, the data collected over three years highlights both progress and persistent challenges in job satisfaction among ITAOs within Agile frameworks. On one hand, improvements were observed in areas such as skills matching, managerial support, and Agile awareness. On the other hand, challenges remain in areas like career-path perspectives and workload management. These results answer to study's main objective: to determine how the Agile practices contribute to or detract from the IT Application Owners' overall satisfaction. Further efforts are needed to address concerns related to career development and workload sustainability.

5. Discussion

The results indicate a series of important improvements in job satisfaction among IT Application Owners (ITAOs) within an Agile context. It was observed that ITAOs reported a better alignment between their abilities and the position's requirements, generating increased job satisfaction. Also, management perceived as a symphony orchestra conductor, turning noise into a living whole of music, repre sented an instrument in the Agile impact on job satisfaction. Through the incorporation of effort, vision and leadership, it manages to accompany the individual instrumental parts into a whole symphony by offering support and guidance. Moreover, an improved awareness of the Agile practices was noted, creating a more cohesive and efficient work culture among ITAOs. With this in mind, these positive trends align with this study's main objective, more specifically to identify specific Agile practices that enhance job satisfaction. Despite these positive trends, several challenges were identified. Limited career advancement opportunities within the Agile frameworks, through the concrete and specific roles' scope and distribution was mentioned as a main concern by ITAOs. Also, high workload dimensions and the pressure to meet Agile deadlines continue to be an important challenge for ITAOs. In this context, by identifying and addressing these challenges, sustainable career development and an increased job satisfaction level for ITAOs can be created and maintained.

Based on this, to answer to the research question: *What is the impact of agile practices on the job satisfaction of IT application owners?*, several arguments can be introduced supporting a positive impact on the job satisfaction of ITAOs in the context of a multinational organisation. More exactly, this study revealed that during the 2021–2024 timeframe (except 2022), the implementation of Agile practices has generally increased job satisfaction for ITAOs. For example, the respondents' agreement on skills matching the ITAO position increased by 13.80%, showing better alignment between ITAOs' abilities and their roles. Furthermore, the managerial support, seen through the ITAOs' lenses, also registered an increase of 9.68%, indicating a strong leadership involvement. Colleagues' support represents another consistent point of this argument as it suggests a solid team dynamic. Agile awareness, an important indicator of the Agile practices' implementation in the ITAOs' spectrum, registered an initial increase of 23.84% with a minor decline appeared in 2024, still reflects a cohesive work culture. On the other hand, the ITAOs' manageable workload levels were reduced by 7.40%, suggesting possible areas of improvement regarding the workload pressures. Also, an initial increase in role value area was identified, followed by a decline, suggesting a need for concrete career advancement opportunities. With this in mind, multiple ITAO's tasks analysed in this study indicated a positive impact of the Agile practices on the ITAOs' overall job satisfaction, such as: skill enhancement (33%), leadership activities (23%), and cross-divisional projects (13%), generating a positive professional growth for respondents. These arguments build the answer of the current research question, that Agile practices positively impact the ITAOs' job satisfaction, but is very important to mention that further efforts are necessary to address challenges Ducu as: workload management and career development opportunities.

During this study, several limitations were encountered. One of them is related to the generalizability aspect, the current findings do not have the validity to be used in any domain; they can be restricted due to the specific sample size and diversity within the multinational banking organization, which might not reflect other industries or cultures. More exactly, cultural influences within the organisation also impacts the employees' mindset as this study is conducted within a concrete and solid organisational culture with unique characteristics that directly impact Agile practices perception and implementation. Based on this, the current findings may not be generalisable to other organisational contexts. Moreover, even if the questionnaire was anonymously distributed, since it was internally shared, some respondents might feel constrained to freely express their perceptions on the researched areas. Also, comparative analysis based on a three-year period has a limitation, despite its ability to observe trends, as these trends could be also influenced by several external factors, such as economic changes or organizational shifts over this three-year period. This limitation challenges the observation of how individuals' job satisfaction and perceptions of Agile practices change over an extended timeframe. In this context, the reliance on valid conclusions about the long-term effects of Agile practices on job satisfaction can be affected. Furthermore, self-reporting bias represents another key limitation as the reliance on this type of data generated through questionnaires may involve subjectivity. More exactly, the study's respondents can consciously or unconsciously provide answers that they believe are socially desirable or aligned with organisational perceived expectations, rather than their inner experiences. Based on this, this limitation can influenţe the study's results and the overall accuracy. Another possible limitation posed by this study is reflected in its findings. They may not be supported, validated by enough external sources, generating challenges on the reliability of the results. In this context, external validation is important as current findings should be compared in different organisational contexts to underline the validity of the results. Moreover, an important limiting factor of this study can be found in the survey design and instrumentation. This may influence the level of data quality. For example: incoherent language, unstructured survey, leading questions, or lack of comprehensive coverage of the study's relevant key aspects. With this in mind, by analysing and adjusting the above mentioned limitations, future research can incorporate a more comprehensive and detailed study on the potential biases and constraints affecting them, including improvement ideas and ultimately contributing to a more robust understanding of the impact of Agile practices on IT Application Owners' job satisfaction. These factors need to be analysed when interpreting the study's findings on the impact of Agile practices on IT Application Owners' job satisfaction. The impact of Agile practices on ITAOs' job satisfaction was analysed through the data captured over the 2021–2024 timeframe. In this context, numerous researchers have also tried to explore and measure the impact of the Agile practices on job satisfaction in the IT industry. For example, a study conducted in 2022 on 260 employees, measured the relationships between Agile work practices and occupational well-being [16]. The results of this study demonstrated that the direct effects of Agile work practices on employees' well-being were not significant, suggesting that the relationship between these elements is only indirect. In a supplementary analysis, the study tested the extent to which the direct and indirect effects developed when a high-performance work system was included. As a result, only the positive relationship between Agile work practices and job resources persisted, but not the relationship with job demands, nor the indirect relationships with well-being. This study is in concordance with the current research paper study, which also suggests that the advantages of Agile practices might be influenced by several factors. Moreover, the current results align with prior academic research concerning the impact of Agile methodologies on job satisfaction area. More exactly, in 2016, John Tripp and his colleagues examined how Agile practices can reshape work processes to increase overall job satisfaction reported at the Hawaii International Conference on System Sciences. In this context, it was observed that Agile methodologies often generate an increased alignment between employees' skills and job requirements, enhancing job satisfaction, fact that is consistent with the current reported experience of ITAOs in this study, who confirmed an improved alignment between their abilities and their position's requirements. This observation supports this study's findings, where ITAOs indicated a strong alignment between their skills and job requirements based on Agile practices. Additionally, in the Fatima Khurram's research focused on job characteristics and Agile practices, it was observed that by improving job autonomy and feedback systems, Agile methodologies can significantly increase job satisfaction. This research paper's symphonic analogy, where management is compared to a conductor orchestrating a harmonious team effort, illustrates how Agile practices create a cohesive and efficient work culture. This concept is also supported by Khurram's findings, which emphasize the importance of collaboration and feedback in Agile teams. Khurram's findings underline the importance of collaboration and communication in the Agile teams, which this research paper's study also identifies as key aspects in job satisfaction. Despite these positive trends, this study also identifies numerous challenges, such as limited career development opportunities within Agile frameworks and high workload demands. These concerns are also echoed in Sidky and Arthur's research, which discovered that while Agile methodologies improve different areas of job satisfaction, they can also lead to stress and burnout if not managed accordingly. This further emphasise the need for concrete actions and efforts to address career development and workload balance challenges within Agile frameworks. Based on this, the current study's findings imply that while Agile practices have significantly increased job satisfaction in certain areas, there is still a need for ongoing efforts to address career development and workload sustainability. In this context, future studies and research are worth focusing on career development programs by introducing a structured career development program concentrated on Agile principles to provide clear advancement paths for ITAOs. Another interesting topic for further research is the analysis of workload management in different types of organizations and the creation of strategies in order to ensure an equilibrated and sustainable work environment. With this in mind, by addressing these areas of interest, organizations can further improve job satisfaction levels and the overall well-being of their workforce, creating a solid bridge between them and one of their most valuable resources: the employees, leading to more effective and sustainable Agile practices.

6. Conclusions

This research analyses the relation between Agile practices and job satisfaction among ITAOs within a multinational organization in the banking industry. The comparative data spanning three years used in this study show significant improvements in the area of job satisfaction, especially through a concrete alignment between ITAO skills, role requirements, managerial support and by shaping an Agile thinking style among employees. In this context, these results demonstrate that Agile practices can serve as catalysts for creating a more satisfying work environment for employees, increasing organizational efficiency. Despite these positives, notable challenges still exist, especially in a dynamic Agile framework, such as: limited opportunities for career development, the pressures associated with heavy workloads and tight deadlines. Addressing these issues is an important aspect of maintaining these positive trends in order to create an efficient work environment. As organizations meet and address the challenges posed by the changes of the digital age, it is important to perceive Agile practices not only as operational frameworks but as integral components of an organizational culture that prioritizes employee satisfaction. In this context, further research should focus on exploring possible career development initiatives and strategies, together with innovative workload management approaches that align with Agile principles. Ultimately, by developing an Agile framework that supports the professional growth and job satisfaction of ITAOs, organizations can work toward a more resilient and malleable workforce equipped to thrive in the face of continuous change. This research contributes to the academic discourse on job satisfaction within Agile frameworks while providing some practical insights that can improve the effectiveness of Agile implementations in banking and beyond, being catalyst documentation between organizations and their workforce.

References

[1] Lameijer, B. A., Boer, H., Antony, J., & Does, R. J. M. M. (2021). Continuous improvement implementation models: a reconciliation and holistic metamodel. *Production Planning & Control*, *34*(11), 1062–1081. *https://doi.org/10.1080/09537287.2021.1974114.*

[2] Bozkus, K. (2023). *Organizational Culture Change and Technology: Navigating the Digital Transformation*. IntechOpen eBooks. *https://doi.org/10.5772/intechopen.112903*.

[3] Brown, T. C., O'Kane, P., Mazumdar, B., & McCracken, M. (2018). Performance Management: A Scoping Review of the Literature and an Agenda for Future Research. *Human Resource Development Review*, *18*(1), 47–82. *https://doi.org/10.1177/1534484318798533.*

[4] Clarivate Analytics. (2021). Web of Science: Job satisfaction – Results overview. https://www.webofscience.com/wos/woscc/summary/8431b79f-fd24-4b5d-9e76-b59a82bc3bde-1e29ab44. Accessed on: 02.09.2024.

[5] Cockburn, A. (2003). People and methodologies in software development. *Faculty of Mathematics and Natural Sciences*.

[6] Congress.gov. (2024). H.R.4986 - 110th Congress (2007–2008): National Defense Authorization Act for Fiscal Year 2008. Retrieved from: https://www.congress.gov/bill/110th-congress/house-bill/4986. Accessed on: 02.09.2024.

[7] Diane, E., Huff, S. L., & Tretiakov, A. (2009). The Impact of Organizational Culture on Agile Method Use. *System Sciences* (January). 1–9. *https://doi.org/10.1109/hicss.2009.436.*

[8] Goodpasture, J. C. (2015). *Project Management the Agile Way, Second Edition: Making it Work in the Enterprise*. Florida: J. Ross Publishing.

[9] Herzberg, F. (1966). *Work and the Nature of Man*. Cleveland: World Publishing Company.

[10] Hoda, R., Noble, J., & Marshall, S. (2012). Self-organizing roles on agile software development teams. *IEEE Transactions on Software Engineering*, *39*(3), 422–444. *https://doi.org/10.1109/tse.2012.30.*

[11] IBM. (2024). *Application Management*. Ibm.com. *https://www.ibm.com/think/topics/application-management.* Accessed on: 02.09.2024.

[12] Jones, M. (2019). Governance and Compliance in IT. *Information Systems Management*, *36*(1), 78–89.

[13] Judge, T. A., & Bono, J. E. (2001). Relationship of Core Self-evaluations Traits – self-esteem, Generalized Self-efficacy, Locus of Control, and Emotional Stability – with Job Satisfaction and Job Performance: A Meta-analysis. *Journal of Applied Psychology, 86*(1), 80–92. *https://doi.org/10.1037/0021-9010.86.1.80*.

[14] Raza, M. (2021). *What's An App Owner? Application Owner Roles & Responsibilities*. BMC Blogs. https://

www.bmc.com/blogs/application-owner/. Accessed on: 02.09.2024

[15] Manifesto for Agile software development. (2020). *https://agilemanifesto.org/*. Accessed on: 02.09.2024.

[16] Rietze, S., & Zacher, H. (2022). Relationships Between Agile Work Practices and Occupational Well-Being: The Role of Job Demands and Resources. *International Journal of Environmental Research and Public Health, 19*(3), 1258. *https://doi.org/10.3390/ijerph19031258.*

[17] Rowland, D., Thorley, M., & Brauckmann, N. (2023). *The Most Successful Approaches to Leading Organizational Change*. (online) Harvard Business Review. *https://hbr.org/2023/04/themost-successful-approaches-to-leading-organizational-change.*

[18] Schultz, H., & Gordon, J. (2011). *Onward: how Starbucks fought for its life without losing its soul*. New York: Rodale.

[19] Schwaber, K., & Sutherland, J. (2020). *Scrum Guide. https://scrumguides.org/scrum-guide.html.*

[20] Serrador, P., & Pinto, J. K. (2015). Does Agile Work? – A Quantitative Analysis of Agile Project Success. *International Journal of Project Management, 33*(5), 1040–1051. *https://doi.org/10.1016/j.ijproman.2015.01.006.*

[21] Spector, P. E. (2012). Industrial and organisational psychology: *Research and practice (6th ed.). Hoboken: John Wiley and Sons.*

[22] Spector, P. E. (2022). Job satisfaction: *From Assessment to Intervention. London:Routledge.*

[23] Stanford Graduate School of Business. (2019). Leading Change and Organisational Renewal. *https://www.gsb.stanford.edu/exec-ed/programs/leading-change-organizationalrenewal.*

[24] Stanford Graduate School of Business. (2024). Digital Transformation: Leading Organisational Change. *https://www.gsb.stanford.edu/exec-ed/programs/digital-transformation.*

[25] Stanford University, 2021. "Sustaining job satisfaction in agile teams: A longitudinal analysis". *Stanford University Press.*

[26] Stettina, C., J., Victor Van Els, Job, C., and Joost, V. (2021). The Impact of Agile Transformations on Organizational Performance: A Survey of Teams, Programs and Portfolios. *In Lecture Notes in Business Information Processing,* 86–102. *https://doi.org/10.1007/978-3-030-78098-2_6.*

[27] Weiss, Howard M. (2002). Deconstructing Job Satisfaction. *Human Resource Management Review,* 12 (2): 173–94. *https://doi.org/10.1016/s1053-4822(02)00045-1.*

[28] Wolf, M. G. (1970). "Nedd gratification theory: A theoretical reformulation of job satisfaction/dissatisfaction and job motivation". *Journal of Applied Psychology*, 54(1, Pt.1), 87–94. *https://doi.org/10.1037/h0028664.*

[29] World Economic Forum (2020). The Future of Jobs Report 2020. (online) Retrieved from: *https://www.weforum.org/publications/the-future-of-jobs-report-2020/. Accessed on: 02.09.2024.*

9 Language as a Sales Tool: The Power of Multilingual Pricing Tags

Pavol Lipták[1,a] *and Filip Kalaš*[2,b]

[1]Department of Marketing, Faculty of Commerce, University of Economics in Bratislava, Bratislava, Slovak Republic, Slovakia
[2]Department of Linguistics and Translation, Faculty of Applied Languages, University of Economics in Bratislava, Bratislava, Slovak Republic, Slovakia

Abstract: In an increasingly globalized world, language barriers are becoming a significant obstacle in retail. This study explores how multilingual product labelling and advanced technologies such as QR codes can contribute to removing these barriers. Based on our research, we found that consumers, value access to information in a language they understand, and that this information has a significant impact on their purchasing decisions. The study found that 73% of respondents support the introduction of multilingual pricing tags in stores. 35% of respondents are willing to pay a higher price for a product with detailed information in a language they understand. Furthermore, the study emphasizes the importance of sustainable and innovative solutions, such as QR codes and mobile applications, which can provide multilingual information while minimizing the environmental impact of printed materials. The research provides new insights into how retailers can use language as a strategic tool to increase sales and build stronger customer relationships. Our findings provide new insights into how retailers can use language as a strategic tool to increase their sales, build stronger customer relationships and eventually decrease environmental footprint.

Keywords: Consumer behaviour, customer decision-making, customer experience, global retail, innovations, language barriers, multilingual pricing tags, QR codes, retail, retail innovation

1. Introduction

In today's digital world retail is constantly changing and evolving. QR codes, augmented reality and personalized mobile apps are changing the way we shop and the need for innovation, particularly in digital technology is confirmed by studies [1, 2] and [3] Even though technology is constantly advancing, language barriers still represent a significant barrier to a seamless shopping experience.

At the same time the increasing use of automation of various activities in retail through human-robot collaboration is confirmed by a recent study [4]. For these innovative approaches to be effective, they need to be implemented in a comprehensive manner, considering the entire supply chain as emphasized by the authors [5].

Our study focuses on how language barriers affect consumer decision-making and what potential modern technologies have to mitigate this problem. Through extensive research we found that consumers increasingly value access to information in a language they understand not only in the form of texts but also through various multimedia elements.

This study aims to investigate the effectiveness of QR codes in providing multilingual product information in retail settings. Drawing on the key findings of a study [6] regarding the increasing consumer demand for multilingual information, we will analyse the potential of these technologies to overcome language barriers and enhance the customer experience. Furthermore, building upon the research [7] and [8], we will explore consumer preferences for these technologies and identify the challenges associated with their implementation in a retail environment. By comparing the effectiveness and feasibility of QR codes, this study will provide valuable insights for retailers seeking to improve their communication strategies and enhance customer satisfaction in an increasingly globalized market.

2. Methodology

Our study adopted a comprehensive approach that combined analysis of existing knowledge and empirical research. Secondary data were obtained through a deep review of the foreign literature. We used Scopus and

[a]pavol.liptak@euba.sk, [b]filip.kalas@euba.sk

DOI: 10.1201/9781003778905-9

Google Scholar databases to identify relevant studies. We then subjected these studies to methods of analysis and inference to extract key findings and theoretical frameworks relevant to our study. By synthesizing these findings, we created a comprehensive picture of the current state of knowledge in the field.

Primary data were collected through an online questionnaire. The questionnaire included both structured and unstructured questions and we used a number of open-ended questions as well as Likert scales that focused on consumers' broader understanding of their requirements and preferences in the retail industry as well as their language skills and ability to obtain information about products abroad.

A combination of random sampling was used to obtain a representative sample of respondents. Random selection ensured that each member of the target population had an equal chance of being included in the sample. Respondents were randomly selected from online panels and contacted via email. A total of 140 respondents between the ages of 18 and 44, most of whom were college-educated residents of regional cities with regular travel experience, participated in the study. We adjusted our sample of respondents for outliers and worked with a sample of 136 respondents in the research. In terms of language proficiency, English was the predominant language, but we also noted proficiency in other languages such as German, French, and Spanish.

The chosen sampling method allowed us to obtain relevant data on the attitudes and preferences of consumers who frequently travel abroad. However, it should be kept in mind that online questionnaires may be rather accessible to more digitally skilled individuals, which may slightly bias the results. Another limitation is that the sample was restricted to Slovak residents, which may limit the generalizability of the results to other countries.

The chi-square test is a statistical method commonly used in data analysis to determine if there is a significant association between two categorical variables. By comparing observed frequencies to expected frequencies, the chi-square test can determine if there is a significant relationship between the variables.

We applied the following formula:

$$x^2 = \sum_i \frac{(O_i - E_i)^2}{E_i}$$

where,

- x^2 Chi-Square value
- O_i Observed frequency
- E_i Expected frequency

The chi-square test helps us answer the above question by comparing the observed frequencies to the frequencies that we might expect to obtain purely by chance. We are almost at the implementing aspect of chi-square tests, but there's one more thing we need to learn before we get there. In order to fully understand the distribution of a variable, both descriptive statistics and a chi-square test are essential tools. Descriptive statistics provide a snapshot of the data, while a chi-square test can reveal important relationships between categorical variables. The normal distribution is a fundamental concept in statistics and is often used to model variables in experiments. We used the method of comparison to compare our results with existing knowledge. By comparing our findings with other relevant study results. We identified similarities and differences in other authors that contributed to a deeper understanding of the issue under study and were able to make relevant recommendations based on them.

3. Results and Discussion

Author Liewkasemsant in his study [9] focuses on the challenges associated with international cooperation using the Thai retail industry as an example. He discusses the issue of language barriers that arise when communicating with foreign language customers within a business. According to the author it is essential to invest in language training for employees especially in English language, which is supported by another study [10, 11] focusing on the Malaysian retail industry.

Liewkasemsant further states that the success of businesses in the international market is closely linked to their ability to attract new customers. This requires constant adaptation to changing market needs and the introduction of new technologies. In this way businesses can better position themselves in a competitive market and meet the expectations of foreign customers.

Interesting findings in the context of communication are presented in a study [12] which focused on the impact of the timing of the use of different language styles in customer interactions. While other research has often emphasized the importance of either a cognitive (focusing on expertise and competence) or affective (focusing on emotion and empathy) approach, this study shows that the best results are achieved by combining both approaches. However, the timing of when these styles are used is key. The beginning of the conversation is the ideal moment to demonstrate expertise and competence which builds trust with the customer. At the end of the interaction, it is again appropriate to use affective language which will strengthen the relationship with the customer and leave a positive impression. Therefore, this research suggests that effective customer communication is not just about what we say, but also when we say it.

The problem arises when the employee does not know the language in which the customer communicates. As Liewkasemsant [9] states, the success of businesses in the international market is closely related to their ability to attract new customers. Therefore, knowledge of multiple languages or at least one world language is key to building trusted relationships with customers from different parts of the world. Although the study by Packard [12] provides valuable insights into how to use language more effectively, it is important to recognize that a fundamental prerequisite for successful communication is mutual understanding which is achieved primarily through shared language. In making these claims we rely on important findings from a study by Pappas [13].

Shopping abroad can be challenging for customers especially if they do not know the local language. Missing or unclear product information can lead to dissatisfaction and reduced sales. Therefore, we decided to investigate what information customers, value most (Figure 9.1).

The survey results clearly point to the importance of language as a key factor influencing consumer behaviour. The chart shows that up to 73% of respondents support the introduction of multilingual price labels in shops. This high proportion indicates that the majority of consumers consider the language barrier to be a significant obstacle to navigating the product range and making purchasing decisions. Multilingual price labels could help significantly to remove this barrier and increase convenience and customer satisfaction.

The findings of this survey confirm the importance of visual communication and the role that price tags play in conveying product information. It is not only the price itself but also other important data such as composition, weight or country of origin. If the consumer does not understand the language in which this information is presented misunderstandings and dissatisfaction may arise. Multilingual price labels could improve the overall quality of communication between the shop and the customer.

While the study by Quinones [14] focuses on the broader context of technology in retail its findings have direct implications for the language barrier. The authors highlight that investment in new technologies such as translation applications, chatbots and virtual assistants can greatly facilitate communication between businesses and customers from different cultural backgrounds.

It is clear from the studies presented that language plays a key role in the consumer decision-making process. While Liewkasemsant's study highlights the importance of language in cross-cultural communication and its impact on building trusting relationships with customers the study on green products [15] focuses on how language influences the perception and evaluation of products. The common denominator of the studies in question is obvious – effective communication based on understanding is the key to success in the marketplace.

In order to make the best use of this knowledge in practice it is necessary to combine employees' linguistic competence with a solid knowledge of the target market. This means not only knowing a foreign language but also understanding the cultural specifics and customer preferences. It is also important to pay attention to the language used on product packaging. Clear, concise and understandable information that resonates with the values of the target group is the key to successful green product marketing [15].

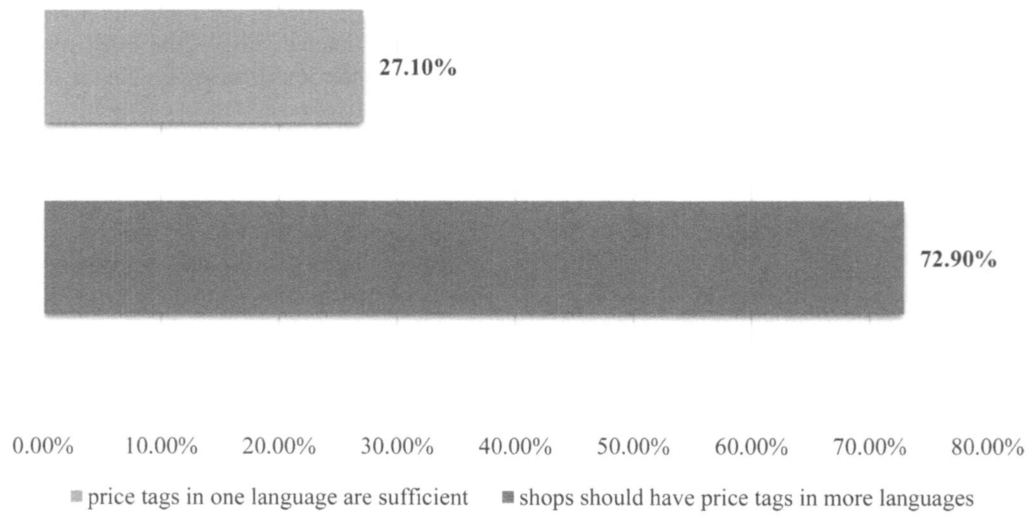

Figure 9.1. Should prices in stores be listed in multiple languages?

Source: The data for this graph was obtained through original data processing of our survey results.

4. Customer Needs in a Multicultural Environment

What information do we look for when we shop abroad? The answers to this question can have a significant impact on the way we present products and communicate with customers. Our research focused on what information is most important to customers when shopping abroad drawing on a literature review [16].

Based on the responses we can conclude that customers most value practical information to help them make decisions when shopping abroad. Their greatest need seems to be for a quick and accurate conversion of prices into their home currency, which would allow them to compare prices of different products more easily. However, in addition to price customers also care about other information about the product such as its composition, country of origin or name in English. This information is particularly important when buying food and other specific products.

Customers would also like price labels to contain multilingual information especially in English which is the international language of trade. Another interesting finding is the interest in additional information such as nutritional values, ecological footprint or specific product characteristics. This suggests that customers want to be increasingly informed and are interested in knowing details about the products they buy.

Based on these findings it would be possible to develop a universal price tag system that would meet the requirements of most customers.

This system should contain basic information such as the price in local currency and in euros, the name of the product in the local language and in English and a brief description of the product. For foodstuffs and other specific products, it would also be useful to include additional details such as composition, country of origin and nutritional values.

For even greater flexibility and personalization technologies such as QR codes could be used to link to websites with detailed product information. Such a feature would provide customers with exactly the information they need while saving space on the price tag itself. Intelligent systems could analyse large amounts of textual data and produce accurate and contextually relevant translations significantly reducing the time and cost associated with manual translation.

5. Consumer Preferences and Purchasing Behaviour

Every consumer has different buying habits and expectations that influence how they make product choices. Quality is important to some; price is important to others, and some are careful to understand everything on price tags and packaging. It is often the language and availability of product information that determines whether a customer leaves satisfied or frustrated.

The results show us that language and the way information is presented are important factors that influence

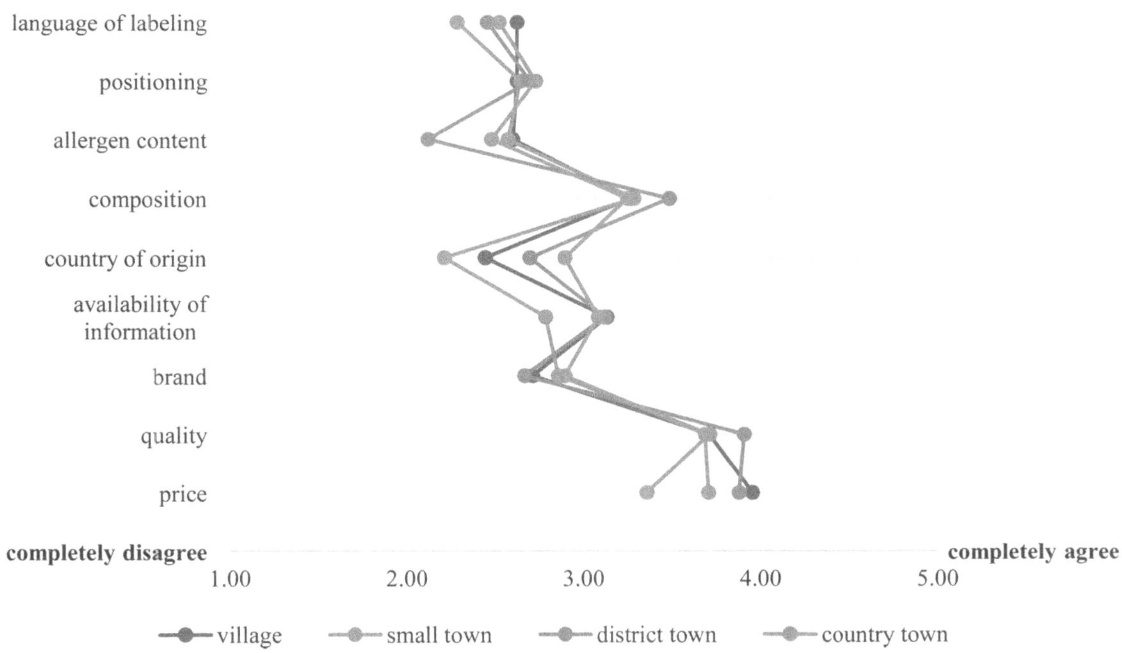

Figure 9.2. The urban-rural divide: What consumers want.

Source: The data for this graph was obtained through original data processing of our survey results.

buying behaviour regardless of whether we are buying food, souvenirs or other specific products.

Figure 9.2 shows us that urban and rural consumers have different expectations when it comes to product information. While people in urban areas prefer modern solutions such as QR codes and apps that allow them to get product details directly on their phone, rural consumers place more emphasis on clear and understandable information directly on price tags.

This difference is probably due to the better availability of technology in cities but also to the higher expectations of urban consumers who are used to quick access to information. In rural areas, there is still a strong emphasis on simplicity and practicality – a price tag that includes basic information can be key to a pleasant shopping experience.

The figure also shows us that consumers' preferences are not just about where they live but also about their individual needs and expectations. We can see that the language of product labels is important across all regions, showing that clear and understandable communication is essential for successful sales. In addition, for urban customers the visual aspect of the information is often important – attractive and detailed labelling can be a critical factor.

Rural consumers on the other hand value simplicity and practicality with a strong emphasis on basic information such as price and ingredients. These findings underline that retailers should create flexible solutions that take into account the diverse needs of their customers while striving to present information in the most comprehensible way for all.

Despite the growing popularity of QR codes in urban areas, their implementation in rural areas still faces a number of significant obstacles. For example, the biggest challenges in these areas may be the low internet coverage, which in the context of QR code use may constitute a barrier to customers who in rural areas often have limited options and are less inclined to learn how to use new technologies. There are a number of ways in which the implementation of QR codes could be extended to these areas:

- Providing free internet connectivity for consumers on-premises could also make it possible to scan QR codes on the spot for customers who do not have access to the internet, either due to poor coverage or a lack of attitude towards the use of new technologies – older people, especially in rural areas, often only use mobile phones or smartphones to make calls and therefore do not have a subscription to the internet.
- An on-site scanner could display information from the database to consumers even if internet coverage is zero. Thus, consumers in rural areas would still be able to access the same information as in large cities, with the only disadvantage for the retailer being some major investment in the equipment and its installation on the premises.
- A third solution, in terms of efficiency of use, would be for consumers to implement NFC chips in price tags, which allow contactless data transfer between the phone and the price tag. The use of chips with this technology would allow customers to have instant access to product information even if they do not have an internet connection, which would increase their satisfaction and simplify their purchasing decision.

The implementation of QR codes and related proposed alternatives in rural areas may represent a significant step forward in several countries. By building and transforming rural environments into 'tourist friendly' areas, it can attract foreign visitors and thus increase sales and revenues.

In Figure 9.3 we can see how often customers visit different retail store formats. Supermarkets are clearly the most visited, with more than half of respondents visiting

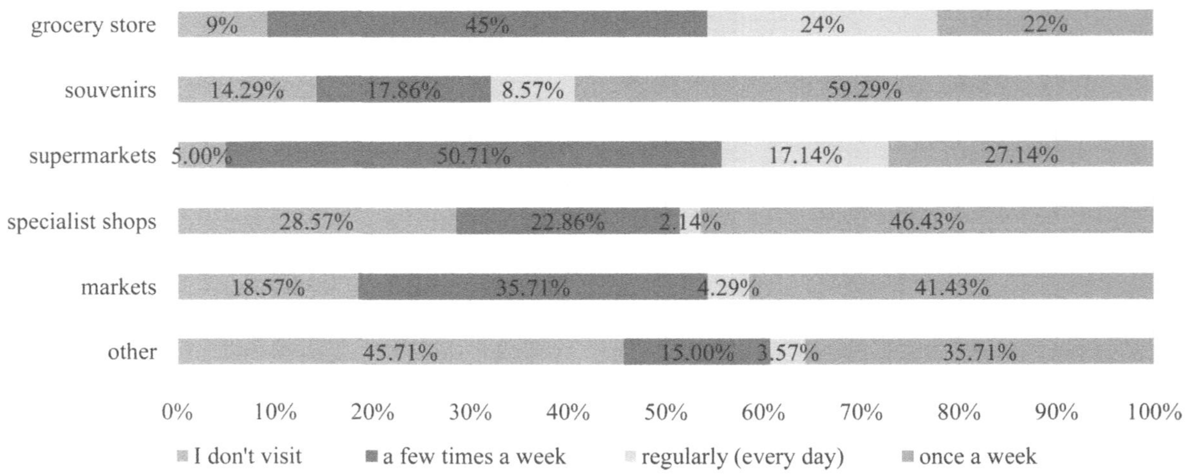

Figure 9.3. Shopping patterns of consumers across different retail formats.

Source: The data for this graph was obtained through original data processing of our survey results.

several times a week. Grocery stores are also popular but with fewer regular visits.

The data on specialist shops and markets is also interesting, where we see that customers visit them either occasionally or once a week. This trend suggests that these formats play a complementary role in shopping, often targeting specific needs such as fresh food or different specialities.

Souvenir shops are logically the least frequented, with the highest percentage of visitors visiting them only occasionally. This pattern of behaviour reflects their specific use, which is not an everyday necessity.

6. Economic Aspects and the Future of Multilingual Solutions

The topic of multilingual solutions can be looked at from several perspectives. In the case of large international chains, it is more effective in the long run to address this idea efficiently – by investing in innovative solutions that will attract customers and increase the competitiveness of the business. In the short term, on the other hand, such solutions require high investments that small local operations cannot afford.

Our study highlights the needs of consumers and shows the trend in which society is moving in the international environment. The survey results clearly indicate that up to 99% of respondents are proficient in at least one world language, with up to 97% of respondents indicating that they are proficient in English. Therefore, if we were to make recommendations also for small local businesses that are visited by foreign customers, we would be able to make recommendations that would cost minimal investment to implement.

Our research brings relevant data to the topic, based on which we are able to set recommendations and suggestions for transforming any retail operation. The data shows that consumers want to be informed and that they demand this information from the retailer. Up to 68% of respondents said that they need to have some information about a product before they buy it abroad, and up to 90% of respondents use some kind of technology (translators, etc.) to search for product information.

Based on the above information, we can conclude that if 99% of respondents know at least one world language, 97% of them know English and up to 90% of respondents use applications to obtain information, because there is not enough information in a language they understand on the store or product, we can suggest a basic recommendation – to provide price tags in at least one world language, specifically in English.

In the case of conventional paper price tags in small stores, there would be minimal costs associated only with the modification and printing of new price tags. However, for larger multinationals, we would recommend the introduction of electronic price tags, where this information could also be multilingual.

Overall, this subsection is supported by our research. Up to 72% of respondents think that all shops should be required to provide information in more than one language, with one in three respondents saying they would be willing to pay a higher price for products for which detailed information is available in a language they understand.

The consumer's view of multilingual price tags is largely about the shopping experience. If the information at the foreign outlet is in a language that the consumer understands, the consumer's shopping experience is enhanced, and it makes the consumer feel more welcome in the country. In the long run, such an approach by retailers can only have a positive impact on company awareness as well as customer loyalty. We did not observe any negative aspects in the introduction of such innovative solutions and no negatives emerged from our survey either.

We provide a comprehensive look at consumer need and suggest relevant recommendations that can be applied and implemented in any part of the world without the need for major investment solutions. However, the future of retailing is facing many big changes, as argued, for example, by Ahamed [17] who stress the importance of collaboration between manufacturers, retailers and consumers in the adoption of new technologies. While the introduction of RFID chips requires an initial investment mainly from manufacturers, collaboration between all stakeholders can bring significant benefits to the entire supply chain. Our study confirms that consumers are willing to support initiatives that contribute to greater awareness, sustainability and transparency.

7. Statistical Testing of Hypotheses

As part of our study, we also decided to measure our respondents using Chi-Square tests, where we set several hypotheses (Table 9.1). For the purpose of our study, we present two hypothesis tests, and in the first test we set the following hypotheses:

H_0: Among the variable *"Can you be deterred from buying if you don't have access to product information?"* and *"How did you react abroad when you saw a price tag whose language you did not understand?"* there is no dependency.

H_1: Among the variable *"Can you be deterred from buying if you don't have access to product information?"* and *"How did you react abroad when you saw a price tag whose language you did not understand?"* there is a dependency.

There is no dependence since the *p* value is higher than the significance level (classically working with $\alpha = 0{,}05$) therefore $0{,}458 > 0{,}05$.

Table 9.1. Chi-square tests

	Value	*df*	*Asymptotic Significance (2-sided)*
Pearson Chi-Square	2,596[a]	3	,458
Likelihood Ratio	2,575	3	,462
N of Valid Cases	115		

[a]1 cells (12,5 %) have expected count less than 5. The minimum expected count is 4,57.
Source: Author.

Table 9.2. Chi-square tests

	Value	*df*	*Asymptotic Significance (2-sided)*
Pearson Chi-Square	5,101[a]	3	,165
Likelihood Ratio	5,347	3	,148
N of Valid Cases	120		

[a]0 cells (0,0 %) have expected count less than 5. The minimum expected count is 5,47.
Source: Author.

Hypothesis testing showed that although we did not find a statistically significant relationship, we cannot conclusively state that consumers are not primarily influenced by language barriers. There may be a weaker relationship that our test failed to capture or there may be another, unmeasurable factor that influences consumer purchasing behaviour.

The Chi-Square test yielded a non-significant result (Pearson Chi-Square = 2.596, df = 3, p = 0.458). The likelihood ratio test also produced a non-significant result (p = 0.462). These findings suggest that there is insufficient evidence to reject the null hypothesis. In other words, we did not find a statistically significant relationship between consumers' reactions to encountering a price tag in an unfamiliar language abroad and their likelihood of being deterred by a lack of product information.

While the Chi-Square test did not reveal a significant association between these specific variables, it is crucial to acknowledge the limitations of this analysis. The lack of statistical significance does not definitively rule out the influence of language barriers on consumer purchasing behaviour. Several factors could explain these findings. The observed relationship between language barriers and consumer behaviour might be subtle or weaker than anticipated, potentially beyond the sensitivity of our current testing methods. Furthermore, unmeasured factors such as cultural differences, economic disparities, or varying levels of consumer literacy could be influencing consumer behaviour and masking the true impact of language barriers. Insufficient sample size or a lack of statistical power in our analysis might also have limited our ability to detect a true, albeit weak, relationship. Additionally, the data used in our analysis may not accurately reflect the true extent of language barriers faced by consumers, as self-reported data on language proficiency might not fully capture the nuances of language use in real-world purchasing situations.

In the second test, we decided to focus on the relationship between travel abroad and access to information (Table 9.2). Therefore, we set the following hypotheses:

H_0: Among the variable *"Would you be willing to pay a higher price for a goods if detailed information about the product was available in a language you understand?"* and *"How often do you travel abroad?"* there is no dependency.

H_1: Among the variable *"Would you be willing to pay a higher price for a goods if detailed information about the product was available in a language you understand?"* and *"How often do you travel abroad?"* there is a dependency.

There is no dependence since the *p* value is higher than the significance level (classically we work with $\alpha = 0{,}05$) therefore $0{,}165 > 0{,}05$.

The second hypothesis testing also showed that the relationship between the variables was not statistically significant, which is positive news from the perspective of our study. This points to the fact that how often people travel abroad does not affect their willingness to pay for better product information.

While the statistical analysis did not reveal a significant association between travel frequency abroad and the willingness to pay a higher price for products with detailed information in a language they understand, the observed trend merits further exploration. This could be due to several factors, such as the limited sample size or the potential influence of other variables not considered in this study, such as income level, education, or travel experience. Further research, incorporating these factors and potentially employing more sophisticated statistical methods, is necessary to fully understand the nuanced relationship between travel experiences, language preferences, and consumer behaviour in international contexts.

Interestingly, although a statistically significant relationship was not confirmed, analysis of the table shows that a slightly higher proportion of respondents who travel abroad more frequently expressed a willingness to pay a higher price for products with detailed information.

In terms of practical implications for retail, the results of our testing suggest that investing in multilingual signage and providing detailed product information can be beneficial regardless of the customer segment the retailer is addressing. Gaining customer trust by providing transparent information can lead to increased loyalty and better brand perception, no matter how often customers travel abroad.

8. Application of QR Codes to Price Tags and Recommendations for Retail

Our research has confirmed that QR codes can significantly improve the customer shopping experience. In line with the research [18], which focused on customers' perceptions of QR codes in the fashion industry, our respondents also appreciated the ease of use of QR codes and the ability to obtain additional product information. These findings suggest that QR codes are not just a "fashion" trend, but that they are a real tool to improve customer satisfaction.

An interesting finding was that the majority of respondents expected QR codes to provide more detailed information about the composition of the products and their country of origin. This finding corresponds with the trend towards sustainable fashion and customer interest in transparency of production processes. In contrast to the study [18], which focused more on the consumer impression of QR codes, our respondents placed more emphasis on the practical usefulness of these tools.

In addition, QR codes offer valuable data for retailers. Scanning the code provides information on what products customers are interested in, how much information they read about them and what next steps they take. This data can be used to personalize marketing campaigns, optimize assortments, and improve the overall shopping experience [19].

The combination of QR codes and artificial intelligence, as described [20] represents a significant step in this direction. This technology enables the creation of personalized and interactive shopping experiences that not only attract customers but also increase their loyalty. It also provides valuable data for operational optimization and enables rapid adaptation to changing market conditions, ensuring the long-term competitiveness of businesses (Figure 9.4).

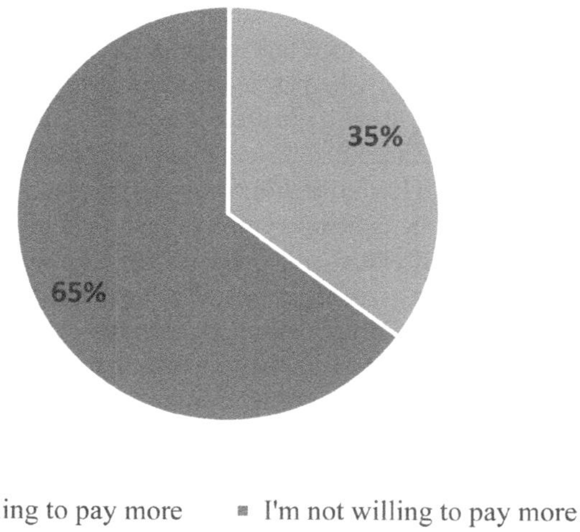

Figure 9.4. Consumers pay premium for product transparency.

Source: The data for this graph was obtained through original data processing of our survey results.

The survey results show that 35% of respondents indicated a willingness to pay a higher price for a product with detailed information in a language they understand. This finding provides an interesting and positive insight into new trends in consumer purchasing behaviour. Although the majority of respondents (65%) did not express this willingness, a third of respondents represent a significant proportion of consumers that cannot be overlooked. This customer segment opens up new opportunities for companies looking to increase the value of their products through transparency and clarity.

The data also shows that more than a third of customers see detailed and clear information as a key aspect of product quality, and that these are consumers who are willing to invest in products that give them a sense of security and confidence. For them, price is not the main factor, but rather the value that clear labelling brings. This trend is particularly important in segments such as food, cosmetics, health products or technology, where details can have a significant impact on the final consumer decision.

For companies, this means an opportunity to target this group and take advantage of their willingness to pay more. Focusing on products with detailed labelling, certified quality and an emphasis on transparency can be an attractive way to increase sales. Personalized marketing that emphasizes the benefits and details of products has the potential to appeal to this group of customers. In addition, packaging innovations that are not only visually appealing but also informative can substantially increase customer trust and satisfaction.

This 35% represents a group that is likely to appreciate not only quality products but also long-term transparency and responsiveness from brands. Gaining this group as loyal customers can mean not only higher profits for companies but also a positive reputation in the marketplace. In today's competitive economy, it is the emphasis on information that can be a significant advantage over competitors.

The results of our research suggest that QR codes will play an increasingly important role in retail. Combining QR codes with artificial intelligence and other digital technologies will create new opportunities for personalized marketing, interactive shopping experiences and improved customer decision-making. Businesses that can harness the potential of these technologies will gain a significant competitive advantage.

9. Cultural Aspects and Limitations

Our findings confirm the importance of cultural factors in influencing consumer preferences for multilingual price tags. Consistent with Hofstede's cultural dimensions theory, we found that consumers in cultures with high levels of individualism tend to prefer the language of the dominant group, whereas in cultures with low levels of individualism, there is a greater emphasis on individual preferences. These results are consistent with the findings of Shahid [21] who highlight the importance of cultural specificities in consumer motivation. In addition to the degree of individualism, other cultural dimensions such as uncertainty avoidance may also have an impact. These factors may influence not only language choice, but also the way consumers perceive the information presented on price tags. Our findings have important implications for marketing practice. When designing multilingual price tags, it is necessary to take into account the cultural specificities of the target market and tailor the communication to resonate with consumers' values and expectations. There is great scope for further research in this area, where cross-cultural differences and connections or even various other pronouncements along Hofstede's dimensions could be explored in greater depth, where intersections could be found across regions and thus recommendations could be personalized to these areas, which could influence consumer attitudes and positively motivate them to buy.

Although our study has provided valuable insights into the impact of multilingual price tags on consumer decision making, it is important to recognize its limitations. The results obtained may be influenced by socially desirable responses and may not be fully generalizable to other cultures and contexts.

Future research should aim to overcome these limitations and to further explore the impact of multilingual price tags on consumer behaviour. An interesting direction would be to explore the potential of augmented reality and virtual reality in this area, where we see that by using these innovative technologies as well as artificial intelligence, it would be possible to create price tags that adapt to individual customer preferences based on their purchase history or other available data.

Probably the most effective way of further research would be to carry out a trial implementation of multilingual solutions, to monitor the changes that occur in consumer preferences and then to analyse the impact on their behaviour, and it would be advisable to take an interdisciplinary approach, where future research would combine knowledge from marketing, psychology and linguistics.

10. Conclusions

Our study has clearly confirmed that multilingual price tagging combined with QR codes represents a significant step forward in improving the customer experience and increasing retail efficiency. We found that customers appreciate the availability of information in a language they understand and are willing to actively use QR codes to obtain additional product information.

Our study reveals that language barriers significantly impact consumer behaviour, particularly when shopping abroad. Consistent with previous research, English emerged as the preferred language for product information. However, our findings also highlight a unique demand for detailed product information, including ingredients, origin, and nutritional value, which may not be as pronounced in other studies. By leveraging digital technologies such as QR codes and mobile applications, businesses can provide multilingual product information in a convenient and accessible format. This approach not only enhances the customer experience but also offers environmental benefits by reducing the need for printed materials. Moreover, digital solutions are scalable and can be easily adapted to different markets and languages. To maximize the benefits and minimize costs, businesses should focus on providing information in a limited number of key languages, train staff to communicate effectively in multiple languages, and continuously monitor customer feedback to refine their strategies. By considering the environmental impact and scalability of their solutions, businesses can make informed decisions that benefit both customers and the planet.

Another promising research direction is the use of QR codes equipped with trackers. These tools could provide valuable data on customer behaviour that could be used to personalize marketing campaigns, optimize inventory and better understand buying habits.

Other directions in which research could continue is to focus on the analysis of cultural preferences in language and communication. Consumer behaviour varies across cultures, so how customers perceive different languages on price tags, what their expectations are in terms of information provision and what their preferences are in terms of innovative solutions is important to find out in terms of further research. Conducting further follow-up studies will allow us to better understand how consumer behaviour is changing and what their expectations are regarding the use of QR codes. In addition, future research should also focus on the environmental and social aspects of QR code use, such as reducing waste in the context of price tags, supporting local communities and protecting personal data. Such a comprehensive investigation will allow us to better understand the potential of QR codes and their impact on consumer behaviour.

Integrating QR codes with augmented reality (AR) and virtual reality (VR) could offer customers a whole new, interactive shopping experience. Imagine a customer using a smartphone to point a camera at a product and get a 3D visualization that would allow them to examine the product or its contents, in detail from every angle, even try it on virtually and compare it to other products.

The use of artificial intelligence (AI) to analyse data collected through QR codes opens up further interesting possibilities. For example, AI could generate personalized product recommendations based on a customer's purchase history or their current searches.

In conclusion, the potential of QR codes is huge. By combining QR codes with other technologies such as trackers, AR, VR or AI, we can create innovative and personalized shopping experiences that will meet ever-growing customer expectations. Our findings suggest that QR codes have the potential to transform retail and open up new opportunities for businesses of all sizes.

Acknowledgment

This article is an output of the research project VEGA – 1/0392/23 "*Changes in the approach to the creation of companies' distribution management concepts influenced by the effects of social and economic crises caused by the global pandemic and increased security risks***" and grant of University of Economics in Bratislava for young teachers, researchers and doctoral students I-24-113-00 / A-24-106/0027-00 "***Artificial intelligence in the humanities and social sciences***".**

References

[1] Calderon-Monge, E., & Ribeiro-Soriano, D. (2024). The role of digitalization in business and management: A systematic literature review. *Review of Managerial Science*, *18*(2), 449–491. https://doi.org/10.1007/s11846-023-00647-8.

[2] Nodirovna, M., & Sharif, A. (2024). E-Commerce Trends: Shaping The Future of Retail. *Open Herald: Periodical of Methodical Research*, *2*(3), 46–49. https://academiaone.org/index.php/6/article/view/637.

[3] Tagscherer, F., & Carbon, C. C. (2023). Leadership for successful digitalization: A literature review on companies' internal and external aspects of digitalization. *Sustainable Technology and Entrepreneurship*, *2*(2), 100039. https://doi.org/10.1016/j.stae.2023.100039

[4] Arora, M., Goel, R., & Singla, J. (2024). Innovation or Intrusion? Examining Employee Willingness to Collaborate With AI-Powered Service Robots in Retail. *Augmenting Retail Reality, Part A: Blockchain, AR, VR, and the Internet of Things*, 97–116.

[5] Hrouga, M., & Sbihi, A. (2023). Logistics 4.0 for supply chain performance: perspectives from a retailing case study. *Business Process Management Journal*, *29*(6), 1892–1919. https://doi.org/10.1108/BPMJ-03-2023-0183.

[6] Hedvall, L. (2023). *Designed QR codes: An innovative way to invoke interaction,* 1st ed.

[7] Ilham, I., Widjaja, W., Sutaguna, I. N. T., Rukmana, A. Y., & Yusuf, M. (2023). Digital Marketing's Effect on Purchase Decisions Through Customer Satisfaction. *CEMERLANG: Jurnal Manajemen dan Ekonomi Bisnis, 3*(2), 185–202.

[8] Paananen, T., Holkkola, M., Makkonen, M., Frank, L., & Kemppainen, T. (2023). *Customers' QR Code Usage Barriers in a Brick-and-Mortar Store: A Qualitative Study*. Paper presented at the Bled eConference, University of Maribor.

[9] Liewkasemsant, S. (2023). *Creating Better Multinational Teamwork: A Thai Retail Business Company Case*. PhD diss., Mahidol University.

[10] Abdullah, B. S., Nawi, N. C., Mustapha, H., & Sbihi, A. (2023). Logistics 4.0 for supply chain performance: perspectives from a retailing case study. *Business Process Management Journal, 29*(6), 1892–1919.

[11] Abdullah, B. S., Nawi, N. B., Zainuddin, S. A., Hassan, A. A., Ibrahim, W. K., Mohamed, A. F., & Zin, M. Z. (2023). Customer satisfaction and sustainable purchasing behaviour via QR code with the mediating role of perceived flow among Malaysian shoppers. *FIIB Business Review, 14*(1), 1–15.

[12] Packard, G., Li, Y., & Berger, J. (2024). When language matters. *Journal of Consumer Research, 51*(3). https://doi.org/10.1093/jcr/ucad080.

[13] Pappas, A., Fumagalli, E., Rouziou, M., & Bolander, W. (2023). More than Machines: The Role of the Future Retail Salesperson in Enhancing the Customer Experience. *Journal of Retailing*, *99*(4), 518–531.

[14] Quinones, M., Gomez-Suarez, M., Cruz-Roche, I., & Díaz-Martín, A. M. (2023). Technology: A strategic imperative for successful retailers. *International Journal of Retail & Distribution Management, 51*(4), doi:10.1108/IJRDM-03-2022-0088.

[15] Tan, F., Li, X., Agarwal, R., Joshi, Y., & Yaqub, M. Z. (2024). Does multilingual packaging influence purchasing in retail segment? Evidence from multiple experiments. *Journal of Retailing and Consumer Services, 79*. doi:10.1016/j.jretconser.2024.103878.

[16] Rajasa, E. Z., Manap, A., Ardana, P. D. H., Yusuf, M., & Harizahayu, H. (2023). Literature Review: Analysis of Factors Influencing Purchasing Decisions, Product Quality and Competitive Pricing. *Jurnal Ekonomi, 12*(01), 451–455.

[17] Ahamed, A., Huang, P., Young, J., Gallego-Schmid, A., Price, R., & Shaver, M. P. (2024). Technical and environmental assessment of end-of-life scenarios for plastic packaging with electronic tags. *Resources, Conservation and Recycling, 201*. doi:10.1016/j.resconrec.2023.107341.

[18] Holkkola, M., Paananen, T., Frank, L., Kemppainen, T., & Makkonen, M. (2023). How Do QR Codes Enhance Customer Experience? Omnichannel Customer Experiences in a Brick-and-Mortar Fashion Store. *Paper presented at the Bled eConference, University of Maribor*. https://doi.org/10.1108/BPMJ-03-2023-0183.

[19] Raji, M. A., Olodo, H. B., Oke, T. T., Addy, W. A., Ofodile, O. C., & Oyewole, A. T. (2024). Real-time data analytics in retail: A review of USA and global practices. *GSC Advanced Research and Reviews, 18*(3), 059–065.

[20] Lu, H. P., Cheng, H. L., Tzou, J. C., & Chen, C. S. (2023). Technology roadmap of AI applications in the retail industry. *Technological Forecasting and Social Change, 195*. doi:10.1016/j.techfore.2023.122778.

[21] Shahid, S., Adil, M., Sadiq, M., & Dash, G. (2024). Why do consumers consume massive products? A cross-cultural investigation through the lens of self-determination theory. *Journal of Retailing and Consumer Services*, *76*, 103607.

10 Urban walkability: Insights from neighbourhood studies in New Delhi

Prateek Dhasmana[a] *and Niva Turna*[b]

Chitkara School of Planning and Architecture, Chitkara University, Rajpura, Punjab, India

Abstract: This paper focuses on walkability in neighbourhood studies and how physical characteristics such as enclosure ratios, human scale, and transparency affect pedestrian liveability in the unplanned Indian metropolis of New Delhi. This paper analyses the conditions affecting walkability in Batla House, Masigarh, and Sarai Jullena in New Delhi. Accessibility of cities means walkability, an aspect of sustainable urbanism whose objective is influenced by the components of city design that determine the walk experiences, safety, health, and social connectivity. The study is centered on several essential attributes including enclosure ratios, human scale, imageability, transparency, and complexity to develop an understanding of how each of the aspects influences – and to what extent – they may impact pedestrian function and comfort. The findings indicate that Sarai Jullena demonstrated the highest walkability, characterized by balanced enclosure ratios, and features diverse land use and activation, interactive ground floor activity elements, and high transparency and building complexity.

In contrast, Batla House exhibited low walkability, with narrow streets, high enclosure ratios, low level of transparency, and a small number of interactive street fronts implying that the pedestrian character is rather restricted. Masigarh achieved a moderate level of walkability, the street contains a blend of residential and commercial activities and balanced values of enclosure but could not match the liveliness of Sarai Jullena. The paper highlights the implications of walkability in the built environment and its importance in creating positive social change, enhancing the quality of life, and preserving the environment from the negative effects of motor cars. Proposed design solutions for these challenges entail maximizing sky exposure to the building and incorporating green areas into the design structure, as well as activating ground level through shops and community areas. The policy recommendations include restricted building altitudes, appropriate building setbacks, and people's involvement in the planning of urban areas. Collectively, the research offers practical lessons for enhancing the health and walkability of urban neighbourhoods for more sustainable urbanism.

Keywords: Enclosure ratios, human scale, neighbourhoods pedestrian experience, sustainable urbanism, urban design, walkability

1. Introduction

Accessibility, most particularly through walking, is a critical measure of achieving sustainable urban environments. It shows the level of accessibility of the pedestrian when it comes to mobility around towns and cities. When meeting essential needs in densely populated cities like Delhi, creating walkable neighbourhoods is not only a question of mobility and accessibility but a pressing social justice and health issue as well as an environmental imperative. States that one can walk from home to commercial hubs of business are presumed to promote daily walking, lower vehicle use, and enhance social relations among the residents [1]. However, walkability in Delhi's neighbourhoods has not remained a planning priority of much importance. Since there are very few to no pedestrian-oriented spaces the general feeling is that it is unsafe to walk around, essential services are almost out of reach, and no chance for social activities to occur.

To overcome these challenges, this research uses an integrated research method that entails qualitative and quantitative research methods. It starts with a literature review to situate different best practices for designing friendly facilities for pedestrians within the context of Delhi. Secondary data was collected using a literature review of existing published articles, follow-up of newspapers and magazines, official reports and documents, and website research. These surveys involved purposively designed questionnaires to capture the perception of pedestrians on the environment, the health effects of walking, and the spatial functionality of streets. Attributes like the amount of Natural Light, Enclosure ratios, and pedestrian density were used to find out the relationship between design and walkability. In doing so, the research presents practical solutions that include details of Delhi's physical

[a]prateek.dhasmana@chitkara.edu.in, [b]niva.turna@chitkara.edu.in

DOI: 10.1201/9781003778905-10

environment based on the analysis of the documented literature as well as the facts collected from the field concerning the connection between urban design features and walkability within various neighbourhood types. In this way, the study seeks to offer approaches for improving pedestrian conditions as well as support the implementation and development of more sustainable forms of city living.

2. Review of Literature

The present literature review was performed systematically. To find related literature, keywords that will be searched for were determined regarding walkability, and other tools such as Sci-space, elicit, and research rabbit were used in keyword probing (Figure 10.1). More related papers were reviewed to identify factors that influence walkability and relevant papers were selected to obtain these factors.

Walkability is an essential element of sustainable urban design and has been investigated in many countries. This paper builds on Jacobs' study, which established the importance of accessible streets in creating active city life [2]. Jacobs noted that pedestrianizing streets improves social interaction and reduces automobile use. This view resonates with Gehl, who argues that when developing cities, small-scale, people-oriented design is needed to counter car-oriented designs [6]. Gehl explains that careful urban planning promotes walking and community interaction.

Ewing and Handy (2009) [7] delved deeper into the concept of walkability which they identified and defined three key components of it: enclosure, human scale, and transparency. Enclosure refers to street width in proportion to building heights, and the sense of definition they create in a space. Human scale is the environmental feature in which such items as paths and street furniture are used, which take into account human proportions and movement pace. Transparency captures the physical openness of the building and its surroundings, such as if the building is visible, if ground floor activities are engaging, and whether there are active frontages. These factors come together in a manner that facilitates creation of places that are friendly for pedestrians and makes walking an appealing alternative.

In light of that, this paper will seek to determine how the factors influencing walkability are different in developing countries such as India. For instance, Pandey states that in India, that people's mobility movement and walkability are curtailed further because the urban areas have been developed with cars and motor vehicles as the primary mode of transport rather than pedestrians [8]. Frequent problems for walkers in that country include non-even pavements, insufficient shading by trees, and poor street lighting. Pandey identifies the debilitating issues within the infrastructure that must be remedied for current pedestrian experiences to improve.

The third defining factor related to walkability is the influence it has on mental wellness. In a study done by Al Hagla [3], inadequate design of pedestrian facilities may turn out to be detrimental to one's mental state as such designs can foster stress, anxiety and isolation. Considering the population density and unregulated expansion of Delhi, Singh's study is very applicable in this case. Zhang emphasize that even minor landscaping such as single trees placed on the sidewalk or small urban parks can serve major wonders for enhancing walkability [9].

International reports further corroborate the effectiveness of policy measures taken to promote walking. For example, an extensive traffic policy focusing on pedestrian zones has been adopted as is common in several European cities including Amsterdam, Copenhagen works like this. These cities illustrate that urban densification and less car consumption can improve healthiness of the built environment. These policy approaches are useful for Delhi, for in this case, improvement of walkability will address social problems which are more of a collective action.

Possibly the most controversial concept pertaining to walkability is how it pertains to urban form. Moughtin suggests that the arrangement of buildings and the design of streets has an impact on walking [10]. Stated otherwise, if the width of the street is equal to or less than the height of the buildings on the side of the street, then the street will be unappealing and hostile in nature due to the lower enclosure ratio. On the other hand, streets built for mixed traffic have greater walking comfort. Hedman, endorses this principle where he argues that limited access to streets reduce the frequency of social interactions amongst people especially women, children and the old persons [11].

The tech boom has also aided the study of walkability. Currently, Geographic Information System (GIS) tools and other spatial analysis aids simplify quantifying walkability and pinpointing areas of improvement. For instance, Rossetti use GIS metrics for analyzing pedestrian networks and their interactions with public transportation systems [13]. These tools can help intervention planning in Delhi, where insufficient planning has led to inadequate interconnectivity in the urban surface for pedestrians.

The broader cultural and climatic conditions is being adopted in walkability studies which is relatively new. For a dense city like Delhi where weather has a great impact on people, design must take into consideration strong sunlight and poor air quality. As Lin points out, adequate shade and ventilation are imperative for on-foot comfort [14]. Strategies to alleviate urban heat islands include growing drought-resistant trees, shading the pavements, and adding water features.

But, even with the available literature on walkability, these changes in Delhi have an uphill task. Some

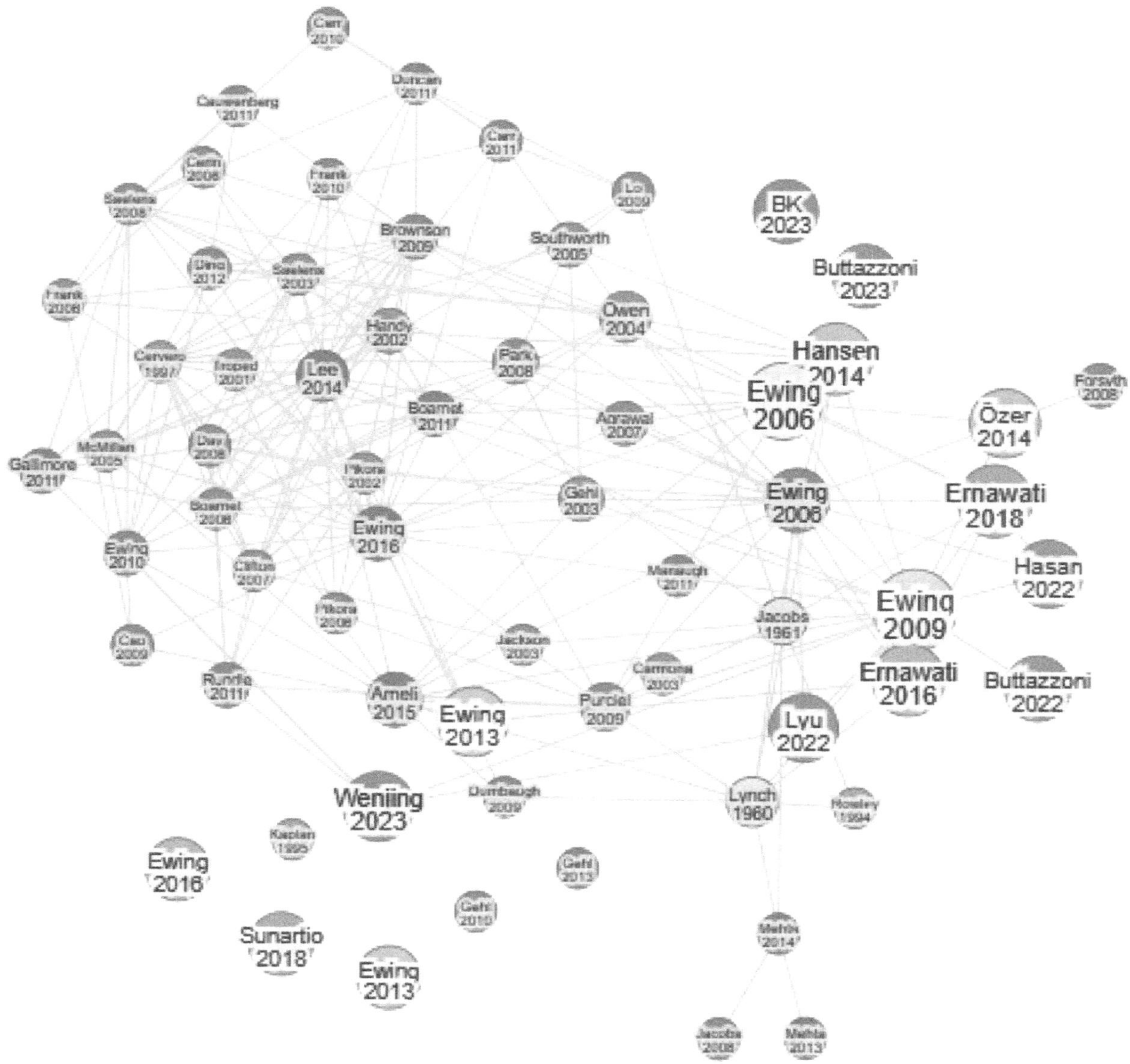

Figure 10.1. Connected papers related to walkability.

Source: Research Rabbit.

projections estimate that India will lose 200 square kilometers of land to informal, or 'pirate' urbanization. These 'missing' areas do not have footpaths, or lighting, or even crossings, which makes walking a safety hazard. Besides, an emphasis on mechanized transportation has resulted in road centric planning that literally vandalizes footpaths, while also interrupting them with trunk roads and overpasses. Solutions require a significant restructuring of how these spaces are planned and built.

This brings us to the notion of 'complete streets' planning, which seeks to cater to people, regardless of if they are walking, cycling, selling on the street or even assembling using the street. Such strategies are consistent with the new urbanism as a form of development that seeks to achieve a mix of use on a given parcel or area, and design that centers on people. In Delhi, these complete streets could change neighbourhoods into busy, vibrant, and accessible places for all.

The United Nations Habitat [5] has noted that streets and roads are valuable sources of assets. Incentives, such as tax breaks for mixed-use properties or green building certifications, can further aid in the implementation of such policies. Similarly, community participation can be useful in displaying support for better pedestrian facilities. Such policies and codes can aid in the achievement of higher walkability within any area. It is the infrastructure policies that aid in walkability enhancement.

Hence, the literature here has been compiled in a manner that it offers a multi-dimensional approach to walkability which allows the user to grasp its structure and consequences to a city's urban growth. Incorporating the street network designs as well as the physical and mental requirements of a pedestrian, these works stress the role of urbanism in providing a suitable environment for pedestrian mobility. This research will form part of a multi-country detailed evaluation of the scope of walkability in Delhi, India and also for the target interventions needed in response to poor urban design.

3. Research Methodology

This research used a mixed-methods approach, combining qualitative and quantitative methods, to evaluate the walkability of three neighbourhood sub-centers in New Delhi: Batla House, Masigarh, and Sarai Jullena (Figure 10.2). The study began with a literature review to identify established walkability measures, including imageability, enclosure, human scale, transparency, and complexity, drawn from existing urban design literature. Qualitative data collection involved field observations and activity mapping to document pedestrian behaviours, street activities, and the influence of design on walkability. Quantitative data was collected through surveys documenting pedestrian counts, flows, and behaviours within the built environment. Activity mapping further illustrated key pedestrian activity associated with specific design elements. Qualitative data analysis involved open coding of field notes, while quantitative analysis considered features such as street width and building height. A comparative analysis of the three neighbourhoods revealed how specific design parameters, including infrastructure, land use, and social practices, affected walkability. This study has some limitations, including the limited study area and the time constraints on data collection, which affected the depth of analysis regarding the built environment's impact on walkability and the ability to develop comprehensive guidelines specific to New Delhi's pedestrian characteristics.

4. Factors Affecting Walkability of Neighbourhoods

This research investigates factors that enhance walkability to support sustainable neighbourhoods and the public realm. Prioritizing pedestrian movement is crucial for urban design and development strategies aimed at improving public spaces, promoting people-friendly city planning, and enhancing social and economic vitality. As urban sustainability becomes increasingly important, walking is gaining recognition as a key mode of transport. While the physical benefits of walking are well-established, it is also an enjoyable, affordable activity that improves individual well-being and life expectancy. The American Journal of Public Health supports the concept of pedestrian-friendly neighbourhoods for increasing individual and collective social capital, linking higher social capital to improved community functioning, as demonstrated in urban settings that blend traditional and modern elements [4].

This analysis uses activity mapping and observational studies, focusing on several factors. Appropriate street enclosure creates a sense of safety for pedestrians, encouraging longer stays. Shorter block lengths reduce perceived walking distances and enhance perceived street connectivity. Street edge conditions also significantly influence walkability. Streets with frequent building entrances and active frontages encourage street use and improve walkability. These findings underscore the importance of building frontages in promoting walkability and emphasize the need for built environments that give pedestrians a sense of control over their streets and public spaces.

Walkable environments contribute to community health, reduce crime, and stimulate economic activity. This paper explores how the built environment influences walking. Everyday activities like walking, talking, eating, and recreation contribute to street vibrancy. Whyte argues that in lively streets, a strong relationship exists between ground-floor building uses and adjacent street

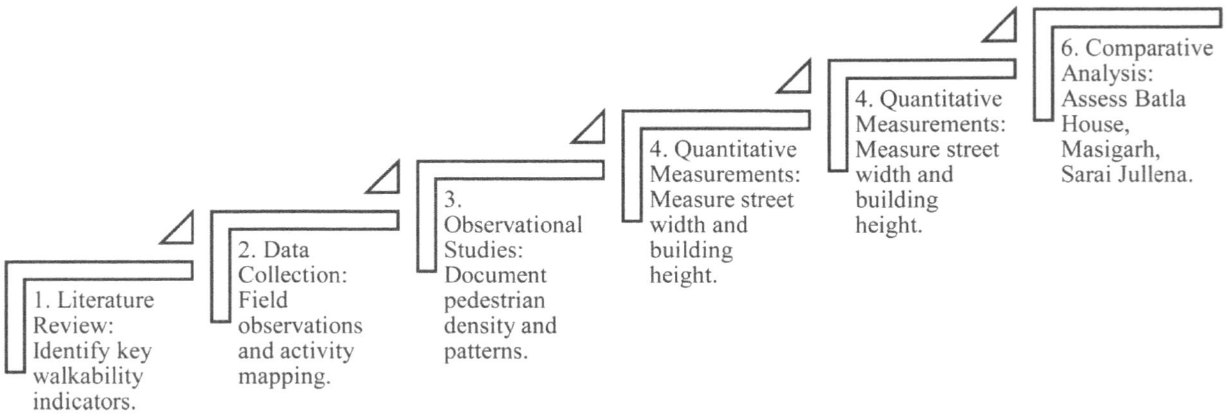

Figure 10.2. Research methodology.

Source: Author.

spaces. He identifies "dead" spaces – such as non-retail businesses, offices, and parking garages – as detrimental to pedestrian activity, while uses like newsstands and restaurants enhance walkability. Whyte introduces the concept of "soft edges," where pedestrians directly interact with ground floors [12]. An ideal "soft edge" features shops with transparent facades, large windows, numerous openings, and interactive displays.

This paper assesses walkability based on urban design elements such as Imageability, Enclosure, Human Scale, Transparency, and Complexity (Figure 10.3). These elements include building positioning, block size, building density, street enclosure, and building diversity. The research questions are: How does urban form influence walking, and what factors mediate this relationship? This involves an in-depth analysis of how various aspects of the built environment affect pedestrian activity in different contexts. A qualitative approach, combining urban form analysis with ethnographic observation, is used to collect data on walking behaviour, considering:

- Pedestrian density and patterns
- Route choices made during walking trips
- Morphological factors influencing walking activity
- The empirical study documented individual walking behaviours by observing these factors. The research was conducted in Mehrauli, a traditional area in rapidly urbanizing New Delhi, India, to identify varying pedestrian behaviours in different conditions

5. Understanding the Walkability in Neighbourhoods of New Delhi - Case of Batla House, Masigarh, Sarai Jullena

The Batla House, Masigarh, and Sarai Jullena were chosen as a case area to conduct a walkability assessment of the neighbourhoods. While Batla House is also an unauthorised colony that has been regularised the other two areas namely Masigarh and Sarai Jullena are notified urban villages. Most of them have a small amount of sky exposure due to the high gross density of the neighbourhood; residential and mixed-use dominate the neighbourhood in almost all regions. Residential buildings are major daughter complexes of G+4 with a total occupancy of nearly 2500 inhabitants. Three different streets were selected for this study, each of which differ in width and other parameters. The widths of streets change from 1.5 meters to 3 meters with most of Batla House streets having only residential usability while Masigarh and Sarai Jullena contain mixed usability streets.

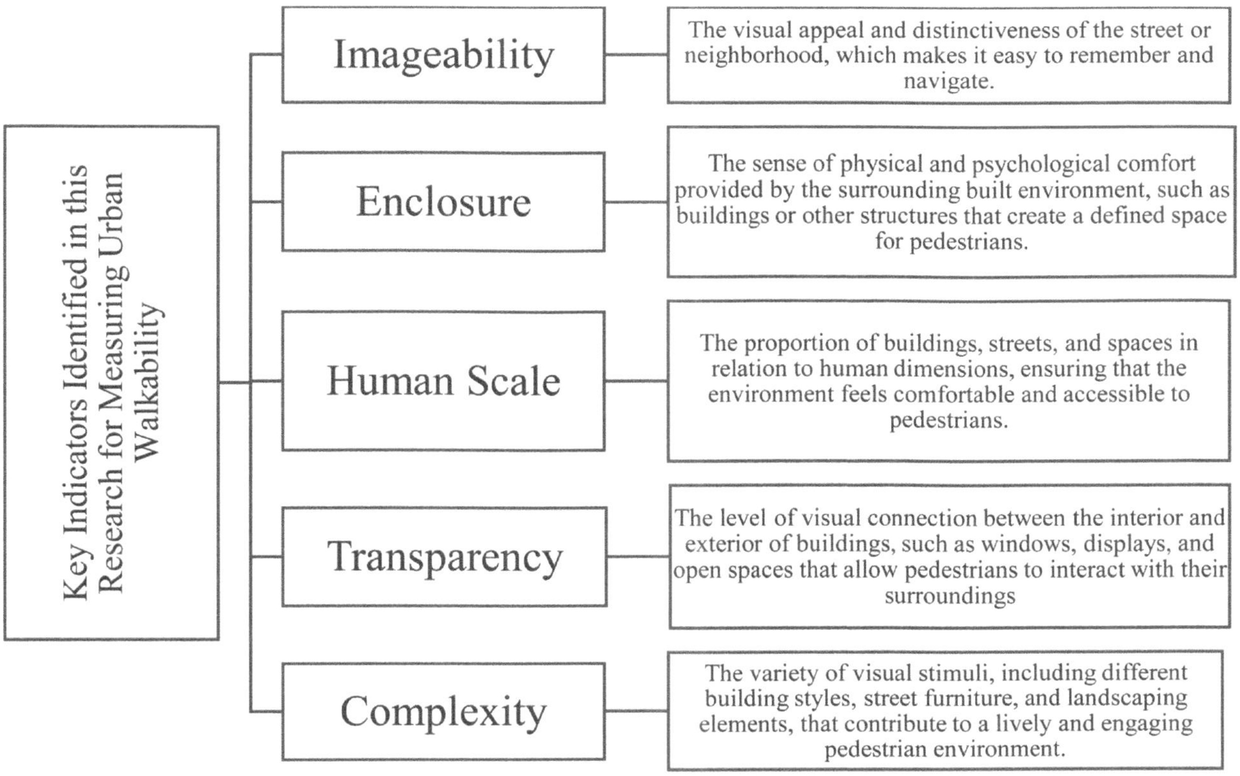

Figure 10.3. Key indicators of walkability.

Source: Author.

6. Comparative Analysis of Batla House, Masigarh, and Sarai Jullena Based on Key Walkability Indicators

The neighbourhoods of Batla House, Masigarh, and Sarai Jullena are analyzed based on five key walkability indicators: Imageability is how easily an object can be visualized, while enclosure refers to how enclosed an area is to the public, and human scale relates to how large the object is about the human body, and transparency is the degree to which each object is see-through, and complexity is how complex the form of each object is (Figure 10.4).

1. **Imageability**
   - **Batla House:** The streets in Batla House have no attractive architectural features to guide the heads and eyes of the pedestrians in this area and therefore are not memorable. Heavy and continuous settlement formation reduces the heterogeneity and activity required for imageability.
   - **Masigarh:** Provides a reasonable level of imageability because there is a mix of commercial and residential buildings and a better-defined street network; however, there are no evident and interesting landmarks.
   - **Sarai Jullena:** This is higher in imageability due to richer variations in the use of the land, sheer glass fronts, and active street fronts, therefore is more distinctive.
2. **Enclosure**
   - **Batla House:** The enclosure ratio is from 1:6 to 1:9 due to the constrained zone width by 1.5–2m width street containing G+4 structures. This forms a sort of covered passage which may be quite constricting or like being in a canyon.
   - **Masigarh:** In Masigarh what has been achieved is a better balance of streets and block width and the height of buildings, the figures shown for the enclosure ratio are 1:3 to 1:4. It is also covered, but it has more free space than Batla House.
   - **Sarai Jullena:** As in Masigarh, the ratio of the enclosure of 1:3 to 1:4 gives a touch of bodying without aggressive confinement. There is more vertical connectivity for pedestrians and the spaces are more permeable for streets.
3. **Human Scale**
   - **Batla House:** Clustering occurs, and despite the significant fabric of buildings present interactive ground floor elements which augment the human scale are fewer. The structures themselves overwhelm street space, and this latter sense alters pedestrians' comfort levels.
   - **Masigarh:** The human scale is moderately better than single-use commercial streets and lower-storey buildings (ground floor+3). Here, once again, the ratio of pedestrians to the environment is more promising than in Batla House.
   - **Sarai Jullena:** The human scale is most evident here, through the integration of active ground

Figure 10.4. Streets of Batla house, Sarai Jullena and Masihgarh.
Source: Author.

floor uses, transparent façades and a great variety of instantly appealing street furniture.

4. **Transparency**
   - **Batla House:** Low visibility mainly because of blank walls and more often residential buildings. The space between the buildings and the streets eliminates the perception of pedestrian crossing largely.
   - **Masigarh:** Moderate transparency; diversity of some mixed-use structures means that some of them are designed with display windows and accessible entrances, while the majority of residential building elevation dominates.
   - **Sarai Jullena:** The highest extent of transparency is evident in the context of the three neighbourhoods. Public first levels are for shops and communication areas with glazed facades affording a visual connection with people on the street.
5. **Complexity**
   - **Batla House:** Little variability in heights of buildings; little to no neighbouring commercial or industrial districts; relatively few differences in housing style, outdoor furniture, or greenery. There are no spectacles on the streets that would add energy to the street.
   - **Masigarh:** Moderate intensity of the competitive influences because of the combining of the land uses, and some variation in the building and place forms and activities. However, the level of detailing as well as the activity level is not as high as that of Sarai Jullena.
   - **Sarai Jullena:** High intensity, a mix of different building forms, myriad land uses, and a strong street frontage. Shops, cafes, and transparent proportions also bring liveliness and distinction to the building with its triangular structure.

Table 10.1 adds that Sarai Jullena scores the highest across all the aspects providing a balanced place that promotes walkability through mixed-use, active street fronts, and moderate perceived enclosure, however, Masigarh scores midway between transparency, complexity, and perceived enclosure. On the other hand, the Batla house having a simple layout, is poorly lit with several blind ends, poorly transparent, and hence very less complexity to the layout scores the lowest, implying a lot of discomfort to people walking around.

Table 10.1. Comparative analysis of 3 neighbourhoods based on key indicators identified

Key Indicators	*Batla House*	*Masigarh*	*Sarai Jullena*
Imageability	Low	Moderate	High
Enclosure	High (1:6–1:9)	Moderate (1:3–1:4)	Moderate (1:3–1:4)
Human Scale	Low	Moderate	High
Transparency	Low	Moderate	High
Complexity	Low	Moderate	High

Source: Author.

7. Findings

The findings reveal that land-use heterogeneity, the degree of enclosure, and ground-floor activity contribute to improved neighbourhood walkability.

This study highlights variations in spatial walkability across Batla House, Masigarh, and Sarai Jullena based on Imageability, Enclosure, Human Scale, Transparency, and Complexity. Imageability was lowest in Batla House due to its predominantly residential character and lack of distinctive features. Masigarh exhibited moderately higher imageability with some mixed-use structures, while Sarai Jullena scored highest due to its vibrant street edges and diverse activities.

Enclosure ratios varied significantly. Batla House had the most confined environment (1:6 to 1:9). Masigarh presented more balanced ratios (1:3 to 1:4), while Sarai Jullena's ratios (1:4 to 1:6) were considered more open, although residents still perceived some enclosure.

Regarding human scale, Batla House performed poorly due to its dense construction, narrow streets, and tall buildings with blank walls. Masigarh was marginally better with relatively active ground-floor activity, while Sarai Jullena exhibited the most effective human scale with varied building heights and pedestrian-friendly elements.

In terms of transparency – the interaction between the built environment and the street – Batla House offered little, with predominantly blank facades and limited openings. Masigarh had shopfronts with some windows and balconies, offering moderate transparency. Sarai Jullena demonstrated the highest transparency, fostering greater pedestrian interaction.

Finally, regarding complexity (the extent of architectural ornamentation and land-use mix), Batla House had simple building structures and lacked street furniture. Masigarh displayed slightly more complex architectural and land-use patterns with some site-to-site variation. Sarai Jullena scored highest in complexity due to its diverse architectural styles, varied land uses, and vibrant street activity.

8. Conclusion and Way Forward

This study establishes a strong relationship between the built environment and walkability, including pedestrian comfort. Sarai Jullena emerged as the most pedestrian-friendly of the studied neighbourhoods due to its balanced enclosure ratios, vibrant street edges, and high levels of imageability, transparency, and complexity. Masigarh offers moderate walkability, with reasonably good enclosure and some opportunities for interaction, but it lacks the inviting, pedestrian-oriented character of Sarai Jullena. Batla House, with its extremely high enclosure ratios, low transparency, and limited interactive street features, is the least walkable and somewhat hostile to pedestrians.

Overcoming obstacles to better walkability requires specific and strategic interventions. Design interventions should address enclosure ratios by reducing excessive building heights or, where feasible, increasing street widths. Design regulations, including those concerning sky exposure ratios and natural lighting, can mitigate the negative effects of extreme enclosure. Introducing green buffers can also positively impact occupants' health by counterbalancing the effects of continuous enclosure. Promoting mixed-use development at the ground floor and using transparent materials like glass in shopfronts, cafes, and community areas enhances legibility and creates a more engaging pedestrian environment. Furthermore, appropriate lighting, attractive street furniture, and enhanced architectural features can revitalize streetscapes and further promote walkability.

Policy implications should include recommendations for controlled building heights, adequate setbacks, and thoughtful urban planning that prioritizes human scale and pedestrian comfort. Educating stakeholders, including developers and residents, about the benefits of walkability and encouraging community participation in urban design processes are also crucial.

These findings demonstrate that a comprehensive approach to these factors can transform a neighbourhood into a healthy and active community.

References

[1] Baobeid, A., Koç, M., & Al-Ghamdi, S. G. (2021, August 26). *Walkability and its relationships with health, sustainability, and livability: Elements of physical environment and evaluation frameworks*. Frontiers. https://www.frontiersin.org/journals/built-nvironment/articles/10.3389/fbuil.2021.721218/full

[2] Jacobs, G. A. (1995). The development of a national plan for disaster mental health. *Professional Psychology: Research and Practice*, *26*(6), 543–549. https://doi.org/10.1037/0735-7028.26.6.543

[3] Al-Hagla, K. (2008). Towards a sustainable neighborhood: The role of Open Spaces. (n.d.-b). *International Journal of Architectural Research*. https://www.researchgate.net/publication/26519154_Towards_a_Sustainable_Neighborhood_The_Role_of_Open_Spaces

[4] Li, S. (2023). A sustainable neighbourhood for the future. *Urbanie & Urbanus - Urban Design for a Sustainable Future: Innovations for the Model City*, (8). https://doi.org/10.55412/08.03

[5] UN Habitat. (2015). *A new strategy of Sustainable Neighbourhood Planning: Five principles - urban planning*. UN. (n.d.). https://unhabitat.org/five-principles-of-neighbourhood-design

[6] Gehl, J. (2011). *Life between buildings using public space*. Washington DC island Press: Scientific research publishing. (n.d.). https://www.scirp.org/reference/ReferencesPapers?ReferenceID=1845563

[7] Ewing, R., & Handy, S. (2009a). Measuring the unmeasurable: Urban design qualities related to walkability. *Journal of Urban Design*, *14*(1), 65–84. https://doi.org/10.1080/13574800802451155

[8] Pandey, D. (2016). *Quantitative and qualitative analysis of walkability of Indian street : A case of lucknow*. (n.d.-a). https://www.researchgate.net/publication/314439028

[9] Zhang, X., Melbourne, S., Sarkar, C., Chiaradia, A., & Webster, C. (2020). Effects of green space on walking: Does size, shape and density matter? *Urban Studies*, *57*(16), 3402–3420. https://doi.org/10.1177/0042098020902739

[10] Moughtin, C. (2003, May 11). *Urban design: Street and square*. Routledge & CRC Press. https://www.routledge.com/Urban-Design-Street-and-Square/Moughtin/p/book/9780750657174

[11] Hedman, R. (2019). *Fundamentals of Urban Design*. Routledge & CRC Press. https://www.routledge.com/Fundamentals-of-Urban-Design/Hedman/p/book/9780918286352

[12] Whyte, W. H. (1980). *The social life of small urban spaces*.

[13] Rossetti, S., Tiboni, M., Vetturi, D., Zazzi, M., & Caselli, B. (2020). Measuring Pedestrian Accessibility to Transport Public in Urban Areas: A GIS-based Discretisation Approach. *European Transport/Trasporti Europei. (n.d.)*. http://www.istiee.unict.it/issues/76-2020

[14] Lin, T. P., Tsai, K.-T., Liao, C.-C., & Huang, Y.-C. (2013). Effects of thermal comfort and adaptation on park attendance regarding different shading levels and activity types. *Building and Environment*, *59*, 599–611. https://www.sciencedirect.com/science/article/abs/pii/S0360132312002703

11 Sustainability leadership: Developing human capital to drive social impact

Arpana Sharma[a]

Managing Partner, PraeEminere Advisory, Dubai, United Arab Emirates

Abstract: In 1992, The United Nations (UN) launched the Conference of the Parties (COP) to tackle climate change. Three decades later, rising temperatures fueled by unsustainable production patterns, consumerism and demands of a growing population continue to alter the nature of industries, communities and the planet. This necessitates a refreshed understanding of businesses as a natural vehicle for embracing social and environmental stewardship at the core of economic growth. The transition implies businesses reconceiving the intersection between corporate performance and society. Social impact in this context is defined in terms of sustaining the well-being of people. Social institutions provide human capital deployed by organizations as production inputs; these individuals are a fundamental component of dynamic and complex social structures – therefore reciprocity. Acknowledging the inter-dependencies, this paper encourages enhancing human resources as a fundamental determinant to catalyze systemic change and societal upliftment. The author undertakes a methodical analysis of the Five Capitals Model, Leadership Theories and Sustainability Leadership (SL) approach to develop human capital through Organizational Learning approach, application of the Triple Bottom Line model to measure outcomes and Creating Shared Value as levers for enabling systemic shifts. The discussion recognizes the lack of a comprehensive SL concept that postulates a cohesive integration of fundamental components that influence positive social impact Thematic evaluation and synthesis of literature leads the author to conclude that SL exhibits social consciousness by assimilating social well-being at the core of a firm's corporate strategy, creates an inspiring vision and develops individuals as change agents. The discussion concludes by highlighting the opportunity for practitioners and researchers to develop consolidated frameworks and a curriculum that aims to establish a systems mindset in developing leaders across all levels of management hierarchies to escalate a cohesive momentum for social impact.

Keywords: Five Capital model, human-capital, living systems, organizational learning, sustainability leadership

1. Introduction

Economic growth reliant on the dominant neo-classical capitalistic theory and narrow definition of gross domestic product (GDP) has proved incapable of managing the equitable distribution of benefits to key factors of production – people and environment. Consequentially, communities have been overlooked and are being challenged by climate change-induced crisis, resource scarcity, environmental degradation, poverty, pollution and social inequality. Research supports: (i) lack of attention on sustainable leadership development theories, (ii) gaps in effective operationalization of corporate sustainability strategy, and (iii) a social responsibility mindset where societal issues sit at the periphery and not at the core. As a result, when sustainability goals are introduced to usual business practice, it creates uncertainty amongst leaders, managers and employees [1]. The assumed trade-offs between economic growth and social progress have been institutionalized through decades of traditional capitalistic leadership choices [2].

Sustainability Leadership (SL) tests common leadership assumptions, proposing that anyone taking responsibility for influencing and acting on sustainability challenges by working "with" rather than "over" others to achieve a common goal qualifies as a "sustainability leader" [3]. Amongst the fundamental traits include the ability to understand the concept of taking whole systems view and focusing on direction, alignment and commitment to influence collaborative action [4]. Businesses are comprehending that long-term competitive advantage relies on their proactive responsiveness to societal challenges [5]. Social Impact is reflected in the leadership's sustainability values that set the foundation for empowering and developing employees as a strategic capability to facilitate and generate a wide-reaching impact across all stakeholders.

Leadership for sustainability takes accountability, navigates the complexity of social issues by effectively

[a]arpana.sharma@praeeminere.com

DOI: 10.1201/9781003778905-11

and authentically communicating the interdependence of business competitiveness, economic growth and societal impact. Also, leading with a "living systems" paradigm, that appreciates the cultural, social and ecological diversity of ecosystems resulting in transparent and open engagement. SL facilitates momentum for large-scale change by inspiring innovation, awareness, creativity, "sustainability-centric" mindsets, inclusivity, collaboration and reflective leadership process at all levels. SL illustrates skills to harness diverse perspectives and optimize conflicts in individual viewpoints to design optimal scalable community-centric solutions. It is important to highlight that a methodical assessment of the context is necessary to determine the most appropriate strategy that will deliver desired outcomes [6].

2. Methodology

In reference to social sustainability, the concept of organizations as transactional or mechanistic machines designed to maximize profitability and shareholder value, requires an essential paradigm shift from a business-as-usual, silo approach towards the concept of viewing these as adapting, dynamic and continually developing living systems that overlap, interact and connect with its surrounding environment [7]. These linkages are dynamic and complex; change in one sphere creates exponential impact in all other realms. The methodology reviews existing literature, establishing the rationale for deploying SL for uplifting human capital as a source for escalating social sustainability and vitally for long-term business viability.

2.1. The concept of human capital (HC)

Post WW II, witnessed a rise in neo-liberalism wherein the delivery of education has been encapsulated as an essential pillar for economic growth, as a medium to deliver the knowledge and technical skills necessary to achieve prosperity. Human capital theory considers education as an important part of a person's income generating abilities. HC theory highlights the role of education in human development; providing people with the ability to enhance their skills which in turn influences their well-being, economic independence, earn a living and improves human right values. At its core, the purpose of education equips human beings to lead a life of dignity and fulfilled potential (page 2 & 3). From the human rights standpoint advocates are firmly rooted in the thinking that the fundamental purpose of education is not to achieve economic development but promote human dignity and therefore societal wellness. Human Capital is acknowledged as a renewable resource essential for growth, innovation and creativity. It is a portable asset that is owned by the employee and not the employer. An organization can enhance the quality of its human capital through training, motivation and infrastructure to improve its competitive advantage and productivity.

2.2. Understanding the five capitals model (FCM)

Traditional business theory offers a nested depiction of economic growth and profitability that overlooks the complexity and inter-relatedness of diverse spheres. Ekins [8] defines wealth creation as a combination of labor, land and manufactured capital for the production of goods and services. Ludwig von Mises) [9] defined economics as an outcome of human choice and action and the result of the way individuals react to conditions in their environment and not as goods and services. A more sophisticated explanation emphasizes that economic growth is a sub-system of human and social resources which in turn is a sub-system of natural planetary resources [10].

The conventional depiction of "Capital" as an asset restricted to financial and manufactured capital is flawed [11]. The FCM provides a systems-macro level view, highlighting Five Capital stocks namely: (i) Natural, (ii) Human, (iii) Social, (iv) Manufactured, and (v) Financial which the social systems draw on. The mutuality between these stocks and the interchange between the five categories has a direct influence on human well-being [9]. Brooks and Ivory [10] purposely replace the word "Capital" with the term "Resources" thereby depicting the FCM model as Five Resources Sustainability (FRS) which rejects the substitutability of the stocks. Therefore, to thrive and develop resilience, it necessitates efforts towards building, protecting, and managing these resources to ensure adaptability to change.

Research has highlighted the fundamental contribution of human's ability to form relationships and social systems, both of which constitute building blocks for economic growth. The social affiliations residing within the human factor encourage people to work together for mutual benefit therefore facilitating a three-way benefit – internally through corporate gain and economic activity, externally through cohesive functional relationships with suppliers and customers, third where society provides businesses a license to operate [10]. Social well-being is often conceived as meeting basic human needs and concerns with social equality and eradicating poverty, human rights issues, employment and enabling just transition [12]. FCM or FRS, offers a framework for organizations to articulate a vision and develop corporate strategies in an integrated way to maximize value distribution across all five stocks [13].

2.3. Social capital in the context of HC

In reference to social sustainability, the concept of organizations as transactional or mechanistic machines designed to maximize profitability and shareholder value, requires an essential paradigm shift from a business-as-usual, silo approach towards the concept of viewing these as adapting, dynamic and continually developing living systems that overlap, interact and connect with its surrounding environment [7]. Within the context of social systems – individuals are inherent to various systems – families, workplaces, professional and social organizations, communities, governments and others. These institutions are embedded in a world that is facing accelerated change, volatility, increasing complexities and uncertainty. Within the sustainability domain, it is important to recognize the impact of investing in human resources and inherent leadership at the individual and group levels as a building block to enhance social impact. Research literature has defined human capital as the source of unique advantages for businesses and economic growth. Theorists define social capital as informal and formal structures that thrive on trust, common values, norms, mutual aid and reciprocity, making communities resilient and adaptive [14]. They are mobilized and accessed for goal-oriented actions aimed at lowering transaction costs and advancement of society which in turn influence the climate of consent and license to operate for businesses and are vital contributors to socio-political stability. Social sustainability acknowledges the critical contribution of human capital as a strategic asset that allows firms to innovate, adapt, network, collaborate and compete.

Scientists [15] are presenting a deeper understanding of the physical, biological, and social systems that are paradoxical networks of dynamic and interconnected activity that cannot be controlled or predicted with a reasonable degree of certainty. [9] in their paper "Human Capital and Sustainability," highlight the welfare and development of human consciousness as the real source of wealth creation and core determinant of social, economic and ecological development. They define human capital as knowledge, skills, attitudes and individual competencies, the capacity for invention, technological advancements, resourcefulness and discovery as well as the collective social and cultural endowments. Fundamentally, societal progress relies on the generation of new ideas, innovation, higher values and attitudes demonstrated by individuals which eventually are accepted and assimilated by social institutions [9]. In their research, they have drawn attention to education at the core of human development and social evolution [9].

Similarly, [11] refer to the stock of skills, knowledge and competencies that are assets of an individual and that the value of human capital is secured by employment and application of these assets versus non-use; the value will increase with education, learning and training. Further a positive correlation between the practical application of human capital together with innovative technology provides companies with a competitive advantage and increases economic growth. This results in good health, resilience, improved work attendance and adaptability of the workforce and consequently within the communities. A fundamental difference between human and social capital is that at the individual level, for example, health and education can be acquired by a single person regardless of what other people do; social capital on the other hand relies on networks built on cooperation and trust [16]. This creates an opportunity to invest in the development of human capital as a conduit for creating social advocates as enablers of a self-perpetuating cycle of social reforms.

2.4. SL theories: literature review

Avery in his book "Leadership for Sustainable Futures – Achieving Success in a Competitive World," defines two types of Capitalism that impact sustainability development and leadership in organizations. The "Anglo/US capitalism" model focuses on profitability and maximizing shareholder value. A leader in this context, can effectively lead linear change that is well-defined, rational and focused on a pre-defined outcome leading the organization [15]. Within this context, the text highlights the disadvantages of short-term profits that ignore stakeholder interests and discourage long term thinking, investing and planning.

The "Rhineland capitalism" model on, the contrary, recognizes the inter-connectedness between business and their community and is therefore concerned with social justice, long-term sustainability, and relationships with its broader network not just shareholders. The literature demonstrates the influence of capitalism on organizational values, priorities and beliefs that inform corporate strategy and ultimately drive decision-making processes [17]. The Rhineland model has a pronounced social dimension with varying forms that include the social market economies which rely on principles of equitable distribution of income and resources, social justice and elimination of poverty. The approach centers on engaging multiple stakeholders in a dialogue and capitalizing on diverse perspectives to co-create solutions that are relevant to the context. Researchers [17] agree that the two forms of capitalism are distinct in their influence on income distribution, innovation, the nature of employment and people's quality of life with a general agreement that Rhineland model is superior.

Avery (17) argues that the widely accepted leadership theory premised in the Anglo/US model fails to bring the quality of life to individuals and societies that is required for sustainability and that its approach to capitalism and business is seriously defective. The narrow belief of deferring to a leader for problem-solving, guidance and direction comes at the cost of rejecting personal accountability, creating a "learned helplessness" that presents an obstacle to enabling a collective and synergistic action required to develop innovative solutions and solve complex problems [15]. As opposed to working with a very narrow definition, leadership for sustainability enables opportunities for people to collectively generate solutions through dialogue, collaboration, exploration, knowledge exchange and presenting diverse perspectives that lead to realistic and relevant action.

Traditional leadership theories propose that human relations and interactions can be controlled, predicted and defined by internal rules. Whereas sustainability leadership recognizes the complexity and dynamism of human relationships that represent attributes of living processes that include adaptivity, resilience, self-renewal, awareness, partnerships and flexibility. Their expanded awareness and holistic view of the interconnectedness of all spheres and that no single action occurs in isolation but is inextricably linked to every other action helps to engage in the genuine process of decision-making with others in the interest of people. This approach recognizes the potential to explore human differences and tap into diverse insights to make smarter, more reliable and responsive choices to tackle sustainability challenges. Thinking holistically creates win-win partnerships and joint strategies to initiate far reaching solutions [15].

SL challenges the status quo of business as usual, they highlight collaboration, inclusiveness, relationships, common purpose and renewed values that embrace the ecological and cultural diversity of natural systems [18] define SL as one who fosters sustainable practices in their society, organizations and drives economic growth. It reinforces creating long-term value while enhancing the quality of life for all stakeholders. Sustainable leaders exhibit core abilities that include innovation, sustainable organizational culture, ethical behaviour, forward looking perspective, human capital development, social and environmental accountability [18].

The role of business is at the core of designing and delivering impactful social equity through advancing human capital. Common SL viewpoint in creating sustainable organizations is to challenge the status quo and recognizing self-responsibility towards individuals, groups and organizations [4]. Sustainability leaders play a catalytic role in a system-wide transformation and co-creating "social impact organisations," that systematically and sustainably aim to resolve local and global community needs. Latiffi and Zulkiffli [4] define SL as "an ability to influence and motivate individual, groups, organization and society by assessing sustainability knowledge into their principles without neglecting experience from the past, so that it can be improved continuously either in present also in future" [4]. UNESCO [3] suggested competencies for SL include: (a) systems thinking, (b) anticipatory, (c) normative, (d) strategic action, (e) collaboration, (f) critical thinking, (g) self-awareness, and (h) integrated problem-solving competencies. Drawing from a cross-cultural perspective these are broadened to include other dimensions such as gender complementarity, collective decision-making, equality and awareness of ancestors and future generations.

2.5. SL leading social impact

2.5.1. Organizational learning (OL)

Organizations lead by Sustainability Leadership are demonstrating conscious and strategic "people-first" policy approaches in securing social prosperity and scaling social impact efforts. Organizations utilize leadership in human capital as rare, non-substitutable and inimitable rare resources who care for all stakeholders. Human resources offer the dynamic capability that allows firms to adapt, develop, re-configure and integrate both internal and external competencies to deal with climate change threats. Leadership for sustainability plays a vital role in developing learning organizations that are concerned with extensive collaboration and systems thinking. SL drives, promotes and influences sustainability values at the individual and organizational levels. They inspire a mindset shift centered around shared vision, valuing employees, social responsibility, amicable labor relations and long-term competitive advantage [18].

The concept of learning organizations as a strategic tool deployed to elevate growth, adaptability and resilience through enhancing human capital, knowledge exchange, learning and capacity building. Fundamental to learning organizations are various components including: (i) commitment to learning, (ii) fostering connections and community, (iii) encouraging employee inclusivity and empowerment, (iv) supporting creativity, innovation and risk-taking, (v) establish a safe working environment, (vi) motivate purpose-driven action, (vii) focus on open, transparent communication and fair governance systems, (viii) engage in future-oriented dialogue with employees and embrace diverse perspectives to resolve issues. Effective OL ultimately improves social performance through human connections with the social systems [18, 19] have highlighted the critical role of SL in institutionalizing a safe work environment that encourages knowledge sharing and open communication conducive to learning. Tangible and intangible manifestations of OL have been illustrated through diverse literature with positive and responsible citizenship behaviour, conscious mindfulness, civic virtue, service quality, innovation, market orientation, active participation and establishing partnerships. Further, an increased learning mindset provides a higher capacity to manage the triple bottom line approaches by providing competencies to create new structures, policies and processes [18].

Research [18] in select ASEAN countries validated the significant influence SL exerts in establishing a thriving OL culture as an enabler of sustainable thinking, knowledge base and orientation to complex sustainability problem solving to climate change threats to communities. Principles of inter-organiztional learning through the integration of knowledge management processes enhances human capital capabilities and create psychological empowerment – a powerful moderator in effective knowledge generation and exchange that extends beyond organizational boundaries and inspires widespread change. OL provides a sense of purpose and willingness within employees to take the initiative and exhibit SL behaviour in their interaction with colleagues, supervisors, stakeholders from local and international communities backgrounds, ethics and locations. SL premised within a firm's human capital promotes climate education and introduces OL as a dynamic capability thus driving sustainability performance and high organizational citizenship behaviours.

The Pandemic is a useful reference in the context of necessitating organizational learning in the short term for both leaders and employees. Strategic shifts were necessary to adapt to changing environments, including pivoting the workforce by adopting effective talent management techniques that included retraining, upskilling and reskilling to align with renewed organizational objectives. To meet new demands emerging from sustainable business practices, OL approach is inevitable to enhance quality of human capital and business competitiveness, to move forward and avoiding the risk of failure.

2.5.2. Taking the triple bottom line approach (TBL)

The concept of TBL provides a strategic accounting framework that measures three dimensions of a company's activities including both profitability and shareholder values on its social, environmental and economic capitals. TBL is a globally accepted model in setting out sustainable development corporate strategies based on three agendas – People, Planet and Profit [20]. Getzner's TBL model highlights the overarching impact of wider environmental quality with social equity and economic benefits as subsystems. Several academicians [20] have identified additional dimensions within the TBL model – institutional, cultural, human values, ethics, technology and world-view. Social dimension encompasses an organization's influence on the people's welfare both employees and community in addressing issues like education, community interaction, charitable causes, fair and ethical practices.

Extant literature proposes the application of organizational learning at the core to meet TBL objectives in turbulent operating environments. Increasing uncertainty implies an enhanced level of OL to meet higher cognitive demands that involve tasks like information analysis, making connections and drawing conclusions which then create conditions for increased interactions that play a central role in quality outcomes related to sustainable performance [18]. TBL lacks a universal standard for calculation which makes it adaptable to the needs of different entities. Anecdotal evidence has established a compelling case for the integration of TBL as a core value within organizations. Within the human resource and social perspective, businesses have identified variables including: (i) average training hours per employee, (ii) career retention, (iii) employee welfare, and (iv) charitable contributions which link directly to some social components for example relative poverty, unemployment, hygiene and health, education standards and gender equality [21].

2.5.3. Creating shared value (CSV)

A concept by Michael Porter and Mark Kramer [2] proposed re-inventing the neo-classical capitalistic model that is increasingly being perceived as the reason for social, environmental and economic problems. The CSV model amplifies the importance of connecting business and society. Three components within the model that create shared value opportunities: (i) re-imagining products and markets, (ii) redefining productivity in the value chain, and (iii) enabling community development [2]. The framework encourages firms to expand their pool of economic gains. It incorporates policy levers and operational practices within the strategic objectives aimed at enhancing organizational competitiveness while uplifting communities in which it operates. Companies like Coca-Cola, Wal-Mart, Johnson and Johnson, Google and Unilever are examples of companies practicing CSV by re-imagining the intersection between corporate and social performance [2].

Sustainable organizations understand the role of CSV in embedding a positive social-business relationship. SL investing in CSV initiatives reflect their ability to appreciate the long-term strategic benefits – foster trust, decrease transaction costs, positive publicity, institutional advocacy, minimize turnover, build a diverse workforce, promote ethical supply-chain management, introduce a moral dimension into policy-making, co-create collaborative solutions attract and retain talent [22].

3. Fındıngs

Mainstream leadership models illustrate top-down decisions that are concerned with accounting for financial profitability in a planned, rational, efficient way to achieve pre-determined outcomes but fail to understand the connectedness of organizations with human, social and natural capitals; sustainability solutions in one domain will impact all other spheres [15]. Leadership for sustainability as presented in this literature is a radically expanded view of traditional leadership traits. It requires individuals in and outside formal positions of power who understand their association within a broader, dynamic human living system of relationships and interdependencies. These everyday leaders across all agencies are committed to taking actions, leveraging the power of human capital and collaborations to drive change and make a positive difference in communities and organizations.

Enhancing human capital through effective utilization, education and training has a direct impact across all social systems that these individuals are part of and feed into. Further, cross-sectoral nature of businesses enables a multiplier impact across their networks. Skills, competencies, and education residing within an individual provide the propensity to mobilize a collective action that becomes the bedrock for social upliftment. Human capital well-being and development play a vital role in reinforcing their impact on economic growth, better governance, health, employment and social control premised on their interrelationship. Quality of communication is at the core of effective transformation. These competencies demonstrated by leaders creates an enabling environment of trust that allows open dialogue, two-way exchange of ideas and perspectives making conversations goal oriented, productive, enriching and focused. The author acknowledges real world challenges that global organizations witness within the diversity of its workforce and intercultural management. In scenarios where diverse perspectives need to be harnessed and negotiated to achieve multinational objectives, cultural differences create a potential for conflicts, bias and operational risks within the organizational, national and social contexts.

The author acknowledges that due to its flexibility, application of the TBL framework can be problematic. Asset owners and Managers profess that firms applying the model perform better present more accurate valuation, demonstrate faster growth and sustain longer than companies that don't consider "People, Planet & Profit". The challenge is that TBL represents just one bottom line by considering the material risks/opportunities across all sectors. TBL has inspired several reporting frameworks including Social Return on Investment (SROI), Global Reporting Initiative (GRI) and ESG (focus on investors and financial analysts on Environmental, Social and Governance features). Its core purpose was to create a shift from traditional capitalism towards systems change by provoking companies to delve into their firm's social, environmental and economic impact and be ready for future markets. In a Harvard Business Review article, Elkington recalled the TBL not because the concept of "people, planet and profit" was inaccurate, but it is the misinterpretation of the word "profit". Companies have exploited this framework as a marketing tool to block corporate accountability, over-inflate their sustainability performance, provide incomplete information, hide greenwashing practices, and justify inaction against sustainability.

The insights presented in this literature are a synthesis of diverse research resources to establish a compelling case for developing sustainable values, consciousness and leadership skills inherent in employees. Human resource empowerment is at the core of proactive responsiveness to address societal challenges, develop adaptive capacity and resilience thus enabling a self-sustaining and scalable solution across diverse stakeholders. SL enabled OL as a dynamic capability, enabling businesses to rapidly configure and leverage resources to meet the requirements of its stakeholders thus being a source of continuing competitive advantage. In the assessment of existing research, the author recognizes the lack of theoretical and conceptual coherence in this domain.

4. Conclusion

SL ability to enhance Human Capital to drive Social Impact relies on diverse conceptual models that should not be treated as mutually exclusive but recognized as synergistic and interlinked. Contextualization of these frameworks and their principles is critical to achieve desired results. A renewed focus on SL models provides information into core competencies, traits, values, behaviours, skills and actions, they lack in presenting a holistic purview and integration with how these aspects are connected and affect social impact.

The author recommends the development of a comprehensive and cohesive leadership model and teaching pedagogy that encourages peer-to-peer learning as presented by OL learning models. Simulated program design centered on real-world sustainability challenges, systems thinking, experiential learning and interdisciplinary approach is critical to developing human capital as strategic resources and change agents for social impact. Insights presented in this paper, provide a comprehensive argument to develop SL premised within human capital as impactful levers to drive and enable top-down, bottom-up and inside-out change that is self-perpetuating and scalable. Demonstrating self-awareness allows leaders to identify areas of weaknesses and pro-actively leverage development tools including training programs, feedback loop, assessments and mentoring to improve their competencies.

Further, structured reporting frameworks are central to ensuring accountability and transparency in sustainable business practices. Theorists have proposed ideas to fine-tune the concept of TBL to reflect societal value. Proposed solutions include replacing "profit" by the word "prosperity" as a more accurate representation of the companies creating economic value for the society. This extends beyond financial gains into creating employment, innovation and education. A standardized approach for example science-based impact measurement, is proposed by investors that incorporates a consistent format for organization's to report on all material issues, foster stronger collaboration between scientists, companies, investors and not for profit and government agencies.

For example, in the instance of automation industry that rely heavily on technology, machinery and specialized skills, SL competencies that ensure equitable integration of technology, collaboration with local partners and supporting communities with technological solutions to resolve issues and access to learning. Enhanced employee engagement through education and incentivization to create a culture that values sustainability can be an effective tool to extend the benefits into the communities. Creating value and its equitable distribution amongst it underlying production resources including talent, suppliers and consumers and the environment will determine the viability of organizations and their ability to remain profitable in the long term.

Within the domain of Organizational Learning, research purports the advantages of distributed decision making and the positive influence of decentralized organizational structure on performance, flow of information, leadership and talent development, fostering innovation by bridging the gap between ideas and execution with tangible results. Referencing to the Resource Based View (RBV) companies can leverage their unique internal resources to enhance competitiveness and strategic impact while facilitating societal wellness.

Decentralized operations for global corporates, enabled by technology fosters an agile cohesive ecosystem. The approach allows firms to empower societies by equipping local teams with the control and autonomy required to meet regional and market conditions, improved customer satisfaction and cross-collaboration while providing conditions for sustainable progress and societal advancement. Companies with SL, operating within local contexts have an opportunity to participate in uplifting whole communities through job creation, education, promoting equality, enhanced health privileges and supporting local economies. Additionally, through environmental stewardship, these leaders ensure their organization are contributing to the preservation and regeneration of ecosystems and biodiversity that provide sustenance to communities that in turn provide firms with talent and human capital to remain competitive.

References

[1] Galpin, T., & Whittington, J. L. (2012). Sustainability Leadership; from strategy to results. *Journal of Business Strategy*, *33*(4), 40–48. *https://*& Slaus, I. (2011), Human Capital and Sustainability. *Sustainability*, *3*(1), 97–154. *https://doi.org/10.3390/su3010097*

[2] Porter, M. E., & Kramer, M. R. (2011). Creating Shared Value, How to Reinvent Capitalism – and unleash a wave of innovation and growth. The Big Idea – *Harvard Business Review*, 5–11. *https://hbr.org/2011/01/the-big-idea-creating-shared-valu*e

[3] Beehner, C., & Norren, D. V. (2021). Sustainability leadership, UNESCO competencies for SDGs, and diverse leadership models. *International Journal of Development and Sustainability, 10*(1), 24–49. Article IJDS21022201 https://isdsnet.com/ijds-v10n1-03.pdf

[4] Latiffi, A. A., & Zulkiffli, N. A. (July 2016). Theoretical Review of Sustainable Leadership (SL). *MATEC Web of Conferences*, *66*(5–6). Article 00045. https://www.researchgate.net/publication/305309626_Theoretical_Review_on_Sustainable_Leadership_SL

[5] Asif, V., & Palus, J. C. (2013). Leadership Strategies for Societal Impact. *Technical Report: Affiliation, Centre for Creative Leadership*, 3–13. *https://www.researchgate.net/publication/310399812_Leadership_strategies_for_societal_impact*

[6] Burns, H., Diamond-Vaught, H., & Bauman, C. (2015). Leadership for Sustainability: Theoretical Foundations and Pedagogical Practices that Foster Change. *International Journal of Leadership Studies, 9*(1), 89–96. ISSN 1554-3145. *https://pdxscholar.library.pdx.edu/elp_fac/45/*

[7] Barnett, M., & Salomon, M. R. (2011). Does it Pay to Be Really Good? Addressing the Shape of the Relationship between Social and Financial Performance. *Strategic Management Journal, 33*(11). doi:10.2307/41679849. *https://www.researchgate.net/publication/228248940_Does_it_Pay_to_Be_Really_Good_Addressing_the_Shape_of_the_Relationship_between_Social_and_Financial_Performance*

[8] Ekins, P. (2000). *Economic Growth and Environmental Sustainability – The prospects for Green Growth*. Routledge (Limited Preview digital ed.). *https://books.google.ae/books?hl=en&lr=&id=wzCEAgAAQBAJ&oi=fnd&pg=PT9&ots=fQRG0RIJd1&sig=gUb991WMSupnUQcvhnbl0JIk_5s&redir_esc=y#v=onepage&q&f=false).*

[9] Jacobs, G., & Slaus, I. (2011), Human Capital and Sustainability. *Sustainability*, *3*(1), 97–154. *https://doi.org/10.3390/su3010097*

[10] Brooks, S. B., & Ivory, S. (2018, September 3–6). *An updated conceptualization of corporate sustainability: Five resources sustainability*. British Academy of Management Annual Conference, Bristol, United Kingdom. *https://www.research.ed.ac.uk/en/publications/an-updated-conceptualisation-of-corporate-sustainability-five-res*

[11] Davidsdottir, B., & Maack, M. (2015). Five capital impact assessment: Appraisal framework based on theory of sustainable well-being. *Renewable and Sustainable Energy Reviews, 50*(2), 1338–1351 *https://www.researchgate.net/publication/279270305_Five_capital_impact_assessment_Appraisal_framework_based_on_theory_of_sustainable_well-being*

[12] Blewitt, J., & Kopnin, H. (2014). *Sustainable Business: Key Issues*. Routledge, doi:10.4324/9781315110172 https://www.researchgate.net/publication/258727756_Sustainable_Business_Key_Issues

[13] Porritt, J. (2020, December). The Five Capitals – a framework for sustainability. *Forum for the Future.* https://www.forumforthefuture.org/the-five-capitals

[14] Schuller, T. (2001). *The Complimentary roles of human and social capital*. Birbeck College, University of London, 2–26. https://www.oecd.org/innovation/research/1825424.pdf

[15] Ferdig, M. A. (2007). Sustainability Leadership: Co-creating a Sustainable Future. *Journal of Change Management*, *7*(1). 26–33. doi:10.1080/14697010701233809 *https://www.researchgate.net/publication/240237712*

[16] Parts, E. (2004) Interrelationships between Human Capital and Social Capital: Implications for Economic Development in Transition Economies; University of Tartu Economics and Business Working Paper No. 2003–24 *https://papers.ssrn.com/sol3/papers.cfm?abstract_id=486946*)

[17] Avery, G. C. (2005). *Leadership for Sustainable Futures: Achieving success in the competitive world*. Edward Elgar Publishing limited, Cheltenham, United Kingdom, 6–9. *https://books.google.ae/books?hl=en&lr=&id=H-o4AgAAQBAJ&oi=fnd&pg=PR1&ots=59fvajJklz&sig=i612kk0v7wYQpNRnf-F00BhY-Tg&redir_esc=y#v=onepage&q&f=false*

[18] Ahmad, N. H., Halim, H. A., & Iqbal, Q. (2020). How does SL influence sustainable performance – Empirical Evidence from Selected ASEAN countries. *SAGE Open*, *10*(4), 3–12. *https://journals.sagepub.com/doi/10.1177/2158244020969394*

[19] Mahmood, M., & Malik, H. (2022). Impact of Authentic Leadership, Sustainable Leadership on Sustainable Growth with mediating Role of Organizational Learning. *Academic Journal of Social Sciences, 6*(1), 48–69. *https://www.academia.edu/103882126/Impact_of_Authentic_Leadership_Sustainable_Leadership_on_Sustainable_Growth_with_Mediating_Role_of_Organizational_Learning*

[20] Correia, S. M. (2019). Sustainability: An Overview of the Triple Bottom Line and Sustainability Implementation. *Article in Journal of Strategic Engineering, 2*(1), 32–34. *https://www.researchgate.net/publication/330057873*

[21] Hall, T. J., & Slaper, T. F (2011). The Triple Bottom Line: What Is It and How Does it Work?. *Indiana Business Review, 86*(1). *https://www.ibrc.indiana.edu/ibr/2011/spring/article2.html*

[22] Menghwar, P. S., & Daood, A. (2021). Creating shared value: A systematic review, synthesis and integrative perspective. *International Journal of Management Reviews*, *23*(4), 466–485.

12 Community development through advocacy and solution-based journalism: The case of *Radio Tilonia*

Avneesh Kumar[1,a], *Soumyadipta Banerjee*[1,b], *and Lakhan Raghuvanshi*[2,c]

[1]Department of Journalism and Mass Communication, Manipal University Jaipur, Jaipur, Rajasthan, India
[2]School of Journalism & Mass Communication, Devi Ahilya Vishwavidyalaya, Indore, Madhya Pradesh, India

Abstract: Community radio stations are known for focusing on the interests of the community. Specifically, community radio stations working in the rural areas strive for highlighting the concerns of the local people and practising solutions-based journalism. Through a case study of Radio Tilonia, this article explores the specific focus of this radio station on community rights and entitlements, through solution-based journalism. To engage and be connected with the local community, the community radio station broadcasts relevant information about government schemes in both Hindi and the local language. This study builds on observations and interviews to showcase the commitment of this radio station in bringing social change. By providing information to the community members about government schemes, the radio station is ensuring that the community members stay informed. This has led to better awareness about government schemes and the community members also receiving information about their rights and entitlements. Thus, this study demonstrates how solution-based journalism and media advocacy by community radio may serve as social change agents and deliver solutions to issues that may daunt members of the community.

Keywords: Community radio in India, Community media, media advocacy, case study, Radio Tilonia, social change agents

1. Introduction

Majority of Indians live in rural areas. The rural sector in India is defined by the government of India as an area (which may be a village or a collection of a village) with a population density of less than 400 people per square kilometre and where the total population doesn't exceed 5000. Also, the general characteristic of a rural population is that more than 25% of the male working population is engaged in agriculture [1]. Fulfilling this criterion is 908.8 million people vis-à-vis 508.37 million who are living in urban or semi-urban areas in India [2]. There is a marked apathy of the mainstream, legacy media toward the rural areas of India in terms of news coverage, resulting in "silencing" the rural populace [3]. This has resulted in the creation of news deserts across large swathes of the rural landscape of India, which aren't serviced by the legacy or corporate media that are based out of the Indian metropolitan cities. This has adversely impacted democratic systems, civic participation, among other effects [4]. This dominant and corporate media system has systematically created a large subaltern population in the rural regions of India where issues, such as agricultural distress, community rights, health facilities, unemployment and so on, are regularly overshadowed by the urban-centric news. This has given rise to alternative forms of media in the regions that try to cover up in the face of severe handicaps [5].

The alternative forms of media, particularly community media, have demonstrated noticeable successes in key developmental parameters such as gender issues and violence against women in the remote rural areas of India that are unreachable to the commercial, city-based Indian news media [6]. Indian commercial and legacy news media, especially the Indian languages media, have been experiencing transformative changes over the last few decades, resulting in rapid expansion in terms of audience, organizations, and markets [7]. However, these changes have failed in making media more pluralistic or audience-centric due to commercialization and cross-media ownership, among other factors [15]. Indian media has also been repeatedly called out for exhibiting bias in its reporting, propagating disinformation and fake news, and making insufficient efforts

[a]avneesh.kumar@jaipur.manipal.edu, [b]soumyadipta@soumyadipta.com, [c]drlakhanraghuvanshi@gmail.com

DOI: 10.1201/9781003778905-12

in asking relevant questions. The experts at the World Economic Forum's Global Risk Report ranked India on top for the perceived risk of pervasion of misinformation and disinformation in the commercial mainstream media [16]. Moreover, survey findings suggest that readers are losing trust in mainstream media in India [17], while on the other hand, community media is thriving and gaining trust among the rural communities of India.

2. Community Radio: Bridging Gaps

Community communication generally depends on the strong participation of the individuals belonging to these communities. To start with, these initiatives emerged because of people's dissatisfaction with the mainstream media [8]. The intention to particularly amplify the voices of specific communities has been instrumental in making these initiatives truly democratic and encouraging integration of local residents into a cohesive community [9]. Outside the legacy media, smaller organizations perform strong journalism even with limited resources and must be studied to understand the changes effected by them at the grassroots level. In their works, several media scholars have highlighted the key role of community media, as alternative media, in empowering small communities, interest groups, social movements, and civil societies [10–12]. Thus, community media fulfils voids left along the way by the legacy media and there is scholarly evidence that communities have chosen their own media over legacy media at times of crises [13].

In India, mainstream media channels feel the pressure of constantly being relevant to the larger audience and a need to constantly acquire readers and expand their consumer base in the country, at a time when literacy and digital adoption both are on an uptick in India. To grab the attention of audiences, they also engage in marketing practices that perpetuate targeting of the young, urban populace living in the cities [14]. In such a scenario, community media, more specifically community radio channels, have gained credibility and acceptance among communities [18]. Community radio in India celebrated 20 years of existence in India and was acknowledged as the "important third tier in Radio Broadcasting, distinct from Public Service Radio broadcasting and Commercial Radio" [19]. This is driven by their existence as community-based, independent from commercialization, and unaffected by the market or the government. They have emerged as the alternative media and have significantly contributed to counterbalancing the hegemonic attitudes of commercial mass media [20]. As an entity established for the service of the community, community radio has given voice to people and has assisted them in expressing their sufferings [20]. Additionally, community radio stations have also contributed towards strengthening the communication rights of people, furthering media democracy and social change [21]. Community radio stations are known for embracing participatory, open, not-for-profit practices, which takes into account only the benefit of the community and not the interests of the owners. [22], contends that community radio is a source of local, neighbourhood-based news, entertainment and information. The voices of local people get a platform through community radio. On this platform, they learn to appreciate each other and assert their local identity. Hence, the existence of a community radio, [23], suggests, is similar to proclaiming that "we may be citizens of a country, but we are residents of a locality."

One of the major functions of community radio in India has been advocacy for the rights of the community members, covering a broad range from women's empowerment, awareness about rights and laws, education, health and preservation of indigenous cultures that are typical to the community it serves. Hence, advocacy is one of the important functions of community radio and has brought positive outcomes in community development, especially in far-flung areas of India that are not served by legacy media [24].

3. Community Media Advocacy: An Interventionist Tool

The interventions of the community media to reinforce positive societal changes have received numerous scholarly affirmations from academicians and professionals alike. Milan (2009) acknowledges the role community media plays as a developmental tool, such as democratization, aiding and supporting social struggles to bridge social gaps and creating awareness. However, the study also accepts the challenges, community media faces due to financial constraints and legal issues to perform the same functions [25]. The Council of Europe (2022), in its report on the effects of community media, conforms to the view that thriving community media is more often an indicator of a healthy, democratically orientated social structure that is dealing with the societal and structural challenges within the community much more effectively [26].

Media advocacy, which is defined as a strategic use of mass media to advance public policy initiatives, is particularly effective in the case of communities [27]. Media advocacy, especially through community media, is regarded as a potent tool to bring about positive changes in society and it works well when used in conjunction with community organizations' outreach and dialogues within the community [28]. The posit about the potency and power of advocacy on community media has received confirmational foundations from world agencies like UNESCO and the World Bank too [22]. Such interventions of community media have shown results during health policy advocacy for public health initiatives [29] and garnered support regarding policy changes that may have widespread impact [30].

There are cases of community media advocacy being used for influencing public policies as well [31]. In this sphere, community media has an inherent advantage over legacy media, as the dependence on journalists from mainstream media limits the ability to reach the policymakers. On the other hand, legacy media's tendency to endorse the elitist theory of democracy also serves as a spanner in the wheel regarding effecting policy changes [32]. In the field of policy advocacy, community media has a distinct edge over legacy and commercial media. During challenging times, community media is seen as a harbinger of inclusivity and a solution provider through its function as an advocate of positive change [33]. Thus, community media, through advocating issues that bring social change, engages and re-engages communities, opening possibilities for the change to take effect [34]. As a result, we may see a trend of advocates emerging within a community that may be a micro-community within a larger community [35].

4. Research Methodology

To understand the role of the community radio station's impact through advocacy and solution-based journalism, the case study method was selected as a research method as most scholars have used the method of single and comparative case studies to understand the rural community at Tilonia village. The Case Study method is also deemed a viable research method to understand different aspects of a community, especially those related to community media [36–38]. Hence, an in-depth case study was determined to be a suitable research method for this study. Radio Tilonia falls under the category of rural stations in India and serves a thriving community of about 7,500 people in about 30 villages, located about 50 kilometres to the north-east of Ajmer city, Rajasthan [39].

To understand the impact of the community radio station's programmes on the community members, semi-structured interviews were conducted with the participants of the community, as it allows for rich qualitative data in areas where human inputs determine results, as in community studies [40].

5. Radio Tilonia: Serving the Rural Community of Rajasthan in India

Tilonia radio station is part of the Barefoot College community programme that serves villages in a range of 500 square kilometres, covering about 110 villages in the Silora Block in Ajmer district of Rajasthan. The community radio started functioning in 2010 and has a reach that covers 30 villages where various community programmes, like night schools and training camps, are undertaken regularly. These community programmes were part of a model grassroots rural development strategy that was initiated in the village on February 5, 1972 with the setting up of a social work research centre against a modest lease amount imposed by the state government of Rajasthan. Over the decades, this community programme has been recognized as one of the most successful rural community development programmes in India [41]. Tilonia village, which the radio station primarily serves, is located in Kishangarh Tehsil of Ajmer district in Rajasthan, where approximately 604 families reside. As per the last census in 2011, the village has a population of 3556, of which 1789 are males and 1767 are females. The female literacy rate of the village is around 44.8% [42].

Radio Tilonia commenced its operations on November 9, 2009 because of the efforts of Raghav Mahto, who established this low-cost station on the premises of the Barefoot College, an NGO established by Bunker Roy, an Indian social activist. Mahto was a radio repairman from Mansoorpur in Vaishali district in Bihar who used to run an unlicensed FM radio station in his hometown that was eventually shut down by the government. He used his earlier experience to set up Radio Tilonia [39].

Several community interventions of the "Barefoot Programme," with the aid of the community radio station boosting their awareness, have been proven to be successful women empowerment intervention models, emulated at several diverse rural locations across the globe [43]. The intervention models have been emulated in 43 countries across Asia, Africa, and Latin America with human change agents like doctors and engineers trained at Tilonia. Notably, many of these training modules are conducted and led by the native women of Tilonia. The training programmes to empower rural change agents to deliver the interventions at different levels and locations are an ongoing activity in Tilonia village. The social change leadership approach at Tilonia was found to be bottoms-up (which includes the change leaders driving change through community radio). Active participation (including in community outreach programmes) was found to be effective as it instilled a sense of pride and resulted in the empowerment of the community members [44].

6. Radio Tilonia: Advocating rights through people-centred journalism

As a community radio station, Radio Tilonia is focused on attaining social change in the community it operates in. The station takes up the issues of villagers, makes people aware of their rights and also engages with the authorities concerned if there is a requirement of grievance redressal.

By practicing journalism through focusing on issues of rights and entitlement of the locals, this community radio station is championing the cause of the community. Their rights and concerns drive the journalism of Radio Tilonia. Thus, in the context of this specific community, the channel makes for a relevant case study. This study is designed to provide the context of Radio Tilonia doing advocacy journalism, highlight their contribution towards the promotion of rights and entitlements, and give a perspective on changes brought about at the grassroots level with people's participation.

On a daily basis, the station delivers seven hours of engaging content for the local community. Typically, their programs revolve solely around the rights and concerns of the local community. However, it also actively promotes local culture and folk music. Thus, traditional artists also receive a platform. Since its inception, the station has been making significant strides. Their programming approach is characterized by an activist style and people-centred journalism. This radio station devotes considerable time to discussing the rights and concerns of the local community. For practicing people-centred journalism, Radio Tilonia frequently features human interest stories. This bottom-up approach bridges the gap between the listeners and the producers of radio programmes. Arti Devi, the station head of Radio Tilonia, explains the approach of the radio station:

> …our engagement with the community is robust as well as responsive. We produce content through a bottom-up, community-oriented approach. People are disappointed with the mainstream media. They consume mainstream media for entertainment, whereas they trust us for being accountable. Our efforts have been fruitful in bringing transparency in local governance. We continuously work towards disseminating awareness about government services and play a critical role in smooth delivery of government services in the local community.

Norat Mal is a local RTI activist and actively helps Aarti Devi manage the radio station. He regularly visits nearby villages, discusses issues with people and endeavours to understand their concerns. By incorporating these discussions in the community radio programs, he brings in diverse perspectives and tries to increase community participation. He adds:

The focus is on the community. Our real strength lies in them. For calling this station a community radio station, we are required to remain connected to the community. And this can only happen when we establish a strong connection with them. This is why I consistently meet them to understand and listen to their problems. We also organize programs and seek community feedback. Accordingly, programs are prepared and broadcast. The effort is to provide them with relevant information and find solutions to their problems.

In its programming, this community radio station demonstrates commitment towards solution-oriented journalism. Regular interaction with the community assists in knowing about local people's experiences and preparing programs. When people require information and support, they contact the radio station and the staff of the station escalates the matter to the authorities concerned. This approach helps foster positive social change. Because of the facility of call-ins to the radio station, people find it easier to reach out and report events or suggest information requirements.

The Indian government has devised several developmental schemes particularly targeted towards the rural communities, such as the Mahatma Gandhi National Rural Employment Guarantee Act, Pradhan Mantri Gram Sadak Yojana, Deen Dayal Upadhyaya Grameen Kaushalya Yojana and so on. Given the large percentage of rural population in this area, the dependence on government schemes is very high. However, information about these schemes is scarcely available to the community. Radio Tilonia makes an important intervention here. The radio station educates the community members on how to avail these schemes from the government, especially the process for application, how to apply and more importantly, how to follow up on an application.

The community radio station also educates the local people about some crucial rights, such as the right to information and its processes, right to food, and right to education, to ensure that the villagers have ample information about these important laws and government initiatives. Programs about these schemes are consistently aired in both Hindi and Marwari, the local language spoken by most people in the community. This ensures a clear an easy reception of the messages. For providing accurate information, the radio station also frequently invites government officers. These guests answer the questions of the listeners and clarify their doubts. Also, these programs enhance the credibility of information while also creating opportunities for dialogue and participation.

7. Information, Access and Accountability

Community radio stations are not allowed to broadcast news bulletins in India. This strict regulation on community radio prevents them from doing direct journalism. However, as [45] points out in her study that these radio practitioners have succeeded in practising journalism by concentrating on providing relevant information and furthering development-related discourse. The specific, local, timely news appearing on community radio stations in India addresses a major concern related to local news coverage not finding space in the mainstream Indian media. The accountability towards the community in the broadcasting of Radio Tilonia is appreciated by listeners. "Their programs are related to the local news requirements. News and information about community rights, agriculture and government schemes are broadcasted by the radio station," adds a listener.

As a community platform, Radio Tilonia has successfully created an informative and accessible space for people. Consequently, people get the opportunity to partake in development communication discourses. In this rural area of Rajasthan, the community radio station actively engages with the local community and aims to make this engagement sustainable and purposeful. Through this empowered mode of participation, the radio station is also providing direct access to radio programming to the local community. The result is the direct impact on the produced content. The broadcaster succeeds in making community-relevant programs, which reflects in how villagers perceive the journalism of Radio Tilonia.

A regular listener of the radio, who generally uses his mobile phone for tuning in to the radio station, points out the specific nature of journalism:

I work as a labourer. I listen to this radio regularly to receive information about our rights. Discussion about government schemes is regularly broadcast. If I face any problem in accessing these schemes, I contact the station to get clarity. Programmes about our rights help us become more aware and provide us the required information.

This is a hyperlocal journalism practice that goes beyond the broader scope of regional or national news and delves into the intricacies of the neighbourhood. The content delivered is essential for community development. Because of the unique interests, concerns, and dynamics of the local population, this kind of journalism is of great importance to the local community. For community development, Radio Tilonia has proven to be an important ally in the promotion and preservation of folk and indigenous culture in a culturally rich village like Tilonia. The community covered by Radio Tilonia is best described as a "marginalised community". Despite being marginalized, the community can be earmarked as resilient for creating sustainable livelihoods for their members (which includes the staff working for the community radio station) through the bottom-up participatory approach.

8. Conclusion

The Indian mainstream media often fall short of delivering relevant information and support. Due to this, people living in the rural areas of the country often only receive inadequate information to make informed decisions. The focus, particularly, on the rights and entitlements of local people is a key aspect of the overall programming of the radio station. Through advocacy and solutions-based journalism, the radio station highlights issues directly affecting the community members. By centering their programs around the needs and voices of the community, the radio station effectively addresses key aspects of community development, fostering local engagement and empowerment. This approach ensures that the station not only informs but also actively contributes to solving issues that matter most to the community. For the local community, Radio Tilonia and its existence matters. For the community members, the radio station is a reliable source of information. Because the radio station also broadcast in the local language, Marwari, listeners find it easy to understand the messages. This also resonates well with the local population and strengthens community identity. The efforts of the radio station have contributed to a more informed, connected, and empowered citizenry.

Acknowledgment

This study was funded by the Enhanced Seed Grant under Endowment Fund 2023–24 received from Manipal University Jaipur.

References

[1] The Government of India. (2013). Rural Indian| National Portal of India. *https://www.india.gov.in/content/rural-indian* (accessed December 29, 2024).

[2] Rathore, M. (2023). India - rural and urban population 2011. Statista. *https://www.statista.com/statistics/621507/rural-and-urban-population-india/* (accessed on December 30, 2024).

[3] Khare, A., & Vikas, R. M. (2022). People's Archive of Rural India (PARI) as an alternative to corporatized media: The public sphere and rural silencing in India. In R. Verma, & D. Vijay (Eds.), *Organizing resistance and imagining alternatives in India*, 213–240. n.p. Cambridge University Press.

[4] Chadha, K., & Linda, S. (2015). The potential and limitations of citizen journalism initiatives. *Journalism Studies, 16*(5), 706–718.

[5] Chamroy, P. (2022). People's Archive of Rural India as alternative media. *Media Asia, 50*(3), 333–354.

[6] Sinha, A. (2022). Community media coverage of gender issues: Struggles and successes in rural India. *Journal of Communication Inquir, 46*(4), 019685992210966.

[7] Chaudhry, L. (2016). Can the digital revolution save Indian journalism? *Columbia Journalism Review. https://www.cjr.org/special_report/india_digital_revolution_startups_scoopwhoop_wire_times.php (accessed December 26, 2024).*

[8] McQuail, D. (1994). *Mass communication theory: An introduction*. London: Sage Publications.

[9] Mesch, G. S., & Wright, J. D. (2015). Community and media. In *International encyclopedia of the social & behavioral sciences*, 332–336. Oxford: Elsevier.

[10] Downing, J. D. H. (2001). *Radical media: Rebellious communication and social movements*. Delhi, India: Sage.

[11] Rodriguez, C. (2001). *Fissures in the mediascape: An international study of citizens media*. New Jersey: Hampton Press.

[12] Carpentier, N. (2011). *Media and participation: A site of ideological-democratic struggle*. Intellect, New Delhi, India.

[13] Birowo, M. A., & Christine H. (2012). Community media and civic action in response to volcanic hazards. In *Chandos Information Professional Series*, 139–53. Chandos Publishing.

[14] Arora, C. (2019). The evolving Indian media market: Succeeding through localisation. *https://reutersinstitute.politics.ox.ac.uk/sites/default/files/2019-09/Chanpreet_Arora_Journalist_Fellow_paper.pdf*

[15] Chadha, K. (2017). The Indian news media industry: Structural trends and journalistic implications. *Global Media and Communication, 13*(2), 139–156.

[16] World Economic Forum. (2024). *Global risks report 2024*. World Economic Forum. *https://www.weforum.org/publications/global-risks-report-2024/* (accessed on December 21, 2024).

[17] Krishnan, A. (2024). India | Reuters Institute for the Study of Journalism. Reutersinstitute.politics.ox.ac.uk. Reuters Institute and Oxford University. *https://reutersinstitute.politics.ox.ac.uk/digital-news-report/2024/india* (accessed on December 26, 2024).

[18] UNESCO. (2007). *Community radio in India*. UNESCO. *https://unesdoc.unesco.org/ark:/48223/pf0000156854* (accessed on December 19, 2024).

[19] Ministry of Information & Broadcasting. (2024). *Celebrating 20 years of community radio in India*. Press Information Bureau. *https://pib.gov.in/PressReleaselframePage.aspx?PRID=2005299* (accessed on December 29, 2024).

[20] Dagron, A. G. (2004). The long and winding road of alternative media. In J. D. H. Downing, D. McQuail, P. Schlesinger, & E. Wartella (Eds.), *The SAGE Handbook of Media studies*, 41–64. Delhi, India: SAGE Publishing.

[21] Malik, K., & Pavarala, V. (2020). Community radio in South Asia: A roadmap for media democracy. In K. Malik, & V. Pavarala (Eds.), *Community Radio in South Asia: Reclaiming the Airwaves*. New Delhi: Routledge.

[22] Coyer, K. (2008). Community media: Scholarship, policy advocacy, and power tools. Items. *Social Science Research Council. https://items.ssrc.org/making-communications-research-matter/community-media-scholarship-policy-advocacy-and-power-tools/* (accessed December 24, 2024).

[23] Dunaway, D. (2002). Community radio at the beginning of the 21st century: Commercialism vs. community power. In J. Nicholas, & P. Ole (Eds.), *Community media in the information age: Perspectives and prospects*, 63–82. New Jersey: Hampton Press Inc.

[24] Nair, P. (2011). Community radio in India: Scripting a new role for development. *Media Watch, 2*(1), 12–19.

[25] Milan, S. (2009). Four steps to community media as a development tool. *Development Practice, 19*(4/5), 598–609.

[26] Council of Europe. (2022). Community media: Contributions to citizens' participation. *Information Society Department*. Council of Europe. https://rm.coe.int/community-media-contributions-to-citizens-participation-en/1680a94cd5.

[27] Wallack, I. (1994). Media advocacy: A strategy for empowering people and communities. *Journal of Public Health Policy, 15*(4), 420–436.

[28] Jernigan, D. H., & Wright, P. A. (1996). Media advocacy: Lessons from community experiences. *Journal of Public Health Policy, 17*(3), 306–330.

[29] Jackson, M., Brennan, L., & Parker, L. (2021). The public health community's use of social media for policy advocacy: A scoping review and suggestions to advance the field. *Public Health, 198*, 146–155.

[30] Holder, H. D., & Treno, A. J. (1997). Media advocacy in community prevention: News as a means to advance policy change. *Addiction, 92*(6), S189–S199.

[31] Dorfman, L. (2007). Using media advocacy to influence policy. In L. Cohen, V. Chavez, & S. Chehimi (Eds.), *Prevention is primary: Strategies for community well-being*, 181–91. San Francisco: Wiley.

[32] Gibson, T. A. (2010). The limits of media advocacy. *Communication, Culture & Critique, 3*(1), 44–65.

[33] Huntsberger, M. W. (2020). Community media in the United States: Fostering pluralism and inclusivity in challenging times. *Interactions: Studies in Communication & Culture, 11*(2), 191–205.

[34] Saeed, S. (2009). Negotiating power: Community media, democracy, and the public sphere. *Development in Practice, 19*(4–5), 466–478.

[35] Ali, C., & David, C. (2015). A community of communities? Emerging dynamics in the community media paradigm. *Global Media and Communication, 11*(1), 3–23.

[36] Har-Gil, A., & Roei, D. (2010). A failed success: A community television case study of the contradictory nature of participation and deliberation. *International Journal of Communication, 4*(0), 21.

[37] Howley, K. (2013). Community media studies: An overview. *Sociology Compass, 7*(10), 818–828.

[38] Johnson, L. R. (2017). *Community-based qualitative research: Approaches for education and the social sciences*. United States: SAGE Publications.

[39] Digital Empowerment Foundation. (2016). *TBI BLOGS: Community radio in a Rajasthan village is using the Internet to empower 50,000 lives*. The Better India. *https://thebetterindia.com/48435/tbi-blogs-tilonia-radio-building-community-awareness-fm/* (accessed on December 23, 2024).

[40] Adams, E. (2010). The joys and challenges of semi-structured interviewing. *Community of Practice, 83*(7), 18–21.

[41] Roy, S. (1987). The Tilonia model. A successful Indian grass root rural development strategy. *Canadian Journal of Development Studies, 8*(2), 355–374.

[42] www.census2011.co.in. (2022). Tilonia village population - Kishangarh - Ajmer, Rajasthan. Census2011.Co.in. 2022. *https://www.census2011.co.in/data/village/91461-tiloniya-rajasthan.html* (accessed on December 24, 2024).

[43] Mininni, G. M. (2017). The "Barefoot Model" of economic empowerment in rural Rajasthan. *Journal of the Indian Ocean Region, 13*(1), 54–75.

[44] Patterson, J., & Kinchington, F. (2024). Learning sustainability at the Barefoot college: Local and global community values in action. *Sustainable Earth Reviews, 7*(1), 16.

[45] Backhaus, B. (2019). News by any other name: Community radio journalism in India. *Journal of Alternative & Community Media, 4*(2), 91–104.

13 An AI-driven IoT framework for monitoring musth in elephants and estrus peaks in livestock: A cost-effective approach to animal management and welfare

Lija Jacob[a], Vijayalakshmi S.[b], Thomas K. T.[c], and Sharon Susan Thomas[d]

School of Sciences, Christ University, Bengaluru, India

Abstract: The largest terrestrial mammal in the world, 'elephants' are valued for their ecological, cultural, and economic significance. However, in male elephants' there is a natural phenomenon called "musth" which frequently results in erratic and hostile conduct, endangering people, other elephants, and property. Elephants play a crucial role in religious festivals and the timber industry in Kerala, India, where accidents involving musth are sadly frequent. The current methods for detecting or predicting the possibility of musth is mostly rely on the experiential knowledge of the mahouts or veterans which is considered as the musth detection techniques in the current scenario and hence this method is insufficient for prompt and precise predictions.

In the proposed research work, an IoT-based integrated warning system driven by artificial intelligence (AI) is proposed to forecast and report musth in domestic elephants. Three modules make up the system: (1) an Internet of Things (IoT)-based data collection module which uses sensors to track important indicators like changes in body temperature, testosterone levels, and behaviour; (2) a deep learning model that has been trained to analyse these parameters and forecast the onset of musth; and (3) a communication module that uses a centralized control system to send warnings to mahouts, owners, and authorities.

The approach uses video analysis, machine learning model training, and ongoing data monitoring to improve forecast accuracy. By facilitating early detection and doing away with the necessity for harsh control measures during musth, the project highlights compassionate care. The outcome of the proposed system includes amended human safety, less property damage, and better elephant care.

Though this research primary focus is on elephants, the proposed methodologies and technologies can be adapted to other mammals, such as goats, for estrus detection. Timely identification of stages like goat estrus is essential for boosting production yields and breeding efficiency in the livestock and poultry industries. With similar IoT sensors and AI-based analytics, the cattle's hormone, temperature, and behavioural changes can be tracked which allows the farmers to improve productivity and breeding schedule. The proposed work not only fills key gaps in wildlife and livestock management, promoting a sustainable ecosystem through technological innovation, but it also improves welfare, lowers property damage, and increases human safety. It promotes productivity gains and economic sustainability for animals. The suggested approach provides scalable and significant solutions for a range of applications in animal management and conservation by encouraging greater awareness and preventative actions.

Keywords: Animal welfare and management, estrus detection, IoT enabled animal monitoring, musth detection, sustainability

1. Introduction

Elephants are the largest land animals now present on Earth. They are known as cultural icons with great importance across the globe. Especially in many states of India. They are well known for their intelligence, social behaviour. Elephants are found mainly in Asia and Africa, They have important roles in maintaining ecosystems and supporting biodiversity. In India, elephants have important religious and economic value. Especially in states like Kerala, they are important in temple festivals and in the timber industry [1].

In the state of Kerala, elephants have great importance in cultural and religious traditions. They often serve as important participants in temple processions and rituals [2]. More than these cultural importance, these large animals are ecologically important animals, supporting regeneration of the forests by helping dispersion of seeds

[a]lija.jacob@christuniversity.in, [b]s.vijayalakshmi@christuniversity.in, [c]thomas.kt@christuniversity.in, [d]sharon.susanthomas@bcah.christuniversity.in

DOI: 10.1201/9781003778905-13

over vast expanses [1]. Even though they have this much important status and the multifaceted roles they play, managing elephants in captivity has some great challenges. It is especially so during the state of musth, which needs careful attention.

Musth is a Hindi word derived from the word mast. The word "Musth" means "intoxicated" or "uncontrollable". In fact, it is a natural physiological state which happens in mature male elephants. This condition is identified by raised levels of testosterone hormone levels. During musth testosterone level can rise up to 60-fold above normal. This leads the animal to have sharp reproductive activity and significant physiological and behavioural changes [3, 12]. Though "musth" is a sign of good health and reproductive vitality, it is also connected with changed and really aggressive behaviour, making even normally demurest elephants potentially dangerous to human and other animals [4]. In the state of Kerala, where there is a large amount of domesticated elephants, musth-related incidents frequently result in human-elephant conflicts, damage to the property, and even human deaths. Many of these cases are well-documented, with cases of elephants in musth causing injuries which even cause loss of life during this period of big aggressive behaviour [5, 7]. To handle these challenges, it needs highly innovative management skills for ensuring the safety of humans as well as the elephants without affecting their ecological and cultural importance.

Just as the musth finding in elephants, prediction of goat estrus can significantly contribute to goat livestock handling if carefully handled. Determining estrus, or heat, in goats is critical for optimizing breeding strategies. If the estrus period is forecasted properly, the goat breeders can maximize conception rates, resulting in a healthier and more productive herd [13]. This can lead to more effective resource management, improved genetic selection, and overall herd health [13].

Early estrus identification promotes synchronized breeding, which can aid in the successful control of breeding schedules while also reducing labor and expenses involved with animal monitoring and management [14]. Moreover, this might help in planning for kidding seasons, ensuring that births occur at appropriate times for both the animals and the availability of supplies [13].

In effect, the ability to accurately forecast goat estrus early on can help livestock farmers improve reproductive efficiency, production, and financial benefits [13, 14].

Physiological and hormonal changes during the about said scenarios provides solid evidence for early detection. Traditional methods of observation and prediction, on the other hand, rely on mahouts' and caregivers' expertise and wisdom. These methods have a low likelihood of accuracy and may fail to provide early warnings, increasing the risk of harm. In today's environment, advancements in the Internet of Things (IoT) and Artificial Intelligence (AI) provide a solid alternative and better answers to this problem.

This work proposes an IoT-based device powered by AI to predict musth in domestic Tuskers. The proposed device will reduce risks associated with musth due to its real-time monitoring, analysis, and prediction. Simultaneously, this device increases the welfare of both elephants and humans. Apart from this, we can adapt the device to a broader applicability to other species like goats, for reproductive state prediction, highlighting its potential impact on livestock management.

This proposal is to develop an IoT-based, AI-powered device to report musth in elephants to the mahouts, caretakers, and owners. The device will monitor various parameters such as hormone levels, body temperature and other behavioural patterns using non-invasive sensors and the data collected by these IoT sensors are analysed with the help of AI algorithms to predict musth and send data to mahouts, caretakers and owners and relevant authorities. This simple device is a strong approach to safety, reducing casualties and ensure welfare for animals

The scope of its application can be extended to other species too. Akin methods can be useful in livestock and poultry, such as detecting estrus in goats. Early detection of estrus is advantageable in improving efficiency in breeding and livestock productivity [16]. Monitoring the hormonal changes, IoT and AI can schedule breeding, for sustainable agricultural practices.

The idea comes up with an AI integrated IoT system that provides an effective approach towards animal management. It improves safety, welfare and enhances musth management. It offers an economical approach for increasing productivity for both humans and livestock. This initiative can solve traditional issues by integrating technology and innovation with economic demands.

Modern research advancements in technology have opened new possibilities for animal monitoring and welfare. Prediction and managing behavioural and hormonal changes in animals with the help of AI integrated IoT sensors is often accurate and promising. Physiological parameters such as body temperature, heart rate etc., of the animal are continuously monitored using non-invasive IoT sensors while AI algorithms analyse these data to detect anomalies to make the predictions Studies have shown that the effectiveness of these approaches in livestock management especially prediction of estrus cycles in cattle and goats have resulted in improved productivity and welfare [6].

The paper is structured as follows: Section 2 provides a review of the literature on elephant conservation. It focuses on the integration of AI and IoT for musth prediction. It then discusses studies on livestock management, especially those aimed at optimizing conditions such as estrus. Section 3 presents the proposed methodology, followed by the experiments conducted and the conclusions drawn from the study.

2. Literature Review

The scenario "Musth" in elephants is a physiological state marked by significant hormonal changes that generate behavioural swings in the animal. Some of the early research, such as that conducted by Poole [4], has shown that elevated testosterone levels causes the initiation of the aggressive and unpredictable behaviour in male elephants during musth. The hormone spike, which can sometimes reach 60 times the typical normal level, is associated with adverse effects such as temporal gland secretions and increased urine dribbling [3]. These physiological changes suggest reproductive wellness. At the same time, present significant animal handling issues due to heightened hostility and difficulty in early prediction of the situations [7].

The handling of domesticated elephants during musth include great risks, especially in regions like the state of Kerala, where elephants are highly into cultural and religious celebrations. Research done by Abraham and Shaji [5] and Nair et al. [8] emphasize the prevalence of human-elephant conflicts during musth episodes, including damage to property, injuries, and life threatening fatalities. These conflicts shows the importance of the necessity of innovative solutions for early detection and intervention.

In recent times, improvement in technology has paved the way for new approaches to manage livestock. The combination of IoT and AI has shown positive results to similar common issues in fields like livestock and poultry. For example IoT devices are used for real time monitoring of environmental conditions, behavioural patterns, and health parameters in livestock [9]. Similarly, AI models have been developed to analyse the data collected using sensors, which detects anomalies in their regular behaviour and gives predictions, enabling timely decision making in the field of animal husbandry [10, 11].

Even though there are existing research works that target livestock, principles and technologies are easily applicable in the field of elephant management. The study by Singh et al. [11] displayed the use of IoT devices integrated with AP Algorithms for monitoring wildlife, giving insights into the scope of this field. These tools can be used to monitor the physiological and behavioural indicators of musth in elephants. It can be a proactive method to reduce the risks.

The use of Internet of Things (IoT) technology in animal management has been a growing research area that seeks to provide innovative solutions to the problem of managing the physiological conditions in animals. For example, IoT applications have been showing its potential in monitoring elephant musth, which is a natural condition found in male elephants that tends to be aggressive due to high levels of testosterone and erratic behaviour. IoT systems can detect physiological indicators by using sensors that measure a combination of body temperature, modified levels of hormones, and living activity indicators, hence the timely interventions reducing the risks to humans, property or even other animals [1, 4]. Likewise, IoT technologies have been used to detect estrus in livestock, such as goats, by monitoring temperature fluctuations, motion patterns and vocalizations. Estrus has to be accurately detected so as to shorten the length of the mating cycle, and the IoT based systems have proved to be efficient and accurate to the traditional approaches applied enhancing productivity and economic benefits [3].

The paper "IoT and Animal Care: A Potential Application in Elephant Musth and Goat Estrus" [18] shows the role of IoT in addressing specific challenges among various other species. It describes how IoT devices can detect and provide real-time monitoring, making them useful tools for managing the animals. This article discusses the benefits and requirements of various devices for increasing animal care, safety, and production. While these technologies have tremendous potential, cost, ethical concerns, and accessibility, particularly in rural regions, must be addressed before broad implementation. This combination of IoT and animal care demonstrates how technology can alter management practices for different species and stakeholders [7].

The purpose of this study was to examine the advantage of artificial intelligence and the Internet of Things approach in animal management and also how it is practiced among the domestic elephants in order to develop means of monitoring musth. Apart from the previous research using behavioural and technological application in animal management, there has been hardly any research proposing the use of the combined efforts on successful ways to reduce musth.

This study aims to bridge the gap by showcasing an IoT and AI driven system adapted to the unique issues of musth in domesticated elephants, deriving from research on similar disciplines. Similarly, the study helped to review estrus monitoring in goats and other animals.

3. Proposed Methodology

The proposed framework leverages IoT technologies, AI algorithms, and real-time reporting to forecast and control crucial behavioural changes in animals, notably elephant musth and goat estrus. This exclusive technology improves animal welfare as well as human safety by combining real-time data collecting, AI-driven predictive modelling, and modern communication technologies. Early detection of musth in elephants helps prevent aggressive behaviour, decrease property damage, and guarantee compassionate care. Similarly, early detection of goat estrus can boost breeding efficiency and production in the dairy and meat industries. This scalable and reliable approach not only lessens the hazards associated with musth but also optimizes cattle reproduction, encouraging sustainable animal management and economic benefits to farmers.

The recommended AI based integrated warning system for elephant musth includes two-phase approach, to accurately predict and manage musth in elephants. Phase 1, the system uses the sensor to monitor physiological indicators, behavioural and testosterone levels. The data is then transmitted to microcontrollers, which then process the data using machine learning model to predict musth. These predictions are passed to associated people or stakeholders through SIM equipped devices, ensuring timely alerts. Phase 2 incorporates a deep learning model which is trained on videos of the elephants' behavioural patterns. Cameras capture real time video, which is then analysed to detect behavioural indicative of musth. This dual phase method not only uses advanced AI and IoT but also includes continuous data collection and model training, resulting in better accuracy in prediction over time.

3.1. System modules

3.1.1. IoT module for data collection

The IoT module employs a network of IoT sensors to monitor the physiological and behavioural parameters of the elephant. The sensors collect:

- *Temperature:* Infrared thermometers or temperature sensors is used to monitor body temperature fluctuations.
- *Hormonal/Temporal Gland Secretion:* Sensors placed near the temporal glands detect secretion levels. Also a camera captures the images of the secretion
- *Urine Dribbling*: Flow sensors analyze frequency and consistency of the urine drib of the animal
- *Behavioural Movements:* Accelerometers detect swaying or aggressive behaviours.

The IoT devices communicate the data to a cloud server in real-time through Wi-Fi or GSM modules. Along with the sensor, a camera can also be placed to capture the images of head swaying and also the presence of secretion from the gland.

3.1.2. AI-based predictive modelling

A deep-learning model can be developed using the behaviour pattern of the animal and the expert inputs. As this is animal healthcare, the experts include the vets, animal owners and the associated agencies. It includes:

- Feature Extraction: Physiological data (testosterone levels, temperature, gland secretion, urine dribbling) and behavioural data (swaying patterns).
- Training: Data from IoT sensors and other inputs such as behavioural patterns and manual inputs captured are fed into the model to identify patterns preceding musth.
- Prediction: The model predicts the onset of musth with high accuracy, issuing alerts before critical stages.

3.1.3. Report generation and alert module

The report generation module ensures timely dissemination of actionable insights about the animal under observation.

- Generates detailed reports on the various reading / observation of the variables under study.
- Sends alerts and warnings via SMS, emails, or app notifications to mahouts, owners, and government officials.
- Real Time monitoring using the mobile application.

3.2. Architecture diagram

The components for the proposed system are as follows:

- IoT Sensors: Collect data on physiological and behavioural indicators.
- Data Transmission: Sensors transmit data via GSM or Wi-Fi to a cloud-based server.
- Cloud Storage: Stores real-time and historical data for analysis.
- AI Model: Processes data, identifies patterns, and predicts musth onset.
- Alerts and Notifications: Sends actionable insights to stakeholders via apps or SMS.

Description

- Input Layer: IoT sensors monitor the elephant's physiological and behavioural parameters. Sensors include:
  - Temperature sensors.
  - Gland secretion detectors.
  - Urine dribbling monitors.
  - Accelerometers.
- Communication Layer: GSM modules and Wi-Fi transmit data securely to the cloud.
- Processing Layer: The cloud server runs AI algorithms to predict musth based on input data.
- Output Layer: Alerts are generated and sent to stakeholders, and detailed reports are stored in the cloud for long-term analysis.

With information obtained from vets, elephant owners, and mahouts, a study on the factors of variation and its variation levels of elephant during the musth season was conducted. The study is currently focusing on factors: temperature and hormonal level and behavioural pattern.

We propose two phases that include three modules, for detecting that the elephant is turning to mush.

Phase 1

1. Sensors in our proposed system should be able to detect changes in the animal's two attributes, which

are listed below. We can determine whether an elephant is in Musth based on a continuous evaluation of these attributes. A significant amount of research is required to determine the actual pattern of changes in these attributes.

- An increase or fluctuation in testosterone levels in elephants approaching Musth.
- Elephants nearing Musth experience an increase/fluctuation in body temperature.

2. Microcontrollers and memory devices shall receive analogue input from the aforementioned sensors and probes and pass it to a trained machine learning/Deep learning model capable of predicting whether the animal is currently approaching Musth or not.
3. A small device equipped with a SIM card can send the information to a centralized control centre or to a group of users such as mahouts, owners, or a government nodal agency.

The data collected from the animals on a regular basis can be used to retrain the Machine/Deep learning model to improve prediction accuracy.

It is based on the decision of the elephant's owner to determine whether the device should be worn for the rest of the elephant's life or just during the high-probability months of Musth. Once in production, the total cost of the product must be within an affordable range.

Phase 2

1. A deep learning model can be created and trained using videos/images of elephants in Musth and elephants that are not in Musth. The videos must be thoroughly preprocessed before they can be used to train the models.
2. A camera placed at the location where the elephant is kept can take video of the animal on a regular basis and send it to the pre-created model in step 1 to predict if the elephant is on the verge of a Musth/not. The knowledge gained from vets and mahouts that once an elephant gets musth, it recurs almost at the same time the following year aids more in this decision.
3. A small device with a sim card can send the details to a centralized control center or to a group of users like mahouts, owners or a government nodal agency.

Figure 13.1 shows the system architecture providing a technical overview of the hardware and software components. The integration of IoT sensors, data collection mechanisms, AI processing pipelines, and the user interface is discussed.

As shown in the figure [1], a similar system can be used for livestock management in applications like goat estrus, where the input factor is the hormonal level, such as progesterone. This system enables real-time monitoring and early detection of reproductive cycles. By integrating AI and IoT, predictive insights can be generated, enhancing breeding efficiency and optimizing livestock production.

3.3. Real world pertinency

Once developed, the system can be adopted by:

- Private Owners/Mahouts: To ensure the safety of elephants and nearby humans.

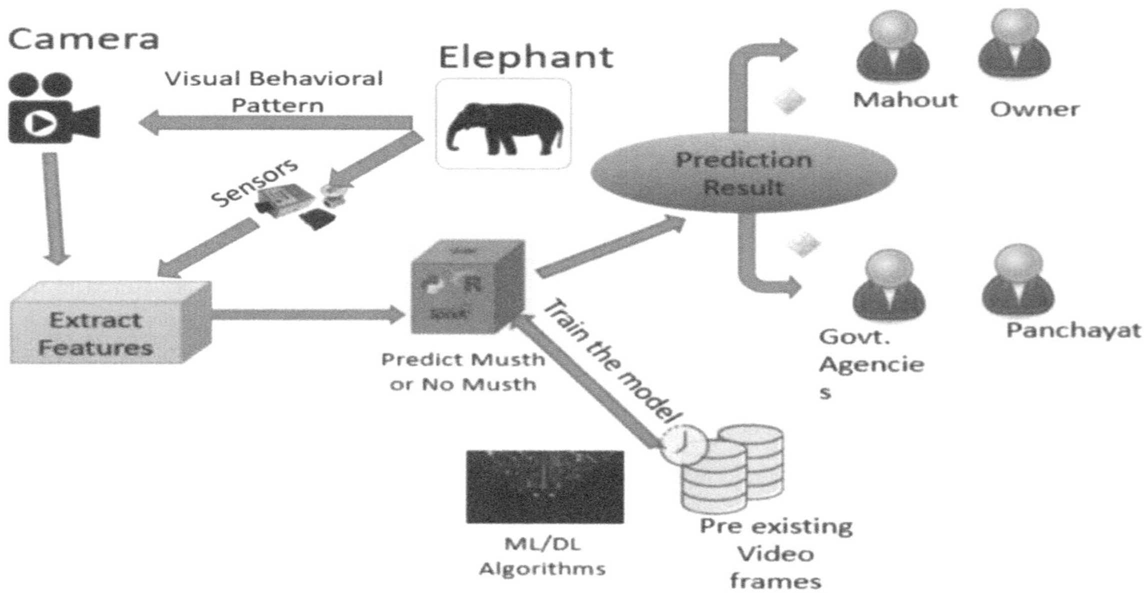

Figure 13.1. Proposed methodology of AI-IoT framework for monitoring elephant musth.

Source: Author.

- Government Agencies: To monitor elephants in public roles (e.g., timber transport, temple parades).
- Industries: To mitigate risks in logging operations involving elephants.

Similarly, the technology aids in the smart health monitoring of animals and the development of a smart warning system, allowing humans to make shrewder and more efficient decisions.

3.4. Scientific and social rationale

Based on literature and interviews with vets and mahouts [2, 6, 7, 18], musth is a gradual process, not a sudden occurrence. Key indicators include temporal gland secretion, urine dribbling, aggression, and a rise in body temperature. The proposed system's predictive capacity surpasses the experiential knowledge of mahouts, offering a scientific, data-driven alternative. Preventative measures can then be implemented, such as isolating the elephant and reducing strenuous tasks.

3.5. Contributions to sustainable development goals (SDGs)

The title "An AI-Driven IoT Framework for Monitoring Musth in Elephants and Estrus Peaks in Livestock: A Cost-Effective Approach to Animal Management and Welfare" aligns well with several Sustainable Development Goals (SDGs) due to its focus on protecting elephants and their habitats while leveraging AI technology for conservation efforts. The proposed work directly contributes to achieving SDG goals, particularly SDG 15, SDG 13, SDG 9, SDG 3, SDG 11 and SDG 17. It highlights the importance of innovative approaches in addressing global environmental challenges while ensuring the well-being of both wildlife and humans [15, 16].

Below is the explanation of the proposed system's contribution to SDG.

1. **SDG 15: Life on Land:** The proposed system for Elephant Conservation focuses on protecting and conserving terrestrial ecosystems, particularly elephants, which are key species in maintaining ecosystem balance. By implementing an AI-based warning system, the project aims to reduce human-elephant conflicts, preserve biodiversity, and promote sustainable land use.
    - **Biodiversity Conservation:** Elephants are keystone species, meaning their conservation has a significant positive impact on their ecosystems [15].
    - **Habitat Protection:** By ensuring the well-being of elephants, the system indirectly supports the protection of their natural habitats [16].
2. **SDG 3: Good Health and Well-being:** Assuring Human Safety-Human-elephant conflicts can result in injury or loss of life. By predicting musth and preventing aggressive behaviour in elephants through AI-based warning systems, the system helps protect mahouts, veterinarians, and local communities from potential harm.
    - **Animal Welfare:** Ensuring the well-being of elephants by reducing stress and preventing injuries during musth periods.
3. **SDG 9: Industry, Innovation, and Infrastructure**
    - **Innovation:** The development of an AI-based warning system requires innovation and advanced technological infrastructure. By utilizing AI and big data, this work promotes sustainable industrial practices and advances infrastructure that supports environmental conservation efforts. Utilizing AI and IoT technologies to create a predictive system represents a significant technological advancement in wildlife management.
    - **Advancements in Infrastructure:** Developing robust data transmission and cloud storage infrastructure to support the system.
4. **SDG 17: Partnerships for the Goals:** The project likely requires collaboration between governments, researchers, AI specialists, conservation organizations, and local communities. Partnerships strengthen the implementation of AI systems and help scale conservation efforts to a wider geographic scope.
5. **SDG 13: Climate Action**
    - **Ecosystem Management:** Healthy elephant populations contribute to the maintenance of their ecosystems, which play a role in climate regulation. The use of AI for monitoring musth (a behavioural state of elephants) helps predict and mitigate human-elephant conflicts, reducing the negative impact on local communities and ecosystems. This leads to better land management practices, minimizing deforestation and promoting sustainable agriculture, contributing to climate action.
    - **Biodiversity:** Protecting elephants helps preserve biodiversity, which is crucial for resilient ecosystems.
6. **SDG 11: Sustainable Cities and Communities**
    - **Human-Wildlife Conflict:** Reducing conflicts between humans and elephants by predicting and managing musth can lead to more harmonious coexistence.
    - **Community Safety:** Enhancing the safety of communities living near elephant habitats.

4. Experiments and Results

4.1. Data collection

The data collection approach for the proposed system began with a questionnaire survey of veterinarians, mahouts, and owners. This approach helped to get various useful information for identifying a significant physiological biomarker of musth in elephants: an increased body temperature above 40°C and the hormonal variation. It has been found through the study that elephants' temperatures gradually rise during musth and then return to normal after a specified number of days (mostly 2 weeks).

4.2. Sensor-based data collection and storage

To monitor this physiological change, temperature sensors are used to measure the elephant's body temperature daily. The measurements are automatically recorded in a database for subsequent analysis. The data collected is analysed on a rolling 10-day basis (e.g., Day 1 to Day 10, Day 2 to Day 11, and so on) using the Daily_Analysis algorithm. This algorithm also performs a statistical t-test to detect the substantial patterns in the temperatures, and the results are stored in the database for later analysis.

Figure 13.2 illustrates a sample questionnaire designed to collect data from veterinarians, owners, and mahouts, providing a robust foundation for system development and validation. Figure 13.3 shows the image of an elephant where there is secretion of the gland.

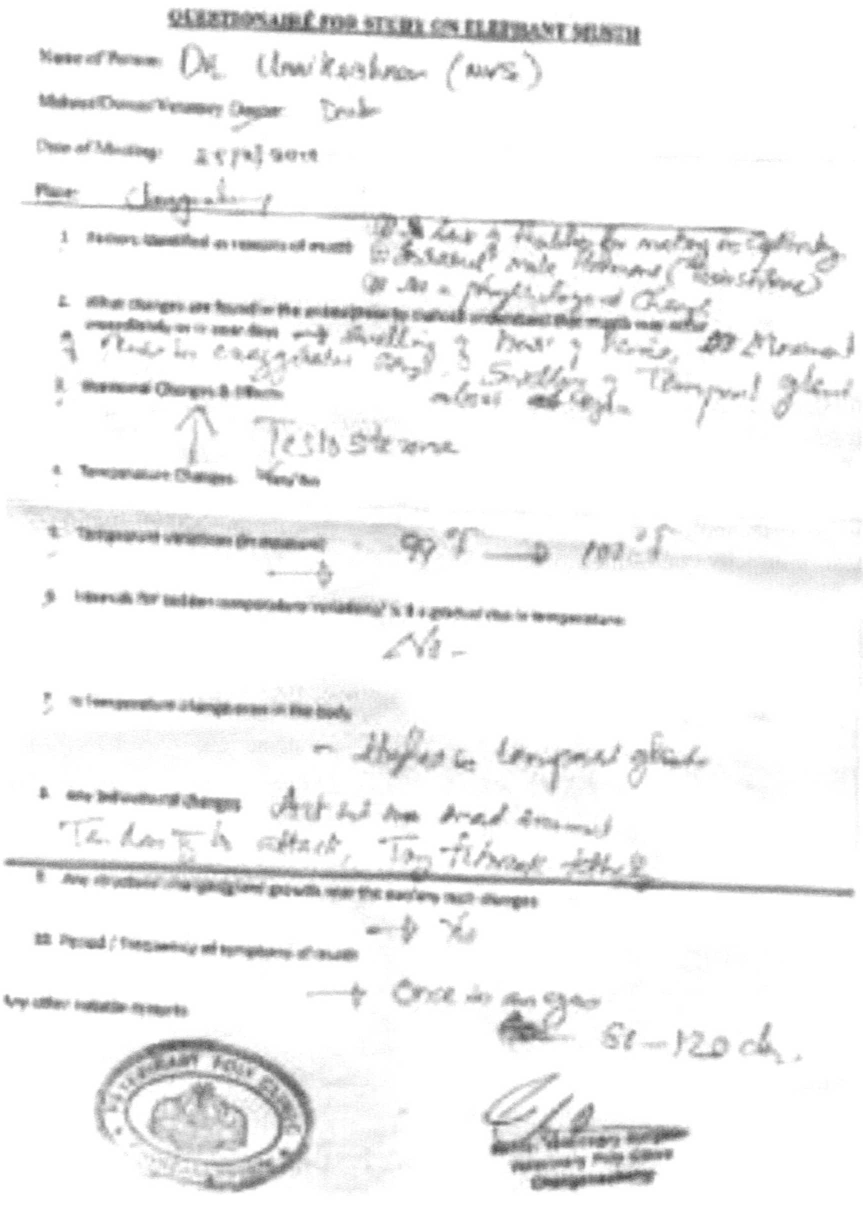

Figure 13.2. Sample questionnaire of data collection about musth in elephants.

Source: Author.

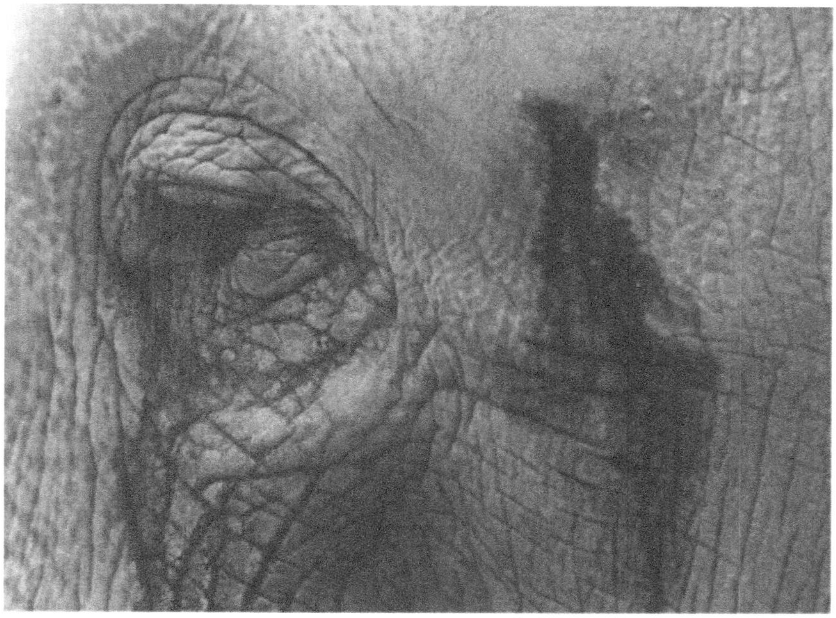

Figure 13.3. Secretion in temporal glands [19].
Source: Author.

The prototype implementation and testing of the proposed system was performed which generated the warning messages in the registered mobile. The effectiveness of the system in predicting musth is evaluated, along with its potential for scalability.

4.3. Applications in livestock management

The idea is an easily adaptable, effective system originally developed to detect the musth in elephants, and can be modified and expanded to use in various other animals for other purposes too. For example, similar to using temperature sensors in elephants, we can accommodate smart collars or ear tags that can monitor various parameters like temperature, heart rate, and hormonal changes. Meanwhile an integrated camera can capture the change in behavioural patterns of estrus. Using this information, a deep learning model trained on livestock activity can predict with maximum accuracy. Utilization of algorithms like Daily Analysis and weekly analysis along with data on previous reproductive cycles can improve the accuracy in the prediction. The system will send real time alerts via mobile applications to the concerned people and make sure that timely information has been passed, which helps in farmers deciding on their breeding resulting in better productivity and efficiency. This automated approach in estrus detection reduces labor and improves conception rates and contributes to animal welfare and sustainable management.

5. Conclusion

A real-time AI-IoT network system for detecting and identifying the likelihood of musth in elephants and goat estrus peaks is proposed in this paper. The recommended system reports the current system restrictions in the prediction of the goat/cattle estrus cycles or the likelihood of the musth occurrence in elephants. Disregarding such grave information can result in calamitous consequences, such as endangered elephants endangering public safety or cattlemen losing money due to missed breeding prospects.

5.1. Challenges

This study have proposed a novel approach for predicting musth in elephants and estrus in goats, addressing a largely unexplored area in animal behaviour research. Due to the limited availability of real-world datasets, we conducted our experiments using synthetically generated or assumed data. While this provided a foundational validation of our methodology, we acknowledge that the true potential of our system can only be fully realized with real, diverse datasets collected from multiple animals through behavioural observations and sensor-based methods. Our research has been conducted with the conviction that, as more empirical data becomes available, the proposed framework can be seamlessly integrated and further refined to yield tangible, verifiable, and practically applicable results. The architecture of the exact DL model which can be practically used can be given only after we are able to collect such data in the next phase of the experiment.

5.2. Conclusion

The proposed approach meets the objective by facilitating monitoring of many animals at the same time, as well as sending out timely and effective alarms whenever unexpected patterns are discovered in the monitored data. The arrangement comprises a wearable wireless sensor device, a mobile unit, a central data centre, a data analysis module, and a warning mechanism. The real time data collected and the perceived risk if itself informed to the stakeholders as alerts via the system. This approach is especially effective for elephants which has to be taken for the public events such as religious festivals or chores such as log hauling, resulting in a considerable reduction in fatalities associated with musth episodes. Recognizing estrus peaks in animal husbandry increases breeding efficiency as well as profitability.

This system's main advantage is the low cost of its implementation due to wearable wireless sensors, software and detection algorithms animal husbandry practices.

5.3. Future scope

In the future, Modifications can be done such as integrating other sensors which can monitor other factors besides hormones and temperature. The accuracy can be improved by incorporating optimized deep learning models. Usage of video and sensor data to integrate a deep learning model augments the technology to examine physiological and behavioural patterns of larger populations of animals by training. This makes it suitable for a wider range of purposes, such as conservation, livestock management and wildlife monitoring. The Deep Learning model can be improved through continuous learning from new data, enabling adaptability in a range of species and environmental conditions. The DL model can be modified by adopting a continuous learning approach based on recent data thereby enhancing adaptability to various species and environmental factors. The proposed system is a cost effective and outstanding, reproductive and behavioural monitoring system for animals, which has the potential to transform the existing animal monitoring systems to an extent that it can help ensure public safety, improve productivity of existing livestock and promote better animal husbandry practices.

Acknowledgment

We gratefully acknowledge the vets, mahouts and owners from whom we took the survey for the study. Our students and faculty members and management who motivated us to do this research.

References

[1] Sukumar, R. (2003). *The Living Elephants: Evolutionary Ecology, Behavior, and Conservation*. Oxford University Press.

[2] Nibha, N. (1997). *Practical Elephant Management - A Handbook for Mahouts.*

[3] Lincoln, G. A., & Ratnasooriya, W. D. (1996). Testosterone secretion, musth behaviour and social dominance in captive male Asian elephants living near the equator. *Journal of Endocrinology*, *151*(1), 117–129.

[4] Poole, J. H. (1987). Rutting Behavior in African Elephants: The Phenomenon of Musth. *Behavioral Ecology and Sociobiology, 20*(3), 157–164.

[5] Benedict, F. G., & Lee, R. C. (1936) Studies on the body Temperature of Elephants. *Physiology*, *22*, 405–408

[6] Maroto-Molina, F., Navarro-García, J., Príncipe-Aguirre, K., Gómez-Maqueda, I., Guerrero-Ginel, J., Garrido-Varo, A., & Pérez-Marín, D. (2019). IoT in Livestock Management: Applications and Challenges. *Computers and Electronics in Agriculture*, *162*, 486–497.

[7] Varghese, S., Jacob, L., & Others. (2015). An experimental study for an IoT-based automated system for early detection and warning on the probability of musth in elephants. *International Journal of Innovative Research in Computer and Communication Engineering, 5*(2).

[8] Nair, S. R., Madhusudan, M. D., & Sukumar, R. (2009). Conflicts between humans and elephants: A case study of southern India. *Conservation and Society*, *7*(2), 78–88.

[9] Wolfert, S., Ge, L., Verdouw, C., & Bogaardt, M. J. (2017). Big data in smart farming – A review. *Agricultural Systems*, *153*, 69–80.

[10] Tian, F., Liu, Y., & Cui, X. (2019). Intelligent livestock monitoring using IoT and AI: A case study. *Computers and Electronics in Agriculture*, *161*, 217–229.

[11] Singh, R., Sharma, A., & Kumar, V. (2021). IoT and AI-based wildlife monitoring system: Insights and future directions. *Sensors*, *21*(4), 1021.

[12] Sengupta, A., Binoy, V. V., & Radhakrishna, S. (2020). Human-elephant conflict in Kerala, India: A rapid appraisal using compensation records. *Human Ecology, 48*(1), 101–109. *https://doi.org/10.1007/s10745-020-00131-2*

[13] Farmingpedia. (n.d.). *How to detect estrus for successful goat breeding programs*. Retrieved December 27, 2024, from *https://farmingpedia.com/how-to-detect-estrus-for-successful-goat-breeding-programs/*

[14] Dawson, L. (2013). Estrus Synchronization in Goats. *Clinical Theriogenology*. https://cdn.ymaws.com/www.therio.org/resource/collection/2CF03851-0A7C-4489-8F1A-8C507FEB205D/2013_v3_022.pdf.

[15] *https://tsavotrust.org/ five-ways-in-which-elephant-conservation-builds-a-sustainable-future-for-the-planet/).*

[16] *(https://herd.org.za/blog/the-making-of-a-sustainable-herd-through-conservation/).*

[17] Akash, A., Hoque, M., Mondal, S., & Adusumilli, S. (2022). Sustainable livestock production and food

security. In S. Mondal & R. L. Singh (Eds.), *Emerging Issues in Climate Smart Livestock Production*, 71–90. Academic Press. https://doi.org/10.1016/B978-0-12-822265-2.00011-9

[18] Jacob, L., & Thomas, K. T. (2018). IoT and Animal Care: A Potential. *Application in Elephant Musth and Goat Estrus,* 292–296. doi:10.1109/ICCONS.2018.8663179.

[19] The Call to Conserve. (n.d.). *What is musth?* Retrieved December 27, 2024, from *https://www.thecalltoconserve.com/wildlife-faqs/what-is-musth#:~:text=Musth%20is%20a%20phenomenon%20in%20bull%20elephants%20that,levels%20can%20increase%20by%20as%20much%20as%20100x.*

14 Elevating precision and performance in football match predictions through advanced XGBoost comparing over KNN algorithmic techniques

Karthik B.[a] and V. R. Vimal[b]

Department of Artificial Intelligence and Data Science, Saveetha School of Engineering, Saveetha Institute of Medical and Technical Sciences, Saveetha University, Chennai, Tamil Nadu, India

Abstract: This paper will concentrate on comparative analysis of the XGBoost and K-Nearest Neighbors (KNN) models in estimating the possibility of football match outcomes in Spanish League. This research seeks to compare the accuracy, precision, recall, F1-score, confusion matrices, and training time of the said models. This work employs the following type of data: historical football match data, the features of which are team statistics, player's performance, and even match outcomes. In this study, the KNearest Neighbors classifier, which is a simple classification algorithm, is compared to XGBoost, a gradient boosting technique. The results show that for the same features and data sets, XGBoost is in fact more accurate and efficient than KNN based on the higher accuracy rate obtained 85.2 for XGBoost and 78.5 for KNN (Vic cont.) Cooccur matrices indicate that XGBoost is precise in identifying win and loss outcomes with low misclassification. Also, something very important that most of the researchers do not look at is time in training, and on this one, XGBoost stands tall and has a better record when it comes to training time in those big data sets. The result shows that the proposed model XGBoost is better than other models for football match prediction.

Keywords: Football match prediction, t, K-nearest neighbors, players performance, XGBoost

1. Introduction

Football which is a sport has grown to become a very complex field in which data science plays a very big role in determining performance and decision-making. Today, forecasts are a natural part of match probability and opportunity prediction, player and in-game performance prediction, and even more – a strategic advantage for the teams and an additional interest for the fans. This infusion of data into decision making has called for high end algorithms in machine learning that can handle big data problems while delivering quality results. The general task of estimating the results of football matches is intrinsically complex because the nature of football is unpredictable. The possibilities for influence are numerous and incalculable: players' injuries and forms, collective psychology, team tactics, weather and other contingent factors [1]. Solving such a complex problem necessitates algorithms that schedule these factors into considerations as well as analyze changing patterns within the game. Thanks to machine learning, sports analysis has ceased to be a difficult task and become rather a collection of reliable predictions based on bigger data analyses. KNN and XGBoost are two methods that have appeared to outcompete the other methods in football match result prediction among the many methods used in machine learning. Algorithms presented herein provide separate advantages, however, they demonstrate different results based on data characteristics and prediction goals [2].

KNN, largely because of ease of understanding and simplicity, works by forecasting results based on data closest to the query. The information about its applicability to different domains also deserves attention because of the simplicity of the method and the absence of serious obstacles to its work. Nevertheless, due to the fact that it relies on proximity-based predictions it is vulnerable to high dimensionality, noise susceptibility and computational intensity especially while trying to predict large rich football datasets that have high features [3]. Still, KNN seems to be unstable with the large amount of data and low accuracy, especially when applied to important events such as football match prediction. As the volume and the complexity of the data, the performance of the algorithm drops to worse and worst, makes the program yield suboptimal results [4]. Large and complex datasets

[a]karthikb4232.sse@saveetha.com, [b]vimalvr.sse@saveetha.com

DOI: 10.1201/9781003778905-14

that define football games presents numerous interactions within team and player performance variables, historical, and present performances, which require algorithms that will navigate these complexities while ensuring a high level of accuracy. XGBoost, however, is one of the powerful machine learning techniques with recent development recognized as one of the best performing algorithms in a variety of machine learning problems. Incorporation of multiple decision trees, and the boosting of these trees enhance accuracy levels while, at the same time reducing overfitting. This makes it especially suitable for use in football match predictions, where complex and correlated attributes are involved and where care must be taken to compute them in a way that results in meaningful values. The functional aspects of this model include handling of missing value, feature importance, and the ability to work from large data sets [5].

XGBoost on the other hand, has a more proactive way of functioning compared to KNN which simply waits for data similarities: XGBoost learns from mistakes as it moves round the decision tree and is able to generate more accurate predictions as a result of this. The fact that it has the capability to work with challenging football datasets is a convincing reason why it is still meaningful in sports analysis, complementing the regular algorithms. Comparisons between KNN and XGBoost in framework of sports analytics show hint at the stronger ability of XGBoost to predict and to solve computationally intensive problems [6]. Previous work has indicated that except for high accuracy, XGBoost runs through a big data set in less time and is therefore of great importance especially for football analyst and researcher. In light of these results, one cannot overemphasize the role of algorithm choice to obtain accurate match predictions. Football prediction data often include a large number of factors, such as players' characteristics, goals, scores, formation, and sometimes psychological characteristics. Also, such datasets are problematic for algorithms unable to differentiate between the necessary and the extraneous. Feature selection strategies make it possible for XGBoost to make smarter decisions than KNN that works mechanistically by comparing proximity [7].

Football predictions do not restrict to pinpointing the team that is likely come out of a match as a winner. They impact betting markets, inform coaches, help in player scouting, and increase levels of fan engagement. The extent to which actual predictions of match results can be made increases the competitiveness of teams by allowing them to highlight vulnerabilities in their strategies. Consequently, enhancing the prediction accuracy retains substantial worth across the different domains of the sport [8]. The purpose of this research is to critically evaluate the efficiency of XGBoost over KNN in football match prediction. This paper seeks to justify the necessity of using XGBoost for solving the challenges which are unique to work on football analysis, through metrics like accuracy, computational speed and flexibility. The findings may be useful for data scientists, sport analysts, and professionals exploring the opportunities of increasing the effectiveness of prediction [9]. In what follows, this paper outlines the method used in implementing the algorithms, provides a description of dataset features, and a comprehensive analysis of the outcome. This paper continues the development of the field of sports analytics and shows, through the comparison of XGBoost to KNN, how the utilization of powerful new machine learning techniques can enhance football match predictions.

2. Literature Review

A.A. Asije's [10] work have suggested that Bayesian analysis should be utilized to predict football match results in Africa. The research applies Bayesian networks, Jeffrey prior, and logistic regression to address the uncertainties and make fine-grained forecasts. Adding elements such as team ability, players' fitness, and game plans, the study strives to enhance reliability of the match outcome prediction. The paper employs data from the 2023 Africa Cup of Nations qualification to explain how Bayesian models generate forecasts based on participative performances and external conditions. Outcomes prove the model efficient since the prediction probability is higher than the base rate. The paper explores a possibility more extensive data analysis of sports in Africa to establish higher cooperation with teams and governing boards.

The research of Gianluca Morciano [11] presents the field of supervised machine learning for the prediction of football players' performance. The evaluation of players above team average is done using four biometric variables and seven performance variables. For model optimization, grid search is utilized for tuning the Random Forest classifier and two whale optimization algorithms of which one incorporates Euclidean distance. The research segregates the players into strikers, midfielders, and defenders because the abilities may differ significantly. Overall, the experiments show that the Random Forest classifier attains an accuracy of over 90% for all the roles. The proposed optimization method provides football teams with substantial and potentially valuable orientations for tactical choices, training, and players' management, in comparison with current approaches.

Abdessatar Ati [12] focuses his researches on the increase in football player selection and performance prediction based on MCDM and machine learning. The study also benefits from the multiple criteria are identified that cover physical, technical, tactical, and behavioural aspects of player selection process. An SLR is performed by identifying 66 articles that meet the inclusion criteria published from 2018 to 2023. It also discusses the merging of MCDM with traditional artificial neural network and random forest techniques for detailed evaluation of performance levels. The purpose is to support the football clubs to improve the process of players' acquisition and to increase the managers and financials productivity. The current proposed hybrid approach is the next step; it will integrate both methodologies for the purpose of offering impartial, evidence-based direction for decision makers who are interested in assembling top talent and enhancing organization's competitive performances.

The work of Chen Zhang [13] suggests the implementation of a football trajectory prediction and a response mechanism in real-time: Temporal Convolutional Networks and spatial channel attention. The model describes the temporal position and movement of players and the ball and immediately provides feedback to coaching processes. Joint trajectory prediction covers the long-term dependence and makes the result more accurate in dynamic environment. The results of experiments demonstrate that established algorithms offer greater prediction accuracy than baseline models with PPA and TPA of 65.85% and 87.12%, respectively. The method can be used for making small purposely adjustments on the field and analyzing the game itself and, thus, is useful for developing with sophisticated sports analysis systems.

This paper by Konstantinos Loukas [14] proposes using Poisson regression model to make football match predictions using historical data. In the analysis, data of the Premier League 2022/2023 is used to make a prediction of the number of goals that each team would be scoring using the Poisson distributions. The dependency which is developed is the dual Poisson regression model for attacking and defensive techniques, home ground influence and other facets of performance. The data have proven that the algorithm yielding high accuracy and frequently, the goal prediction varies with the actual goal by one goal only. They provide suggestions for the prediction and analysis of quantitative evaluation of sports business, betting markets, and the fans. Consequently, the study centers the model's feasibility and speed; coupled with suggestions for altering the analysis for the proper zero-inflation to enhance precision.

3. Materials

From Kaggle, there is a dataset known as "Football Matches of Spanish League" which compiles extensive records of matches in La Liga the top football division in Spain. It elaborates the match dates, teams and scores and other performance analysis data. The data have collected for multiple seasons so that the team performance comparison can be made over time. Those include home and away teams, goals, wins, draws, and losses of a particular match. This structured data gives a good starting point of baseline data for modeling and statistical analysis. It is ideal for use in other operations that are standard in the field of machine learning such as classification and regression. To this end, this study employed this dataset in training and assessing the performance of the applied XGBoost and KNN algorithms with the aim of enhancing match outcome forecasts.

4. Methodology

4.1. Preprocessing techniques

Dataset Acquisition: This research uses the dataset known as 'Football Matches of Spanish League' available on Kaggle. The relevant dataset includes the matches in La Liga and such data as the names of the teams, the dates of the matches, scores and performance indicators reflecting goals, results, and field conditions (home or away matches). The first process is about to upload such dataset into a proper context for data handling and analysing (as an example, utilizing Python alongside with Pandas) (Figure 14.1).

Data Cleaning: Handling took time since data cleaning involves managing missing values, correcting errors, numerical and categorically abnormal values as well as data conversion. In this paper, you NULL or missing values for critical features such as goals scored, match results, or team names is accepted in this paper by imputing them or by deleting all the records in the dataset containing the missing data, depending on their extent.

Feature Engineering: To enhance the predictive power of the model, new features might be created based on existing data. For example, we can derive additional variables such as:

- Goal Difference: The difference between goals scored by the home and away teams.
- Team Strength: A derived metric based on past performance (e.g., average goals scored or conceded).
- Win/Loss Streaks: A binary variable indicating whether a team is on a winning or losing streak.
- Home/Away Advantage: A feature indicating whether a team is playing at home.

Categorical variables, such as team names, need to be encoded into numerical representations using methods like one-hot encoding or label encoding.

Data Splitting: Precisely, the entire dataset is divided into the training and testing data subsets. Conventionally, the split is 80-20 based on which 80% of the data set is used for the model's training while 20% is used in determining the model's performance. They fix the problem of evaluating the model on data that it has been trained from, as it helps to use data that it never saw.

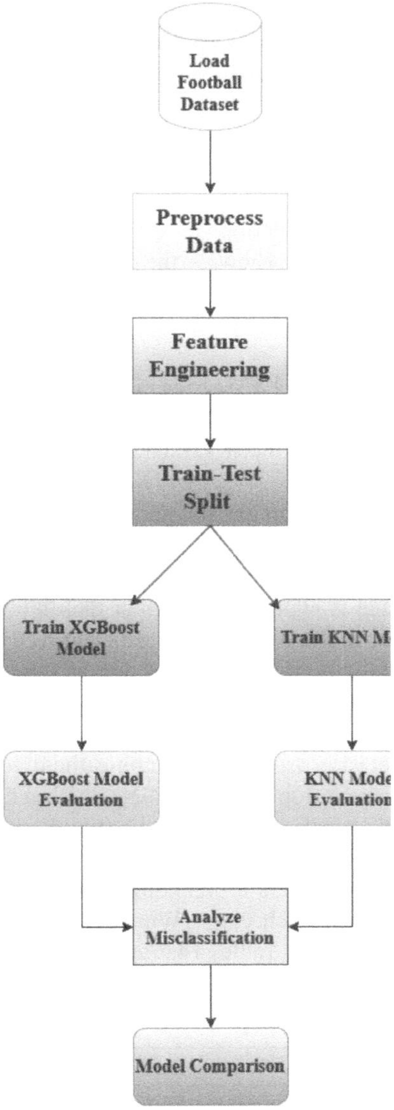

Figure 14.1. Flow of proposed work.

Source: Author.

4.2. Model training

In the model training process, we focus on two machine learning algorithms: Specifically, explorations of model type have included XGBoost (Extreme Gradient Boosting) and K-Nearest Neighbors (KNN). The following outlines the training stage of both models with the use of different mathematical concepts, and the equations in those concepts as follows:

4.3. XGBoost (Extreme Gradient Boosting)

Step by Step XGBoost is an ensemble learning model under Gradient Boosting technique. It develops a number of trees /control and decision/ where the next tree rectifies the mistakes made earlier by the previous tree. Training process is the process of adjusting or minimizing the loss function by boosting the residual errors iteratively.

4.4. Objective function in XGBoost

The objective function of XGBoost consists of two components:

- Loss Function (L): Measures the error between the predicted and actual values.
- Regularization Term (Ω): Penalizes the complexity of the model (e.g., the depth of trees) to avoid overfitting.

The overall objective function is:

$$L(\theta) = \sum_{i=1}^{N} L(y_i, y_i) + \lambda \sum_{j=1}^{T} \Omega(f_j) \tag{1}$$

Where:

- y_i is the actual outcome (label) for data point iii,
- $y^\wedge_i$ is the predicted outcome for data point iii,
- λ is the regularization parameter,
- f_j represents the *j*-th tree in the ensemble.

4.5. Loss function (L)

The most commonly used loss function for regression in XGBoost is the squared error loss:

$$L(y_i, y_i) = (y_i - y_i)^2 \tag{2}$$

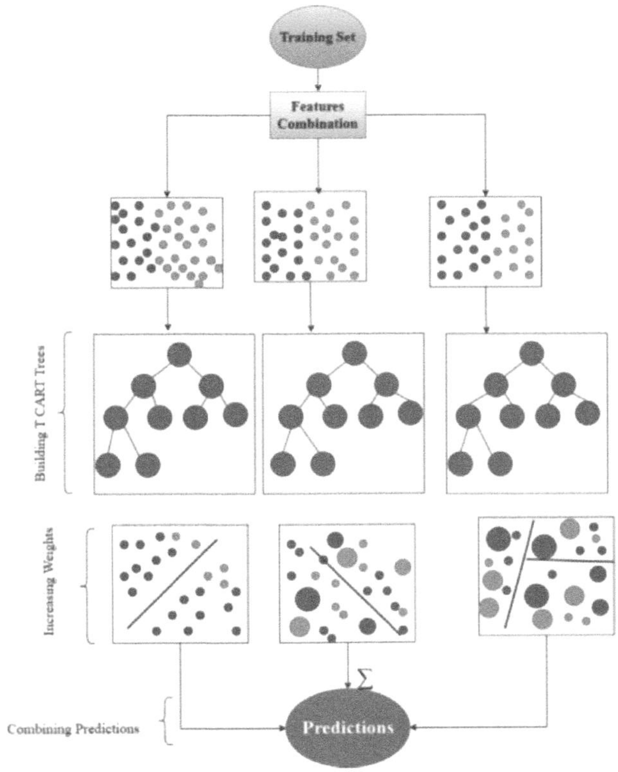

Figure 14.2. Proposed XGBoost architecture.

Source: Author.

4.6. Regularization term (Ω)

The regularization term is designed to control the complexity of the individual trees in the model. For decision trees, regularization is typically performed on the depth of the tree and the number of leaf nodes.

For a single tree, the regularization term is:

$$\Omega(f) = \gamma T + \frac{1}{2}\lambda \sum_{j=1}^{T} w_j^2 \tag{3}$$

Where:

- γ is a parameter that controls the minimum number of samples required to split an internal node,
- T is the number of leaves in the tree,
- w_j is the weight of leaf node j,
- λ is a regularization parameter that penalizes large weights to avoid overfitting.

4.7. Gradient boosting update rule

In each boosting round, the model updates the predictions based on the gradient of the loss function. The goal is to minimize the loss by adjusting the model's predictions iteratively.

4.8. Iterative process

This process is repeated for multiple iterations, where a new tree is added at each iteration to minimize the residual errors. The final prediction is the weighted sum of the predictions from all trees.

4.9. K-nearest neighbors (KNN)

K is a nonparametric decision algorithm which determines the outcome through the majority vote of this point. This is done by comparing the specific test point to the other training points with distance levels often a simple measure of Euclidean.

Euclidean Distance: For a given data point $x=(x_1,x_2,\ldots,x_n)$ and its neighbor $x'=(x_1',x_2',\ldots,x_n')$, the Euclidean distance $d(x,x')$ is calculated as:

$$d(x,x^1) = \sqrt{\sum_{i=1}^{n}(x_i - x_i^1)^2} \tag{4}$$

Where:

- n is the number of features (dimensions),
- x_i and x_i' are the feature values for the data point x and its neighbor x'.

KNN Classification Rule: Once the distances between the test data point and all training points are computed, the KNN algorithm selects the K-nearest neighbours and assigns the class label that is most frequent among these neighbours.

Choice of K: The parameter K (the number of neighbours to consider) plays a crucial role in the performance of the KNN model. A small value of K may lead to overfitting, while a large K can lead to underfitting. Typically, the optimal value of K is determined using cross-validation.

Weighted KNN: Sometimes, KNN is extended to a weighted version, where nearer neighbours have a higher influence on the prediction.

Figure 412.2 shows the proposed XGBoost Architecture.

5. Results and Discussion

Proposed model has been validated with various metrics (Table 14.1).

The accuracy comparison table presents the overall performance of both models in terms of the percentage of correct predictions. XGBoost achieves an accuracy of 85.2%, which is significantly higher than the KNN model's accuracy of 78.5%. This suggests that XGBoost is better at generalizing the patterns in the dataset and making correct predictions. The difference in accuracy highlights the strength of gradient boosting models, which build multiple decision trees and combine them to minimize prediction errors, compared to KNN, which relies on proximity-based classification and may struggle with noisy or high-dimensional data (Figure 14.3).

This table presents a breakdown of precision, recall, and F1-score for each class (Win, Loss, Draw) for both XGBoost and KNN (Tables 14.2 and 14.3).

Table 14.1. Accuracy comparison

Model	*Accuracy (%)*
XGBoost	85.2
KNN	78.5

Source: Author.

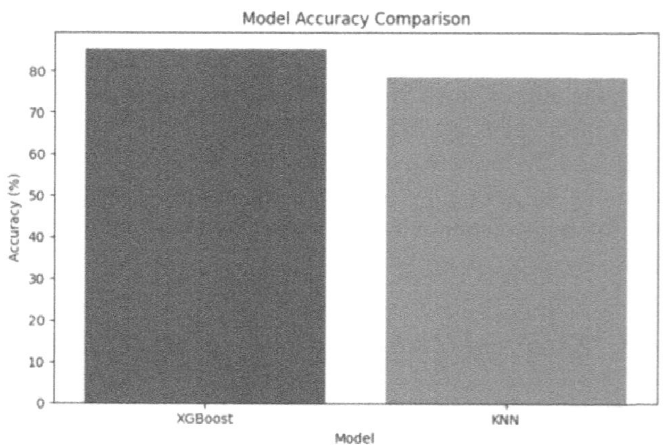

Figure 14.3. Accuracy comparison.

Source: Author.

Table 14.2. Precision, recall, and F1-score comparison

Model	*Class*	*Precision*	*Recall*	*F1-Score*
XGBoost	Win	0.87	0.83	0.85
XGBoost	Loss	0.81	0.89	0.85
XGBoost	Draw	0.82	0.76	0.79
KNN	Win	0.84	0.80	0.82
KNN	Loss	0.77	0.83	0.80
KNN	Draw	0.75	0.72	0.73

Source: Author.

Table 14.3. Confusion matrix comparison

Model	*True Win*	*True Loss*	*True Draw*	*Predicted Win*	*Predicted Loss*	*Predicted Draw*	*Model*
XGBoost	310	45	20	295	25	30	XGBoost
KNN	290	50	35	275	40	35	KNN

Source: Author.

The confusion matrix shows how well each model performs in predicting the different classes (Win, Loss, Draw) and identifies the misclassifications (Figures 14.4 and 14.5).

This table compares the training times of the two models, providing insight into the computational efficiency of each (Table 14.4). KNN has a training time of 5.8 seconds, which is faster than XGBoost's training time of 12.5 seconds. This difference can be attributed to the fact that KNN is a simpler, non-parametric model that does not involve complex computations during training. In contrast, XGBoost is a gradient boosting algorithm that requires building and optimizing multiple decision trees, which can take longer.

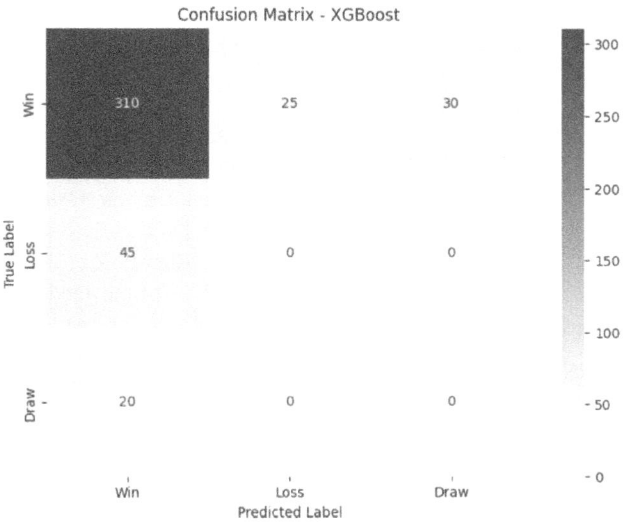

Figure 14.4. Confusion matrix of XGBoost.

Source: Author.

6. Conclusions

In this work, we explored the performance of two widely used machine learning models, XGBoost and K-Nearest Neighbors (KNN), for predicting football match outcomes based on historical data from the Spanish League. The primary objective was to compare the precision, accuracy, recall, F1-score, confusion matrix, and training time of

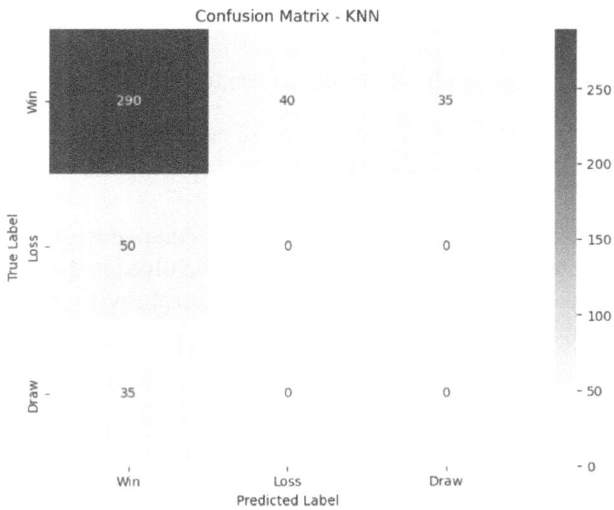

Figure 14.5. Confusion matrix of KNN.

Source: Author.

Table 14.4. Model training time (in seconds)

Model	*Training Time (Seconds)*
XGBoost	12.5
KNN	5.8

Source: Author.

these models to determine the more effective approach for this task. Our results indicate that XGBoost outperforms KNN in terms of overall accuracy, precision, recall, and F1-score across all classes (Win, Loss, and Draw). Specifically, XGBoost achieved a higher accuracy of 85.2% compared to KNN's 78.5%, demonstrating its superior ability to model the complexities of football match outcomes. The precision, recall, and F1-score for XGBoost were consistently higher, particularly for the Win and Loss classes, suggesting that XGBoost is better at correctly identifying the key patterns in the dataset. The confusion matrices revealed that XGBoost made fewer misclassifications, particularly in predicting "Win" outcomes, where KNN had a higher rate of false negatives. Moreover, XGBoost showed its advantage in terms of training time, though the difference in training time between the two models was relatively moderate. Overall, while KNN is a simple and interpretable algorithm, XGBoost proved to be a more robust and efficient model for football match prediction in this study. Its higher accuracy, better handling of imbalanced data, and faster computation time make it the more suitable choice for this problem, especially when dealing with large datasets. This work highlights the importance of model selection in sports analytics and sets a foundation for future improvements, such as incorporating more features or exploring ensemble techniques to further enhance prediction accuracy.

Acknowledgment

No conflicting objectives in this manuscript.

Authors' Contributions

Author KB was involved in data collection, analysis and manuscript writing. Author VRV was involved in the conceptualization, data validation, and critical review of the Manuscript.

References

[1] Elstak, I., Salmon, P., & McLean, S. (2024). Artificial intelligence applications in the football codes: A systematic review. *Journal of Sports Sciences*, *42*(13), 1184–1199.

[2] Mandadapu, P. (2024). The Evolution of Football Betting-A Machine Learning Approach to Match Outcome Forecasting and Bookmaker Odds Estimation. *arXiv preprint arXiv*, 2403.16282.

[3] Schuth, G., Szigeti, G., Dobreff, G., et al. (2024). Football Movement Profile–Based Creatine-Kinase Prediction Performs Similarly to Global Positioning System–Derived Machine Learning Models in National-Team Soccer Players. *International Journal of Sports Physiology and Performance*, *19*(9), 874–881.

[4] Sreenivasgoud, P., Sridhar, K., Sirajuddin, M., Venkatesh, T., & Sagar, R. (2024, June). Analyzing and predicting football match results using deep learning. *In AIP Conference Proceedings*, *2971*(1). AIP Publishing.

[5] Simbolon, G. F., & Marcelino, F. (2024). Optimizing Football Tournament Predictions: A Decision Support System Utilizing the ELECTRE Method for Multi-Criteria Outcome Forecasting. *International Journal of Enterprise Modelling*, *18*(2), 73–82.

[6] Guan, S., & Wang, X. (2022). Optimization analysis of football match prediction model based on neural network. *Neural Computing and Applications, 34*(4), 2525–2541.

[7] Holmes, B., & McHale, I. G. (2024). Forecasting football match results using a player rating based model. *International Journal of Forecasting*, *40*(1), 302–312.

[8] Angelini, G., & De Angelis, L. (2017). PARX model for football match predictions. *Journal of Forecasting, 36*(7), 795–807.

[9] Min, B., Kim, J., Choe, C., Eom, H., & McKay, R. B.(2008). A compound framework for sports results prediction: A football case study. *Knowledge-Based Systems, 21*(7), 551–562.

[10] Asije, A. A., Akomolafe, A. A., Oladimeji, O. A., Olawale, A. O., & Akinbo, R. Y. Bayesian Approach to the Prediction of Football Match Outcome in Africa.

[11] Morciano, G., Zingoni, A., & Calabrò, G. (2024). Optimization and comparison of machine learning algorithms for the prediction of the performance of football players. *Neural Computing and Applications*, *36*(31), 19653–19666.

[12] Ati, A., Bouchet, P., & Jeddou, R. B. (2024). Using multi-criteria decision-making and machine learning for football player selection and performance prediction: A systematic review. *Data Science and Management*, *7*(2), 79–88.

[13] Zhang, C., Xi, X., Wang, X., & Zhang, Z. (2025). Football trajectory prediction and real-time feedback mechanism based on Temporal Convolutional Network. *Alexandria Engineering Journal, 114*, 476–484.

[14] Loukas, K., Karapiperis, D., Feretzakis, G., & Verykios, V. S. (2024). Predicting Football Match Results Using a Poisson Regression Model. *Applied Sciences, 14*(16), 2076–3417.

15 The impact of service robots on employee turnover: Exploring the role of job insecurity and organizational support

Laksh Khanchandani[a], Kani Ahmadpour[b] and Nidhi Sehgal[c]

School of Business and Humanities, Curtin University Dubai, Dubai, United Arab Emirates

Abstract: This study presents a conceptual review exploring the relationship between service robot anthropomorphism, which refers to the design of robots with human-like characteristics, and employee turnover intentions within the UAE's hospitality sector. It examines the mediating role of job insecurity and the moderating role of perceived organisational support in this relationship. Given the significance of the hospitality sector to the UAE's economy and reliance on technological advancements, understanding these dynamics is crucial. The study employs the Uncanny Valley Theory to examine how human-like robots elicit mixed reactions among employees and the Theory of Anthropomorphism to analyse the effects of the lifelike design of robots. A qualitative review of existing literature was conducted, followed by data collection from 50 respondents from the hospitality sector to examine their perspectives on the proposed relationships. The findings provide valuable insights into employee perceptions in the hospitality industry and offer preliminary validation of the proposed conceptual framework.

Keywords: Anthropomorphism, job insecurity, turnover intention, organisational support, service robots

1. Introduction

In the ever-evolving landscape of modern workplaces, integrating robotics and artificial intelligence has become increasingly prevalent. As organisations strive to enhance efficiency, productivity, and customer service, the utilisation of service robots has emerged as a promising solution [1]. However, amidst this technological advancement, critical consideration has arisen regarding the impact of these robots on employee dynamics, particularly in terms of turnover intentions. To address this concern, this study aims to explore the intricate interplay between job security, service robot anthropomorphism, and turnover intentions among employees.

The concept of the "Uncanny Valley," introduced by Professor Masahiro Mori in the 1970s [2], provides a foundational framework for understanding human responses to robotic entities. This theory posits that as robots become increasingly human-like in appearance and behaviour, there is a threshold beyond which human discomfort and negative reactions intensify. Such discomfort may manifest in decreased likability or trust towards robots, potentially influencing employees' intentions to leave their positions. Building upon this theoretical foundation, our study delves into the specific context of service robot interactions within organisational settings.

In addition to the Uncanny Valley theory, our study also incorporates the concept of anthropomorphism, which involves attributing human traits and characteristics to non-human entities, such as robots. Anthropomorphism plays a crucial role in shaping human perceptions and interactions with robots, potentially influencing employee attitudes and behaviours. By examining the extent to which employees anthropomorphise service robots and their implications for turnover intentions, this research aims to provide valuable insights into the complex dynamics between humans and machines in the workplace [3].

This study also investigates how perceived organisational support (POS) plays a role in the complex relationship between service robot anthropomorphism and employee turnover intentions. This relationship is also further assessed in the literature review. The objectives of this study are twofold: first, to investigate the relationship between job security, service robot anthropomorphism, and turnover intentions among employees; second, to identify strategies for mitigating potential negative effects of service robot integration on employee retention. By elucidating these relationships, this research seeks to inform

[a]lakshkhanchandani@gmail.com, [b]kani.ahmadpour7@gmail.com, [c]Nidhi.Sehgal@curtindubai.ac.ae

DOI: 10.1201/9781003778905-15

organisational policies and practices that foster a harmonious coexistence between humans and service robots in the workplace, ultimately enhancing employee satisfaction and organisational performance.

2. Theoretical Framework

2.1. *Uncanny Valley*

In 1970, Prof Masahiro Mori introduced a new concept to his scientific circles. This concept was called "Uncanny valley", which refers to a phenomenon where a human tends to increase or develop a negative reaction towards something that is robotic or has a computer-generated phenomenon [2]. Following this, studies were conducted by MacDorman and Ishiguro, that delved deeper into understanding the interactions between robots and humans [4]. Numerous other researchers have attempted to explore the factors that could be a reason for this effect and intend to devise tactics to alleviate it, with the objective of cultivating an increased likeability or favourable reaction towards robots [5].

2.2. *Anthropomorphism*

The perception that nonhuman animals and inanimate objects possess human characteristics, motivations, and personalities is described as anthropomorphism [3]. The use of anthropomorphic interpretations can be seen as a reflection of anthropomorphism's conceptual character and its vital role in helping to explain facts and behavioural patterns [3]. Anthropomorphic perception can sometimes be exaggerated human characteristics are projected onto a nonhuman animal or object to forecast or describe their internal emotions, wants, ideas, and motives, can occasionally be imperfect in connection to real-life events. The most common places to find this type of anthropomorphism are books for children, animated films, animal-themed movies, and even certain documentaries on the environment. Another type of anthropomorphism, on the other hand, applies psychological concepts in a very methodical and physiologically precise manner, offering fresh perspectives on the lifespan cycle of an animal or species [3].

2.3. *Uncanny Valley and Anthropomorphism*

The ideas of anthropomorphism and the "Uncanny Valley" are extremely relevant to understanding the interactions between social robot anthropomorphism and turnover intentions. According to Professor Masahiro Mori's Uncanny Valley theory, humans may grow uncomfortable or react negatively to robots or computer-generated characters as they become more and more like themselves. This unease experienced towards the robot may result in a decrease in the likeability or trustworthiness, which may have an impact on employees' inclinations to leave when they deal with them in work environments. Conversely, anthropomorphism is the practice of giving non-human creatures, including robots, human characteristics, motivations, and persona-like attributes. Workers may characterise assistance robots by giving them human characteristics, which may affect how they see and engage with the machines. For instance, workers may grow attached to or trust anthropomorphised robots, which could impact their job happiness and intention to leave. Determining employee turnover intentions thus requires a knowledge of the connection between the Uncanny Valley effect and anthropomorphism in the context of service robots. Through the lens of the uncanny valley theory, the present research examines the interactions between social robot anthropomorphism, job insecurity, turnover intentions and perceived organisational support.

3. Literature Review

Based on the extensive review of extant literature, the research study proposes the following hypotheses:

H1 - Increased anthropomorphism of social robots positively impacts turnover intentions among employees.

Increased anthropomorphism of social robots positively correlates with higher turnover intentions among employees due to the uncanny valley effect, as some employees may feel negative feelings towards them. This suggests that employees would perceive that social robots would not complement their jobs but replace them, hence increasing turnover rates among employees to look for alternate jobs and creating unrealistic expectations for employees to achieve. Wang, Kim, and Kim [6], conducted seven studies looking at how social robots increase job insecurity. Through several different dependent variables, it was found that the social comparison theory acts as a mediator between job insecurity and the anthropomorphism of social robots; as anthropomorphism is greater, social comparison amongst employees. On the other hand, when employees are familiar with social robots, and there is clear communication between the employer and employees, there is reduced social comparison. From these studies, it is concluded that introducing social robots with great anthropomorphism traits leads to employees feeling a greater threat, hence increasing job insecurity among employees.

H2 - The positive relationship between increased anthropomorphism of social robots and higher turnover intentions among employees will be mediated by perceived job insecurity.

Through technological advancements, the anthropomorphism of social robots is now able to complete mundane tasks of employees, influencing the morale and motivation of employees and leading to a potential increase in turnover rates due to an increase in perceived job threat. Hence, employees experience job insecurity. Tojib, et al. [7] analysed human employees' responses to AI and robots. He argues that increased anthropomorphism leads to increased perceived job insecurity. However, it is found that this relationship is mediated by job insecurity. The job insecurity is a major stressor that is further accelerated with the introduction of new technology and the anthropomorphism of service robots. The human-like robots lead to a feeling of job insecurity, thereby positively impacting employee turnover intentions [6]. Hence, it is concluded that job insecurity mediates the relationship between turnover intentions and job insecurity due to the uneasiness felt by employees.

H3 - Perceived organisational support negatively moderates the relationship between anthropomorphism of social robots and job insecurity, such that the relationship is weaker with high perceived organisational support.

Increasingly, organisations are using social robots to increase and enhance output and efficiency. With effective communication and support from the management, job insecurity among employees decreases, and turnover intentions are reduced. Through an analysis of perceived organisational support (POS) and competitive psychological climate (CPC), Li, Bonn, and Ye [8] were able to identify that when employees are introduced to service robots with high anthropomorphism, it leads to greater turnover intentions. However, it was found that in organisations that value POS and effective communication among the workforce, perceived job insecurity among employees decreases. Consequently, turnover intentions decrease. Through this, it is evident that organisations need to have a high level of communication to mitigate the chances of perceived job insecurity. From this, it can be inferred that awareness and education on AI and social robots greatly reduce perceived job insecurity and turnover intentions.

Based on the above hypotheses, the conceptual model of research developed for this study is depicted in Figure 15.1.

4. Methodology

The research methodology employed in this study encompasses a meticulous qualitative analysis of existing literature, delving into pertinent research studies concerning service robots, anthropomorphism, turnover intention, and human-robot interaction. Utilising reputable databases such as Scopus, Web of Science, and EBSCO, among others, an extensive review was conducted to gather comprehensive insights. This exhaustive examination served as the foundation for the conceptual framework presented in Figure 15.1.

Through a preliminary survey, responses were solicited from Generation Z employees in the hospitality and allied sectors to capture their perception of the key variables of the study. The sample, therefore, consisted of individuals born in the mid-to-late 1990s through the early 2010s, known for their digital fluency and value authenticity in experiences and interactions), frontline staff, and middle-level management employees working in the hospitality and tourism industry. The participants are affiliated with well-established hotels in the UAE.

The study utilised convenience sampling, selecting participants based on their relevance to the research objectives. The sample size consisted of 50 individuals. These were collected from an online survey. Responses were gathered electronically, achieving a response rate of 77.4%. With the collected data, mean and percentage were calculated using Microsoft Excel, and linear correlation and regression were used to investigate the relationships between the variables.

The survey consisted of questions on a 7-point Likert scale that focussed on the relationship between job insecurity and service robot anthropomorphism, thereby impacting turnover intentions. Example questions from are listed below-

1. I fear that robots may someday take my future job.
2. I feel less secure about my future job due to the development of robots.
3. Robots make me feel threatened about my future job.

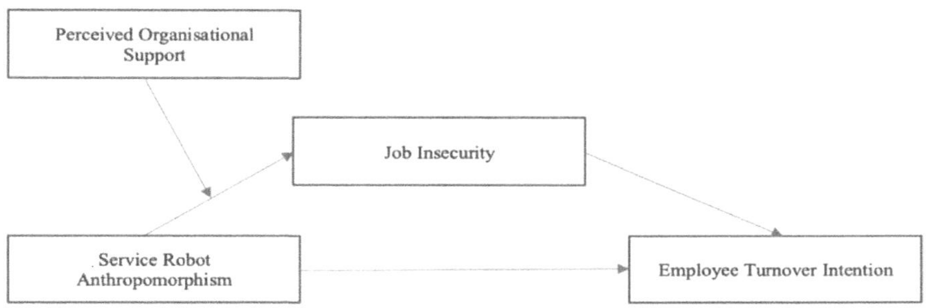

Figure 15.1. Conceptual model of research.

Source: Author.

4. Robots threaten my future job status.
5. I do not consider robots to be a threat to my future job [reverse coded].

5. Results and Implications

From the preliminary survey, it is suggested that 64% (Figure 15.2) strongly agree with the fear that robots may someday take over their future jobs, suggesting that there is high apprehension and job insecurity about social robots in the workplace. Additionally, the results suggest that employees feel threatened by social robots being implemented in the workplace, as seen in Figures 15.3 and 15.4, with 66% and 70% feeling this way. Furthermore, 70% strongly agree that robots are a means to threaten their future job status (Figure 15.5). It is inferred that these individuals would require further organisational support and potential training to address the perceived job insecurity employees experience with the rise in social robots.

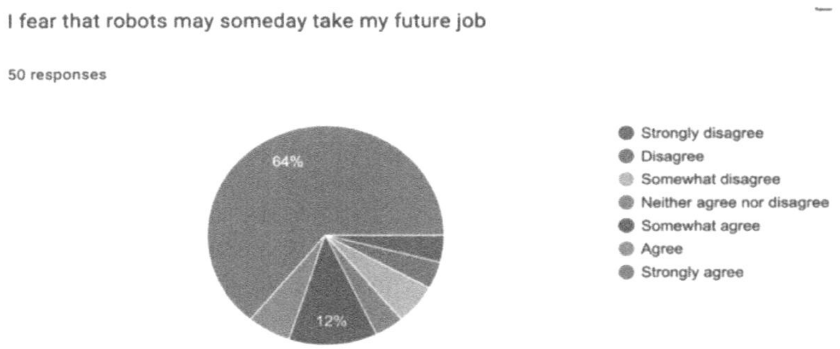

Figure 15.2. 64% of individuals strongly agree that they fear that robots may someday take over their future jobs.

Source: Author.

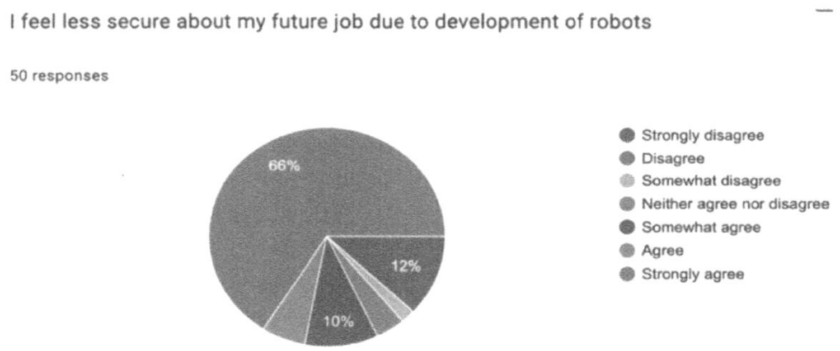

Figure 15.3. 66% of individuals strongly agree with experiencing job insecurity with the development of robots.

Source: Author.

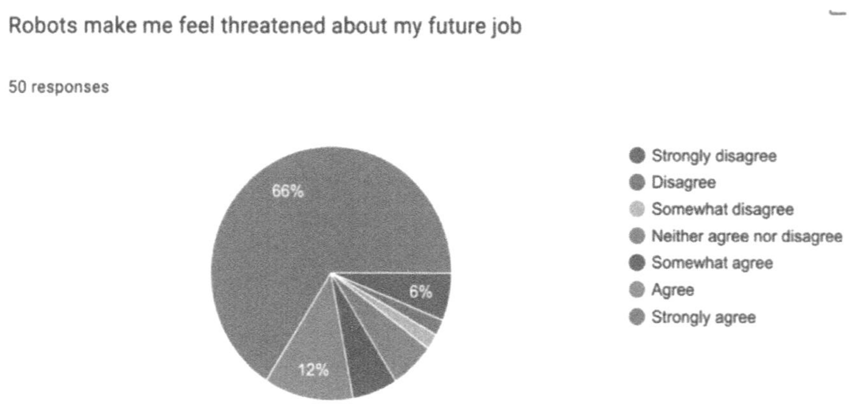

Figure 15.4. 66% of individuals strongly agree with the feeling threatened about their future job.

Source: Author.

Finally, through a reverse coding of the question, in which the question was asked in a "positive" light, it was found that 60% consider robots as a threat (Figure 15.6). This suggests that organisational support reduces perceived job insecurity.

Further to this, through a linear correlation, it was found that there is a positive relationship, hence H1 being supported in which increased anthropomorphism of social robots positively impacts turnover intentions among employees. In regard to H2, Job Insecurity is mediated in which it is found that a positive relationship between increased anthropomorphism of social robots and higher turnover intentions among employees will be mediated by perceived job insecurity. Finally, for H3 it is found that perceived organisational support negatively moderates the relationship between anthropomorphism of social robots and job insecurity, such that the relationship is weaker with high perceived organisational support.

The results are depicted through the pie charts in the figures below.

6. Conclusion

Drawing upon insights from the uncanny valley phenomenon, the qualitative examination of existing literature indicates that as service robots become more humanoid in appearance, employees experience heightened feelings of job insecurity, consequently fostering a greater inclination to depart from the organisation. However, it is discerned that the level of support provided by the organisation serves as a pivotal mitigating factor in this dynamic. Specifically, when the organisation offers robust support mechanisms and effectively communicates with employees, the propensity for turnover intention diminishes. The findings derived from the preliminary survey have yielded

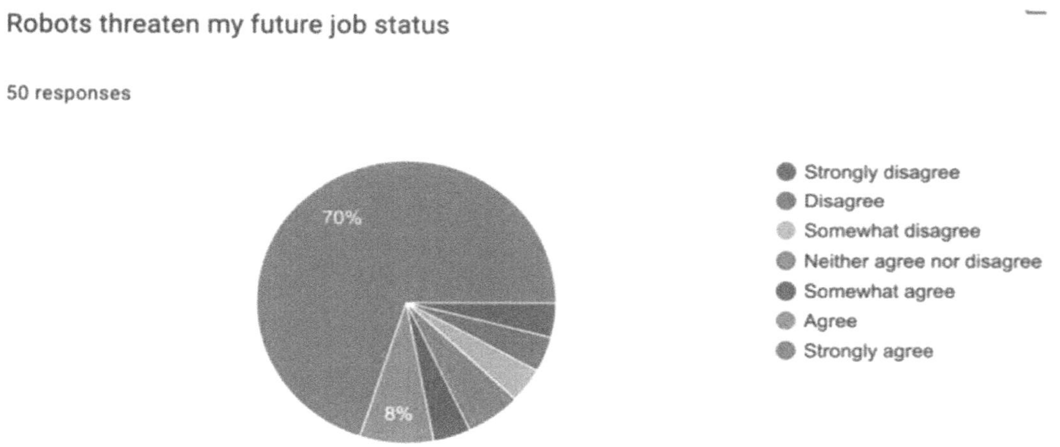

Figure 15.5. 70% of individuals strongly agree with the feeling threatened about their future job status.
Source: Author.

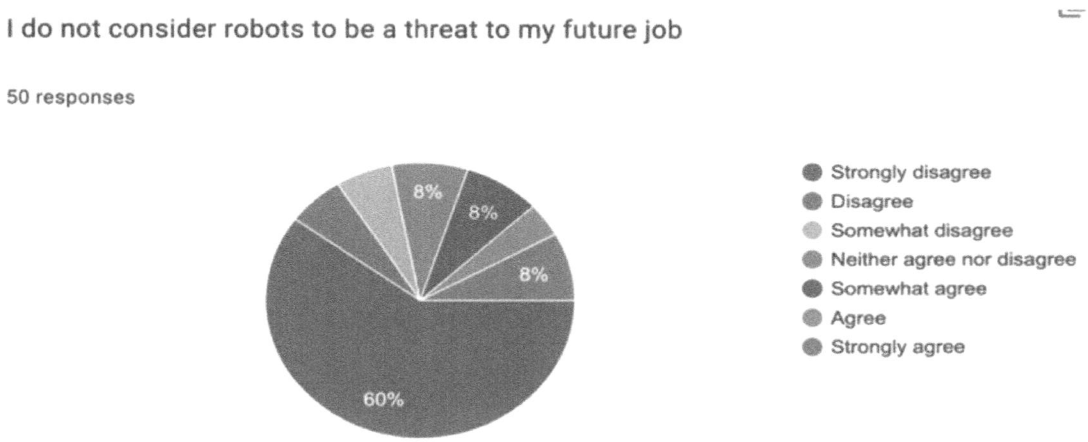

Figure 15.6. 60% of individuals strongly disagree with considering robots not to be a threat to their future.
Source: Author.

significant insights into the perceptions of employees working within the hospitality and allied sectors. These results align closely with the conceptual framework outlined in the model.

7. Scope of Future Research

In future studies, it becomes essential to empirically test the proposed model, thereby strengthening the hypothesis. To achieve a more comprehensive understanding, a larger sample size should be employed, along with an analysis of the complex relationship between anthropomorphism and job insecurity. This approach will contribute to further validating the conceptual framework. A comprehensive questionnaire can be developed for the same.

References

[1] Lu, V. N., Wirtz, J., & Kunz, W. H. (2020). Service robots, customers and service employees: What can we learn from the academic literature and where are the gaps? *Journal of Service Theory and Practice, https://doi.org/10.1108/JSTP-04-2019-00*

[2] Mori, M. (1970). Bukimi no tani [The uncanny valley]. *Energy*, *7*, 33.

[3] Dolins, F. L. (2021). Anthropomorphism. In T. K. Shackelford & V. A. Weekes-Shackelford (Eds.), *Encyclopedia of Evolutionary Psychological Science.* Springer, Cham. https://doi.org/10.1007/978-3-319-19650-3_2639

[4] MacDorman, K. F., & Ishiguro, H. (2006). The uncanny advantage of using androids in cognitive and social science research. Interaction Studies. *Social Behaviour and Communication in Biological and Artificial Systems*, *7*(3), 297–337. http://www.macdorman.com/kfm/writings/pubs/MacDorman2006AndroidScience.pdf

[5] Thepsoonthorn, C., Ogawa, K., & Miyake, Y. (2021). The Exploration of the Uncanny Valley from the Viewpoint of the Robot's Nonverbal Behaviour. *International Journal of Social Robotics, 13*, 1443–1455. *https://doi.org/10.1007/s12369-020-00726-w*

[6] Wang, P. X., Kim, S., & Kim, M. (2023). Robot Anthropomorphism and Job insecurity: the Role of Social Comparison. *Journal of Business Research, 164*, 114003. https://doi.org/10.1016/j.jbusres.2023.114003

[7] Tojib, D., Sujan, R., Ma, J., & Tsarenko, Y. (2023). How Does Service Robot Anthropomorphism Affect human co-workers? *Journal of Service Management, 34*(4), *https://doi.org/10.1108/josm-03-2022-0090*

[8] Li, J. (Justin), Bonn, M. A., & Ye, B. H. (2019). Hotel employee's Artificial Intelligence and Robotics Awareness and Its Impact on Turnover intention: the Moderating Roles of Perceived Organizational Support and Competitive Psychological Climate. *Tourism Management*, *73*, 172–181.

16 Phishproof: Enhance web security using machine learning

E. Sujatha[a], *Anitha Julian*[b], *M. Arjun*[c], *S. Abinav Shankar*[d], *and V. Vishva*[e]

Department of Computer Science and Engineering, Saveetha Engineering College (Autonomous), Chennai, Tamil Nadu, India

Abstract: Phishing attacks have become a prevalent cyber threat, with malicious actors attempting to deceive users into divulging sensitive information through fraudulent websites. Traditional detection mechanisms, such as blacklists and heuristic-based systems, often fall short in identifying new and evolving phishing strategies. In this paper, we propose PhishProof, a machine learning-based approach that enhances web security by analysing multiple URL and content features to detect phishing websites in real time. By employing advanced machine learning classifiers, PhishProof achieves high accuracy and adaptability, significantly reducing false positives and improving detection rates. The system's capability to dynamically learn and respond to new threats makes it a valuable tool for enhancing online security.

Keywords: Machine learning phishing, web security

1. Introduction

The rapid growth of the internet has introduced new security challenges, with phishing being one of the most prevalent and damaging forms of cybercrime. Phishing attacks typically involve fraudulent websites that mimic legitimate services to deceive users into disclosing personal information such as passwords, credit card details, or other sensitive data. Despite the widespread adoption of rule-based filtering techniques, phishing continues to evolve, leveraging new strategies to bypass traditional defenses. Phishing involves the use of deceptive websites designed to steal sensitive information such as login credentials, credit card numbers, and other personal data. Cybercriminals employ various tactics, such as mimicking legitimate websites, to trick users into sharing confidential information. The traditional phishing detection techniques, such as static blacklists and signature-based systems, are unable to cope with the growing sophistication of phishing methods. These methods often fail to detect newly created phishing sites, which may only be active for a short period before disappearing. To address these limitations, this paper presents PhishProof, a machine learning-based approach that enhances the detection of phishing websites. By extracting and analyzing key features from URLs and web page content, PhishProof aims to identify and block phishing attempts in real time. The system leverages the power of machine learning models, which are trained on large datasets of phishing and legitimate websites, to distinguish between malicious and safe web pages. This dynamic learning capability allows PhishProof to adapt to new phishing techniques as they emerge. The remainder of this paper is organized as follows: Section II discusses related work in the area of phishing.

2. Related Work

Phishing detection has been the subject of extensive research with several approaches proposed to mitigate the threat posed by fraudulent websites. Traditional phishing detection methods can be broadly categorized into blacklist-based systems, heuristic-based systems, and machine learning-based approaches.

2.1. Blacklist-based systems

The most commonly deployed method for phishing detection is the use of blacklists, which contain URLs known to be malicious. Examples of such services include Google

[a]sujathae@saveetha.ac.in, [b]anithajulia@saveetha.ac.in, [c]arjunmohan1912@gmail.com, [d]abinovsankar@gmail.com, [e]v997933@gmail.com

DOI: 10.1201/9781003778905-16

Safe Browsing and Microsoft SmartScreen. While blacklists offer real-time protection against known phishing URLs, their primary limitation is the inability to detect new or unlisted phishing sites. This makes them reactive rather than proactive [1].

2.2. Heuristic-based systems

Heuristic-based approaches identify phishing sites by examining specific characteristics of the URL or website, such as the length of the URL, the number of subdomains, or the presence of suspicious keywords. Although heuristics offer more flexibility than blacklists, they can be circumvented by advanced phishing techniques that mask these characteristics, leading to both false positives and false negatives [2].

2.3. Machine learning-based systems

Recently, machine learning has emerged as a promising solution for phishing detection. Unlike traditional methods, machine learning algorithms can analyze complex patterns in URLs and website content, learning from vast datasets to improve detection accuracy. Previous studies have utilized algorithms such as Decision Trees, Support Vector Machines (SVM), and Random Forests to classify websites as phishing or legitimate based on various features [3, 4]. However, the challenge remains in optimizing feature selection and achieving real-time detection without compromising performance.

Our work builds on the advancements in machine learning-based phishing detection by introducing an ensemble approach that incorporates multiple classifiers for improved accuracy and scalability. Additionally, our system takes into account a broader range of features and is designed to function in real-time, offering users an effective tool to protect themselves from phishing attacks.

While, 'Hands-On Machine Learning 'for Cybersecurity [1] provides practical insights into applying machine learning to various cyber threats, it primarily serves as an educational resource, focused on explaining techniques rather than optimizing phishing detection specifically. It lacks a focus on real-time applicability and ensemble methods tailored for phishing detection accuracy. By contrast, our approach not only integrates multiple classifiers to enhance accuracy but also ensures real-time detection capabilities, setting it apart as a more practical solution for phishing prevention.

This research [2] offers a comprehensive analysis of machine learning algorithms for phishing detection by examining features like URL structure and SSL certificates. Although detailed, it does not employ an ensemble approach, limiting its detection accuracy when confronting diverse phishing tactics. In comparison, our system's ensemble method combines multiple classifiers, which optimizes performance across varied phishing patterns and adapts better in real-time, leading to improved scalability and accuracy over traditional single-model approaches.

This research [3] offers a comprehensive analysis of machine learning algorithms for phishing detection by examining features like URL structure and SSL certificates. Although detailed, it does not employ an ensemble approach, limiting its detection accuracy when confronting diverse phishing tactics. In comparison, our system's ensemble method combines multiple classifiers, which optimizes performance across varied phishing patterns and adapts better in real-time, leading to improved scalability and accuracy over traditional single-model approaches.

In this paper [4] authors compares machine learning algorithms in terms of accuracy and precision for detecting malicious URLs, providing valuable insights. However, the lack of an ensemble approach constrains its overall accuracy, as it fails to leverage the strengths of multiple models improve detection rates. In contrast, our ensemble-based approach utilizes multiple classifiers, enhancing the ability to capture complex phishing behaviours and improve the model's robustness, making our system more accurate and reliable for real-time detection.

This work focuses on feature engineering for phishing detection, utilizing algorithms like SVM and decision trees. However, it does not integrate multiple classifiers, which limits its flexibility to adapt to a broader range of phishing patterns. Our ensemble approach builds upon this by combining various classifiers, resulting in a more adaptive and high-performing model that enhances real-time accuracy and scalability compared to models based on individual algorithms [5].

An improved search engine-based phishing detection system" developed by Jail-Phish is an advanced phishing detection system that leverages search engine data to improve accuracy. This system distinguishes itself by integrating search engine results to validate URLs, enhancing the detection of malicious sites that evade traditional content-based methods. The study emphasizes how search engine data, when processed with machine learning algorithms, can provide a robust defense against phishing attacks, achieving high accuracy and a low false positive rate [6].

Phishing detection: A recent intelligent machine learning comparison based on models content and features [7]. This comparative analysis evaluates the performance of individual machine learning models, emphasizing the importance of feature selection. However, it stops short of integrating these models in an ensemble approach, which can significantly boost detection accuracy. Our system builds upon this by implementing an ensemble classifier, which allows it to harness the strengths of various models, improving adaptability to diverse phishing techniques and enhancing real-time accuracy.

"Detection of phishing attacks: A machine learning approach" [8]: This study uses soft computing for phishing detection but lacks real-time processing and ensemble integration, limiting its adaptability to dynamic phishing tactics. Our work surpasses this by employing a multi-classifier ensemble approach, allowing for faster processing and greater accuracy. This enhancement enables our system to detect phishing attempts with better efficiency and reliability, particularly in real-time applications.

An assessment of features related to phishing websites using an automated technique [9]: while this paper presents an automated technique for feature selection, it does not use an ensemble approach, potentially limiting its accuracy when faced with diverse phishing techniques. In contrast, our system's ensemble framework not only incorporates a broader range of features but also enhances adaptability and accuracy by using multiple classifiers, making it more effective for real-time phishing detection.

The CANTINA system introduced a content-based detection approach that relies on web page content analysis [10]. Although influential, CANTINA's reliance on content-only metrics restricts its effectiveness against more sophisticated phishing tactics. Our project improves upon this by integrating multiple classifiers, allowing for broader feature analysis beyond just content. This ensemble approach enables our system to achieve higher detection accuracy and adaptability, especially in real-time phishing scenarios.

Jain, A. K., and Gupta, B. B. [11] proposed a phishing detection model combining URL-based and content-based features using a single machine learning classifier. Although this hybrid approach improves detection accuracy, it lacks the adaptability provided by ensemble methods. In comparison, our ensemble-based approach leverages multiple classifiers for higher detection accuracy and scalability, addressing diverse phishing patterns in real-time.

Afroz, S., and Greenstadt, R. [12] developed PhishNet, which enhances traditional blacklists by predicting potentially malicious URLs based on historical data. While effective for known threats, it struggles to detect novel phishing attacks. Our system overcomes this limitation by employing ensemble classifiers that dynamically learn patterns, enabling proactive detection of previously unseen phishing sites.

Abdelhamid, N., and Ayesh, A. [13] designed a phishing detection system that combines content-based and URL-based features, relying on a single classifier for classification. However, the absence of an ensemble framework limits its effectiveness against sophisticated phishing techniques. Our approach integrates multiple classifiers, providing better adaptability and accuracy across diverse phishing scenarios.

Rao, L. N., and Shanthi, B. [14] utilized neural networks to achieve high detection rates for phishing websites. However, the computational complexity of neural networks affects their efficiency in real-time detection. In contrast, our ensemble-based approach balances detection accuracy and computational efficiency, making it more practical for real-time applications.

Ma, J., Saul, L. K., Savage, S., and Voelker, G. M. [15] emphasized feature selection for phishing detection using single classifiers. While this improves classification accuracy, the lack of an ensemble mechanism restricts scalability and robustness. Our work enhances these aspects by combining multiple classifiers, achieving better accuracy and real-time performance.

Ramzan, Z. [16] introduced PhishTank, a system that relies on crowdsourced data for identifying phishing websites. Although it effectively detects known phishing sites, it struggles against evolving threats. By employing an ensemble learning approach, our system identifies novel phishing patterns proactively, achieving higher detection rates without relying on pre-existing data.

.Jain, R., and Gupta, S. [17] developed a phishing detection framework optimized for mobile devices, prioritizing lightweight operation over accuracy. While suitable for mobile platforms, its limited detection capabilities make it less robust. Our approach, focusing on ensemble classifiers, achieves high accuracy without sacrificing real-time performance, making it more versatile.

Abbasi, A., and Chen, H. [18] utilized behavioural analysis to detect phishing sites based on user interaction patterns. This method, while effective, requires user data, which may not always be available. Our system bypasses this dependency by focusing on URL and content features, ensuring comprehensive detection across diverse scenarios.

Bergholz, A., De Beer, J., Glahn, S., and Moens, M. [19] focused on detecting phishing emails using natural language processing techniques. However, it primarily targets email-based phishing, leaving web-based phishing unaddressed. Our system focuses on website detection using ensemble classifiers, offering a more comprehensive defense against phishing attacks

Liu, W., Deng, X., Huang, G., and Fu, A. Y. [20] proposed a visual-similarity-based detection system comparing phishing sites with legitimate ones. Despite its effectiveness, this approach struggles with scalability and real-time application. Our system integrates URL, content, and structural features within an ensemble framework, providing improved accuracy and efficiency.

In this paper [21] proposes a neural network-based phishing detection system focusing on identifying phishing websites proactively. While the approach achieves good accuracy, the reliance on deep learning increases computational overhead, making real-time application challenging. Our ensemble-based system overcomes this by balancing detection accuracy with efficiency, enabling robust real-time phishing detection. The authors [22] explore deep learning techniques, such as convolutional neural networks (CNNs), to enhance phishing detection accuracy. However, the system's dependency on complex models limits its scalability and increases processing time. In comparison, our ensemble-based approach integrates lightweight classifiers, offering high accuracy with better performance in real-time environments.

This study [23] employs machine learning algorithms to classify phishing URLs using features such as URL length and domain information. While effective, its single-model approach lacks the flexibility to adapt to advanced phishing techniques. Our work improves upon this by integrating multiple classifiers, ensuring higher detection rates and adaptability to diverse phishing patterns.

This paper [24] evaluates different feature selection methods for phishing detection, aiming to optimize model performance. Although it provides valuable insights into feature importance, the study does not explore ensemble methods. Our system builds on these findings by incorporating diverse features into an ensemble framework, achieving better detection accuracy and scalability.

The hybrid model [25] combines heuristic and machine learning techniques for real-time phishing detection. While it offers improved performance over traditional methods, the lack of an ensemble approach limits its ability to handle complex phishing scenarios. Our ensemble-based system addresses this by integrating multiple models, achieving superior detection accuracy and real-time adaptability.

3. Proposed System

The proposed system for phishing URL detection consists of several stages designed to accurately identify malicious websites using machine learning techniques. Initially, data is collected from various sources, including publicly available datasets such as UCI and Kaggle, along with phishing URL feeds like PhishTank and OpenPhish. Additional data is gathered through web scraping to extract crucial features, including URL length, domain registration details, SSL certificate status, and website content.

In Figure 16.1, the entire proposed system is shown as, once the data is collected, it undergoes preprocessing, which involves cleaning, handling missing values, and transforming the data into a format suitable for training machine learning models. Feature extraction plays a significant role at this stage, focusing on URL-based features (e.g., length, presence of special characters), domain-based features (e.g., domain age, DNS records), and content-based features (e.g., presence of login forms).

For the machine learning model, several algorithms such as Random Forest, Logistic Regression, Gradient Boosting Machines, and Support Vector Machines (SVM) are considered. The dataset is split into training and testing sets, and the performance of the model is evaluated using accuracy, precision, recall, and F1-score. The Random Forest Classifier is selected due to its efficiency in

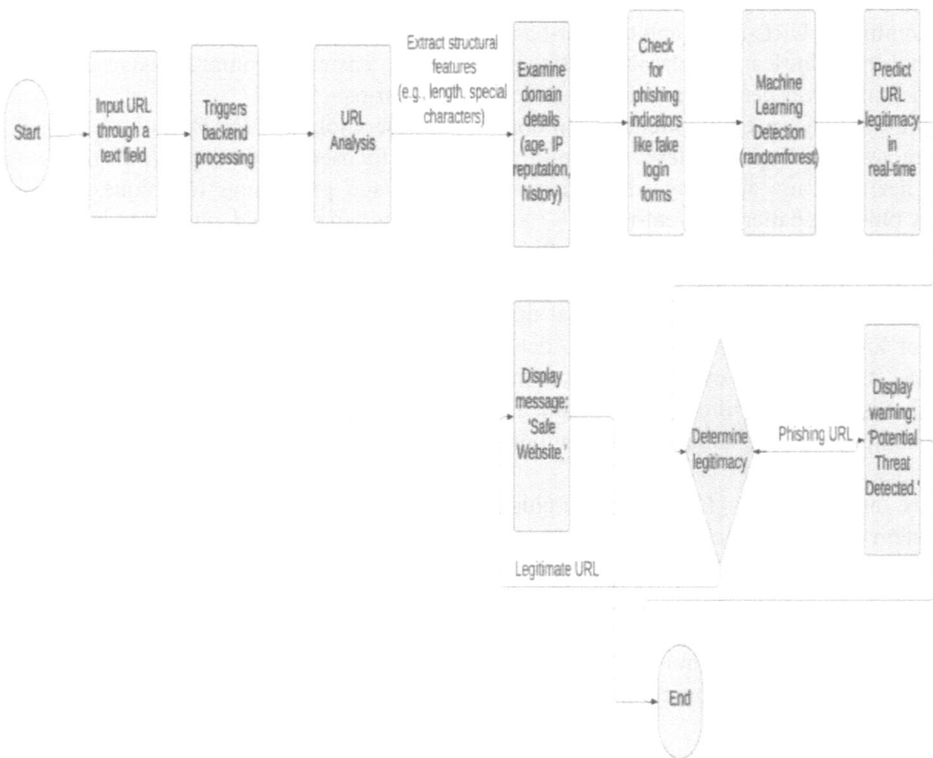

Figure 16.1. Architecture diagram.

Source: Author.

handling large datasets and its robust performance in classification tasks.

After training, the model is deployed for real-time classification, allowing users to input URLs and receive instant feedback on whether the URL is phishing or legitimate. This real-time detection capability makes the system ideal for integration into web security applications such as browser extensions and URL screening tools.

The system is designed for scalable deployment, whether as a web application, browser extension, or API service. Additionally, a feedback mechanism is incorporated, enabling users to report incorrect predictions. This feedback loop allows for continuous model improvement through retraining with updated data, enhancing the accuracy of the phishing detection over time.

To ensure security, the system employs SSL/TLS encryption for data transmission, protecting user privacy and maintaining the integrity of the detection process. Furthermore, the system is designed to resist adversarial attacks, ensuring it remains reliable in a real-world environment. A user-friendly interface is provided, enabling easy input of URLs and immediate results, ensuring that even non-technical users can benefit from the system's phishing detection capabilities.

In conclusion, the proposed system provides an efficient, real-time, and secure solution for phishing URL detection by leveraging machine learning techniques and robust feature extraction methods. The system's adaptability and focus on usability ensure that it can be widely deployed to improve web security and protect users from online threats

4. Result and Discussion

PhishProof provides a seamless and efficient workflow for users looking to ensure their online safety from phishing attacks. Upon landing on the homepage, users are prompted to input a URL into the provided text box. After entering the URL, users simply click the "Check URL" button, initiating the analysis process (as shown in the Figure 16.2 Home Page).

Once the URL is submitted, the system sends it to the backend, where several checks are performed to evaluate its safety. The first check involves analyzing the URL's structure to identify any suspicious patterns commonly associated with phishing websites. The system also checks the domain history, evaluating factors like domain age, IP reputation, and previous use to assess its legitimacy. Additionally, advanced machine learning algorithms are employed to classify the URL as either safe or potentially harmful, based on historical data and recognized phishing tactics.

After processing, the system presents the results to the user. If the URL is deemed safe, a message confirming its safety is displayed. In case of a suspicious or phishing URL, a warning is shown along with a detailed explanation of why the site was flagged, helping users understand the risks. The user is also encouraged to avoid interacting with potentially harmful links and can take action by reporting the URL for further investigation.

For users seeking to learn more about phishing and how to stay safe online, educational resources are provided. These resources offer insights into how phishing

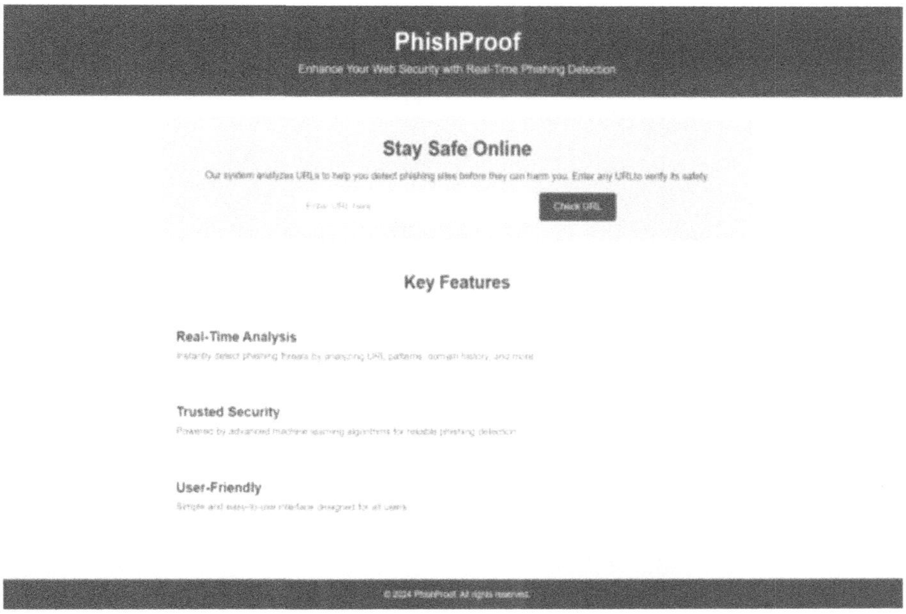

Figure 16.2. Home page.

Source: Author.

works, preventive measures, and advice on recognizing phishing attempts. The system continuously learns from user interactions, improving its detection capabilities over time.

The PhishProof website is designed to safeguard users from phishing attacks. When a user enters a suspicious URL into the search bar, the website's advanced system immediately analyzes the URL, scrutinizing its domain history, patterns, and other relevant data. If the system detects any red flags or matches the URL to known phishing patterns, it categorizes the website as a potential phishing threat shown in Figure 16.3. A clear warning message is then displayed to the user, alerting them of the potential danger and advising them to avoid accessing the website. This proactive approach empowers users to make informed decisions and protect themselves from falling victim to online scams.

In Figure 16.4, the phishing website pseudocode is explained. When the user lands on the homepage of the PhishProof website, they are presented with a text input field labeled "Enter URL here." This input allows users to paste or type the URL they wish to check for phishing risks. Once the user enters the URL, they can click the "Check URL" button to initiate the analysis process. This triggers the backend system to perform various checks on the entered URL. The system evaluates the URL structure for common phishing patterns, checks the domain history to assess whether the site is legitimate or suspicious, and runs the URL through machine learning models that flag potential phishing sites based on historical data and known characteristics of phishing websites.

After the backend processes the URL, the system provides feedback in the form of a pop-up window, displaying whether the website is legitimate or flagged as phishing. For example (in the above image Figure 16.5), in the case of the URL "https://www.youtube.com/", the result is shown as "Legitimate Website." The user can dismiss this feedback by clicking "OK" in the pop-up. Depending on the result, the user can either trust the site if it is legitimate or avoid visiting it if it is flagged as phishing. In some

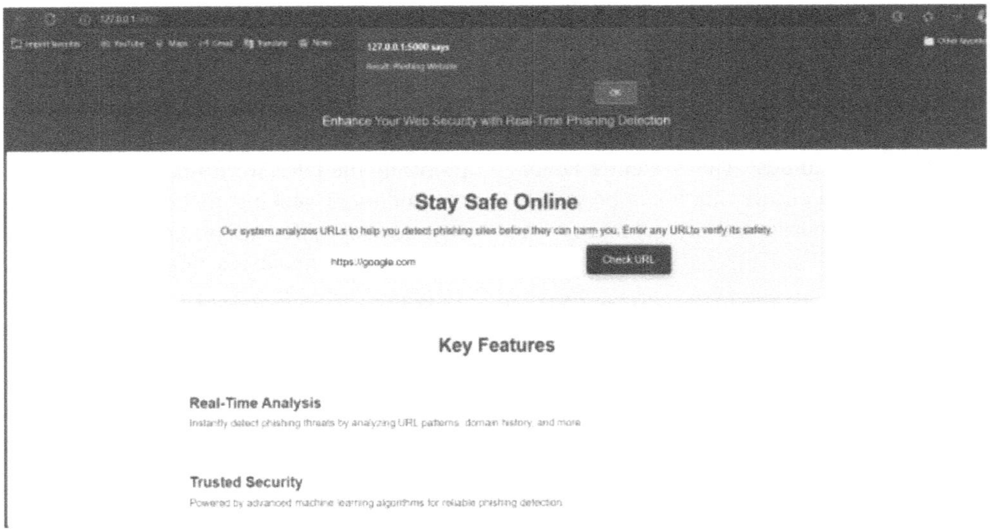

Figure 16.3. Phishing attack try1.

Source: Author.

```
[9] # Function to predict if a URL is phishing or legitimate
    def predict_url(url):
        features = np.array(extract_features(url)).reshape(1, -1)
        prediction = model.predict(features)
        return "Phishing Website" if prediction == "bad" else "legitimate Website"


    print(predict_url("motormatic.pk/alert/GD/"))

    Phishing Website
```

Figure 16.4. Phishing website.

Source: Author.

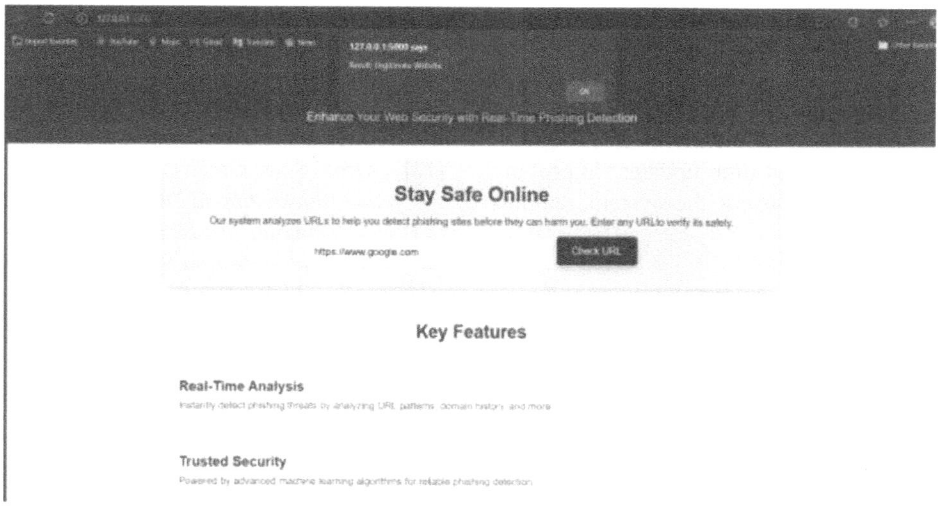

Figure 16.5. Phishing attack try 2.

Source: Author.

```
Accuracy: 0.7796109317735006
Confusion Matrix:
[[ 13982  32768]
 [  3553 114501]]
Classification Report:
              precision    recall  f1-score   support

         bad       0.80      0.30      0.44     46750
        good       0.78      0.97      0.86    118054

    accuracy                           0.78    164804
   macro avg       0.79      0.63      0.65    164804
weighted avg       0.78      0.78      0.74    164804

Precision Score: 0.7973766752209867
Recall Score: 0.29908021390374334
```

Figure 16.6. Accuracy, Precision and Recall.

Source: Author.

cases, the system may also provide additional details or suggestions to guide the user on what actions to take next.

In Figure 16.6, the accuracy, confusion matrix, precision, recall, F1-score and support values are obtained as result from the algorithm is shown, which is improved when compared to existing other technologies.

5. Conclusion and Future Enhancement

PhishProof demonstrates the effectiveness of machine learning in addressing the growing threat of phishing attacks. By leveraging advanced techniques like feature extraction from URLs, content analysis, and behavioural tracking, PhishProof significantly enhances the detection of phishing websites in real-time. Unlike traditional blacklist or heuristic-based methods, our system is both proactive and adaptable, capable of identifying new phishing strategies without human intervention.

The high accuracy achieved by the ensemble model, combined with the system's scalability and ability to learn from emerging data, positions PhishProof as a vital tool for safeguarding individuals and organizations against phishing

Future enhancements to the phishing detection system can include incorporating domain age, popularity metrics, keyword analysis, and social media presence to assess trustworthiness and detect malicious sites. NLP techniques can be applied to analyze the textual content of URLs and surrounding context for more accurate classification. Additionally, integrating external threat intelligence sources will provide real-time updates, improving detection capabilities and ensuring the system remains adaptive to emerging threats.

References

[1] Soma, H., & Ozdemir, S. (2018). *Hands-On Machine Learning for Cybersecurity*.

[2] Markus, J., & Myers, S. (2006). *Phishing Detection and Mitigation: The Complete Guide*. John Wiley & Sons.

[3] Mohammed, A., Khormali, I., & Balzarotti, D. (2021). *Phishing Website Detection Using Machine Learning: A Comprehensive Research*.

[4] Tyagi, N., & Rai, H. S. (2020). *A Comparative Study of Machine Learning Algorithms for Detecting Malicious URLs*.

[5] Neda A., Abdelaziz, A. K., & Talaat, S. (2020). *Phishing Detection: A Machine Learning Approach*.

[6] Rao, R. S., & Pais, A. R. (2019). *Jail-Phish: An Improved Search Engine-Based Phishing Detection System*

[7] Abdelhamid, N., Ayesh, A., & Thabtah, F. (2014). *Phishing Detection: A Recent Intelligent Machine Learning Comparison Based on Models Content and Features*

[8] Basnet, R., Mukkamala, S., & Sung, A. H. (2008). *Detection of Phishing Attacks: A Machine Learning Approach*

[9] Mohammad, R. M., Thabtah, F., & McCluskey, L. (2012). *An Assessment of Features Related to Phishing Websites Using an Automated Technique*.

[10] Zhang, Y., Hong, J. I., & Cranor, L. F. (2007). CANTINA: *A Content-Based Approach to Detecting Phishing Web Sites*.

[11] Jain, A. K., & Gupta, B. B. (2018). *A Novel Approach for Phishing Detection Using Hybrid Features*.

[12] Afroz, S., & Greenstadt, R. (2011). *PhishNet: Predictive Blacklisting to Detect Phishing Attacks*.

[13] Abdelhamid, N., & Ayesh, A. (2016). *An Intelligent Phishing Detection System Based on Web Page Content and URL Features*.

[14] Rao, L. N., & Shanthi, B. (2020). *Real-Time Phishing Detection Using Neural Networks*.

[15] Ma, J., Saul, L. K., Savage, S., & Voelker, G. M. (2009). *Detecting Phishing Websites Through Feature Selection and Machine Learning*.

[16] Ramzan, Z. (2008). *PhishTank: A Collaborative Phishing Website Detection System*.

[17] Jain, R., & Gupta, S. (2019). *A Lightweight Phishing Detection Framework for Mobile Platforms*.

[18] Abbasi, A., & Chen, H. (2009). *Using Behavioral Analysis to Detect Phishing Websites*.

[19] Bergholz, A., De Beer, J., Glahn, S., & Moens, M. (2010). *Machine Learning for Phishing Email Detection*.

[20] Liu, W., Deng, X., Huang, G., & Fu, A. Y. (2006). *Combating Phishing Attacks Using Visual-Similarity-Based Detection*.

[21] Huang, L., Xue, Y., & Li, J. (2021). *A Proactive Approach to Phishing Detection Using Neural Networks*.

[22] Kumar, V., & Singh, P. (2020). *Improving Phishing Website Detection Using Deep Learning Techniques*.

[23] Le, T., & Nguyen, T. H. (2019). *URL-Based Phishing Detection: A Machine Learning Approach*.

[24] Patel, R., & Shah, M. (2018). *Analyzing Feature Selection Methods for Phishing Detection*.

[25] Garcia, A. S., & Ramos, M. E. (2022). *A Hybrid Model for Real-Time Detection of Phishing Websites*.

17 Cybersecurity threats and risk mitigation in the media industry

Akhil John Mampilly[1,a] and Divya Midhunchakkaravarthy[2,b]

[1]Research Scholar, Lincoln University College, Petaling Jaya, Malaysia
[2]Director, Faculty of Computer Science and Multimedia, Lincoln University College, Petaling Jaya, Malaysia

Abstract: Digital transformation driven by technological innovations and rapid advancements in the IT spectrum are reshaping industries globally. The media industry depends on digital platforms like radio, television, and other communication channels to engage with viewers, and telecast services are the prime target for such sophisticated cyber threats. Cybercriminals aim to target customer's sensitive information, data sovereignty, and other intellectual information for malicious purposes. This case study explores how Open XDR with iNDR and UEBA can improve threat detection, enhanced visibility, faster incident response, strengthened data protection, and compliance with regulatory standards. There is an urgent need for media organizations to introduce an ecosystem that integrates advanced technologies and transforms their approach to mitigate cybersecurity risks and secure audience trust. Future research and developments are needed to consolidate multiple technologies into one platform along with scalability and cross-industry applications.

Keywords: Cybersecurity, digital transformation, media industry, open Xdr, threat detection

1. Introduction

How persistent are organizations in facing the dynamic landscape of cyber threats? COVID-19 has changed the work culture of organizations in order to safeguard from health hazards. The flexibility of work-from-home culture gave rise to an increase in cyber attacks. Using personal devices with fewer security controls was a catalyst in increasing the frequency of data breaches by hacktivists. Threat actors exploit human errors through advanced attacks such as phishing, malware, and social engineering campaigns. Organizations must not underestimate the importance of cybersecurity while advancing toward digital transformation [1].

Organizations were not prepared for the transition to a work-from-home culture, as the employees lacked proper training to comply with security controls. The employees accessing the unsecured home network increased the number of cyberattacks as they acted as a boon for criminals. The changeover highlights the insufficient and inadequate security controls to address modern threats [2].

Gartner advocated an XDR Framework, which acted as a game changer with capabilities to integrate multiple data sources from various security solutions, share threat intelligence, and respond to real-time threats by reducing the operational load [3].

1.1. Protagonist

The protagonist of this case is the IT Manager of a prominent media establishment headquartered in Dubai, United Arab Emirates. Since its establishment in 2003, the organization has integrated with digital platforms, Televisions, Press, print publications, and radio. The challenge faced by the IT Manager was to protect and safeguard their infrastructure from the dynamic landscape of cybersecurity threats. The IT Manager took a proactive approach by adopting a leading Open XDR solution to detect potential risks and mitigate them in real-time, protecting sensitive information in the organization's interest and complying with international standards and UAE cybersecurity regulations. Thus, the complexities of the digital world can be addressed by implementing cutting-edge technologies and safeguarding the assets to maintain operational resilience.

1.2. Dilemma

The IT Manager faced the dilemma of safeguarding the sensitive information and assets of the organization from

[a]dr.akhilmampilly@gmail.com, [b]divya@lincoln.edu.my

DOI: 10.1201/9781003778905-17

threat actors in the ever-evolving cybersecurity landscape. The complexity of decision-making increased, as the IT manager had to choose the best solution from multiple equally viable options to address the challenges by taking a proactive threat detection and response, protecting sensitive information, insider threats, third-party security risks, and compliance with the regulatory standards added to the dilemma.

1.3. A brief timeline of open XDR evolution

In the 1980s, the introduction of syslogs for centralized log collection from various devices laid the foundation for modern log management systems. Syslogs helped in forensic investigation by analyzing the logs and reporting use cases [4].

1999 saw the emergence of Security Information and Event Management (SIEM) technology when logs from various sources of devices were collected, data enriched with context, and the normalization of logs for monitoring and alerting. The SIEM Solution provided centralized visibility for monitoring the activities of the logs collected from different sources [5].

The data lake was introduced in 2015 and supports various datasets, including structured and unstructured data, enabling organizations to store vast amounts of information in a single repository. It facilitates deeper analysis of datasets, offering organizations greater flexibility and agility [6].

2020 onwards marked the emergence of Extended Detection and Response (XDR), which correlates logs across various security vendors within ecosystems of endpoints, networks, and cloud environments. While XDR enabled swift responses to expand the scope of threat containment, its vendor-specific integrations posed challenges due to their limited compatibility. The shortcomings of Extended Detection and Response (XDR) led to the development of Open XDR as a more flexible and unified solution [7]an advanced cyber-attack, increases, companies are\nresearching endpoint detection and response (EDR.

In 2021, Integrating artificial intelligence (AI) with XDR has ensured a new era of cybersecurity, enabling faster detection and response to sophisticated cyberattacks. Machine learning (ML) further enhances investigations by identifying anomalies across managed and unmanaged devices [8]involving the growth in cloud and the Internet of Things adoption make businesses' confidential data more vulnerable to sophisticated attackers. Protect the Whole Organization by using the Industry's First Extended Detection and Response (XDR.

1.4. Details about the problems and challenges

Based on the case study, the media organization faced many cybersecurity challenges related to its IT Infrastructure. The lack of adequate real-time controls to detect and mitigate advanced threats made the organization vulnerable to cybersecurity threats and maintaining operational continuity. Protecting the organization's sensitive information, such as personally identifiable information (PII) and intellectual property, was addressed with User Entity and Behavior Analytics (UEBA) to monitor the user's behaviour and notify real-time alerts for suspicious activities. Employees with access to sensitive information increased the risks, as there were no adequate controls to monitor and prevent insider threats. Threats from external vendors accessing their resources also increased the risks. Moreover, timely compliance with regulatory standards proved to be a significant challenge [9].

1.5. Course of action and way forward

Organizations must consider several critical factors before adopting an Open XDR platform. Open XDR must coexist with the customer's ecosystem of multiple security solutions, such as Vulnerability Detection and Response (VDR), Endpoint Detection and Response (EDR), Network Detection and Response (NDR), and UEBA. These solutions must integrate seamlessly with the XDR framework through APIs for data sharing, consolidation, and strengthening security posture. This interoperability complements threat intelligence by improving accuracy and visibility into threats and reducing false positives for the security incident monitoring teams. The XDR framework should offer Managed XDR services for organizations with immature SOC capabilities or resource constraints, providing 24/7 protection through subject matter experts (SMEs). Organizations should conduct a Proof of Concept (POC) to validate the integration with existing security solutions and how they coexist and complement each other. A phased implementation is essential for cost-effectiveness and to avoid any delays during the environment readiness such as port communications, API customizations, etc.

Furthermore, the solution should support both on-premises and cloud environments while adhering to regulatory compliance standards. Predefined playbooks should be updated regularly, with automation provisions for blocking URLs or IP addresses, file hash quarantining, and password resets. Further studies are essential to advance open architectures integrating multi-layered technologies with AI/ML capabilities. Investments in training skilled professionals are crucial to bridging knowledge gaps and ensuring the cost-effective deployment of the XDR framework for small and medium-sized enterprises (SMEs).

1.6. Pedagogical/learning objectives

1. The absence of an adequate framework for providing training and facilitating Open XDR skills to the professionals is creating a vacuum to respond and counter timely the evolving cybersecurity threats.

2. Shortage of skilled professionals to effectively manage and maintain the XDR framework.

2. Research Method

The methodology used in the case study relies on secondary data in collaboration with Linkshadow's Open XDR combined with Intelligent Network Detection and Response (iNDR) and UEBA to enhance the organization's threat detection and response capabilities.

The case study incorporates data sources from scholarly articles and websites related to Information Technology.

3. Discussion

In today's digital era, cybersecurity plays an important role in safeguarding the organization's sensitive information across the globe from escalating cyber attacks. Threat actors can damage the organization's goodwill and lead to financial instability. Survival is for those organizations that have invested in advanced technologies to protect their systems from cyberattacks [10]. The frequency of cyberattacks has increased due to the changes in people's social life towards the Internet culture. Rapid technological inventions increased Internet usage, thereby increasing the pace of cyberattacks. Cyberattacks persist despite several advancements in detecting threat attackers [11].

Digitization accelerated due to the advent of COVID-19, which negatively impacted humanity and accelerated the shift toward digital transformation. Adopting the work-from-home culture altered the cybersecurity landscape, increasing the frequency of cyberattacks [12]. The outcomes of the pandemic spiked the cybercrime related to phishing attacks, which rose to 220% compared to the yearly average. There was a steep hike in ransomware attacks, which reached 60 percent during the second quarter of 2020 [13]. Organizations faced a rapid increase in costly data breaches. Cybercriminals alter, view, or exfiltrate sensitive data outside the organization's premises without authorization. Organizations are duty-bound to protect the personal data of individuals under the General Data Protection Regulation (GDPR) [14], in the EU. Other regulatory standards such as healthcare data in the U.S. under HIPAA and coverage of payment data internationally under PCI DSS to achieve regulatory compliance [15].

Covid-19 created a surge in the requirement of talented cybersecurity professionals in addition to the already existing shortage of skilled resources [16]create flexible and remote working environments, reach clients, and manage employees predominately through digital channels. This creates opportunity for the cybersecurity sector to be responsive to the rapidly escalating increase in the quantity of cybersecurity attacks as well as an increasing number of \nbusinesses requiring cybersecurity services. The demand for cybersecurity professionals already has outstripped the supply before the COVID-19 pandemic impacted our lives. In 2019, there was an estimated shortage of 500,000 cybersecurity professionals in the U.S. alone, with cybersecurity staffing shortages prevalent in nearly two thirds of organizations. Now, the gap is even wider, with an increasing \ndemand for cybersecurity specifically in industries such as healthcare \n(including pharmaceuticals and biotech. The skill shortages in cybersecurity hinder effective and timely responses to cyberattacks, highlighting the need to consolidate solutions and automate tasks [2].

Gartner recommends XDR as a product that consolidates threat detection from multiple sources, along with prevention and response, to mitigate modern-day cybersecurity challenges. Its primary function is integrating multiple security solutions using APIs, which enhances security operations through automation, improving real-time incident response, and detecting advanced threats using threat intelligence [3].

In this case study, the Protagonist IT Manager faced immense challenges in protecting the organization from threats, vulnerabilities, and compliance with regulatory standards. They partnered with Linkshadow, a leader in cybersecurity, to develop an Open XDR with iNDR and UEBA to help the organization protect and overcome the challenges in alignment with its strategic goals.

3.1. Potential solution

The IT Manager of a leading media organization adopted an Open XDR framework comprising iNDR and UEBA as a unified platform to address their cybersecurity challenges. They partnered with a leading cybersecurity provider, aligning with the vision and strategic goals of the organization.

Open XDR tool provides a unique platform to detect and protect against advanced, sophisticated cybersecurity threats such as zero-day attacks, ransomware, and more. It offers a team of specialists to deploy the solution in customer environments with minimal effort. An active product development team for custom integrations, project management, and solution architecture supports it [17].

The security strategy ecosystem includes Open XDR Technology, which comprises iNDR and UEBA. This unified platform addresses the risks associated with the dynamic cyber threat landscape by providing advanced threat detection capabilities, real-time monitoring, and actionable insights to enhance organizational security posture.

The iNDR solution ingests traffic from switches or TAP solutions, covering North-South and East-West traffic. It analyses network anomalies, identifies threats, and alerts security teams while responding to advanced cyber threats in real time. UEBA prevents insider threats by monitoring activities from contractors, suppliers, and third-party vendors. It provides visibility into user behaviour, detects suspicious activities, and generates real-time alerts to mitigate potential risks [9].

3.2. Audience for the case

The audience for this case includes professionals in the media industry, cybersecurity practitioners, researchers, and academicians. They focus on the strategic vision of organizations to consolidate technologies into a unified platform to counter cybersecurity threats.

3.3. Level of difficulty

This case study has a moderate level of difficulty.

4. Suggested Research Questions for Discussion

Safeguarding digital assets and infrastructure is of paramount importance to all organizations. Practical and comprehensive mechanisms to counter cybersecurity threats are limited in the present digital era. Most of the solutions are point-point, vendor-specific, or siloed, with limited visibility and slow response times. A unified and consolidated approach, such as Open XDR, which integrates diverse data sources, is emerging as a critical need in cybersecurity and raises questions on the following:

1. How can Open XDR be architected to integrate and mitigate threats from multiple data sources effectively?
2. What is the importance of implementing more sophisticated and accurate threat detection mechanisms?
3. What skill sets and training programs are required to implement Open XDR and manage its operations effectively?
4. How effective is Open XDR in reducing Mean Time to Detect (MTTD) and Mean Time to Respond (MTTR) as key performance metrics to counter cyber threats?
5. How can Open XDR be implemented as a cost-effective solution for SMEs?
6. What environmental readiness factors are needed for SMEs before adopting and customizing Open XDR?

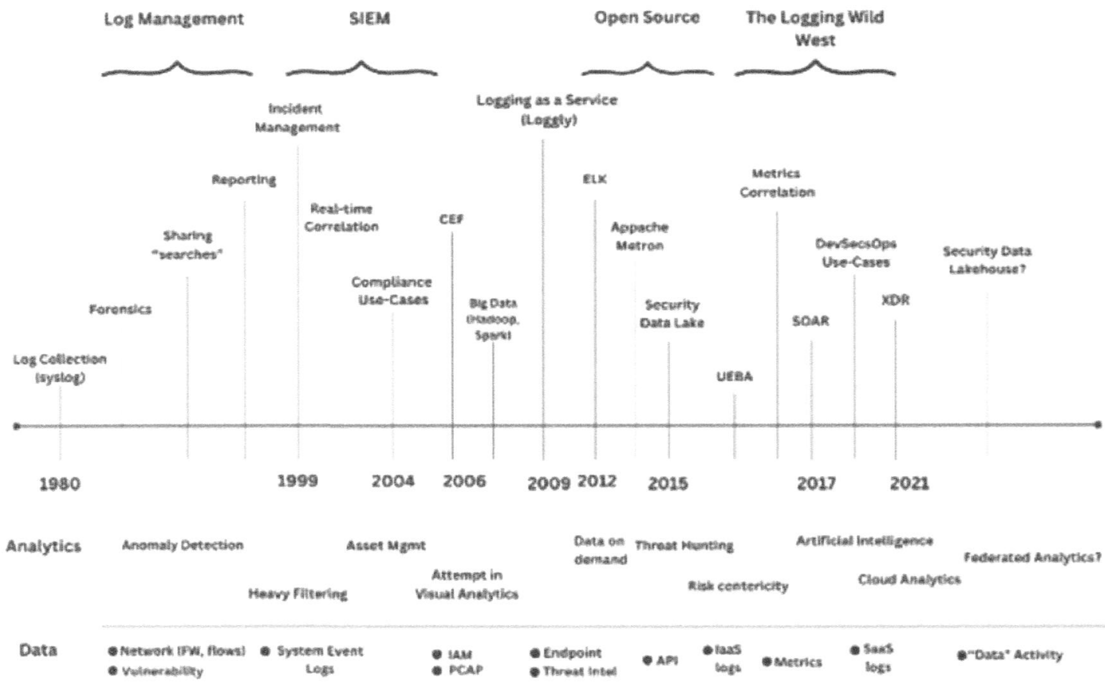

Figure 17.1. Timeline of open XDR evolution.

Source: Martiny, R. (2021). A logging history lesson – From syslogd(8) to XDRTechnology. Recreated on January 11, 2025, from https://raffy.ch/blog/2021/06/08/a-logging-history-lesson-from-syslogd8-to-xdr/.

5. Mandatory/Suggested Reading

- Name of the Book: Extended Detection and Response (XDR) For Dummies, Cisco Special Edition
- Author: James Sullivan
- Publisher: John Wiley & Sons, Inc.
- Release Date: 2022
- ISBN: 978-1-119-84558-4

5.1. Figures

See Figures 17.1–17.3.

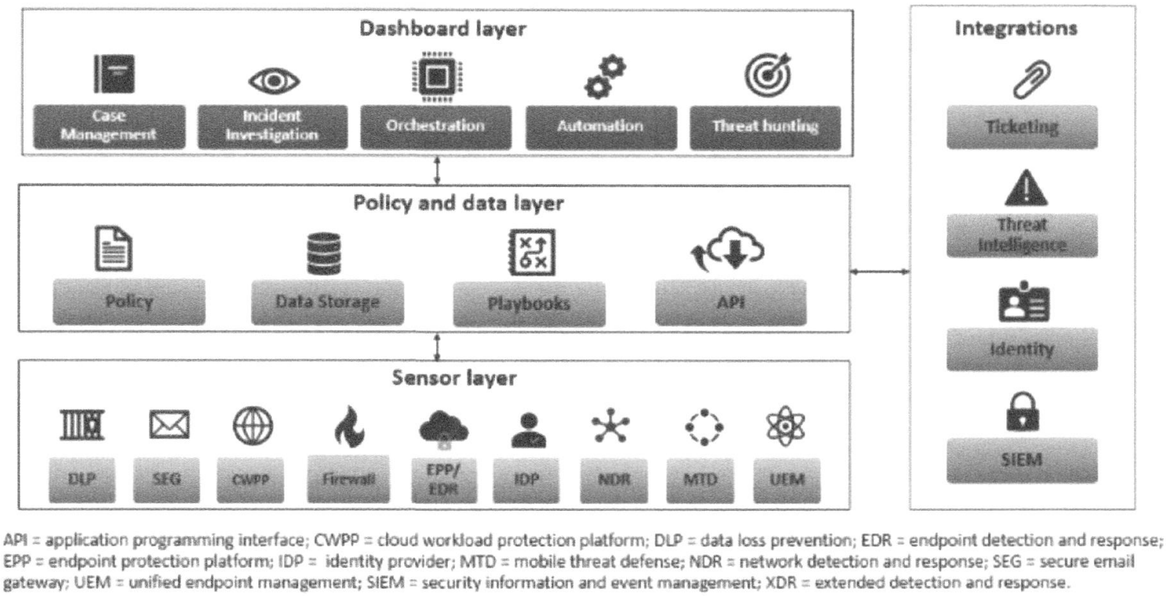

Figure 17.2. Timeline of XDR core components: An overview of the core components of the XDR framework.

Source: Gartner (2024). *A Market Guide for Extended Detection and Response.* Recreated on January 14, 2025, from https://www.gartner.com/en/documents/5859979.

Figure 17.3. Open XDR technology: A comprehensive overview of Linkshadow Open XDR solution.

Source: Linkshadow (2025). Technology Overview. Retrieved January 11, 2025, from https://www.linkshadow.com/technology.

6. Conclusion

Using the case study method, the IT Manager of a leading media organization encountered challenges in countering cyber threats driven by reforms and transformations in the IT industry. Traditional cybersecurity solutions proved inadequate in securing digital assets, sensitive customer data, and other critical information against attacks. IT Manager adopted game-changing measures in implementing an Open XDR solution integrating with iNDR and UEBA to transform the organization's security posture. The technology provided advanced threat detection, increased visibility, and compliance with regulatory standards. Open XDR enabled the media organization to mitigate the risks and enabled the vision of operational resilience. However, further studies are needed to consolidate the integration of multiple security solutions into a unified platform with AI/ML capabilities.

Acknowledgment

This case study would not have been possible without the mentors' invaluable support and guidance, whose cooperation and insights significantly contributed to the research.

References

[1] Atstāja, L., Rūtītis, D., Deruma, S., & Aksjoņenko, E. (2021). Cyber Security Risks and Challenges in Remote Work Under the COVID-19 Pandemic. *European Proceedings of Social and Behavioural Sciences.* *doi: 10.15405/epsbs.2021.12.04.2.*

[2] Bispham, M., Creese, S., Dutton, W., Esteve-González, P., & Goldsmith, M. (Dec. 2022). An exploratory study of cybersecurity in working from home: problem or enabler? *Journal of Information Policy*, *12*, 353–386. *doi: https://doi.org/10.5325/jinfopoli.12.2022.0010.*

[3] Lintemuth, T., Firstbrook, P., Lawson, C., & Ahlm, E. (Oct. 2024). Market Guide for Extended Detection and Response. Gartner, [Online]. Available. https://www.gartner.com/en/documents/5859979

[4] Marty, R. A Logging History Lesson – From syslogd(8) to XDR. *A Logging History Lesson – From syslogd(8) to XDR*. [Online]. Available: *https://raffy.ch/blog/2021/06/08/a-logging-history-lesson-from-syslogd8-to-xdr/*

[5] LópezVelásquez, J. M., Martínez Monterrubio, S. M., Sánchez Crespo, L. E., & Rosado, D. (2023). Systematic review of SIEM technology: SIEM-SC birth. *International Journal of Information Security*, *22*, 691–711. *doi: https://doi.org/10.1007/s10207-022-00657-9.*

[6] Sawadogo P., & Darmont, J. (2021). On data lake architectures and metadata management. *Journal of Intelligent Information Systems*, *56*(1), 97–120. *doi:https://doi.org/10.1007/s10844-020-00608-7.*

[7] Lee, S. J., Jeon, S. E., & Lee, I. G. (2024). A machine learning-enhanced endpoint detection and response framework for fast and proactive defense against advanced cyber attacks. *Soft Computing*, *28*, 7807–7821. *doi: https://doi.org/10.1007/s00500-024-09727-7.*

[8] George, A. S., George, A. S. H., & Baskar, D. T. (2021). XDR: The Evolution of Endpoint Security Solutions-Superior Extensibility and Analytics to Satisfy the Organizational Needs of the Future. *International Journal of Advanced Research in Science, Communication and Technology (IJARSCT)*, *8*(1), 493–501. *doi: 10.5281/zenodo.7028219.*

[9] LinkShadow, LinkShadow: Leading Media Company Case Study. LinkShadow, 2025. [Online]. Available: https://www.linkshadow.com/assets/case-study/LinkShadow-Leading-Media-Company-Case-Study.pdf

[10] Zaid T., & Garai, S. (2024). Emerging Trends in Cybersecurity: A Holistic View on Current Threats, Assessing Solutions, and Pioneering New Frontiers. *Blockchain in Healthcare Today*, 7. doi: *https://doi.org/10.30953/bhty.v7.302.*

[11] Aslan, Ö., Aktuğ, S., Ozkan-Okay, M., Yilmaz, A., & Akin, E. (2023). Comprehensive Review of Cyber Security Vulnerabilities, Threats, Attacks, and Solutions. *Electronics*, *12*, 6. *doi: https://doi.org/10.3390/electronics12061333.*

[12] Lallie H. S., Shepherd, L. A., Nurse, J. R. C., et al. (2021). Cyber security in the age of COVID-19: A timeline and analysis of cyber-crime and cyber-attacks during the pandemic. *Computers & security*, 105. *doi: https://doi.org/10.1016/j.cose.2021.102248.*

[13] Fichtenkamm, M., Burch, G., & Burch, J. (Apr. 2022). Cybersecurity in a COVID-19 World: Insights on How Decisions Are Made. *ISACA Journal*, *2*(2), 10.

[14] Cremer F., Sheehan, B., Fortmann, M., et al. (Feb.2022). Cyber risk and cybersecurity: a systematic review of data availability. *The Geneva Papers on Risk and Insurance - Issues and Practice*, *47*(3), 698–736, doi: *https://doi.org/10.1057/s41288-022-00266-6.*

[15] Ahuja, A. (2024). *A Detailed Study on Security and Compliance in Enterprise Architecture*, 1. [Online]. Available: *https://papers.ssrn.com/sol3/papers.cfm?abstract_id=5114289*

[16] Ouellette, M., & Deppa, (2020). *The Impact of COVID-19 on the Cybersecurity Sector*. ICF, [Online]. Available: *https://www.apprenticeship.gov/sites/default/files/impact-of-covid-19-on-cyber-security-industry.pdf.*

[17] LinkShadow, LinkShadow iNDR Ratings Overview. Linkshadow, 2025. [Online]. Available: *https://www.gartner.com/reviews/market/network-detection-and-response/vendor/linkshadow/product/linkshadow-indr.*

18 AI based digital academic assistance for supporting University students

Faizal Hajamohideen[1,a], *Karthikeyan Subramanian*[1,b], *Viswan Vimbi*[1,c], *Noushath Shafee*[2,d], *Rihab Zaid Al Mamari*[1,e], *Manar Ahmed Al Mamari*[1,f], *and Nouf Mohammed Al Balushi*[1,g]

[1]College of Computing and Information Sciences, University of Technology and Applied Sciences (UTAS), Suhar, Sultanate of Oman, Oman
[2]Department of Computer Science, College of Science, Sultan Qaboos University, Sultanate of Oman

Abstract: UTAS voice assistant is very important because it organizes the life of the university student and helps them focus on their studies, which makes it easier for them to gain better time because of this audio application. The problem is that some university students are unable to balance university studies and their personal lives, especially when they student is under study circumstances such as fatty materials, Low rate, or even lack of academic focus. And to solve this problem the application was created to solve many of the problems faced by the university student, for example, time, tests without awareness (the student does not know them), the teacher, and the educational system. UTAS voice assistant will help many students solve their study problems, organize, and gain more time. The aim of this research is to create an application that can balance the various subjects that the student chooses within his study plan. And because this application is the optimal and advanced solution for university students. UTAS voice assistant this category serves students in various scientific universities, and it is expected that many students in their various disciplines will turn out to use this application that is able to organize and understand everything that goes on in the student's mind. The project also contributes to achieving many goals in the educational sector in general, which increases the demand for the application and its application to school students. Also, even many companies must include it within the company's system to help employees. This project will improve very positive attitude for the university student, which reflects his practical performance in various professional lives, and it will also greatly serve the foundation year students at the university, as most students do not understand the new system, the study plan, the materials, or the rate, which is easy for the students able to understand.

Keywords: Advising, applied sciences, deep learning, innovations in digital assistance, voice

1. Introduction

A voice assistant is a type of voice-enabled artificial intelligence that is becoming integral to our daily lives. This study examines the effects of voice assistant personality traits on consumer experience. It shows that voice interactions with a voice assistant that incorporates functional intelligence, sincerity, and creativity empower consumers to take control of their voice interactions VA (voice assistants) include Apple's Siri, Amazon's Alexa, Google Assistant, Microsoft Cortana, and among smart speaker offerings are Amazon's Echo, Google's Home, and Apple's Home. VA enables users to navigate, listen to music, send text messages, control smart home devices, and more [10]. The aim of this research is to create an application that is able to solve the problems of university students and try to facilitate the study, which consists of: the study plan, time, calculating and raising the GPA, everything related to the study schedule, teachers, and evaluating teachers through the application. It also allows the student to view the old tests and Abstracts, and everything related to student materials. There are studies looking for new variables that aid in creating better acceptance models for new technologies using psychological science and behavioural theories. HCI is an essential idea that needs to be taken into account in AI-based systems. The importance of HCI has increased significantly in recent years as computers have ingrained themselves into almost every aspect of our existence. As everything around, us becomes digital and unwittingly integrated with interactive computing services that make our daily lives more exciting, effective, and practical, HCI will become even

[a]Faizal.hajamohieen@utas.edu.om, [b]Karthikeyan.Supramanian@utas.edu.om, [c]Vimbi.Viswan@utas.edu.om, [d]n.shaffi@squ.edu.om, [e]s2017293005@utas.edu.om, [f]s2018293038@utas.edu.om, [g]s2018293041@utas.edu.om

DOI: 10.1201/9781003778905-18

more crucial in interactive systems. The early emphasis of HCI has been on how to create interaction and implement interfaces for systems that go beyond simply providing the required computational functionalities. One of the primary characteristics of VASs is interaction, which people value more in modern society due to their uses. In 5 fact, the interaction in VASs goes beyond the basic interaction between a person and a computer and is increasingly resembling human relationships. In this research, we employ SET (Social Exchange Theory) to comprehend this novel form of contact. According to SET explains the patterns of human relationships and social interaction. The partnership involves the two parties having vague, open-ended responsibilities to one another. Any social exchange connection can be categorized as high-quality or low-quality based on its level of regard, commitment, and confidence [22].

2. Problem Statement

Each application, whether highly skilled, has pros and cons, which leads to the non-acceptance of the target group for this scientific project, such as the sound is not clear, the answer being inaccurate, the confusion in the application, and the lack of correct data. As Iahoual and Frejus said In order to better understand how voice assistants (VA) are used and assess the effectiveness of verbal exchanges in real-world settings, we performed an in-home survey of six homes in domestic and commuting contexts. The actions of oversight, verification, diagnosis, and problem-solving were seen in the videotaped notes and conversations. These tasks not only took up a lot of time but also slowed down the residents' other. But we, as university students, need correct information that the student bases on in his university life, for example, the clarity of the voice, the accuracy of the application, the name of the building, the number of the hall, the name of the professor, the name of the subject, and information about the subject. UTAS voice assistance provides great support and organizes time. It also works to enhance the student's ability to study and arrange his priorities in terms of accuracy and time. He also acquires many important information. activities. The VAs was supposed to make it easier to complete a second, concurrent job, but they actually got in the way. These mistakes can lead to desertion, but the findings showed a paradox of use: the residents overlooked and accepted these mistakes while still claiming the vocal system as their own.

3. Literature Review

There are many applications that are identical to our application, such as:

3.1. Google Now

Intelligent Personal Assistants (IPAs), which are now a commonplace commodity, frequently exhibit a high degree of variation in their engagement philosophies. For instance, Apple's Siri is heavily promoted while Google Now is advertised as having no personality at all [6]. Based on beauty and psychological state reactance, we evaluated user personality profiles and their choice of Apple's Siri, Google's Now, or Microsoft's Cortana. Analysis showed that a person's choice for an IPA is influenced by their personality characteristics. Individual trait preferences are addressed, and typical descriptions for followers of various IPAs are provided. The outcomes can be used to suggest IPAs that are especially suited to a user's psychological description. The research ends with several suggestions for the [15]. A comprehensive user model sits at the core of any customization tool, like Google Now. Users can be understood in a variety of ways, from their basic past to smaller-scale dimensions like interests, locations, tastes, etc. We will talk about various user comprehension models [16]. As we move from comprehension to application, we will discuss two general uses of Google Now: information suggestions and guided investigation. From the standpoint of information search, we will concentrate on such uses. In reaction to a question or, in the extreme, in a query-less application, information recommendation then takes the shape of biasing information retrieval. We will explore the roles that personalization and guided discovery play in the general declaration of user purpose that rests somewhere in between, such as an interest in food. Considering the often-spectacular failure of prior efforts to establish a virtual identity [18].

3.2. Cortana

The creators of Siri have cautiously established their goals. The first release, scheduled for this year, will be targeted at smartphone users and will only carry out a limited range of tasks, like assisting with making eatery reservations, tracking a trip, or organizing weekend plans. Users can use natural language to type or voice instructions, and the software will infer their meaning from the environment. Due to Siri's connections to numerous online services, a brief conversation with it can complete a number of minor chores that ordinarily call for multiple website visits. For instance, a user can ask Siri to locate a reasonably cost Chinese eatery in a particular area of the city and make On April 2, 2014, Microsoft made Cortana, the voice-activated digital helper integrated into Windows 10 and Windows Phones, available to all Android phone owners in a public beta [19].

It is named after Cortana, a fictional artificial intelligence from the Microsoft Halo video game series. Its growth began in 2009 when Zig Serafin was hired as general manager. [5] Cortana is made to assist with task completion. It is useful for a variety of tasks, including obtaining weather predictions, setting up reminders, making jokes, writing emails, locating files, and conducting online searches. For 13 different nations, it has eight different dialects. Without even having to ask her, it helps us recall things we've mentioned in our letters that we might do [4].

In order to accomplish this miraculous accomplishment, Cortana makes use of a Microsoft interpreter backend. A cloud-based automated translation tool is provided by Microsoft Translator Speech API. The primary goal of Microsoft Translator is to provide translation in order to overcome linguistic barriers. Bing, an ASP.NET-developed online search engine, is used by it. The natural processing skills of Cortana 8 come from Tellme Networks, which Microsoft acquired in 2007, and are combined with a semantic search database named Satori.

Its main goal is to give data more meaning and to combine logical concepts with stronger conceptual concepts that are familiar to us from the field of artificial intelligence. The purpose is to offer high level modeling primitives as a core component of a data model to make it easier to depict situations in the actual world [21].

There are stages that are necessary for voice recognition:

- **Signal processing:** This technology is used throughout the entire audio processing process, from analog to digital conversion to the addition of filters or amplitude control. About Cortana, it allows pulling the data from signals to transform it into understandable words.
- **Speech detection:** This step is crucial because it is where the real classification is carried out. The series of feature vectors is then translated into a list of words. Using techniques like Dynamic Time Warping, this is accomplished. The method that assesses similarity between two temporal patterns that may differ in speed is called dynamic time warping [20, 29].

3.3. Robin

Although there are frequently numerous classes in real world issues, many learning algorithms are inherently binary, meaning they can only distinguish between two classes [11]. The reasons for this may be constraints imposed by the hypothesis language (e.g., linear discriminants or support vector machines), the learning architecture (e.g., neural networks with single output nodes), or the learning framework (e.g., many rule learning algorithms are tailored towards concept learning, that is, the problem of learning a concept description from positive and negative examples) [12–14]. There are two principal approaches for applying such algorithms to multiclass problems: one approach is to generalize the algorithms has, for example, been done for support vector machines or boosting [27].

Using binarization methods the multiclass issue is broken down into a number of binary problems. One of the most common classes binarization approaches is to learn separate concept descriptions for each individual class, that is, to form a series of problems, one for each class, where all examples of this class are regarded as positive examples, while all other exam-c 2002 Fürnkranz [27]. ples are regarded as negative. The groups of neural networks and support vector machines have recently begun to pay attention to the alternative class binarization method known as pairwise classification. The fundamental concept is to learn a classifier for each pair of classes, use only training examples for these two classes, and ignore all other classes in order to limit a multi-class issue to numerous two-class problems [34] every other. In this paper, we will, on the one hand, evaluate the technique – which we name round robin binarization – for inductive rule learning algorithms and show that it is significantly more accurate than the ordered and unordered (one-against-all) techniques that are currently used for rule 10 learning algorithms like Ripper [35]. On the other hand, we offer a thorough study of the approach's intricacy and demonstrate that learning the learning problems of a single round robin can be done more quickly than learning the learning problems of the traditional one-against-all method [37, 39]. Despite the fact that this study is independent of the fundamental learning algorithm, we demonstrate that the edge grows with costlier students. Our experimental data support the theory findings. Evaluation [8].

With mixed findings, we will examine the characteristics of round-robin classification as a general ensemble method. While the technique can, on average, lower C5.0's error, the gains fall short of those of boosting. However, Ripper does benefit more from a simple round robin learning and bagging combo. We will then talk about a few more important characteristics of round-robin classification, such as its appropriateness for parallel applications, potential workarounds for its inefficiency during classification, and its understandability [9].

3.4. Top assistant

The purpose of this research was to investigate how judge placement affected how well-qualified referees and assistant referees made decisions during international matches. The 2009 Federation Internationale de Football Association (FIFA) Confederations Cup match analyses looked at 380 foul play occurrences and 165 offside scenarios. When noting the events, the officials' average rate of error was 14% [40]. The middle region of the field, where the assistant referee's cooperation is restricted, had the lowest error percentage, which was attained when showing the incidents from a distance of 11 to 15 meters. On the other hand, this percentage peaked (23%) during the final 15 minutes of the match [17].

The backup refs had a 13% error percentage [33]. The backup referee's location accuracy of the offside judgment was unaffected by proximity to the offside line. When the assistant officials observed the offside scenarios from an angle between 46 and 60°, the likelihood of making the wrong call was 11 decreased. The second half of the events saw twice as many incorrect offside rulings as the first [28]. Football referees' weekly schedules should include perceptual-cognitive training classes tailored to the rules of the game to lower the total error rate [7].

3.5. Genie

The Human Genome Project is expected to produce two Mbases of data per day for the next seven years, according to current projections. It is critical to create novel tools for annotation and study of genomic DNA because of the high rate. This novel variety of content sensor combines data from various sources to assess the likelihood of a sequence [lo] by integrating the evidence [1].

The probability is then determined using this analysis. Because components can be added or removed as needed, this quick and easy technique promotes a modular strategy to creating an efficient gene finding system. A content monitor can simply have components added or removed [2].

In spite of the fact that indigo's colour is highly reliant on its surroundings, it is blue in the majority of circumstances [38]. I give a summary of the theories put forth to explain why indigo's absorption at such long wavelengths for such a tiny molecule is unusual. A plausible qualitative answer could be offered using the conventional valence-bond method. Differently sophisticated molecular orbital techniques offer a more thorough, quantitative account, and several theories have been put forth using these models [40]. The idea that the crucial structural element in determining colour is founded on the cross conjugated "Hchromophore" notion is frequently put forth. It is described as two symmetrically linked merocyanine chains in a second, related description. According to a different hypothesis, the fundamental chromophore is possibly the aza counterpart of two linked anti aromatic cyclopentadienyl ions. The hues of indigo and indirubin, a red isomer, have been successfully quantified using PiSYSTEM, a commercial quantum mechanics software [3].

3.6. Andy android emulator:

Andy is an Android emulator that allows you to run Android apps and games on your computer. It was developed by an American company called Android, which was founded in 2011. Andy is designed to provide a complete Android experience on your computer, with features like multi-touch support, full 14 Android UI customization, and integration with your computer's hardware, including the microphone and camera [23, 30]. This means that you can use Andy to play games, use social media apps, or do any other task that you would normally do on an Android device. In addition to running Android apps, Andy also allows you to install and run the Google Play Store on your computer, which gives you access to a vast library of apps and games [31]. Andy is free to download and use, and it is available for both Windows and macOS operating systems. It has received mixed reviews from users, with some praising its performance and features, while others have reported issues with bugs and stability [32, 36].

3.7. Dragon Mobile Assistant:

Dragon Mobile Assistant is a virtual assistant and voice recognition app designed for mobile devices [40]. It was created by Nuance Communications, the same company responsible for Dragon NaturallySpeaking software for desktop computers [24]. Dragon Mobile Assistant is engineered to assist users with completing tasks on their mobile devices by utilizing voice commands, eliminating the need to type or tap on the screen. It allows users to give commands such as making phone calls, sending text messages, setting reminders, searching the web, playing music, and more. Additionally, it provides information such as weather updates, sports score, and news headlines [25].

To comprehend and react to user requests, Dragon Mobile Assistant employs natural language processing and advanced speech recognition technology. It is accessible for both iOS and Android devices and is free to download from the respective app stores. The app has been positively reviewed for its accuracy and user-friendliness [26]. The Figures 18.1 and 18.2 demonstrates the differences among Alexa, Siri, Google, and UTAS voice assistants in a number of areas, including the voice command to start them, the ability to distinguish between one or more users by voice, the location of Internet searches, and the answer field.

The table compares the academic capabilities of Alexa, Siri, Google, and UTAS voice assistants and demonstrates how they differ from each other in terms of advising, registered courses, staff details, timetables, and room locations. Alexa, Siri, and Google only have a timetable feature, which depends on the study table in the phone's calendar. In contrast to UTAS voice assistants, it is capable of including advising, registered courses, staff information, timetables, room locations, and other features.

4. Research Methodology

- When students start to get distracted, especially new students, they get immediate help without wasting time.

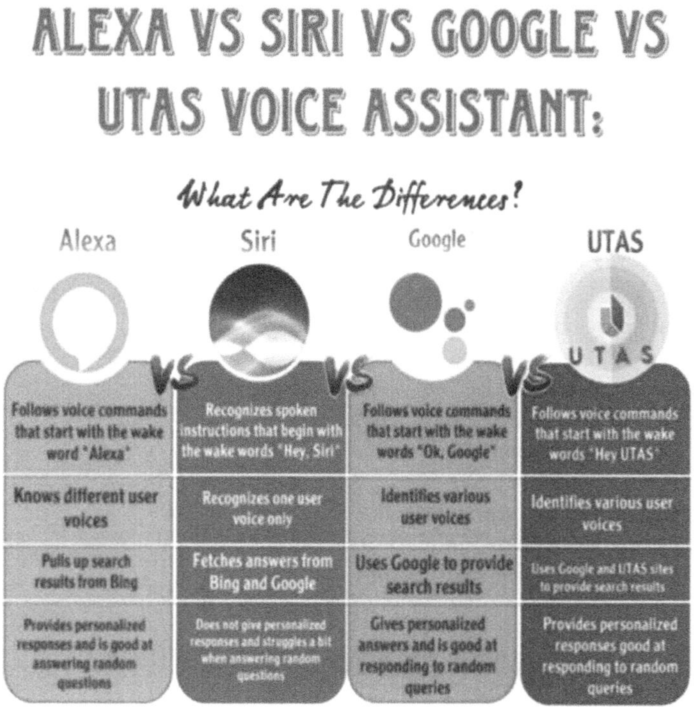

Figure 18.1. The differences between Alexa, Siri, Google, UTAS voice assistant in general way.
Source: Author.

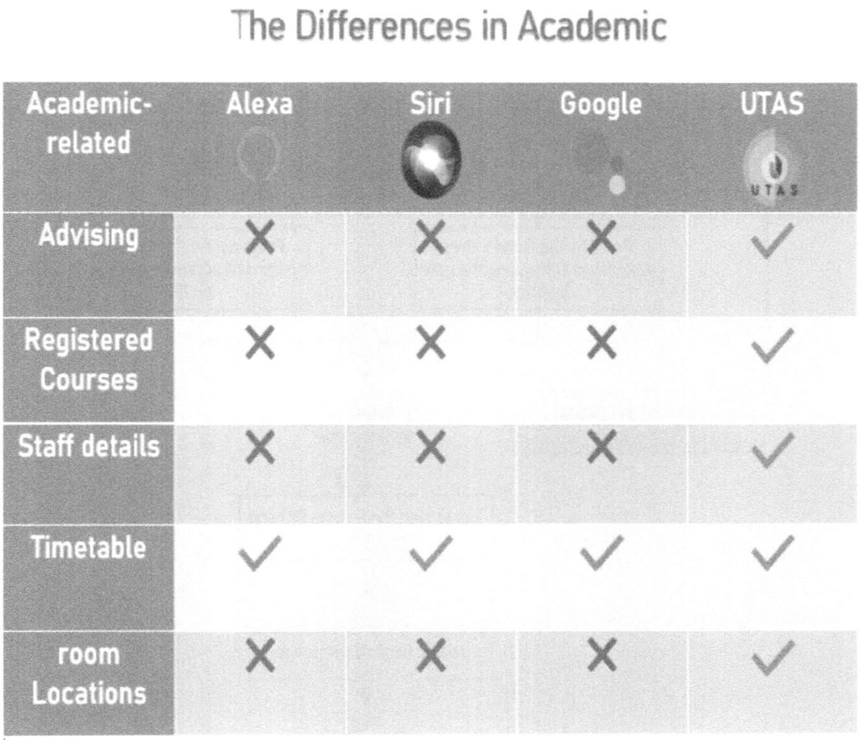
The Differences in Academic

Academic-related	Alexa	Siri	Google	UTAS
Advising	✗	✗	✗	✓
Registered Courses	✗	✗	✗	✓
Staff details	✗	✗	✗	✓
Timetable	✓	✓	✓	✓
room Locations	✗	✗	✗	✓

Figure 18.2. The difference between Alexa, Siri, Google, UTAS voice assistant in academic area.
Source: Author.

- UTAS voice assistant tips they need to increase will, not despair, and love to study.
- Finding the study schedules for doctors and students as soon as possible to know the office hours of doctors in less than a second.
- Know the students who are participating in the same lecture as you.
- It informs about the number of hours and the number of materials remaining for each student when needed, which helps to organize time and good study management.
- It is connected to the university email of the students and doctors in order to make it easier for students and doctors to send and receive emails.
- Organizing student time, setting study hours, and reminding students of important tests and activities to prepare for it.
- UTAS tips the voice assistant for each student to raise his competitive rate, and to start taking interest in studying by studying first to get a result that satisfies the student.

The Figure 18.3 shows the UTAS voice assistant logo contains the University of Technology and Applied Sciences (UTAS) logo, the name of the university as it relates to university matters such as advertising, registered courses, staff details, timetables, and room locations, and a circle coloured in shades of blue denoting energy and excitement that are in the application.

Figure 18.4 depicts a flow chart of the communication process, the UTAS voice assistant application work when the user starts open the app in their phone. First the program need to checks whether the user is male or female by

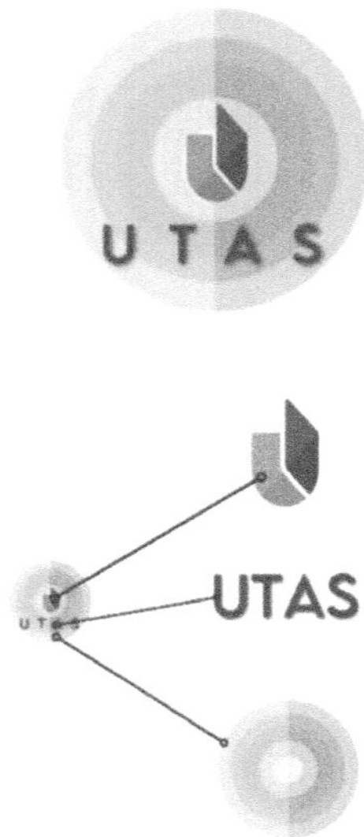

Figure 18.3. Logo of UTAS voice addistant.

Source: Author.

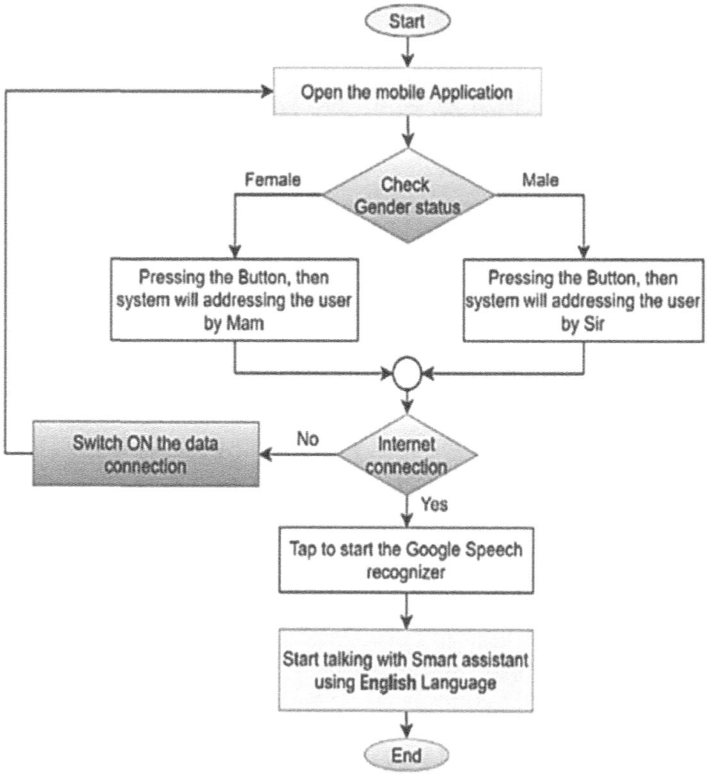

Figure 18.4. A flow chart of the communication process.

Source: Author.

showing a list that allows the user to choose his gender. When the user chooses his gender be pressing whether male or female the system directly will addressing the user by Sir or Mam. Secondly the system will start searching for the internet connection. If the connection not found, the connection data will be closed and return to the beginning. But if the system found the internet connection, a speech recognition button will appear, then the user can speak and ask freely but in English language only.

In this Figure 18.5, the UTAS voice assistant features, it is divided into three sections: the section for the first advice:

Figure 18.4 UTAS voice assistant application work when the user starts open the app in their phone. First the program need to checks whether the user is male or female by showing a list that allows the user to choose his gender. When the user chooses his gender be pressing whether male or female the system directly will addressing the user by Sir or Mam. Secondly the system will start searching for the internet connection. If the connection not found, the connection data will be closed and return to the beginning. But if the system found the internet connection, a speech recognition button will appear, then the user can speak and ask freely but in English language only.

In this Figure 18.5, the UTAS voice assistant features It is divided into three sections: the section for the first advice: by giving advice that contains instructions and how to raise the average and from aids by the teacher. Plan: It contains the study schedule and is divided into the time at which the lecture begins, the name of the subject, the room number, and the professor. All short tests and activities, whether with the teacher or the student, are included under the name of the subject. The last evaluation is the evaluation through the evaluation of the master through the subject.

5. Conclusion and Future Work

In conclusion, The objective of this project is to support students in their academic endeavors so that they can complete their university degrees more easily and independently. The following describes the benefits of the proposed system:

1. This system's primary goal is to serve as a proactive guidance system for students, whether they are at risk or not. It will also make it simpler for students in Oman's universities and colleges to calculate their

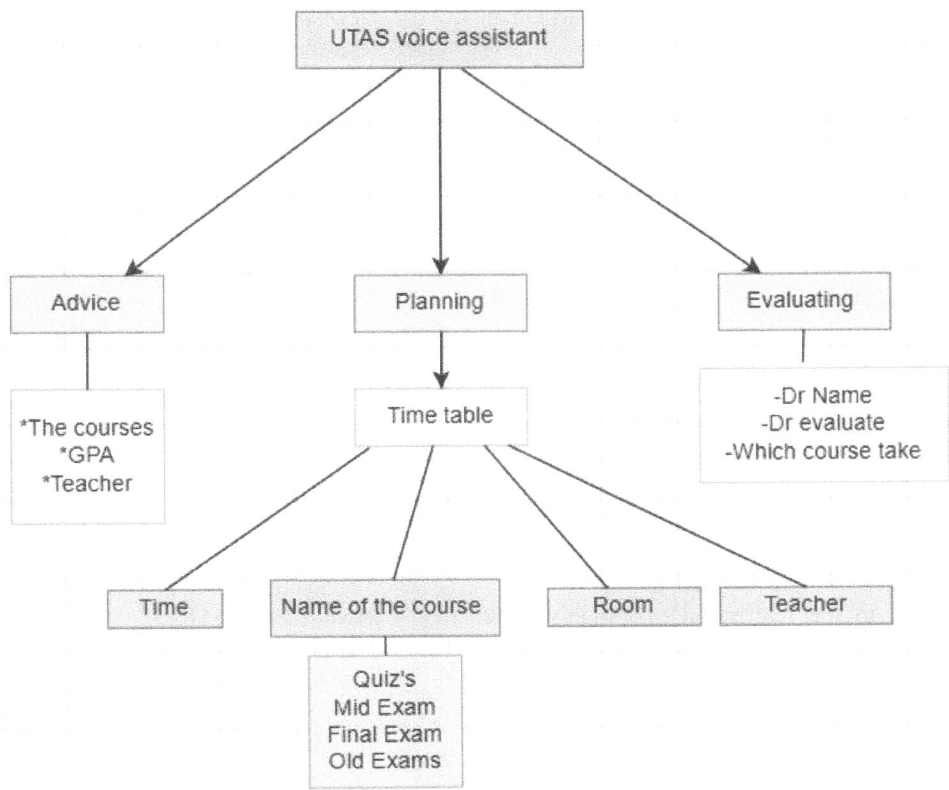

Figure 18.5. UTAS voice assistant features.

Source: Author.

GPA and other possible grades to reach a particular objective or cumulative rate for each student.

2. After selecting the courses, he/she wants to register for, students will see several sample schedules of the academic courses they want before opening the course registration on the university's website. These schedules will be generated by artificial intelligence algorithms that can calculate and coordinate the time periods for courses.
3. this system will leverage artificial intelligence, which results in speedier activities such as calculating the student's remaining course load and scheduling study time, saving time and effort for students, staff, and stakeholders in Oman. Moreover, it uses AI algorithms to arrange simple and complex operations for students that would otherwise take hours to complete by humans.
4. The technique informs the student of the timing of the exams and important appointments so that he may attend them at the proper time since often students forget the exam times or the dates of the university activities.
5. The system will suggest and notify the student of the number of remaining courses and the need to take them in order to reduce the accumulated courses and lateness, addressing the issue of students' non-compliance with the study plan in universities in Oman and their tardiness by a number of years.
6. Close interaction between students and professors is facilitated by the student's knowledge of the professors' evaluations, office location, and courses they teach from our application.
7. As planned the future work as stated below,
   - Time management for students and avoiding waste.Full awareness of the student regarding their study plan. Improving students' self-confidence.
   - Students' sense of responsibility for their university education.
   - Create Strong student engagement in their studies, which results in higher grades and GPU.
   - Improve a low rate of students asking professors and advisors for assistance with course registration and scheduling. And low rate of student absence from lectures and exams.
   - Contribute to the realization of Oman's 2040 vision by deepening the field of ML and deep learning.

References

[1] Curtiss, S., Fromkin, V., Krashen, S., Rigler, D., & Rigler, M. (1974). The linguistic development of Genie. *Language*, 528–554.

[2] Curtiss, S. (2014). *Genie: A psycholinguistic study of a modern-day wild child*. Academic Press.

[3] Reese, M. G., Eeckman, F. H., Kulp, D., & Haussler, D. (1997, January). Improved splice site detection in Genie. In *Proceedings of the first annual international conference on Computational molecular biology* (pp. 232–240).

[4] Christie, R. M. (2007). Why is indigo blue? *Biotechnic & Histochemistry*, *82*(2), 51–56.

[5] Blackburn, R. S., Bechtold, T., & John, P. (2009). The development of indigo reduction methods and pre-reduced indigo products. *Coloration Technology*, *125*(4), 193–207.

[6] Balfour-Paul, J. (2012). *Indigo in the Arab world*. Routledge.

[7] Mallo, J., Frutos, P. G., Juárez, D., & Navarro, E. (2012). Effect of positioning on the accuracy of decision making of association football top-class referees and assistant referees during competitive matches. *Journal of Sports Sciences*, *30*(13), 1437–1445.

[8] Fürnkranz, J. (2002). Round robin classification. *The Journal of Machine Learning Research*, *2*, 721–747.

[9] Shprintzen, R. J. (1992). The implications of the diagnosis of Robin sequence. *The Cleft Palate-Craniofacial Journal*, *29*(3), 205–209.

[10] Naone, E. (2009). TR10: Intelligent software assistant. *Technology Review, Mar.-Apr*, *200*(2).

[11] Hausman, C., Nebeker, A., McCreary, J., & Donaldson Jr, G. (2002). The work life of the assistant principal. *Journal of Educational Administration*, *40*(2), 136–157.

[12] Ehrenbrink, P., Osman, S., & Möller, S. (2017, November). Google now is for the extraverted, Cortana for the introverted: investigating the influence of personality on IPA preference. *In Proceedings of the 29th Australian Conference on Computer-Human Interaction* (pp. 257–265).

[13] Thakur, S. (2016, September). Personalization for google now: user understanding and application to information Recommendation and exploration. In *Proceedings of the 10th ACM Conference on Recommender Systems* (pp. 3–3).

[14] Simas, C., Larson, H. J., & Paterson, P. (2021). Saint Google, now we have information!: A qualitative study on narratives of trust and attitudes towards maternal vaccination in Mexico City and Toluca. *BMC Public Health*, *21*(1), 1170.

[15] Carr, N. (2008). Is Google making us stupid? *Teachers College Record*, *110*(14), 89–94.

[16] Hoy, M. B. (2018). Alexa, Siri, Cortana, and more: An introduction to voice assistants. *Medical reference services quarterly*, *37*(1), 81–88.

[17] Bhat, H. R., Lone, T. A., & Paul, Z. M. (2017). Cortana-intelligent personal digital assistant: A review. *International Journal of Advanced Research in Computer Science*, *8*(7), 55–57.

[18] Kepuska, V., & Bohouta, G. (2018, January). Next-generation of virtual personal assistants (microsoft cortana, apple siri, amazon alexa and google home). In *2018 IEEE 8th annual computing and communication workshop and conference (CCWC)* (pp. 99–103). *IEEE.*

[19] Yang, S., Lee, J., Sezgin, E., Bridge, J., & Lin, S. (2021). Clinical advice by voice assistants on postpartum depression: cross-sectional investigation using Apple Siri, Amazon Alexa, Google Assistant, and Microsoft Cortana. *JMIR mHealth and uHealth*, *9*(1), e24045.

[20] Zhu, X., & Dragon, L. A. (2016). Physical activity and situational interest in mobile technology integrated physical education: A preliminary study. *Acta Gymnica*, *46*(2).

[21] Nguyen, Q. N., & Sidorova, A. (2017). AI capabilities and user experiences: a comparative study of user reviews for assistant and non-assistant mobile apps.

[22] Hamdan, K., & Amorri, A. (2016). Mobile learning devices to assist dyslexic students to improve their English reading proficiency. In *INTED2016 Proceedings* (pp. 8201–8213). IATED.

[23] Ortmanns, S., & Haiber, U. (2018). The Mobile Cognitive Assistant: Bridging the Gap between In-Car and Outside-the-car Experiences. *Studientexte zur Sprachkommunikation: Elektronische Sprachsignalverarbeitung,* 1–6.

[24] Labský, M., Kunc, L., Macek, T., Kleindienst, J., & Vystrčil, J. (2014, April). Recipes for building voice search UIs for automotive. In *Proceedings of the EACL 2014 Workshop on Dialogue in Motion* (pp. 28–32).

[25] Teng, S. Y., & Wen, C. Y. (2017). A study on common Android emulators and anti-forensic message-hiding applications. *Forensic Science Journal*, *16*(1), 1–11.

[26] Litkowski, K., & Smołka, J. (2018). Performance comparison of an emulator and physical Android mobile device based on chess algorithm. *Journal of Computer Sciences Institute*, *6*, 77–81.

[27] Oliveira, L. C. C. A. D. (2022). *Comparative study of techniques for detecting emulators on Android devices* (Bachelor›s thesis).

[28] Forecast, A., & Sigernes, F. (2024). Aurora Forecast 3D 8.4.

[29] Maiyana, E. (2018). Pemanfaatan android dalam perancangan aplikasi kumpulan doa. *Jurnal Sains dan Informatika: Research of Science and Informatic*, *4*(1), 54–65.

[30] Khatri, P. (2019). Forensic analysis of a virtual android phone. In *Communication, Networks and Computing: First International Conference, CNC 2018, Gwalior, India, March 22–24, 2018, Revised Selected Papers* (p. 839).

[31] Kaplan, A., & Haenlein, M. (2019). Siri, Siri, in my hand: Who's the fairest in the land? On the interpretations, illustrations, and implications of artificial intelligence. *Business Horizons*, *62*(1), 15–25.

[32] Hong, G., Folcarelli, A., Less, J., Wang, C., Erbasi, N., & Lin, S. (2021). Voice assistants and cancer screening: A comparison of Alexa, Siri, Google Assistant, and Cortana. *The Annals of Family Medicine*, *19*(5), 447–449.

[33] Canbek, N. G., & Mutlu, M. E. (2016). On the track of artificial intelligence: Learning with intelligent personal assistants. *Journal of Human Sciences*, *13*(1), 592–601.

[34] Panyako, D., & Rorie, L. (1987). The changing role of the assistant principal. *NASSP Bulletin*, *71*(501), 6–8.

[35] Oleszewski, A., Shoho, A., & Barnett, B. (2012). The development of assistant principals: A literature review. *Journal of Educational Administration*, *50*(3), 264–286.

[36] Vladimir L. Uskov, R. J. (2020). *Smart Education and e-learning 2020*. UK: Springer Singapore. *Smart Education and e-Learning: SpringerLink*

[37] Mieczysław L. Owocl, A. S. (2021, Feb 11). Artificial Intelligence Technologies in Education: Benefits, Challenges and Strategies of Implementation, 3–7.

[38] Brewer, R., Pierce, C., Upadhyay, P., & Park, L. (2022, July 20). *An Empirical Study of Older Adult's Voice Assistant Use for Health Information Seeking*. ACM Digital Library. https://dl.acm.org/doi/abs/10.1145/3484507

[39] Elghaish, F., Chauhan, J. K., Matarneh, S., Rahimian, F. P., & Hosseini, M. R. (2022, August 1). *Artificial intelligence-based voice assistant for BIM data management. ScienceDirect.* https://www.sciencedirect.com/science/article/pii/S0926580522001935

[40] Alboaneen, D., Saffar, D., Alqahtani, A. S., & Alamri, L. P. (2021, December 1). *Smart information desk system with voice assistant for universities. ResearchGate. https://www.researchgate.net/profile/Dabiah-Alboaneen/publication/354176340_Smart_information_desk_system_with_voice_assistant for_universities/links/ 6129a8f638818c2eaf64a2b5/ Smart-information-desk-system-with- voice-assistant-for-universities.pdf.*

19 Unmasking digital impostors: A machine learning framework for social media profile detection

Uma Kuppusamy[1,a], *Sandeep M.*[1,b], *Thirumurugan Shanmugam*[2,c], *and Ramaprabha K. P.*[3,d]

[1]School of Computer Science Engineering and Information Systems, VIT University, Vellore, Tamil Nadu, India
[2]University of Technology and Applied Sciences, Suhar, Oman
[3]School of Computer Science and Engineering, Vellore Institute of Technology, Chennai, Tamil Nadu, India

Abstract: The fast boom of social media has revolutionized global communique, but it has also led to the proliferation of faux profiles, posing extensive dangers including identity theft, incorrect information, and on-line fraud. This work gives a system getting to know-based totally framework for detecting and reporting fake social media profiles. The device leverages key functions, which include follower-buddy ratios, account age, and posting frequency, to differentiate among legitimate and fraudulent debts. Multiple system studying fashions, along with Random Forest, Logistic Regression, and XGBoost, had been trained and evaluated on datasets of valis and pretend profiles. Among these, XGBoost achieved the nice performance with an accuracy of 99.47% and a great ROC-AUC rating of 1.000. The version changed into deployed as a user-pleasant internet application, allowing real-time profile class and imparting actionable insights for investigative businesses. The proposed framework automates the historically guide system of fake profile detection, drastically enhancing accuracy and performance. This research contributes to enhancing online safety by supplying a Scalable and reliable solution for preventing fake social media profiles. Future work includes integrating extra superior models and increasing the device to locate other kinds of on-line fraud.

Keywords: Artificial Intelligence, automated detection, data preprocessing, fake social media profiles, feature engineering, fraud detection, machine learning, random forest, social media security, XGBoost

1. Introduction

In the recent modern years, the fusion of deep learning and computing has transformed ophthalmology, making it possible to diagnose eye diseases like cataracts with remarkable accuracy. Cataracts, which cause cloudiness in the eye's lens, can lead to significant vision loss or blindness if not caught early. Traditional methods for diagnosing cataracts often depend on the expertise of trained ophthalmologists, a luxury that isn't always available, especially in underserved areas. With advancements in deep learning, we now have tools that not only speed up the diagnostic process but also improve its accuracy and reliability.

However, even with these advancements, there's still a gap in understanding which deep learning models work best for cataract detection. outputs from various convolutional neural networks (CNNs) were assuring in analysing the fundus images. A thorough comparison of different CNN architectures has been very helpful in the areas with limited access to eye care. By recognizing the best deep learning model and addressing the gaps. This study targets to address the existing gap by doing a comparative analysis of three widely used convolutional neural network (CNN) models – ResNet50, ResNet101, and VGG19 – utilizing the Ocular Disease Intelligent Recognition (ODIR) dataset. The main objective is to examine the effectiveness of these models in detecting cataracts and to explore strategies for enhancing their accuracy.

The study highlights on three key aspects: first, evaluating the execution and reliability of ResNet50, ResNet101, and VGG19 in cataract detection; The next stop is improving the preprocessing methods by implementing Contrast Limited Adaptive Histogram Equalization (CLAHE) to improve the image contrast and converting grayscale images to the RGB format for good model compatibility;

[a]uma.kuppusamy@vit.ac.in, [b]sandeep.m2022@vitstudent.ac.in, [c]thirumurugan.shanmugam@utas.edu.om, [d]ramprabha.kp@vit.ac.in

DOI: 10.1201/9781003778905-19

and third, optimizing data augmentation methods to enable more effective learning while mitigating overfitting.

This study focuses to develop a more accurate and effective cataract detection system, particularly beneficial for regions with limited access to eye care system. By utilizing the advanced image processing methods, this research looks to enhance early diagnosis, eventually contributing to improved eye healthcare outcomes for underserved populations.

2. Related Works

With the fast increase of fake accounts on social media, security and privacy issues have developed dramatically on applications such as Facebook, Twitter, and Instagram. Fake accounts are mostly used to spread misinformation, phishing, and social engineering attacks. Security Researchers have focused on many different detection and prevention methods, including statistical analysis, machine learning, and deep learning models [1, 7].

The old studies focused on assessing the user behaviour, content patterns, and metadata to differentiate between real and fake profiles [8, 15]. Machine learning techniques such as Random Forest, SVM, Decision Trees, and Naïve Bayes have verified to be useful in detecting fake accounts with a high ratio of accuracy. Deep learning models, specifically CNNs, have modernized the detection of fake accounts further by analysing multimodal data, including text, images, and user activities [2, 5, 14].

Modern methods are combining AI-driven models like Deep Profile which use CNN for automatic feature extraction, where, making the detection highly accurate. Further, hybrid models combining multiple classifiers and preprocessing methods have been suggested to refine the verification processes. Future research work includes upgrading the multilingual analysis, feature selection, and GAN-based and explainable AI-based real-time detection systems [3, 11].

These developments help improve the security of social media, minimize the impact of malicious activities, and ensure user privacy [4, 6] (Figure 19.1).

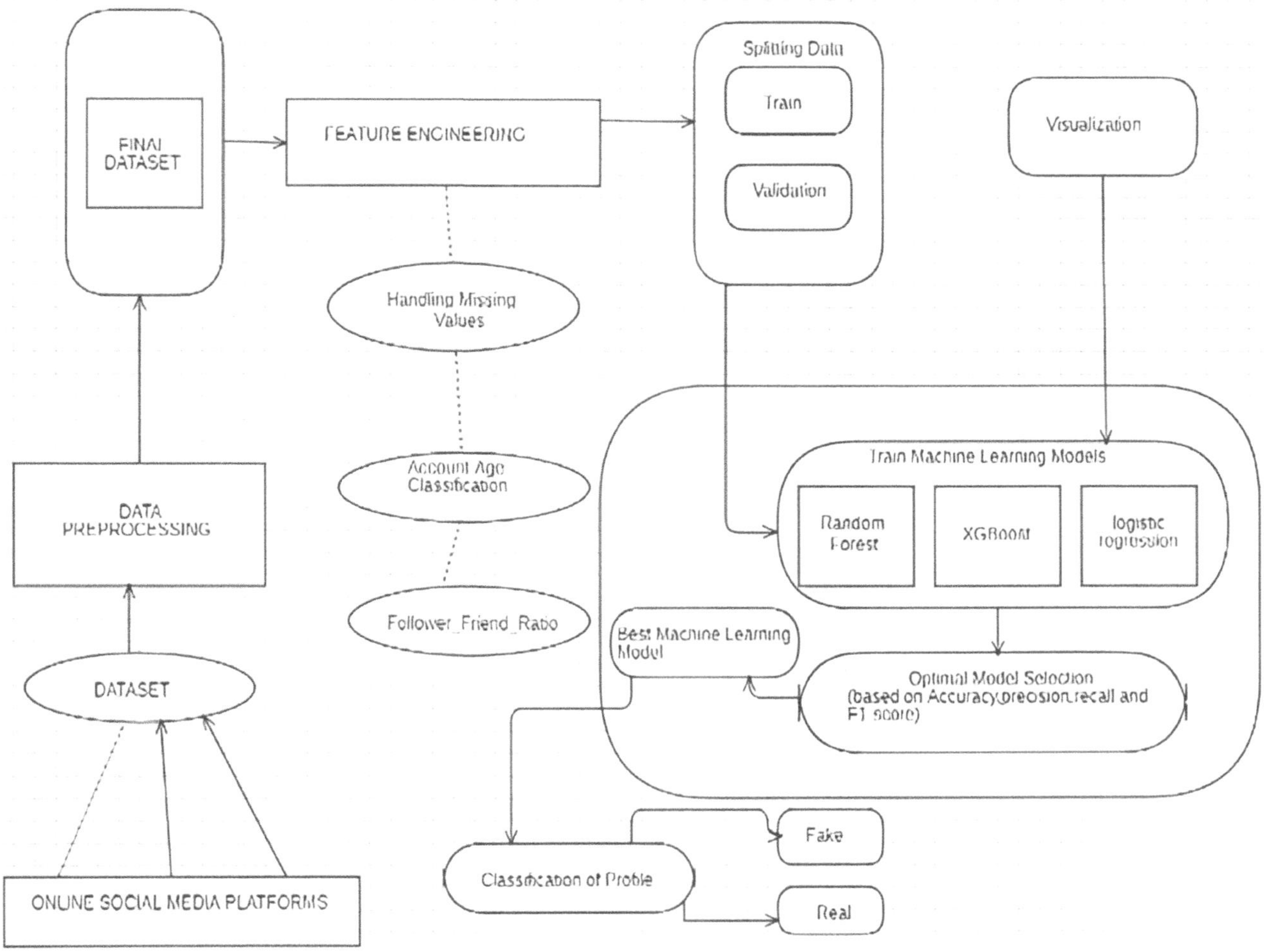

Figure 19.1. Proposed system architecture.

Source: Author.

3. Methodology

The fake social media profile detection system follows a structured approach involving data collection, preprocessing, feature extraction, model training, and deployment [12, 13]. The proposed system architecture is given in the Figure 19.1.

Data Collection and Preprocessing: Data was collected from various social media sites, both actual and fake accounts. Important features were followers, friends, account age, posting frequency, and engagement metrics. Missing values were imputed, numerical features normalized, and categorical data encoded. Outliers were detected and corrected to ensure data integrity.

Feature Extraction: Important features were engineered to enhance the accuracy of the model:

Follower – Friend Ratio – identifies the abnormal behaviour of users.

Account age – Fake accounts tend to be comparatively newer.

Posting Frequency – Identifies the bot-like action.

Engagement Metrics – Authenticity in interactions is seen.

Profile Completeness Fake profiles contain less information required.

Machine Learning Models: Three models have been tested on the dataset.

Random Forest Classifier: It is one of the methods of ensemble approach that reduces the overfitting as shown in Figure 19.2.

XGBoost (Extreme Gradient Boosting): A high-performance boosting algorithm with regularization as shown in Figure 19.3.

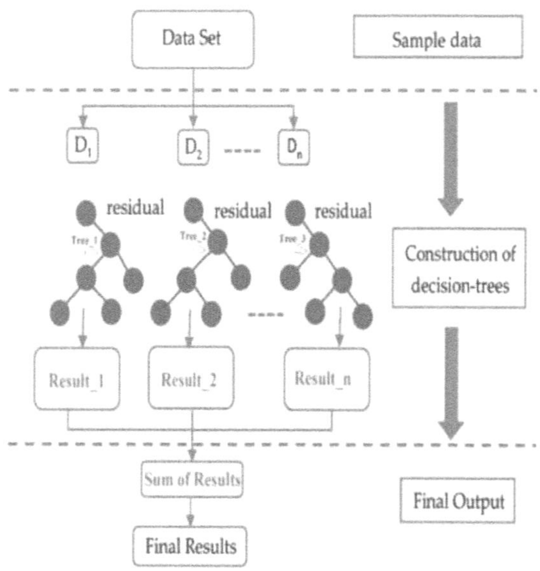

Figure 19.2. Random forest architecture.

Source: Author.

Logistic Regression: An easy-to-interpret binary classification model as shown in Figure 19.4.

The models were educated and examined on an eighty-20 train-check break up of the dataset. Hyperparameter tuning turned into executed the usage of grid seek to identify the ultimate settings for every model, maximizing their performance [10].

Model Selection and Deployment: The model was trained on an 80-20 split; XGBoost resulted in the best accuracy (99.47%) and was thus deployed. A web-based application had been developed to give the real time prediction with visual insights for user friendly analysis.

Evaluation Metrics: To assess the model's effectiveness several metrics such as precision, recall, accuracy, and F1-score are derived.

Accuracy: Accuracy refers to the correctness in all details and statements provided. It indicates how close is the result to the true value.

$$Accuracy = \frac{TP+TN}{TotalPredictionsTrue} \quad (1)$$

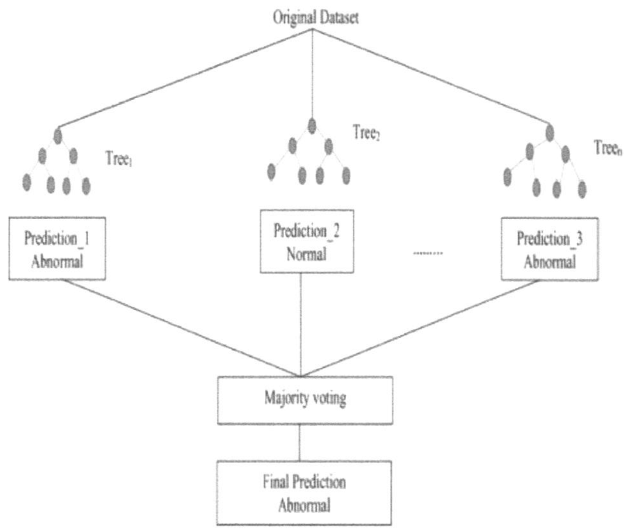

Figure 19.3. XGBoost architecture [20].

Source: Author.

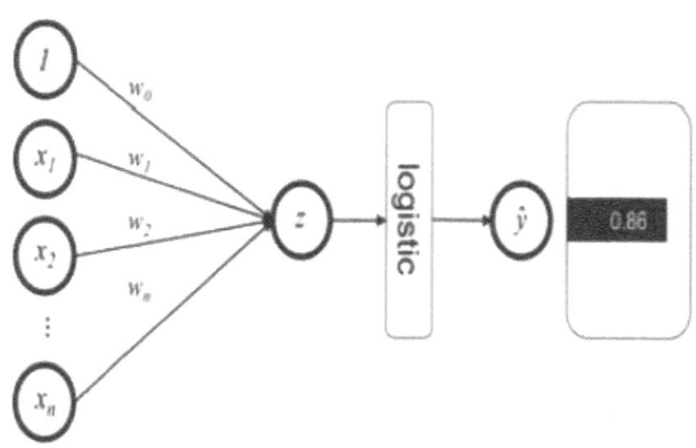

Figure 19.4. Logistic regression architecture

Source: Author.

Table 19.1. Comparison of results with pretrained ML models

Performance Metrics	*Random Forest*	*XGBoost*	*Logistic Regression*
Accuracy	0.992908	0.994681	0.989362
Precision	1.000000	1.000000	0.977695
Recall	0.984791	0.988593	1.000000
F1-Score	0.992337	0.994264	0.988722
ROC-AUC	0.999994	1.000000	0.999987

Source: Author.

Recall (Sensitivity): Recall measures the ability of the model; To determine all the true positive instances.

$$Recall = \frac{TP}{TP+FN} \quad (2)$$

Precision: Precision is the ratio of true positive estimations out of all the positive estimations made by the model.

$$Precision = \frac{TP}{TP+FP} \quad (3)$$

F1 Score: A single metric which combines the precision and recall attributes; which offers a balanced evaluation of model performance.

$$F1 = 2x\frac{PrecsionxRecall}{Precsion+Recall} \quad (4)$$

Confusion Matrix: The confusion matrix gives a overall view on the model's performance by showing the counts of TP, FP, TN and FN. It assists in the computation of durable performance metrics such as recall, specificity, accuracy, and precision. The visual representation facilitates says about the comparison and interpretation of classification results, which allowing for a deeper understanding of the model performance.

4. Result Analysis

This segment compares three machine learning models, namely about the Random Forest, XGBoost, and Logistic Regression, for the job of fake social media profile detection. The dataset had 1,481 rows and 35 features in it. The data was divided into 80:20 ratio for training and validation. Hyperparameter tuning was done through grid search to optimize model performance.

XGBoost showed perfect accuracy at 99.47% and perfect ROC-AUC score at 1.000, meaning nearly flawless classification performance. Random forest was very close at 99.29%. Logistic Regression showed a slightly reduced score at 98.94% but high recall.

Figures 19.5(a), 19.5(b), and 19.5(c) depict the confusion matrices for each model. XGBoost had the most balanced classification with high accuracy and minimal errors. Logistic Regression had perfect recall but minor

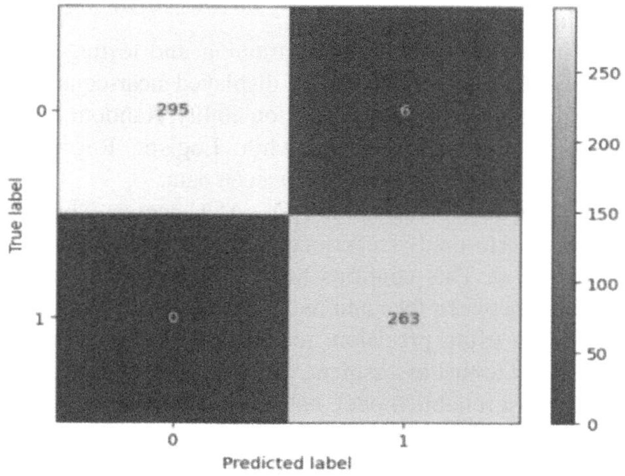

Figure 19.5(a). Confusion matrix for logistic regression.

Source: Author.

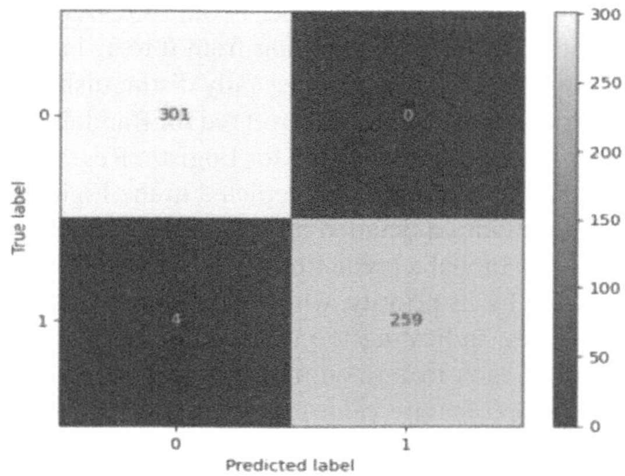

Figure 19.5(b). Confusion matrix for random forest.

Source: Author.

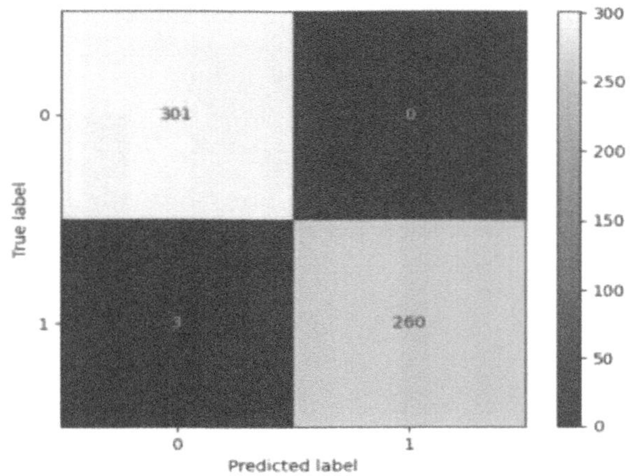

Figure 19.5(c). Confusion matrix for XGBoost.

Source: Author.

false positives, while Random Forest had high precision but slightly lower recall.

Figure 19.6 compares the training and testing accuracy of the models. XGBoost displayed near-equal values, highlighting its generalization ability. Random Forest exhibited minor overfitting, while Logistic Regression showed efficient adaptation to unseen data.

Figure 19.7 presents the ROC-AUC scores, where all models performed exceptionally well, reaching values close to 1.0. This confirms their effectiveness in distinguishing between fake and real profiles. However, further evaluation using precision, recall, and F1-score remains crucial for robust assessment. Overall, XGBoost emerged as the most reliable model, balancing precision and recall effectively while avoiding overfitting. This study confirms its suitability for real-time fake profile detection.

Figures 19.6. and 19.7. compares the receiver performance characteristic – area under the curve (ROCAUC) scores of three machine learning models: random forest, XGBoost, and logistic regression A key performance metric for binary classification tasks is the ROC-AUC score represented on the y-axis ranging from 0 to 1. Each sample is displayed on the x-axis, visually distinguishing their scores by colour-coded bars above: red for Random Forest, black for XGBoost, and purple for Logistic Regression.

The SHAP summary plot depicted in the Figures 19.8 and 19.9 provides a detailed picture of the feature contribution to the model's predictions. The y-axis lists the factors ordered by its priority, while the x-axis represents the SHAP values, indicating the magnitude and direction of the effect of each feature on model output points are coloured based on feature values on, with red that represents the high values and blue representing low values. Key parameters such as follower-friend-ratio, lang-it, followers count, account-age-days show considerable variability among SHAP values, and reveal their strong influence on the model's measures for example, blue dots. Forecasts are often changed negatively. Factors such as location Everywhere and other SHAP values close to zero exhibit a negligible effect on model output, indicating inefficiency This analysis clarifies the internal performance of the model, providing valuable insight into factors a stimulates its predictions, thereby enhancing the interpretation of the results for research purposes.

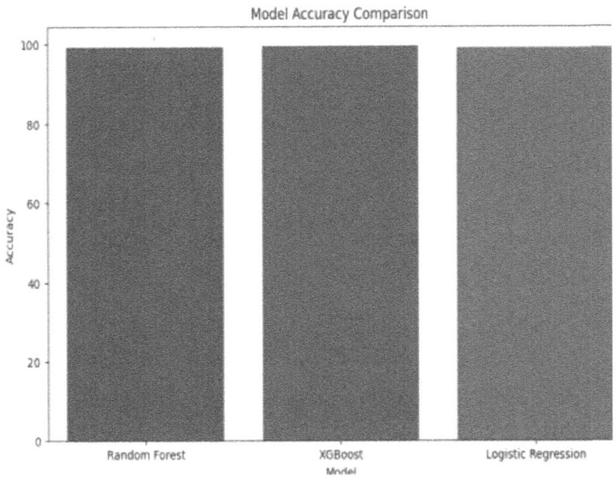

Figure 19.7. Model accuracy comparison.

Source: Author.

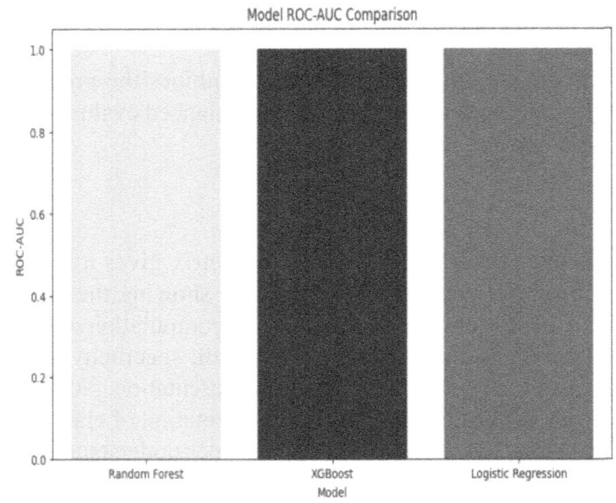

Figure 19.8. Model ROC-AUC comparison.

Source: Author.

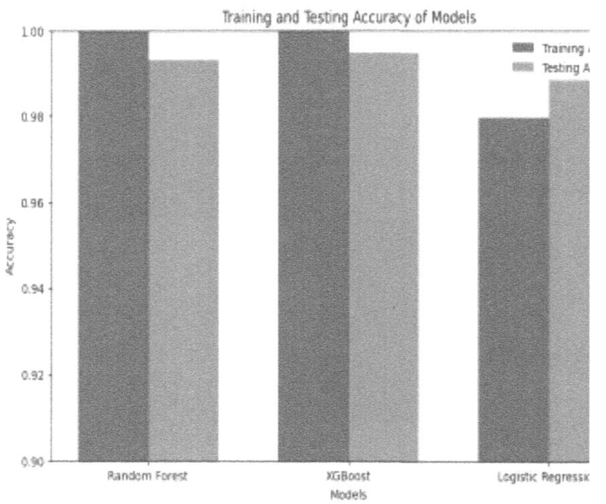

Figure 19.6. Training and testing accuracy of models.

Source: Author.

5. Limitations and Future Scope

Several challenges had been encountered in the course of the development system. Ensuring the quality and diversity of statistics was important, as biases or gaps may want to impact model performance. Class imbalance, a commonplace trouble in fraud detection, changed into

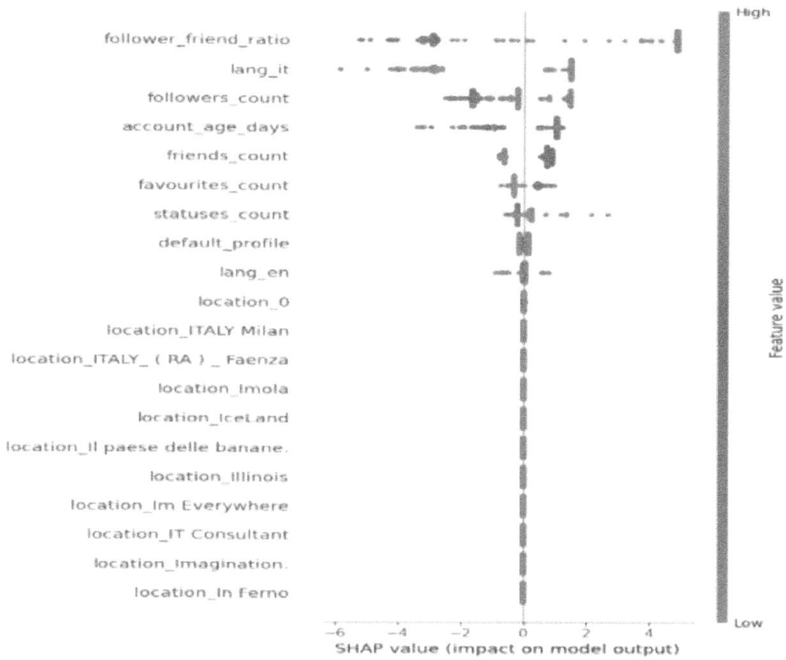

Figure 19.9. SHAP explanation of XGBoost model.

Source: Author.

addressed using oversampling and below-sampling strategies. Additionally, the ever-evolving strategies of fake profile creators gift an ongoing challenge, necessitating everyday updates and retraining of the model to hold its effectiveness. Future work will focus on integrating advanced machine learning models such as deep learning to further upgrade of accuracy. There are also plans to expand the system's ability to detect other types of online fraud, such as phishing and counterfeits. These upgrades will strengthen the role of the system in securing social media platforms and combating cybercrime.

6. Conclusion

Social media fake profiles have brought risks such as identity theft, frauds, or misinformation. In this study, a machine learning approach is utilized to detect the fake accounts using follower-friend ratios, age of the account, and posting frequency. Out of the many tested models, it was XGBoost that proved to be the best with 99.47% accuracy and a perfect ROC-AUC score of 1000, making it very suitable for real world applications. The system's integration into a user-friendly web tool enhances its practicality, enabling real time detection and reducing manual verification efforts, Future improvements include incorporating deep learning, expanding detection capabilities, and continuously updating models to counter evolving fraud tactics. This approach contributes to a safer online environment.

References

[1] Roy, P. K., & Chahar, S. (2020). Fake profile detection on social networking websites: A comprehensive review. *IEEE Transactions on Artificial Intelligence*, *1*(3), 271–285.

[2] Joshi, U. D., Vanshika, Singh, A. P., Pahuja, T. R., Naval, S., & Singal, G. (2021). Fake social media profile detection. *Machine Learning Algorithms and Applications*, 193–209.

[3] Romanov, A., Semenov, A., Mazhelis, O., & Veijalainen, J. (2017, April). Detection of fake profiles in social media – Literature review. *In International conference on web information systems and technologies* (vol. 2, pp. 363–369). *SCITEPRESS.*

[4] Conti, M., Poovendran, R., & Secchiero, M. (2012, August). Fakebook: Detecting fake profiles in online social networks. *In 2012 IEEE/ACM International Conference on Advances in Social Networks Analysis and Mining* (pp. 1071–1078). IEEE.

[5] Goel, S., Guha, A., Kuppusamy, U., Shanmugam, T. (2023). Survey on Artificial Intelligence and Its Applications. In H. Selvaraj, G. Chmaj, D. Zydek (Eds.), *Advances in Systems Engineering.* ICSEng 2023. Lecture Notes in Networks and Systems, vol 761. Springer, Cham. https://doi.org/10.1007/978-3-031-40579-2_48

[6] Aditya, B. L., & Mohanty, S. N. (2023). *Heterogeneous social media analysis for efficient deep learning fake-profile identification.* IEEE Access.

[7] Elyusufi, Y., Elyusufi, Z., & Kbir, M. H. A. (2019, October). Social networks fake profiles detection based on account setting and activity. In *Proceedings of the 4th international conference on smart city applications*, 1–5.

[8] Chinnasamy, P., Ayyasamy, R. K., Subramaniam, S., Sangodiah, A., Iftikhar, A., & Kiran, A. (2024, July). Fake social media profile identification and report using machine learning. *In 2024 International Conference on Signal Processing, Computation, Electronics, Power and Telecommunication (IConSCEPT)* (pp. 1–5). IEEE.

[9] Kaur, R., Singh, S., & Kumar, H. (2021). An intrinsic authorship verification technique for compromised account detection in social networks. *Soft Computing*, *25*, 4345–4366.

[10] Casu, M., Guarnera, L., Caponnetto, P., & Battiato, S. (2024). GenAI mirage: The impostor bias and the deepfake detection challenge in the era of artificial illusions. *Forensic Science International: Digital Investigation, 50*, 301795.

[11] Khan, A. A., Chen, Y. L., Hajjej, F., et. al., (2024). Digital forensics for the socio-cyber world (DF-SCW): A novel framework for deepfake multimedia investigation on social media platforms. *Egyptian Informatics Journal*, *27*, 100502.

[12] Wu, W., Ghazali, M., & Huspi, S. H. (2024). *A Review of User Profiling Based on Social Networks*. IEEE Access.

[13] Sangher, K. S., Singh, A., & Pandey, H. M. (2024). LSTM and BERT based transformers models for cyber threat intelligence for intent identification of social media platforms exploitation from darknet forums. *International Journal of Information Technology, 16*(8), 5277–5292.

[14] Perera, A., & Fernando, P. (2024). Cyberbullying detection system on social media using supervised machine learning. *Procedia Computer Science*, *239*, 506–516.

[15] Xing, L., Li, S., Zhang, Q., Wu, H., Ma, H., & Zhang, X. (2024). A survey on social network's anomalous behavior detection. *Complex & Intelligent Systems*, 1–16.

20 Economic impact: Unraveling the dynamics between Bitcoin values and India's growth for its sustainability

Aditi Wani[a], Lawrence Bansode[b], Avichal Sharma[c], Lija Jacob[d], and Savithri M.[e]

Department of Data Science, Christ (Deemed to be) University, Pune, Lavasa Campus, India

Abstract: This research investigates the relationship between cryptocurrency values, specifically Bitcoin, and economic growth in India using an Autoregressive Distributed Lag (ARDL) model. Analysing data from 2010 to 2023, the study incorporates GDP, Bitcoin prices, and trading volume. Descriptive statistics, correlation analysis, unit root tests, and cointegration bounds tests are employed. The ARDL model reveals significant long and short-term effects of cryptocurrency prices and volume on GDP. Diagnostic tests confirm model robustness, indicating a lack of serial correlation and heteroscedasticity. The Vector Error Correction Model (VECM) framework detects short-term directional links between variables through causality tests. The research contributes insights into the complex dynamics of cryptocurrency impacts on economic growth.

Keywords: ARDL model, Bitcoin, cointegration, cryptocurrency, economic growth, GDP, India

1. Introduction

In the evolution of finance, cryptocurrencies have grown to be a significant phenomenon that is attracting the attention of scholars, decision-makers, and investors alike. The decentralized nature of cryptocurrencies, along with their potential for financial inclusion and technological innovation, have led to their rapid expansion throughout the economy. Concerns concerning the possible effects of cryptocurrency markets on stability and economic growth are raised by their speculative and unstable nature, especially in times of disaster.

The need for a decentralized currency free from centralized control emerged in the wake of the financial crisis. With its controlled manufacturing rate and guaranteed quantity, Bitcoin emerged as the answer. With businesses from a variety of industries using Bitcoin to settle bills, it is even being heralded as the next great thing after the Internet as its popularity soars.

Cryptocurrencies have garnered a lot of interest lately because of their potential to drastically change banking institutions. The emergence of cryptocurrencies such as Bitcoin and Ethereum has brought about a substantial shift in the global economic environment and sparked debates about their potential impact on traditional economies. India is a fast-developing country that has also been impacted by the rise of cryptocurrencies. It is still necessary to research how the price of bitcoin affected India's economic expansion during a long period of time (Figure 20.1).

The purpose of the study is to look into the connection between long-term economic growth and cryptocurrency values. The impact of market liquidity, investor sentiment, governmental policies, and macroeconomic circumstances on cryptocurrency values will be examined. The subsequent influence on the expansion of the global economy will be analysed. By considering these factors, insight into potential risks and opportunities associated with cryptocurrencies in the future can be gained by policymakers and market participants (Figure 20.2).

Several research works have examined the relationship between cryptocurrencies and economic growth, highlighting the benefits and drawbacks of each. As an illustration, [1] found a positive correlation between the market capitalization of cryptocurrencies and economic expansion, suggesting that cryptocurrencies may serve as a substitute investment avenue to promote economic expansion. However, some studies, like [2], have highlighted the

[a]aditi.wani@msea.christuniversity.in, [b]savi3.ram.dach@gmail.com, [c]avichal.sharma@christuniversity.in, [d]lija.jacob@christuniversity.in, [e]bansode.lawrence@msds.christuniversity.in

DOI: 10.1201/9781003778905-20

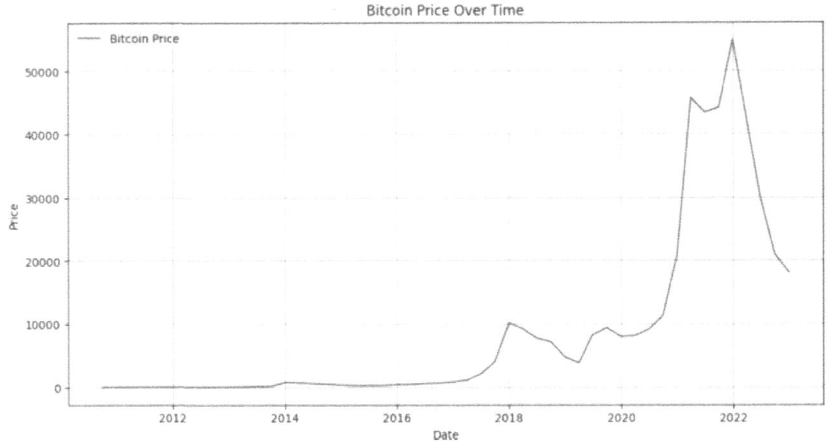

Figure 20.1. Bitcoin Prices over the time period of study.

Source: Author.

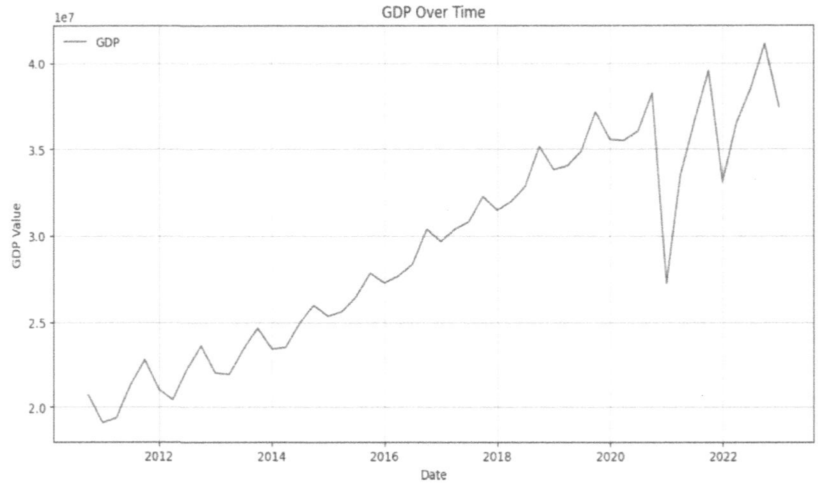

Figure 20.2. GDP indicator over the time period of study.

Source: Author.

speculative nature and potential risks of cryptocurrencies, highlighting the need for additional research.

This study will complement and progress previous research by focusing specifically on the relationship between cryptocurrency prices and economic growth through the ARDL model. Through an analysis of these occurrences, the study hopes to provide information on the robustness and potential vulnerabilities of cryptocurrency markets as well as their implications for general economic growth and stability.

The goal of this research is to investigate bitcoin values in detail and how they affect economic growth in the long run. By examining the relationships between underlying variables, economic growth indicators, and cryptocurrency values, this study aims to expand on the body of knowledge. It also seeks to inform market players and regulators on the possible ramifications of cryptocurrencies in future.

Following is the remainder of the paper: The history of cryptocurrencies and their links to economic development are examined in the second section. The analytical approach is described in Section 3 of the article. The results of the data analysis are presented in Section 4. The Causality test is performed in Section 5. Forecasting model is discussed in Section 6 Conclusions and recommendations are included in Section 7.

2. Review of Literature

This study's literature review will be divided into two essential sections, each of which will examine the relationship between the variables under investigation and relevant earlier studies. These sections will go into great detail about the origins and development of cryptocurrencies in India, and how closely cryptocurrency trends relate to GDP. This structured method seeks to offer a thorough grasp of the intersections between cryptocurrencies and economic indicators.

2.1. The development of cryptocurrencies

In the distant past, India was at the forefront of a technological revolution. At the start of the digital era, people were enthusiastically embracing the wonders of the internet. When chances arose and the nation's economy expanded, a group saw a chance to redefine money for progressive individuals. They held the opinion that digital currencies, or cryptocurrencies, might drastically change how people save, trade, and invest their money. Thus began the incredible journey of creating cryptocurrency in India.

Early in the 2010s, tech-savvy individuals worldwide quickly developed an interest in Bitcoin, the first decentralized cryptocurrency. With a large population and a growing digital sector, India soon became a haven for bitcoin aficionados. Demand for cryptocurrencies increased as more individuals became aware of these digital assets' potential.

From barter to fiat currencies, the evolution of payment systems has been significantly impacted by the emergence of cryptocurrencies [3]. As a result of advancements in technology and financial economics, cryptocurrencies are gaining popularity because to their capacity to execute real-time transactions with electronic histories [4]. While conventional economics has always acknowledged the value of money, cryptocurrencies – which resemble both fiat money and gold – adding a new degree of complication [5]. As a way to allay fears and suspicions stemming from erratic fluctuations in the financial system, digital currencies have emerged [6]. This is a revolutionary move toward a cashless system of exchange [7].

Digital currencies known as cryptocurrencies are freely accessible and unregulated by financial authorities or governments. They represent a break from conventional financial institutions and are managed electronically using an advanced peer-to-peer encryption system based on blockchain technology [8, 9, 11]. With its many benefits, Nakamoto's 2008 [10] launch of Bitcoin, which made use of blockchain technology, has had a major influence on how modern finance develops [12]. The general cryptocurrency industry is growing as a result of recent patterns showing investors' attention shifting away from Bitcoin and towards other up-and-coming cryptocurrencies.

2.2. Cryptocurrency and GDP

Although GDP and cryptocurrency are two different ideas, there are many connections between them. Cryptocurrency is a type of virtual or digital money that is secured by encryption. The GDP, or gross domestic product, is the total monetary or market worth of all completed goods and services produced inside a country's borders over a specific period of time [11].

Cryptocurrencies have a variety of effects on GDP. The first thing they can do is measure the pace of money, or the rate at which commodities and services are exchanged for money. This may result in faster economic expansion. Second, cryptocurrencies have the potential to draw in foreign investment, which raises GDP. Third, new sectors and jobs can be generated by cryptocurrency.

But cryptocurrency may potentially be detrimental to GDP [13]. For instance, they may cause the financial markets to become more volatile and uncertain. This may deter consumption and investment, which would slow economic growth. Cryptocurrencies can also be used for illicit purposes including tax evasion and money laundering. The economy may also suffer from this. The connection between GDP and cryptocurrencies is intricate and constantly changing. Remember that there are other indicators of economic well-being besides GDP. Other key aspects to take into account include environmental sustainability and income disparity [14].

3. Data and Methodology

3.1. Dataset description

The examined dataset is intended to encompass a broad array of factors associated with quarterly price changes in cryptocurrencies, with a specific emphasis on prominent cryptocurrencies such as Bitcoin (Table 20.1). Additionally, the dataset incorporates quarterly volume fluctuations corresponding to Bitcoin, which have been converted. Data collection spans quarterly intervals from 2010 to

Table 20.1. Variables description

Variables	*Description*	*Source*
GDP	The gross domestic product, or GDP, is a measure of the value of all goods and the supply and demand of financial activities within the economy. It is adjusted for inflation. This is the dependent variable in the research that will demonstrate India's economy's growth.	investing.com
Log of Quarterly prices of Bitcoin	The daily prices of Bitcoin represent the closing values of the cryptocurrency in the financial markets, reflecting the market sentiment and valuation of Bitcoin on a day-to-day basis.	investing.com
Log of Quarterly Volume fluctuations	Daily volume fluctuations refer to the variations in the trading activity of Bitcoin, specifically the changes in the total number of Bitcoin units traded within a single day, providing insights into the liquidity and market participation in the cryptocurrency.	investing.com

Source: Author.

2023, rendering it adequate for long-term analysis. To gain insights into the growth dynamics of the nation, the GDP of India is included as a crucial element in the dataset. The primary utility of the dataset lies in its capacity to assist in recognizing and assessing new trends in the bitcoin industry. The original source of the data is the reliable platform investing.com, ensuring the dataset's validity for in-depth scientific examination. E-views software has been employed to conduct this econometric analysis.

In this analysis, the abbreviations follow the lin-log approach, where the dependent variable GDP is considered linear, and logarithmic transformations are applied to the independent variables. The abbreviations used are as follows [15]:

GDP = Economic growth of India

LPRICE = log of price of bitcoin

LVOLUME = log of volume of bitcoin

The empirical framework for this particular paper is specified as:

$$GDP = f(LPRICE, LVOLUME) \tag{1}$$

3.2. Methodology

The distributed lag autoregressive model is used in this study to evaluate how Bitcoin prices, in particular, affect India's economic expansion. The analysis also considers the significance of India's GDP and the amount of Bitcoin trades.

- The short- and long-term connections between variables are examined using a time-series econometric technique known as the ARDL model.
- It can handle time series data that is both stationary and non-stationary, which makes it appropriate for economic data analysis.
- The dynamics of the linkages between trade volume, GDP, and cryptocurrency prices can be captured using the ARDL model.
- Pre-processing: If necessary, pre-processing will be done on the GDP, trade volume, and cryptocurrency price returns to guarantee stationarity and consistency.
- Model Specification: We will build an ARDL model with GDP as the dependent variable and cryptocurrency price returns and trading volume as the independent variables.
- Estimation and Analysis: To identify the long- and short-term associations between variables, the ARDL model will be estimated for each event period. The results will then be analysed.

This research supports consistency of model using normality test, serial correlation test, and heteroskedasticity test.

The ARDL model estimation approach comprises the subsequent steps to analyse the influence of bitcoin price and volume on economic growth [15]:

1. Unit root test, for stationary of variables.
2. Cointegration test.
3. Long-run and Short-run Estimates
4. Diagnostic Tests
5. Causality Test

As the ARDL is not an ideal method for establishing causal linkages, Granger causality tests are employed in this study. These tests are transformed into Vector Error Correction Models (VECM) to account for both short- and long-term dynamics. The VECM framework, incorporating an error-correction term (ECT-1), is utilized to identify short-term causal relationships, following the methods proposed by Engle and Granger. A significant, negative ECT coefficient at a 0.05 significance level would indicate a noteworthy rate of adjustment towards equilibrium, offering insights into the sensitivity of the bitcoin market to financial crises. In cases where long-term cointegration is absent, the VAR technique is employed to assess short-term Granger causality, facilitating the identification of relationships between cryptocurrency prices and the potential impact on economic growth.

Furthermore, machine learning techniques are utilized to predict GDP by fitting a model based on the dependent and independent variables. This approach enables an analysis of whether GDP for a country can be predicted through cryptocurrency prices and volume. The data is trained and tested, and performance is evaluated using Mean Squared Error. The actual vs. predicted GDP values are also visualized for further analysis.

4. Results and Discussions

4.1. Descriptive statistics and correlation analysis

To comprehend the paradox of plenty hypothesis, the investigation commences with an examination of basic statistics and correlations before delving into a more intricate study. The initial step involves the presentation of a table (Table 20.2), displaying straightforward and concise numbers concerning all the pertinent variables. This table provides a visual summary, facilitating a clearer understanding of the fundamental information regarding these variables before undertaking a more thorough empirical analysis.

Table 20.3 offers a succinct overview of the relationships among the variables under examination in this paper. Primarily, it serves as a swift reference that encapsulates the interconnections between various factors in our study, enhancing the ease with which readers can discern patterns and associations within our data (Figure 20.3).

4.2. Unit root test

Prior to performing co-integration tests in time series analysis, it is critical to assess stationary behaviour of the variables. One often used technique for this is the Augmented Dickey-Fuller test. The process is comparing alternative hypothesis (H1), which states that a variable lacks a unit root and is stationary, to null hypothesis (Ho), which states that a variable has unit root and is non-stationary. Systematically applying the ADF test to each variable allows the determination of their respective orders of integration, a crucial step for subsequent co-integration analysis. This ensures the robustness and reliability of our time series modelling.

Table 20.2. Descriptive statistics

	GDP	*LPRICE*	*LVOLUME*
Mean	29263766	6.534798	16.24449
Median	29007400	6.647219	15.70409
Maximum	41123600	10.91152	24.5007
Minimum	19091100	−2.30259	12.7903
Std. Dev.	6169768	3.391823	2.191705
Skewness	0.073831	−0.79372	1.737929
Kurtosis	1.779823	2.858181	7.388703
Jarque-Bera	3.147158	5.291868	65.29647
Probability	0.207302	0.070939	0
Sum	1.46E+09	326.7399	812.2243
Sum Sq. Dev.	1.87E+15	563.7189	235.3751
Observations	50	50	50

Source: Author.

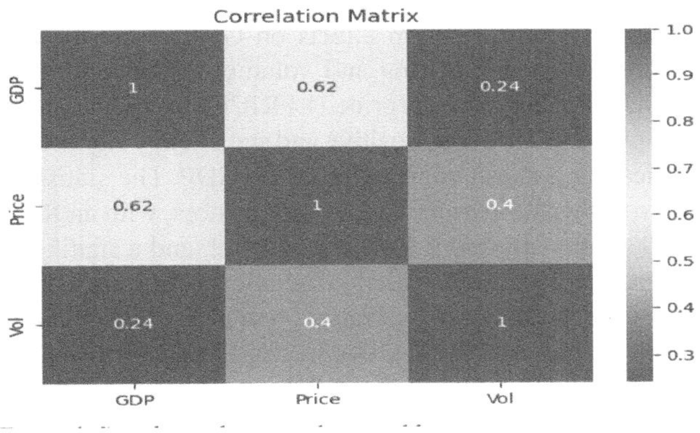

Correlation	*GDP*	*LPRICE*	*LVOLUME*
GDP	1	0.888964	0.679049
LPRICE	0.888964	1	0.573883
LVOLUME	0.679049	0.573883	1

Figure 20.3. Correlation between the variables.

Source: Author.

Augmented Dickey-Fuller (ADF)

Stationary tests were initially performed in both original levels and subsequent first differences for all variables to determine the existence of order of integration and unit root for each. GDP and LPRICE show stationarity at the first difference level, indicating that they are integrated of order one (I(1)), according to the results, as shown in Table 20.4. When LVOLUME, on the other hand, exhibits stationarity at the levels, it is integrated of order zero (I(0)). These results offer crucial information on the characteristics of the variables, directing further investigations and guaranteeing that suitable modeling approaches are used in accordance with the variables' individual integration qualities.

4.3. Co-integration testing results

The results of the ARDL cointegration boundaries test are shown in Table 20.5. An important indicator is the F-test, whose predicted outcomes imply that the research variables are cointegrated. When the calculated F-test value is less than upper bound criteria at significance levels of 1% and 5%, cointegration is confirmed. Essentially, these findings inform our comprehension of long-term correlations between the variables being studied and offer critical evaluation of their common patterns and interdependencies, especially at the designated significance levels.

The results from the Cointegration Bounds Test, detailed in Table 20.5, suggest a nuanced interpretation. The F-statistics for various combinations of the variables indicate cointegration. Specifically, the model with variables GDP, LPRICE, and LVOLUME (F (GDP/LPRICE, LVOLUME)) yields a significant F-statistic of 9.863, exceeding the upper bounds at both 1% and 5% significance levels. This suggests the presence of a single cointegrating equation. However, for the models F (LPRICE/GDP, LVOLUME) and F (LVOLUME/LPRICE, GDP), the F-statistics (2.866 and 2.090, respectively) fall below

Table 20.3. Unit root test

Variables	*Levels*		*1st Diff*		*Order of Integration*
	t-stat	*P-value*	*t-stat*	*P-value*	
GDP	−2.36	0.3945	−11.301***	0.000	I (1)
LPRICE	−1.424	0.8403	−5.555***	0.0002	I (1)
LVOLUME	−5.117***	0.0007	—	—	I (0)

**level of significance at 5% ***level of significance at 1%

Source: Author.

Table 20.4. Results of cointegration bounds test

Model for Estimation		*F-Statistics*	*Critical Value Bounds*	*I (0) Bound*	*I (1) Bound*
F (GDP/LPRICE, LVOLUME)	ARDL (4,1,2)	9.863***	1%	3.88	5.3
F (LPRICE/GDP, LVOLUME)	ARDL (4,5,4)	2.866*	5%	2.72	3.83
F (LVOLUME/LPRICE, GDP)	ARDL (3,2,6)	2.090	10%	2.17	3.19

Note: ***, **, and * signify rejection of the null hypothesis at the 1%, 5% and 10% significance levels, respectively.
Source: Author.

Table 20.5. Long-run and short-run outcomes under the ARDL approach

Variables	*Coefficient*	*Std. Error*	*t-Statistic*	*Prob.*
Long term Estimation				
LPRICE	1258731	216402.7	5.816	0.0000
LVOLUME	1397765	138659.3	10.080	0.0000

R^2	*0.6934*
Adj R^2	0.6462
Durbin-Watson Stat	1.909
F-Statistic	9.8636
Prob (F-Statistic)	0

Source: Author.

Table 20.6. Summary of the results obtained from long-term and short-term Autoregressive Distributed Lag approaches

Variables	*Coefficient*	*Std. Error*	*t-Statistic*	*Prob.*
Short term Estimation				
GDP (−1)*	−0.4851***	0.2152	−2.2538	0.0002
LPRICE (-1)	610633.9*	310077.4	1.9692	0.0564
LVOLUME (−1)	678082.3**	259252.5	2.6155	0.0128
D (GDP(−1))	−0.296**	0.1107	−2.672	0.0111
D (GDP (−2))	−0.475***	0.112	−4.245	0.0001
D (GDP(−3))	−0.603***	0.1068	−5.644	0.000
D (LPRICE)	−424078.2	472570.3	−0.8973	0.3753
D (LVOLUME)	562031***	152715.2	3.680	0.0007
D (LVOLUME (−1)))	−369543**	163168.6	−2.2648	0.0295
ECT (−1)	−0.485***	0.0868	−5.584	0.0000

Note: ***, **, and * indicate significance at the 1%, 5% and 10% significant levels, respectively.
Source: Author.

the upper bounds at 1% and 5%, implying a lack of long-term cointegration in these cases. These findings guide our understanding of the relationships among the variables and help in determining the appropriate modeling approach for subsequent analyses.

4.4. Long-run and short-run estimates

A detailed summary of the results obtained from long-term and short-term Autoregressive Distributed Lag approaches is given in Table 20.6. This dual viewpoint includes both an analysis of the short-term, temporary effects and the long-term relationships between variables across time. The findings provide important new information about the dynamics of the variables under study and provide a more sophisticated picture of how they interact in more immediate and long-term contexts. The table, which presents the results from both temporal dimensions, aids in the comprehensive understanding of the complex linkages uncovered by the ARDL methodology in the research study.

The ARDL model estimates show that there are notable short- and long-term effects on GDP from volatility in cryptocurrency pricing and volume. In the long term, the coefficients for log price (LPRICE) and log volume (LVOLUME) are both positive and statistically significant, indicating a substantial influence on GDP. The statistical tests further support the model's robustness, with an R2 of 0.6934, an Adjusted R square of 0.6462, and a significant F-statistic of 9.8636. Serial correlation is not present, as indicated by the Durbin-Watson score of 1.909. In short term, lagged values of GDP, LPRICE, and LVOLUME, along with their first differences, contribute significantly to GDP variation. The adjustment towards equilibrium is also shown by the negative and significant error-correction term (ECT (-1)). These results collectively suggest a comprehensive understanding of the dynamic relationships and influences of cryptocurrency on Economic growth of the country.

4.5. Diagnostic tests

Three vital diagnostic tests – 1. Normality Test 2. Serial Correlation LM Test 3. Heteroscedasticity Test are systematically employed to assess the robustness of the model. These tests provide crucial insights into the adequacy of the model's assumptions and the reliability of its predictions.

The Normality Test evaluates whether the residuals conform to a normal distribution, ensuring the validity of statistical inferences. Our test indicates that our model deviates from normality. The Serial Correlation LM Test

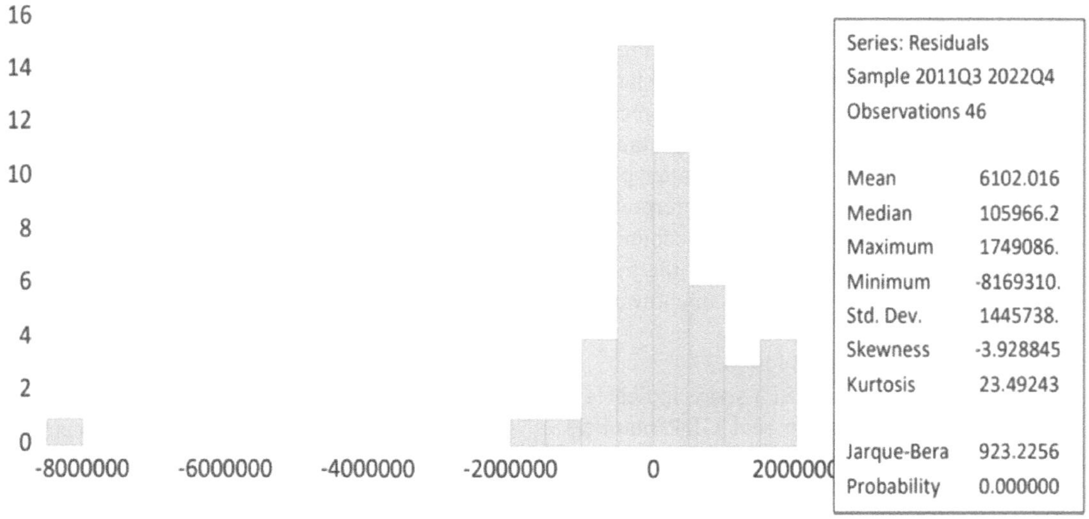

Figure 20.4. Normality test.

Source: EViews.

examines the presence of autocorrelation in the residuals, verifying the independence of observations. In this case, no serial correlation or autocorrelation is detected, as evidenced by the serial correlation test results yielding a p-value better than 0.05.

Simultaneously, the Heteroscedasticity Test scrutinizes whether the variability of residuals remains constant, validating the model's predictive precision. Finally, we do not have enough information to rule out homoscedasticity as the null hypothesis because the Breusch-Pagan-Godfrey test for heteroscedasticity produces a p-value of observed R squared larger than 0.05.

Collectively, these diagnostic tests enhance the model's analytical rigor and refine its predictive capabilities (Figure 20.4). Despite the non-normality of residuals, the estimated model is considered robust and reliable, as the assumption of normality is typically not required for Ordinary Least Squares (OLS) estimation; its primary application lies in hypothesis testing [16, 17].

5. Causality Test

The evaluation of possible directional relationships between the research variables is made possible by the existence of cointegration. Table 20.7 provides a concise summary of the short-term causal linkages between the variables that are being examined by the Vector Error Correction Model (VECM). A targeted investigation of the direct effects and interdependencies between the components under study is made possible by this analytical framework. This makes it possible to comprehend how variations in one element within the co-integrated framework may instantly affect other variables in a more nuanced way.

6. Forecasting

In the analysis, a linear regression model is developed with independent variables such as cryptocurrency prices (Price) and trading volume (Volume), and machine

Table 20.7. Long Run and short-run causality estimates

Dependent Variable			*Independent variable*
	ΔGDP	*ΔLPRICE*	*ΔLVOLUME*
ΔGDP	-------	0.81086	11.2945*
ΔLPRICE	0.73965	-------	1.41550
ΔLVOLUME	0.31135	1.18960	-----------

Note: ***, **, and * indicate significance at the 1%, 5% and 10% significant levels, respectively.
Source: Author.

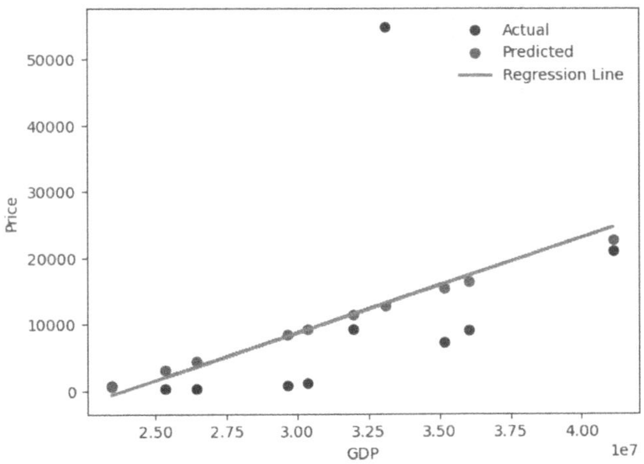

Figure 20.5. Actual vs Predicted GDP.

Source: Author.

learning is employed to estimate a nation's GDP. After the dataset is sorted, it is divided into training and testing sets. The former is used to train the model, whereas the latter is used to assess its performance. GDP values are forecasted using the fitted model, and the accuracy of the predictions is measured using Mean Squared Error. A scatter plot is used to visualize the results, which improves interpretability and sheds light on how well the model accounts for variations in GDP caused by the dynamics of the bitcoin market. This offers insightful viewpoints on how these processes might affect economic growth.

Mean Squared Error: 31021640544925.77

The high mean square error (MSE) score indicates a significant discrepancy between the real GDP numbers and the conclusions of the linear regression model. This implies that the model's capacity to precisely forecast GDP based only on cryptocurrency prices and volume is constrained from an economic standpoint. Although the volume and price swings of cryptocurrencies might add to the unpredictable nature of economic growth, accurate GDP forecasting requires more than these variables

7. Conclusion

This study provides a thorough understanding of the intricate relationship between the growth of the Indian economy and the prices of cryptocurrencies, especially Bitcoin. The model's calculations indicate that fluctuations in the price and volume of cryptocurrencies have a major short- and long-term effect on India's GDP. Diagnostic tests ensure that the model is reliable and accurate in its predictions. Causality tests show the dynamic interactions that take place inside the economic system in addition to the short-term directional links between the variables. These results add important new information to the growing corpus of research on the financial effects of cryptocurrencies. This information may be used by market players and policymakers to make informed decisions that take into account the effects of various cryptocurrency factors on economic growth. The study's findings warn against depending just on cryptocurrency prices and volume for accurate forecasting, emphasizing the necessity for a thorough grasp of the complex elements impacting GDP.

Future research directions could explore more in-depth policy implications as the cryptocurrency landscape develops. Some of these might include determining how cryptocurrencies affect or exacerbate financial crises, creating a comprehensive regulatory framework for macroeconomic indicators, and weighing their relative importance to traditional stock markets in determining India's economic trajectory.

References

[1] Bouri, E., Gabr, A., & Jouini, O. (2017). The impact of cryptocurrency on economic growth, Finance. *Research Letters*, *25*, 18–23.

[2] Dyhrberg, H., et al. (2010). The impact of cryptocurrencies on the financial system stability: A review of the literature. *In The Routledge companion to money and finance, 20, N. Kaushal, Ed. Hern, A*, 1–20.

[3] Elwell, M. R., & Elwell, K. R. (2013). The evolution of money: From barter to bitcoin. *In The Routledge companion to money and finance*, 1–23.

[4] Brezo, J. M., & Bringas, P. M. (2012). The impact of cryptocurrencies on the financial system. *The Journal of Business Ethics*, *105*(2), 289–299.

[5] Sas, M. I., & Khairuddin, S. (2015). The role of cryptocurrencies in the future of finance. *Journal of Accounting and Finance*, *56*, 1–11.

[6] Shahzad, S. A., Zaidi, S. A. H., & Mirza, S. M. (2018). The impact of cryptocurrencies on the financial system stability: A review of the literature. *Journal of Risk Management*, *21*(6), 1074–1095.

[7] Wang, J., Li, J., & Li, X. (2019). The impact of cryptocurrencies on economic growth and stability: A review of the literature. *International Review of Financial Economics*, 64.

[8] Carrick, J L. (2016). The economics of cryptocurrencies. *Review of Financial Studies*, *29*(10), 2961–3001.

[9] Haq, M., Ahmed, S., & Khan, A. (2021). The impact of cryptocurrencies on the financial system: A review of the literature. *Journal of Risk Financial Management*, *14*(11), 1–20.

[10] Hern, A. (2013). *Bitcoin: What it is and why it matters*. New York Times.

[11] Kaushal, N. (2016). The future of cryptocurrencies. *In The Routledge companion to money and finance*, 204–224.

[12] Corbett, S. (2010). Bitcoin: An anonymous digital currency. *SSRN Electronic Journal*, *16*(1), 1–20.

[13] Hung, J. (2023). The impact of cryptocurrencies on the economy. *Journal of Economic Perspectives*, *37*(1), 1–20.

[14] Umar, M., Shahzad, F., Ullah, I., & Fanghua, T. (2023). A comparative analysis of cryptocurrency returns and economic policy uncertainty pre- and post-Covid-19. *Research in International Business and Finance*, *65*, 101965.

[15] Examining the Relationship between Economic Growth, FDI and Trade: VAR and Causality Analysis.

[16] Studenmund, H. A. (2016). *Using econometrics: A practical guide*, 7th edition. Pearson.

[17] Bhat, M. A. (2021). *Trade linkages among BRICS countries with special reference to India*.

21 Advancing sustainable fraud detection in finance: A comprehensive survey of AI-driven techniques, innovations, and challenges

Dina Abdelnaser Mohammed[1,a] *and Anjitha Mary Paul*[2]

[1]Student, Department of Computing, British Applied College, Umm al Quwain, UAE
[2]Lecturer, Department of Computing, British Applied College, Umm al Quwain, UAE

Abstract: This paper examines the transformative impact of artificial intelligence (AI) on fraud detection in the financial sector, detailing the shift from rule-based methods to advanced AI techniques like deep learning. It reviews recent studies, highlighting AI's role in enhancing detection efficiency and promoting sustainability through optimized resource use. Key issues such as data imbalance, scalability, and evolving fraud patterns are addressed. The paper emphasizes real-time processing, explainable AI (XAI), and adaptive learning models to improve transparency, accuracy, and responsiveness. It advocates for continued innovation and collaboration to combat sophisticated fraud while safeguarding data privacy and regulatory compliance.

Keywords: Sustainable AI-driven fraud detection, financial fraud, deep learning, graph neural networks, real-time fraud detection, explainable AI, adaptive learning, data imbalance, sustainability in fintech, regulatory compliance

1. Introduction

Financial fraud poses a major threat to global financial stability, especially as digital technologies and online transactions expand. Traditional rule-based detection systems, once effective, now struggle to counter increasingly sophisticated fraud tactics. This limitation has driven the adoption of artificial intelligence (AI) for more adaptive and robust detection methods.

Sustainability has become essential in fraud detection, emphasizing not only improved effectiveness but also greater efficiency and reduced environmental impact. AI enhances sustainability by automating decision-making, minimizing resource use, and improving accuracy. These advances not only protect personal and institutional assets but also reinforce trust in financial systems and support global goals for social and environmental well-being.

2. Real-World Incidents of Financial Fraud

The integration of AI into fraud detection is essential in addressing the growing complexity of financial fraud. Real-world cases demonstrate the limitations of traditional methods and the potential of AI to enhance detection and prevention.

2.1. *Massive online banking fraud*

Fraudsters exploited a major U.S. bank using synthetic identities, causing losses of tens of millions. Traditional systems failed to detect the fake accounts, while AI-driven behaviour analysis could have identified early anomalies [22].

2.2. *Credit card skimming operations*

An international syndicate used ATM-installed skimmers across Europe to clone cards. AI tools analyzing transaction velocity and location anomalies could have detected this activity more swiftly than manual monitoring [23].

2.3. *Wire transfer fraud in corporate finance*

A corporation lost $45 million through a phishing scam targeting financial officers. AI systems with natural language processing (NLP) could have flagged suspicious email content before the transfer occurred [24].

[a]2210025@acuq.ae, banjitha.p@bacu.ae

DOI: 10.1201/9781003778905-21

2.4. Insurance claims fraud

A European insurer employed machine learning to analyze claim patterns, successfully identifying fraudulent submissions and saving millions. AI detected anomalies in data that conventional methods missed [25].

3. Traditional Approaches

3.1. Rule-based systems

Rule-based systems apply predefined criteria to flag potentially fraudulent transactions. They are valued for their simplicity and transparency but lack adaptability, requiring frequent updates to remain effective. This often leads to high false positives, mistakenly blocking legitimate transactions and impacting user experience [1, 5–7, 12].

3.2. Statistical models

Statistical models, such as logistic regression and Bayesian networks, analyze historical data to detect fraud patterns. They are effective for known fraud types but struggle with novel or complex schemes, limiting their effectiveness in rapidly evolving fraud landscapes [3, 5–7].

4. AI-Driven Techniques

4.1. Supervised learning models

Trained on labeled datasets, supervised models – such as decision trees, SVMs, and neural networks – detect fraud by learning patterns from historical data. They are effective when past data reflects future cases [1, 3, 4, 6, 9, 10, 13].

The graph in Figure 21.1 illustrates an SVM classification model, where a decision boundary separates two classes by maximizing the margin between support vectors.

The diagram in Figure 21.2 shows a decision tree, with a root node, decision nodes, and leaf nodes, representing hierarchical decision paths for classification.

4.2. Unsupervised learning and anomaly detection

In contrast to supervised learning, unsupervised learning models identify anomalies without labeled data, making them valuable for detecting new fraud types. Techniques like clustering and isolation forests detect irregular patterns that traditional systems might miss [6, 7, 10–12].

The scatter plot in Figure 21.3 depicts clustering of data points into three groups, based on feature similarities.

The diagram in Figure 21.4 demonstrates an Isolation Forest, where anomalies (dark blue) are identified through fewer partitions, unlike normal points (light blue) which lie deeper in the trees.

4.3. Hybrid models

Hybrid models leverage the strengths of both supervised and unsupervised learning techniques to enhance fraud detection capabilities. By integrating these approaches, hybrid models can quickly adapt to new and changing types of fraud with minimal need for manual retraining, offering a flexible and robust solution for modern fraud detection challenges [1, 2, 4].

5. Workflow of AI-Driven Fraud Detection

The following workflow diagram (Figure 21.5) details the sequential process for implementing AI-based fraud detection systems:

1. **Data Collection:** Gathering transactional and contextual data from financial systems.

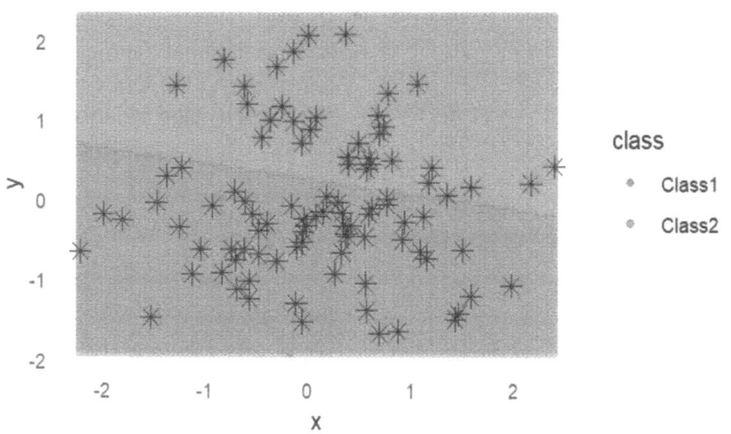

Figure 21.1. Representation of a support vector machine (SVM) classification model.

Source: Author.

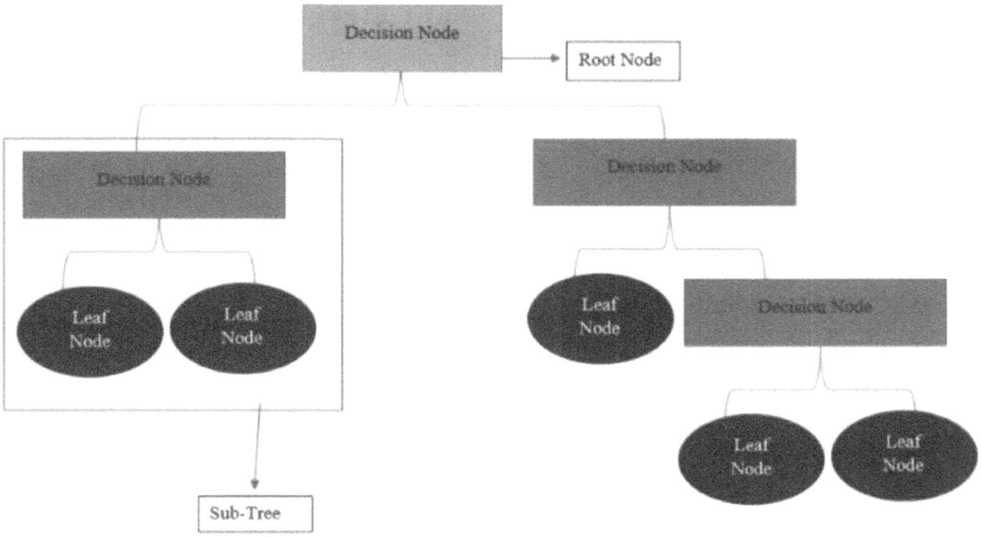

Figure 21.2. Structure of a decision tree model.

Source: Author.

Figure 21.3. Clustering of data points using unsupervised learning.

Source: Author.

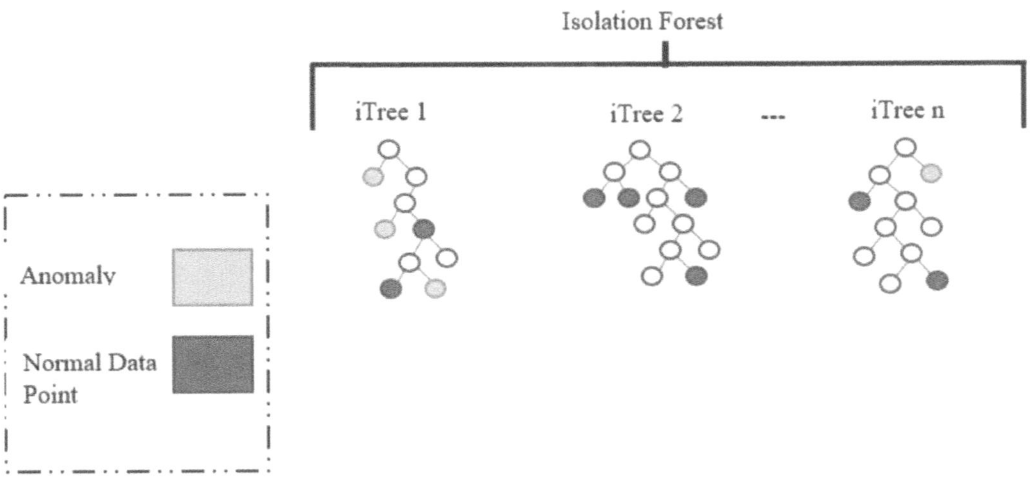

Figure 21.4. Isolation forest for anomaly detection.

Source: Author.

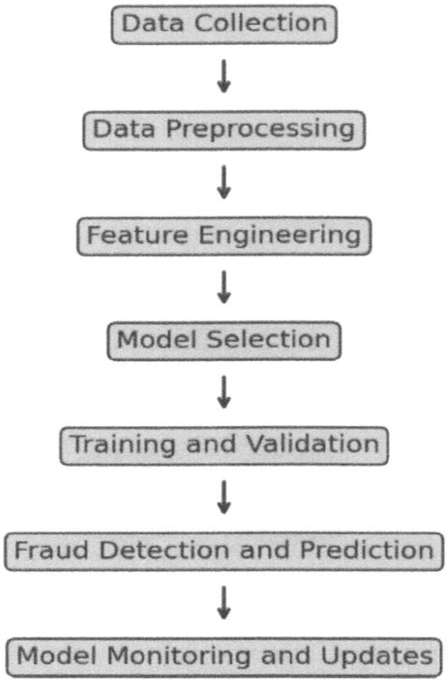

Figure 21.5. Workflow of AI-driven fraud detection.

Source: Author.

2. **Data Pre-processing:** Clean and organize raw data to ensure consistency and quality.
3. **Feature Engineering:** Extract and select key features relevant to detecting fraud.
4. **Model Selection:** The right AI/ ML model is chosen.
5. **Training and Validation:** The model is trained on labeled datasets and validated for accuracy.
6. **Fraud Detection and Prediction:** Deploy trained models to identify and predict fraudulent activity.
7. **Model Monitoring and Updates:** Continual monitoring and updating of the model to handle new fraud patterns.

6. Emerging Innovations

6.1. Graph neural networks (GNNs)

GNNs excel in fraud detection by modeling the complex, relational nature of financial data. They represent users and accounts as nodes and transactions or communications as edges, capturing broader context and subtle patterns that traditional models often miss. GNNs are adaptable and scalable, allowing real-time updates to graph structures without full retraining. This leads to better detection of evolving fraud schemes, fewer false positives, and improved integration of diverse data types – making GNNs a key technology for future fraud detection systems [5–7].

The diagram in Figure 21.6 illustrates how nodes update their embeddings by aggregating information from neighbours through hidden layers with activation functions (e.g., ReLU), resulting in graph-level predictions for fraud detection.

6.2. Real-time processing frameworks

To prevent fraud instantly, real-time systems analyze transactions as they occur. These frameworks minimize delays, reduce financial loss, and enhance response speed – key advantages for modern financial security systems [2, 4, 15].

6.3. Explainable AI (XAI)

XAI enhances transparency in AI decision-making by providing clear, interpretable insights into model outputs. This is critical for user trust, error identification, and compliance with financial regulations, especially in high-stakes scenarios [9, 12].

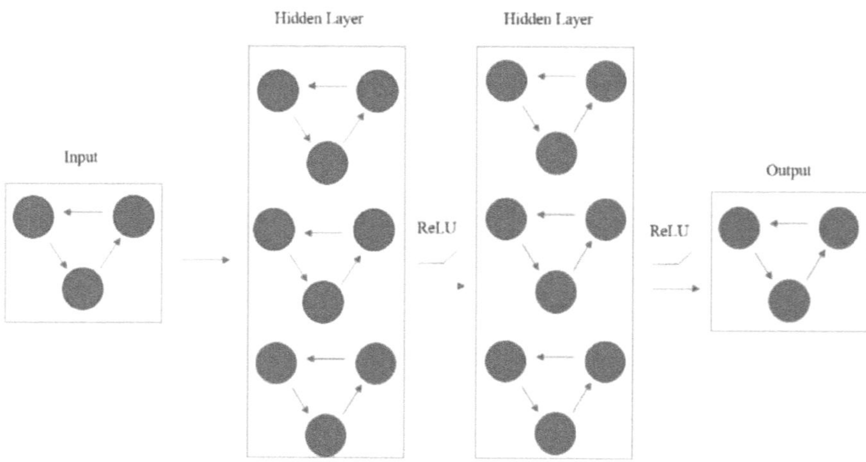

Figure 21.6. Graph neural network (GNN) architecture.

Source: Author.

The diagram in Figure 21.7 depicts a shift from opaque deep learning models to interpretable pipelines, where tools explain AI decisions in human-understandable terms, aiding usability and trust in fraud detection applications.

7. Comparative Analysis

In this section, we undertake a comprehensive comparative analysis of prominent studies in AI-driven fraud detection. The objective is to illustrate how various methodologies have evolved to meet the increasing demands for accuracy, scalability, and efficiency in financial fraud prevention. Table 21.1 encapsulates the key approaches, advantages, and limitations identified in the reviewed literature.

The comparative analysis shows AI's transformative role in fraud detection through supervised, unsupervised, deep learning, and hybrid models. Deep learning techniques (GNNs, CNNs, LSTMs) handle complex patterns well but require significant resources, while hybrid models improve adaptability but face challenges in real-time use. Real-time frameworks reduce losses yet raise privacy and compliance concerns. Sustainable AI approaches using resource-efficient methods are promising but rely on data quality and scalability. Overall, AI boosts fraud detection accuracy and adaptability, though issues like computational load, privacy, and regulation remain. Future work should focus on building efficient, transparent, and sustainable systems.

8. Statistical Metrics Analysis

AI-driven fraud detection models show strong performance across key metrics such as precision, recall, F1-score, accuracy, and ROC-AUC. These indicators help evaluate effectiveness and limitations across different contexts (Table 21.2).

The reviewed studies use metrics like accuracy, precision, recall, F1-score, and ROC-AUC to evaluate AI fraud detection models. While these models improve accuracy and adaptability, issues like high false positives, computational demands, and scalability persist. Deep learning methods (e.g., GNNs, CNNs, TCNs) offer high precision (90%+) but require significant resources. Models balancing precision and recall reduce false positives but may miss rare fraud cases.

ROC-AUC scores are generally strong (>0.90), though performance can drop in unstructured or large datasets. Explainable AI (XAI) boosts transparency and compliance but adds complexity. Sustainable AI models aim to maintain performance while minimizing resource use, though they depend on data quality and scalability. Future research should enhance scalability, efficiency, and transparency for wider adoption.

9. Key Findings of the Studies

The surveyed papers provide diverse insights into AI applications for fraud detection, emphasizing sustainable innovation in financial technologies:

9.1. Improved accuracy

Studies [1, 3, 4, 6, 9] report improved accuracy due to advanced ML/DL models that interpret complex data and detect subtle fraud patterns. These improvements reduce false positives/negatives, saving time and resources and enhancing sustainability.

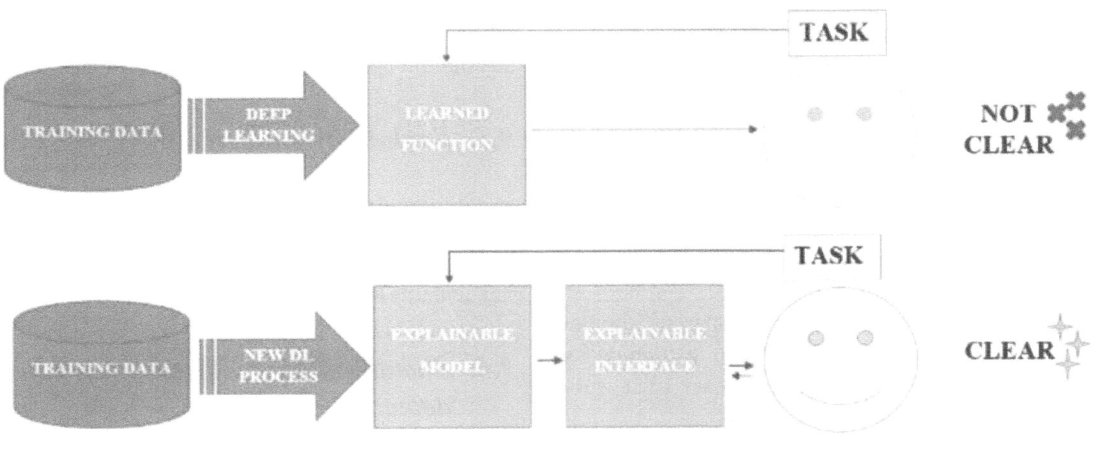

Figure 21.7. Framework for explainable artificial intelligence (XAI).

Source: Author.

Table 21.1. Comparative analysis of the studies

Study	*Technique*	*Key Advantage*	*Limitation*
[1]	Supervised Learning	Enhances precision in skewed data	May not generalize across different types of data sets
[2]	Hybrid Models (Random Forest, Isolation Forest)	Effective in anomaly detection in credit card transactions	Requires substantial computational resources
[3]	Deep Learning	High accuracy in detecting enterprise financial fraud	Can be complex to implement and maintain
[4]	Supervised Learning	Broad application in finance fraud detection	Sometimes produces high false positive rates
[5]	Unsupervised Learning (Isolation Forest),GNNs	Captures complex patterns effectively	High computational demands
[6]	Deep Learning, Real-Time Processing Frameworks	Reduces false positives significantly	Struggles with data privacy issues
[7]	Deep Learning	Accurately identifies patterns, anomalies, and signs of fraud	Overfitting can occur with limited data diversity
[8]	Unsupervised Learning (Clustering, Isolation Forest)	Provides extensive review and recent advances	Focuses more on theory than practical implementation
[9]	Explainable AI, Supervised Learning	Enhances transparency in fraud detection methods	Implementation complexity increases
[10]	Deep Learning	Superior accuracy over traditional methods	Requires high-quality, extensive training data
[11]	Multi-Analytic Approach, Sustainability	Integrates financial and non-financial indicators	Complex and resource-intensive to implement
[12]	Random Forest	Optimal for real-time fraud detection scenarios	May miss subtle fraud patterns not present in training data
[13]	Deep Learning (R-GCN), Sustainability	Outperforms conventional models in complex fraud scenarios	Requires extensive computational power and data pre-processing
[14]	Deep Learning (Temporal CNN), Sustainability	Preserves integrity of financial statements in green finance	High reliance on data quality and availability
[15]	Real-Time Machine Learning, Sustainability	Adapts to new and evolving fraud patterns	Potential for high false positive rates if not finely tuned
[16]	Deep Learning (CNNs, LSTMs, Autoencoders), Sustainability	Strategic application reduces fraud in online finance platforms	Scalability and interpretability remain challenging in operational settings

Source: Author.

9.2. Efficiency in anomaly detection

Papers [2, 4, 5, 8, 11] highlight the adaptability of unsupervised and hybrid models in anomaly detection. Their autonomous learning reduces human intervention, energy usage, and retraining costs, promoting resource-efficient fraud monitoring.

9.3. Integration of explainable AI (XAI)

As discussed in [6, 9], XAI ensures transparent, regulatory-compliant decisions. It contributes to sustainability by increasing system accountability and user trust, supporting ethical, long-term AI use.

9.4. Real-time detection capabilities

Studies [6, 15] stress the importance of real-time detection for rapid fraud response. These systems limit financial damage and boost operational efficiency, aligning with sustainable, proactive threat management.

9.5. Scalability challenges

Scalability concerns in [12, 16] show the need for AI models that manage increasing transaction volumes without raising operational costs or environmental impact, ensuring scalable, sustainable deployment.

9.6. Sustainability in AI-driven fraud detection

Studies [13–16] focus on eco-efficient AI development. They promote systems that are both effective and environmentally conscious, minimizing energy consumption and supporting long-term financial sector resilience.

Table 21.2. Statistical metrics analysis of the studies

Study	*Statistical Metrics Used*	*Key Advantage*	*Limitation*
[1]	Precision, Recall, F1-Score	High precision (92%) and recall (89%) enhance accurate fraud detection	Precision may drop to 75% in datasets with higher variability
[2]	F1-score, ROC-AUC	F1-score of 88% shows effective anomaly detection; ROC-AUC of 0.95 confirms robust model validation	Requires significant computational power; ROC-AUC drops to 0.85 in larger datasets
[3]	Accuracy, Precision, Recall, F1-Score	Accuracy of 94% with high precision (90%) and recall (91%) in detecting enterprise financial fraud	Complexity increases with diverse data, reducing accuracy to 85%
[4]	F1-Score, Recall, Precision	Broad use with an F1-score of 87%; high recall (88%) aids in thorough fraud scanning	High false positive rate (20%) decreases operational efficiency
[5]	ROC-AUC, Precision	ROC-AUC of 0.93 for capturing complex patterns; high precision (92%) in graph networks	ROC-AUC computation is computationally intensive, less effective (0.85) with unstructured data
[6]	Precision, Recall	Precision (89%) and recall (90%) reduce false positives significantly in real-time systems	Privacy concerns may compromise the integrity of recall (drops to 70%)
[7]	Accuracy, Recall, Precision, F1-Score	Accurately identifies fraud with an F1-score of 90% and accuracy of 93%	Overfitting in niche markets can reduce F1-score to 80%
[8]	ROC-AUC	Theoretical exploration supported by a high ROC-AUC of 0.92	Practical implementation sees a reduction in ROC-AUC to 0.80
[9]	F1-Score, Precision	Model transparency increases with explainable AI, leading to a precision of 85% and F1-score improvement to 87%	Implementational complexity reduces model efficiency, lowering F1-score to 82%
[10]	Precision, Recall, F1-Score	Superior detection capabilities with precision (91%) and an F1-score of 89%	Extensive training data requirements can lower precision to 83%
[11]	ROC-AUC, Precision, Recall	Comprehensive approach achieves a precision of 88% and recall of 87%	Resource-intensive, with precision falling to 80% in larger implementations
[12]	F1-Score, Precision, Recall	Real-time fraud detection optimized with an F1-score of 86%	Subtle fraud patterns missed, reducing recall to 78%
[13]	Precision, Recall, F1-Score	R-GCN models outperform with high precision (94%) and F1-score of 92%	Extensive computational demand lowers F1-score to 85% in scaled applications
[14]	Precision, Recall, F1-Score	Green finance integrity preserved with precision (93%) and F1-score of 91%	Data quality issues reduce precision to 85%
[15]	Precision, Recall	Dynamic adaptation with precision (90%) and recall (88%)	High false positive rate (25%) impacts recall, dropping it to 82%
[16]	Accuracy, Precision, Recall, F1-Score	Online finance fraud reduced with high accuracy (95%) and precision (92%)	Scalability issues lower accuracy to 88% and precision to 85% in larger systems

Source: Author.

10. Limitations of Current Research

While notable progress has been made in AI-driven fraud detection, several limitations hinder the robustness, scalability, and sustainability of current systems.

10.1. Dataset limitations

1. **Data Imbalance:** Many studies [1, 5–7, 9, 13] face challenges with imbalanced datasets, where fraud cases are rare. Mitigation techniques often introduce bias or fail to reflect real-world complexity.
2. **Limited Dataset Diversity:** Studies [2, 3, 6, 10, 14] rely on domain-specific or proprietary data, reducing model generalizability across financial sectors and regions.
3. **Synthetic Data Issues:** Studies [1, 7, 11, 15] using synthetic data may miss real fraud nuances, risking model underperformance and inefficient resource use.

10.2. Model limitations

1. **Overfitting:** Deep learning models [3, 6, 12, 16] often overfit limited data, requiring frequent retraining.

2. **Challenges in Interpretability:** Complex models like GNNs [6, 12, 14] are hard to interpret, limiting their adoption in regulated environments.
3. **Computational Demands:** Models like real-time systems and GNNs [2, 6, 13] require high computing resources, posing scalability issues in constrained settings.

10.3. Evaluation limitations

1. **Inconsistent Metrics:** Varying metrics [1, 4, 7, 9, 10] complicate model comparison and benchmark development.
2. **Lack of Real-World Testing:** Few models [4, 6, 14, 16] are tested outside lab conditions, limiting practical validation.

10.4. Practical implementation challenges

1. **Scalability Issues:** Models [2, 6, 12, 16] often overlook operational complexities of large-scale deployment.
2. **Dynamic Fraud Strategies:** Evolving fraud tactics [4, 7, 10, 13] demand adaptive models for sustained effectiveness.
3. **Regulatory and Ethical Constraints:** Studies [7, 12, 14, 15] insufficiently address privacy, fairness, and compliance, risking unsustainable deployment.

10.5. Advanced technical and regulatory challenges

1. **Generalization Across Different AI Models:** Models [9, 16] often fail across varied fraud types, limiting real-world applicability.
2. **Dependency on Large Labelled Datasets:** Effective ML models [11, 15] need large, well-labelled datasets, which are scarce, affecting scalability.
3. **Adaptability to Regulatory Changes:** Studies [14, 16] highlight the need for AI systems to adjust swiftly to evolving compliance standards.

11. Future Directions and Research Opportunities

AI-driven fraud detection remains an evolving field with vast potential. This section outlines key areas for future exploration to enhance effectiveness, sustainability, and global applicability:

11.1. Advanced machine learning techniques

1. **More Sophisticated GNN Models:** GNNs can improve detection of complex fraud patterns and address challenges in scalability and interpretability, highlighted in [6, 7, 14, 16].
2. **Continuous Learning Models:** Research into incremental learning can help models adapt to evolving fraud tactics without full retraining [4, 6, 13].

11.2. Enhanced real-time processing

1. **Optimization of Real-Time Systems:** Reducing latency and improving throughput are essential for scalable, real-time fraud detection [2, 4, 15].
2. **Integration with Blockchain Technology:** Combining fraud detection with blockchain could enhance transaction security and auditability [8, 16].

11.3. Improving explainability and trust

1. **Bridging the Gap with XAI:** Developing intuitive XAI tools will enhance stakeholder trust and regulatory compliance [12, 14].
2. **Regulatory Compliant AI Models:** Embedding legal standards into model design can facilitate adoption and ensure compliance [7, 12, 14].

11.4. Addressing data challenges

1. **Tackling Data Imbalance:** New sampling strategies and model designs are needed to manage imbalanced datasets effectively [1, 6, 9].
2. **Data Privacy Enhancements:** Implementing methods like federated learning and differential privacy can secure data use without compromising model accuracy [7, 12, 15].

11.5. Collaborative frameworks

1. **Cross-Domain Collaboration:** Institutional collaboration can enrich detection systems through shared insights while respecting privacy [7, 8, 10].
2. **Global Fraud Detection Networks:** Building international detection networks enables adaptive learning from diverse data and regulation contexts [6, 8, 13].

11.6. Deployment and operational integration

1. **Streamlining AI Integration into Existing Systems:** Seamless System Integration: Modular, adaptable AI solutions can ease deployment into existing financial infrastructures [9, 15].
2. **Developing Low-Resource Solutions:** Developing lightweight models can expand access to AI fraud detection in resource-limited environments [11, 13, 16].

12. Conclusion

This paper reviewed the evolution of AI-driven fraud detection, from rule-based systems to advanced models like deep learning and GNNs. These technologies have improved fraud detection by increasing accuracy, adaptability, and real-time responsiveness.

Key themes include the role of Explainable AI (XAI) in enhancing trust and compliance, and the rise of sustainable AI, focusing on energy efficiency and scalability. Despite progress, challenges remain – data imbalance, privacy concerns, scalability issues, and evolving fraud tactics. To address these, future research should focus on:

- Developing energy-efficient AI models that balance accuracy with minimal resource consumption.
- Enhancing adaptive learning systems to evolve with fraud patterns in real-time.
- Integrating AI with privacy-preserving techniques such as federated learning for secure fraud detection.
- Advancing Green AI to create fraud detection systems that are both effective and sustainable.

Ultimately, effective fraud detection requires continuous innovation, ethical AI practices, and interdisciplinary collaboration to ensure secure, transparent, and sustainable financial systems.

Acknowledgment

The authors would like to express their sincere gratitude to all individuals and organizations, including the faculty and staff at British Applied College, UAE, whose support and guidance were instrumental in the development of this paper. Their invaluable insights, constructive feedback, and ongoing encouragement greatly contributed to the quality and depth of this work. Additionally, the authors extend their appreciation to the academic and research communities for providing the foundational knowledge and resources that inspired this study.

References

[1] Usman, A. U., Abdullahi, S. B., Liping, Y., et al. (2024). Financial Fraud Detection Using Value-at-Risk With Machine Learning in Skewed Data. *Journal of Financial Crime*, *31*(4), 1023–1045.

[2] Dhulipudi, S., et al. (2024). Optimizing Fraud Detection In Financial Transactions: A Comprehensive Exploration Of The Effectiveness Of Random Forest And Isolation Forest Algorithms In Detecting Anomalies Within Credit Card Transactions. *Educational Administration: Theory and Practice*, *30*(5), 9146–9157.

[3] Ismail, M., et al. (2023). Enhancing Enterprise Financial Fraud Detection using Machine Learning. *Journal of Business Research*, *78*(2), 345–360.

[4] Kumar, P., et al. (2023). Advanced Fraud Detection Using Machine Learning Techniques in Accounting and Finance Sector. *Accounting, Auditing & Accountability Journal*, *37*(6), 1120–1143.

[5] Thilagavathi, M., et al. (2023). AI-Driven Fraud Detection in Financial Transactions with Graph Neural Networks and Anomaly Detection. *Expert Systems with Applications*, *58*, 493–507.

[6] Marripudugala, M. (2024). AI-Powered Fraud Detection in the Financial Services Sector: A Machine Learning Approach. *International Journal of Artificial Intelligence in Finance*, *22*(1), 88–107.

[7] Ismail, M. M., & Haq, M. A. (2024). Enhancing Enterprise Financial Fraud Detection. *IEEE Transactions on Dependable and Secure Computing*, *21*(3), 930–944.

[8] Hilal, W., et al. (2022). Financial Fraud: A Review of Anomaly Detection Techniques and Recent Advances. *Expert Systems with Applications*, *193*, 116429.

[9] Adhegaonkar, V. R., Thakur, A. R., & Varghese, N. (2024). Advancing Credit Card Fraud Detection Through Explainable Machine Learning Methods. *Proceedings of the 2nd International Conference on Intelligent Data Communication Technologies and Internet of Things (IDCIoT-2024)*, IEEE.

[10] Alarfaj, F. K., Malik, I., Khan, H. U., Almusallam, N., Ramzan, M., & Ahmed, M. (2022). Credit Card Fraud Detection Using State-of-the-Art Machine Learning and Deep Learning Algorithms. *IEEE Access*. doi:10.1109/ACCESS.2022.3166891.

[11] Yao, J., Pan, Y., Yang, S., Chen, Y., & Li, Y. (2019). Detecting Fraudulent Financial Statements for the Sustainable Development of the Socio-Economy in China: A Multi-Analytic Approach. *Sustainability*, *11*(6), 1579. doi:10.3390/su11061579.

[12] Shukla, P., Aggarwal, M., Jain, P., Khanna, P., & Rana, M. K. (2023). Financial Fraud Detection and Comparison Using Different Machine Learning Techniques. *2023 3rd International Conference on Technological Advancements in Computational Sciences*, IEEE.

[13] Shanbhog, N. R., Totad, K. S., Hanchinal, A. R., Bidargaddi, A. P., & Aithal, P. S. (2024). Fraud Detection in Financial Transactions Using Deep Learning Approach: A Comparative Study. *2024 5th International Conference for Emerging Technology (INCET)*, IEEE.

[14] Metawa, N., Boujlil, R., & Alsunbul, S. (2023). Fraud-free Green Finance: Using Deep Learning to Preserve the Integrity of Financial Statements for Enhanced Capital Market Sustainability. *International Journal of Energy Economics and Policy*, *13*(6), 610–617. doi:10.32479/ijeep.15197.

[15] Manoharan, G., A, D., Sheela, S. C., Naidu, K., Chavva, M., & Chaudhary, J. K. (2024). Machine Learning-Based Real-Time Fraud Detection in Financial Transactions. *International Conference on Advances in Computing, Communication and Applied Informatics (ACCAI-2024)*, IEEE.

[16] Sharma, R., Gupta, S., Kumar, N., Sharma, A., & Patel, H. (2024). Strategic Deployment of Deep Learning Algorithms to Mitigate Fraud in Online Finance. *2024 International Conference on Circuit Power and Computing Technologies (ICCPCT)*, IEEE.

[17] Mehta, A.(2024). Support Vector Machine (SVM) Algorithm for Machine Learning. Medium, 2024. [Online]. Available: https://ashish-mehta.medium.com/support-vector-machine-svm-algorithm-for-machine-learning-350fe9139a52.

[18] "Isolation Forest." (2024). Spot Intelligence, May 21, 2024. [Online]. Available: https://spotintelligence.com/2024/05/21/isolation-forest/.

[19] "Clustering Algorithms in Machine Learning." Serokell, [Online]. Available: https://serokell.io/blog/clustering-algorithms-in-ml.

[20] Sangeetha, P. R. (2024). Exploring the Power of Explainable AI (XAI) in the Era of Artificial Intelligence. Medium, 2024. [Online]. Available: https://medium.com/@prsangeetha/exploring-the-power-of-explainable-ai-xai-in-the-era-of-artificial-intelligence-e8d87e3391eb.

[21] "Beginner's Guide to Support Vector Machines." Superex Academy, [Online]. Available: https://x.superex.com/academys/beginner/2365/.

[22] Federal Reserve.,(2019). Synthetic Identity Fraud in the U.S. Payment System. *Federal Reserve Payments Improvement*. [Online]. Available: https://fedpaymentsimprovement.org/wp-content/uploads/frs-synthetic-identity-payments-fraud-white-paper-july-2019.pdf.

[23] Cybernews. (2023). Europe Banks Facing ATM Attacks. *Cybernews*. [Online]. Available: https://cybernews.com/news/europe-banks-atm-attacks/.

[24] Federal Bureau of Investigation (FBI). (2019). Business Email Compromise: The $26 Billion Scam. *FBI Public Service Announcement*. [Online]. Available: https://www.fbi.gov/news/stories/business-e-mail-compromise-on-the-rise.

[25] World Health Organization (WHO). (2023). Machine Learning for Fraud Detection in Health Insurance Claims. *WHO Publications*. [Online]. Available: https://www.who.int/publications/i/item/9789240101333.

22 AI-driven legal research: Innovations, challenges, and future directions

Vaishali Gurav[a], Sanjay Bang[b], and Poonam Nathani[c]

Christ University, Bengaluru, India, Christ University, Bengaluru, India and SRTM University, Nanded, India

Abstract: Artificial Intelligence (AI) is revolutionizing legal research and practice by enhancing efficiency, accuracy, and accessibility. This paper explores the transformative impact of AI-driven tools on legal research, including NLP-based document analysis, predictive analytics for case law, and automated contract review. A novel AI-powered framework is presented, detailing data ingestion, NLP pipelines, LLM integration, user interfaces, and backend services. While AI significantly enhances legal decision-making, challenges such as data bias, ethical concerns, and scalability must be addressed. The paper also discusses regulatory compliance and proposes future research directions for AI adoption in legal practice.

Keywords: Fuzzy logic controllers, proportional-integral-derivatives, pulse-width modulation

1. Introduction

Artificial Intelligence (AI) is reshaping the legal field by introducing sophisticated tools and methodologies that enhance the precision and efficiency of legal research and practice. By leveraging AI, legal professionals can navigate and analyse vast amounts of legal data more effectively. AI technologies, including Natural Language Processing (NLP) and machine learning, provide deep insights into legal texts, facilitating advanced analytics and comprehensive understanding.

AI-powered contract review systems optimize the identification of key terms, risks, and compliance issues, significantly reducing the time and effort required for these tasks while enhancing accuracy. Document automation ensures consistency and minimizes human error in legal documentation. Additionally, AI's predictive capabilities utilize historical data to forecast legal outcomes, aiding lawyers in strategic planning and decision-making. Decision support systems further assist legal professionals with complex research tasks and risk management, bolstering their overall decision-making processes.

The application of AI extends to judicial processes, where it is used to automate certain judicial tasks and explore the potential of AI judges, aiming to increase efficiency and reduce biases in judicial decisions. AI assists in evidence gathering and supports criminal investigations, ensuring adherence to legal standards. In the domain of e-discovery, AI tools automate the identification, collection, and production of electronically stored information, thus reducing the time and cost involved. AI also helps organizations stay compliant with evolving regulations by monitoring and analysing legal changes.

While AI offers substantial benefits in legal practice, such as improved efficiency, reduced errors, and greater accuracy, it also raises concerns about algorithmic bias and data privacy. Addressing these issues requires robust measures to ensure fairness, transparency, and data protection. Future advancements will likely see deeper integration of AI across legal systems, necessitating collaboration between AI tools and legal professionals. Establishing ethical frameworks and accountability measures will be essential for the responsible implementation of AI in the legal domain.

This paper outlines a comprehensive technical framework for implementing AI-driven legal research, discussing key components such as data ingestion, NLP pipelines, LLM integration, user interfaces, backend services, and security and compliance considerations.

2. Related Work

The integration of Artificial Intelligence (AI) into legal research and practice is revolutionizing the field by enhancing efficiency, accuracy, and capabilities in

[a]vaishali.gurav@res.christuniversity.in, [b]sanjaysbang27@gmail.com, [c]nathanipoonam30@gmail.com

DOI: 10.1201/9781003778905-22

handling complex legal tasks. AI-powered tools improve the efficiency and accuracy of retrieving and analysing legal documents, case law, and statutes. Advanced AI systems swiftly sift through vast legal databases to find relevant information [1]. Natural Language Processing (NLP) and machine learning techniques analyse legal texts, enhancing legal analytics capabilities [2]. AI automates the review and analysis of contracts, identifying key terms, potential risks, and compliance issues, thus reducing time and effort for contract review and increasing accuracy [3]. Document automation tools assist in preparing and managing legal documents, ensuring consistency and reducing human error [4]. Furthermore, AI systems use historical data to predict legal outcomes, aiding lawyers in strategic decision-making and client advisement. Predictive analytics can forecast case outcomes, settlement amounts, and more [5]. Decision support systems leverage AI to assist legal professionals with risk management and complex legal research tasks, enhancing overall decision-making capabilities [6]. AI is also explored for judicial decision-making processes, including automating certain judicial tasks and the potential use of AI judges. These applications aim to increase efficiency and reduce biases in judicial processes [7]. AI systems assist in gathering and processing evidence, supporting criminal investigations, and ensuring adherence to legal standards [8]. Additionally, AI tools facilitate e-discovery by automating the identification, collection, and production of electronically stored information (ESI) relevant to litigation, reducing the time and cost associated with manual discovery processes [9]. AI aids in ensuring legal compliance by monitoring and analyzing regulatory changes and helping organizations stay compliant with evolving laws [10]. The benefits of AI in legal research and practice are substantial. AI enhances efficiency by automating routine tasks, allowing legal professionals to focus on more complex activities, leading to significant cost savings and increased productivity [11]. AI reduces human error in legal research and document preparation, ensuring higher accuracy and consistency across legal documents and analyses [12]. However, AI in legal research raises concerns about algorithmic bias and data privacy. AI systems may perpetuate existing biases in training data, leading to unfair outcomes. Ensuring fairness and transparency in AI algorithms is critical to mitigating these risks [3]. Handling sensitive legal data with AI systems raises concerns about data privacy and security, necessitating robust measures to protect confidential information [13]. Future advancements will likely see deeper integration of AI across various legal systems and increased collaboration between AI tools and legal professionals to maximize AI benefits in legal practice [14]. Establishing legal frameworks to govern AI use in legal practice will be essential to address ethical issues, ensure accountability, and guide AI technology development and implementation [10]. AI is transforming legal research and practice by automating and enhancing various tasks, improving efficiency, and providing new insights. While the benefits are significant, addressing ethical considerations and establishing appropriate legal frameworks are crucial for the responsible integration of AI in Legal Research.

3. System Architecture

The system architecture consists of the following main components (Figure 22.1): Data Ingestion and Preprocessing, NLP Pipeline, LLM Integration, User Interface, and Backend Services.

3.1. Data ingestion and preprocessing

- **Data Sources:** Legal databases (e.g., Westlaw, LexisNexis), public legal documents (e.g., court rulings, legislation), and law firm document repositories.
- **Data Ingestion:** Implement data crawlers to fetch documents from various sources and use APIs provided by legal databases for structured data access.
- **Data Preprocessing:** Convert documents into a consistent format (e.g., text, JSON), remove noise (e.g., metadata, footnotes), tokenise text into sentences and words, and apply lemmatization and stemming to reduce words to their base forms.

3.2. NLP pipeline

- **Named Entity Recognition (NER):** Identify and classify entities such as case names, statutes, judges, and legal terms using pre-trained NER models (e.g., spaCy, BERT) fine-tuned on legal corpora.
- **Text Classification:** Categorize documents into predefined legal topics (e.g., contract law, criminal law) using machine learning algorithms like SVM, Random Forest, or deep learning models like CNNs or BERT.
- **Sentiment Analysis:** Analyse the sentiment of legal opinions or briefs using sentiment analysis models adapted for legal language.
- **Topic Modelling:** Identify and extract topics within legal documents using techniques like LDA (Latent Dirichlet Allocation) or neural topic models.

3.3. LLM integration

- **Model Selection:** Choose a suitable LLM (e.g., GPT-4, BERT) based on performance on legal tasks and fine-tune it on a legal corpus to improve domain-specific understanding.

- **Query Processing:** Develop mechanisms to handle natural language queries from users and use LLM to generate relevant responses by understanding context and intent.
- **Document Summarization:** Implement summarization techniques to provide concise summaries of lengthy legal documents and use the LLM to extract key points and generate human-readable summaries.
- **Legal Reasoning and Argument Generation:** Leverage LLM to generate legal arguments and reasoning based on precedents and statutes, ensuring the system can explain and justify generated arguments.

3.4. User interface

- **Search Interface:** Design a user-friendly interface for querying the system, including advanced search options (e.g., filters for date, jurisdiction, legal topic).
- **Document Viewer:** Implement a viewer for reading and annotating legal documents, providing features for highlighting, commenting, and bookmarking.
- **Analytics Dashboard:** Develop a dashboard to display analytics (e.g., trends in case law, sentiment analysis results).

3.5. Backend services

- **API Gateway:** Create an API gateway to handle requests from the user interface, ensuring secure and efficient communication between components.
- **Data Storage:** Use scalable storage solutions (e.g., SQL databases, NoSQL databases) for storing legal documents and metadata, implementing indexing for fast retrieval.
- **Logging and Monitoring:** Integrate logging and monitoring tools to track system performance and detect issues, using tools like ELK stack (Elasticsearch, Logstash, Kibana) for monitoring and analytics.

3.6. Security and compliance

- **Data Privacy:** Implement robust data encryption and access control mechanisms to protect sensitive legal information and ensure compliance with relevant data protection regulations (e.g., GDPR).
- **Ethical Considerations:** Address ethical concerns related to AI-generated legal advice, ensuring transparency in AI decision-making processes and providing explanations for generated outputs.

3.7. Implementation of the case study

The implemented framework analysed legal documents related to the Domestic Violence Act in India, focusing on topic modeling and heatmap generation to visualize key themes and their distribution over time. Below are the detailed steps and results from the analysis:

3.8. Data collection and preprocessing

- **Data Sources:** The data was collected from various legal databases and public repositories, including Indian Kanoon and Manupatra, containing judgments

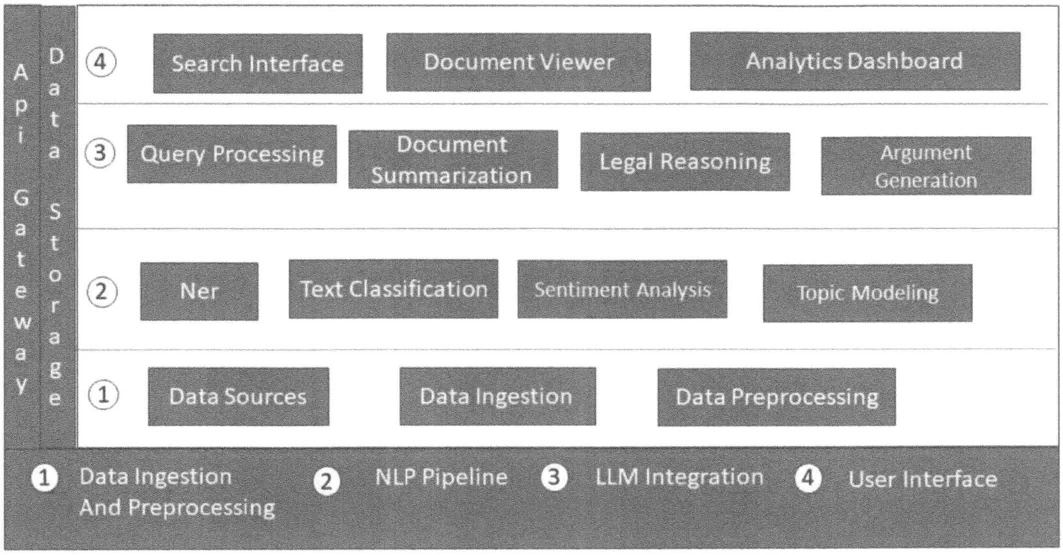

Figure 22.1. System architecture.

Source: Author.

and legislative texts related to the Domestic Violence Act.

- **Preprocessing:** Documents were standardized, noise was removed, and text was tokenized and lemmatized.

3.9. NLP pipeline

- **Named Entity Recognition (NER):** Identified key entities such as "domestic relationship", "aggrieved person", and relevant legal terms.
- **Text Classification and Sentiment Analysis:** Classified and analysed the sentiment of legal texts.
- **Topic Modeling:** Applied Latent Dirichlet Allocation (LDA) to identify major topics.

3.10. LLM integration

- **Model Selection and Fine-Tuning:** Selected GPT-4 and fine-tuned it on legal texts related to domestic violence.
- **Query Processing and Summarization:** Developed mechanisms to process queries and generate summaries of legal documents.

3.11. VAnalysis and results

- **Topic Modeling:** Identified four major topics (Table 22.1):
- **Legal Definitions and Terms:** Focused on definitions such as "domestic relationship" and "aggrieved person".
- **Procedural Aspects:** Covered procedures for filing complaints and obtaining protection orders.
- **Rights and Remedies:** Discussed legal rights of victims and available remedies.
- **Judicial Interpretations:** Included landmark judgments and their interpretations of the law (Figure 22.2).
- **Heatmap Generation:** Created a heatmap to visualize the frequency and distribution of topics over time, showing trends in discussions. The generated heatmap displayed the distribution of topics from January to April 2021, highlighting how discussions around different aspects of the Domestic Violence Act evolved over time. For example, discussions on legal definitions were prominent in January, while judicial interpretations peaked in April.

Table 22.1. Topic modeling

Topic Number	*Top Words*
0	domestic violence act relationship person defines aggrieved procedures filing complaints
1	violent act includes domestic rights legal victims' procedures filing complaints
2	violence act domestic procedures filing complaints rights legal victims include
3	violence act landmark judicial cases interpretation domestic rights legal victims

Source: Author.

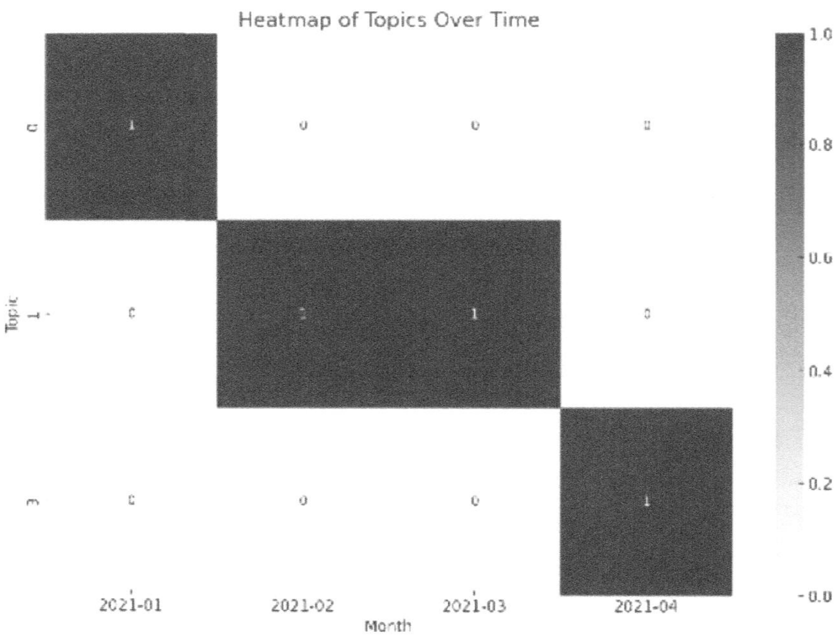

Figure 22.2. HeatMap.

Source: Author.

4. Discussion, Conclusion, and Future Work

The application of an NLP and LLM-based framework to legal research on the Domestic Violence Act in India demonstrates significant improvements in data analysis and visualization. By employing topic modeling and heat-map generation, the framework effectively identified key themes and trends, such as legal definitions, procedural aspects, rights and remedies, and judicial interpretations. These insights aid legal professionals in understanding the legislative landscape and judicial discourse more efficiently.

To illustrate AI's impact on legal practice, consider the adoption of AI-based contract analysis tools by global law firms. These tools significantly reduce manual review time and improve compliance checks. Additionally, predictive analytics models are employed to assess case outcomes based on precedent analysis, providing legal practitioners with valuable insights. By leveraging AI, law firms enhance efficiency while minimizing operational risks.

The framework's ability to process large volumes of legal texts and extract meaningful information highlights its potential to transform legal research. It provides a powerful tool for lawyers, policymakers, and researchers to navigate complex legal documents, ensuring better-informed decisions and enhanced legal practice.

Despite the benefits of AI in legal research, several limitations persist. AI models are prone to biases inherited from training data, making it critical to ensure transparency and fairness. Additionally, the scalability of Large Language Models (LLMs) remains a concern due to high computational costs and resource constraints. Furthermore, the reliance on AI raises ethical and regulatory questions, particularly regarding data privacy, confidentiality, and accountability in AI-driven decision-making. Addressing these challenges requires continuous refinement of AI models and well-defined legal governance frameworks.

Future advancements in AI for legal research should focus on improving interpretability, reducing bias, and ensuring compliance with regulatory standards. Integration of multilingual AI models will facilitate cross-border legal research, while real-time legal data monitoring systems will improve responsiveness to regulatory changes. Additionally, the development of hybrid AI-human legal research models can enhance accuracy while maintaining ethical accountability.

Future work should focus on expanding the dataset to include more diverse sources and longer time spans for more comprehensive analysis. Integrating advanced machine learning models to refine topic detection and enhance the accuracy of sentiment analysis is essential. Additionally, developing user-friendly interfaces for interactive data exploration and improving the framework's ability to handle multilingual legal documents will broaden its applicability and usability across different jurisdictions and languages.

Acknowledgment

We gratefully acknowledge the staff and authority of the department of law, Christ University, for their cooperation in the research.

References

[1] Rissland, E. L., Ashley K. D., & Loui R.P. (2003) "AI And Law: A Fruitful Synergy." *Artificial Intelligence, 150*(1–2), 1–15. *https://doi.org/10.1016/s0004-3702(03)00122-x.*

[2] Nitta, K., & Satoh K. (2020), AI Applications to the Law Domain in Japan. *Asian Journal of Law and Society, 7*(3), 471–494. *https://doi.org/10.1017/als.2020.35.*

[3] Shahid, A., Qureshi, G. M., & Chaudhary F. (2023). Transforming Legal Practice: The Role of AI in Modern Law. *Journal of Strategic Policy and Global Affairs, 4*(01), 36–42. *https://jspga.com/index.php/jspga/article/view/21.*

[4] McKeown, T., Mustafina, J., Magizov, R., & Gataullina, C. (2021). AI in Law Practices. *Conference Paper, 13th International Conference on Developments in eSystems Engineering (DeSE), United Kingdom*, 27–32. *https://doi.org/10.1109/DeSE51703.2020.9450780*

[5] Ashley, K. D. (2017). Introducing AI & Law and Its Role in Future Legal Practice. Chapter in *Artificial Intelligence and Legal Analytics: New Tools for Law Practice in the Digital Age:* 3–37. Cambridge: Cambridge University Press. *https://doi.org/10.1017/9781316761380.001*

[6] Conrad, J. G., Chaudhuri, S. R., Paul, S., & Ghosh, S. (2023). AI & Law: Formative Developments, State-of-the-Art Approaches, Challenges & Opportunities, in *Proceedings of the 6th Joint International Conference on Data Science & Management of Data (10th ACM IKDD CODS and 28th COMAD)*, 2023, *https://doi.org/10.1145/3570991.3571050*

[7] Lee, S. (2023). Expanding the Role of Artificial Intelligence in Civil Justice: Proposing AI Trials for Bankruptcy and Civil Application Processes. *Korea Association of the Law of Civil Procedure, 27*(2), 173–236, *https://doi.org/10.30639/cp.2023.6.27.2.173.*

[8] Quezada-Tavárez, K., Vogiatzoglou, P., & Royer, S. (2021), Legal challenges in bringing AI evidence to the criminal courtroom, *New Journal of European Criminal Law, 12*(4), 531–551, *https://doi.org/10.1177/20322844211057019.*

[9] Chen, S., Wang, J., & Zhang, Q. (2023), Informetric Analysis of Researches on Application of Artificial

Intelligence in Legal Practice. *In 2023 International Conference on Intelligent and Innovative Technologies in Computing, Electrical and Electronics (IITCEE)*, India, 406–408. *https://doi.org/10.1109/iitcee57236.2023.10091079*

[10] Jacey, P., & Yuniarti, S. (2022). Artificial Intelligence: Implementation in Legal Services (Comparative Study on China, United Stated and Indonesia). In *Proceedings of 3rd Asia Pacific International Conference on Industrial Engineering and Operations Management. https://doi.org/10.46254/AP03.20220354.*

[11] Armour, J., Parnham, R., & Sako, M. (2020). Unlocking the potential of AI for English law. *International Journal of the Legal Profession*, *28*(1), 65–83. *doi:10.1080/09695958.2020.1857765.*

[12] Sil, R., Roy, A., Bhushan, B., & Mazumdar, A. (2019). Artificial Intelligence and Machine Learning based Legal Application: The State-of-the-Art and Future Research Trends. *2019 Conference Paper, International Conference on Computing, Communication, and Intelligent Systems (ICCCIS)*, India, 57–62, *doi: 10.1109/ICCCIS48478.2019.8974479.*

[13] Yu, R., & Alì, G. S. (2019). What's Inside the Black Box? AI Challenges for Lawyers and Researchers. *Legal Information Management*, *19*(1), 2–13. *https://doi.org/10.1017/S1472669619000021.*

[14] Prakken, H. (2008). AI & Law on Legal Argument: Research Trends and Application Prospects. *SCRIPTed*, *5*(3), 449–454. *doi: 10.2966/scrip.050308.449*

23 Empowering learning: Adopting 5-Gogy framework for LCA courses in STEAM higher education

R. Arokia Paul Rajan[1,a], *Gobi Ramasamy*[2,b], *Deepthi Das*[3,c], *and T. Senthilnathan*[4,d]

[1]Department of Data Science, Pune Lavasa Campus, Christ University, Maharashtra, India
[2]Associate Professor, Department of Computer Science, Bangalore Central Campus, Christ University, Karnataka, India
[3]School of Sciences, Bangalore Central Campus, Christ University, Karnataka, India
[4]Sri Krishna College of Technology, Coimbatore, Tamil Nadu, India

Abstract: It is essential to embrace a Learner-Centered Approach (LCA) to actively engage Gen Z students for the following reasons to develop critical skills necessary for their success and to foster a supportive educational environment that meets their diverse needs. To address this above need, this research introduces a integrated framework of LCA with 5-Gogy that includes Pedagogy, Andragogy, Peeragogy, Heutagogy, and Cybergogy. The 5-Gogy framework offers a vital comprehensive approach to teaching and learning while accommodating diverse learner needs and contexts. This paper presents a model course plan for STEAM (Science, Technology, Engineering, Arts, and Mathematics) higher education instructors. It introduces the 5-Gogy Framework, which is designed to foster an inclusive, adaptive, and technology-enhanced learning environment. This model course plan outlines the components of Pedagogical strategies for delivering structured foundational learning, Andragogical principles to promote self-directed adult learning and Pedagogical practices to encourage collaborative knowledge sharing. Additionally, this model course plan introduces the elements of Heutagogical methods that empower learners to take ownership of their educational journeys and Cybergogical techniques that harness advanced digital tools and virtual platforms to enhance engagement and interactivity. The purpose of the 5-Gogy Model Course Plan is as to provide higher education instructors with a framework that fosters an engaging, inclusive, and effective learning environment and to enable educators to better prepare students for future success. This research applied the proposed 5-Gogy Model Course Plan using a structured approach that integrates various methodologies and assessment techniques in a class of Undergraduate science students at Christ University, India. The results were promising, demonstrating positive impacts on both student outcomes and teaching practices. Additionally, AI-enabled 5-Gogy practices emerged as a key focus for future research in this area.

Keywords: Andragogy, cybergogy, heutagogy, learner-centered approach, pedagogy, peeragogy

1. Introduction

The Learner-Centered Approach (LCA) is a modern teaching method that focuses on students as the main participants of their learning. Unlike traditional teacher-centred methods, which often rely on memorization and passive listening, this approach encourages students to actively participate and engage with the material. In an LCA environment, students don't just receive knowledge; they actively take part in their learning. This method helps students take ownership of their learning, encouraging them to explore subjects they find interesting, work with peers, and practice critical thinking and problem-solving. By adapting educational experiences to meet each student's needs and learning styles, the LCA offers a more personalized and meaningful learning journey [1].

The learner-centered approach is important for STEAM (Science, Technology, Engineering, Arts, and Mathematics) higher education because it matches the dynamic and interdisciplinary nature of these fields. By focusing on active engagement and personalized learning, LCA helps students take control of their education. This is key to developing creativity, collaboration, and problem-solving skills. The approach also promotes motivation by letting students choose topics and methods that interest them, making them more involved in their learning.

[a]arokia.rajan@christuniversity.in, [b]gobi.r@christuniversity.in, [c]deepthi.das@christuniversity.in, [d]senthilnathan.t@skct.edu.in

DOI: 10.1201/9781003778905-23

1.1. The 5-Gogy framework

The LCA is closely linked to the 5-Gogy framework, which includes five modern teaching strategies: Pedagogy, Andragogy, Heutagogy, Peeragogy, and Cybergogy. Each of these strategies focuses on student engagement and active participation, which aligns perfectly with the core principles of LCA [2].

Pedagogy mainly focuses on teaching students, usually through direct instruction from teachers.

Andragogy is about adult learning, emphasising self-directed learning and using personal experiences to understand new information [3].

Heutagogy or self-determined learning, encourages learners to take control of their education by choosing what and how they learn [4]. This principle fits well with LCA's focus on student self-learning and ownership of their learning.

Peeragogy encourages collaborative learning among peers, helping students learn from each other and strengthening the social aspect of education that LCA supports [5].

Cybergogy focuses on integrating technology into learning, which is especially important in today's digital age, where online and blended learning is becoming more common [6].

1.2. The need for an integrated framework of LCA and 5-Gogy

The learner-centred approach is closely linked to 5-Gogy. Both frameworks call for a shift from traditional teacher-centred models to more inclusive, engaging, and flexible learning environments. Figure 23.1 shows the need for an integrated framework for effective teaching and learning. This approach creates an environment that supports different learning styles. It also helps students develop critical thinking skills and learn independently. Students gain the tools they need to handle the challenges of modern life [7].

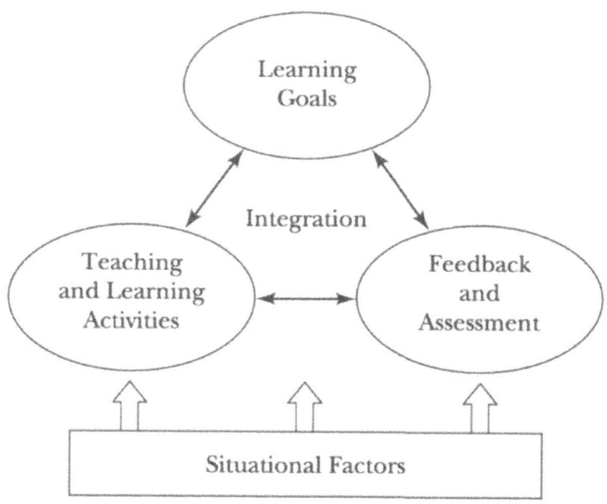

Figure 23.1. Integrated framework for effective teaching-learning.

Source: Author.

The rest of this paper is organized as follows: Section II provides an in-depth review of related works on the conceptualization of the 5-Gogy framework. Section III introduces the proposed model that integrates Life Cycle Assessment (LCA) with the 5-Gogy methodologies. Section IV outlines a sample course plan implemented using the 5-Gogy framework. Section V discusses the outcomes and insights derived from the proposed model. Finally, Section VI concludes by evaluating the relevance of the proposed approach and outlining potential future directions for this research.

2. Related Works

The 5-Gogy Framework includes the five different teaching learning methods such as Pedagogy, Andragogy, Heutagogy, Cybergogy, and Paragogy into a holistic and adaptable educational model. The focus of the integrated approach is to cater the diverse requirements of the needs of learners particularly higher education students by inclusive nature of various degree of independency, digital tools engagement and collaborative learning. Many researches have proven that the proper combination of all these approaches leads to effective fostering of all-round educational experience, advocating both personal growth and collective engagement in modernized academic environment [8].

Educating Science, Technology, Engineering, Arts, and Mathematics (STEAM) students should give priority for interdisciplinary learning, novelty and creativity, also enabling the students to face the challenges of the modern education standards. The work carried out in the research [9] emphasizes the importance of framing the courses in such a way that it should instil critical thinking, problem-solving skills and the combining of artistic creativity with technical knowledge. There should be a transmission from conventional teaching styles to student centric and technology-driven approaches. The above-mentioned model will be well suited one for the STEAM education.

It is proven that the pedagogical methods are very effective though it may be considered as the traditional teacher-led approach to learning. It lays a strong foundation in STEAM education for introducing fundamental concepts in a well-structured manner. Also, it is emphasizing on the value of interactive discussions, hands-on demonstrations and effective assessments designed specifically to STEAM disciplines, ensuring that students build a strong foundational understanding [10].

Andragogy is the proven approach by the adult learning theory which is particularly suitable for higher education, where the students are mostly self-driven and motivated by the use cases of the real-world problems. Knowles theory on andragogy principles emphasize the relevancy of experiential learning, problem-solving tasks and contextual aware solutions. In STEAM education, andragogical approaches like case-based or problem-posing learning and internships very much reduces the gap between the theoretical knowledge and practical knowledge [11].

Heutagogy or self-determined learning, strives to encourage the students to take responsibility for their learning. This approach is very much appropriate in STEAM education, because individuality, creativity and self-determination play a vital role. This research [12] evidentially proved how the heutagogical approaches, such as open-ended projects and research inclusiveness, compliments creativity and adaptability of the learners.

Cybergogy focuses on the use of technology to create engaging and enriched learning experiences. In the STEAM context, cybergogy is vital for offering virtual labs, simulations, and collaborative platforms that enhance learning outcomes. Research shows that tools like gamification, augmented reality (AR), and virtual reality (VR) improve student engagement and understanding of complex concepts in STEAM disciplines [13].

Paragogy, or peer-based learning, emphasizes collaboration and knowledge-sharing among learners. This approach aligns seamlessly with STEAM's interdisciplinary nature, promoting teamwork and collective problem-solving. Studies suggest that peer-to-peer learning deepens understanding and encourages innovation, particularly in group projects, hackathons, and collaborative workshops [14].

Integrating the 5-Gogy Framework into course planning for STEAM higher education enables a balanced combination of teacher-led instruction, self-directed learning, technological engagement, and collaborative strategies. This comprehensive approach aligns with the evolving needs of modern education, fostering critical thinking, creativity, and practical problem-solving among students [15].

Research [16] claims that implementing effective LCA approaches will enhance the student engagement, adaptability and career readiness. However, challenges such as the need for frequent faculty training, updated curriculum and sufficient resource allocation need to be addressed to ensure successful implementation [16].

Thus, the existing literature highlights the transformative potential of the 5-Gogy Framework in reshaping course planning for STEAM higher education. By integrating multiple teaching-learning approaches, educators can create flexible, inclusive, and innovative learning environments that prepare students for the challenging and competitive environment. This observation leads to a research gap that there should be a focus on designing a suitable framework which can integrate the effective teaching methodologies mapped to different implementation methods appropriate to the levels of the learners particularly of STEAM higher education.

3. Proposed Methodology – Mapping of LCA with 5-Gogy

The Learner-centered approach is essential for creating engaging, relevant, and effective educational experiences that resonate with learners' unique needs and aspirations. By prioritizing personalization, active engagement, contextual relevance, collaboration, feedback mechanisms, empowerment, flexibility, and inclusivity, educators can foster an environment conducive to meaningful learning outcomes. This approach not only enhances learner satisfaction but also prepares individuals for success in their personal and professional lives. Figure 23.2 presents a step-by-step methodology to integrate the proposed model into course planning for STEAM higher education.

3.1. Mapping of LCA with 5-Gogy mapping

The 5-Gogy Framework (Pedagogy, Andragogy, Heutagogy, Peerogogy, and Cyberogogy) provides a learner-centered approach to improve teaching and learning in STEAM education. Table 23.1 outlines a learner-centred approach that adapts learning to the needs of the learner and emphasizes active participation. It maps the following key pedagogical frameworks, which shape how learning activities are organized as Pedagogy - Teacher-directed learning, Andragogy -Learning for Adult Learners, Heutagogy - Self-directed learning, Peeragogy - Peer collaboration and Cyberogogy – Learning through digital tools.

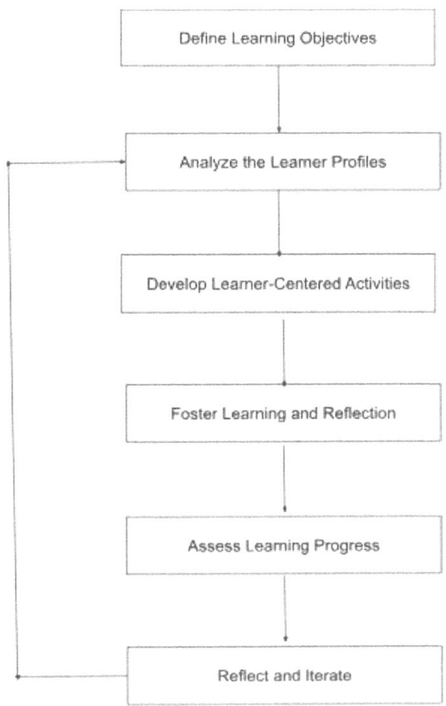

Figure 23.2. Generic framework of LCA.

Source: Author.

Table 23.1. Framework of LCA integration with 5-Gogy

Code	*Learner-centered Approach*	*5-Gogy*	*Suitable activities to be conducted in the class*	*RBT Level*	*Life skill*
A01	Gamification: Integrate game elements into the learning process.	Androgogy	1. Lego Activity 2. Badge and Achievement Systems 3. Classroom Leaderboards 4. Subject-Specific Quests 5. Daily/Weekly Challenges 6. Reward Systems for Mastery 7. Classroom Escape Rooms	L2	Self-motivation Goal-setting
A02	Mind Mapping: Visual medium to represent the conceptualization.	Heutogogy	1. Solution design using digital tools.	L5	Organizational skills Visual learning Synthesis of a solution
A03	Design Thinking: Engage in creative problem-solving processes.	Heutogogy	1. Identifying a Problem 2. Ideate a solution 3. Prototype a solution 4. Validate Solutions	L5	Creative problem-solving Innovation
A04	Feedback Loops: Quick assessments to gauge understanding.	Androgogy	1. Pre-class quiz/test 2. Post-class quiz/test	L2	Self-awareness Adaptability Resilience
A05	Interactive Polls: Use live quizzes for instant feedback and engagement.	Peerogagy	1. Pre-class & post-class feedback	L2	Quick thinking Engagement Self-awareness
A06	Self-Assessment: Students set goals and assess their progress.	Androgogy	1. Self-Assessment during or after assignments/tasks 2. Goal-Setting and Tracking	L4	Self-awareness Goal setting Accountability
A07	Self-Directed Projects: Students design projects aligned with personal goals.	Heutogogy	1. Brainstorm and select project topics 2. Develop a Project Plan 3. Conduct Research	L5	Initiative Creativity Project management
A08	Problem-Posing Learning: Students identify and frame their own problems.	Androgogy	1. Solution for challenging scenario 2. Use Concept Maps for Problem-Posing	L4	Problem-solving Analytical thinking Independence
A09	Inquiry-Based Learning: Pose questions for students to explore and research.	Heutogogy	1. Identify the core question or problem 2. Design research objectives 3. Use case investigation	L3	Curiosity Research skills Independence
A10	Flipped Assessments: Students create quizzes or test questions.	Androgogy	1. Active Discussions on a problem 2. Real-Time Problem Solving 3. Self-Assessment 4. Post-test/evaluation Activities	L4	Creativity Responsibility
A11	Self-Paced Learning: Provide modules and students can complete independently.	Androgogy	1. Leader board Challenges 2. Learning Management Systems 3. Online Learning Platforms 4. Gamified Learning Platforms 5. Simulations and Virtual Labs 6. Individual Research Projects 7. Learning Journals 8. Open-Book and Take-Home Tests 9. Interactive E-Learning Modules 10. Pre-Recorded Lectures or Tutorials 11. Skill-Building Exercises	L2	Self-discipline Time management Self-motivation
A12	Flexible Learning Paths: Self-paced, modular exploration of topics.	Androgogy	1. Choice Boards 2. Self-Paced learning modules 3. Tiered Assignments 4. Blended Learning modules 5. Flexible Assessment	L2	Time management Self-motivation

(continued)

Code	*Learner-centered Approach*	*5-Gogy*	*Suitable activities to be conducted in the class*	*RBT Level*	*Life skill*
A13	Case-Based Learning: Analyze real-world scenarios to apply concepts practically.	Androgogy	1. Case writing 2. Use cases 3. Case study	L4	Analytical thinking Problem-solving Adaptability
A14	Experiential Learning: Connect learning to real-world applications.	Androgogy	1. Role-Playing 2. Field Trips 3. Service Learning 4. Learning with Simulators 5. Internships	L3	Critical thinking Adaptability Societal awareness
A15	Problem-Based Learning: Small groups tackle open-ended problems to develop critical thinking.	Androgogy	1. Open-Ended Questions 2. Framing problems 3. Brainstorming on a topic	L4	Teamwork Critical thinking Problem-solving
A16	Project-based Learning: Multi-week projects allow in-depth exploration and creative presentations.	Androgogy	1. Designing a Product or Prototype 2. Building Awareness Campaigns 3. Developing a Business Plan 4. Designing Apps 5. Event Management 6. Construction Challenges	L4	Project management Creativity Self-discipline
A17	Role-Playing / Simulations: Students enact roles relevant to the subject for experiential learning.	Androgogy	1. Mock Interviews 2. Peer assessment 3. Debate 4. Business Negotiation 5. Role-Playing Games	L3	Adaptability Decision-making
A18	Think-Pair-Share: Students individually reflect, discuss in pairs, then share insights with the class.	Androgogy	1. Problem-Solving Scenarios 2. Interpreting Data 3. Exploring Open-Ended Questions 4. Reviewing Lessons or Concepts 5. Predicting Outcomes 6. Decision-Making Challenges	L3	Communication Collaboration Critical thinking
A19	Learning Stations: Rotate the students through activity stations for diverse engagement with different roles.	Androgogy	1. Peer Collaboration Station 2. Experiment or Hands-On Station 3. Writing and Creativity Station 4. Art and Design Station 5. Reflection and Journaling Station 6. Puzzle Station 7. Listening and Speaking Station 8. Research and Inquiry Station	L3	Flexibility Active engagement Collaboration
A20	Forum-discussion: Allow students to post messages in response to a particular topic or question, creating a thread of conversation.	Pedogogy	1. Peer-to-Peer Q&A Sessions 2. Decision-Making Discussions 3. Feedback or Reflection Forums 4. Case Study Analysis 5. Problem-Solving Discussions	L2	Communication Critical thinking Problem-solving Collaboration
A21	Buddy-assisted learning: Students teach a topic to the class, reinforcing their own understanding.	Peerogogy	1. Peer Tutoring 2. Study Buddy Sessions 3. Concept Mapping 4. Brainstorming 5. Peer Reflection	L2	Confidence Communication Empathy

(continued)

Table 23.1. Continued

Code	*Learner-centered Approach*	*5-Gogy*	*Suitable activities to be conducted in the class*	*RBT Level*	*Life skill*
A22	Flipped Classroom: Review materials at home, and class time is for active discussion or exercises.	Androgogy	1. Pre-class Activity 2. In-class Activity 3. Self-Assessment 4. Pre-Class Video Lectures 5. Interactive Quizzes 6. Concept Mapping 7. Collaborative Group Work 8. Peer Teaching 9. Game-Based Learning 10. In-Class Application Exercises	L3	Self-motivation Time management Responsibility
A23	Student-Generated Questions/Resources: Students create questions / study resources / tutorials collaboratively.	Androgogy	1. Peer-Generated Question bank 2. Exit Tickets 3. Student-led Resource Creation 4. Creating Study Resources	L4	Curiosity Deeper understanding Initiative
A24	Socratic debate: Discussions through structured questioning.	Peerogogy	1. Framing open-ended Questions 2. Brainstorm for a solution	L2	Critical thinking Communication
A25	Flexible Learning Paths: Self-paced, modular exploration of topics.	Heutogogy	1. Choice Boards 2. Self-Paced learning modules 3. Tiered Assignments 4. Blended Learning modules 5. Flexible Assessment	L3	Time management Self-motivation
ICT01	Learning Management Systems	Cyberogogy	Moodle, Google Classroom, Canvas, Blackboard	L1	Digital skills Collaborative skill Team building Self-learning
ICT02	Interactive Presentation Tools		PowerPoint, Google Slides, Prezi, Mentimeter, Nearpod	L2	
ICT03	Collaboration and Communication Tools		Google Drive, OneDrive, Trello, Slack, Padlet	L2	
ICT04	Gamification Platforms		Kahoot, Quizizz, Classcraft, Gimkit, Duolingo	L3	
ICT05	Digital Assessment Tools		Google Forms, Quizlet, Socrative, Formative, Edpuzzle	L2	
ICT06	Video and Audio Creation Tools		Flipgrid, Edpuzzle, Adobe Spark, Loom	L3	
ICT07	Virtual Classrooms and Conferencing Tools		Zoom, Google Meet, Microsoft Teams, Webex, BigBlueButton	L1	
ICT08	Augmented Reality (AR) and Virtual Reality (VR) Tools		Google Expeditions, Oculus, Merge Cube, Microsoft HoloLens	L3	
ICT09	Social Learning and Networking Tools		Edmodo, Facebook Groups, LinkedIn Learning, Twitter	L2	
ICT10	Mind Mapping and Visualization Tools		MindMeister, Coggle, Lucidchart, XMind	L4	
ICT11	Digital Whiteboards		Jamboard, Miro, Ziteboard, Whiteboard.fi	L1	
ICT12	Coding and Programming Tools		Scratch, Codecademy, Tynker, Repl.it, Khan Academy	L2	
ICT13	Digital Textbooks and e-Learning Resources		OpenStax, Kindle, iBooks	L1	
ICT14	Digital Collaborative Tools		Lucidchart, Trello, Asana, Miro, Padlet	L1	

Source: Author.

The activities are aligned with the levels of Revised Bloom's Taxonomy (RBT) as follows: Remembering, Understanding, Applying, Analyzing, Evaluating, and Creating. These levels guide the development of cognitive skills, progressing from basic knowledge to more complex problem-solving. The frameworks and activities foster essential skills like critical thinking, collaboration, self-regulation, and creativity. This ensures a personalized learning experience that progresses from basic understanding to advanced innovation.

There is a coding convention used in Table 1 for the mapping purpose in the course plan. Also, the cyberogogical tools listed in Table 23.1 are a sample ones but not the exhaustive list.

3.2. Implementation of the model

Based on the proposed methodology, a sample course plan was designed and implemented for the Advanced Software Engineering course offered to second-year Bachelor of Computer Applications students of an Higher Education institute in the Bangalore city of India. The study was conducted during the even semester of the academic year 2023–24, comparing a course delivered without LCA and one integrated with LCA using the 5-Gogy methodology. Table 23.2 presents the Micro Course Plan developed and implemented as part of this experiment.

4. Results and Discussions

A learner-centred approach leads to better student engagement and improved academic performance. It helps to develop critical thinking, problem-solving, and collaboration skills. Students take more ownership of their learning, benefiting from personalized and inclusive experiences that meet diverse needs and encourage lifelong learning. This approach also boosts confidence, satisfaction, and accountability while promoting active participation and self-directed growth. Success can be measured through higher assessment scores, increased participation, positive feedback, and noticeable changes in behaviour, such as teamwork and leadership.

4.1. Results

A comparison between the Non-LCA course and the LCA course with 5-Gogy applied shows clear improvements across key metrics. Attendance increased from 77% to 81% shown in Figure 23.3, indicating higher student engagement in the LCA course. The average CIA marks rose from 69% to 76% shown in Figure 23.4, suggesting better academic performance, likely due to the effectiveness of the 5-Gogy teaching methodology. The feedback score improved from 7/10 to 8.2/10 presented in Figure 23.5, reflecting greater student satisfaction with the course structure and delivery.

Table 23.2. Sample micro course plan implemented with the proposed model

COURSE PLAN		
Unit & Topic details	Week	Mapping format: Unit No-Topic No: 5-Gogy code-Activity No.
Unit-1: Introduction to Advanced Software Engineering U1-T1: Software reuse - Component-based software engineering - Distributed software engineering Service-oriented architecture.	Week 1 20–23, November 2023	U1-T1: A13-2; ICT02 ICT04
U1-T2: - Embedded software - Aspect-oriented software engineering - Using High-Level Conceptual Data Models for Database Design-Naming Conventions, and Design Issues Introduction to Advanced Databases U1-T3: - Subclasses, Super classes, and Inheritance	Week 2 25–30, November 2024	U1-T2: A03-2; U1-T3: A15-3; ICT02 ICT10
Unit-2: Software System Modeling - Normalization, File Organization and Indexing U2-T1: Models: Context – Interaction - Structural – Behavioural - Model driven engineering – Architectural design decisions - architectural views – Architectural patterns – Application architectures - Design Guidelines for Relation Schemas.	Week 4 09–14, December 2024	U2-T1: A03-2 U2-T1: A13-3; ICT02 ICT10 ICT11
U2-T2: Functional Dependencies - Normal Forms Based on Primary Keys-Second and Third Normal Forms-Boyce-Codd Normal Form - Multivalued Dependency and Fourth Normal Form - Join Dependencies and Fifth Normal Form U2-T3: Inference Rules, Equivalence and Minimal Cover-Properties of Relational Decompositions - Nulls and Dangling Tuples.	Week 5 16–20, December 2024	U2-T2: A13-2 U2-T3: A15-3 ICT02 ICT14

Source: Author.

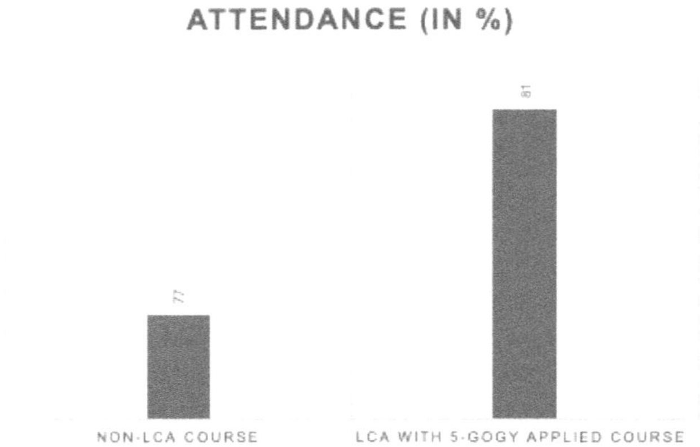

Figure 23.3. Regularity of the students.

Source: Author.

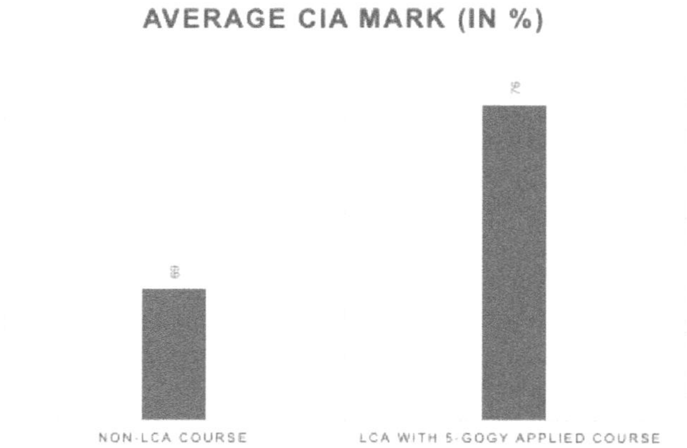

Figure 23.4. Performance of the students.

Source: Author.

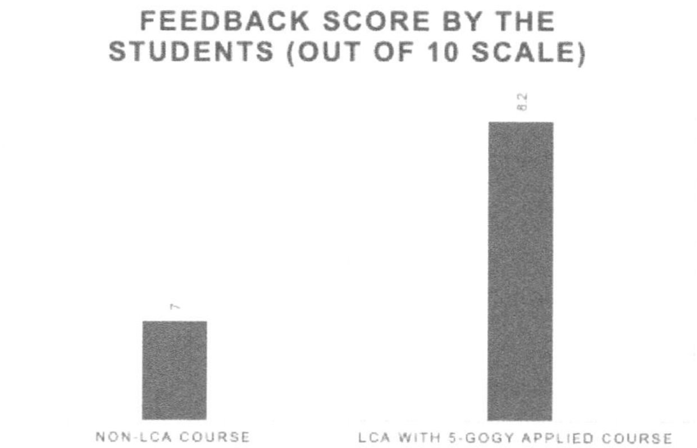

Figure 23.5. Satisfaction of the students.

Source: Author.

Overall, the LCA course with 5-Gogy applied demonstrates strong potential for enhancing engagement, learning outcomes, and satisfaction, making it a valuable approach to adopt.

4.2. Discussion

The effectiveness of teaching can be measured by student learning outcomes, such as academic performance, the ability to apply knowledge and participation in class activities. The key factors include using diverse teaching strategies, creating an inclusive classroom and gathering regular student feedback. The better improvement can be achieved through the quality of assessments, the relevance of teaching methods and the use of technology to enhance learning. Also, this model can bring a long-term impacts like the development of critical thinking, career success and a greater satisfaction from the stack holders.

5. Conclusions

This research emphasizes the importance of adopting the 5-Gogy framework. The framework includes Pedagogy, Andragogy, Peeragogy, Heutagogy, and Cybergogy. It is an effective model for meeting the diverse learning needs of Gen Z students in STEAM higher education. The proposed course plan creates an inclusive, adaptive, and technology-driven learning environment. It also provides educators with practical strategies and tools to improve teaching effectiveness and student engagement. The experimental implementation with undergraduate science students at Christ University, India, showed promising results. The results proved that increased learner engagement, enhanced development of critical skills and the adoption of innovative teaching practices.

This research emphasizes the importance of comprehensive frameworks in helping students succeed in real-world challenges. It also helps achieve institutional goals. This research is a valuable contribution to the evolving field of higher education. Future research will focus on integrating AI-enabled 5-Gogy practices. This approach offers a transformative direction, allowing for personalized, data-driven learning experiences. It will further enhance the effectiveness of education.

References

[1] Tzenios, N. (2022). Learner-Centered Teaching. *International Research Journal of Modernization in Engineering Technology and Science*, *4*(12), 950–958. *https://doi.org/10.13140/RG.2.2.36641154О*

[2] Joshi, A. (2021). Understanding "5 Gogy": Pedagogy, Andragogy, Peeragogy, Heutagogy, and Cybergogy. *Cummins College Bulletin on Engineering Education*, *1*(1), 1–10.

[3] Sandberg, P. (2018). Various ways of understanding the concept of andragogy. *Cogent Education*, *5*(1), 1496643. *https://doi.org/10.1080/2331186X.2018.1496643*

[4] Blaschke, L. M. (2012). Heutagogy and lifelong learning: A review of heutagogical practice and self-determined learning. *The International Review of Research in Open and Distributed Learning*, *13*(1), 56–71. *https://doi.org/10.19173/irrodl.v13i1.1076*

[5] Yadav, S. K. (2020). Peeragogy: A nascent approach of digital age. *Indian Journal of Educational Technology*, *2*(2), 1–10.

[6] Wang, M., & Kang, M. (2006). Cybergogy for engaged learning: A framework for creating learner engagement through information and communication technology. *In* M. Spector (Ed.), *Planning for two transformations in education and learning technology*, 225–239. Lawrence Erlbaum Associates Publishers.

[7] Tzenios, N. (2022). Learner-Centered Teaching. *International Research Journal of Modernization in Engineering Technology and Science*, *4*(12), 950–958.

[8] D'Souza, R. (2024). Heutagogy: A new "gogy". *Journal of Research Initiatives*, *8*(4), Article 3.

[9] Manikutty, G., Sasidharan, S., & Rao, B. (2022). Driving innovation through project-based learning: A pre-university STEAM for Social Good initiative. *arXiv preprint arXiv:2211.01998*.

[10] Reid, N., & Wilkes, J. (2016). Addressing the challenges of teaching STEM disciplines in higher education. *Higher Education Pedagogy, 1*(1), 24–35.

[11] Taylor, E. W., & Laros, A. (2014). Researching the transformative dimensions of andragogy in higher education. *Adult Education Quarterly, 64*(4), 351–369. https://doi.org/10.1177/0741713614543177

[12] Blaschke, L. M. (2012). Heutagogy and lifelong learning: A review of heutagogical practice and self-determined learning. *The International Review of Research in Open and Distributed Learning, 13*(1), 56–71. *https://doi.org/10.19173/irrodl.v13i1.1076*

[13] Wang, F., Wu, H., & Chen, N. (2021). Exploring the impact of gamification and AR/VR technologies on STEAM learning outcomes. *Interactive Learning Environments, 29*(7), 1–18. *https://doi.org/10.1080/10494820.2021.1889784*

[14] Corneli, J., Danoff, C., Pierce, C., Ricuarte, F., & Snow MacDonald, L. (2015). Paragogy: Synergizing individual and organizational learning. *Peeragogy Handbook,* 3rd Edition.

[15] Knowles, M. S., Holton, E. F., & Swanson, R. A. (2015). The adult learner: *The definitive classic in adult education and human resource development* (8th ed.). Routledge.

[16] Leigh, E., & Blaschke, L. M. (2020). Digital transformation and the role of the 5-Gogy Framework in higher education. *Educational Technology Research and Development, 68*(4), 1–15.

24 A survey on language speaking disabilities of non-native speakers: Insights and applications of Artificial Intelligence

Shaheena Jaleela Faizal[1,a], Kawkab Abdulaziz Al Balushi[2,b], and Faizal Hajamohideen[3,c]

[1]Department of Language Studies, Sohar University, Oman
[2]Department of Preparatory Studies, University of Technology and Applied Sciences (UTAS), Suhar, Sultanate of Oman, Oman
[3]Department of IT, College of Computing and Information Sciences, University of Technology and Applied Sciences (UTAS) Suhar, Sultanate of Oman, Oman

Abstract: Speaking the mother tongue is a fundamental right of any human being, and it is an epidemic impediment when communicating with other language speakers. It is widely understood that English is a worldwide spoken language. Many people struggle to cope, especially when speaking and reading essays. Good reading skills are acquired through a person's ability to decode essential speech units. It starts from childhood when people are getting disabled in learning, perhaps not acquiring the learning ability properly. Some exceptional cases are the disabilities that occur in learning delays in terms of auditory processing disorder and difficulty in verbal working memory that prevent learning of new languages. Though many researchers discuss eliminating learning disability, language adaptability is lacking in some ways due to the critical influences of the mother tongue. This paper debates the various survey explorations to eliminate language impairment and depicts the statistics of the usage of other languages contrary to English. Also, this study determines the e-learning avenue to remove the deficiency of non-native language. It categorizes and charts the population of different languages, speaking people against the English language. Likewise, this paper explores the numerous tools used, including artificial intelligence, to combat language snags, such as mobile and desktop-based applications used by non-native speakers. In conclusion, this study records the key to overcoming the Speaking Disability for Non-Native Orator.

Keywords: Applied sciences, e-Learning, innovations in english language, language disability, native speakers, non-native speakers, speaking

1. Introduction

English is a universally articulated language. Many people grieve to cope with it, especially when reading essays. Good study skills are also acquired from a person's ability to decode essential speech units. Rapid naming also plays an important role, describing the ability to name things like colours and objects quickly. Psychological tests for academic and language skills should be used to evaluate kids, encouraging them from childhood to learn the worldwide language. This is the age when people get disabled from learning. Disability occurs due to learning delays, auditory processing disorder, and difficulty in verbal working memory.

Language disability disappears when small children practice more extensive assessments than lectures typically offered during the school period. Some people do not learn the language because it is against their cultural prospects. Some factors can improve the world; since "God has given us mouth," people can individually talk to the counsellor or the class teacher about their problem in their own language. So, they can give us a sincere and creative solution. Regular support of setting a new standard in teaching and group meetings leads to perfection.

Trying to provide specific accommodations that students believe will support their progress. Teachers keeping track of students' progress see where most students need to benefit.

Speaking directly to international students or international students requesting support and understanding, what are their challenges in accepting them? Starting a creative flow of solutions and accessing higher implementation of extra subjects for students in unique ways would bring the world to shine.

[a]244717@students.su.edu.om, [b]sohkawkab@utas.edu.om, [c]faizal.h@gmail.com

DOI: 10.1201/9781003778905-24

2. Literature Review

Research has identified disabilities in speaking and writing languages remarkably in English-speaking non-native speakers; it is stated as a continuum of difficulties related to comprehending and using language [1].

The previous research suggested that occasionally, learning disabled in a foreign language class turned out to be those school children who were not previously spotted with a learning disability [2].

Another study concludes that perhaps a child exhibits delays in their native language development, struggles with literacy skills in their native language, and has specific language impairments in both contexts.

A learning disability might be suspected if factors such as challenges with the native language and English (e.g., phonological issues), a family history of reading difficulties, and minimal improvement after suitable interventions are observed [3, 12].

Recent researchers say that the brilliant procedure of the described data on disabilities signifies rectified starters. However, they use the word threaten to describe persons with specified difficulties in foreign language courses in the classroom. However, limited studies show that with accurate instructional changes, pupils with a language learning disability can succeed in learning a foreign language. For example, this assessment conducted a study to determine if multisensory structured language (MSL) training was superior to other methods of teaching at-risk learners [4].

Ganschow and Schneider [5] offer recommendations for teachers working in an inclusive foreign language classroom based on eight MLS principles:

1. Multisensory (teaching using visual, auditory, tactile, and kinesthetic strategies),
2. Repetitive (providing opportunities for practice and review),
3. Structured (direct and explicit teaching of language patterns in a logical progression),
4. Sequential (from simple to complex),
5. Cumulative,
6. Alphabetic/Phonetic (teaching sounds and letter-sound patterns from most frequent to least frequent),
7. Metacognitive (helping students to think about language concepts and to explain them in their own words),
8. Analytic/Synthetic (breaking multi-syllable words apart and returning them together) [12, 13].

2.1. AI and language disabilities

Technological tools are often used to support individuals with language difficulties, particularly non-native speakers. They assist in enhancing pronunciation, grammar, and fluency by offering specific feedback and facilitating opportunities for language practice.

For example, certain applications evaluate speech patterns to deliver feedback on pronunciation, grammar, and fluency, enabling users to enhance their speaking abilities. Moreover, virtual tutors and interactive chat platforms offer a conducive environment for language practice, promoting steady progress in confidence and proficiency. Tools incorporating natural language processing can also assist in identifying specific areas where learners struggle, making it easier for educators to implement tailored instructional strategies. By leveraging these AI technologies, we can create a more inclusive and supportive learning environment, allowing individuals with language disabilities to enhance their communication skills effectively [14].

They also highlighted that significant challenges for students with language learning difficulties may arise due to numerous differences between their first language and the new language they are trying to learn. It is suggested that foreign language teachers often receive training and education designed to shape them into "ideal learners," capable of mastering language skills – such as pronunciation, reading, writing, speaking, and listening – through consistent exposure and practice [5, 6].

Teachers frequently face challenges in distinguishing students who are learning English as a foreign language and experiencing difficulties from those with actual learning disabilities. Without timely identification and suitable instructional strategies, these challenges may worsen, leading to a growing disparity in academic achievement between these students and their peers [12]. An article discussing language learning disabilities in university students offers a checklist of indicators that can assist in identifying students who may be at risk. General signs include struggling with quizzes and tests despite consistent attendance and completion of assignments; frequent confusion during lessons, characterized by either excessive silence or over-questioning; feelings of frustration leading to disruptive behaviour, such as aggression toward the teacher, due to difficulties in understanding course material; and requiring extended time to complete tasks, often working at a slower pace than peers. Students are easily distracted and need help following the teacher's directions [7]. A professor in 1987 conducted research on factors influencing success in foreign language learning and examined variables related to foreign language learning disabilities in a group of university students with learning disabilities. The study found that the results from the MLAT were significant as both predictive and diagnostic indicators [8]. While some teachers worry that implementing these suggestions might make their classes less engaging, researchers emphasize that strategies aimed at enhancing language clarity and comprehensibility benefit all English language learners, including those without learning disabilities [9].

The article studies the relationship between success in learning a foreign language and language aptitude, measured using the MLAT. Opinion of debater results showed a strong correlation between language learning achievement and aptitude. However, they concluded that further research is needed in this field, specifically in measuring language aptitude, learner profiles, individual differences, ability differences on particular language-studying tasks, and the influence of different tasks on various learners [10].

3. Methodology

This research depicts the evolution of each perfect data provided according to the survey of non-native English speaking disability. Through the content, the describer reviews that many applications and e-learning apps can be used to improve the deficiency relating to language learning. It also determines the various statistics relating to the top plus largest English native countries and depicts the statistics of the usage of other languages contrary to the English language. Also, this study regulates language communication in different non-native languages (Table 24.1).

It categorizes and projects a population of different languages, speaking people against the English language. Likewise, this paper explores the numerous tools used to combat language snags, such as mobile and desktop-based applications used by non-native speakers. In conclusion, this study records the possibility of overcoming the Speaking Disability of a NonNative Orator.

3.1. Data analysis

The work of Methodology is presented in the form of statistics

As shown in the chart depicted in Figure 24.1, the native speaker is less than the non-native speaker who speaks non-native languages. This is one reason the language of native speakers is declining. Also, Figure 24.1 shows that the non-native speaker population frequently seeks other languages due to migration, job orientation, skill learning, and business communication.

In the US, the Grammarly app ranks first for keywords such as "never notice," "negated," "Oxford comma," "ax," and "what is metaphor." These words have a higher capacity volume: nearly 90,000 searches.

Improvements in this dealing can appear trendy on school websites, where teachers advocate for students to use the Grammarly app to improve their skills and broaden their knowledge.

The schools are unlikely to prepare this by chance, as Grammarly has communicated with institutions across the US and the world to promote its useful device to students. Some of those schools appear on the website.

4. Result Discussion

When people find it challenging to learn a new language, they find a new alternative to learning the same. People's choices vary depending on their ability to learn from different unique apps provided on the internet. Relations between people's mindsets are one, besides some learning apps. It can be worthy as well as valuable for a starter.

Table 24.1. AI tools for supporting language learning and overcoming disabilities

Tool Name	*Description*	*Usage*	*Citation*
Duolingo	A mobile and web-based application for language learning through gamified lessons.	Users can engage in daily practice through interactive exercises to build vocabulary and grammar skills.	[15]
Babbel	A language learning platform offering courses in various languages focusing on conversation.	Encourages speaking and listening practice with real-life dialogues to enhance fluency.	[16]
Rosetta Stone	A comprehensive language learning software emphasizing immersion and visual learning.	Users learn through pictures and sounds, enhancing associative memory for vocabulary.	[17]
Speech Ace	An online speech evaluation tool that provides feedback on pronunciation and fluency.	Users practice speaking and receive real-time feedback to improve their speaking skills.	[18]
Quizlet	An educational tool using flashcards and games to aid memorization and learning.	Helpful for vocabulary enhancement and test preparation; users can create custom study sets.	[19]
HelloTalk	A language exchange app that connects users with native speakers for conversational practice.	Facilitates real-time chat and voice exchanges, promoting language practice in a social context.	[20]
FluentU	A language learning platform using realworld videos like music videos and movie trailers.	Users learn vocabulary and grammar through context, improving comprehension and speaking skills.	[21]

Source: Author.

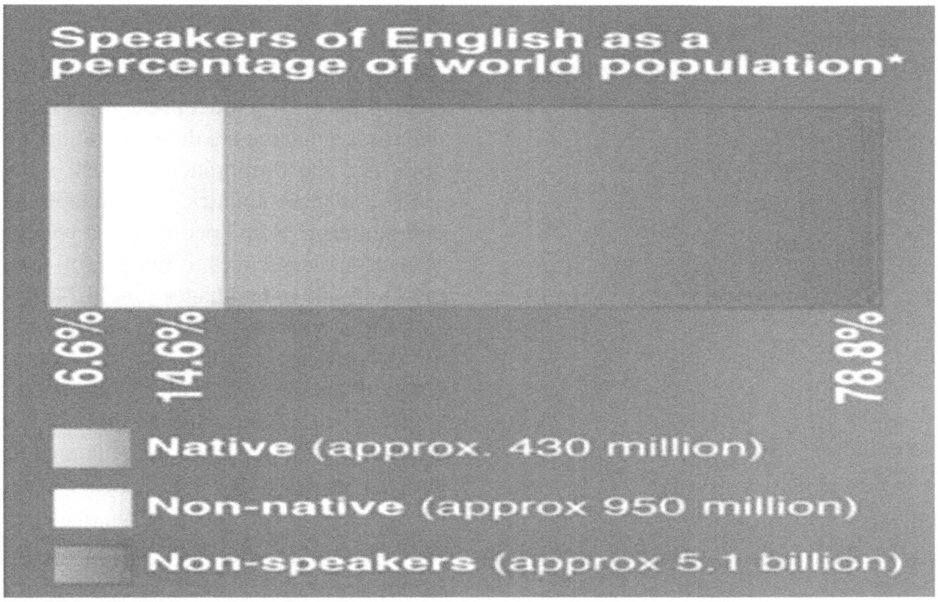

Figure 24.1. Non-native speakers in the world population.

Source: Author.

Many websites provide answers for the same. The population is enriched when people use such apps.

Different languages can be preferred words/languages for non-native speakers in many countries. The highest and lowest speaking countries in the world depict the enrichment of our global languages. Many videos and network-based learning include whiteboard collaboration for writing, learning from different, far tutors' lectures, and translating phrases and sentences (Table 24.2).

In the above chart (Figure 24.2), we have figured out that people preferred seven language applications in the previous history. These types of apps include Memrise, LinguaLift, Duolingo, HelloTalk, Mindsnacks, Busuu, Babbel and TripLingo.

English, Chinese, Hindi, French, Arabic, and Spanish languages are primarily used in all the preferred applications available in the store. There are masses of users for this application, about a million. The languages desired by most people are English, Chinese, Hindi, Spanish, French,

Table 24.2. Language learning apps and their populations

Language App	*Population*
Memrise	40,000,000
LinguaLift	264,765
Duolingo	20,000,000
HelloTalk	10,000,000
Mindsnacks	2,732,516
Busuu	50,000,000
Babbel	1,000,000

Source: Author.

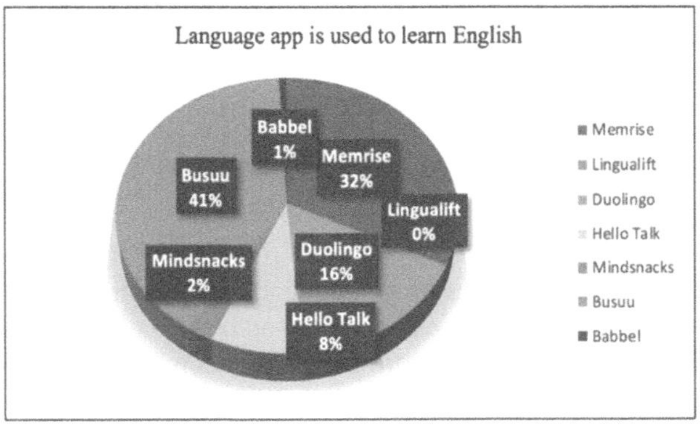

Figure 24.2. Language app is used to learn English.

Source: Author.

Arabic, Russian, and many more. As per the data, English is a significantly more endured language than other languages. Statistics show Memrise is 32% used for a foreign language; henceforth, Busuu 40%, Duolingo 16%, Hello Talk 8%, Mindsnacks 2%, Babble 1%, and Lingualift. People use the application Memrise to learn French, Spanish, German, and Japanese.

There are almost 1121 million English language speakers, which is in contrast to other non-native languages (Table 24.3).

This statistic shows that 1121 million non-native speakers of English are used orally globally (Figure 125.3). The data provided for English and Chinese show slight differences. Hindi and Spanish are half a million more than expected in the other languages provided. Other languages

Table 24.3. Native language Orators (in Millions)

Native Language	*Orators (in Millions)*
English	1121
Chinese	1107
Hindi	534
Spanish	513
French	285
Arabic	274
Russian	265
Bengali	262
Portuguese	236
Indonesian	198

Source: Author.

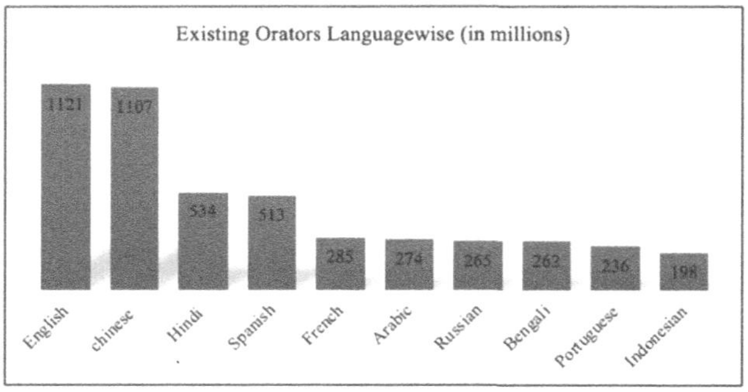

Figure 24.3. Existing Orators language-wise (in millions).

Source: Author.

determined to be the first language for all native states lessen to nearly a quarter of a million by 300 or less. This shows that people are more attracted to communicating in English than their mother language.

In all states of the United States, the Philippines and the United States of America is the largest user of their language. Henceforth, English has remained in all states.

E-learning is a broad term for using electronic tools to obtain and develop knowledge that changes attitudes and behaviours. It includes several teaching tactics and approaches.

E-learning allows starters to learn from anywhere and at any time as long as the learner has access to the equipment required for the learning process [12]. It can be internet-based,

1. CD-ROM
2. Network-based includes videos, texts, virtual environments, and animations

English is the leading language on the internet. Nearly 54 proportion of content on the internet is in English. Russian, at six proportion, is a distant second. (The data concerns 10 million websites with the most traffic.) [11] Countries that are preferring English have equally high and lowest percentages (Table 24.4).

People prefer English to the top 7 nationals worldwide (Figure 24.4). The most popular states that use English as their first language are the United States, the United Kingdom, and the Philippines. English is the least preferred subject in these countries, and people use it as their second language. Some people use a wide range of speaking phrases and sentences in English by translating them into their non-native languages (Table 24.5).

Well-populated countries such as the aforementioned are boosted in economy and development in a massive level of language learning (Figure 24.5). Recent studies have used data acquired from different sources and approved by designers of many language faculty in different universities.

Table 24.4. Top English-speaking countries

Countries	*Population (in Millions)*
United States	231
United Kingdom	60
Australia	17
Canada	20
New Zealand	4.8
Ireland	4.8
Philippines	90

Source: Author.

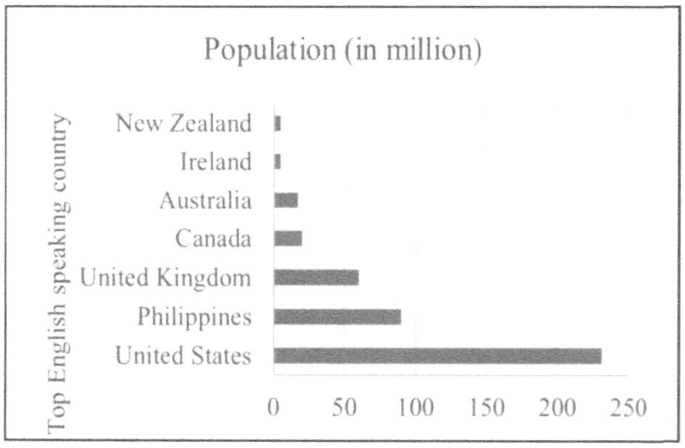

Figure 24.4. Top English-speaking country (in millions).

Source: Author.

Table 24.5. Largest English-speaking countries

Countries	*Population (in Millions)*
United States	231
United Kingdom	60
Philippines	90

Source: Author.

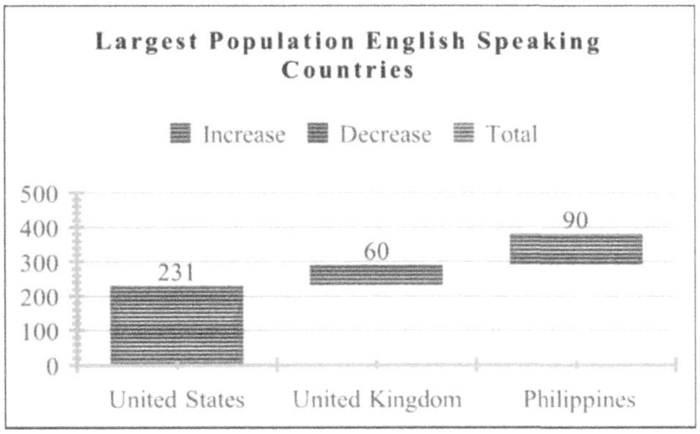

Figure 24.5. Largest population with English speaking countries.

Source: Author.

5. Conclusion

This research taught the disabilities faced by non-native speakers. Also, it creates a healthy debate about the various survey explorations to eliminate language impairment. The aforementioned illustrations are statistics on using other languages contrary to English. Also, this study evolves the e-learning avenue to remove the deficiency of non-native language. It classifies the importance of using e-learning tools to remove difficulties in other language-speaking people against the English language. Likewise, this paper explored the numerous tools used to combat language snags, such as mobile and desktop-based applications used by non-native speakers.

This study records the possible strategies to overcome the Speaking Disability for Non-Native Speakers.

References

[1] Newhall, P. (2012). Language-Based Learning Disability: What to Know. *Retrieved October 2016.* From http://www.ldonline.org/article/56113/

[2] Schwarz, R. (1997). Learning Disabilities and Foreign Language Learning. *Retrieved October 2016.* From http://www.ldonline.org/article/6065

[3] Spear-Swerling, L. (2006). Learning Disabilities in English Language Learners. *Retrieved October 2016.* From http://www.ldonline.org/spearswerling/Learning

[4] Ela, W. (2021). A Correlation Between Student's SpeakIng Anxiety And Speaking Achievement At The Second Semester of English Department Students of Unisma. *https://core.ac.uk/download/386298882.pdf*

[5] Ganschow, L., & Schneider, E. (2006). Assisting Students with Foreign Language Learning Difficulties in School. *Retrieved October 2016.* From http://www.ldonline.org/article/22725/

[6] Ortiz, A. (2001). English Language Learners with Special Needs: Effective Instructional Strategies. Retrieved October 2016. From http://www.ldonline.org/article/5622/

[7] DiFino, S., & Lombardino, L. (2004). Language Learning Disabilities: The Ultimate Foreign Language Challenge. *Foreign Language Annals*, *37*(3), 390–400.

[8] Gajar, A. (1987). Foreign language learning disabilities: The identification of predictive and diagnostic variables. *Journal of Learning Disabilities, 20*(6), 327–330.

[9] Brown, D., & Ford, K. (2007). Communication Strategies for All Classrooms: Focusing on English Language Learners and Students with Learning Disabilities. Retrieved October 2016. From http://www.ldonline.org/article/19260/

[10] Ivancevi˘ c-Otanjac, M. (2016). Nastava stranih jezika za u´cenike sa˘ tesko˘ cama u njihovom usvajanju. Specijalna Edukacija i Rehabilitacija.´ https://doi.org/10.5937/specedreh15-12071

[11] Koissaba B.R. Ole, (January 2014). E-learning Principles and Practices in the Context of Indigenous Peoples: A comparative Study bkoissa@Clemson.edu, *International Family and Community Studies*, Clemson University.

[12] E-learning principles and practices in the context of education with special reference to indigenous Peoples: A study. *https://doi.org/10.5281/zenodo.240280*

[13] Ela, W. (2021). A correlation between students' speak-Ing anxiety and speaking achievement in the second semester of English department students of unismA. *https://core.ac.uk/download/386298882.pdf*

[14] Smith, R., & Jones, A. (2019). AI Tools for Writing: Exploring the Impact of Grammarly on Language Learners. *Language Education in Asia*, *10*(2), 140–156.

[15] Duolingo. (n.d.). Retrieved from https://www.duolingo.com

[16] Babbel. (n.d.). Retrieved from *https://www.babbel.com*

[17] Rosetta Stone. (n.d.). Retrieved from *https://www.rosettastone.com*

[18] Speech Ace. (n.d.). Retrieved from *https://www.speechace.com*

[19] Quizlet. (n.d.). Retrieved from *https://www.quizlet.com*

[20] HelloTalk. (n.d.). Retrieved from https://www.hellotalk.com

[21] FluentU. (n.d.). Retrieved from *https://www.fluentu.com*

25 Integrating sustainability with smart technologies: The pathway for a resilient 21st century environment

Chidambaram N.[1,a], *Akshaya A. V. R.*[2], *John Steward Raj J.*[3], *and Sathish Kumar*[3]

[1]Associate Professors, School of Business & Management – BBA CHRIST University, Bangalore, India
[2]Assistant Professor, School of Arts & Humanities – Department of English & Cultural Studies CHRIST University, Bangalore, India
[3]Associate Professor MBA, Department of Business, Dr NGP Institute of Technology, Coimbatore, Tamil Nadu, India

Abstract: In this 21st century, sustainable development has become an essential need characterized by formerly unheard-of environmental problems and fast technology breakthroughs. Our research investigates the potential of merging sustainability with smart technology if we are to create a strong and rich future. This paper shows how smart technologies may solve important challenges such as pollution, resource depletion, climate change, and biodiversity loss using sophisticated systems including artificial intelligence (AI), big data analytics, and machine learning (ML), the Internet of Things (IoT), etc. Examining the ecological, social, financial, and technical aspects of this integration, the research shows how well it may improve resource efficiency, slow down the pace of climate change, support social fairness, and increase world cooperation. By means of a comprehensive literature analysis and pragmatic investigation, the study shows how data analytics, prediction models driven by artificial intelligence, and IoT enabled sensors may enhance environmental monitoring, maximize resource management, and encourage sustainable behaviours. Case studies of smart grids, energy-efficient infrastructure, and waste management systems highlight the transforming possibilities of these technologies. Among the subjects the paper addresses – data security, interoperability, and environmental impacts – also discussed are ethical innovation and stakeholder cooperation. This study emphasizes the possibility of combining smart technology with sustainability to build a future free from environmental damage, financially feasible, and socially inclusive.

Keywords: Artificial Intelligence (AI), biodiversity conservation, climate change mitigation, global collaboration, Internet of Things (IoT), resource efficiency, smart technologies, social equity, sustainability

1. Introduction

The 21st century stresses the importance of combining sustainability with the use of creative clever technology. The judicious use of resources to satisfy present demands without sacrificing the capacity of next generations to satisfy their own defines a sustainable environment. It is essential to include sustainability into many industries and society constructions as technological developments redefine them. This integration guarantees environmental preservation, guarantees effective management of resources, and strengthens resistance to climate change, therefore paving the path for a sustainable and rich future.

Maintaining ecological equilibrium depends critically on both technology and environmental interaction. By means of real-time data and predictive insights, the Internet of Things (IoT) and artificial intelligence (AI) can significantly monitor, safeguard, and control ecosystems. These technologies may provide fresh methods of habitat protection, species extinction prevention, and ecosystem monitoring and conservation.

A good environment backed by smart technology immediately benefits human well-being and technical advancement. Intelligent systems lower pollution and exposure to harmful materials by means of efficient waste management systems and air pollution sensors, therefore fostering health-friendly surroundings and access to pure air, safe water, and nutritious food.

Achieving sustainability depends on innovative solutions helping to mitigate climate change. Projects using

[a]chidambaram.n@christuniversity.in

DOI: 10.1201/9781003778905-25

renewable energy help lower greenhouse gas emissions and maximize energy utilization; examples of these are smart grids and artificial intelligence-based energy management systems. By reducing waste, supporting recycling, and thus promoting responsible consumption patterns, advanced technologies include IoT-enabled resource monitoring systems and AI-based supply chain optimization help to enhance resource efficiency.

Innovative solutions driven by economic growth may coexist with sustainability to propel sectors like smart infrastructure, clean technologies, and renewable energy. Inclusive and fair development depends critically on including all stakeholders – including under-represented groups – in decision-making.

Realizing a sustainable and strong worldwide future depends on global responsibilities as well as cooperative technologies. Ensuring the health and well-being of current as well as future generations depends on the creative technology and sustainability being integrated. In these two respects, synergy responds to environmental preservation, public health, adaptation to climate change, effective resource use, economic growth, social justice, and world stewardship.

1.1. The imperative of sustainability in the 21st century

The 21st century stresses how important it is to combine technology with ecology to protect the earth. This integration guarantees environmental preservation, efficient use of resources, and climate resilience, therefore opening the path for a wealthy future. AI and the IoT can greatly monitor, preserve, and manage ecosystems, so preserving habitat, preventing species extinction, and so monitoring and conserving ecosystems. By means of effective waste management systems and air pollution sensors, smart technology reduces pollution and exposure to hazardous materials, therefore benefiting human well-being and technological growth.

Reaching sustainability calls for creative ideas to slow down global warming including smart grids, renewable energy initiatives, and artificial intelligence-based energy management systems. Modern technologies improving resource efficiency include IoT-enabled resource monitoring systems and AI-based supply chain optimization. Fair and inclusive development relies on including all stakeholders – including under-represented groups – into decision-making.

Global responsibilities and cooperation technologies will define a strong and sustainable international future. Integration of creative technology with sustainability is essential to guarantee the health and welfare of present and next generations. Synergy answers environmental preservation, public health, climate change adaptation, efficient resource use, economic development, social justice, global stewardship.

2. Review of Literature

The research on sustainability and smart technology exposes growing agreement on the need of using present technologies to solve environmental problems. Research is on in IoT in real-time monitoring of the environment [1], artificial intelligence in forecasting for climate change [2] and data analytics in resource management improvement [3]. Moreover underlining the importance of sustainable practices in waste reduction, energy management, and urban design are studies by Batty et al. [4]. Attaching the United Nations Sustainable Development objectives (SDGs) [5] is deemed to rely heavily on the integration of these technologies with goals for sustainability.

Dealing with social, environmental, and financial problems of the twenty-first century calls for combining smart technology with sustainability. Emphasizing the ecological, technical, and social aspects of this integration, this review examines the current research on the topic. Defining the research are major topics including the link between environment and technological advances, climate change mitigation, resource efficiency, economic growth, social equality, and global cooperation. The literature underlines how clever technology has transformed capacity to help sustainability and resistance against global environmental problems.

2.1. Ecological and technological interdependence

There is much to say in literature on the link between technological development and environmental processes. The world runs as a cohesive system where the energy of ecosystems determines ecological equilibrium. Modern technologies like AI and the IoT are very essential for both surveillance of ecosystems and their management. Neumann and Emanuel [6] claim that IoT-enabled sensors as well as artificial intelligence-driven analytics give real-time data on conditions in the environment, hence helping proactive conservation strategies. Most importantly for halting species extinction and safeguarding of natural ecosystems, these advancements enable tracking of habitat conditions, biodiversity, and ecological health [7].

Slowing down the loss of biodiversity has been very effective using artificial intelligence-augmented monitoring and satellite pictures. Real-time observation of sensitive species and their environments is offered via GPS animal tracking and artificial intelligence-based identification methods [8]. These developments guide policy decisions and management strategies based on data-driven insights, therefore helping conservation initiatives. The literature emphasizes the significance of integrating these ideas into ecosystem management to assure the continuous resilience of natural resources.

2.2. Climate change mitigation through smart solutions

Among other things, climate change affects ecosystems, the economy, and human health; it is therefore the main issue of the twenty-first century. The results highlight the need for intelligent technology in lowering greenhouse gas emissions and strengthening climate resilience. Smart grids and artificial intelligence driven energy management systems (IPCC), [9] among initiatives in renewable energy will help to lower dependency on fossil fuels and improve energy efficiency. These technologies help solar and wind power to be included into current energy systems, therefore lowering carbon footprints among other renewable energy sources.

Predictive analytics and IoT-enabled climate monitoring systems provide real-time temperature variations, sea-level elevation data, and frequency of extreme storms. These tools help companies to create appropriate mitigating strategies and change with the times [7]. By estimating the effects of climate change on ecosystems, artificial intelligence-enhanced climate models help governments develop policies that increase resilience. Particularly in the industrial sectors, the study underlines the need of carbon capture and storage (CCS) technology in reducing greenhouse gas emissions [6].

2.3. Resource efficiency through advanced technologies

Maintaining ecological balance and assuring their availability for future generations depends on sustainable use of natural resources. According to the literature, smart technology is absolutely necessary in increasing resource efficiency and waste reduction. Artificial intelligence and IoT-enabled resource monitoring systems promote very effective supply chain optimization in this environment [10]. These technologies provide real-time resource usage monitoring which supports the implementation of corrective action by helping to find inefficiencies.

In agriculture, precision farming techniques consist of artificial intelligence-driven irrigation systems that improve water, fertilizer, pesticide usage efficiency and drone-based crop monitoring. These methods lower the environmental impact of agricultural activities at once while raising crop yields [11]. In similar lines, smart water management systems monitor water quality and usage in tandem with IoT sensors and artificial intelligence analytics, hence maintaining safe and clean water supplies. The findings highlight how important these technologies are for encouraging environmentally friendly water use, hence reducing the water scarcity.

2.4. Economic development through innovative solutions

Especially in the development of green technologies and businesses, smart technology combined with sustainability shows significant financial possibilities. The findings highlight how important smart infrastructure, clean technologies, and renewable energy are for driving economic growth and creating green jobs [12]. Among other renewable energy sources, switching to solar and wind power has created employment in operation, maintenance, and installation.

Modern transport systems and energy-efficient buildings among smart infrastructure alternatives improve operational efficiency and assist to save expenses. These technologies help to boost economic growth and raise resilience against environmental stress [7]. The research underlines how crucial circular economy solutions – including recovery of resources and recycling – are in reducing waste and supporting environmentally beneficial consumer behaviour. These techniques provide income possibilities and help to reduce the environmental effect of industrial activity.

2.5. Social equity and access to technology

The literature highlights the need of guaranteeing social justice all via the use of smart technology. Especially underprivileged and marginalized communities, everyone should be able to live in a smart and sustainable environment. Innovations in urban design incorporating inexpensive housing and energy-efficient infrastructure enhance conveniently available sustainable living [6]. These solutions aim to decrease energy expenditures and enhance quality of life for families with low incomes.

The application of the smart setting still suffers a major obstacle from the digital divide. The research underlines the need of initiatives for fair access to smart technology and services [12]. Attaching including and fair development means integrating all stakeholders – especially marginalized groups – in processes of decision-making. The results underscore how crucial capacity-building programs and education are in increasing technical literacy and supporting the adoption of sustainable practices.

2.6. Global collaboration and technological innovation

Global environmental problems include diminishing resources and climate change call for international collaboration as well as the development of universal technical standards. The studies underscore how crucial global frameworks – such as the UN's Agenda for Sustainable Development Goals (SDGs) – are in promoting cooperative efforts and technology development [9]. These systems provide a whole stage for using smart technology to handle social, economic and environmental problems.

Blockchain technology, for instance, encourages openness in the trade of carbon and emissions monitoring, therefore supporting the implementation of world agreements such the Paris Agreement [7]. Real-time monitoring of global environmental data made possible by IoT networks helps create data-informed policies and operations. The studies underscore the need of cooperative platforms for information flow and cooperative decision-making, which are more necessary for reaching environmental goals.

2.7. Challenges and unresolved issues

Smart technologies have transforming power even if their utilization brings varied challenges. Data security and privacy are among the main issues as thorough data gathering and management in automated systems expose vulnerabilities of unauthorized access and data breaches [12]. To help to address these problems, the study underlines the requirement of robust encryption methods, access limits, and authentication mechanisms.

Standardisation and interoperability provide major challenges as the integration of many smart devices from various manufacturers usually raises problems about compatibility [6]. Many aspects of smart environments rely on effective communication and cooperation, which is inhibited by absent defined protocols. To help smart technology grow, the literature emphasizes the requirement of open standards and scalable architecture.

Still unresolved are the ecological consequences of smart technology, particularly with respect to energy consumption and growth of electronic waste. The study underlines the need for sustainable materials, effective recycling systems, and circular economy models fit for smart gadgets [11]. Dealing with these challenges calls for a multidisciplinary approach including government collaboration, business organizations, colleges and universities, and civic society.

3. Research Methodology

Investigating how smart and sustainable technology could collaborate to solve social, environmental, and economical concerns is the goal of the research method. The strategy is meant to provide a thorough awareness of how smart technology might assist fair development by means of resource management, decrease climate change, optimize resource management, and so enhance sustainability initiatives. Using thematic coding of interview transcripts and literature, the qualitative research design aims to find significant themes and patterns, offering a complete knowledge of how smart technologies can support sustainability initiatives, lower climate change, optimize resource management, and promote fair development. The paper examines how intelligent technology and sustainability could interact to address financial, social, environmental, and technological challenges.

3.1. Research design

The research looked at how smart technology may be combined with sustainability using a descriptive and exploratory approach. Analysing the complex relationships of natural systems, technological advancement, and socioeconomic factors calls for this approach as perfect. The study consists of two main phases:

3.2. Phase 1: Literature review and theoretical framework development

This stage involves a thorough review of the present literature in order to identify important ideas, challenges, and opportunities in the combination of smart technology with sustainability. Theoretically, ecological interdependence, technological innovation, and sustainable development build the framework.

3.3. Phase 2: Empirical analysis

This stage emphasizes the compiling and analysis of main data to support the theoretical framework and provide useful information. To look at how smart technology could help to improve sustainability, the empirical research gives qualitative approaches like case studies and expert interviews top priority.

3.4. Data collection methods

The research offers a complete analysis by means of secondary data collecting approaches.

3.5. Secondary data collection

Secondary data comes from government publications, industry studies, academic publications, and international frameworks such the United Nations Sustainable Development Goals (SDGs). Peer-reviewed research on sustainability and smart technology – for example, Neumann & Emanuel, 2018 [6], Sassen, 2019 [7] – are primary sources. Reports from organizations range from the World Economic Forum to the Intergovernmental Panel on Climate Change (IPCC) [9]. Case studies on the use of smart technology in fields like urban design, energy consumption control, and preservation of biodiversity.

3.6. Data analysis techniques

The research employs qualitative analysis techniques to interpret the collected data.

3.7. Qualitative analysis

Theme analysis runs over qualitative information gathered from case studies and expert interviews. This means identifying recurring motifs, trends, and understanding of how smart technology and sustainability should be combined. Main subjects are: o ecological and technological connectivity.

- Solving climate change using creative ideas.
- Economic progress and effective resources.
- Social equity and technology availability.

This study offers necessary insights for legislators, academics, and practitioners by clarifying how smart technology might be used to improve sustainability using qualitative research approaches.

3.8. Research objectives and goals

The following objectives and aims guide the research, which reflects the main goal of combining sustainability with smart technologies:

1. **Understanding Environmental Issues through Technology Lenses**
   - To investigate how IoT and artificial intelligence technology could help us better understand environmental problems like resource depletion, declining biodiversity, and climate change.
   - Developing Sustainable Smart Technologies and Innovations
   - To look at the development of sustainable-fostering new technologies like smart waste management systems, energy-efficient infrastructure, and renewable energy systems.
2. **Assessing Environmental and Technological Impacts**
   - To investigate the environmental and technical implications of human activities, products, and policies using methodologies such as environmental impact assessments and life cycle assessments.
3. **Informing Policy Development with Empirical Evidence**
   - To provide scientific facts to back up the development of policies combining sophisticated technology with sustainability.
4. **Facilitating Behavioural Change with Smart Technologies**
   - To look at how smart technology could affect customer behaviour and support of environmentally friendly lifestyles.
5. **Increasing Resilience and Adaptation with Smart Solutions**
   - To investigate how smart technologies – including IoT networks and predictive analytics – might raise community resilience to environmental challenges.
6. **Encouraging Stakeholder Collaboration through Technological Platforms**
   - To look at how technologically driven platforms could encourage collaboration across many stakeholders – including scientists, legislators, and local residents.

3.9. Analysis

According to the studies, smart technology combined with sustainability has major advantages in many different spheres. By giving real-time environmental element data, IoT-powered devices provide proactive resource management. By helping to improve the accuracy of climate predictions, AI-driven prediction models enable fast responses. Data analytics helps to better distribute resources, lowers waste, and increases efficiency. Emphasizing their capacity to create strong and sustainable ecosystems, case studies reveal the clever use of smart grids, better waste management techniques, and environmentally friendly transportation choices.

The twenty-first century defines unmatched environmental challenges including climate change, resource depletion, loss of biodiversity, and pollution. These issues are exacerbated by fast urbanization, industry, and population growth. Along with these problems, technology developments – especially in the domains of AI, the IoT, and big data analytics – offer revolutionary answers. Emphasizing their help to create a rich and robust future, this paper looks at the confluence between smart technology and sustainability. The seven primary objectives of the research determine the structure of the study and enable one to connect the provided facts with them.

3.10. Understanding environmental issues through technology lenses

The first objective is using contemporary technology can help us to better understand environmental issues like climate change, biodiversity loss, pollution, and resource depletion. Particularly IoT and artificial intelligence, smart technologies provide real-time data and forecast insights that enable legislators and researchers to identify patterns and create focused solutions.

4. Climate Change and Global Warming

Driven by the rising greenhouse gases (GHGs) including carbon dioxide (CO2), methane (CH4), and nitrous oxide (N2O), climate change is a key concern of the twenty-first century. IoT sensors, satellite-based climate monitoring systems, and AI-driven climate models provide real-time data on sea-level rise [9] temperature variations, and severe storm incidence among modern technologies. These instruments help one to build reasonable mitigation solutions and to grasp the extent of climate change.

Predicting how ecosystems might be affected by climate change helps AI-augmented models to create preemptive actions reducing vulnerabilities. IoT-enabled sensor networks provide real-time monitoring of greenhouse gas emissions, hence optimizing energy consumption and include renewable energy sources [7].

4.1. Biodiversity loss

Decline in biodiversity brought on by habitat destruction, pollution, and climate change puts the ecological stability under danger. Among other technologies, remote sensing, GPS animal tracking, and AI-driven biodiversity monitoring systems offer real-time data collection on species movement, habitat conditions, and ecosystem health. These technologies assist in support of conservation initiatives by offering data-driven insights that shape policy choices and management techniques [8].

AI-driven identification technologies enable conservationists to design more targeted preservation strategies by recognizing vulnerable species and following invading species. Projects aiming at sustainable forest management and regeneration benefit from real-time data on illicit logging activity and deforestation made feasible by IoT-enabled environmental monitoring devices.

4.2. Pollution and resource depletion

In its many forms, pollution seriously compromises ecosystems and human health. IoT sensors and artificial intelligence-based analytics are among smart technologies that provide real-time monitoring of air and water quality, therefore allowing prompt reaction to lower pollution. Smart air quality monitoring systems enable urban planners to choose greener energy sources and transit by pointing out pollution hotspots [11].

One of the main problems is the overall depletion of resources like minerals, forests, water, and tools. IoT-enabled resource monitoring systems and AI-driven supply chain optimization tools increase resource efficiency by cutting waste and helping recycling. By methods of sustainable development, these technologies enable to protect natural resources therefore ensuring their availability for following generations.

4.3. Development of sustainable smart technologies and innovations

The second objective is the creation of innovative smart technologies advancing environmental sustainability. This covers developments in sustainable materials, energy-efficient infrastructure, renewable energy sources, and clever waste management techniques.

4.4. Renewable energy systems

Reducing greenhouse gas emissions depends on renewable energy projects incorporating smart grids and artificial intelligence-driven energy management systems. Smart networks help to improve the integration of solar and wind power, hence lowering reliance on fossil fuels. Examining energy usage patterns, AI-powered energy management solutions help to optimize energy use and reduce carbon footprints [6].

4.5. Energy-efficient infrastructure

Energy efficiency of smart technology is transforming urban infrastructure. By optimizing lighting, heating and cooling based on real-time occupancy data, IoT-enabled building management systems lower energy waste. Data analytics is how smart cities improve service delivery, lower running costs, and allocate resources more effectively.

4.6. Smart waste management systems

Smart waste management systems improve garbage collection and recycling processes by utilizing IoT sensors and analytics powered by artificial intelligence. The technologies in question play a significant role in minimizing the environmental impact associated with waste disposal, aiding in the reduction of littering, and enhancing recycling processes. Waste bins equipped with IoT technology monitor their fill levels and schedule pickups according to demand. Additionally, AI-driven sorting systems improve the operational efficiency of recycling facilities.

4.7. Assessing environmental and technological impacts

Third objective is the evaluation of how policies, products, and human actions affect many spheres of the environment and technology. Using life cycle assessments (LCAs), environmental impact assessments (EIAs), and data-driven ecological models, one evaluates these effects.

5. Life Cycle Assessments

From purchase of raw materials to disposal, life cycle assessments (LCAs) look at the environmental effects of goods and activities all through their whole lives. Through their evaluation of the environmental impact of their industrial operations, AI-driven life cycle assessments enable businesses to find inefficiencies and apply sustainable practices.

5.1. Environmental impact assessments

Environmental impact assessments look at how legislation and initiatives could, going forward, change the ecosystem. By means of previous data analysis and future projection, AI and machine learning (ML) technologies assist to improve the accuracy of environmental impact assessments (EIAs). AI-driven prediction models enable lawmakers to design appropriate mitigation plans by evaluating how climate change might affect ecosystems.

5.2. Data-based ecological models

Big data analytics underlie data-based ecology models to replicate ecosystem processes and forecast the effects of human activities. Supporting evidence-based decision-making, these models provide important light on habitat destruction, resource depletion, and biodiversity loss.

5.3. Informing policy development with empirical evidence

The fourth objective is to provide scientific data to direct the development of policies embracing innovative technologies and sustainability. Monitoring, evaluating, and strengthening environmental laws all depend on research.

5.4. Smart environmental policies

Data-informed insights used in smart environmental strategies help to further sustainable development. Real-time data on greenhouse gas emissions from IoT-enabled climate monitoring equipment lets governments carry out focused carbon reduction programs. Predictive analytics enabled by artificial intelligence help legislators create adaptable plans and project the consequences of climate change.

5.5. Regulatory frameworks

The fast advancement of technical innovation often surpasses current regulatory structures. Research offers empirical information to substantiate the formulation of policies that tackle the distinct difficulties of smart settings. Blockchain technology improves transparency in carbon trading and emissions monitoring, hence aiding the execution of international accords such as the Paris Agreement.

5.6. Facilitating behavioural change with smart technologies

The fifth objective underlines the need of understanding the dynamics of human behaviour and using smart technologies to support sustainable practices. With real-time feedback and incentives, smart technologies – such as waste reduction systems and energy management systems – affect consumer behaviour.

5.7. Energy management systems

Real-time energy consumption monitoring made possible by smart energy management systems encourages energy-conserving behaviours. Smart meters connected by the Internet of Things provide consumers thorough understanding of their energy use, therefore enabling the identification of areas for saving.

5.8. Waste-saving systems

Smart trash pickup and recycling systems use IoT devices and AI-powered data to make the process better. These systems provide consumers instant feedback on waste generation, which encourages them to adopt environmentally friendly behaviours such composting and recycling.

5.9. Increasing resilience and adaptation with smart solutions

The sixth objective is to design smart and strong mechanisms enabling communities to address environmental issues like climate change. By supplying real-time data and early warning systems, smart technologies – including IoT networks and predictive analytics – improve community resilience.

5.10. Climate monitoring and disaster preparedness

Real-time data on temperature variations, severe storm events, and sea-level elevation made possible by IoT-enabled climate monitoring equipment Using this information, predictive analytics systems help communities to foresee natural disasters, therefore enabling preemptive approaches and risk reduction.

5.11. Ecosystem-based approaches

Ecosystem-based solutions increase the resilience of natural systems by means of modern technologies. By tracking species migratory and habitat status, AI-driven biodiversity monitoring tools support ecosystem restoration and conservation projects.

5.12. Encouraging stakeholder collaboration through technological platforms

The seventh objective is to encourage teamwork among many groups, such as scientists, lawmakers, business leaders, and people in the community. Technology-driven platforms encourage information flow and group decision-making, therefore enabling the implementation of smart solutions addressing local and worldwide environmental problems.

5.13. Collaborative platforms

Using IoT, artificial intelligence, and big data analytics, cooperative systems make real-time data exchange and decision-making possible. Blockchain technology, for instance, improves openness in carbon trading and emissions monitoring, therefore promoting global climate change mitigating cooperation.

5.14. Community involvement

Smart technologies enable local people to take part in procedures of decision-making. IoT-enabled citizen science projects, for example, let individuals of communities' record data on air and water quality, therefore aiding evidence-based decisions.

6. Conclusion

A strong and sustainable environment for the twenty-first century depends on the mix of modern technologies and sustainable behaviours. Technologies such artificial intelligence, data analytics, and the Internet of Things help to manage world issues including climate change, resource depletion, and pollution worldwide. By means of resource efficiency and environmental factor control, these technologies improve social fairness and economic progress. Effective use of smart technology depends mostly on ethical concerns, ingenuity, and teamwork. A good future depends on guarantees of data security, interoperability, and fair access to technology. A sustainable future depends on cooperation among public agencies, businesses, and individual stakeholders.

Integration of IoT, AI, and data analytics improves resource management efficiency, lowers the effects of climate change, and promotes fair development by means of these channels. Successful use of smart environments depends on addressing issues like environmental effect, interoperability, and data security. Modern technology may be used under ethical values, creative ideas, and cooperation to build a strong and sustainable future for every person.

Modern technologies combined with sustainable practices enhances quality of life and helps to preserve the surroundings. Complying with this double goal helps to guarantee a technologically sophisticated and environmentally sustainable society and thus advancing social equality. Going ahead, a coherent plan stressing innovation, teamwork, and a shared vision for a sustainable future is crucial.

References

[1] Atzori, L., Iera, A., & Morabito, G. (2010). The Internet of Things: A survey. *Computer Networks, 54*(15), 2787–2805. *https://doi.org/10.1016/j.comnet.2010.05.010.*

[2] Rolnick, D., Donti, P. L., & Kaack, L. H., (2019). Tackling climate change with machine learning. *arXiv preprint arXiv:1906.05433.*

[3] Manyika, J., Chui, M., Brown, B. et al. (2011). *Big data: The next frontier for innovation, competition, and productivity*. McKinsey Global Institute.

[4] Batty, M., Axhausen, K. W., Giannotti, F., et al. (2012). Smart cities of the future. *The European Physical Journal Special Topics, 214*(1), 481–518. *https://doi.org/10.1140/epjst/e2012-01703-3*

[5] United Nations. (2015). *Transforming our world: The 2030 Agenda for Sustainable Development*. United Nations General Assembly.

[6] Neumann, J. E., & Emanuel, K. A. (2018). Climate change and its impacts on ecosystems and human health. *Nature Climate Change, 8*(6), 531–540. *https://doi.org/10.1038/s41558-018-0182-1*

[7] Sassen, S. (2019). *Cities in a world economy*. Sage Publications.

[8] Rees, W. E., & Wackernagel, M. (2013). The ecological footprint and sustainable development. *Ecological Economics, 45*(3), 321–332. *https://doi.org/10.1016/S0921-8009(03)00088-6*

[9] IPCC. (2018). Global warming of 1.5°C. Intergovernmental Panel on Climate Change.

[10] Song, X., & Zegeye, E. (2017). Resource efficiency and sustainable development. *Journal of Cleaner Production, 142*, 1–10. *https://doi.org/10.1016/j.jclepro.2016.10.0*

[11] Rocha, J. C. (2018). Pollution and its impacts on ecosystems and human health. *Environmental Science & Technology, 52*(12), 6543–6550. *https://doi.org/10.1021/acs.est.8b01236*

[12] Batty, M. (2018). *Inventing future cities*. MIT Press.

26 Innovation in communication protocols: Impact and effectiveness in professional settings

G. Gandhi Mathi[1,a] and R. Abilasha[2,b]

[1]Research Scholar, Department of English, Holy Cross College (Autonomous), Nagercoil-4. Affiliated to Manonmaniam Sundaranar University, Abishekapatti, Tirunelveli, Tamil Nadu, India
[2]Assistant Professor, Department of English, Holy Cross College (Autonomous), Nagercoil-4. Affiliated to Manonmaniam Sundaranar University, Abishekapatti, Tirunelveli, Tamil Nadu, India

Abstract: Communication is a vital skill that encompasses various aspects of verbal and non-verbal methods including written communication, visual communication, and interpersonal communication. Verbal communication plays a significant role in professional settings during interviews and business meetings. Non-Verbal communication involves conveying messages without the usage of words. In professional settings, communication plays a pivotal role in how one understands and interacts with others. It fosters a positive and healthy work environment. Considering the lack of communication skills among youths as one of the major impediments to success, Tamil Nadu Skill Development Corporation (TNSDC) has funded programmes to improve the soft skills of the youths. In Kanyakumari district over 17% of graduates are unemployed (Proportion Unemployed) This paper throws spotlight on the significance of effective communication that underline some strategies to enhance efficiency, security, and adaptability in different professional settings.

Keywords: Communication, listening, non-verbal, pronunciation, speaking, verbal

1. Introduction

Communication is the act of transmitting information, complex ideas, and feelings, either verbally or non-verbally. It involves expressing one's ideas and understanding others', requiring a sender and a receiver. It can occur between two individuals, in small groups, or in larger teams and effective communication demands concentration and attention. "India is a leading hub for software development, boasting a vast pool of English-speaking, technically skilled professionals, making it an ideal destination for IT outsourcing" (p. 9289) [11].

In this paper, a quantitative research approach was employed to examine the impact of strong communication skills on teamwork, work efficiency, and negotiation skills. The primary objective is to understand the patterns of communication in professional settings and identify ways to enhance them.

2. Review of Literature

George and Alexandru Marius [1], highlighted in their study "The Role of Communication in Enhancing Work Effectiveness of an Organization" asserts that communication and management are crucial for business success. The study also sheds light on how company management communicates with employees. Effective communication between employers and the employees is essential for coordinating professional activities. The paper concludes that communication is an effective management tool in professional settings, helping achieve the company's objectives.

Daniela Vogel, Marco Meyer and Sigrid Harendza [2] explored the significance of communication in medical encounters in their paper "Verbal and non-verbal communication skills including empathy during history taking of undergraduate medical students" The assessment revealed that undergraduate medical students' verbal communication correlated significantly with their non-verbal communication but not with their empathy. However, their empathy correlated significantly with their non-verbal communication.

Dr. Bushra Sumaiya and et al in their paper "The Role of Effective Communication Skills in Professional Life," explored the significance of effective communication skills in the workplace, identifying common barriers and proposing strategies to overcome them. It also emphasized that effective communication is pivotal for professional

---

[a]gandhimathi2312@gmail.com, [b]abilasha.r@holycrossngl.edu.in

DOI: 10.1201/9781003778905-26

success, highlighting the importance of active listening. The study underscores the need for graduate programs to prioritize communication skills development.

Carolyn Henzi Plaza and Suzzana Windon, in their article "Effective Communication in the Workplace," examine the benefits of effective communication in professional settings and provide practical strategies to enhance communication skills. It also explores communication planning strategies and guidelines for both senders and receivers. The authors highlight that effective workplace communication lifts job satisfaction and productivity.

3. Verbal Communication

This mode of communication includes spoken and written words to convey the intended message and are essential to communicate the message clearly and concisely. Humans share knowledge and express ideas and thoughts verbally and non-verbally. "There has been a steady fall in performance regarding their language skills. This poses a serious threat" (p. 204) [3]. Verbal communication allows one to exchange ideas, thoughts, and emotions through words. In non-verbal cues, speakers convey messages through facial expressions, appropriate hand gestures, and body language. Effective listening leads to effective communication. Intrapersonal, Interpersonal, Small group communication and public communication are the four types of verbal communication.

Intrapersonal: Communication occurs within oneself that takes place within the brain. Examples – Decision making and day dreaming

Interpersonal: Communication happens between two or more people.

Examples – Communication between two friends and between mother and a son

Small Group Communication: Interaction occurs with a purpose. It happens between three or more people for academic purpose, task completion, group discussions. Examples – Conference calls and feedback sessions

Public Communication: Speaker transfers information to a majority of people. Examples - Election Campaign and through mass media.

4. Fundamentals of Verbal Communication

The process of communication includes encoding and decoding. Encoding means the process of creation of message by the sender. Verbal and non-verbal cues take place in encoding. In decoding the receiver decodes the meaning of the message after interpreting it by observing the body language, facial expressions, gestures, emotions.

Completeness: The message conveyed by the sender has to be complete. The sender's message is expected to be complete containing all necessary information, facts, and answers to all the questions the listeners ask. Completeness in information build trust, enhances understanding that reduces misunderstandings and leads to better outcome in personal and professional settings.

Correctness: It means the accuracy of the words and figures used for communication. The message needs to be free from grammatical errors, punctuation, and spelling.

Consideration: The act of considering the preferences, feelings from the receiver's point of view. It focuses more on "You."

Clarity: Communication must be precise and concrete using simple language, proper punctuation, and facial expressions avoiding ambiguous terms.

Conciseness: Communicating messages in brief and to the point eliminate irrelevant details. It is the sole procedure of effective communication.

Courtesy: Use of expressions that shows respect and appreciation from both the sender and the receiver fosters a positive environment.

Concreteness: Use of solid facts and figures for transferring information lead to concreteness. The use of real-life examples, charts, graphs, descriptive adjectives, and adverbs emphasize on the points that helps listeners remember the information for long time.

Tone and Volume: The quality and loudness of the voice convey the attitude and emotions of the sender. It stresses the important points and adds meaning to the message.

Pronunciation and Vocabulary: Pronunciation of the words should be clear, distinct, and understandable for the targeted audience. The choice of words is expected to be appropriate to convey the message precisely.

4.1. Training project

Table 26.1 highlights the key economic drivers, key partners, job roles, target group, training target people, cost of training for the project "Training for Soft Skills and English Communication." In the tabular column given above column 1 mentions the job roles "Training for Soft Skills and in spoken English." In Column 2 the "NSQF level" is mentioned as 2 and in Column 3 NSQF code is mentioned as MEP/N9995 & MEP/N9993. In Column 4 "cost category" is mentioned as 3. In column 4, the "duration of training (Hours)" is mentioned as 180 hours[40] In column 5 "target group" is highlighted as graduates who have completed courses from Degree Colleges, Engineering Colleges. In column 6, 'training target people' is mentioned as 4000 and in the 7th column "cost of training (₹ Crores)" is mentioned as ₹3.1 Crores. The Assessment costs (₹1,000 per Assessment) is ₹0.4 Crores and in total government has provided ₹3.5 Crores to bridge the skill gaps of the youth.

Table 26.1. Training for soft skills and English communication

Name of the Project: Training for Soft Skills and English Communication
Key Economic Drivers: Lack of communication skills has been identified as a major contributor towards unemployment of the youth in District
Key Partners: British Council

Column 1	*Column 2*	*Column 3*	*Column 4*	*Column 5*	*Column 6*	*Column 7*	*Column 8*
Job Roles	*NSQF Level*	*NSQF Code*	*Cost Category*	*Duration of Training (Hours)*	*Target Group*	*Training Target (People)*	*Cost of Training (₹ Crores)*
Training for Soft Skills and in spoken English	4	MEP/ N9995 & MEP/ N9993	3	180 hours[40]	Graduates who have completed courses from Degree Colleges, Engineering Colleges	4,000	₹3.1 Crores
Total Training Costs						4,000	₹3.1 Crores
Assessment Costs (₹1,000 per Assessment)							₹0.4 Crores
Total							₹3.5 Crores

Abbreviation:
National Skills Qualification Framework (NSQF)
Key Considerations:
- Soft skills especially, communication skills, interpersonal skills, work ethics etc., has been identified as a major contributor towards the low employability for the youth. In addition, the IT-ITES Sector / Tourism & Hospitality sectors have highlighted the requirement for good communication skills in English.
- Kerala's Additional Skill Acquisition Program and Andhra Pradesh's Employability Skill Centers are models that have similar components of Soft Skill and English Communication

Source: Author.

4.2. Non-verbal communication

Non-Verbal communication plays a significant role in day to day lives. It is referred as "a process in which communicators use the natural features of their bodies to deliver information and express specific meaning instinctively to the other communicator" (p. 90) [8]. It involves conveying messages without the usage of words. Messages conveyed through non-verbal cues plays a pivotal role in how one understands and interacts with others. "Nonverbal cues convey care, honesty, and attentiveness" [12].

4.3. Types of non-verbal communication

- **Facial Expressions:** It is one of the most universal forms of non-verbal communication. Chad notes that "using common expressions makes speakers sound more natural and less artificial" [6]. Countless emotions such as happiness, sadness, anger, surprise, anxiety are often expressed through facial movements.
- **Eye Contact:** Maintaining Eye contact is one of the powerful tools during the process of communication. It can convey a range of emotions and intentions, from attentiveness to aggression. Eye contact helps to identify if the message conveyed is true or not.
- **Paralanguage:** Paralanguage includes the activities that happens in the vocal elements that accompany speech, such as tone, pitch, volume, and speaking rate. These elements support the verbal message and can modify the meaning of verbal messages.
- **Gestures:** Gestures involve movements of the hands, arms, or other parts of the body to convey messages or emphasize speech. It helps in avoiding misinterpretation.
- **Body Language:** Body postures such as standing, sitting, walking, holding hands express confidence, fear, openness. It plays a great during communication.
- **Proxemics:** Proxemics implies the use of personal space in communication. The distance maintained in interactions can indicate the levels of comfort, intimacy, or authority.
- **Haptics:** Physical touch is another significant non-verbal communication. Communication through touch can convey a variety of messages and emotions, depending on the context and relationship between individuals.

4.4. Significance of non-verbal communication

- **Communicate Emotions:** Non-verbal communication often conveys emotions more precisely than words. Facial expressions, paralanguage, and body language can effectively express feelings like happiness, sadness, anger, and surprise.

- **Strengthen Relationships:** Eye contact, touch, and body language play significant roles in establishing trust, and rapport. Non-verbal communication is crucial in developing and maintaining relationships.
- **Cntradicting Verbal Messages:** Non-verbal cues can sometimes contradict verbal messages and reveal true feelings or intentions. Facial expressions and posture help understand the true feelings.
- **Perceptions:** Non-verbal communication shapes how others perceive of an individual. "Culture and Society influence nonverbal behaviour and how it is understood" (p. 208) [9]. Confident body language, appropriate facial expressions, and good posture can create a positive impression.
- **Cultural Understanding:** Non-verbal communication varies across cultures. Being aware of and understanding the cross-cultural interactions can prevent misunderstandings. It enhances the communication and show respect for other cultures.
- **Enhance Interaction:** Effective use of non-verbal cues, such as appropriate facial expressions, and active listening signals, can enhance the interaction from classrooms to business meetings.
- **Empathy and Understanding:** Non-verbal communication can convey empathy and understanding through a sympathetic look, a comforting touch, or simply being physically present. It helps enhance the relationship and communication.

Non-verbal cues help the visual and kinesthetic learners, understand, and retain information easily. "Nonverbal cues are a crucial, yet often overlooked, aspect of communication" (p. 173) [7]. Using visual aids, demonstrations, and body language can enhance learning for these individuals.

5. Communication in Different Professional Settings

- **Meetings:** Formal communication takes place in business meetings. In meetings formal language is used to express ideas logically. Meeting starts with an agenda, the speaker articulate strong points, and conclude with a summary. Active listening, clarity, time constraints and open feedback are significant. Listening and speaking skills plays an essential role in business meetings.
- **Interviews:** Language proficiency is crucial for an interviewer or interviewee. Formal language and professional tone are used. Non-verbal cues like body posture, facial expression add supplement to the verbal communication. Clear and concise question answer, confidence in tone and language choice are essential during the interview process.
- **Presentations:** Both verbal and non-verbal communication strengthen the presentations and public speaking. The choice of engaging topics, storytelling, visual aids is important to keep the audience engaged during presentations and public speaking. Regular practice before the actual presentation boosts confidence and enhances communication. Positive body language, face to face conversation, practice sessions, clarity, and brevity help reinforce the message strongly.
- **Customer Service:** Polite and respectful language strengthen customer relationships. Straightforward and empathetic dialogue during customer inquiries create good customer experience. Clear communication avoiding unnecessary tangents and actionable advice are the agenda for favourable customer service. Conversing in professional tone, responding promptly, offering solutions and taking responsibility for the inconveniences enhance the reputation of the organization.
- **Educational Settings:** Verbal communication in educational settings build relationships between teacher-students, parent-teachers and strengthen relationship in the different other institutions. Both formal and informal communication is pivotal in school settings. Communication style varies at every educational level. Interactive sessions, feedback sessions for teachers, students, group discussions, motivate and encourage learners. Creating a sympathetic and empathetic environment in school settings fosters a good environment for the growth of the students.
- **Client Communication:** Effective communication skill is necessary to build rapport with a company and its customers that involves competence, confidence, positive body language, while attending phone calls and responding to emails during communication with clients for mutual understanding. Bedi suggests that "communicative approaches enable learners to apply skills in professional settings" (p. 48) [5]. Organizational skills with clear knowledge on the subject, active listening and responding to the queries build trust and enhance strong professional relationships.

6. Strategies

Employers who have good subject knowledge and effectively convey ideas with appropriate facial expressions and body language help in getting the intended outcome. "Literature is a powerful tool in language learning by fostering critical thinking and broadening perspectives" (p. 188) [10]. Effective verbal and non-verbal communication are essential in professional settings to convey ideas with clarity and brevity.

- **Develop Listening Skills:** Actively listening to the speaker without interrupting the flow of communication is significant. Focusing completely on the speaker and simultaneously noting down vital points would be helpful to recall the gist. Summarizing the content and giving feedbacks at the end also would be beneficial for both the speaker and the listener.

- **Effective Nonverbal Cues:** Non-verbal cues enhance the transfer of ideas. Face to face conversation with listener make the communication more engaging. Use of positive facial expressions and appropriate hand gestures might emphasize the points strongly.
- **Clarity and Concise:** Use of strong points and structured sentence help in conveying the messages precisely. Use of complex sentence and unnecessary tangents could be misunderstood easily. Sticking to main points and passing it with clarity can be effective during verbal communication.
- **Tone and Style:** Tone has to be formal in business meetings, interviews, client communication. Tone can be moderate during casual conversation. During lectures and meetings, the speaker has to make sure that the voice is audible and words delivered at a moderate pace and the pronunciation of words need to be clear to all the listeners. Moreover, appropriate tone and style add relevance to the situation to connect with the audience.
- **Use of Technology:** With the emerging technologies for learning, the speaker could utilize technology effectively to enhance the communication. Speaker needs to ensure if the audio or video works correctly before the online or offline technical session. The use of power point slides, use of relevant videos aids in communicating the content efficiently. Effective verbal communication is significant on online meeting platforms like Microsoft Teams, zoom, google meet.
- **Practice Sessions:** Practice thoroughly before the actual presentation boosts the confidence of the speaker. Practicing in front of the mirror can alleviates the pressure and motivates to speak up boldly. Consecutively, knowledgeable speaker on the topic concerned would answer follow up questions raised by the listeners.
- **Feedback:** Feedback sessions at the end of the lecture or meetings is beneficial for both the speaker and the audience. Valuable feedbacks pave way for speakers' growth. Speakers have to accept both criticisms and appreciations equally and respond promptly to the questions raised. If the answer is unknown, the speaker should not overlook the question instead could ask for permission and answer it during the next lecture or meeting.

Strategies for effective verbal communication significantly enhances effective interactions between colleagues, officials, administrative members leading to build strong personal and professional relationship.

7. Advances in Technology

a) **Unified Communication (UC)**: Streamlines multiple communication tools including voice, video, and text communication into one platform.
b) **Cloud-based communication:** Facilitates effortless, secure, and scalable communication, while reducing costs and increasing flexibility.
c) **AI-Powered Chatbots**: Streamlines customer support, providing swift and personalized responses that optimize communication workflows.
d) **Virtual Reality:** Fostering teamwork and innovation through immersive virtual meetings and shared workspaces.

8. Conclusion

Effective communication is the keystone of successful teamwork, collaboration, and rapport-building among employers. Effective workplace communication "minimizes miscommunication risks" [4]. In today's fast-paced professional landscape, excelling in communication is crucial for maintaining a healthy work environment, fostering positive relationships, and achieving business objectives. By emphasizing the importance of effective communication and providing actionable strategies for improvement, this research paper aims to empower professionals to excel in their roles and drive business success.

References

[1] Bucăţa, G., & Rizescu, A. M. (2017). The role of communication in enhancing work effectiveness of an organization. *Land Forces Academy Review*, *22*(1), 49–57. 10.1515/raft-2017-0008.

[2] Vogel, D., Meyer, M., & Harendza, S. (2018). Verbal and non-verbal communication skills including empathy during history taking of undergraduate medical students. *BMC medical education*, *18*(1), 157. https://doi.org/10.1186/s12909-018-1260-9

[3] Abilasha, R., & Ilankumaran, M. (2018). English language teaching: challenges and strategies from the Indian Perspective. *International Journal of Engineering and Technology (IJET)*, *7*(3), 202–205. 10.14419/ijet. v7i3.6.14970.

[4] Barnard, D. (2019). The Importance of Soft Skills. https://virtualspeech.com/blog/importance-soft-skills

[5] Bedi, K. K. (2010). Communicative Approach to Soft Skills: Its Relevance and Implementation. *The*

Journal of English Language Teaching, *48*(1). ISSN 0973-5208.

[6] Chad. (2013). English Expression: The Importance of Learning Expressions. https://reallifeglobal.com/english-expressions/

[7] Dash, B. B., & Davis, K. (2022). Significance of non-verbal communication and paralinguistic features in communication: A critical analysis. *International Journal for Innovative Research in Multidisciplinary Field*, *8*(4), 172–179. doi:10.2015/IJIRMF/202204029.

[8] Guan, Y. (2004). Nonverbal communication and college English teaching. *Jing Ji Shi, 02*, 90–91.

[9] Hess, U. (2016). Nonverbal communication. *Encyclopedia of mental health*, *2*(3), 208–218. doi:10.1016/B978-0-12-397045-9.002184.

[10] Ilankumaran, M., & Deepa, P. (2018). Teaching literature enhances communication skills–a study with special emphasis on poetry. *International Journal of Engineering & Technology*, *7*(3.6), 187–191.

[11] Premalatha, T. R. (2019). Development of Education in Kanyakumari District. *Scholarly Research Journal for Humanity Science & English Language, Online ISSN 2348-3083, SJ IMPACT FACTOR 2017: 5.068, www.srjis.com Peer Reviewed & Referred Journal*, *7*(34).

[12] Segal, J., Smith, M., & Robinson, L. (2025). Body Language and Non-Verbal Communication Communicating Without Words. Help Guide.org.https://www.helpguide.org/articles/relationships-communication/nonverbal communication.htm

[13] Skilling for the Future Skill Gap Assessment & Action Plan for Tamil Nadu District Skill Development for Tamil Nadu District Skill Development Plan for Tamil Nadu. (2019). *Tamil Nadu Skill Development Corporation*, 52.

27 Cartoons for enhancing speaking skills

Susmitha Sharu R.[1,a] *and R. Abilasha*[2,b]

[1]Research Scholar, Department of English, Holy Cross College (Autonomous), Nagercoil-4. Affiliated to Manonmaniam Sundaranar University, Abishekapatti, Tirunelveli, Tamil Nadu, India
[2]Assistant Professor, Department of English, Holy Cross College (Autonomous), Nagercoil-4. Affiliated to Manonmaniam Sundaranar University, Abishekapatti, Tirunelveli, Tamil Nadu, India

Abstract: English as a language has developed over ages. English Language Teaching (ELT) is the process of teaching English to non-native English speakers. In the 21st century, social media and cartoons have made it easy for learners to learn speaking skills smoothly. Cartoons play a pivotal role in the lives of children, who grow watching them. It acts as a knowledge provider wherein it entertains and keeps the kids engaged. It serves as a platform in edutaining the learners. This paper emphasizes on how cartoons function as a promising stand in enhancing speaking skills of the learners. The study also differentiates the impact of using cartoons as a tool in improving the speaking skills of the learners. This quantitative study comprises thirty learners as experimental group respondents. The learners were imparted with vocabulary and phrases in order to enhance their speaking skills through verbal classes. The results were collected through a pre-test followed by their exposure to cartoons such as Oswald and Scooby Doo!. To observe their acquisition to new words and short phrases, a post-test was conducted and the results were analyzed. A noticeable change is observed in the post-test results based on the usage of cartoons.

Keywords: Cartoons, edutainment, English language teaching, learners, social media, speaking skills

1. Introduction

Learning of any language requires effort and concentration. Language plays a crucial role in every individual's life as it helps in maintaining a good rapport with individuals. It helps in conveying ideas and thoughts without misinterpretation. It acts as a bridge for sharing emotions. English is learnt as a second language in India. English is considered a global language and therefore it is essential for an individual to possess good language skills to survive in any situation across the world. Teaching and learning of English is the need of the hour, since it has emerged as a global language. The significant skills of English Language Teaching are listening, speaking, reading and writing. Imparting the four language skills of learning have endured changes over time.The basic aspect of ELT is to enhance learners' language skills.

1.1. Research question

Are cartoons an effective learning tool in enhancing learners' speaking skills?

1.2. Objectives

The paper discusses

- cartoons as an effective tool for language acquisition.
- the role of cartoons in enhancing speaking skills.

1.3. Hypothesis

Cartoons act as an effective aid in promoting speaking skills of the learners.

2. Review of Literature

Sandamali Gamage [1] in "Cartoons as an Authentic Supplementary Teaching Tool in English as a Second Language Classrooms" states the usage of cartoons in shaping the language skills among learners of English as the second language, especially speaking skills. The empirical study demonstrates that majority of the students energetically participated in the assigned tasks related to cartoons and the learners also established a positive perception towards the use of cartoons.

Le Thi Thuy Nhung [2] in "Impacts of using cartoons as an instructional tool in English communicative skills of young learners of a Vietnamese primary school" throws light on the impact of cartoons in the learning process. The study was conducted among the fifth grade learners who were divided into control group and experiment group. The learners in the experiment group were taught similar

[a]sharukumar108@gmail.com, [b]abilasha.r@holycrossngl.edu.in

DOI: 10.1201/9781003778905-27

lessons which included cartoons as a medium. The observations after the examination revealed significant changes among the learners in the experiment group compared to that of the control group. The study further recommends the usage of cartoons in classrooms for effective participation of students.

Ceren Duran [3] in "Improving the Speaking Skill of Primary School Students Instructed in a Multigrade Class through Cartoons" speaks about the impact of cartoons on the learners with speaking disability. The result of the study discloses learners' ability to speak confidently, forming sentences, usage of new vocabulary, increased conversation and improved pronunciation. It also reveals the adjustment in tones, sounds and a positive change towards the psychological dimensions of the learners' speech.

Jaisy Yasmin Alphariyadi [4] in "How Cartoon Can Improve Speaking Skill" deals with the effectiveness of cartoon based learning in enhancing speaking skills. A qualitative method was undertaken by the researcher and it is found that learners' level of confidence has improved so as their knowledge towards technology. The paper also suggests that cartoons aid in the teaching-learning process when used appropriately.

3. Evolution of Learning

Learning has experienced significant transformations over the centuries. In the past, learners often sought knowledge from gurus, gaining insights into various aspects of life. This approach has evolved, leading to the development of homeschooling, formal schools and distance education. There existed a period when educational institutions were temporarily closed during the pandemic which gave raise to admittance of social media into education. The rise of social media has introduced many effective ways to acquire skills. Social media could be utilized effectively for a brighter future. Almost anything could be learned through these platforms, including new languages and language skills. English language proficiency could also be improved by engaging the contents of social media and even cartoons.

3.1. Cartoons

Cartoons are loved by people of all ages. It has been a part of childhood. Every individual carries a sweet memory associated with cartoons. It is a great form of entertainment and also it could be a great platform to enrich language skills. Cartoons that are produced in United Kingdom provide the viewers with the experience of the actual British life. These cartoons could be effective in the learning process only when they are watched in English. The sole purpose of implanting cartoons into learning is to impart English language skills among kids without making them lose interest in learning. The UK produced cartoons such as Oswald [5] and Teletubbies help the audience learn new vocabulary and short phrases and so do Scooby-Doo! and The Powerpuff Girls that are produced in America. These cartoons provide the learners not only with new glossary and wordings, but also enrich the pronunciation with proper accent and voice modulation. In fact, there are people who assure that cartoons have created a greater impact on their English language proficiency.

3.2. Oswald

Oswald is a television educational series for pre-school children (Figure 27.1). The title character Oswald is a blue octopus that lives with a pet dog Weenie. The series follows the day-to-day life experiences of Oswald. It edutains the children and provides them with an optimistic outlook on life. The colourful picturization and the thoughtful whimsical dialogues of the characters attract the young learners. It also focuses on the British accent in a simple and comprehensive manner as it is a UK produced series. Though it has been long since the series has been released, it holds a unique place in the hearts of the learners who have grown watching it and it is also suggested for kindergarteners to learn simple English.

3.3. Scooby-Doo!

Scooby-Doo! [6] is an American series that revolves around solving mysteries with four friends and their pet Scooby Doo (Figure 27.2). The series is known for its visual presentation and spookiness that keeps the kids involved. Conversational skills could be improved through this series. It also offers the audience with new words and catchy phrases irrespective of the American accent.

4. Methodology

Thirty two students of classes I and II were randomly chosen for the study. They were given verbal classes on

Figure 27.1. Oswald.

Source: Author.

Figure 27.2. Scooby-Doo!

Source: Author.

vocabulary and word phrases. The students were later exposed to the above mentioned cartoons. There was a huge difference between the authentic teaching and cartoon blended learning. The students were able to understand the words easily, pronounce the words in proper accent and use the words appropriately. The learners were able to speak and frame phrases in both the methods of teaching, but through cartoon blended learning, the effectiveness of learning process stays longer. The following are the results of the study.

5. Results

Table 27.1 reflects the initial and the increased activity in pre-cycle, cycle I and cycle II. Column one indicates the cycles. Column two shows the observations of typical classroom learning (Pre-cycle), Cartoons embedded learning (Cycle 1) and teaching speaking skills through cartoons (Cycle II) in percentages. Column three displays the overall results of Pre-cycle, Cycle I and Cycle II. It is clearly evident from the table that there is a transformation in the learners' skills. Table 27.2 provides details of the developed speaking skills of the students.

Table 27.2 displays the improved analysis of speaking skills among the learners. Column 1 indicates the average value, improved speaking skills, number of students who have improved and the category. Columns 2, 3 and 4 exhibit the improved analysis of Pre-cycle, Cycle I and Cycle II respectively. The results clearly provide that cartoons have helped the learners in refining their speaking skills, including vocabulary and short phrases.

Figure 27.3 diagram shows the results of improved speaking skills among the students. It is evidenced that cartoons when used as an instructional tool, helps the learners learn things easily and effectually.

Table 27.1. Increased activity in pre-cycle, cycle I and cycle II

Activities	*Observation (%)*	*Result*
Pre-cycle	53	Fair
Cycle I	75	Good
Cycle II	99.2	Very Good

Source: Author.

5.1. Analysis

Cartoons act as a game changer in today's world, where social media and AI tools rule. Children are glued to television series and movies. The series and movies that are entertaining and intriguing attract the audience. Cartoons are the sources that provide the audience with entertainment and knowledge. The study reveals that the students who are exposed to the regular teaching learning process exhibited great transformation when they are introduced to cartoons as an instructional tool. The impact of cartoons in enhancing the learner's speaking skills is evident from the results obtained.

5.2. Recommendations

- Implementing cartoons as a part of learning material might help the learners to develop speaking skills.

Table 27.2. Improved speaking skills of learners

Aspect	*Pre-cycle*	*Cycle I*	*Cycle II*
Average Value	67.74	74.87	82.26
Improved Speaking Skills	28.12	53.12	96.87
Number of Students Who have improved	9	17	31
Category	Was not improved	Somewhat improved	Was successful

Source: Author.

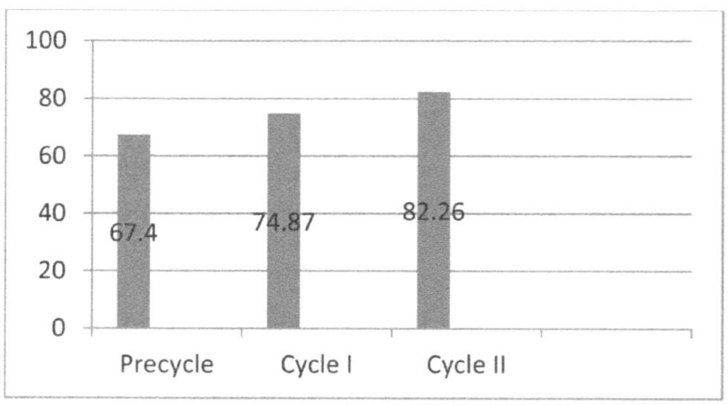

Figure 27.3. Improved speaking skills of learners.

Source: Author.

- The educators are to be aware of the accurate usage of cartoons for a desired outcome.
- There is a minimal need for strong technical skills in applying cartoons into the process of learning.

6. Conclusion

Teaching-learning process is made easy using the technologies and social media. Cartoons boost the process in an effective manner. The role of cartoons in shaping the language expertise is significant as it makes the method of learning stress-free. It develops the learners' confidence and boosts the conversational skills. The students who face discomfort during public speaking could be rectified using cartoons. It creates a joyous environment and eliminates the anxiety of the young learners, which in turn reflects in their psychological and personal growth. This study thus discloses that edutainment in the form of cartoons is welcomed by majority of the students, since their basic need for entertainment is left undisturbed during the learning process.

References

[1] Gamage, S. (2019). Cartoons as an Authentic Supplementary Teaching Tool in English as a Second Language Classrooms. *Advances in Language and Literary Studies*, *10*(1). https://files.eric.ed.gov/fulltext/EJ1216993.pdf.

[2] Nhung, L. T. T. (2020). Impacts of using cartoons as an instructional tool in English communicative skills of young learners of a Vietnamese primary school. *Ho Chi Minh City Open University Jour. of Science*, *10*(2), 78–86. *https://ideas.repec.org/a/bjw/socien/v10y2020i2p7886.html#:~:text=The%20findings%20show%20the%20English,watching%20cartoons%20in%20English%20classes.*

[3] Duran, C. (2021). Improving the Speaking Skill of Primary School Students Instructed in a Multigrade Class through Cartoons. *Participatory Educational Research (PER)*, *8*(4), 44–63. *https://eric.ed.gov/?id=EJ1300871.*

[4] Alphariyadi & Jaisy Yasmin. (2024). How Cartoon Can Improve Speaking Skill. *Fonologi: Jurnal Ilmuan Bahasa dan Sastra Inggris*, *2*(3). *https://www.researchgate.net/publication/382936906_How_Cartoon_Can_Improve_Speaking_Skill.*

[5] Oswald (TV Series 2001–2003). (2024). *IMDb*, *https://images.app.goo.gl/hcbhukmQkegsiNFy5.*

[6] Scooby-Doo (Franchise). (2023). *TV Tropes*, *https://images.app.goo.gl/u7N6VCfKAgTdr9vb9.*

28 Innovative strategies for teaching English to learners with learning disabilities

S. Sajna Beevi[1,a] *and R. Abilasha*[2,b]

[1]Research Scholar, Department of English, Holy Cross College (Autonomous), Nagercoil-4. Affiliated to Manonmaniam Sundaranar University, Abishekapatti, Tirunelveli, Tamil Nadu, India
[2]Assistant Professor, Department of English, Holy Cross College (Autonomous), Nagercoil-4. Affiliated to Manonmaniam Sundaranar University, Abishekapatti, Tirunelveli, Tamil Nadu, India

Abstract: Teachers play a vital role in moulding the intellectual experiences of students with academic challenges. This study investigates the competency of teachers in identifying and understanding the various requirements of second language learners for their academic and personal growth. Teachers are expected to frame an inclusive classroom environment that helps students to foster their self-esteem. This involves differentiating instruction, utilizing assistive technologies, and engaging in continuous assessment and feedback. For that, teachers have to be knowledgeable and approachable to converse with parents, caretakers, and other members closely associated with the challenged learners. The paper also emphasizes on the selected learning disability like dyslexia and the eminence of teachers' competency in fostering a positive learning environment where teaching and learning can thrive better. For the study, data were collected from fifty secondary school students from two different streams like commerce and science through questionnaire. By equipping teachers with the necessary tools and technology to handle the needs of these students, the quality of learning may be improved.

Keywords: Competence, disability, dyslexia, inclusivity learners, second language, teachers

1. Introduction

In the current educational scenario, varying from the traditional teaching methods, a thorough understanding of each student's strength and encountering their challenges in their learning journey is mandatory. Nowadays, children face numerous challenges like attention deficiency, slow process of acquiring knowledge, and unexplained stress due to internalized and externalized difficulties. In this circumstance, teachers play a major role to embracing learners with specialized strategies to confront their needs. Teachers must be proficient in handling these special students with differentiating instruction, incorporating with assistive technologies and understanding alternative ways to access the content. Moreover, deep evaluation and timely feedback are mandatory to monitor the progress of learners; accordingly teachers can generate strategies to meet students' specific needs both inside and outside the classroom.

1.1. Role of teachers

Teachers have to be eminent in addressing the specific needs and issues faced by the language learners with learning disability (LD). Such students not only find it difficult to cope with acquiring a new language but also in writing, reading, and processing information etc. With the well-equipped usage of tools, techniques and mindset, teachers can transform the challenges faced by learners into opportunities for personal and academic growth and equip them to realize their capabilities. Moreover, patience and emotional support are equally important in strengthening the confidence of learners with LD, as these children need extra care and guidance to actively engage in classroom exercises [3]. Teachers can also promote communication skills by generating a suitable atmosphere, where learners feel relaxed while practising their skills without fear of judgement. Through personal interaction, teachers can develop individual learning plans, handle the specific needs of each student, and make them resourceful.

2. Literature Review

In the article titled, "Awareness of Learning Disabilities Among Elementary School Teachers", Menon, Seema K. P. [5] stated that, apart from their gender and teaching backgrounds, the tutors involved in this analysis have minimal knowledge of specific learning disabilities. This

[a]sajnahameed278@gmail.com, [b]abilasha.r@holycrossngl.edu.in

DOI: 10.1201/9781003778905-28

is due to the lack of sufficient training to handle students with learning disabilities. The article concludes that controlling mental and social harm requires proper training based on the special needs of teachers in handling dyslexic learners, then only they will better be able to identify and manage dyslexic learners in their classroom.

Juhri Abdul Muin, Riyanto and Satriyo Budi Wibowo [1], in their article "Teacher Competencies for Dyslexia Students" focuses on identifying teachers' competency in dealing with dyslexic students. This study emphasized the importance of providing special training to understand dyslexic students, and argued that without proper backup, teachers may fail to catch-up the needs of not only dyslexic learners but also those with other educational challenges. This article analyzes various surveys to strengthen the study. The results indicate that teachers play an important role in handling the dyslexic students through proper training to effectively assist learners with disabilities.

3. Teachers Competency Required for Addressing Academic Challenges

- Understanding Learning Disabilities - Knowledge of various learning disabilities (e.g., dyslexia, dysgraphia, attention deficit hyperactivity disorder) and their impact on students' academic performance.
- Ability to identify and assess students with learning difficulties and provide appropriate interventions.
- Use of Differentiated Instruction to meet the diverse needs of students.
- Capability to handle lessons, tasks, and assessments related to individualized learning styles and abilities.
- Ability to manage classroom using unique techniques to create a structured and supportive environment.
- Effective use of Assistive Technologies and understanding how to integrate these tools effectively into the learning process.
- Regularly collaboration with learners to monitor their progress.
- Emotional sensitivity to understand the challenges and struggles of learners.
- Adaptability and problem-solving skills.
- Commitment to engage in continuous learning to stay updated on the best practices for addressing academic challenges.

4. Identifying Dyslexic Learners

Dyslexia is a learning disability in which learners have difficulty to understand and using language for reading, writing, listening and speaking. This partially affects their ability to recognize and process written text. In second language acquisition, dyslexic students may struggle more than learners with general language difficulties. Dyslexia can overlap with the typical complications of learning a new language. Through certain signs, teachers can diagnose dyslexia separately from other general learning disabilities [2]. Dyslexic second language learners may regularly struggle with reading, mainly with decoding words, spelling patterns and sounds of letters even with substantial practice. It also leads to slow reading fluency, mispronounciation of words, and difficulty in recalling new vocabulary. In that view, typical English language learners who constantly improve their language exposure while dyslexic students may fail to attain all the tasks. Early identification is vital along with timely interventions like specialized strategies to improve overall learning experience for dyslexic learners.

5. Early identification and Diagnosis

Early detection and diagnosis of dyslexia are essential in maintaining prompt support to learners and restrict long-term academic barrier. Through identifying the early signs like difficulty in writing, spelling and letter recognition, allows teachers and specialists to mediate before these challenges terribly affect a student's learning journey. Fawcett (2008) stated that "The problems faced by many dyslexic children are by no means confined to reading and spelling. There appears to be a general impairment in the ability to perform skills automatically, an ability thought to be dependent upon the cerebellum" [4]. For dyslexia, signs may include difficulty with phonological awareness, confusion with same-sounding words and slow reading progress. Early diagnosis through assistive technologies, personalized instruction and accommodations assures that learners obtain the support they need to develop their reading and writing skills, fostering both academic and cognitive success.

6. Instructional Strategies for Inclusive Environment

1. Tailored instruction to meet the expectation of individuals with various teaching methods (auditory, visual, kinaesthetic)
2. More access with the availability of visual aids.
3. Scaffold learning to provide an extra support to gain and build confidence.
4. Positive reinforcement to reduce the psychological challenges.
5. Provide flexible writing options
6. Contextualized learning connected with the real-life situations, helps to enhance the comprehension and language skills.

7. Collaborate learners with their peers in a group or pair.
8. Provide frequent practice and repetition to reinforce learning, and engage them with varied activities like games, interactive sessions, role-playing etc.

7. Assistive Technology

Assistive technology (AT) plays a vital part in upholding second language learners with learning disabilities by providing specific tools to reinforce their learning experience and language acquisition.

- **Text-to-Speech Software:** This technology convert written text into spoken words, assisting learners in understanding difficult context in a better way. It is a suitable tool for dyslexic learners, allowing them to hear the textual context read aloud.
- **Video Content with Subtitles:** Video contents with running captions help learners to enhance their listening as well as reading skills simultaneously, which will easily access the cognitive part of learners as well.
- **Applications like Duolingo and Rosetta:** These applications offer various interactive and engaging features for learning a new language. They can be easily adapted to meet the needs of learners with diverse learning disabilities.

8. Professional Development (PD) Programs for Teachers

To develop the teachers' competency in handling the learning disability students, it is essential to engage them in Professional Development (PD) programs that promote their skills and effectiveness in supporting diverse learners. Effective PD programs have to be connected with the key features of understanding learning disabilities, instructional patterns, multisensory teaching practices etc. In collaboration with parents and specialists, teachers can use assistive technologies to access and address the needs of learners with learning disabilities. There are numerous formats for PD, like online courses for teachers, workshops, the latest research on disabled learners and peer observations etc. Teachers can foster a more inclusive and suitable atmosphere to all learners through a well-structured and comprehensive program.

9. Objective of the Study

The objective of the study is to identify the difficulties faced by the dyslexic second language (L2) learners and to assess teachers' competence in fostering their self-esteem through suitable training with assistive technologies.

A questionnaire consisting of eight questions was administered to learners to gather their response.

1. Do you find it difficult to spell or recognize new words?
2. Do you get confused by similar looking letters when reading?
3. Do you struggle with pronouncing complex words?
4. Do you find it easy to use of visual aids to understand reading materials?
5. Do you feel that your teacher understands your learning difficulty?
6. Do teachers use different strategies to support your learning?
7. Do you feel happy when you receive feedback from your teacher?
8. Do you feel that your teacher creates a supportive and inclusive classroom?

10. Hypothesis

H1 - Dyslexic L2 learners tutored by trained teachers exhibit a broad progress in reading rather than the untrained teachers.

H2 - Teachers who obtain assistive coaching are able to identify and address dyslexia at its earlier stage than untrained teachers.

H3 - Dyslexic L2 learners under the guidance of trained educators shows long term academic improvement.

11. Data Analysis

A survey was conducted using a random sampling method. A questionnaire was used to collect data from a secondary school students in the maths and science group at Government Higher Secondary School, Trivandrum. The study focused on dyslexia and how teachers support students with learning challenges. A total of fifty students from two different academic streams participated in the study. The questionnaire included eight questions about dyslexic learners and teachers' ability to handle learning difficulties in the classroom.

Students were asked to respond by selecting one of five options: strongly agree, agree, neutral, disagree, or strongly disagree. The results reveals that both academic and personal growth of students rely on teachers' skills. A competent teacher can boost the confidence and self-esteem of students with learning difficulties, especially those learning a second language.

The Table 28.1 a provides an in-depth analyzes of fifty secondary school students from two different streams towards their opinion on dyslexia. The first variable is

Table 28.1. L2 learning with dyslexia students

S. No	*Question items*	*Strongly Agree*	*Agree*	*Neutral*	*Disagree*	*Strongly Disagree*
1.	Difficult to recognise and spell new words	39	4	5	1	1
2.	Difficult to read	32	14	4	0	0
3.	Struggle with complex words	36	12	2	0	0
4.	Confuse similar looking words	40	10	0	0	0

Source: Author.

Table 28.2. Teachers competency

S. No	*Question items*	*Strongly Agree*	*Agree*	*Neutral*	*Disagree*	*Strongly Disagree*
1.	Teacher understands learning difficulty	26	14	8	1	1
2.	Used different strategies	30	12	7	1	0
3.	Feedback from teacher	21	19	10	0	0
4.	Supportive and inclusive classroom	31	14	5	0	0

Source: Author.

targeted to observe the difficulties of students to spell and recognize new words. Among the fifty students, thirty-nine strongly agree that they struggle to spell new words, four agreed, five remained neutral, while one disagreed and another strongly disagrees. The second variable is to check out the difficulties in reading. Thirty-two students strongly agreed with this challenge, fourteen agreed, and four remain neutral, whereas none opted for disagree or strongly disagree. The third question is meet to examine students view on struggle with complex words. The highest number of thirty-six students opted for strongly agree, while twelve students stand along with agreed, two opt to be neutral and none of the student ready to choose the option disagree and strongly disagree. The fourth variable is intended to look at student's view on confusion with similar words. The highest count, forty students strongly agreed that they got confused with similar words, ten students have opted for agreed, none of the student choose neutral, disagreed, and strongly disagreed.

The Table 28.2 provides an in depth analyzes of fifty secondary school students from two different streams regarding the importance of teacher's competency in handling learners with learning disabilities. The first variable is intended to analyse the understanding level of teachers towards the difficulties of learners. Among fifty students, twenty-six students strongly agreed, fourteen opt for agreed, eight students opted for neutral and one goes with disagree and one stands with strongly disagree. The second question regards the different teaching strategies to handle the learning disabilities. Thirty students opted to have strongly agreed, twelve students opt for agreed, eight take the option neutral and one goes with disagreed and no one choose for strongly disagree. The third variable aims to verify the student's opinion on getting feedback from teachers helps to improve their skills. Twenty-one students have opted for strongly agree, whereas nineteen students stand with the option agreed, ten opt to be neutral and none of the student ready to choose the option disagreed and strongly disagree. The fourth variable is to check out the opinion of students on whether teacher use new strategies to create supportive and inclusive classroom. The highest number of thirty-one students strongly agreed, fourteen students have opted for agreed, five students choose neutral, none of the student choose disagree and strongly disagree.

12. Conclusion

In conclusion, this study highlights the necessity of providing proper skills and knowledge to develop teachers' competency in handling students with learning disabilities. Teachers must be trained to understand the specific challenges faced by the individual learners in acquiring a second language. By thorough understanding of their issues, teachers can implement evidence-based practices and create an inclusive atmosphere that fosters the academic and personal growth of affected students. With the right tools and technology, teachers can thrive dyslexia in a better way in their language. Developing this type of competency and commitments to their profession will not only promote teachers professional growth and but also ensure that learners receive a meaningful support. In the end, this approach will upgrade the entire educational community, promote inclusivity and contribution to overall success in learning.

References

[1] Abdul, Juhri., et. al., (2020). Teacher Competency for Dyslexic Learners, *Universal Journal of Educational Research*, 8 (3), 904–908.

[2] Alley, G. R., Deshler, D. D., & Warner, M. M. (1979). Identification of learning-disabled adolescents: A Bayesian approach. *Learning Disability Quarterly*, 2(2), 76–83.

[3] Bryan, T., (1974). An observational analysis of classroom behaviours of children with learning disabilities. *Journal of Learning Disabilities*, 7(1), 26–34.

[4] Fawcett, A. J., & Nicolson, R. I. (2008). Dyslexia and the cerebellum. The SAGE handbook of dyslexia, 77–98.

[5] Menon, Seema K.P.Awareness of Learning Disabilities among Teachers of Primary Schools. *Online Journal of Multidisciplinary Research,* 2(2), 78–83.

29 The impact of technology-enhanced language learning tools on vocabulary acquisition in EFL learners: A comparative study of mobile applications versus traditional classroom methods

Shaheena Jaleela Faizal[1,a], *Kawkab Abdulaziz Al Balushi*[2,b], *and Faizal Hajamohideen*[3,c]

[1]Department of Language Studies, Sohar University, Oman
[2]Department of Preparatory Studies, University of Technology and Applied Sciences (UTAS) Suhar, Sultanate of Oman, Oman
[3]College of Computing and Information Sciences, University of Technology and Applied Sciences (UTAS) Suhar, Sultanate of Oman, Oman

Abstract: This study investigates the impact of mobile-assisted language learning (MALL) tools on vocabulary acquisition among English as a Foreign Language (EFL) learners, comparing their effectiveness to traditional classroom methods. This research uses a mixed-methods design to analyze pre- and post-test scores, participant feedback, and learning outcomes. Findings reveal that although both methods promote vocabulary learning, mobile applications offer more personalized learning experiences and increase greater learner autonomy. Implications for technology integration in EFL contexts conclude the paper.

Keywords: English as a foreign language (EFL), innovative mobile-assisted language learning (MALL), language learning tools, learning outcomes EFL contexts, vocabulary acquisition

1. Introduction

The rapid development of technology has barely left any aspect of education untouched, and language learning is no exception. Vocabulary acquisition is one of the most fundamental parts of EFL education, since it underpins learners' abilities to communicate effectively and comprehend linguistic nuances. Traditionally, vocabulary learning has relied on classroom based methods, including rote memorization, teacher-guided instruction, and collaborative peer activities. But the advent of mobile technologies brings new dimensions into this process through dynamic, accessible, and personalized learning with mobile applications. MALL has lately gained greater attention for its potential to complement or even supplant conventional educational practices. Vocabulary acquisition applications often involve gamified components, spaced repetition, and contextual learning, which may be appealing to a variety of learner requirements and preferences. On the other hand, direct interaction, immediate feedback, and social dimensions of learning in the traditional classroom provide deeper cognitive engagement. This study compares the efficiency of mobile applications and traditional classroom practices in EFL vocabulary acquisition. It will explore their respective relative strengths and potential synergies in addressing the following critical research question: To what extent do mobile applications enhance vocabulary acquisition compared with traditional classroom methods, and in what ways can the two approaches be integrated to optimize learning outcomes?

2. Past Studies

2.1. Mobile-assisted language learning (MALL)

MALL represents a shift from the traditional ways and methodology towards technology-enhanced methodologies in language learning; and thus, vocabulary acquisition is no exception. The integration of mobile apps into language

[a]244717@students.su.edu.om, [b]sohkawkab@utas.edu.om, [c]faizal.h@gmail.com

DOI: 10.1201/9781003778905-29

learning has been supported by their ready accessibility, portability, and efficiency in meeting individual learner needs. The apps often make use of multimedia flashcards, gamification, and spaced repetition algorithms, which actually are designed to promote engagement and retention. Kukulska-Hulme and Viberg 2018 stress that mobile apps hold a collaborative potential, enabling learners to connect in peer-based activities both socially and in language learning [4, 5]. Lin, Warschauer, and Blake (2021) go further to say that MALL creates personalized and adaptive opportunities for learning by which learners can progress at their own pace, perhaps with heightened motivation and superior outcomes than traditional instruction [5].

MALL has, however, also shown in shortcomings: Chen and Hsu 2021 detail that some of the shortcomings involve inconsistency in app quality, inadequate teacher participation, and other complications brought on by mobile use. Therefore, though MALL indeed offers an opportunity for advancement in learning, carefulness may be necessary in its use for EFL teaching [1].

2.2. Traditional classroom instruction

Traditional classroom instruction is still the backbone of EFL education when it comes to vocabulary acquisition. Zimmerman 1997 describes the historical development in teaching vocabulary, including learning by context, repetition, and explicit instruction [12]. These techniques have been developed and perfected over many years and are also underpinned by research showing their effectiveness in improving both recognition and productive vocabulary. According to Richards, the facilitation by the teacher and the provision of immediate feedback by them, such corrections of errors and, thus refine their understanding [7]. Besides, classroom environments do foster social interaction and collaborative learning surely necessary in language acquisition. Despite these advantages, traditional methods lack the flexibility and interactivity possible with MALL. Learners of different proficiency levels or learning styles may have difficulty keeping pace with structured classroom activities.

2.3. Theoretical underpinnings of vocabulary acquisition

Schmitt 2010 claims that developing inventiveness, recognition, and retention are all important components of the multidimensional process that is required to learn a language [8]. Strong vocabulary development requires exposure, meaningful insights, repetition, and interaction with context-rich materials. Mobile apps align with these principles by offering spaced repetition and multimedia contexts that enhance learning [11]. Similarly, traditional classrooms utilize contextualized teaching and collaborative exercises to deepen understanding and retention [6].

2.4. Comparative studies on MALL and traditional methods

Research comparing MALL with traditional classroom instruction has remained limited but insightful. Chwo et al. 2018 reported that learners using mobile apps performed better in retention, as the tools were either gamified or interactive in nature [2]. However, Sung et al. 2016 believe that by integrating the social and cognitive aspects of language acquisition, traditional classroom training can provide an expanded learning environment [10]. Thus, there is a growing trend of incorporating cells into classrooms to create blended learning settings. Stockwell 2020 comments that each of these hybrid models naturally has the potential to have maximum advantages from both approaches, by which learners will benefit properly from the structured guidance of tutors and the flexibility of mobile learning [9].

3. Methodology

The methodology to be undertaken in this study will compare the effectiveness of MALL and traditional classroom instruction in vocabulary acquisition among EFL learners.

This research employs a mixed-approaches strategy, including quantitative pre- and post-tests with qualitative feedback from 60 intermediate level EFL learners aged between 18–24 were recruited from a Sohar University language program. The participants were also randomly assigned into two equal groups of 30 from a class:

1. The Mobile App Group, or MALL for short, created a smartphone application specifically for vocabulary learning. To improve interest and retention, it combined multimedia support, spaced repetition, and gamification. Because the learning process was self-paced, users could access lessons at any time and from any location.
2. Classroom Group: This group enjoyed traditional classroom-based vocabulary learning, provided by an experienced teacher in the form of direct instruction, collaborative peer activities, and written exercises. The learning sessions in this condition were performed within a structured and interactive setting where real-time feedback was presented, along with further opportunities for students discussion.

3.1. Mobile application overview

Three essential characteristics were included in the mobile application employed in this study to help in building vocabulary:

1. *Flashcards:* To provide students with holistic input, the multimedia flashcards included pictures, audio

pronunciations, and sample phrases. This approach is supported by findings by (Chwo 2018), who indicated that multimedia aids in reinforcing word meaning and context [2].

2. *Gamified Exercises:* Vocabulary quizzes with scoring systems, badges, and rewards sustained the motivation of the learners. Gamification strategies in learning have been observed to enhance engagement and achieve better outcomes by making the process even more interactive and appealing for learning by Kukulska-Hulme and Viberg 2018 [4].
3. *Spaced Repetition Algorithms:* The application calculates time-efficient intervals for reviewing learned vocabulary with increased long-term retention using spaced repetition algorithms. Indeed, Webb 2007 drew on the advantages of repetition to improve both recognition and productive knowledge of vocabulary [11]. Figure 29.1 depicts the workflow of the mobile application, showing how learners progressed through flashcards, gamified quizzes, and review sessions using spaced repetition. Best practices are the mobile assisted language learning that reflects this methodical blending of motivation, retention, and multimedia techniques [3].

3.2. *Traditional classroom methods*

Through collaboration and contextualization of learning activities, the classroom instructions used a structural approach to vocabulary acquisition (Table 29.1). Instructional methods were based on established EFL teaching practices following Richards 2015, Zimmerman 1997 [7, 12] (Figure 29.1).

1. *Teacher-Led Exercises:* The teachers gave explicit instruction on the target vocabulary; that is, explaining what the word means, giving examples, and how to use it contextually. According to Nation 2001 [6], the guided practice allowed students to clear up any confusion related to the subject and receive prompt feedback, both of which are essential for vocabulary retention.
2. *Group Discussions:* Learners were involved in peer collaboration activities, including group discussions and role-playing, in which they were expected to use target vocabulary actively in meaningful contexts. This form of collaborative learning is congruent with the theories that emphasize the role of social interaction in language acquisition Richards 2015 [7].
3. *Printed Materials:* These classroom sessions themselves consisted of word lists, example sentences, and practice worksheets that had been specifically prepared to match the standard EFL curriculum, allowing the learners to practice recognition and productive vocabulary skills in a structured way Webb 2007 [11]. This was then put into some sort of structured approaches which drew upon the expertise of a teacher and peer dynamics promoting vocabulary learning. Also, this traditional classroom incorporated holistic approach to vocabulary acquisition with a

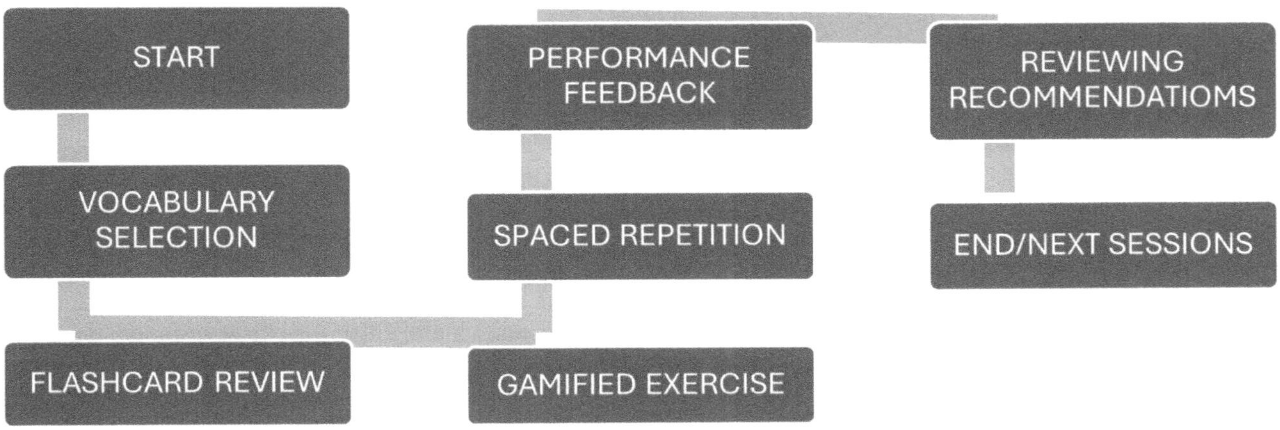

Figure 29.1. Workflow of the mobile application.

Source: Author.

Table 29.1. Participant demographics and language proficiency

Group	*Number of Participants*	*Age Range*	*Gender Distribution (M/F)*	*Language Proficiency Level*
Mobile app group	30	18-24	12/18	Intermediate
Classroom group	30	18-24	14/16	Intermediate

Source: Author.

meaningful explanation, peer interaction, and contextual materials, on the other hand, juxtaposed to an individualist use in the mobile learning tools.

3.3. Vocabulary acquisition measures

This was measured by using two types of assessments before and after the intervention:

1. *Recognition Test:* Multiple-choice questions to test the learners' recognition of vocabulary meaning.
2. *Productive Test:* Fill-in-the-blank exercises in which test takers are supposed to produce target vocabulary in the sentences.

4. Data Collection Procedures

The research began with a pre-test that took place in Week 1. Both groups were pre-tested on their vocabulary knowledge to establish a baseline of comparison in both the mobile app and classroom groups. These tests were recognition and productive vocabulary sets to ensure that both groups were equal in this aspect. During the succeeding six weeks, that is, Weeks 2–7, the mobile-app group used an assigned vocabulary learning application for 30 minutes daily. It enabled features that learners could employ for individualized active vocabulary preparation, including gamified activities, multimedia flashcards, and spaced repetition algorithms.

Participants were able to concentrate on their own language recall difficulties while moving at their own speed thanks to this methodical and self-directed approach. The classroom group attended three structured 90-minute sessions each week. These sessions were conducted by an experienced EFL instructor and incorporated teacher-led explanations, discussion in collaborative groups, and exercises based on printed vocabulary materials. The activities had a focus on contextual learning and peer interaction, enhancing a supportive environment for developing vocabulary. During Week 8, both groups participants took the same post-test on vocabulary acquisition as the pretest (Tables 29.2 and 29.3).

In addition, participants submitted reflective journals of their learning experience, and focus group discussions were conducted to collect qualitative feedback on the holistic understanding of the effectiveness of each instructional method. Quantitative data analysis was done through paired t-tests to determine gains both pre- and post-test. Qualitative data from journals and focused groups were thematically analyzed for insights into user experiences and preferences.

Table 29.2. A hypothetical chart showing the sequence of activities in a classroom setting

Sequencing of Classroom Activities	*Description*	*Visual Representation*
1. Collaborative Brainstorming	Students share prior knowledge and experiences.	Group of students with speech bubbles
2. Group Discussions	Exploring different perspectives and building ideas.	Students sitting in a circle or around a table
3. Hands-On Projects	Applying understanding through collaborative tasks.	Students working on a project together
4. Instructor Facilitation	Teacher guiding discussions and maintaining focus.	Teacher interacting with students
5. Reflection and Presentation	Groups present findings and get peer feedback.	Students presenting to the class

Source: Author.

Table 29.3. Vocabulary test format

Test Type	*Number of Items & Scoring Criteria*	*Example Item*
Recognition Test	20 items Correct meaning selection	Select the correct meaning for "ubiquitous".
Productive Test	20 items Contextual accuracy	Complete the sentence: "He felt when the truth came out."

Source: Author.

5. Results

With a mean improvement of 6.4 points in post-test scores, participants in the mobile app group showed more vocabulary improvements than those in the classroom group, which showed a mean improvement of 3.7 points.

The difference in significant (p ¡ 0.05), according to statistical analysis, suggesting that mobile-assisted learning improved word recall and retention in the study setting.

The mobile app group's superior performance aligns with research highlighting the efficacy of mobile-assisted language learning (MALL) for vocabulary acquisition [5], 11]. The app's integration of gamified exercises and spaced repetition likely contributed to better retention, as these techniques have been shown to support long-term memory consolidation Chwo et al. 2018, Godwin-Jones 2019 [2–3]. The quality insights were MAG reported enjoying the autonomy and flexibility provided by the app. Features such as immediate feedback and gamified elements were particularly engaging, fostering sustained motivation [1, 4].

Lastly, for students who appreciated the teamwork and social connection that come with conventional approaches. A supportive environment was established through peer discussions and teacher direction, which is consistent with research by Nation 2001 and Richards 2015 on the significance of social dynamics and context in language learning [6–7]. This supports the findings of Stockwell 2020 [9], who found that mixed approaches can maximize results by combining the advantages of both approaches.

6. Advantages of Mobile Application and Strengths of Traditional Methods

The study gives support to earlier studies by highlighting the benefits of mobile-assisted language learning (MALL) for vocabulary acquisition. MALL provides individualized learning pathways that let students concentrate on specific areas of difficulty and advance at their own speed. This findings support Chen and Hsu 2021 [1], who pointed out the flexibility of mobile apps enables them to accommodate a range of student demands and preferences.

Gamification is yet another important advantage. According to the study from Chwo et al. 2018, the incorporation of gamelike components, such as challenges, rewards, and scoring systems, improves motivation and engagement, two factors that are essential for long-term learning. Students in the mobile app group emphasized how these features promoted regular usage and made vocabulary practice for fun. The spaced repetition of the algorithms included in MALL provided strong evidence for Webb 2007 emphasis on repetition for retention. These platforms allow systematic review and strengthen long-term memory (Table 29.4).

MALL also facilitates autonomy, a key factor in adult language learning. Learners reported feeling empowered by the ability to control their learning schedule and progress, reflecting Godwin-Jones 2019 observations about the importance of flexibility in mobile learning environments [3].

Social connection and teacher assistance were the foundation of the classroom-based instruction's strengths. Participants placed a high priority on cooperative activities, including roleplays and group discussions. Peer contact is encouraged by these techniques, which is crucial to vocabulary practice in relevant settings. According to Richards 2015 [7], these kinds of exchanges aid language learners in honing their abilities and gaining self-assurance when using the language in everyday situations (Figure 29.2). An instructor's presence guaranteed prompt feedback to address mistakes and clear up any misconceptions regarding the lesson. This is a major benefit of classroom instruction since students follow the teacher's guidance, claims Nation 2001 [6].

Furthermore, in keeping with Zimmerman 1997 emphasis on contextualized instruction, the planned format of class sessions made sure that students were exposed to vocabulary in a variety of context-rich tasks [12].

The findings suggest that the benefits of both systems might be combined in an integrative strategy that blends MALL with traditional classroom methods. By providing

Table 29.4. Comparison of pre-test and post-test results across groups

Group	*Pre-Test Mean (SD)*	*Post-Test Mean (SD)*	*Mean Improvement*
Mobile App Group	12.3 (2.4)	18.7 (1.9)	6.4
Classroom Group	12.5 (2.6)	16.2 (2.3)	3.7

Source: Author.

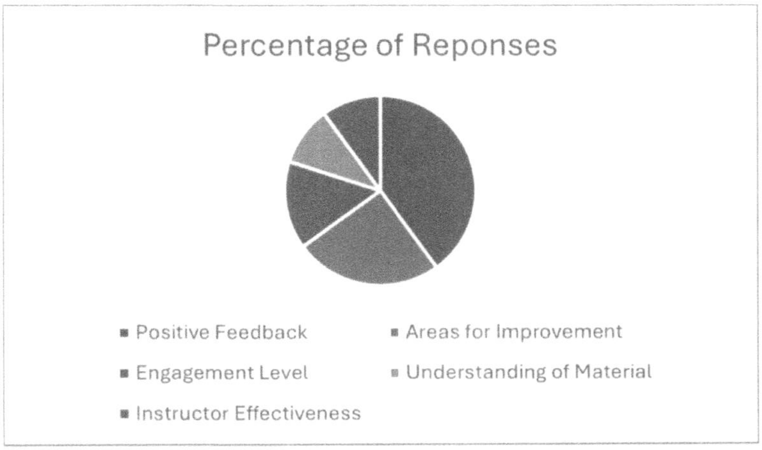

Figure 29.2. Percentage of responses on class observation.

Source: Author.

additional practice opportunities outside of scheduled sessions, mobile apps can improve classroom education and promote hybrid learning environments, claims Stockwell 2020 [9].

These models might take use of MALL's personalized and gamified features while maintaining the collaborative and feedback-driven benefits of the classroom. To reinforce usage in social and contextual contexts, students could employ classroom-based discussions and exercises after using a mobile app for initial vocabulary acquisition and review. According to Lin, Warschauer Lin et al. 2021, this combination can maximize results by improving both individual learning efficiency and collaborative engagement [5].

7. Limitations

There are a number of constraints to take into account, despite the fact that this study provides useful information regarding the benefits of mobile applications for EFL vocabulary development.

First, the results might not be as broadly applicable as they could be given the limited sample size. Second, the study time was too short to assess long-term language retention or consistent learning patterns. Third, the MALL group's performance may have been impacted by participant disparities in technological expertise and mobile application proficiency. Additionally, useful, pre- and post-tests failed to capture subtle word choice or context-dependent learning.

8. Implications for Practice

The results imply that teachers can enhance conventional approaches to EFL instruction by integrating mobile applications. Personalized learning experiences, increased student autonomy, and improved engagement are all possible with mobile-assisted language learning (MALL) solutions. However, teacher and student training programs are crucial for a successful integration.

To get the most out of apps, teachers should become familiar with their features and pedagogical approaches. Students require instruction on how to effectively use apps to supplement what they learn in class. In addition, striking a balance between technology and in-person communication guarantees that the benefits of both approaches are utilized. Future curriculum development should look into blended models that mixes the adaptability and creativity of mobile applications with the interactive nature of classroom instruction in order to create a more dynamic and inclusive learning environment.

9. Conclusion

The methods for the routine classroom techniques and mobile applications work in tandem to support EFL students' vocabulary learning. While traditional classroom approaches offer structured education, real-time feedback, and collaboration opportunities, mobile applications improve student autonomy, engagement, and accessibility.

According to the results, a more balanced and productive learning environment can be produced by utilizing the benefits of both modalities in an integrated strategy. Instructors can meet the requirements of a variety of learners, maximize retention, and foster meaningful language learning experiences by fusing technology with conventional pedagogical approaches. Future studies should examine long-term effects and improve hybrid models to improve EFL vocabulary learning even further.

References

[1] Chen, X., & Hsu, H. (2021). Mobile-assisted language learning: A systematic review. *Computer Assisted Language Learning*, *34*(1–2), 1–25.

[2] Chwo, G. S. M., Marek, M. W., & Wu, W. C. V. (2018). Learning vocabulary through apps. *Journal of Educational Technology & Society*, *21*(2), 30–42.

[3] Godwin-Jones, R. (2019). Emerging technologies: The evolving roles of mobile apps in language learning. *Language Learning & Technology*, *23*(2), 6–11.

[4] Kukulska-Hulme, A., & Viberg, O. (2018). Mobile collaborative language learning. *ReCALL*, *30*(1), 14–24.

[5] Lin, C.-H., Warschauer, M., & Blake, R. (2021). Mobileassisted language learning for english vocabulary acquisition. *International Journal of Mobile and Blended Learning*, *13*(2), 15–31.

[6] Nation, I. S. P. (2001). *Learning vocabulary in another language*. Cambridge University Press.

[7] Richards, J. C. (2015). *Key issues in language teaching*.Cambridge University Press.

[8] Schmitt, N. (2010). *Researching vocabulary: A vocabulary research manual*. Palgrave Macmillan.

[9] Stockwell, G. (2020). *Mobile language learning in context*. Routledge.

[10] Sung, Y.-T., Chang, K.-E., & Liu, T.-C. (2016). The effects of integrating mobile devices with teaching. *Educational Technology & Society*, *19*(3), 269–283.

[11] Webb, S. (2007). The effects of repetition on vocabulary knowledge. *Applied Linguistics*, *28*(1), 46–65.

[12] Zimmerman, C. B. (1997). Historical trends in second language vocabulary instruction. In *Second language vocabulary acquisition*, 5–19.

Appendices

(a) Mobile Application Features

The mobile application used in the study incorporated the following key features:

- Flashcards with multimedia content
- Multimedia flashcards and game-based vocabulary tests
- Algorithms along with spaced repetition

(b) Educational Resources for Classrooms

The control group received instruction in a traditional classroom using the following materials and activities:

- Textbook-based vocabulary lessons
- Vocabulary worksheets and exercises
- Instructor-led vocabulary discussions and presentations

The researchers drew from a variety of relevant sources to inform the design and execution of this comparative study on the impact of technology-enhanced language learning tools, specifically mobile applications, on vocabulary acquisition among EFL learners.

30 Hardware accelerators using FPGA for low earth orbit space debris detection using deep neural network models

D. Somasundaram[a] and Nila R.[b]

Department of Micro and Nano electronics, School of electronics Engineering, Vellore institute of Technology, Vellore, Tamil Nadu, India

Abstract: The sustainability and safety of space operations are seriously threatened by the growing quantity of space objects (SO), debris, and satellite constellations in Low Earth Orbit; these issues must be handled carefully and effectively to prevent collisions. An array of radar and radio-telescopes that detect and track, so presently addresses space situational awareness. However, a significant portion of space debris is made up of little metallic items that are extremely challenging to find. The advantages of employing deep learning (DL) architectures for radar observations-based small space object detection are illustrated by the authors. Range-Doppler maps from a TIRA radio telescope simulation have been used as inputs for object detection by taking advantage of DNN frameworks. The candidate locations are then carefully positioned inside the optical image sequences. Using the acquired image sequences and simulated data, the experiment is carried out. The findings demonstrate the effectiveness of the suggested approach in estimating and eliminating background and its high detection probability for low SNR space debris. For sophisticated algorithms, specialized accelerators still have substantial FPGA design costs. The suggested paper's study focuses on new high-level synthesis (HLS) methods that enable developers to increase abstraction and reduce design costs for deep learning accelerators, especially for applications that represent space. To do this, the open-source HLS tool NNgen is used to create four distinct hardware accelerators of convolutional neural network models for space-based debris identification (ResNet, SqueezeNet, DenseNet, and TinyCNN). After being installed on a reconfigurable Xilinx XCZU programmable logic module, the acquired hardware accelerators are evaluated for latency, resource usage, and inference performance.

Keywords: Debris, deep learning, field programmable gate array, hardware accelerators

1. Introduction

Space debris, also referred to as space junk, is the term used to describe non-operational, man-made objects that orbit the Earth. This category covers a wide range of objects, including defunct rocket stages, dormant satellites, and pieces from collisions or explosions in space [1].

The chance of collisions with this junk increases as more satellites and probes are sent into orbit. Space missions, satellite operations, and even human safety are seriously at danger under this scenario. Thus, keeping an eye on space debris is crucial to reducing these risks and guaranteeing the long-term sustainability of space initiatives. The main goal of this kind of monitoring is to precisely trace the location, path, and characteristics of debris items in Earth's orbit. Space debris has become a significant issue for astronomers and space operators in recent years. According to the European Space Agency, there are over 130 million pieces of debris with a diameter of less than 1 cm, 1 million with a diameter between 1 and 10 cm, and 36,500 pieces with a diameter greater than 10 cm [4], the majority of which are traveling at speeds of over 15,700 miles per hour [5]. As a result, even the smallest debris could cause a space disaster, and preventing it is essential to the success of future space missions [6]. An organized approach to the issue of space debris. Identifying, preventing, and removing. We will concentrate on the detection of space debris in this study.

Additionally, AI-enhanced monitoring systems make it easier to analyse large volumes of observational data, which improves debris object tracking and identification. These AI-powered solutions also boost operational effectiveness and promote international cooperation and responsibility in space exploration. They help satellite operators and space agencies proactively manage collision risks by providing real-time risk assessments and predictive analytics, which

[a]somasundaram.d@vit.ac.in, [b]nila.r2023a@vitstudent.ac.in

DOI: 10.1201/9781003778905-30

lowers the possibility of catastrophic events and protects vital space assets. Nonetheless, for the good of all people, this progressive approach strengthens structures for space administration and encourages international cooperation. Space situational awareness is much improved by the use of AI in space debris monitoring, but space traffic management is also improved, which represents a huge achievement in this sector.

In this paper, open-source HLS tool NNgen is used to create four distinct hardware accelerators of convolutional neural network models for space-based debris identification. Our method's integration of a wide range of Deep Learning algorithms to evaluate the suggested model's performance is one of its main features. Thus, the method is twofold: utilizing the same information, a classification is done to determine the type of debris and concurrently characterize its size.

Therefore, we use thorough metrics to assess the model's performance while it runs on an FPGA board in this work. Figure 30.1 depicts the pipeline for development. Pre-processing involves training the network using the 32-bit floating point space debris dataset, followed by a quantization procedure to produce an 8-bit integer model, specifically in the Xilinx model (.xmodel) format. The instructions that the Deep Learning Processing Unit (DPU) on the target FPGA board is supposed to carry out are then included in the quantized model. For testing, we lastly install the built model on ZCU104. The ZCU104 has two B4096 DPU cores and operates at 300MHz.

2. Convolutional Neural Network Accelerator

Multiple computing layers are stacked to extract and classify features in the CNN algorithm. In order to create feature maps highly abstract representations of the input visual data modern CNNs employ a very deep hierarchy of layers. This allows them to attain their exceptional accuracy. To increase energy efficiency, Chip focuses on two primary strategies: 1) minimizing data transportation and 2) taking use of data statistics. This transfers each given CNN shape's calculation onto the PE array. It may be rearranged to fit various forms and maximizes energy efficiency. The high-dimensional convolutions are the main computation in the CNN layers. A layer creates the output features by adding up the partial sums after applying filters to the input features to extract embedded characteristics. Furthermore, the filtering results are subjected to a 1-D bias.

2.1. Pre-processing

This paper's neural network was modeled after CDRNet [5], a CNN for 3D semantic meshing in real time. This extracts the CDRNet's core, which functions as a 2D feature extractor and comprises the initial 35 Conv2d layers. In order to improve accuracy, the neural network is further strengthened using MnasNet [6] for image classification tasks up to 52 Conv2d layers. The model's input is a 32 × 32 RGB picture from the CIFAR-10 dataset [7], which was trained on 50,000 training images over 30 epochs with a batch size of 100 and a learning rate of 0.001. Ten thousand more photos are utilized for testing. Using Nvidia RTX with CUDA 11.4, the process is carried out on an Intel® Core™ i7 to get the performance operating on the CPU and GPU.

In this proposed method as shown in the Figure 30.2. FPGA serves as the foundation for the preprocessing accelerator's architecture. The categorization accelerator deploys CNN on FPGA using the Xilinx xDNN library [2, 3]. The two accelerators communicate with the server's CPU over the Xilinx PCIe and exchange data via UltraScale+ GTH/GTY transceivers. To set these hardware elements and manage the complete end-to-end operation, we installed a C-based control application on the CPU. The input image that has been encoded is kept on a server disk in our system. Through PCIe DMA, the JPEG data is sent to the pre-processing accelerator via DRAM under CPU control. Sequential image decoding, image block

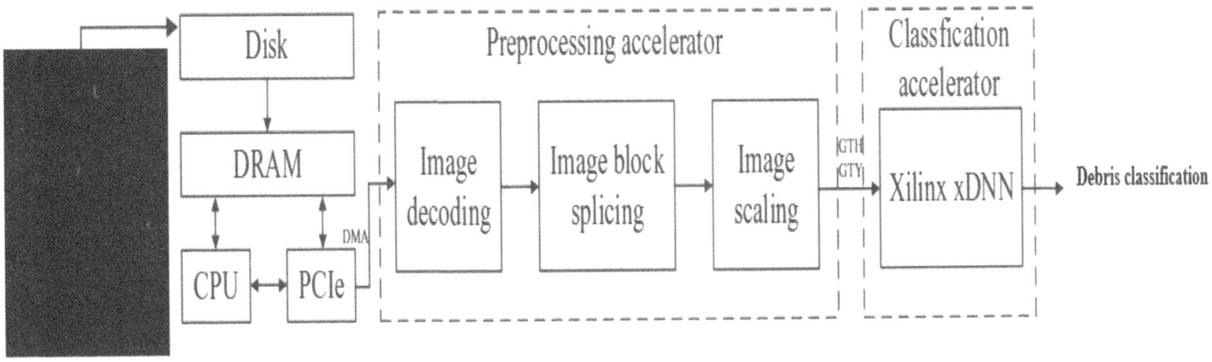

Figure 30.1. Proposed method.

Source: Author.

splicing, and image scaling are used to process JPEG. The raw picture data that satisfies the neural network input is subsequently output by the pre-processing accelerator. To fully extract features, the classification accelerator receives the raw picture data. Ultimately, the debris categorization results are returned under CPU control.

The hardware architecture of proposed accelerator as shown in Figure 30.3. The input buffer, which is managed by the C-based pre-processing controller and decoding controller, reads the debris input picture data in the DDR4 on the chip in accordance with the line, eliminating redundant information that is unrelated to pixels, like 0xFF00, etc. Discrete wavelet transform (DWT) decoding, inverse zigzag, Huffman decoding, and dequantization are then carried out. The YCbCr2RGB module converts the image data into RGB data after it has been decoded. Image block splicing is followed by writing the resultant image blocks into DDR4. The entire raw image is scaled to fit CNNs tensor input after being read from DDR4 using the Xilinx scaling IP. DWT provides a practical way to segregate signals based on low and high frequency using 2D matrix transformation from the space domain to the time domain. The original image's content information is preserved in the low-frequency sub-band, which also concentrates the image's energy.

$$WT_{\varphi}(j) = \frac{1}{\sqrt{mn}} \sum_{x=0}^{m-1} \sum_{y=0}^{n-1} I(x,y)\ \varphi_j(x,y) \qquad (1)$$

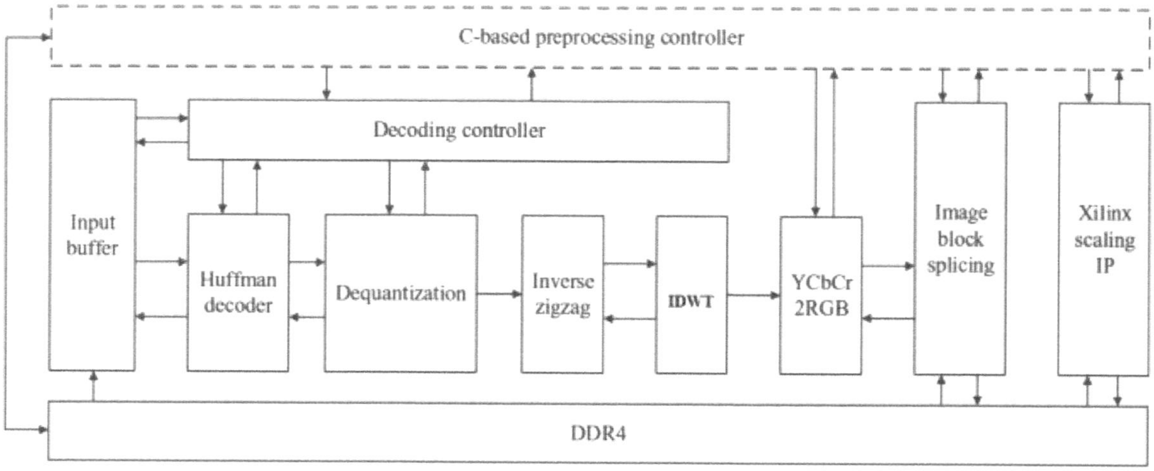

Figure 30.2. Proposed architecture.

Source: Author.

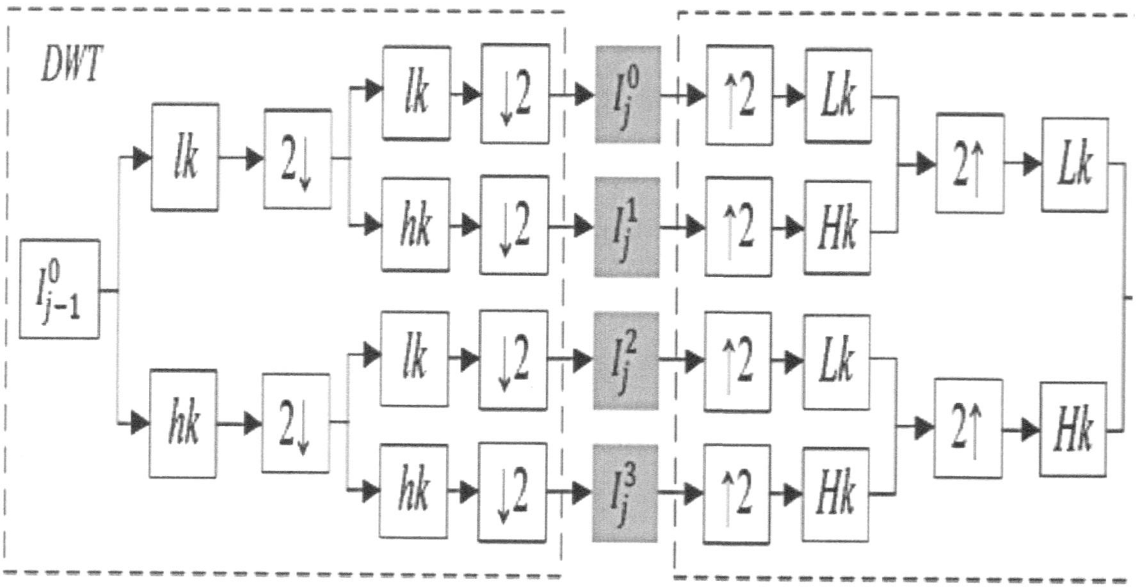

Figure 30.3. DWT and IDWT.

Source: Author.

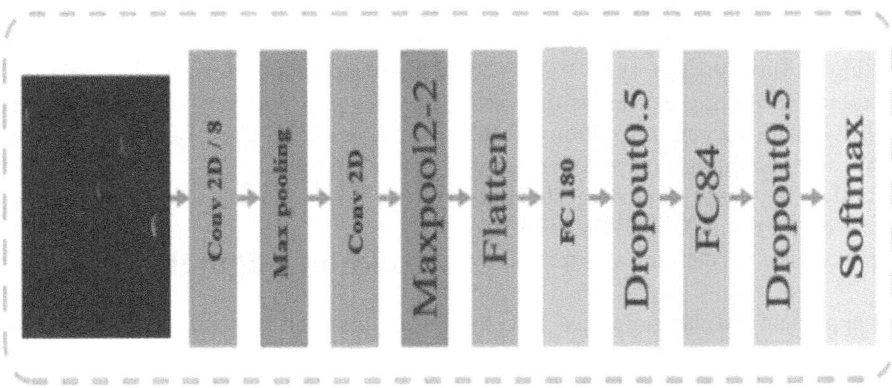

Figure 30.4. CNN for debris detection.

Source: Author.

The high-frequency information is maintained in the vertical and horizontal directions, respectively, via the vertical and horizontal sub-bands. In the diagonal direction, high-frequency information is maintained via the diagonal sub-band. Because various debris sizes have variable chroma subsampling during JPEG batch processing, the MCU's size fluctuates constantly. We created an adaptable picture block to handle an MCU's data in order to solve this problem. To ensure the accelerator's universality, the adaptive image block constantly modifies the block's size based on the picture's various chromaticity sampling. DWT structure through a pipeline with four stages. This work replaces the floating-point multiplication operation with the shift addition structure, based on the concept of [2]. We created a DWT structure with a seven-stage pipeline that can process an 8x8 image block in 16 clock cycles in order to balance speed and resource utilization.

Data can be cached using (1) a control unit, (2) a FIFO, (3) a Ping-Pong buffer, (4) a select unit, and (5) a multiplexer. Only employing FIFO for data caching, however, will use up too many block RAM resources and have an impact because of the chip's restricted block RAM.

A convolutional neural network model based on the LeNet5 architecture, the space debris identification network is used to detect space debris. Immediately following the extraction of the potential areas from the picture sequences. Many false alerts brought on by stars can be avoided.

The only samples used in the space debris detection job are noise and space debris. The majority of its characteristics are low-level ones, such points and edges. It only takes two convolutional layers to do this task. Figure 30.4, depicts the network model structure. 64 X64 is the network's input size. To maintain the output's size, the convolution method employs zero padding. The vanishing gradient issue is successfully avoided by using the rectified linear units (ReLU) as the activation function. Additionally, the accuracy and computation cost of this function are balanced. Later, there is a pooling layer that employs a pooling kernel. Convolution kernels with zero padding are used in the second convolution layer to maintain the output's size. The function of activation is ReLU. The convolution layer is followed by a pooling layer with a 2X2 pooling kernel, after the convolution layer, a fully connected neural network classifier comes next. The first step involves employing a flattening layer to transform a two-dimensional matrix into a one-dimensional matrix. Later on, a hidden layer of 120 neurons is employed, with ReLU serving as the activation function.

3. Results and Discussion

Batch size: The batch size is often a multiple of two (02); examples include 16, 32, 64, and so on. We fixed the remaining network hyper parameters and trained our CNN model with several batch size values (64, 128,256) in order to determine the ideal value. The trained network's performance changes across 100 epochs for various batch-size values. We can observe that the model converges more quickly with a batch size of 64. Because of this, we used batches of 256 images to train the model. The debris images are implemented in the pre-processing

Table 30.1. Performance comparison

Metrics	*Intel Xeon 2.3 GHz 14 nm*	*Nvidia Geforce 12 nm*	*Xilinx XCZU*
Frames per sec	15.98	421.56	482.40
Speedup	1X	22.39X	27.07X
Power (W)	130.6	162.6	83.56
Energy efficiency	47.03X	3.45X	2X

Source: Author.26/04/23

accelerator for classification using FPGA. In this study, we build RTL using Verilog and convert the source code to the bitstream using Xilinx Vivado (v2019.2). The input picture dataset and the Kaggle dataset as the validation set. 50,000 JPEGs with varying resolutions (from 80×60 to 3657×2357) and sampling compression techniques make up the collection. We test our suggested pre-processing accelerator on a 16 nm XCZU7EV-chip. We synthesize our pre-processing accelerator at a frequency of 250 MHz.

The GPU-based approach and our suggested FPGA-based hardware accelerator achieved 2.93 and 2.62 times acceleration, respectively, as compared to the CPU-based implementation following optimization. Using the effective hardware architecture created in Section 4, our suggested FPGA-based hardware accelerator improves performance. We contrast the three solutions' energy efficiency, however. We found that our suggested FPGA-based hardware accelerator lowered the energy usage for each preprocessing frame of a debris image by 27.07 times when compared to the CPU and 4.21 times when compared to the GPU. The efficiency with which our suggested FPGA-based hardware accelerator can finish picture preprocessing is demonstrated by all of these performance outcomes.

Table 30.1 displays the outcomes of the suggested approach. First, the performance of the GPU implementation and the end-to-end FPGA accelerator has increased by 22.39 times and 27.07 times, respectively, in comparison to the CPU-based version. The throughput of FPGA accelerators is higher than that of GPU versions. Second, the energy consumption of our suggested FPGA-based hardware accelerator is 2.88 times lower than that of the GPU and 46.03 times lower than that of the CPU for each debris image classification.

4. Conclusions

Overall, a FPGA-based debris image pre-processing accelerator to increase image classification's overall throughput and energy efficiency. We can speed up the non-convolutional processing of debris pictures prior to feature extraction with our pre-processing accelerator. Four hardware architectures – adaptive image block, DWT, image block buffer, and image block self-location – are used in the design. We use the Xilinx XCZU7EV to develop and test our pre-processing accelerator. It achieves 0.019 J/F of energy efficiency and 889.47 FPS of throughput.

Acknowledgment

Authors like to extend sincere thanks to Vellore institute of technology, Vellore for travel support.

References

[1] LeCun, Y., Bengio, Y., & Hinton, G. (2015). Deep learning. *Nature, 521*, 7553, 436–444.

[2] Girshick, R.., Donahue, J., Darrell, T., & Malik, J. (2014). Rich feature hierarchies for accurate object detection and semantic segmentation. *In Proceedings of the IEEE conference on computer vision and pattern recognition,* 580–587.

[3] Li, T. Y., Zhang, F., Guo, W., Shen, J. L., & Sun, M. Q. (2022). An FPGA-based JPEG preprocessing accelerator for image classification. *Journal of Engineering*, 919–927.

[4] Lavin, A., & Gray, S. (2016). Fast Algorithms for Convolutional Neural Networks. IEEE Transactions on Pattern Analysis and Machine Intelligence, *38*(10), 4013–4021.

[5] Chen, Y., Luo, T., Liu, S., et al. (2015). DaDianNao: A Machine-Learning Supercomputer. Proceedings of the IEEE, *103*(11), 2019–2034.

[6] Ghaderizadeh, S., Abbasi-Moghadam, D., Sharifi, A., Zhao, N., & Tariq, A. (2021). Hyperspectral image classification using a hybrid 3D-2D convolutional neural networks. IEEE Journal of Selected Topics in Applied Earth Observations and Remote Sensing, *14*, 7570–7588.

[7] Waheed, A., Goyal, M., Gupta, D., Khanna, A., Hassanien, A. E., & Pandey, H. M. (2020). An optimized dense convolutional neural network model for disease recognition and classification in corn leaf. Computers and Electronics in Agriculture, *175, 105456*.

31 Exploring the efficiency of hybrid energy systems with solar power: Integration and management perspectives

Vanya Arun[1,a], *S. P. Dwivedi*[2,b], *Asha V.*[3,c], *Ginni Nijhawan*[4,d], *and Hassan M. Al-Jawahry*[5,e]

[1]Department of Electrical & Electronics Engineering, IILM University, Knowledge Park II, Greater Noida, India
[2]Lloyd Institute of Engineering & Technology, Knowledge Park II, Greater Noida, Uttar Pradesh, India
[3]Department of Computer Applications, New Horizon College of Engineering, Bangalore, India
[4]Lovely Professional University, Phagwara, India
[5]Department of Computers Techniques engineering, College of Technical Engineering, The Islamic University, Najaf, Iraq

Abstract: Hybrid systems demonstrate significant improvements in energy utilization and transmission network utilization, with a 72% improvement. These systems effectively store energy, meet electricity demands, reduce CO2 emissions, and offer cost savings, making them suitable for remote areas. This study evaluates the integration of various renewable energy sources, focusing on hybrid systems to enhance energy efficiency, sustainability, and cost-effectiveness. The study assesses the performance and potential of hybrid photovoltaic-thermal (PV-T) collectors, the impact of hybrid wind and solar systems on mitigating drought conditions, and innovative solar power plant designs. Hybrid energy sources like solar, fuel, and wind are becoming increasingly popular in green energy initiatives. However, environmental concerns and power backup networks remain critical. Hybrid devices, such as PEMFC, are essential for maintaining energy stream stability. Artificial intelligence power monitoring is possible in certain situations. The growing need for renewable energy is affecting smart microgrid networks. The review highlights the benefits of hybrid energy systems in reducing greenhouse gas emissions, improving transmission network utilization, and providing reliable energy solutions for both urban and rural areas. The findings suggest that optimizing hybrid renewable energy systems can significantly contribute to global energy security and sustainability goals.

Keywords: GHG, hybridization, integration, management, renewable energy, solar energy

1. Introduction

Increased integrating energy from renewable sources into the built environment may be achieved through the use of solar energy. With efficiency ratings as high as 70%, hybrid photovoltaic-thermal (PV-T) collectors can meet more than 60% of the city's heating and 50% of its cooling needs. Considerable energy savings can be achieved by combining vapour-compression devices with heat pumps or absorption refrigeration systems. Using a probabilistic weather generator, [1] examines how wind, solar, and hybrid energy affect India's drought and concludes that wind causes droughts that are more severe. It also looks at how wind-solar hybridization balances short wind energy periods. In many regions, hybridization is more advantageous than relying only on solar or wind energy; South India is one such region. It is suggested that minimizing regional level renewable droughts requires robust inter-regional grid connections [1]. A revolutionary concentrating solar energy plant employing quartz crystalline solar power & alcohol hydrolyzed is suggested to convert all forms of light into electricity. Through thermal chemistry & photovoltaics, it divides the incoming solar energy and produces solar syngas for solid oxide fuel cells. This type of system offers a wide range of applications and is highly competitive. The system produces 1532 W of light at an achievable effectiveness of 26.4% while it operates at its maximum dispatching capacity of 80% [2]. The optimal

[a]vanyaarun@gmail.com, [b]spdwivedi@gmail.com, [c]asha.gurudath@gmail.com, [d]ginni.nijhawan@gmail.com, [e]hassanaljawahry@gmail.com

DOI: 10.1201/9781003778905-31

design for large-scale hydro-photovoltaic-wind hybrid systems is examined in [2], which focuses on 3080 carefully selected sites worldwide. The results showed that there is a total installed capacity of 1699 GW, and that the percentages of energy generated by wind, solar, and hydropower are 67%, 20%, and 13%, respectively. The region with the most promise is Asia-Pacific. The combination of solar and wind power results in a 72% increase in transmission network utilization efficiency. By 2040, 3900 GW additional PV and wind energy may be produced [3]. In 2019, almost half of the electricity generated in Brazil's Northeast was generated by solar and wind power. The complementary nature of wind and solar energy in the area is examined in [3], along with how this might lessen the erratic character of natural resources. It is revealed that a hybrid generator combining solar, wind, and storage may meet demand for electricity while storing just 6% of yearly energy [4]. Global effort to cut greenhouse gas emissions is now necessary due to climate change. Renewable power (RE) is marketed as a solution in the Paris Agreement and the Sustainable Energy for All program. Yemen, a country rich in renewable energy resources, has few feasibility assessments. In order to electrify rural areas in Shafar, Yemen, an off-grid renewable energy system is examined, and RE technology is evaluated. To optimize and perform an analysis of sensitivity of the system, the hybrid optimization framework for electrical renewable (HOMER) is employed. Based to the study in [5], Yemen should use a hybrid strategy to fulfill the objectives of both the SE4All initiative and the Paris Agreement at the same time [5]. Hybrid wind, solar, along with battery energy system for Jamshoro, Sindh, Pakistan, for stand-alone usage. Solar energy sources generate power and store energy in batteries. Weather and actual load demand are utilized to verify the system's functionality. The system produces the greatest power in the summer, generating 77.88% and 22.12%, respectively. It is suitable for remote rural areas and reasonably priced. Future efforts may combine the device with the electrical grid [6]. The optimization tool HOMER (Hybrid Optimization of Multiple Energy Resources) stands as one of the most popular solutions for determining hybrid energy systems. The tool evaluates different system elements such as solar PV and wind turbines together with batteries and diesel generators to achieve optimal distribution together with cost reduction. This paper is organized as follows: Section 2 presents the Mathematical analysis Section 3 gives an overview of integration techniques for hybrid solar power systems, discussing energy storage strategies and grid interactions. Section 4 introduces control methodologies such as fuzzy logic and high-order sliding mode control. Section 5 describes the simulation setup, HOMER modeling, and PSO optimization process. Section 6 gives the heat coletation Section 7 discusses the results, including performance analysis and sensitivity studies. Finally, Section 6 presents the conclusions and future research directions.

2. Homer Framework for Hybrid Energy Optimization

The HOMER optimization has several key elements of input data that it requires:

- Solar Irradiance (kWh/m²/day) – Location-specific radiation data
  Wind Speed measurements occur at the rate of meters per second based on historical meteorological records obtained from specific geographical areas.
  The operating electricity usage follows a pattern called Load Demand Profile (kW) where it shows power consumption during each hour.
- Battery Parameters – Capacity, Depth of Discharge (DoD), and State of Charge (SOC) limits
- Diesel Fuel Cost ($/L) – Used for economic viability analysis

The Renewable Energy Penetration value stands for the percentage of renewable energy present within the energy network.

The energy dispatch optimization process along with system sizing optimization is implemented through an iteration-based system by HOMER. All system configurations feasible to the system are evaluated using the determination of Net Present Cost (NPC) and Levelized Cost of Energy (LCOE) along with Renewable Energy Fraction to identify the superior system configuration.

2.1. Particle swarm optimization (PSO) for energy dispatch

The power dispatch between energy sources gets enhanced through PSO by using a dynamic adjustment algorithm. The following algorithm procedure must be executed:

- The first step generates decision variable values randomly for solar power and wind power and batteries alongside diesel generator power distribution.
- The fitness function selection includes lowering life cycle energy cost while enhancing renewable power generation.
- The particle motion is updated through a combination of inertia weight and acceleration coefficients.
- Check constraints such as battery SOC, load balance, and grid stability.
- Continue running the algorithm until the determined cost goals alongside efficiency excellence are reached.

Table 31.1 investigates the possibilities of hybrid solar energy systems, such as those that use PV-T collectors,

Table 31.1. Comparative analysis of renewable energy systems and applications

Focus	*Key Points*	*Location*	*Performance Metrics*	*System Configuration*	*Challenges/Notes*
Hybrid PV-T Collectors	• Systems using PV-T collectors for solar energy can get 70% or more efficiency. • 15–20% electrical efficiency. • Over 50% of thermal efficiencies.	Europe (Seville, Rome, Madrid, Bucharest)	• 60% of heating and 50% of cooling demands for urban households • Levelised cost of energy: 0.06–0.12 €/kWh	• Connected to absorption refrigeration equipment or pumps for heating	• High temporal resolution needed for accurate simulations (TRNSYS results)
Renewable Energy Droughts in India	• Stochastic Weather Generator Analysis of Energy Droughts • Wind-droughts more intense than solar-droughts	India (South India, Rajasthan)	• Hybridization benefits are regionally dependent.	Sturdy interregional grid interconnections are necessary to lessen the effects of droughts.	• Simulated long time series (5000 years)
Full Spectrum Solar Conversion	• Concentrated solar power system using parabolic trough collector. • Monocrystalline silicon photovoltaics for visible and near-infrared sunlight. • Methanol decomposition for solar syngas.	-	• Solar power: 1532 W • Solar power efficiency: 26.4%	• Combines PV power and thermochemical power	• High competitiveness and potential for large-scale application
Large-Scale Hydro-PV-Wind Hybrid Systems	• Potential to improve flexibility with multiple renewable sources. • Examines 3080 global sites.	Global	• Total potential installed capacity: 1699 GW • Electricity generation: 4348 TWh/	• Combination of hydropower, PV, and wind power	• Fluctuation ratios 78–99% lower than independent systems
Wind and Solar Complementarity in Brazil	• Complementary nature of wind and solar generation. • Energy storage reduces resource intermittency issues.	Brazilian Northeast	• Daily Pearson's Correlation Coefficient: -0.51	• Storage capacity: 6% of annual generation	• Energy curtailment analysis shows up to 11% reduction in transmission capacity demand
RE Feasibility in Yemen	• Feasibility of off-grid renewable power systems for rural electrification.	Yemen (Shafar, Hajjah province)	• CO2 emission reduction: 70% (PV/wind/diesel) • Cost of energy (COE) reduction: 30% (PV/wind) • Cost of energy (COE) reduction: 45% (PV/wind/diesel)	• Hybrid system (PV/wind/diesel) - Superior robustness to RE variability	• Recommendations for hybrid system deployment to achieve Paris agreement targets and SE4All initiatives
Stand-Alone Hybrid Wind/Solar/Battery System	• Proposed for remote rural areas. • Power management control strategy presented.	Pakistan (Jamshoro, Sindh)	-Wind energy: 77.88% -Solar energy: 22.12%	• Wind and solar as power sources. • Battery for energy storage.	• Future integration with power grid suggested.

Source: Author.

which have efficiency ratings of at least 70%. It also covers the opportunities and problems associated with these systems, including the possibility of large-scale hydro-pV-wind hybrid systems, the complementary nature of solar and wind energy in Brazil, the regionally dependent droughts in India, and the viability of off-grid renewable power systems for Yemeni rural electrification. A standalone hybrid wind, solar, and battery system with a power management control method and potential grid interconnection is also presented in the studies for isolated rural locations. Figure 31.1 shows visual representation of the integration of solar, wind, and storage with the smart grid.

3. Mathematical Models for Fuzzy Logic and High-Order Sliding Mode Control

3.1. Fuzzy logic controller (FLC) for hybrid system optimization

The membership function for power allocation is defined as:

$$\mu = \frac{1}{1+e^{-k(P-P_O)}} \quad (1)$$

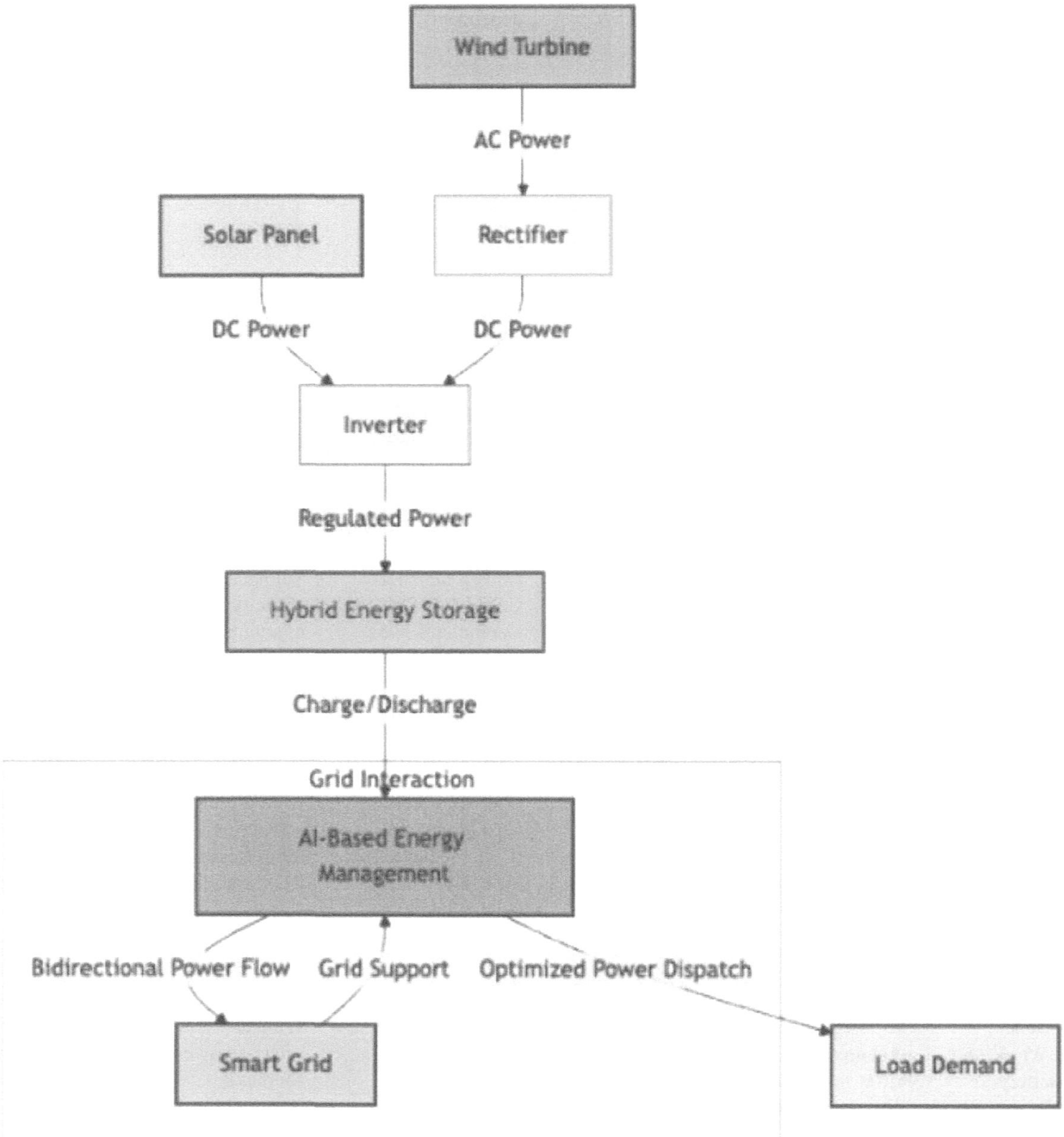

Figure 31.1. A visual representation of the integration of solar, wind, and storage with the smart grid.

Source: Author.

The expression defines the value of the membership function using parameters P, P0 and k for power input, setpoint and scaling factor respectively. The fuzzy rule base implements the following optimization procedure for power delivery: A dual condition exists which specifies charging of the battery when both solar generation remains elevated and the load demand stays below minimum value. When solar generation is low but wind power is high the system should use wind-generated electricity. The activation of diesel generator becomes necessary when both renewable sources provide low output.

3.2. High-order sliding mode controller (HOSMC)

For dynamic power balancing, a HOSMC model is implemented:

$$S = e + \lambda e \tag{2}$$

$$S = -KS^{n} \tag{3}$$

The controller uses e as error term alongside λ as control parameter together with K to achieve fast error reduction. Such operational control decreases power frequency fluctuations and strengthens electrical grid reliability. The system will assess performance indicators including power quality index (PQI) with transient response time and total harmonic distortion (THD).

4. Integration Techniques for Solar Power

Combining solar energy with storage technology can enhance energy supply and minimize fluctuations in grid flow. Summertime afternoons and nights are often when peak power demand happens, while solar energy output is at its lowest. When the sun isn't shining, storage helps solar energy contribute to the supply of power. It also helps equal out differences in solar energy flow caused by the season, time of day, clouds, dust, haze, and obstacles. In order to better integrate solar energy into the energy landscape, energy storage can be situated close to or co-located with solar energy systems. The development and contemporary use of Concentrated Solar Power (CSP) technology for the production of clean energy is examined in [7]. It draws attention on their track record in both technology and business, as well as the potential for hybridization with fossil fuels and continuous operation. The most widely used CSP technology is parabolic trough (PTC), which has been used successfully in more than 28 of business-related operations. On the other hand, because of their better performance, subsequent endeavours are moving toward alternative CSP technologies. While Parabolic dish, towers power, & Fresnel collector technologies have proliferated in under-construction projects, PTC has become less common in operating projects [7]. Technologies like smart grids provide fresh possibilities for optimization and forecasting. Solar power projections are necessary for sophisticated network management solutions as solar power usage rises. It presents a novel vectors autoregression framework-based 6 h advance estimation method as produces probabilistic forecasts for household PV and secondary substation levels. Within Évora, Portugal, there are 44 micro-generation unit & Ten main power plants in the evaluation case [8]. Utility-scale solar power projects can be optimally located by using multicriteria decision-making (MCDM) and geographic information systems (GIS). In order to generate the maximum electricity while reducing project costs, the model takes into consideration combined technical and economic aspects. Each site's LSI model produces six distinct groups. [9] presents a case study of Saudi Arabia based on real meteorology and legal data. Findings show that 16% of the research area could be used for PV plant deployment, with the north and northwest offering the greatest possible locations. In order to meet global energy, environmental, and sustainability requirements, renewable energy sources (RES) are essential. Overcoming technological obstacles is necessary to include RES into the energy mix. The goal of optimizing compatibility across RES systems both geographically and temporally is the development of a methodology. According to an example, compatibility may be greatly increased by making a 10% sacrifice. The technique looks at potential changes that might be made during the installation of PV systems [10]. A potential method for thermochemical energy storage (TCES) that provides long-term storage in a small volume is the Ca-Looping (CaL) process. The use of the CaL technique to store concentrated solar power (CSP) is investigated in [11]. The CO2 closed loop is used as a suggested integrated approach to decouple heat from the solar source and temperatures higher than 550°C. Using sustainable beginnings such native limestone, this leads to high plant global efficiency and long-term storage capacity [11]. Integration costs, such as grid balancing, more flexible thermal plant operation, and decreased capital inventory utilization, are incurred when solar and wind powered generators are incorporated in electrical networks. A methodology is suggested in [12] to examine and measure these expenses, predicated on the electricity's marginal economic worth. This study concludes that lower capital utilization is the main factor contributing to integrating costs, and with elevated rates of penetration can reach 50% of generating costs [12]. Least-squares optimization is proposed to Numeric Climate Forecasting method for hourly-averaged power output from solar systems. The approach is assessed using information from two Californian non-tracking plants between 2011 and 2014. The method's adjustments for systematic errors in the irradiation prediction are demonstrated by the results, which provide a relative root mean square error (RMSE) of 10.3%–14.0% and forecast skill of 13%–23%. The daily PO is over predicted by more than 40% over a three-year period [13].

5. Solar Integrated Hybrid System Monitoring and Control Technologies

Solar, fuel, and wind energy are the main choices for green energy initiatives, which are starting to become a feasible source of electricity in the following ten years. While wind turbines, fuel cells, and photovoltaic systems have outperformed expectations, environmental considerations and power backup networks remain critical. Although it has a tiny membrane existence and a high cost, the PEMFC, a reversible power storage device, has demonstrated success in early efficiency. Power quality problems and oscillations may arise from the intricate link between load demand and renewable energy supply. In order to preserve energy stream stability, hybrid devices must be utilized. In certain situations, artificial intelligence power monitoring is possible. The need for renewable energy is growing as a result of growing energy costs, nuclear safety concerns, climate change, and loss in the electrical system. Managing electricity is complicated in smart microgrid networks since they rely on hybrid energy sources. New fuzzy logic controller and high order sliding mode algorithms are used for controlling a smart DC-microgrid. To maximize energy from renewable sources and enhance power quality, the controller controls source-side converters. Compared to intelligent fractional-order and PID controllers, the suggested controller generates more electricity from wind, photovoltaic, tidal, and load [14]. A hybrid automated transfer switch (ATS) system is the goal of [15] in order to solve the problem of power outages brought on by PLN power failures. Using the Polish government & a solar panel, the device allows for remote android monitoring. A 20-watt solar cell will be employed in the system test for the study. Results after ten hours of radiation in sunny weather are displayed with accuracy and precision values of 96.13%, 95%, and 16.84% in terms of electricity savings [15]. Solving the global energy problems is possible with the use of sunlight to produce power. The greatest choice for boosting efficiency, cost-effectiveness, tracking accuracy, & ease of installation is a solar tracker (ST). Both single & quadruple axes there are two different types of ST. For these devices to be optimized and avoid tracking errors, complex specifications are required. In general, double axis ST improves energy return over fixed PV panels by around 40%. It uses dynamic closed loop feedback control to do this. Large systems reduce costs and resource use. Optimizing software and hardware energy-saving settings at an early stage of system development can prevent material waste and unnecessary energy use [16]. It intends to determine whether a hybrid electrical system (HES) that combines gasoline, solar, or battery power can successfully implement a mixed dispatch control method using HOMER software. Based on CO2 emissions of 27,678 kg/year, the results demonstrate that the combined dispatch control strategy performs best in terms of net current cost and energy cost.

However, variations in important parameters such as battery minimum state of charge, time step, solar radiation, fuel price, and load growth significantly affect how well the system works [17]. This suggests an improved home energy management system (OHEMS) that enhances the functionality of the conventional grid by incorporating energy storage devices (ESS) and renewable energy sources (RES) into demand-side management (DSM) operations. By synchronizing home appliances and ESS in reaction to market pricing, the system reduces power expenses. The system's performance is evaluated in the [18] using MATLAB simulations, and the findings show that integrating RES with ESS reduces peak-to-average ratio and power costs. It outlines an experimental method for lowering Solar temperatures at Taxila, Pakistan, using phase change material and nanofluid. The hybrid PVT system worked best for a 40LPM flow rate & 0.1 vol% nanoparticle content. The greatest PV temperature drops were 23.9°C, 16.1°C, and 11.9°C; in compared to typical PV, those heat drops followed by gains in electric effectiveness of 23.9%, 22.7%, and 9.1%. The nanofluid-based hybrid PVT/PCM system showed 17.5% higher thermal efficiency as well as to an overall increase in efficiency [19]. Energy independence, environmental concerns, with the prohibitive price of burning petroleum makes clean energy technology essential. After 2020, the EU wants to see 20% of the total use of energy come from sources that are renewable. The use of building integrated photovoltaic (BIPV) while constructing combined solar/thermal (BIPV/T) systems has grown in popularity recently. In terms of energy generation, nominal power, efficiency, type, and performance assessment methodologies, the study conducted in [20] examines BIPV and BIPVT applications. Increasing system efficiency through ventilation and developing novel thin-film technologies for building integration are among the study topics [20].

6. Emerging Trends in Technology and Management of Solar Integrated Hybrid System

In order to construct hybrid renewable energy systems (HRESs) for rural electrification, an innovative approach is presented in [21]. It combines particle-swarm optimization. This is a demand-supply management (DSM) to create an off-grid hybrid PV-solar-diesel-battery system intended for residential structures in arid regions. In order to optimize the system, the total net present cost (TNPC) is minimized while taking the widespread use of green power sources and reliability level into account. According to the findings, energy demand and TNPC might have cut through seven percent or 18%, accordingly, using PV-Li-ion or entirely green power (RF) designs [21]. Employing composite Salt collectors, the study in [22] examines the techno-economic performance of solar combined heating, cooling, and power (S-CCHP) systems. The model estimates repayment timeframes based on real energy usage, investment expenses, и both energy prices. According to the findings, a 1.68-the Ministry of Work and S-CCHP installation that has 16.7-each year amortization period will satisfy 20.9%, 55.1%, or 16.3% of the annual space-heating, cooling down, and electrical demands on the campus. Also, the system relocates 911 tons of CO2 annually [22]. Utilizing the Extended Modified Downhill algorithm, the study examines what size is best of a photovoltaic/wind/biomass hybrid system with and without energy storage. The system is comprised of 1.79 MW PV, 2 MW wind, and 0.92 MW biomass systems, all of which have an overall value that is close below zero. At the region's Technical University's Northern Cyprus's Center. The system achieves a power costing 0.1626 $/kilowatt with an energy use proportion of 99.59% [23]. An ideal off-grid solar PV, fuel cell, and diesel generator power system for a university facility is presented in [24]. The concept seeks to replace the petroleum products that are connected with the grid with a cleaner, renewable energy source. The system meets the demands on electricity with experiencing an outage by providing 73% renewable energy, 24% fuel cell energy, and 3% diesel generator energy [24]. This full utilization of each sunlight captured at PV, which is while a fairly modest collecting reducing flow-rate may provide an increased acceptance relative to overall family power needs while greater greenhouse gas deposits over little UV quantities as well as moderate temperature conditions, according to an economic study about hybrid PV/solar-thermal (PVT) systems for distributed electricity and hot-water provision in a London home. Throughout the course its 20-year lifespan, this system produced 2.3-Megawatt energy annually, proved an impressive 1.0 Kw on annual water heating capacity, and reduced CO2 emissions by 16.0 tons. The study also looks at the economics of PVT technology and concludes that, after a 20-year period, with an electricity-only Feed-In Tariff (FIT) support rate of 43.3 p/kW h, the system will survive [25]. The goal of this work is to use a particle swarm optimization to create a mathematical model for a hybrid CCHP plant that includes solar thermal collectors plus photovoltaic panels. The combined approach is most effective to decrease carbon dioxide emissions & use of electricity, according to test findings conducted on a Georgia hotel building using the model. However, because of it large start-up cost, the yearly total costs are higher [26]. It examines fifteen operational hydrogen energy storage systems, ranging in size from lab-scale to full-scale and continuously running. Even though these are technically possible, they need to significantly lower costs in order to be appealing to businesses. The cost per unit of energy is impacted by certain components' inadequate energy efficiency under actual use. Long-term battery backup with hydrogen is still a popular option, and as intermittent renewable energy sources become more prevalent in power systems, hydrogen technology may advance and become more affordable. Hybrid systems – which mix hydrogen with technology for short-term storage like batteries and super capacitors – are the best option [27].

Utilizing DSM with Particle Swarm Optimization, Table 31.2 focuses on optimizing off-grid HRES for residential structures in dry regions. Significant cost and CO2 emission reductions are shown by the results. In addition, table looks at the techno-economic performance of S-CCHP systems, hybrid system sizing, and off-grid power system optimization for university buildings. The economic viability of PVT systems, hybrid CCHP systems with solar power, and distributed energy systems is also examined in the study. Compared to traditional CCHP, the findings demonstrate superior energy savings and CO2 reduction but higher yearly expenditures because of the initial investment.

7. Correlation Heatmap

Correlation heatmap shows the relationship between **solar irradiance, fuel cost, battery capacity, and LCOE**. It depicts that which variables **strongly affect the cost** of hybrid energy systems. A visualization of major variables appears in the correlation heatmap to show the interplay between solar irradiance and fuel cost and battery capacity & Levelized Cost of Energy (LCOE). LCOE decreases when solar irradiance increases according to the heatmap analysis. The higher the fuel prices are the stronger the positive connection becomes between fuel costs and LCOE. Battery capacity demonstrates a negative effect on LCOE because increased storage capabilities lower costs by integrating more renewable energy and decreasing fossil fuel use. The heatmap clearly presents quantitative insights about variable input effects on energy costs which enables better assessment when monitoring system performance under changing weather conditions. The solar irradiance together with fuel cost and battery capacity data are displayed through various probability distribution graphs obtained from running multiple Monte Carlo simulations. The frequency of solar irradiance demonstrates normal

Table 31.2. Comparative analysis of hybrid renewable energy systems: objectives, methods, and outcomes

Objective	*Optimization/ Modeling Method*	*Key Performance Metrics*	*Results Summary*	*Economic Feasibility*	*Environmental Impact*	*Challenges/ Limitations*
Optimize off-grid HRES for residential buildings in arid environments	DSM with Particle Swarm Optimization	TNPC, Reliability, RE Penetration	TNPC reduced by 18%, energy demand reduced by 7%, RF increased from 15% to 63% with DSM	High, with significant cost reduction using DSM	CO2 emission reduction by 57% with lower RF	Initial investment, technology integration
Investigate techno-economic performance of S-CCHP systems	Transient system model	Payback Time, CO2 Displacement	1.68-MWp S-CCHP covers 20.9% heating, 55.1% cooling, 16.3% electrical demands, 16.7 years payback	2.7 times higher payback than PV-only system	Displaces 911 tons CO2/year	Roof-space limitation, higher initial cost
Determine optimal size for hybrid system with/without storage	Generalized Reduced Gradient algorithm	FR, DSF, NPV	System achieves 99.59% FR, 98.86% DSF, COE $0.1626/kWh	NPV $\geq$ 0, COE $0.1626/kWh	High autonomy, potential for polygeneration	Significant excess energy production
Optimize design/ performance of off-grid power system for university building	Hourly calculations, optimization/ control methodologies	Renewable fraction, GHG emissions, COE	66.1% renewable fraction, COE $92/MWh, 24 kg CO2/MWh emissions	Economically feasible at $92/MWh	Low GHG emissions, environmentally friendly	Dependence on fuel cell and diesel
Techno-economic analysis of PVT systems for distributed energy	System model, economic analysis	Coverage of energy demands, CO2 emission savings, payback period	51% electrical demand coverage, 36% hot water demand coverage, 11.2 years payback with FIT	11.2-year payback with FIT, reduced by RHI	16 tonnes CO2 reduction over 20 years	High initial cost, need for policy incentives
Develop and optimize hybrid CCHP system with solar	Particle Swarm Optimization	PESR, CO2ERR, ATCSR	Best mode: FEL-ECR, PESR 36.15%, CO2ERR 53.73%, ATCSR 4.16%	Higher annual costs due to initial investment	Better energy-saving and CO2 reduction than conventional CCHP	High initial investment, cost of hybrid system

Source: Author.

distribution where 1000 W/m² acts as its mean value and the changes exceed or fall below 20% of this value to depict actual solar energy availability patterns. The values within the 800 to 1200 W/m² interval represent the majority of data points which reflect traditional weather-induced variations. Such unpredictable changes affect how energy is produced because they modify the operational performance of the hybrid system. The normal distribution model for fuel cost shows that prices can fluctuate from $0.80 to $1.20 per liter which presents financial uncertainties for the system operation. The diversity of operational costs depends directly on fuel prices because higher fuel expenses result in increased operational expenses for the hybrid system. The battery capacity distribution shows alternating potential storage ranges from 80 kWh to 120 kWh. Higher storage capacity improvements lead to more stable power systems and fuel independence alongside lower cost of energy. The results of the sensitivity analysis prove that solar power optimization leads to substantial energy cost reductions thus requiring increased solar collection efficiency. Data shows that diesel fuel price fluctuations represent a significant danger for hybrid energy systems requiring new strategies to decrease their dependence on diesel generators. Enhanced energy stability and decreased costs become achievable because extended battery storage capacity provides continuous electricity availability against any fluctuations in renewable energy production. Such research discoveries enable the development of reliable hybrid systems with reduced operational costs while maintaining energy stability because they represent key aspects for future renewable integration (Figures 31.2 and 31.3).

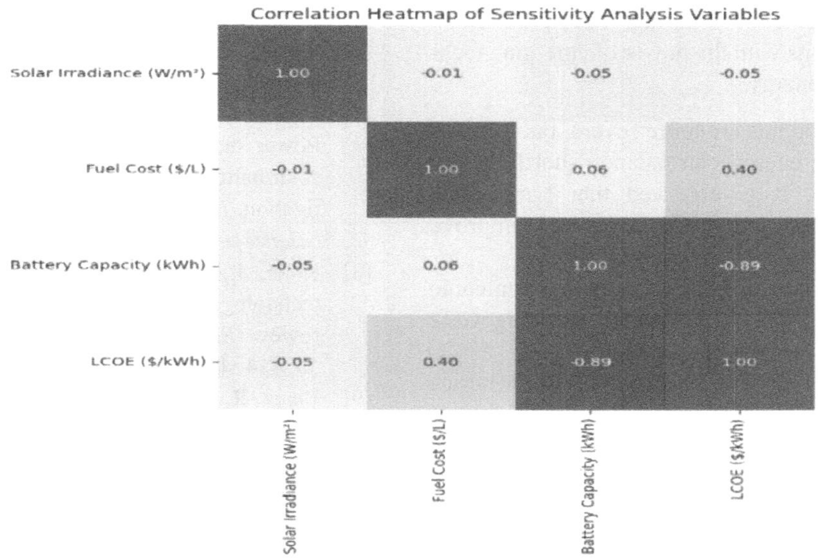

Figure 31.2. Corelation heat map.

Source: Author.

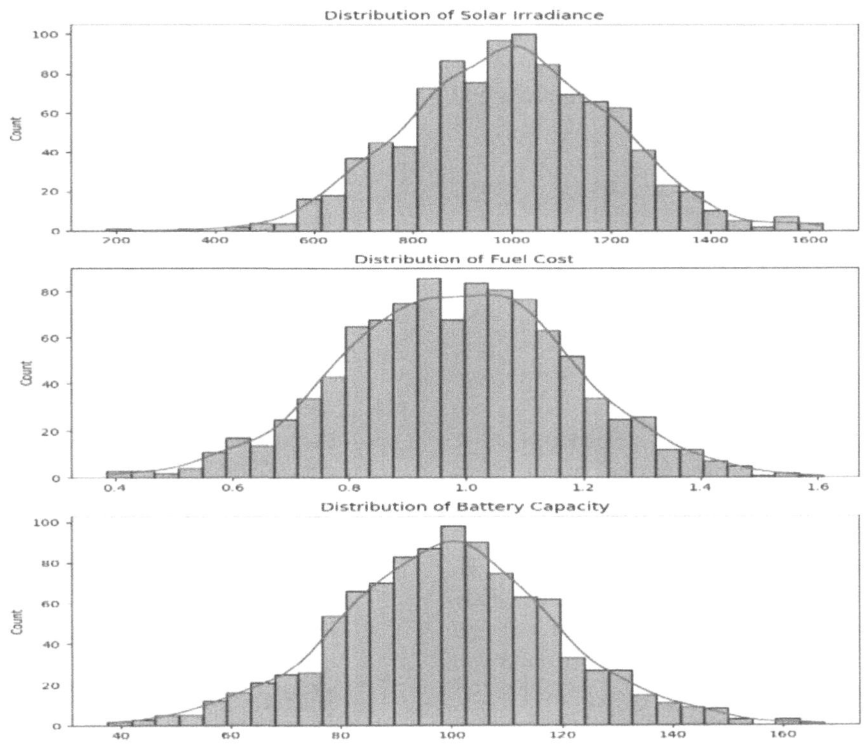

Figure 31.3. Probability distribution graphs.

Source: Author.

8. Conclusion

The findings of this study prove there are significant benefits to be reaped from integrating hybrid renewable energy systems, especially three-resource systems that include solar, wind, and thermal technologies. These hybrid systems have high potential for efficiency, associated cost savings, and reduction of greenhouse gases emission. This analysis clearly shows the cushioning role hybridization plays in energy shortfalls and improving energy security in both urban and remote areas. Hybrid renewable energy systems can significantly contribute to global sustainability objectives through the optimization of system configurations with the power of emerging technologies for resilient energy.

a. Wind-induced droughts are more severe, but hybridization with solar energy can balance shortfalls and mitigate impacts. It is observed that Large-scale hydro-photovoltaic-wind hybrid systems improve transmission network utilization by 72%.
b. Hybrid systems in remote areas provide sustainable and cost-effective energy solutions, reducing CO2 emissions and improving energy security.
c. Advanced control methods and smart grids are critical for optimizing the performance and reliability of hybrid renewable energy systems.
d. High initial investments, the need for robust policy support, and technical integration issues present significant challenges in the widespread adoption of hybrid renewable energy systems.

The adoption of innovative technologies and advanced control methods further enhances their performance and feasibility for both urban and rural applications. The findings highlight the necessity of continued research and optimization to fully harness the benefits of hybrid renewable energy systems, paving the way for a sustainable and secure energy future.

References

[1] Ramos, A., Maria, A. C., Ilaria, G., James, F., & Christos, N. M. (2017). Hybrid photovoltaic-thermal solar systems for combined heating, cooling and power provision in the urban environment. *Energy Conversion and Management*, *150*, 838–850.

[2] Gangopadhyay, A., Seshadri, A. K., Sparks, N. J., & Toumi. R. (2022). The role of wind-solar hybrid plants in mitigating renewable energy-droughts. *Renewable Energy, 194*, 926–937.

[3] Xing, X., Fan, S., Wanjun, Q., Yu, X., & Hui, H. (2022). Numerical simulation and experimental study of a novel hybrid system coupling photovoltaic and solar fuel for electricity generation. *Energy Conversion and Management, 255*, 115316.

[4] Wang, Z., Xin, W., & Qiaofeng, T. (2021). Potential assessment of large-scale hydro-photovoltaic-wind hybrid systems on a global scale. *Renewable and Sustainable Energy Reviews, 146*, 111154.

[5] Campos, R. A., Lucas, Rafael do N., & Ricardo, R. (2020). The complementary nature between wind and photovoltaic generation in Brazil and the role of energy storage in utility-scale hybrid power plants. *Energy Conversion and Management, 221*, 113160.

[6] Ajlan, A., Chee, W. T., & Abdirahman, M. A. (2017). Assessment of environmental and economic perspectives for renewable-based hybrid power system in Yemen. *Renewable and Sustainable Energy Reviews, 75*, 559–570.

[7] Mahesar, S., Mazhar, H. B., Ghulam, S., et al. (2018). Power management of a stand-alone hybrid (wind/solar/battery) energy system: An experimental investigation. *International Journal of Advanced Computer Science and Applications, 9*(6).

[8] Khan, J., & Mudassar, H. A. (2016). Solar power technologies for sustainable electricity generation–A review. *Renewable and Sustainable Energy Reviews, 55*, 414–425.

[9] Bessa, R. J., Artur, T., Cátia, S. P. Silva, & Vladimiro, M. (2015). Probabilistic solar power forecasting in smart grids using distributed information. *International Journal of Electrical Power & Energy Systems, 72*, 16–23.

[10] Al Garni, H. Z., & Awasthi, A. (2017). Solar PV power plant site selection using a GIS-AHP based approach with application in Saudi Arabia. *Applied Energy, 206*, 1225–1240.

[11] Kougias, I., Sandor, S., Fabio, M. F., Thomas, H., & Katalin, B. (2016). A methodology for optimization of the complementarity between small-hydropower plants and solar PV systems. *Renewable Energy, 87*, 1023–1030.

[12] Chacartegui, R., Alovisio, A., Ortiz, C., Valverde, J. M., Verda, V., & Becerra, J. A. (2016). Thermochemical energy storage of concentrated solar power by integration of the calcium looping process and a CO2 power cycle. *Applied Energy, 173*, 589–605.

[13] Hirth, L., Ueckerdt, F., Ottmar, & E. (2015). Integration costs revisited–An economic framework for wind and solar variability. *Renewable Energy, 74*, 925–939.

[14] Soliman, M. S., YoucefBelkhier, Nasim, U., AbdelyazidAchour, et al. (2021). Supervisory energy management of a hybrid battery/PV/tidal/wind sources integrated in DC-microgrid energy storage system. *Energy Reports, 7*, 7728–7740.

[15] Audia, W., Yulkifli, Y., Mairizwan, M., & Rinaldi, A. (2022). Automatic Transfer Switch System Design on Solar Cell–Grid Hybrid Based on Android Application. *EKSAKTA: Berkala Ilmiah Bidang MIPA*, *23*(04), 266–283.

[16] Nsengiyumva, W., Chen, S. G., Hu, L., & Chen, X. (2018). Recent advancements and challenges in Solar Tracking Systems (STS): A review. *Renewable and Sustainable Energy Reviews*, *81*, 250–279.

[17] Aziz, A. S., Tajuddin, M. F. N., Mohd Rafi, A., et al. (2019). Energy management and optimization of a PV/diesel/battery hybrid energy system using a combined dispatch strategy. *Sustainability, 11*(3), 683.

[18] Patel, M. R., & Beik, O. (2021). *Wind and solar power systems: design, analysis, and operation*. CRC Press.

[19] Hassan, A., Abdul Wahab, Muhammad Arslan Qasim, et al. (2020). Thermal management and uniform temperature regulation of photovoltaic modules using hybrid phase change materials-nanofluids system. *Renewable Energy*, *145*, 282–293.

[20] Biyik, E., Mustafa, A., ArifHepbasli, Mehdi, S., et al. (2017). A key review of building integrated photovoltaic (BIPV) systems. *Engineering Science and Technology, an International Journal, 20*(3), 833–858.

[21] Lupangu, C., & Bansal, R. C. (2017). A review of technical issues on the development of solar photovoltaic systems. *Renewable and Sustainable Energy Reviews*, *73*, 950–965.

[22] Herrando, M., Antonio, M., Pantaleo, K. W., & Christos, N. M. (2019). Solar combined cooling, heating and power systems based on hybrid PVT, PV or solar-thermal collectors for building applications. *Renewable Energy, 143*, 637–647.

[23] Al-Ghussain, Loiy, Adnan, D., A., Ahmad, M. A., & Mohamed A. M. (2021). An integrated photovoltaic/wind/biomass and hybrid energy storage systems towards 100% renewable energy microgrids in university campuses. *Sustainable Energy Technologies and Assessments, 46*, 101273.

[24] Ghenai, Chaouki, & MaamarBettayeb. (2019). Modelling and performance analysis of a stand-alone hybrid solar PV/Fuel Cell/Diesel Generator power system for university building. *Energy, 171*, 180–189.

[25] Eteiba, M. B., Shimaa, B., Samy, M. M., & Wael, I. W. (2018). Optimization of an off-grid PV/Biomass hybrid system with different battery technologies. *Sustainable Cities and Society, 40*, 713–727.

[26] Yang, G., & Xiaoqiang, Zhai. (2018). Optimization and performance analysis of solar hybrid CCHP systems under different operation strategies. *Applied Thermal Engineering, 133*, 327–340.

[27] Egeland-Eriksen, T., Amin, H., & Sabrina, S. (2021). Hydrogen-based systems for integration of renewable energy in power systems: Achievements and perspectives. *International Journal of Hydrogen Energy, 46*(63), 31963–3198.

32 Scalable and sustainable customer service chatbot with AWS Lex and AWS Lambda for AI solutions

Gandam Sairam[a], Ande Dileep Sai[b], Naga Venkatasiva Nikhil Maradani[c], Jujjavarapu Sujan Chowdary[d], and Annapurani K.[e]

Department of Networking and Communications, SRM Institute of Science and Technology (SRMIST), Kattankulathur, Chennai, Tamil Nadu, India

Abstract: Customer service chatbot explains about the uses of both the Amazon Lex and AWS Lambda to implement the chatbot by highly relying on the NLU service, so that the chatbot could translate possibly a user input in natural language to a conversational interface. AWS Lambda is the back-end of service, executing custom logic, allowing retrieval of data and enabling integration with APIs. These AWS services together support scalable, flexible, and cost-effective solutions for the automation of multiple channels of customer interaction that include web, mobile, and messaging platforms. To this end, we here advance a scalable and sustainable chatbot solution providing the highest degree of customer service automation through the synergy of Amazon Lex and AWS Lambda. In contrast to conventional chatbots, the solution is HIPAA-compliant (e.g., industrial security standards) as a matter of course by virtue of embracing serverless computing for efficiency and cost-effectiveness.

Keywords: Amazon lambda, Amazon lex, API application programming interface, Chatbot, HIPAA compliance, NLU natural language understanding

1. Introduction

Developing and building the conversational bots, using Amazon Lex and AWS Lambda uniquely recognized for their exceptional scalability and flexibility, and also, they can integrate with numerous other solutions available in the Amazon Web Services (AWS) ecosystem [1]. This is the advanced natural language understanding or NLU service of Amazon that allows a developer to design and implement such capability creating chatbots that are capable of understanding the inputs given through them comprehensively and thereby accurately interpreting them. To make it possible to add support for real-time responses besides interaction, developers can avail of any backend logic to be processed real time through AWS Lambda on the basis of processing given. This enables businesses to design smarter solutions of customer services, powered with continuous availability 24/7, with an always personalized dialogue, along with easy and prompt reply on user queries and this study emphasize the user experience of chatbots and the importance of interaction design for good and perfect communication with customer and system [2]. Research also prove that chatbots are very effective in service recovery: they can promptly respond to customer complaints and restore trust in the brand [3].

While as fast as the pace of AI-powered customer service chatbots has been, current solutions aren't part of enterprise infrastructure, scalable, or security-compliant (e.g., HIPAA). Previous-generation chatbots are often plagued by the lack of real-time conversational depth, resulting in less-than-optimal user experiences. In this paper, a new chatbot architecture using Amazon Lex and AWS Lambda is introduced that goes beyond such constraints to provide a scalable, flexible, and secure conversational front-end for enterprise applications.

2. Literature Review

2.1. *Chatbots for customer service*

A design architecture forms one of the crucial constituent parts that shape up to form chatbots. The design architecture basically determines all such important

[a]ramgandam24@gmail.com, [b]dileepsaiande2207@gmail.com, [c]nikhilmaradani@gmail.com, [d]chowdarysujan27@gmail.com, [e]annapook@srmist.edu.in

DOI: 10.1201/9781003778905-32

aspects, such as a whole thing's functionality in terms of scaling up or scaling down according to demand and at the same time also how it is going to behave with the user. In their research, consider the architectural framework and numerous algorithms needed for the purposes of effective conversational agents for interaction and engaging in meaningful conversations with users [4]. Whereas other work describes customer support advantages of chatbots, other work lacks real-world deployment figures to analyze chatbot behavior under high loads.

2.2. Serverless computing and AWS lambda

Serverless computing fundamentally serves to abstract away and simplify all of the many infrastructure management tasks that are typically required in a conventional cloud computing environment, often involving intricate setups and maintenance responsibilities. AWS Lambda, which is widely regarded as one of the foremost leaders in the rapidly evolving field of serverless computing, provides developers with an exceptional capability that allows them to execute their code directly in reaction to any event that occurs, all without the necessity of provisioning or taking responsibility for managing any servers on their own [5]. Other work describes rule-based or intent-based chatbots, whereas this work describes a hybrid approach with NLU enrichment and real-time AWS Lambda execution [6].

2.3. Amazon Lex and development of chatbots

Amazon Lex is a disruptive technology that offers developers the complete set of tools designed uniquely to make it easier to create conversational interfaces, capable of working with text-based and voice-based interactions seamlessly [7]. This allows businesses to integrate sophisticated as a completely managed service. It utilizes the technique of natural language understanding to interpret and understand details from the input given by the users. According to [8] "Amazon Lex has its integration capabilities seamlessly spread through all kinds of applications-it really shows both its flexibility and scalability and effectively enables developers to create chatbots with several applications within different kinds of applications [9]".

Natural Language Understanding is the ability of chatbots to process, analyze, and interpret user inputs at a high level of effectiveness [10]. Their study examines the many challenges that surface when there is a need to recognize implicit customer intent in conversations [11].

Customer input
↓
(speech-to -text/text input)
↓
Natural Language processing(NLP)
↓
Amazon Lex(Dialog Management)
↓
Amazon LAMBDA(Business Logic)
↓
External API's/Database Access
↓
Response generation(Test/Voice)
↓
Customer feedback Loop

A related area of research emphasizes on a framework, technological basis and strategic role of intensifying the customer interaction by using customer service chatbots. Rai and Bagde point out that proper selections of frameworks and platforms have crucial importance in developing correct chatbots [12]. This work is a comprehensive guide while designing a chatbot because it emphasizes on important things like NLP as well as machine learning-a base to provide intuitive yet responsive customer interaction [13].

The Amazon Web Services is one of the parties involved in developing Bot requirements. It demonstrates how the suite of Artificial Intelligence and ML tools of AWS facilitates scalability and good user system processes. Such technologies can be exploited by an organization to design chatbots to answer complex questions from customers, thereby ensuring quality and efficiency in services rendered [14]. Other work lacks descriptions of HIPAA compliance and security aspects of AI-powered customer support solutions, which this paper attempts to fill [15].

3. Proposed Methodology

Customer service chatbot through Amazon Lex that uses natural language understanding and talks to users; hence, it is very apt for automating business functions, such as answering frequently asked questions or processing transactions. Amazon Lambda acts as the back-end logic in this system, which can make a chatbot run business logic, connect with databases, or call APIs dynamically. For reaching wider channels including SMS and voice, Twilio can be easily integrated with a flexible communication option. In Figure 32.1 shows how Amazon CloudWatch would ensure smooth operation because the service delivers real-time monitoring, logging, and alerting for both chatbot performance as well as system health. Together, these services present a highly scalable, efficient, and adaptable chatbot solution.

3.1. Amazon Lex design phase

Project scope identified objectives and requirements that would give shape to defining what this chatbot was intended for: audience, use case, functionality like service scope, for instance, querying something or account info, as well as design flow in conversation. In Figure 32.2 Lex analyzes user interactions and AWS services like Lambda, DynamoDB, and CloudWatch in order to ensure scalability, reliability, and cost-effectiveness. The speech and intent of the chatbot are dynamically refreshed from actual user input in real time and are therefore adaptive to changing customer queries. Amazon Lex's internal machine learning algorithm adjusts intent detection over time so that accuracy improves from real-world usage patterns.

3.2. Implementation phase

It encompasses the deployment of the designed AWS Lex bot. During this step, the developer designs the bot; defines its intents, slots, and utterances; and programs AWS Lambda with back-end functionality, such as database queries. It supports multimodal interaction and can run in web sites, native mobile apps, or platforms like Slack and Facebook Messenger. The chatbot processes live data streams, maintaining real-time user interaction. Customer queries are dynamically processed and resolved based on

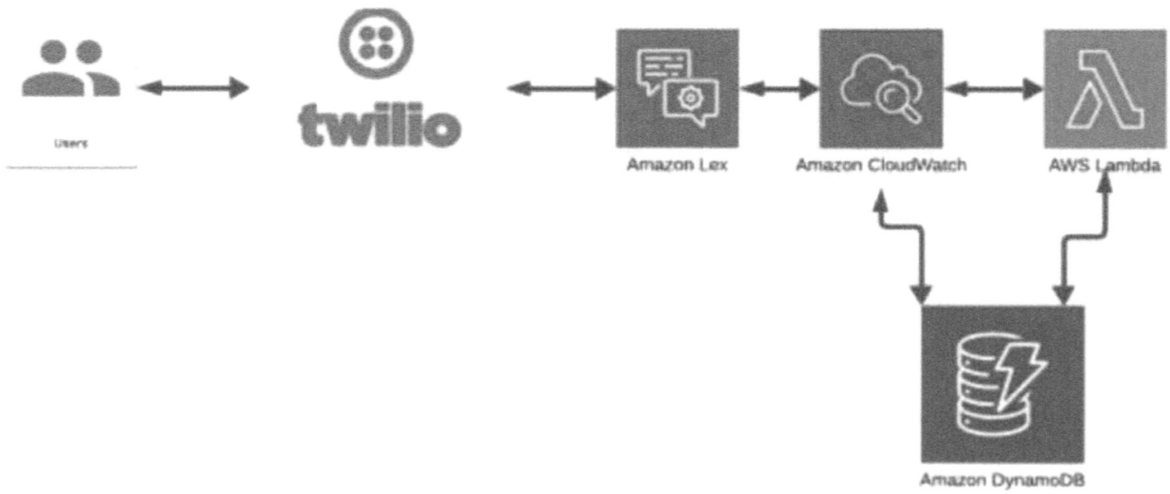

Figure 32.1. Chatbot design.

Source: Author.

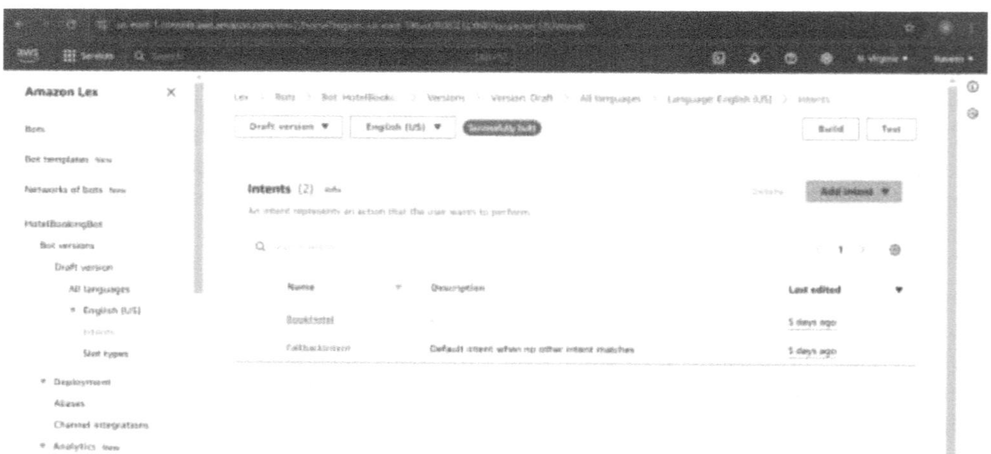

Figure 32.2. Lex Design phase.

Source: Author.

conversation flow. Backend processing for data retrieval, validation, and external API calls is accomplished by AWS Lambda as and when needed. Amazon CloudWatch tracks chatbot usage to enable monitoring and incremental performance improvement against user action.

3.3. Intents

Intents are goal-oriented representations of the user. From Figure 32.3 for hotel booking, different Intents were used. We will make use of the main one:

BookHotel Intent: Hotel room booking.

3.4. Intent examples

BookHotel

Sample sentences:

"Book me a room in a hotel".

"I want a room." "Can I book a hotel reservation?"

3. Integration phase

It is integrated with other systems and contains a database for customer service. The access to user and chat log data is made through Amazon DynamoDB. Custom logic for retrieval of customer data or payment processing is done by AWS Lambda. External APIs are available through API Gateway. This introduces machine learning services as Amazon Comprehend for analysis and multilingual capabilities through Amazon Translate to enhance the user experience.

3.5. Definition of hotel booking slots

Slots are defined as the particular pieces or segments of information that the bot must obtain from the user in order to successfully accomplish the booking request. Each individual slot will directly be related to a certain entity, which may encompass different categories such as date of stay or type of room requested (e.g., date, room type).

CheckIn or checkout Date: The date the user wants to check in or check out to their hotel room (e.g., "2024-12-10").

RoomType: This is the type or category of room the user requires, which includes room options like deluxe, super deluxe, king or queen.

NumberOfGuests: This is the count of people who are now booking the room.

HotelLocation: This is the town or region where the hotel is located, such as "New York".

3.6. Testing phase

Security testing follows the rules and regulations, as for instance HIPAA in healthcare chatbots.Performance of the chatbot is tracked in real-time measures of evaluation. Response time is tracked against a <3 seconds threshold, which is quick processing of queries. Accuracy of intent detection is tracked dynamically in terms of Amazon Lex's natively tracked metrics, with a 85%+ accuracy threshold being maintained through continuous interaction. User satisfaction is tracked through live harvesting of feedback, for example, sentiment analysis and explicit ratings of user interactions.

3.7. Amazon lambda design phase

The first step of the development process focuses on the gaining of a deep understanding about the basic capabilities and architecture design principles that form AWS

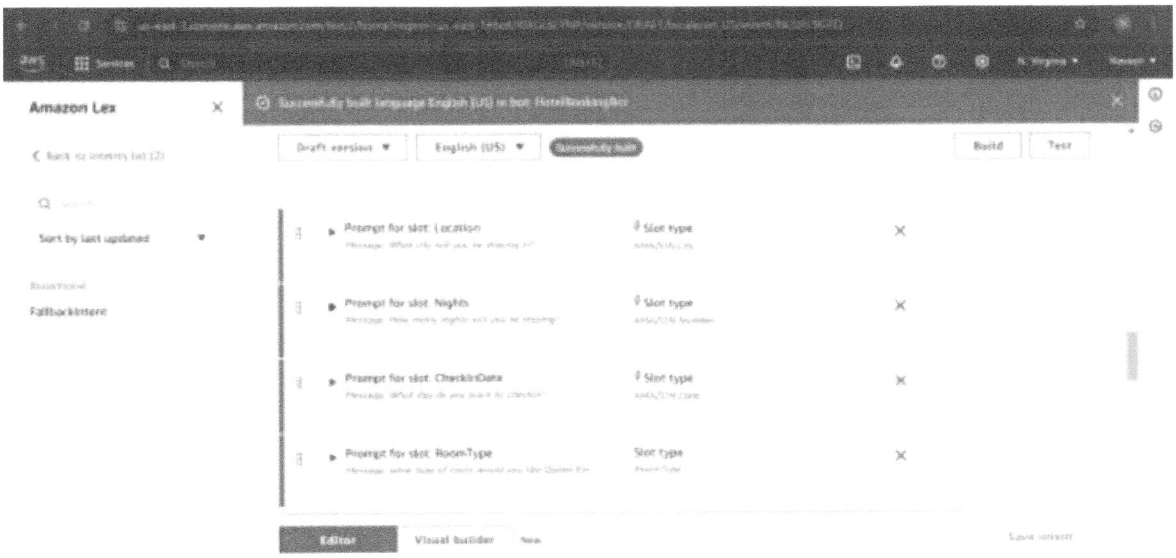

Figure 32.3. Lex Implementation phase.

Source: Author.

Lambda. In this phase, a thorough and meticulous review is conducted on the in-depth documentation and various resources available relating to AWS Lambda, which relates to its seamless integration with other prominent AWS services including Amazon API Gateway, DynamoDB, and S3 among others.

In Figure 32.4 it also describes the critical role of selecting specific use cases for AWS Lambda, which has its basis in real world applications and scenarios, like event-driven architectures that responds to occurrences, microservices that enable modular application developments, or automated tasks aimed at streamlining operations as well as enhancing efficiency. A complete system design is created very carefully so that the interconnection of Lambda with many other services is carried out very smoothly. This integration is carried out so that it meets some special requirements and standards, such as scalability, cost-effectiveness, and reliability.

3.8. *Implementation phase*

The implementation phase of development is that in which code is written in one or more of the programming languages supported by AWS Lambda. Such programming languages are supported and include the very popular Python, Node.js, and Java, among others. Examples of such events include incoming HTTP requests and the uploading of files. Besides the feature lists, this is actually quite a powerful monitoring and logging setup powered by Amazon CloudWatch; it has been specifically put together in a way where it accurately monitors the execution of the Lambda functions themselves, observes error rates, and thus keeps an overview of health operation as shown in Figure 32.5.

3.9. *Lambda function flow*

Verify Room Availability: An SQL query will be called on a predefined database or external API to make sure that there are rooms to rent for the dates needed. The Lambda function is intended to handle and run the logic that is required for checking room availability, processing any reservations that may be made, and returning the appropriate responses that are needed by the users.

This table holds key information such as user name, type of room to be booked, dates related to booking and other relevant information we would require.

Name Table: HotelBookings
Key: UserID (String)
Columns: RoomType, BookingDate.

3.10. *Testing phase*

In this particular stage of evaluation, a series of exhaustive tests are carried out meticulously to test both the performance as well as the reliability of AWS Lambda. In Figure 32.6. Lambda helps to deploy tests code and manage load, cost efficiency in detail take prominence. Load testing simply means invoking Lambda functions with varying traffic conditions so as to measure response times, and overall service stability properly.

3.11. *AMAZON DynamoDB*

AWS DynamoDB is truly an all-inclusive and multidimensional approach that really relates theoretical knowledge. The first stage in this complex process is conducting a very detailed and broad literature review

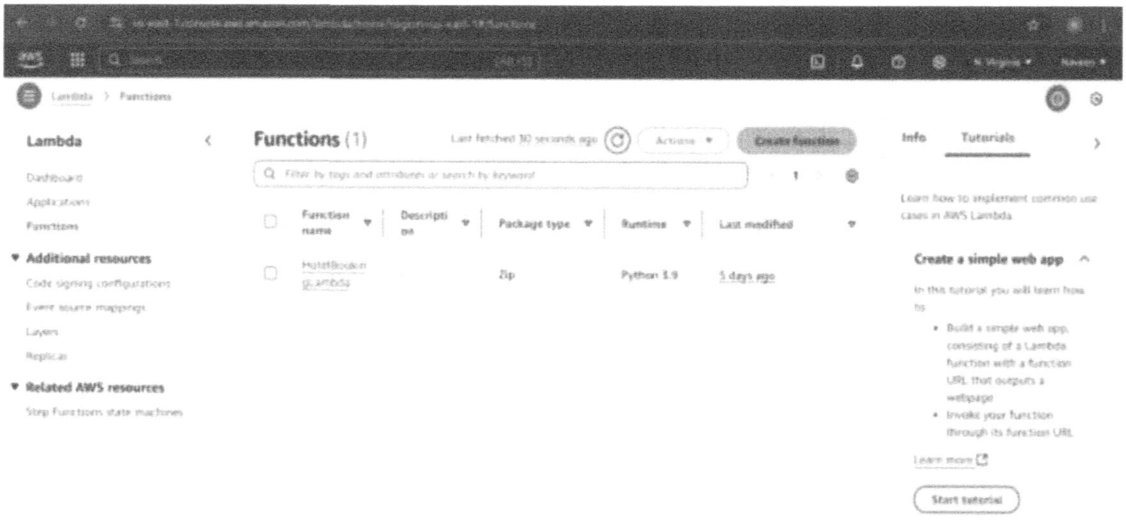

Figure 32.4. Lambda design phase.
Source: Author.

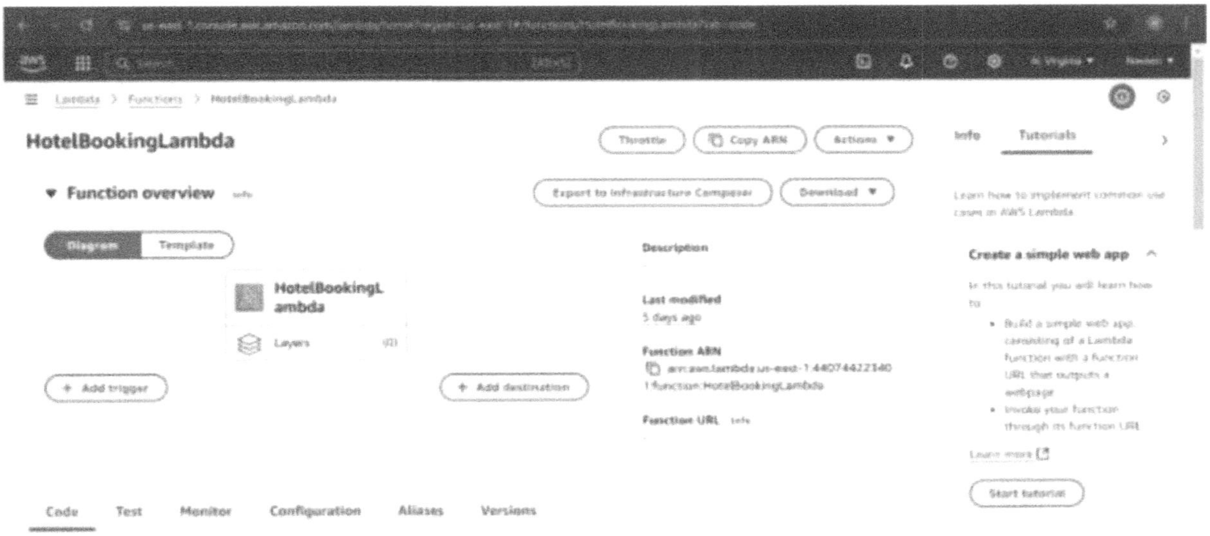

Figure 32.5. Lambda implementation phase.

Source: Author.

Figure 32.6. Lambda testing phase.

Source: Author.

that will help understand the fundamental architecture, distinctive features. DynamoDB with other AWS services, including AWS Lambda, API Gateway, Amazon S3 integrated to find out whether it is possible in the framework of computing serverless architecture. Further still, by using several tools, among which, besides AWS CloudWatch and DynamoDB Streams are several third-party benchmarking tools widely used in industry circles, benchmarks of data, with comparisons of related statistics between DynamoDB and a set of comparable databases.

4. Results and Discussion

The process of room bookings for the user-also one of the key design targets based on this research study-being created as an interactive, efficiency tool whereby users would look at comparisons of Responsive time provided on the service and be capable to make reservations whenever required in the system. The basic feature above was augmented along with the chatbot being armed with its capability of sourcing real-time data via utilization of a number of different APIs retrieved from a couple different hotels. Also, it has been designed deliberately to support and address a wide variety of methods of communication, be it text-based interactions or voice-based communications (Figure 32.7).

4.1. Performance metrics

4.1.1. User interaction rate

This is what it passed through: a total of 10 users in a closely controlled environment that was custom-built for this test evaluation. From Figure 32.8 we can clearly see that the goal was primarily to determine the level of user engagement and overall user satisfaction with the performance of the chatbot. Every one of these users had been given the task to search for a hotel room in a particular area, for several specific dates, and the chatbot dealt with a number of requests in the process.

4.2. Serverless architecture and scaling

The chatbot could scale dynamically and efficiently based on changes in demand levels with the use of AWS Lambda. This characteristic is very valuable in the hotel industry, as demand can change drastically due to season or special events. The serverless model made sure that the

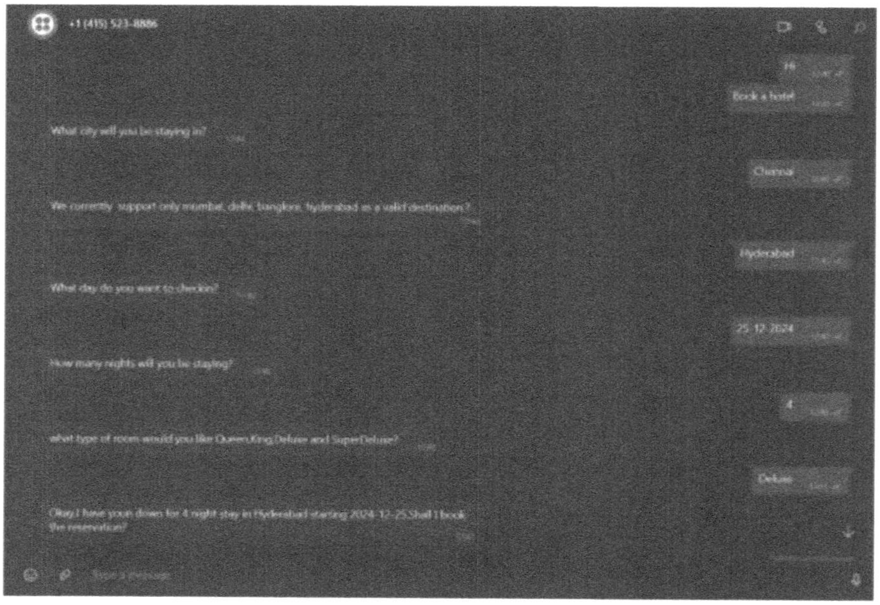

Figure 32.7. Twilio output.

Source: Author.

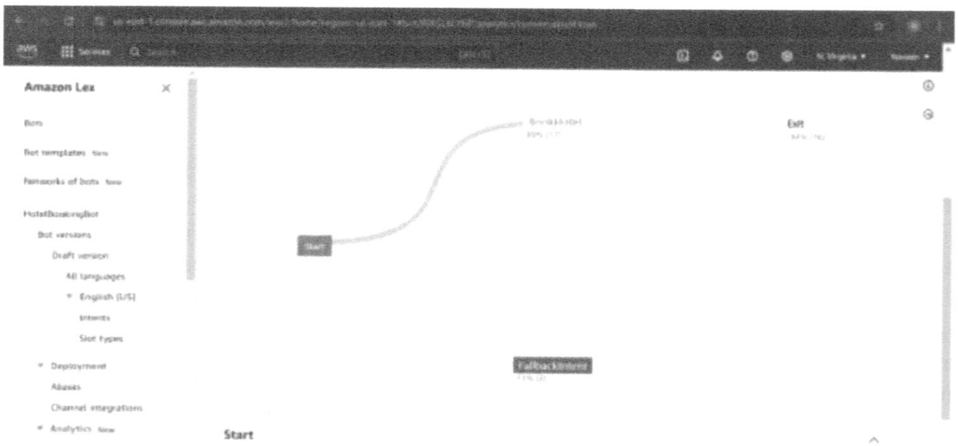

Figure 32.8. User interactions for Chatbot.

Source: Author.

system was able to handle increased traffic loads during peak times without compromising performance and ensuring that the response time remained fast and reliable.

5. Conclusion

This customer service hotel booking chatbot marks a big step toward the efforts at making improvement to the guest experience in the hotel reservations in a seamless manner. Amazon Lex and Lambda to supply the best possible chatbot so that one can handle a series of questions from the customers concerning booking their reservations, suggestions personalized based on specific requirements, hence reducing the dependability of human intervention that was usually required to be done so that routine things could be accomplished.

The studies have demonstrated that chatbots provide many advantages, including 24/7 access, personal service, and faster responses, all of which are meant to deliver a seamless guest experience. Another key factor is that chatbots are easy to scale up without diminishing quality, making it an attractive solution for hotels trying to enhance the delivery of services and the satisfaction of their customers.

This is a very developed technology built, particularly within a domain mainly booking hotels and managing significant amounts of sensitive personal information so that the security feature of the chatbot has to be significantly improved and enhanced and brought up to considerably more robust and sophisticated security solutions.

Acknowledgment

I gratefully acknowledge my co authors, staff, and authority of the networking and communications department for their cooperation in the research.

References

[1] Williams, S. (2018). *Hands-OnDesign chatty interfaces with Alexa skills and Amazon Lex for personalized conversational and voice user interfaces for your aws echo devices and web platforms*. Packt Publishing Ltd.

[2] Haugeland, I. K. F., Folstad, A., et al. (2022). Understanding the user experience for bots. *161*, Art. no. 102788.

[3] Agnihotri, A., & Bhattacharya, S. (2024). Efficiency and effectiveness of bots. *International Journal of Information Management*, *76*, Art. no. 102679.

[4] Chakrabarti, C., & Luge, G. F. (2015). Architecture, algorithms, and evaluation metrics for artificial conversations in user service bots. *42*(20), 6878–6897.

[5] Hu, Y., with Sun, Y. (2023). Understanding the impact of internal and external anthropomorphic cues of customer service bot. *7*(3), Art. no. 10047.

[6] Jones, C. L. E., Hancock, T., Kazandjian, B., & Voorhees, C. M. (2022). Engaging the Avatar: The effects of authenticity signals during chat-based service recoveries. *Journal of Business Research*, *144*, 703–716.

[7] Pawlik, Ł., Boksa, M. P., et al. (2022). A method for improving bot effectiveness by recognising implicit customer intent in contact centre conversations. *143*, 33–45.

[8] Rai, J. H., & Bagde, P. O. (2024). Bulldig bots for frame working. *AIPs Conference Proceeding*, *3180*(1), AIP Publishing.

[9] Sierszen, A., & Drabek, D. (2024). Understanding AIML on AWS. *INTED 2024 Proceedings*, IATED.

[10] Chattaraman, V., Ross, K., et al. (2024). Smart Choice? Evaluating AI-powered mobile decision bots for decision-making. *183*, Art. no. 114801.

[11] Chumpitaz Terry, Alessandro, Liliana Yanqui Huarocc, & Burga-Durango, D. (2023). Artificial intelligence for technological customer service. Cham: Springer Nature Switzerland.

[12] Cordero, J., Barba-Guaman, L., & Franco Guamán, F. (2022). Use of bots for MSME. *Applied Computing and Informatics*, 2022.

[13] Dash, M., & Bakshi, S. (2019). Study of customer chatbots in hospital industry. *International Journal on Customer Relations*, *7*(2), 27–33.

[14] Chauhan, S., & Arora, D. (2023). Developing of cloud services of voice assistance using AWS. *2023 2nd International Conference on Applied Artificial Intelligence and Computing" (ICAAIC)*. IEEE.

[15] Nsaif, Wassem Saad, Saleh, et al. (2024). Chatbot development: work and assistances metrices. *The Eurasia Proceedings of Science Technology Engineering and Mathematics*, *27*, 50–62.

33 Exploring blockchain-powered data security in salesforce CRM: Applications in supply chain transparency

Shalini Polamarasetti[1,a], *Naga Tirumala Rao Chillapalli*[2,b], *Rachit Gupta*[3,c], *and Venkata Sai Manoj Pasupuleti*[4,d]

[1]Sr Salesforce Developer, SS&C Technologies, USA
[2]Manager of computer science, Macy's, United States (USA)
[3]Product manager, Guardian Life, United States
[4]Computer science, Apple Inc, United States

Abstract: Due to expanding complexities, data security and supply chain operations have reached an all-important level where many depend on overall operation management through CRMs, most of which are centralized systems. However, data security integrity assurance and the protection of all transactions are key challenges. Salesforce CRM- the widely used, leading management suite-has to solve for all data maintained about customer and supply chains. To improve some of the considerable limitations presented by this approach, Blockchain technology's decentralized and immutable yet crystal-clear framework allows huge hopes of offering a fundamental capability transformation for Salesforce CRM. This paper presents integrating blockchain technology into Salesforce CRM to enhance data security and supply chain transparency. This study starts by analyzing the key features of blockchain, such as providing tamper-proof records and enabling the real-time traceability of assets. The second one assesses some existing data security measures in Salesforce CRM, mentioning possible vulnerabilities blockchain can handle. Realistic use cases of product provenance tracking, fraud prevention, and intelligent contract automation are discussed to explain the transformation this integration is capable of. These latter sections also discuss technical incompatibility issues, cost considerations, and ways to comply with the regulations. Results indicated that blockchain-powered Salesforce CRM will likely bring a sea change in supply chain functions regarding data security, stakeholder trust, and conformance to changing regulatory standards. Further research directions have been suggested to develop scalability and cross-industry applications.

Keywords: Blockchain, CRM, CRM integration, data security, decentralized systems, fraud prevention, product provenance, regulatory compliance, sales force, smart contracts, stakeholder trust, supply chain transparency, traceability

1. Introduction

The supply chain business is now much more complex due to globalization, customers' changing aspirations, and technological innovation that is taking place very rapidly. The management of these challenges is facilitated by advanced Customer Relationship Management software like Salesforce CRM that maintains operational effectiveness, logistics control, and decision-making on facts. However, these software programs leave themselves vulnerable to cyber-attacks and data corruption by consolidating vast amounts of business-critical information like customers' information, supplier deals, and transactions. Cyber-attacks, phishing scams, ransomware, and insider attacks have revealed critical weaknesses of old CRM protection measures that compromise operational continuity, financial health, and investor/stakeholders' trust.

Traditional security features such as encryption, role-based access control (RBAC), and firewalls lack absolute protection and visibility of CRM data. Centralized data storage is also a weak point that can be accessed by unauthorized people, manipulated by malicious individuals, or breached throughout the system. CRM software also lacks real-time traceability or immutable audit trails, resulting in fraudulent transactions, manipulated supplier information, or poor visibility of goods along the supply chain. Without secure, auditable, and transparent processes, businesses

[a]shalini.research14@gmail.com, [b]visittiru@gmail.com, [c]rachit.swastik97@gmail.com, [d]venkatasaimanojp@gmail.com

DOI: 10.1201/9781003778905-33

can't form trust or fulfill compliance mandates like GDPR or HIPAA [1, 2].

Blockchain technology offers a groundbreaking solution by introducing decentralization, immutability, and real-time data integrity to CRM systems. Unlike centralized databases, blockchain is developed on a distributed ledger where data is encrypted and synchronized on numerous nodes, eliminating centralized loss or theft of data risks. The immutability of blockchain transactions makes transactions irreversible after they have been committed, meaning that no changes can be added or removed, eliminating fraud and unauthorized modification. Besides, smart contracts can automate business transactions on Salesforce CRM, ensuring compliance with transactions on pre-agreed terms and eliminating intermediaries' roles. With blockchain on Salesforce CRM, businesses can significantly enhance supply chain visibility, reinforce data protection, and foster actors' trust, opening doors to efficient and secure digital spaces [2–4].

1.1. Overview of salesforce CRM and its role in supply chain management

Salesforce CRM has undergone capability development to make efficient supply chain operations available to all businesses. Comprehensive enhancement with advanced tools, such as real-time inventory tracking and handling customer interactions, will help software development in a company and enable it to coordinate operational tasks smoothly to fulfill customer orders. It achieves this through big data management and analytics that will allow an organization to keep tabs on supply chain activities to predict customer demand while making data-driven decisions necessary to meet the dynamic changes in the market. Indeed, businesses need adaptability to survive in competitive and fast-moving industries [2–6].

Salesforce CRM would work at the hub in the supply chain, where converged data from different sources are collected, analyzed, and joined together for reporting. The result of all these consolidations would provide real visibility into those key supply chain metrics: the level of inventory, delivery time, and supplier performance. These could identify inefficiencies that may be used to reduce costs and improve customer satisfaction. Further, Salesforce CRM enhances collaboration across the supply chain, integrating data of stakeholders, manufacturers, and distributors to ensure smooth communication and coordination [4, 5, 8].

1.2. Importance of transparency and data security in supply chain operations

In today's globalized economy, transparency and data security are the foundation of a strong and reliable supply chain. Transparency means that all stakeholders securely access correct, timely information about the origin, movement, and status of goods throughout the supply chain. This visibility is essential in making operations efficient, ethical, and compliant with industry standards. In industries dealing with such sensitive products as pharmaceuticals, food, and electronics, traceability is more than an advantage; it's regulated. Consumers and regulators require verifiable proof that the product meets quality, safety, and ethical sourcing standards, making transparency a prime factor in maintaining trust and compliance [4].

In this case, data security protects sensitive supply chain information against unauthorized access, breaches, or tampering. Supply chains manage a vast amount of information, which includes supplier contracts, customer information, and all transaction records. A leak could affect supply chains, breach the privacy of their customers, and lead to a significant loss on several levels for the businesses. For example, cyberattacks on supply chain networks can bring production to a standstill, delay shipments, and erode the trust between stakeholders involved in such a supply network: suppliers, manufacturers, and consumers [3].

1.3. Blockchain technology as a solution for secure and transparent data handling

It has become clear that blockchain technology is decentralized, immutable, and transparent and could provide novel solutions to these chronic data security and transparency challenges beset supply chains. Unlike other centralized databases where data is stored in one spot, blockchain works on a distributed ledger, with information duplicated and synchronized across different nodes on a network. By design, this makes blockchain resistant to tampering and unauthorized changes, as the consent of participants in an entire network would be needed to accomplish any tampering. Its immutability means the recorded data can never be deleted or changed. Hence, in a highly fair and permanent manner, records of transactions are provided [3, 5].

The impact of blockchain in supply chain management has great potential. It allows one to trace the movement and conditions of goods in real-time, thus guaranteeing more accountability and visibility in ways that are not currently possible. This can be done because it makes tracking products for their genuineness easy by recording all transactions involved in the supply chain, from sourcing raw materials to final delivery. This is especially invaluable in industries such as pharmaceuticals and luxury goods, where there's a high risk related to counterfeited products. Besides, blockchain enables supply chain workflow automation by smart contracts - self-executing agreements running under the conditions of predefined rules, reducing reliance on intermediaries and minimizing delays and errors [2–4].

1.4. Research objectives

The core of the research lies in integrating blockchain technology into Salesforce CRM for supply chain transparency and data security. It includes:

- Research blockchain capabilities and their applicability to supply chain operations.
- Review the current security framework of Salesforce CRM and suggest enhancements.
- Propose the framework that will integrate the blockchain with Salesforce CRM.
- Evaluating the benefits and challenges of the proposed integration.

The research, therefore, finds how some of the fundamental challenges at every supply level on Salesforce CRM can be worked around with the blockchain's powered version and lay a platform for many future studies concerning data security and transparency.

2. Understanding Blockchain Technology and its Relevance to Data Security

2.1. Advantages of blockchain for data integrity and transparency

Blockchain technology is better positioned to solve two of the most fundamental challenges of supply chain operations: data integrity and transparency. By design, blockchain ensures that data entered into the system is valid, reliable, and tamper-proof; it eliminates the possibility of fraud or tampering. This is important in supply chain management, where minor discrepancies can lead to severe operational disruption or heavy financial losses. Blockchain transparency, through its system of shared ledgers, facilitates stakeholders' real-time access to the movement, origin, and status of goods. This level of transparency has helped develop trust and a sense of accountability among partners in the supply chain [2–4].

As a result, blockchain allows end-to-end traceability, which has a fundamentally appreciable value in many industries that require high regulation compliance and product authenticity. This might, for example, make it possible to trace where parts are different or how something went through several changes from the farm to being delivered to the table and not just keep its quality but keep it safe because of actions taken right then and there due to some form of recall or contamination issues. Similarly, in the pharmaceutical field, blockchain ensures that drugs are genuine by tracking every movement of them, both in their production and distribution. Added to automation capabilities, it is ideal for smart contracts: it enhances supply chain transparency and ensures data integrity [4].

2.2. Connection between blockchain and salesforce CRM

Integrating blockchain with Salesforce CRM opens a new frontier into the transformation of supply chain management, leveraging the complementary strengths of both technologies. Salesforce CRM is a powerful platform for managing customer interactions and operational data with tools to streamline supply chain processes like inventory tracking, order management, and performance analytics. However, its realization means centralization in its storage; hence, with centralization, various forms of vulnerabilities can widely exist, including breach susceptibility, tampering, or inefficiency in multi-agent settings. Blockchain technology brings this challenge to a benign minimum by providing tamper-proof and transparent decentralization architecture in data management [5–9].

With blockchain integration, Salesforce CRM can enhance the accuracy and authenticity of data using distributed ledgers. Transacted data recorded on a blockchain is immutable and verifiable, meaning that all supply chain participants have one version of the truth they can trust. This would reduce disputes and improve collaboration since stakeholders can confidently depend on the integrity of the data shared. For instance, it can record key supply chain events, such as production milestones, shipment status, and delivery confirmation, on the blockchain. It serves as an auditable, tamper-proof record for each transaction [6].

The blockchain feature in smart contracts further adds value by automating mundane tasks and enforcing predefined agreements. In this case, confirmation of delivery for goods can automatically trigger payment to suppliers, thus avoiding delays and reducing human errors. Real-time traceability on the blockchain also aligns with the visibility that Salesforce CRM emphasizes: tracking the movement of goods, verifying provenance, and ensuring regulatory compliance. Both create a strong, secure solution to the emergent demands of transparency, efficiency and trust in supply chain management. This enables organizations to optimize operations while protecting sensitive data and cultivating deeper stakeholder relationships [7].

2.3. Blockchain integration with salesforce CRM (Technical Details)

Integrating blockchain technology within Salesforce CRM requires effortless integration of Salesforce CRM's cloud-based ecosystem with blockchain networks' distributed environment. Salesforce API is key to making this integration possible by offering an intermediary that relays encrypted data between Salesforce and the blockchain. The integration uses RESTful APIs and Salesforce Apex triggers to post transactional data, customers' history, and supply chain activity onto a distributed ledger, ensuring data integrity, real-time monitoring, and added protection. Middle-ware products such as Mulesoft or Hyperledger Fabric SDK can also make interoperability executed without disruptions, allowing Salesforce to write and read blockchain network data in structured form.

2.4. Types of blockchain suitable for CRM

Selecting the proper blockchain framework is essential to making CRM integration scalable, secure, and compliant. Two blockchain options that are well-adapted to Salesforce CRM are

1. Hyperledger Fabric:
   - Permissioned blockchain suitable for business
   - Enhanced security and confidentiality through only legitimate players' authority to authorize transactions
   - Smart contract integration using Chaincode that makes automation of contract execution within Salesforce processes possible.
   - Fast transaction times compared to public blockchains, making it ideally suited for real-time CRM use
2. Ethereum:
   - Public blockchain that is extremely smart contract-enabled
   - Ideal for multi-stakeholder decentralized trust models where suppliers, producers, and retailers have interactions without central authority
   - Supports ERC-20 tokenization and ERC-721 tokenization, which can be used to tokenize reward schemes and trace assets on Salesforce CRM.
   - Higher transaction costs and processing times due to a proof-of-work (PoW) or proof-of-stake (PoS) consensus mechanism.

Hyperledger Fabric is most likely to be sought after for enterprise-level CRM integration due to its compliance, restricted access, and throughput attributes, along with blockchain's immutability and decentralization features.

2.5. How smart contracts automate transactions within salesforce CRM

A smart contract is a digital contract on the blockchain that automatically executes actions on pre-agreed terms. Salesforce CRM can automate key activities of the supply chain using smart contracts.

- **Supplier Payments:** The smart contract on blockchain automatically triggers payment on confirmation of order update by the supplier using Salesforce.
- **Fraud Prevention:** Supplier identification and client orders are validated on the blockchain, minimizing fraudulent transactions.
- **Regulatory Compliance:** The compliance rules built into smart contracts ensure that only compliant transactions that have been validated are recorded within Salesforce CRM.
- **Product Provenance Tracking:** The blockchain tracks goods movement in real-time, making each product life cycle transparently traceable through to delivery

2.6. Workflow diagram of blockchain-salesforce CRM integration

Below is a workflow chart visually representing how Salesforce CRM is integrated into a blockchain network (Figure 33.1).

CRM uses blockchain technology, detailing how efficiently and securely data flows through software. The process is initiated within Salesforce CRM, where supplier history, supplier files, and history of supplies are tracked. Salesforce API relays data to the middleware (e.g., Mulesoft or Hyperledger SDK), which bridges Salesforce's centralized environment and distributed blockchain network. The blockchain network (e.g., Hy-perledger or Ethereum) writes transactions on an un-tamper-able ledger, ensuring data visibility and integrity. When a transaction fulfills predetermined conditions, smart contracts automatically act, verifying compliance and initiating actions like supplier payables, update of stock, or fraud identification. After verification, the transaction is permanently logged on the blockchain, ensuring responsibility and maintaining trust. The validated history of transactions is relayed to Salesforce CRM, updating supplier history and ensuring that each supplier or client has real-time, un-tamper-able facts. Finally, supplier and client interactions are relayed back into the system, enabling real-time monitoring and optimization of supply chain processes. The integration effectively secures data, makes it transparent and automated, and eliminates intermediaries while increasing efficiency and CRM-based supply chain management trust.

3. Overview of Salesforce CRM and Current Data Security Frameworks

3.1. Salesforce CRM in supply chain management

Salesforce CRM is the leading solution in the market, catering to customer relationship management, but it has

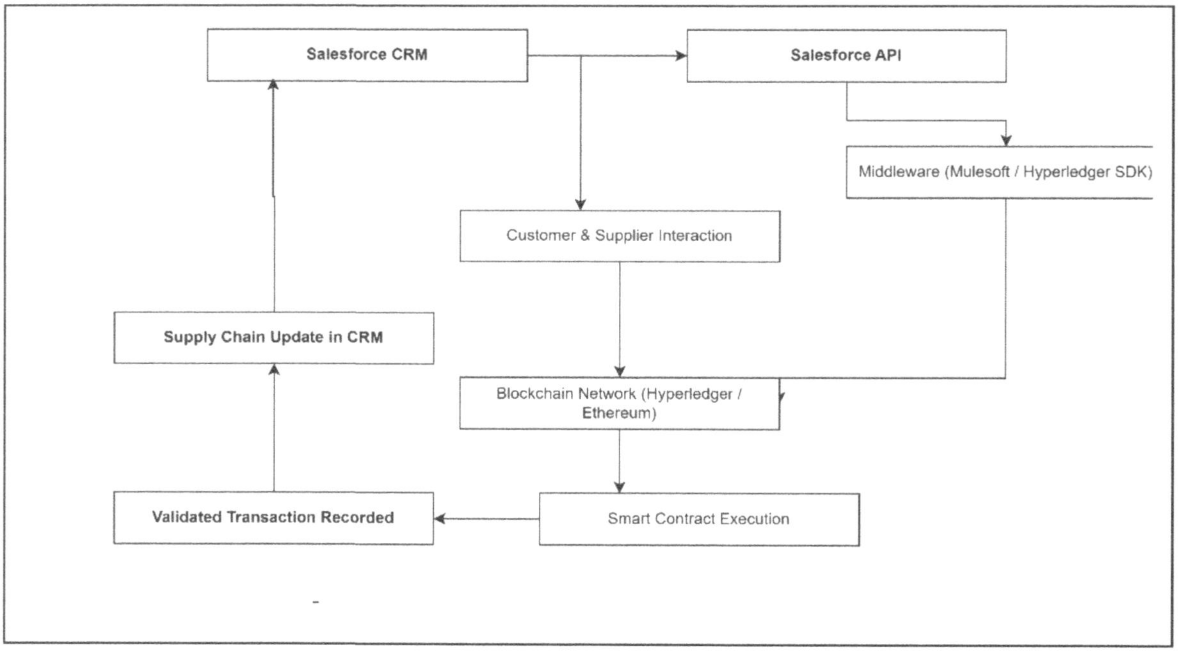

Figure 33.1. Diagram of blockchain-salesforce CRM integration.
Source: Author.

grown significantly, including the supply chain management processes. The cloud architecture it provides enables an organization to consolidate and manage the data coming from various operations for greater collaboration and efficiency. Salesforce CRM ensures better communication amongst those taking part in supply chain management and better tracking of orders and shipments to view the actual inventory in real time. It can also connect various departments with external partners for increased performance, enabling an organization to optimize its supply chain and respond better to a market with changed demands [9, 10].

It improves the visibility and coordination of sales force CRM along the network through an all-around suite of tools ranging from Sales Cloud and Service Cloud to Einstein Analytics. For such huge tasks, supplier relationship management enables them to trace the movement of goods and forecast demand patterns through AI-driven analytics. This is important because, with globalization, supply chains deal with a very complex enterprise of operation that must be reliable, scalable, and flexible at every corner.

3.2. Key features that support supply chain processes

Salesforce CRM is a robust suite of features that address the critical segments of supply chain management, such as solutions that enable organizations to iron out the processes and increase productivity. One positive attribute is inventory management. Based on its centralized data storage, Salesforce CRM manages and tracks the inventory level that can be spread around different locations in real time. That ensures supply levels meet demand and reduces the likelihood of any situation that would cause problems in operational inefficiency around stockouts or overstocking. Salesforce enables companies to monitor the current status of each order placed through every part of order life, up to delivery. This creates visibility and reduces delays or errors interfering with supply chain operations [10].

The strength of engagement in customer dealings is also one of the best features of Salesforce CRM. It has provided functionalities regarding customer inquiries, service issues, response time management, and so on to make them happen promptly and precisely. And with it, all go a long way to cementing the relationships between any business and its respective clients, thus keeping satisfaction levels at the top. Besides, the Salesforce CRM allows the integration of third-party systems, such as ERP solutions and third-party logistics providers, into the system. These integrations provide a shared ecosystem for supply chain operations through which seamless information exchange and collaboration at every touch point of the supply chain may be allowed [12].

3.3. Enhancing salesforce CRM with blockchain

It creates a transformation opportunity for integrating blockchain technology, which will address the inadequacies of the present data security frameworks within

Salesforce CRM. Blockchain architecture is decentralized and immutable, reliant upon central storage with single points of failure entirely avoided. Blockchain distributes data across nodes where no single entity holds complete control over the information, even harder from an attack standpoint. Moreover, blockchain provides more data protection through cryptographic mechanisms, making all transactions secure and verifiable [5–9].

It also enhances blockchain, which creates more transparency and builds trust in supply chain operations by providing a shared ledger visible to all the stakeholders. The result is a single source of truth where participants can always verify consistency in data and track the movement of goods across a supply chain. Additionally, smart contracts could be used to automate processes such as releasing payments and confirming orders, which is part of the blockchain, which cuts down on manual intervention and reduces errors. Such shall be the case that when blockchain integrates with Salesforce CRM, a forceful system emerges, locking the sensitive data while allowing more excellent collaborations and efficiencies across supply chain networks.

Salesforce CRM-Blockchain integration is like a basket of benefits, including overcoming challenges. On the organizational level, the solution must solve many technical challenges concerning system compatibility, data migration, and scalability. On the other hand, blockchain added value to Salesforce CRM: enhanced data security, stakeholder trust, and operational efficiencies. Blockchain has the potential to transform into an essential addition to Salesforce CRM, allowing supply chains to be safer and more transparent [8, 9].

3.4. Case studies in blockchain technology within CRM systems

Integrating blockchain technology within CRM systems has also demonstrated real success in enhancing the visibility of the supply chain, protecting data, and reducing fraud. The most well-known real-world application is Walmart's partnership with IBM's Food Trust blockchain network, where it strives to improve its food's traceability along its supply chain. Without blockchain, tracing sources of contaminated food products took nearly seven days. With blockchain, the company can trace where its food originated in 2.2 seconds, considerably improving response times on recalls of contaminated food products. The blockchain network digitally tracks every activity in the food movement, making each product's history – from farm to shelf – immutable and transparent. The use of blockchain has significantly reduced fraud, streamlined the management of its inventory, and created consumer confidence in product authenticity.

Another successful blockchain use case within CRM and supply chain is that of BMW's PartChain initiative. The company utilizes blockchain technology to ensure greater visibility of its supply chain, making each automotive part and raw material authentic and sourced ethically. With blockchain integration, BMW tracks part movement throughout its suppliers, eliminating fake components within its manufacturing process. It has created a 30% reduction in disputes within its supply chain and a significant reduction in false claims by suppliers. The visibility provided by blockchain also brought greater supplier compliance and responsibility for regulation standards, making its supply chain processes efficient and secure.

A third real-world use is that of the largest shipping company in the world, Maersk, which had TradeLens, a blockchain-based system developed by IBM, integrated into its business. Global shipping processes rely heavily on paper, which is inefficient and fraud-prone without blockchain. With blockchain, shipping transactions have been digitized by Maersk, allowing players to track shipments in real-time. Thus, custom clearance times have been reduced by up to 40%. Paper handling costs have dropped by 20%, indicating how blockchain-based supply chain solutions enhance efficiency while reducing fraud levels.

These examples establish that integrating blockchain into CRM-based supply chains makes it much safer, transparent, and operationally effective. With greater business use of blockchain-based CRM, fraud reduction, compliance management, and automation of supply chains will only improve, driving innovation across business spheres.

4. Regulatory and Legal Compliance Issues

One issue is that the regulatory environment for blockchain adoption is in its formative stages. This engenders uncertainty for organizations considering integrating the technology with Salesforce CRM. Not all jurisdictions are created equal regarding legal frameworks around data privacy, digital transactions, and blockchains. This makes compliance very complicated for global supply chains. For example, with strict data protection laws such as GDPR, the immutability of blockchain goes in contrast to deletion or modification requirements upon the request of a subject. Similarly, many other industries, like healthcare and financial services, have particular regulatory standards with which blockchain systems must also be designed and compliant, adding more complexity [13–19].

4.1. Cybersecurity threats and privacy concerns

While blockchain technology has robust security features at the heart of the design, in integrating the former with

Salesforce CRM, sources of cybersecurity threats and the introduction of potential privacy violations abound. In a practical field, vulnerabilities can occur at every juncture-most, predominantly in middleware between Blockchain and Salesforce. This can compromise a leak in vital data at many levels in supply chain processes to unauthorized users, thus completely disrupting operations. Further, the reliance on blockchain on smart contracts introduces another cause for vulnerability. Attackers can leverage smart contract code vulnerabilities to result in unauthorized transactions or theft of sensitive information [12, 16].

While blockchain's transparency inherently helps increase trust in systems, it may inadvertently expose sensitive data if its access controls are poorly thought through. Supply chain data can include proprietary information, customer information, and transaction records, which must remain confidential. Without proper access controls, the aspect that makes blockchain transparent-the ledger-may allow unauthorized parties to access sensitive information and, consequently, damage stakeholders' business operations and privacy.

4.2. Recommendations for overcoming challenges

Implementation challenges in blockchain-powered Salesforce CRM are of a strategic and phased nature. Technically speaking, selecting the right blockchain platform that matches the operational needs should be the prime focus of any organization. Many of the integration issues get resolved with the choice of permissioned blockchains that have more security and scalability. Collaboration with experienced technology partners and using available blockchain-Salesforce integration tools could reduce complexity and smooth the process. Performance testing and optimization of the integrated system should be regularly performed to meet scalability and efficiency requirements [12, 16].

Financial concerns can also be lessened by adopting a pilot-first concept, where blockchain would ultimately be implemented in focused circles of the supply chain with hypothetical value to be shown in wider-scale deployment. It includes the ability to measure revenue and fix problems at a minimum scale before full-scale commercialization. Grants, deals, or consortium blockchains are other ways to reduce costs. In addition, to overcome such resistance, the business could develop a culture of innovation, invest in education and training, and share decision-making mechanisms with major stakeholders. Demonstrating success stories and even workshops can emphasize in front of major stakeholders the realistic benefits of integrating blockchain into a business application [11, 12, 15, 18].

5. Conclusion and Future Directions

The integration of blockchain technology into Salesforce CRM is a revolutionary way of enhancing the protection of data, visibility of the supply chain, and investor confidence. The study identifies blockchain's capability of providing tamper-proof evidence, real-time traceability, and intelligent contract automation that significantly prevents fraud and wastage of CRM-based supply chain processes. However, though blockchain is complete with benefits, scalability, compliance, and cost of implementation are critical parameters that must be balanced for its use on a universal scale.

Future research must focus on scalability solutions to improve blockchain performance within high-volume CRM environments. Layer 2 protocols, such as state channels and sidechains, promise to process transactions off-blockchain but leave the leading blockchain network secure. Hybrid blockchain designs combining permissioned and public blockchain designs can also enhance data privacy, performance, and compliance with business CRM use case regulations. A critical research avenue is exploring how AI can be combined with blockchain-based CRM. AI-based analytics can leverage blockchain's unchanging data history to provide predictive insight, fraud discovery, and automated decision-making, making overall CRM processes more effective.

Another essential ongoing research priority is conducting cost-benefit analyses of blockchain use within CRM and supply chain management to determine its financial viability. While blockchain increases automation and protection, there is also a requirement to balance installation costs, power consumption, and investments in supporting facilities against real benefits. To foster wide-scale use, the trick will be to set up universal metrics for measuring ROI, operational efficiencies, and compliance expenses. With developing technology, innovation around interoperability, private-preserving protocols, and distributed identity management will continue to set the fate of blockchain-enabled CRM solutions.

Acknowledgment

I gratefully acknowledge the friends, staff, and researchers in sales force and CRM for their inspiration in this paper.

References

[1] Blockchain (February 2025). Powered Data Security in Salesforce CRM: Applications in Supply Chain Transparency. *Google Books.* Accessed *https://books.google.com/books?hl=en&lr=&id=CbkIEQAAQBAJ&oi=fnd&pg=PA89&dq=Blockchain-Powered+Data+Security+in+Salesforce+CRM+Supply+Chain+Transparency*

[2] Neway, Abegaz Sahilu. (February 2025). Digital Supply Chain: Navigating the Future Operation. *Google Books,* 2024. Accessed *https://books.google.com/books?hl=en&lr=&id=V5swEQAAQBAJ&oi=fnd&pg=PA*

9&dq=Blockchain-Powered+Data+Security+in+Salesforce+ CRM+Supply+ Chain+Transparency.

[3] Chang, Y., Iakovou, E., & Shi, W. (2020). Blockchain in Global Supply Chains and Cross-Border Trade: A Critical Synthesis of the State-of-the-Art, Challenges, and Opportunities. *International Journal of Production Research, 58*(7), 2082–2099.

[4] Wang, Z., Zheng, Z., Jiang, W., & Tang, S. (2021). Blockchain-Enabled Data Sharing in Supply Chains: Model, Operationalization, and Tutorial. *Production and Operations Management, 30*(7), 1965–1985.

[5] Habib, G., Sharma, S., Ibrahim, S., Ahmad, I., Qureshi, S., & Ishfaq, M. (2022). Blockchain Technology: Benefits, Challenges, Applications, and Integration of Blockchain Technology with Cloud Computing. *Future Internet, 14*(11), 341.

[6] Morkunas, V. J., Paschen, J., & Boon, E. (2019). How Blockchain Technologies Impact Your Business Model. *Business Horizons, 62*(3), 295–306.

[7] Chillakuri, B., & Attili, V. P. (2022). Role of Blockchain in HR's Response to New-Normal. *International Journal of Organizational Analysis, 30*(6), 1359–1378.

[8] Kargacier, C. (2021). Benefit and Cost Analysis of Blockchain Technology in the Supply Chain and Monitoring in the Automotive Industry. *Doctoral dissertation, Politecnico di Torino. https://webthesis.biblio.polito.it/17716.*

[9] Dheenadhayalan, V., & Vijai, C. (February 2025). Contemporary Research in Commerce and Management. *Sankalp Publication*. Accessed https://books.google.com/books?hl=en&lr=&id=mPa6EAAAQBAJ&oi=fnd&pg=PA1&dq=Blockchain-Powered+Data+Security+in+Salesforce+CRM+Supply +Chain+Transparency.

[10] Sipek, M., & Žagar, M. (2021). Educational Aspects of Trustless Systems and Their Feasibility in Academia and Industry. *In EDULEARN21 Proceedings*, 11106–11110. IATED. *https://library.iated.org/view/SIPEK2021EDU.*

[11] Agrawal, K., Aggarwal, M., Tanwar, S., Sharma, G., Bokoro, P. N., & Sharma, R. (2022). An Extensive Blockchain-Based Applications Survey: Tools, Frameworks, Opportunities, Challenges, and Solutions. *IEEE Access, 10*, 116858–116906.

[12] Gupta, D. G., & Jain, V. (2023). Use of Artificial Intelligence with Ethics and Privacy for Personalized Customer Services. In Artificial Intelligence in Customer Service: *The Next Frontier for Personalized Engagement,* 231–257. Cham: Springer International Publishing. *https://link.springer.com/chapter/10.1007/978-3-031-33898-4_10.*

[13] Takawira, B., Pooe, D., & Samuels, A. Emerging Technologies in the Pharmaceutical Supply Chains: A Systematic Review of Industry 5.0 Challenges. *ResearchGate. https://www.researchgate.net/publication/385760438_Emerging_Technologies_in_the_Pharmaceutical_Supply_Chains_A_Systematic_Review_of_Industry_50_Challenges.*

[14] Basumatary, A., & Joshi, S. (2022). Adoption of Blockchain in Trade Finance and Its Impact on Financial Decision Making. In 2022 *International Conference on Decision Aid Sciences and Applications (DASA),* 556–559. IEEE. *https://ieeexplore.ieee.org/abstract/document/9765150.*

[15] Aithal, P. S., & Aithal, S. (2019). Digital Service Innovation Using ICCT Underlying Technologies. *In Proceedings of International Conference on Emerging Trends in Management, IT and Education,* 33–63. *https://papers.ssrn.com/sol3/papers.cfm?abstract_id=3484105.*

[16] Aggarwal, P., & Manaswi, K. (January 2023). An Integrated System of Blockchain and Corporate Governance - Does It Matter?: A Review. *CPJ Law Journal, 447. https://www.researchgate.net/publication/376957431_CPJ_Law_Journal__Issue_2_NATO*

[17] Jain, V. (2023). Use of AI With Ethics and Privacy for Personalized Customer Services. *ResearchGate. https://www.researchgate.net/publication/373202738_Use_of_Artificial_Intelligence_with_Ethics_and_Privacy_for_Personalized_Customer_Services.*

[18] Chitra, M., Surianarayanan, R., Mahamuni, V. S., Mohammed, S., Keno, M. T., & Boopathi, S. (2025). Study on Cloud Computing-Empowered Small and Medium Enterprises. *In Essential Information Systems Service Management*, 189–220. IGI Global. *https://www.igi-global.com/chapter/study-on-cloud-computing-empowered-small-and-medium-enterprises/357940.*

[19] Bucci, D. (2019). The Use of Blockchain Technology in the Fashion Industry and Its Impact on Sustainability. *Politics, https://www.politesi.polimi.it/handle/10589/175527.*

34 Optimizing business processes with hyper-automation: A case study on salesforce flow in enterprise operations

Shalini Polamarasetti[1,a] *and Harshini Gadam*[2,b]

[1]Sr Salesforce Developer, SS&C Technologies, USA
[2]Computer science, Illinois Institute of Technology, USA

Abstract: Hyper-automation has rapidly emerged as an enterprise optimization strategy, enabling balance in efficiency, scalability, and agility. This paper looks into Salesforce Flow, a low-code automation capability on the Salesforce platform, and its place in enterprise hyper-automation. Salesforce Flow enables organizations to automate repetitive tasks, accelerate decision-making, and build more cohesive interdepartmental teams, thus allowing them to address operational inefficiencies and better adapt to dynamic market demands. This research looks at the hyper-automation theoretical framework. It sets the scene for a concrete discussion of Salesforce Flow: an overview of its core enablement features, including workflow orchestration, decision logic, and system integrations. Major business use cases were identified to provide insights into how Salesforce Flow helps optimize different enterprise practices, such as customer experiences, employee onboarding processes, and complex workflows or approval processes. The paper details how an optimal hyper-automation strategy can be designed with exceptional support for process analysis, articulation of goals, and integration strategies. Cost savings, time reduction, and minimization of errors are metrics showing the potential of hyper-automation in driving operational excellence sustainably. The discussion also carries challenges and lessons learned during hyper-automation initiatives that provide actionable insights into best practices for enterprises.

Keywords: Automation strategy, customer experience, business process optimization, cost savings, decision-making automation, employee on boarding, enterprise operations, error minimization, hyper-automation, low-code automation, operational efficiency, sales forceflow, scalability, system integration, workflow orchestration

1. Introduction

Hyper-automation is a business process optimization process fueled by emerging technologies such as AI, RPA, and low-code platforms to set up automated processes that function autonomously. While automation is generally siloed to discrete tasks, hyper-automation integrates processes within business units to ensure integration, real-time decision-making, and better operational productivity. Despite greater use, business houses continue to experience siloed processes, non-integration processes within business units, and inefficient processes that weigh processes, incur unnecessary expenses, and introduce defects through human interventions. Such ineptness is generally fuelled by old-fashioned legacy systems, siloed silos of data, and the use of manual approvals that introduce bottlenecks that make businesses non-agile and unresponsive. The challenge of scaling automation to numerous business processes also worsens things, making it increasingly difficult for companies to stay efficient within a fast-evolving digital environment [1].

Unlike basic automation, which focuses on and aims at isolated tasks, hyper-automation looks at the big picture: it optimizes whole processes so businesses can realize tremendous gains in efficiency, customer satisfaction, and lower operational costs. By applying workflow orchestration, machine learning, and decision analytics, hyper-automation removes repetitive tasks, improves accuracy, and speeds up essential processes. The growing adoption of hyper-automation across industries underlines its importance as an enabler of strategic business transformation in the digital era [2, 3].

1.1. Relevance of salesforce flow

Salesforce Flow is one of the key powerful enablers within the Salesforce ecosystem that drives hyper-automation forward for the modern enterprise. Being a low-code platform, Salesforce Flow allows users to create and automate

[a]shalini.research14@gmail.com, [b]harshivik05@gmail.com

DOI: 10.1201/9781003778905-34

even the most complex workflows without deep programming knowledge. It enables guided workflows, real-time decision-making, and seamless integrations with other enterprise systems. Salesforce Flow could be an excellent fit for hyper-automation efforts since it bridges the gap between technology and business users by fueling collaboration and innovation within teams [2].

Salesforce Flow empowers enterprise operations to automate lead generation, customer support workflow, invoice processing, or an approval hierarchy mechanism. Low code enables it to help a business adapt or scale fast to the continuously evolving objectives. It allows Salesforce Flow to integrate with external systems in support of artificial intelligence and hyper-automation. With the ability to automate repetitive tasks, optimize decision-making, and foster collaboration, Salesforce Flow shows just how important it is in achieving hyper-automation [3].

1.1.1. Research gap and contribution of the study

Although hyper-automation is gathering steam across most business domains, no systematic body of literature investigates its actual use through low-code interfaces like Salesforce Flow. The existing literature generally focuses on theoretical treatments of automation architectures or case studies of AI-driven automation without taking the actual use of hyper-automation within business processes of business houses into view. Little is also investigated on how hyper-automation can improve cross-functional collaboration by unifying diverse business units, departments, and external systems within a single integrated automation framework.

This study fills this gap by discussing how businesses can utilize Salesforce Flow to introduce hyper-automation, automate processes, and enhance operational effectiveness. Through real-world use case exploration, automation benefits vs limitations analysis, and best practice guidelines on how to deploy, this research adds to business automation strategies literature. The findings will also be helpful to organizations that aim to scale automation, make informed decision-making, remain compliant, save money, and simplify operational processes.

This research contributes to advancing academia on hyper-automation by addressing these critical gaps. It presents valuable business insight to business leaders, IT practitioners, and decision-makers who aim to drive organizations' digital transformation.

1.2. Scope of the paper

This paper explores how enterprise operations can leverage the full power of hyper-automation by using Salesforce Flow. In contrast to literature strictly linked to organizational boundaries, the paper adopts a higher perspective. It highlights some general principles, strategies, and effects of using Salesforce Flow to implement hyper-automation. Given this, a review of the concept of hyper-automation is considered in light of theory and practice: how to perform flows with Salesforce, along with the opportunity to take an example in the different business spheres.

The scope of this research covers the most important subjects related to hyper-automation, including process analysis, the design of workflows, and system integration. The paper illustrates how Salesforce Flow solves these pain points by mapping common ones within an enterprise- including customer support inefficiencies, approval process delays, and isolated workflows. Furthermore, best practices are provided for applying Salesforce Flow with scalable and sustainable business outcomes. This holistic approach ensures that the findings and recommendations apply to various industries and organizational contexts.

1.3. Purpose and objectives

The paper provides insight into the hyper-automation being made using Salesforce Flow. The critical analysis of features and functionalities is targeted to indicate this tool's positioning in developing optimized enterprise operations and ensuring the highest quality of operational outcomes. This also tries to fill the theoretical, conceptual understanding, and operational practice gap by detailing actionable guidelines for a business undertaking any hyper-automation initiative.

The specific objectives of this paper include:

- To define Hyper-automation and its significance in modern enterprises.
- To explore the capabilities and features of Salesforce Flow as a Hyper-automation tool.
- To analyze key use cases of Salesforce Flow in automating and optimizing business processes.
- To evaluate the impact of hyper-automation on operational efficiency, scalability, and cost-effectiveness.
- To identify best practices, challenges, and lessons learned from Hyper-automation projects.

The paper seeks to achieve these objectives by enabling businesses and professionals with the required knowledge and tools to leverage Salesforce Flow for trans-formative operational improvements. It also highlights the broader implications of hyper-automation and calls on organizations to make innovative technologies part of their strategic imperatives.

2. The Role of Hyper-automation in Enterprise Operations

2.1. Concept of hyper-automation

Hyper-automation is a paradigm shift in how the enterprise looks at business operations, going beyond the automation of an isolated task to incorporating advanced technologies like AI, machine learning, and robotic process automation. Automation of complex end-to-end processes and hyper-automation optimize efficiency and reduce human intervention to guarantee that processes are consistent and error-free. This all-inclusive approach eliminates departmental inefficiencies and creates a smooth and harmonious operational framework [1–7].

Hyper-automation focuses on scalability and adaptability, arguably the two most essential features for any business. It leverages AI and machine learning to comb through millions of data sets, deriving action items from insights at warp speed for decision-making. These enable the enterprise to quickly adjust to the shifting market conditions, customers, and operations. That is how hyper-automation allows the enterprise to be competitive and agile in those industries that demand speed and precision [1–3].

Besides all that, continuous improvement is also one of the hallmarks of hyper-automation. Such intelligent systems learn and evolve continuously, find a process for finding process bottlenecks, implement improvements on them, and incrementally refine workflows to arrive at operations efficiently achieved and aligned with ever-changing organizational goals. Most importantly, hyper-automation fosters innovation in that much more people and time now can be spent working more on strategic tasks than on mundane, repeat activity tasks humans do [3].

Hyper-automation for large enterprises is more of a strategic need nowadays than an evolution of technology. While seamlessly bridging the gap between technology and business processes, it provides robustness with flexibility in the system. Thus, hyper-automation enables the enterprise to improve efficiency and operational costs while encouraging innovation toward the company's long-term success. This approach will allow organizations to stay competitive in today's highly competitive business world [4].

2.2. Key components

Hyper-automation is all about several key technologies coming together to mutually enable the seamless knitting of frictionless automation across the length and breadth of enterprise processes. One of the integral components, AI provides a firm grounding for predictive analytics, NLP, and intelligent decision-making. AI trudges through mountains of datasets to identify patterns, provide forecasts of what can subsequently happen, and then allow recommendations that will make innovations in workflows proactive. Upon integrating AI into strategies surrounding hyper-automation, each enterprise will transition from reactive operations to more predictive and prescriptive models. It also increases the speed and accuracy of decisions [5].

RPA automates repetitive and rule-based tasks with precision and consistency, complementing AI. RPA is particularly good at high-volume activities like data entry, invoice processing, and system updates, all of which reduce the burdens on human employees. Combining RPA with hyper-automation initiatives helps an organization free itself from inefficiencies, minimize errors, and ensure mundane tasks get done fast and accurately to free employees for higher-value work requiring creativity, judgment, and strategic thinking [6].

Low-code platforms like Salesforce Flow powered the hyper-automation through more programmable and adaptive workflows. The low-code platforms democratized the competencies for automation throughout departments, enabling business users to easily design, implement, and manage automated processes. Non-skilled end-users can create automation with minimal programming skills. To sum it up, this low-code development tool is democratizing the expertise of automation across departments with its drag-and-drop user interface composed of pre-assembled components for further innovative collaboration. Integrating AI, RPA, and low-code platforms creates an end-to-end hyper-automation ecosystem wherein enterprise workflows are effective, scalable, flexible, and supportive of fully realizing organizational objectives [7].

2.3. Challenges facing the enterprise

Today, a host of operational challenges stands between a modern enterprise and its march toward efficiency and competitiveness. Siloed information lies at the heart of such challenges: critical business knowledge scattered over various disconnected data platforms hinders collaboration, delays decisions, and brings partial and inconsistent insight. This reduces operational efficiency and diminishes the organization's potential for timely response to change either in the market or customer demands. Considering the ability to reach data on a unified basis in real-time, this may well be counted among the principal obstacles enterprises face in the quest for agility within dynamic business environments [8].

Other high priorities are the dependencies on ineffective manual workflows that are inefficient, delaying, and inviting human errors. Outdated processes predominate for many businesses, needing repetitive data entry and the approval of documents or reports. These manual workflows decrease productivity and divert irreplaceable human resources from strategic, high-value activities. Large-scale operations usually compile small inefficiencies that create giant operational bottlenecks, adding costs and delays to significant business outcomes [9].

Therefore, hyper-automation ties together data systems, interdepartmental collaboration, automation of manual-intervention-heavy tasks, and higher-end technologies all in one. For example, it can iron out sales and customer support by interlinking dispersed tools into one single window of customer interaction management. Therefore, it enhances process visibility for speedy and accurate completion of tasks to create more internal efficiency and customer satisfaction. The transformed approach helps enterprises overcome their operational challenges and conduct business in a unified way in this growing competitive and complex marketplace.

2.4. Overview of salesforce flow

Salesforce Flow is a big player in the Salesforce ecosystem for low-code automation. It can smooth out and scale business processes. Having minimal requirements for coding experience, it provides organizational teams with drag-and-drop ease of designing and implementing automated workflows. It will let nontechnical and technical users do that, basically democratizing automation, whereby entire departments in an enterprise all get involved in process optimization. Salesforce Flow automates routine tasks like approvals, notifications, and information updates for businesses, freeing employees to focus on higher-value activities that drive growth and innovation [3–9].

What stands out about Salesforce Flow is its ability to administer such a complex workflow through departments and systems. This could involve automating a customer onboarding process and bringing together the sales, support, and operations teams as one seamless process for the customer and employee. It allows decision-making as part of workflows to adapt dynamically to specific situations through logical conditions and rule-based actions. Such flexibility will ensure that processes remain working correctly and relevant in an often fast-changing business context. Integration of various departments and systems, Salesforce Flow works towards silo avoidance by developing cross-functional cooperation [4].

Salesforce Flow is integrative: businesses can hook it to other Salesforce products and third-party tools. This nature of integrations guarantees that workflows will stay out of the Salesforce bucket and into every technology stack at an organization. It draws data from CRM systems, ERP platforms, and analytics packages to provide an integrated view updated in near real-time. It offers smooth integration, hence improving visibility and decision-making by ensuring different applicable systems are working in harmony for the benefit of the enterprise.

Besides, Salesforce Flow is designed to grow and keep up with your company's needs and the ever-changing development of modern challenges presented, for instance, in significant enterprise operations. This may range from scaling automation abilities to meet burgeoning demands to working out workflows due to changes dictated by regulatory requirements- all the agility your company will need is found in the flow. The quest for continuous betterment means corporations thus iterate and fine-tune their processes over time to do their best continually. As it finally integrates ease of use, cross-functional capability, and adaptability, Salesforce Flow will become the cornerstone of leveraging hyper-automation in enterprise environments [3, 5, 7, 9, 13].

3. Case Studies

3.1. Case study 1: Automating customer service by causeway technologies

Causeway Technologies, a software company that serves the construction industry, had great difficulty managing effective customer support requests. With its diverse products that meet distinct industry requirements, managing case creation and resolution has been problematic due to inconsistent customer information and ineffective manual processes. The company sought to rectify this by using Salesforce Flow to create a dynamic case form integrated within its Experience Cloud portal. The automation permitted customers to submit cases with tailored questions corresponding to the product that customers were using, allowing the support teams to have all pertinent information immediately. The form also allowed customers to embed supporting documentation, screenshots, and critical files, eliminating follow-on emails asking customers to provide supporting documentation or screenshots. Consequently, the support group was much better able to triage and process cases much earlier, cutting wait times by considerable amounts. The streamlined process maximized customer satisfaction and internal productivity by eliminating the give-and-take needed to gather outstanding information. The initiative created tangible reductions in resolution times, better productivity from its support group, and a better overall customer experience, making clear how hyper-automation through Salesforce Flow can foster operational excellence within its customer service function.

3.2. Case study 2: The Mike Morse law firm - legal workflow efficiency optimization

Mike Morse Law Firm, America's leading practice of personal injury law, had its case management processes weighed down by inefficiencies that impacted its capability to provide prompt and effective legal services to customers. Case managers and paralegals had conventionally had to track case updates by hand, follow up on documentation, and ensure compliance with legal deadlines, leading to unnecessary administration burden and delay risks. The company workflow had to be streamlined by implementing Salesforce Flow to automate routine case management processes. The automation ensured that suitable workflows were triggered when opening each case, including automated documentation generation, assigning the case to respective legal teams, and reminding them of deadlines. Salesforce Flow also incorporated AI-based analytics to provide insight into case progress, allowing lawyers and paralegals to allocate tasks better. The productivity impact of automation was phenomenal – productivity levels within the company increased by 35%, enabling case managers to dedicate more resources to client engagement activities than administration activities. Automation also reduced operational costs by eliminating unnecessary hand-based activities and avoiding delay risks through non-achievement of deadlines. By leveraging hyper-automation through Salesforce Flow, Mike Morse Law Firm successfully streamlined its processes, enhanced client servicing, and streamlined legal case handling, establishing that automation can have a phenomenal turnaround on legal practice processes.

3.3. Case study 3: Automating student retention and administrative processes of Texas Tech university

Texas Tech University, a top-notch educational institution, handled students' data hands-only within many siloed systems. With students' data distributed throughout diverse departments, the school had no easy task flagging students likely to need academic care and intervention proactively. The school also had administration inefficiency in handling students' files, financial aid requests, and course enrolment, leading to unnecessary delay and frustration for students and professors alike. The school resolved its issues using Salesforce Flow to link and automate critical department processes. The integration brought together well over eight discrete systems, offering each student a complete, real-time educational experience within one screen view. Automated processes were created to flag students exhibiting signs of risk, such as falling GPAs or incomplete enrolment, allowing advisors to act proactively. The school also automated financial processes, eliminating turnaround times and ensuring students received what they needed on time. The school had noticeable increases in retention and graduation levels, along with better operational efficiency within its administration processes. The automation power of complex processes streamlined processes and gave students a better experience, making hyper-automation key within learning institutions.

4. Designing an Enterprise-Ready Hyper-Automation Strategy

4.1. Analyzing current processes

Hyper-automation strategies require in-depth knowledge of the existing business processes to identify and understand workflows, systems, and interdependencies driving daily operations. Workflow mapping gives an organization a clear picture of its operational landscape, underlining the areas of inefficiency, redundancy, and bottlenecks. Without this foundational knowledge, it's hard to target the right processes for automation or measure the impact of hyper-automation initiatives.

To better understand processes, stakeholders across the enterprise should collaborate. Employees directly part of these workflows provide great views on pain points, dependability on tasks, or where delays keep happening. Process mapping, value stream analysis, and time-motion studies help document the workflow and introduce quantitative insight into their performance. Other visualization tools, such as a flowchart or process diagram, enable further clarity about the sequence and any interrelationship among tasks, making pinpointing inefficiencies in their operations more straightforward [3, 5, 7, 9, 13].

An essential feature of this analysis is the determination of processes that are suitable for automation. The ideal candidate would be repetitive, rule-based tasks with high rates of errors or those tasks that require much manual intervention. Examples might include data entry, approval of documents, or other customer inquiries that follow predictable patterns. Processes that consume quite a lot of time and resources without adding proportional value make them prime targets for Hyper-automation. In addition, identifying processes where delays directly impact customer satisfaction or business outcomes would provide further prioritization for automation efforts [3, 5, 7, 9, 13].

The result of this analysis should be a comprehensive catalogue of the current workflows, replete with metrics like processing time, error rates, and resource utilization. This data guides not only the selection of automation targets but also acts as a baseline against which the impact of the hyper-automation effort is evaluated. An enterprise lays the foundation for a successful hyper-automation strategy by investing time in analysing current processes.

4.2. Setting automation goals

After deeply analysing the current workflow, clear and quantifiable automation objectives should be defined. These objectives guide the strategy for hyper-automation and allow alignment with higher-order priorities at the organizational level. Objectives need to determine the outcome to be expected from the automation: increased efficiency, reduced costs, improvement in customer satisfaction, or greater scalability. By defining such objectives at the outset, enterprises ensure their hyper-automation initiatives deliver value in concrete form. It does so by identifying those processes that have the highest automation potential. High-impact processes either directly affect business outcomes or most need improvement. For instance, automating customer service workflows may reduce response times and result in better customer retention, while smoothing invoicing will speed up cash flow with fewer errors. Enterprises should consider other processes viewed as compliance risks or requiring intensive manual intervention; automating them will reduce risks and improve accuracy [8, 9].

One must go step by step in setting goals. Rather than trying to automate all processes at once, organizations should prioritize initiatives based on feasibility, impact, and resource availability. It is an incremental approach that enables businesses to deliver quick wins to demonstrate the value of hyper-automation while still building momentum for larger and more complex projects. An enterprise, for example, could start with automating data entry tasks while subsequently moving to automating end-to-end workflows spanning several departments [10].

Besides, setting up the goals involves determining key performance indicators that will help the organization measure the success of reaching those goals. Key metrics include process completion time, error rates, cost savings, and other tangible proofs of automation's impact. Customer satisfaction scores, employee productivity, and process scalability can also indicate success. Relating automation goals to specific key performance indicators will enable organizations to track their progress, identify areas for improvement, and communicate the benefits of hyper-automation to stakeholders [3, 5, 7, 9, 13].

4.3. Best practices in salesforce flow implementation

Salesforce Flow can be one of the most powerful ways to implement hyper-automation. The results, however, will depend on best practices being followed in the design and deployment. Among the first considerations is to design for reuse. Building workflows modularly and creating reusable actions will reduce some of the time and resources needed when automating more business processes in the future [12].

For instance, the approval flow in expense requests can be turned into one concerning purchase orders or contract approvals. This modularity boosts efficiency and consistency among the diverse workflows. Another best practice is to keep the workflow design simple. While Salesforce Flow can enable complex automation, all users should intuitively understand the workflow. The too-complex design may lead to higher errors, maintenance difficulties, and user frustration. Enterprises should aim to make workflows robust yet straightforward, with clear decision points and minimum unnecessary steps [9].

Testing becomes a key companion for any attempt at effective Salesforce Flow. Businesses should go out on extensive testing before deploying automated workflows into production to ensure the flow's functionality, accuracy, and reliability. The Test should cater to all possible test scenarios, including edge cases and exception tests, given that one wants to ensure the automation performs as prescribed under every circumstance. Indeed, another key component is inviting to use it among end-users to gather constructive feedback on usability and further improvements [10].

While detailing is another main constituent for best practices, well-documented workflows, configuration details, and decision logic make such automation reproducible and provide transparency. Knowledge transfer ensures that it goes smoothly at any time or changes; having complete records for every part of an implementation involving Flow would contribute more to clear cuts in maintenance updates due to changing circumstances in business.

Finally, continuous monitoring and optimization are critical to realize the full value of Salesforce Flow. Once workflows go live, it is of the essence that an organization routinely revisits its performance against a set of predefined KPIs and makes necessary changes. For example, if automation causes a workflow bottleneck due to unforeseen data dependencies, the workflow should be updated or more system integrations added. This ensures that Salesforce Flow is ever-improving in implementation and aligned with business objectives to maintain value [11, 12].

4.4. Considerations on integrations

The main strength of Salesforce Flow is its ability to integrate with other systems; hence, it is the core of extended hyper-automation. Seamless integration requires a lot of planning and proper execution. A business must identify which systems and applications need to work in tandem and that Salesforce Flow can connect to them.

These systems include customer relationship management, enterprise resource planning, human resource management systems, and analytics solutions. Among the key factors to successful integration are data consistency and synchronization. Enterprises should establish standards for data so that all integrated systems use compatible formats and structures. For example, if Salesforce Flow automates workflows that involve pulling customer data from a CRM system and updating records in an ERP platform, consistency in data cannot afford to be wrong or duplicated [9, 10].

This would enable data interchanges between systems using either middleware or APIs, allowing the workflow to work seamlessly across the enterprise. Besides this, designs also have to consider security and compliance: Since most automated workflows include the access of sensitive data, including customer information or financial records of customers, it becomes imperative that the security is tight. Permissions, access control, and access management tools are supported out-of-the-box within

Salesforce Flow. Still, the overall strategy for encryption, auditing, and compliance has to come from the organizational level to protect your data. For industries with significant private data elements, like healthcare and finance, conformance to a regulatory data protection framework such as GDPR or HIPAA has many critical intersections.

Another consideration has to do with scalability: as the enterprise's requirements change, so too do the needs and desires of an enterprise that may want to eventually add more systems to a Salesforce Flow solution or bring more excellent capabilities with the system as time goes by. Being able to envision scalability helps ensure that growth can be afforded without significant integration architecture makeovers at the proper time. The design workflows leverage standardized APIs or, in a modular manner, for adding new integrations when one needs to extend them easily [7–9].

A focus on training and support means the teams themselves can understand how to manage and maintain integrations. With appropriate training in Salesforce Flow integrative capabilities and involvement in the design, businesses can make the right decisions to help build internal competencies and reduce their dependence on external consultants. Being proactive in such a fashion dramatically adds to successful integration; it equips the teams for the changing tide of technological advancement and business needs.

Coupled with these ways of doing process analysis, setting goals, implementing Salesforce Flow, and planning integrations, an enterprise can develop a hyper-automation strategy that produces results that can be measured. Done thoughtfully, hyper-automation allows organizations to simplify operations, increase collaboration, and ensure long-term growth amidst the ever-growing competitiveness in business [12].

5. Conclusion and Recommendations

5.1. *Key insights*

Hyper-automation can be considered a game-changing approach to enterprise operations, better-streamlining workflows, reducing costs, and increasing agility. In addition, with advanced technologies such as AI, RPA, and low-code platforms like Salesforce Flow, organizations can automate end-to-end complex processes, make better decisions, and utilize optimal resources. Specifically, Salesforce Flow is a low-code, modularly designed platform that can easily integrate, making it an ideal cornerstone for hyper-automation initiatives. The case studies and use cases explored here have demonstrated how, besides varnishing inefficiencies, hyper-automation drives innovation, scalability, and improved customer satisfaction. Such benefits outline hyper-automation as an enabling technology that will be important to strive for operational excellence in a modern enterprise landscape.

5.2. *Best practices*

Smooth Implementation of hyper-automation using Salesforce Flow can only be achieved by a well-framed strategy and keeping in mind certain best practices:

- Detailed Process Analysis: The existing processes need a critical review to identify inefficiency that could lead to prioritization in automation opportunities.
- Incremental Implementation: Adopting phased implementation, starting with those items that will have an 'impact' to win more quickly and build momentum about more significant projects.
- Design for Modularity: Modular design in workflows using reusable components, which can be scalable as per the needs of the business.
- Extensive Testing: These workflows must be extensively tested for their reliability on different scenarios and configurations before deployment.
- Continuous Monitoring and Optimization: Promptly analyse the key performance indicators to continuously upgrade the workflow to meet business objectives.
- Stakeholder Engagement: Early engagement with employees and leadership will ensure collaboration and minimize resistance to change. This is necessary to ensure that priorities within the organization will be aligned.
- Training and Support: Allow the teams to learn through training in the capability of Salesforce Flow to enable practical usage and create a culture of innovation.

Following these practices, adopting Salesforce Flow will enable any organization to unlock full value and ensure success, essentially hyper-automatic.

5.3. *Future of hyper-automation*

The future of hyper-automation is all set to undergo significant evolution as a series of emerging technologies and trends continue to reshape the landscape. Key developments will include:

- **AI-powered Insights:** With deeper functionalities in AI, hyper-automation can predict trends, optimally adjust to processes dynamically, and show real-time actionable recommendations.
- **End-to-end Automation Ecosystems:** Integration with IoT, blockchain, and edge computing extends the practice of hyper-automation among supply chains, logistics, and operational ecosystems.

- **Human-AI Collaboration:** Advanced AI tools will start to support human decision-making and the ability of employees to work with much more strategic and innovative jobs because automation is doing the repetition.
- **Accessibility:** Low-code tools like Salesforce Flow enable companies of any size to take on process automation, even with minimal technical resources.
- **Automation of Regulatory Compliance:** Due to automation, there will be more emphasis on compliance. In addition, the ever-changing nature of compliance requirements within highly regulated industries like finance and healthcare calls for more dedicated efforts toward regulatory compliance.

These emerging trends may signal that continuous hyper-automation will keep pushing the tide of innovation and competitiveness. It will help organizations stay competitive in an increasingly complex, highly speeded-up marketplace.

Acknowledgment

I gratefully acknowledge the friends and researchers in business hyper-automation research for their inspiration.

References

[1] Ceelho, R. F., Concer, F., & Martins, D. C. (2009). A study of the basics of DC-DC converters applied in maximum power point tracking power. *Electronics*, 673–678.

[2] Chihchiang, H., & Shen, C. (1998). Study of maximum power tracking techniques and control of DC/ DC converters for photovoltaic power systems. *Power Electronics Specialists Conference*, *1*, 86.

[3] Stokes, J., & Sohie, G. R. (n.d.). Implementation of PID controllers on the Motorola DSP56000/ DSP56001. 1–84.

[4] Coelho, R. F., Concer, F. M., & Martins, D. C. (2010). Analytical and experimental analysis of DCDC converters in photovoltaic maximum PowerPoint Tracking applications. *IECON 2010 - 36th Annual Conference of the IEEE Industrial Electronics Society*, 2778–2783.

[5] Altas, H., & Sharaf, A. M. (2007). A generalized direct approach for designing fuzzy logic controllers in Matlab/Simulink GUI Environment. *International Journal of Information Technology and Intelligent Computing*, *1*(4), 1–27.

[6] Radak, B., Mahanta, C., & Gogoi, A. K. (2019). DSP-based photovoltaic hardware development is used to control voltage and current. *IEEE 3rd International Conference on Recent Developments in Control, Automation & Power Engineering*, 1–104.

[7] Radak, B., Mahanta, C., & Gogoi, A. K. (2015). MPPT of solar photovoltaic cell using perturb & observe and fuzzy logic controller algorithm for Buck-Boost DC-DC converter. *International Conference on Energy, Power and Environment: Towards Sustainable Growth (ICEPE)*. 87–92.

[8] Wu, Y., Zhang, B., Lu, J., & Du, K. L. (2011). Fuzzy logic and neuro-fuzzy system: A systematic introduction. *International Journal of Artificial Intelligence and Expert Systems (IJA)*, 47–80.

[9] Sharaf, M., & Sahin, M. E. (2011). A novel photovoltaic PV-powered battery charging scheme for electric vehicles. *ICEAS IEEE Conference*, India, 176–192.

[10] Reshmi, R., & Babu, S. (2013). Design and control of DC-DC converter using hybrid fuzzy PI controller. *International Journal of Research in Engineering and Technology*, *1*(3), 73–78.

[11] Mohan, N., Undulant, T. M., & Robbins, W. P. (1995). *Power Electronics*. John Wiley, 1–820.

[12] Kuo, B. C. (1995). *Automatic control systems*. New Jersey: Prentice-Hall, 1–189.

[13] Masoum, M. A., Dehbonei, H., & Fuchs, E. F. (2002). Theoretical and experimental analyses of photovoltaic systems with voltage and current-based maximum power-point tracking. *IEEE Transactions on Energy Conversion*, *17*(4), 514–522.

35 Predictive customer engagement: Exploring the role of AI in salesforce marketing cloud for multi-channel campaigns

Shalini Polamarasetti[1,a], *Harshini Gadam*[2,b], *and Hemadri Ravilla*[3,c]

[1]Sr Salesforce Developer, SS&C Technologies, Boston, Massachusetts, USA
[2]Computer science, Illinois institute of technology, Chicago, USA
[3]Computer science, Anna University, Chennai, India

Abstract: Predictive customer engagement is becoming one of the foundational elements of modern marketing because it allows brands to anticipate specific customer needs and offer personalized experiences. Therefore, this paper has reviewed the role of artificial intelligence within the Salesforce Marketing Cloud in optimizing multi-channel campaigns. Using AI-powered tools like Einstein AI, SFMC enables companies to gain insight into customer behaviour, predict how customers will act, and send targeted content across email, SMS, social media, and more. The study will examine how AI enhances segmentation, mapping the customer journey, and real-time decision-making to drive more personal engagement. It also discusses, to some extent, several main challenges organizations face when they try to deploy AI in their marketing functions, namely in terms of technical challenges, ethical hurdles, and issues of organization. By incorporating case studies and performance metrics regarding key engagement indicators like click-through rates and conversions, the study presents the impact of AI-driven predictive engagement on enhancing efficiency in marketing and customer satisfaction and guaranteeing measurable ROI. Yet, it also underlines the need for businesses to overcome existing challenges and adopt best practices for AI's ethical and practical use. In the end, this research concludes with the trends in the future of AI for marketing and its potential to further revolutionize predictive customer engagement strategies.

Keywords: Predictive customer engagement, artificial intelligence, salesforce marketing cloud, multi-channel campaigns, Einstein AI, customer journey mapping, personalization, predictive analytics, marketing efficiency, customer behaviour, data-driven marketing, ROI analysis

1. Introduction

Predictive customer engagement will revolutionize the face of digital marketing in the modern era, as it has been helping brands meet their customers' needs, preferences, and behaviours through data-driven insights. Unlike traditional reactive approaches, predictive engagement deals with proactive measures whereby businesses use advanced analytics to predict customer action and shape their interactions. This transformational approach will thus enable marketers to deliver personalized experiences that touch the heart of their target audience for more connectedness, besides lifting customer satisfaction and loyalty [1, 2].

Predictive engagement is all about analytics on historical and real-time data. This data-driven approach uncovers patterns and trends that enable businesses to predict future behaviours, such as the likelihood of purchase, the risk of churn, or preferred channels for communication. These insights drive more effective marketing strategies, such as personalized product recommendations, timely promotional offers, or content that aligns with individual preferences. Therefore, predictive engagement adds value to customers and brands by increasing overall efficiency in marketing. In the high competition and over-saturation that characterizes today's digital marketplace, predictability and expectation have become a lot about differentiation for the customer. With increasingly high expectations, modern-day consumers expect a brand to address their unique needs and provide consistent, contextual relevance across all touchpoints. Failure to live up to such heightened expectations will lead to disengagement and lost opportunities as customers move toward competitors who can offer better personalized experiences [3, 4].

Predictive customer engagement, then, is a substantial competitive advantage, placing brands not just responsive but intuitive to the needs of their customers. Its role in

[a]shalini.research14@gmail.com, [b]harshivik05@gmail.com, [c]Hemadrirn@gmail.com

DOI: 10.1201/9781003778905-35

modern marketing strategies is continuously growing and already securing its place among the most vital drivers of long-term business success [3].

1.1. Multi-channel campaigns in SFMC

Multichannel campaigns involve the delivery of marketing messages and experiences across multiple channels, including email, SMS, social media, and web applications. These are important in today's digitally connected world, as every customer interacts with brands using these touchpoints. Multichannel campaigns have been designed in SFMC to ensure seamless and consistent communication across all touchpoints. Its centralized platform lets the marketer keep the messages consistent and personalized for each customer, according to his preference. It ensures that the customers get a continuous and contextually relevant experience, irrespective of their channel. SFMC's multichannel capability means more than just being on multiple platforms; it means better and more integrated personalization of customer journeys [5].

Advanced capabilities in SFMC include Journey Builder and Data Cloud, which truly enable omnichannel campaigns that speak to customer behaviours down to near real-time. It allows capturing and analyzing data from many sources; personalization is assured, and each touch falls at the right time. This integrated approach would reinforce customer engagement, build trust, and engender brand loyalty because it represents one uniform, meaningful experience catered to the needs of each individual. Therefore, the multi-channel campaigns in SFMC are a well-engineered mix of technology and strategy that allows brands to reach their audiences effectively in today's dynamic digital ecosystem [1–5].

1.2. Objectives of the research

The study will, therefore, go deep into the role of AI within Salesforce Marketing Cloud and its impacts on predictive customer engagement. The key objectives are:

- To show how AI is used to leverage multi-channel marketing campaigns.
- To assess the efficiency of AI-powered tools in driving improvement in customer engagement metrics.
- To analyze real-world case studies that demonstrate successful applications of predictive engagement.
- To identify the challenges and limitations associated with the implementation of AI in marketing.
- To provide insight into the future of trends and best practices for leveraging AI in multi-channel campaigns.

In this journey, the research attempts to add to the rapidly increasing literature on AI's transformational power in digital marketing.

2. The Role of AI in Predictive Customer Engagement

2.1. Predictive analytics and its relevance to engagement

Predictive analytics is one of the significant cornerstones of AI that enables businesses to use historical and real-time data to forecast behaviours and outcomes that may occur in the future with their customers. The capability unlocked by predictive analytics enables machine learning algorithms that weed out patterns and trends from highly complex data, thereby gaining essential insights that marketers utilize in their effective decision-making with better precision. This has turned out to be a capability for enabling customer engagement redesign. It allows businesses to anticipate what customers need and like and proactively take necessary steps to offer everything from personalized recommendations to predicting the risk of churn or optimization of purchase journeys. Where predictive analytics identified a customer was likely to abandon his shopping cart, timely interventions through personalized discounts or follow-through emails re-engaged them. It provides a pre-emptive capability to act, heightening customer satisfaction while assuring marketing resources are used much more efficiently [6–8].

The real value in predictive analytics is turning this raw information into actionable insight, moving brands past general, one-size-fits-all approaches. Facilitating stronger audience segmentation helps marketers refine their ways to appeal with more targeted messaging and offers toward specific groups of users. This is very significant nowadays, in that through digital, there comes an expectation of timely relevance in every interaction. Predictive analytics also ensures that resource allocation is efficient in that marketing dollars and effort are utilized on initiatives that generate impact. With improvements in engagement metrics like click-through rates, conversions, and retention, predictive analytics accelerates immediate results. It fuels better, long-term customer relationship scenarios where return on investment is maximized [8–10].

2.2. AI technologies in salesforce marketing cloud

Salesforce Marketing Cloud embeds the latest AI technologies to revolutionize marketing strategies and allow predictive customer engagement. Behind so many innovative solutions stands Einstein AI: a robust set of AI-powered capabilities, each aimed at enhancing every part of the marketing process. Einstein AI utilizes predictive analytics to make sense of mountains of customer data and unlock actionable insights into customer behaviours, preferences, and even next steps. It will also let marketers run highly personalized campaigns that resonate with every customer.

For example, Einstein Email Recommendations uses machine learning algorithms to recommend products or content based on past interactions and predicted preferences. Einstein Segmentation dynamically groups audiences of similar traits, enabling marketers to tailor their messaging better. This places Einstein AI at the core of driving actionable insights in SFMC that can enhance the customer experience and increase engagement. AI technologies on the SFMC platform are more than just analysis of data; execution with it is smoother because that drudgery automates some tasks, allowing marketers to finally rise well above mere repetition and dive deeper into creative and strategically oriented activities [8–10].

2.3. *Enhancing personalization, segmentation, and journeys*

AI will change the face of personalization from simple customization to highly personalized experiences that align precisely with each customer's exact behaviour, preference, and history. This level of precision enables marketers to create more relevant and meaningful interactions. For example, AI dynamically tailors a website's content to a customer's history, shows targeted email offers based on past purchases, or recommends products that interest them. These hyper-personalized experiences have helped create closer customer bonds and driven engagement metrics like click-through rates and conversions. AI guarantees that personalization will evolve through real-time data analysis, with each customer relevant to every interaction between customers. Segmentation and journey mapping are two other highly critical areas in customer engagement that are completely revolutionized with AI [8–12].

With Einstein AI, for example, marketers working in Salesforce Marketing Cloud can create dynamic audience groups that change with the shift in customer behaviour and preference. Unlike static segmentation, dynamic segmentation ensures campaigns stay relevant and effective at hooking customers' latest insights. In addition, AI enhances customer journey mapping on Journey Builder by enabling marketers to design multichannel experiences that evolve with each customer's interactions. Whether clicking on an email, browsing a website, or engaging with a social media post, AI ensures the journey is cohesive and responsive. This adaptability will help create a seamless and enjoyable experience throughout the touchpoints, building customer trust and loyalty while optimizing engagement outcomes [10, 11].

2.4. *AI-driven insights impacting engagement metrics*

AI-powered insights have a material impact on customer engagement metrics and, therefore, have a ripple effect on other KPIs such as click-through rate, conversion rate, and customer retention. For instance, AI-powered content recommendations improve email open and click-through rates by ensuring customers receive messages relevant to their interests. Predictive analytics can also be used for ad targeting so that the right campaigns reach the proper audience at the right time and improve conversion rates. AI amplifies customer retention by identifying customers who are in danger early so that brands can immediately apply retention strategies, such as personalized offers or loyalty rewards. Real-world examples show bottom-line value for AI-driven insight: businesses using AI within SFMC report increased engagement, higher revenue, and improved customer satisfaction. It analyzes the continuous improvement of performance metrics, strategy refinement, and AI that can keep engagement efforts efficient and aligned with business objectives [10].

AI has revolutionized predictive customer engagement by enabling a brand to shift from reactive to proactive marketing strategies. It allows marketers to present their customers with personalized, effective, and scalable experiences through advanced analytics, seamless integration of SFMC tools, and real-time decision-making. As more firms adopt AI-powered ways, the full realization of higher engagement and proper customer relationships starts to be seen [11–13].

3. Multi-Channel Campaigns in Salesforce Marketing Cloud

3.1. *Defining multi-channel campaigns for modern businesses*

Multichannel campaigns are many-sided marketing strategies that use multi-platforms in emails, SMS, social media, mobile applications, and websites for proper customer engagement. These are designed to meet today's consumers' evolving expectations, who interact with a brand across touchpoints during their buying journey. This enables companies to deliver a consistent and relevant message through all channels for cohesive customer experiences. For instance, a customer may browse a particular product on social media, receive an email with an offer for the same product, and finally be reminded via SMS as one cohesive and convincing journey. This alone increases the possibility of securing the customer's attention, trust, and familiarity with the brand due to continuity across varied touchpoints. The value of multichannel campaigns lies in unified single-customer journeys [11–13].

By coordinating the marketing across these touchpoints, businesses could more effectively lead customers through vital stages such as awareness, consideration, and decision. For example, a company can create interest on social media, nurture the lead with long-form information via email, and then send a promo code that's near expiration via SMS. This orchestrated approach ensures customers get the right message at the right time to enhance engagement and drive conversions. In today's competitive marketplace, running multi-channel campaigns with the customer is inevitable, given that every business wants to remain relevant [12].

3.2. Integration of AI in multi-channel functionalities

Artificial Intelligence dramatically expands the multi-channel capabilities of SFMC, adding to it the dimensions of advanced analytics, automation, and hyper-personalization. Equipped with tools such as Einstein AI, marketers can leverage predictive analytics to anticipate customer behaviours and preferences so that the communications are not only timely but contextually relevant. For instance, AI can analyze past and real-time data to determine the best timing to send emails or the best channels to reach segments of customers. This ensures that messages are delivered when they're most likely to resonate with audiences, thus yielding better open rates, click-through rates, and overall engagement. With AI analyzing all the customer interactions dynamically, every touch point integrates to form a coherent and meaningful journey to improve the customer's experience. AI smoothened multi-channel marketing, automating tasks too complex for humans, thereby scaling their business without losing quality and personalization [12, 13].

For example, AI-powered tools automatically create personalized content for emails, SMS, or social media posts from information about customers. Messaging automatically changes in real time as customer interactions continue to evolve. This reduces manual effort in managing campaigns and liberates marketers to think about strategy and creativity. The integration of AI ensures consistency, impact, and actionability across all channels to drive more intelligent decision-making in campaigns. AI changes the game in multichannel marketing because it makes a process far more effective and efficient by incorporating predictive analytics, automation, and personalization. In this way, AI can allow businesses to engage their customers en masse with relevance and personalization [13].

3.3. Case studies of successful multi-channel campaigns

Real examples show the impact AI-driven multichannel campaigns create within the Salesforce Marketing Cloud. One example could be how a global retail brand used SFMC's Journey Builder combined with Einstein AI to create an omnichannel customer journey across e-mail, SMS, and socials. It will look into customers' history of purchases and browsing behaviour and send recommendations of goods personally, with special offers; therefore, 20% of sales have increased. Another example could be a financial services company that, using SFMC, combined email and mobile notifications to onboard new customers. By predicting its customers' preferences using AI, the company created a personalized communication method that reduced customer churn by 15% in the first three months. These case studies showcase the potential for AI and SFMC to drive effective results, improve customer experiences, and ensure business growth on multi-sector campaigns [13, 14].

The capability to manage and optimize multi-channel campaigns, primarily when further powered by AI, places Salesforce Marketing Cloud as an integral tool in the modern enterprise. In conjunction with AI insights, powerful tools enable SFMC to help brands create personalized, seamless, and impactful experiences at all customer interaction touchpoints. This functionality, embedded within well-rounded marketing strategies, allows companies to continue competing in the dynamic digital space [13].

4. Challenges in Implementing AI for Predictive Engagement

4.1. Technical barriers: Data silos and integration complexities

Among the biggest challenges in implementing AI for predictive engagement is solving fragmentation, more popularly known as silos-of customer data. An organization gathers immense data across various touchpoints, including websites, mobile apps, email campaigns, and physical store interactions. However, these datasets are usually stored across different platforms and systems that lack interoperability, preventing the creation of a unified customer profile. This fragmentation prevents the AI algorithms from achieving a helicopter view of customer journeys, thereby reducing their ability to predict, either partially or with reduced accuracy. For instance, an AI model engaged in the forecasting of purchasing behaviour would fail to incorporate key knowledge if the data of in-store purchases remained locked and unanalyzed in silos. Integrating AI systems with existing infrastructure also faces enormous technical difficulties [14].

Most organizations still function on legacy systems, which provide no room for modern AI tools. The usually rigid, inflexible, often less scalable, or relatively low computational power systems block the effective integration of the AI models. Upgrades to more advanced platforms, such as Salesforce Data Cloud, involve tremendous investments in three major components: time, resources, and technical acumen. Businesses may need to implement new data management systems, cloud solutions, and APIs to unify data and ensure seamless platform connectivity.

If not addressed, breaking down data silos and modernizing the infrastructure will pose a technical challenge to fully realizing the potential of AI in predictive engagement, which will, if these challenges stay reconsidered, undermine the AI-driven marketing strategies' accurate correctness of effectiveness. Indeed, barriers to unlocking the transformative gains of AI demand investment into advanced data platforms, integrative solutions, and effective workforce collaboration [13, 15, 16].

4.2. *Ethical concerns: Privacy and data security*

AI-driven personalization in predictive engagement raises several critical ethical concerns, especially regarding customer privacy and data security. Making predictions with a high degree of accuracy for enabling personalization requires enormous volumes of personal information, from browsing behaviour to purchasing history to location. However, customers have become conscious of their digital footprints and want more knowledge about their data collection, storage, and usage. Any abuse of that, or even the appearance of exploiting such information through unauthorized sharing or advertisement to the users without their consent, eats into that trust and builds a reputation crisis for the businesses. Besides that, regulatory mechanisms presented by GDPR and the California Consumer Privacy Act have levied severe compliance burdens to protect personal data and privacy, with intense legal and operational demands upon organizations. Severe penalties arising from non-compliance with regulations further call for responsible data handling in AI-powered marketing. Data security breaches may affect AI systems, adding other business challenges [15, 16].

Such situations further create the possibility of cyberattacks in the form of breaches or hacking, leading customers' financial and personally identifiable information to fall into malicious agents' hands. This results in economic damage, destroying the bottom line consumers' confidence with brand damage. This ranges from encryption of data in use, securing APIs, and real-time threat monitoring. Besides the security concerns, companies will also have to implement ethics in AI by providing transparent consent mechanisms for customers, easy access to their data, and avenues for opting out. A key consideration is the balance between personalization of customers' experiences and privacy considerations if trust is to be developed and success achieved sustainably using AI for predictive engagement [15–17].

4.3. *Organizational challenges: Skills gaps and resistance*

While implementing this predictive engagement through AI workflows, the requirement is to recruit a talented workforce to design, monitor, and improve these seamlessly; however, most organizations face this growing and acute skills gap. In addition, creating and maintaining machine learning models requires highly competent resources such as data scientists and machine learning engineers to keep the AI models functional; thus, attracting talent becomes pretty challenging since market demand outweighs supply. Besides the merely technical competencies, staff in marketing, sales, and customer service also need training in using AI-powered tools for, among other things, predictive analytics, dynamic content creation, and automation workflows. No teams can integrate AI in today's workflows without correctly being trained and educated on those tasks. Of course, such deficiency would contribute to inefficiency and possibly the loss of great opportunities. Indeed, such an absence is one of the key drivers behind the delay in adaptation processes in accelerating the use of artificial intelligence and holding back your company from unleashing its absolute full power. Most barriers to integrating AI-driven workflows are related to resistance to change [13, 15].

Traditional employees may perceive the utilization of AI as threatening because they might feel that it will take away their jobs or that AI is not reliable enough. Decision-makers may also resist investing in AI because of perceived risks or uncertainty about its return on investment. Overcoming this resistance requires organizations to create an innovative culture and communicate that AI is meant to enhance human capabilities, not replace them. The clear articulation of real value derived from AI transparency regarding efficiency, higher personalization, and improved customer outcomes will likely gain trust and acceptance. Furthermore, investing in the workforce's upskilling and collaborative AI solutions that integrate seamlessly with the current workflows empowers the employees. It paves a smooth way toward AI-driven operations [15–17].

5. Impact Assessment: Measuring the Success of AI in SFMC Campaigns

5.1. *Key performance indicators for AI-driven campaigns*

To measure the success of AI-driven campaigns in SFMC, key performance indicators or KPIs that reflect the contribution of predictive engagement strategies must be considered. The common ones include e-mail open rates, CTR, and conversion rates, giving an idea of how well your campaigns engage your audience toward desired actions. It will be taken to the very end, hyper-personalized content by AI-powered tools like Einstein AI, in tune with consumer taste and preference, and this is while the timing is optimized for better engagement of the campaign. Predictive analytics will show you exactly when to email or reach those customer segments for higher engagement levels. More sophisticated KPIs, such as CLV, churn prediction accuracy, and sentiment analysis scores, give a better feel for how well the campaign performs over the longer term. CLV projects the customer's overall value in their relationship with a business, while churn prediction informs a business of future risks in customer attrition. Powered by AI, Sentiment analysis translates customer feedback into emotional resonance on campaigns and offers qualitative insights beyond numerical metrics [12–18].

These KPIs will also enable the business to gauge how effective the AI-powered campaigns are working and where their improvements lie. Continuous analysis ensures that strategies stay aligned with organizational goals and enables marketers to optimize their campaigns for better customer relationships over time. These KPIs show concrete business benefits of applying AI to multichannel marketing activities [12–18].

5.2. *Traditional vs. AI-enhanced engagement metrics*

Traditional customer engagement would involve static segmentation and broad messaging strategies that cannot enable personalization, hence failing to connect with the diverse audience segments. These campaigns involve predefined customer groups and generic content that does not adapt to individual preferences or real-time behaviours. Therefore, all the engagement metrics for traditional campaigns are relatively lower. Examples are low click-through rates or conversion rates because these have been ways to communicate products or services sought from organizations by today's consumers. Traditional processes are labour-intensive to plan and execute, leaving little bandwidth to make creative or strategic changes. By contrast, AI-driven campaigns through SFMC utilize next-generation technologies, including predictive analytics and dynamic content personalization, to make interactions more relevant and engaging [12, 13].

AI enables real-time decisions, where the campaign automatically adjusts to every customer's behaviour and preference. For instance, it can determine which communications channel works best for a customer: email, SMS, or social media, through which the message will be best conveyed efficiently. These capabilities drive CTRs upwards, increase conversion rates, and improve engagement. Meanwhile, AI-driven automation reduces the manual workload by granting marketers more time for creative and strategic work. The following comparison underlines the power of AI to show just how much it further increases marketing performance by being able to personalize at scale while optimizing resources for top-tier customer engagement [12, 14].

Table 35.1 compares marketing through traditional and AI-based methods in Salesforce Marketing Cloud. The AI-based process easily outperforms its traditional counterpart regarding personalization, engagement rates, and ROI. With its ability to harness predictive analytics and real-time information, AI makes campaigns more efficient and targeted in their effects with higher click-through and conversion rates. AI-based marketing also reduces human effort through automation and allows marketers to focus on creativity and strategy. The table highlights the real-life benefits of merging marketing with AI in terms of better customer experience, optimized resource allocation and utilization, and measurable business growth, demonstrating the revolutionary potential of marketing through AI.

5.3. *ROI analysis: Improving efficiency and effectiveness*

ROI is a crucial metric to determine the success of an AI-driven campaign, and Salesforce Marketing Cloud

Table 35.1. Comparative analysis of traditional marketing vs. AI-driven marketing in salesforce marketing cloud

Metric	*Traditional Marketing (Non-AI)*	*AI-Driven Marketing (SFMC with Einstein AI)*	*Percentage Improvement (%)*
Email Open Rate	15%	28%	86.70%
Click-Through Rate (CTR)	4%	8.50%	112.50%
Conversion Rate	2%	5%	150%
Customer Retention Rate	60%	75%	25%
Customer Lifetime Value (CLV)	$500	$800	60%
Churn Prediction Accuracy	65%	85%	30.80%
Personalization Accuracy	Low (Static Segmentation)	High (Dynamic Segmentation with AI)	Significant Improvement
Time Spent on Campaign Management	12 hours per week	6 hours per week	−50%
ROI (Return on Investment)	150%	300%	100%
Customer Satisfaction Score	70%	85%	21.40%

Source: Author.

does contribute a lot in that regard with its advanced capabilities in AI. First, AI enhances efficiency through automation, automating mundane tasks like audience segmentation, content personalization, and scheduling campaigns. These get done faster and more accurately with AI systems, including Einstein AI. These are, in essence, jobs that require many manual operations but will be reduced. Automation can cut operational burdens, allowing marketers to pay closer attention to strategic and creative decisions behind the campaign to heighten their power further. AI auto-creates customized content for emails and ads, tailoring each piece to whom it speaks, significantly improving engagement with very little work required by the marketing team. Other essential features of AI would include predictive analytics, which will enhance the ability of the business to apportion its resources more appropriately since, with this feature, one will be able to see who is a high-value customer and can make offers tailor-made for them [11, 13, 18].

For example, AI can be applied to consumer behaviour analysis to filter out which customers would most likely purchase or respond to a particular campaign. This helps businesses yield a better conversion rate without investing resources in untargeted marketing campaigns. The targeting approach ensures that each dollar contributes more significantly toward generating revenue, maximizing ROI. Real-time analysis of data by AI means continuous optimization of the campaigns for marketing to be ever timely correct in terms of audience preference and changing dynamics of the market. Besides saving costs and better targeting, AI-driven insights increase customer satisfaction and long-term profitability. A business can relate well with its customers by providing relevant and timely content for better loyalty and repeat business [11, 13, 18].

Along with that, the fringe benefits of reduced costs, coupled with increased efficiencies, round off the final push for better customer retention - all pointers of how AI optimization would fundamentally change the paradigm of marketing ROI. Let unmatched customer experiences driven by continuous AI improvements across SFMC ensure business profitability and competitive success in the most vibrant markets [11, 13, 18].

5.4. Summary of research findings

It epitomizes how AI would bring a lot of change to predictive customer engagement, and even more so in the multi-funnel capability of SFMC. AI-powered tools, like Einstein AI, make it easier for companies to analyze their customer data to predict customer behaviour and engage with customers in personalized ways on a real-time basis through email, SMS, or social media, among others. The research underpins the benefits derived from AI campaigns: efficient processing, increased engagement rates, and more significant ROI. It also flags challenges such as technological barriers, ethical concerns, and organizational resistance, which must be overcome to realize AI's potential ultimately. The findings indicate that AI enhances multichannel campaigns and lays a foundation for hyper-personalized customer experiences that drive loyalty and retention.

5.5. Final thoughts on AI's revolutionary potential

The potential of AI in making predictive customer engagement is very high. It helps companies drive meaningful experiences with impact at scale by combining data-driven insights with advanced automation and personalization capabilities. Technology keeps developing, and therefore, integrating AI into the platform will raise the potential of SFMC in predicting and meeting customer needs. On the other hand, companies adopting the AI-driven marketing strategy will have a substantial competitive advantage, creating a closer and long-lasting relationship with customers for their businesses to grow sustainably. Yet, the path of fully realizing the potential of AI is genuinely one of overcoming current obstacles and adopting a forward-looking approach. Finally, AI represents a powerful catalyst in transforming predictive customer engagement, empowering brands to thrive in an ever-customer-centric digital landscape.

References

[1] Carlos, M., & Sofía, G. (2022). AI-Powered CRM Solutions: Salesforce's Data Cloud as a Blueprint for Future Customer Interactions. *International Journal of Trend in Scientific Research and Development, 6*(6), 2331–2346.

[2] Rane, N., Choudhary, S., & Rane, J. (2024). Artificial intelligence and machine learning in business-to-business (B2B) sales and marketing: A review. Available at SSRN 4842575.

[3] Chillapalli, N. T. R., & Murganoor, S. (2024). The Future of E-Commerce Integrating Cloud Computing with Advanced Software Systems for Seamless Customer Experience. *Library Progress International, 44*(3), 22124–22135.

[4] Sripathi, M. (2025). The Future of MarTech. In *Advancing the Marketing Technology (MarTech) Revolution* (pp. 113–152). IGI Global Scientific Publishing.https://www.igi-global.com/chapter/the-future-of-martech/364595

[5] Rainsberger, L. (2023). Sales technology: An ocean of possibilities. In *Digital transformation in sales: How to turn a buzzword into actual sales practice–A 21-step guide* (pp. 189–267). Wiesbaden: Springer

Fachmedien Wiesbaden.https://link.springer.com/chapter/10.1007/978-3-658-38887-4_4

[6] Darvidou, K. (2024). Omnichannel Marketing in the Digital Age: Creating Consistent, Personalized and Connected Customer Experiences. *Technium Business and Management, 10*, 34–54.

[7] Sadrnia, L. (2023). The Future of Marketing: How Predictive Modeling Optimizes Campaign Strategies. *iBusiness, 15*(4), 249–262.

[8] Wolniak, R., & Grebski, W. (2023). The application of business analytics in personalized customer experience. Scientific Papers of Silesian University of Technology. Organization & Management/Zeszyty Naukowe Politechniki Slaskiej. Seria Organizacji i Zarzadzanie, (182). https://managementpapers.polsl.pl/wp-content/uploads/2023/12/182-Wolniak-Grebski-2.pdf

[9] Naslednikov, M. (2024). The Impact of Artificial Intelligence on Customer Relationship Management (CRM) Strategies. https://www.theseus.fi/handle/10024/858753

[10] Kähönen, S. (2020). A case study: marketing automation in digital multi-channel customer experience management. https://lutpub.lut.fi/handle/10024/160739

[11] Vidani, J. (2024). Artificial Intelligence (AI) A Boon for Marketing. Available at SSRN 4849856.https://papers.ssrn.com/sol3/papers.cfm?abstract_id=4849856

[12] Gupta, A. (2023). Salesforce CRM Cloud: Crafting Tailored Solutions through Advanced Engineering. https://www.espjeta.org/Volume3-Issue1/JETA-V3I3P109.pdf

[13] Kusasi, F., & Tiyasiningsih, E. (2024). Implementation of Artificial Intelligence in Customer Relationship Management and Its Implications. https://www.researchgate.net/profile/Firmansyah-Kusasi/publication/383859380_Implementation_of_Artificial_Intelligence_in_Customer_Relationship_Management_and_Its_Implications/links/66dd6007fa5e11512ca8e354/Implementation-of-Artificial-Intelligence-in-Customer-Relationship-Management-and-Its-Implications.pdf

[14] Gupta, A. Salesforce CRM Cloud: Crafting Tailored Solutions through Advanced Engineering. https://www.espjeta.org/Volume3-Issue1/JETA-V3I3P109.pdf

[15] Kalimuthu, M., Jith, R., Sripriya, V., Savarimuthu, A., Ravinder, D., Ali, M., & Herath, R. (2025). Intelligent Process Automation and Its Implications for the Marketing Industry. In *Advancements in Intelligent Process Automation* (pp. 413–434). IGI Global. https://www.igi-global.com/chapter/intelligent-process-automation-and-its-implications-for-the-marketing-industry/358040

[16] Lehton, S. (2024). Exploring the role of marketing automation in fostering online engagement in business-to-business settings. https://stax.strath.ac.uk/concern/theses/s1784m32c

[17] Joshi, R., Nair, V., Singh, M., & Nair, A. (2021). Leveraging Natural Language Processing and Predictive Analytics for Enhanced AI-Driven Lead Nurturing and Engagement. *International Journal of AI Advancements, 10*(1).

[18] Abdul-Yekeen, A. M., Kolawole, M. A., Iyanda, B., & Abdul-Yekeen, H. A. (2024). Leveraging Predictive Analytics to Optimize SME Marketing Strategies in the US. *Journal of Knowledge Learning and Science Technology* ISSN: 2959-6386 (online), *3*(3), 73–102.

36 Exploring the influence of remote work on employee productivity and job satisfaction in the Canadian technology industry

Jasmeen Kaur[1,a], *Mehroz Nida Dilshad*[2,b], *and Nidhi Sehgal*[3,c]

[1]International Business University, Toronto, Canada
[2]Faculty of Business, International Business University, Toronto, Canada, University of Liverpool, UK
[3]School of Business and Humanities, Curtin University, Dubai, UAE

Abstract: The COVID-19 pandemic has accelerated the adoption of remote work and changed many current workplace dynamics, testing common assumptions about productivity and job satisfaction. The study examines the impact of working from home on these factors in the technology industry of Canada. The Job Demands-Resources Model informs this study, in which a synthesis of secondary data is derived from academic articles, industry reports, and government publications, including Statistics Canada. The findings of the study reveal that productivity and job satisfaction are facilitated by flexibility and robust IT infrastructure, however, persisting challenges such as technostress, blurred boundaries between work and life, and communication gaps pose persistent barriers. While flexibility emerged as one of the key drivers of employee satisfaction, excessive digital monitoring and inadequately managed workloads resulted in disengagement and a performance decline. The paper addresses these challenges by making active recommendations through the adaptation of hybrid work models, investment in advanced IT infrastructure, managerial training programs, and initiatives to balance life at work.

Keywords: Employee productivity, job satisfaction, remote work, technology industry

1. Introduction

The COVID-19 pandemic has accelerated the shift toward telework-the most dramatic change the workplace has seen in recent memory [1]. From being an amenity, working from home became the rule. This transformation reshaped industries across the globe [4]. As organizations adjusted to this new reality, working remotely turned out to be complex phenomena with benefits such as more flexibility but also drawbacks like a technological stressor [5]. This shift has changed the dynamics of work in industries such as technology, where innovation and collaboration are very critical. Statistics Canada reports that the percentage of Canadians working from home increased from just 4% pre-pandemic to over 30% during its peak, underscoring the scale of this transformation [2].

Despite these developments, the specific implications for the Canadian technology industry remain underexplored. While existing studies highlight the dual impact of remote working-boosting productivity and making people happier-all over the world, little attention has been paid to nuances such as the specificities of industry contexts [1]. For instance, whereas flexibility is widely accepted as a factor in facilitating satisfaction, its interaction with the organizational issues of IT infrastructure and managerial support needs to be further researched, especially in the Canadian tech industry [2].

By combining knowledge from industry sources, academic literature, and statistical data, this study seeks to close this knowledge gap by investigating the dual effects of remote work on worker satisfaction and productivity in the Canadian tech sector. This study examines how job demands, such workload and cooperation requirements, interact with resources, like flexibility and IT support, to influence employee experiences, guided by the Job Demands-Resources (JD- R) Model [3]. The objective of this study is to investigate the bidirectional influence of remote work on productivity and job satisfaction in the Canadian tech industry. Based on the JD-R Model, this research investigates which job demands-collaborative requirements and workload-and which job resources-finally fully developed IT infrastructure and managerial support-interact in shaping the experiences of employees. Through the triangulation of findings from existing

[a]jkaur.0266@myibu.ca, [b]nidadilshad@gmail.com, [c]nidhissehgal@gmail.com

DOI: 10.1201/9781003778905-36

literature, industry reports, and Statistics Canada, this research aims to gauge the different factors that enhance or hinder productivity and satisfaction in remote work arrangements. It also aims to study unique challenges in the Canadian tech sector, such as maintaining innovation and team cohesion in remote environments.

2. Literature Review

The literature review focuses on the relevant academic articles, industry reports, and government data. Statistics Canada reports detail an increase in working from home precipitated by COVID-19 and highlight the differential impact on work-life balance, productivity, and personal well-being.

3. Work-from-Home Trends in Canada

Statistics Canada gives some fundamental insights into the rise of remote work due to the COVID-19 pandemic, with home workers jumping from 4% pre-pandemic to 30% at its peak. This shift also underlines immense difficulties in industries like tech, which thrive on in-person innovation. While the report shows work-life balance improvements for many employees, it also raises productivity concerns, especially in jobs that require ongoing teamwork [2]. These trends frame the Canadian tech industry as one pivotal focus in studying the dual impacts of remote work on productivity and job satisfaction. Remote work adoption increased dramatically during the pandemic, with rates rising from 4% to 30% [2].

The Dais Report (2022) [2] adds to this, considering employee experiences during remote work conditions, particularly in Canada. It shows how flexible work arrangements have increased employee engagement, and subsequently job satisfaction, but also warns about too much reliance on digital monitoring tools-as that could erode employee autonomy, leading to lower satisfaction. This is a qualitative enriching perspective added to that from Statistics Canada, entailing the value of autonomy and engagement in shaping successful remote work experiences.

4. Flexibility, Autonomy, and Performance

Felstead and Henseke [1] confirm that autonomy and flexibility are the leading guarantees of productivity and job satisfaction. According to their data, workers who manage to control their schedule tend to show better performances and to report higher levels of job satisfaction. At the same time, they warn that badly organized remote work might bring some negative effects, such as task fragmentation and disengagement. This realization is particularly relevant in the technology sector, where a balance must be struck between autonomy and effective communication to maintain performance and well-being.

5. Sector-Specific Insights: The Role of IT Infrastructure

The systematic review by Costa et al. [5], featured in MDPI, presents IT infrastructure as key to unlocking productivity in work-from-home settings. The review shows that industries in which technological tools are well developed have an easier transition to home office mode, while others are seriously hampered in their operations. This thus signifies the importance of the study on remote work within the Canadian tech industry, given that it has greater access to IT resources.

Pansini et al. [6] discuss the utilization of information and communication technology (ICT) tools in smart working. According to them, though these tools promote collaboration, they cause overload if not managed properly. In this respect, their findings also resonate with Buonomo et al. [3], who have used the JD-R Model to discuss how technostress is affecting workers. Conclusions from their findings show that job resources, like flexibility and IT support, enhance performance, while excessive demands result in burnout. IT infrastructure can make or break a remote work environment by enhancing productivity and collaboration or making an environment.

6. Research Methodology

The study uses systematic literature review (SLR) to comprehensively analyze the impact of remote work on productivity and job satisfaction within the technology industry in Canada. Studies were filtered using predefined inclusion and exclusion criteria regarding their relevance to the research objectives and the Canadian tech context. This methodological rigor aligns with the JD-R framework, ensuring focused analysis on job demands - for example, workload and collaboration needs-and resources, such as flexibility or IT infrastructure.

7. PRISMA Flowchart

PRISMA Flowchart The source selection procedure was demonstrated using a PRISMA flowchart. An effective way to illustrate the transparency of study identification and filtering is using a graphic like this. As seen from Figure 36.1, the search strategy was systematic and allowed the inclusion of studies that were particularly relevant to the twin issues of the effects of remote work on job satisfaction and productivity.

This flowchart shows a systematic process for identification, screening and selecting relevant studies that are included in this research.

8. JD-R Model Application

The theoretical framework on which this study is based is the Job Demands-Resources Model. This model is selected for the study because it has the capacity to analyze job demands and resources, and how their interactions impact employee's outcomes regarding productivity and satisfaction.

1. **Job Demands:** The needs concerning workload, level of teamwork required, and technological overload were taken into consideration. High job demands without resources to off-set the demands will bring the motivation and job satisfaction down.
2. **Job Resources:** Resources such as supervisory support, IT infrastructure, and flexibility are analyzed to determine the extent to which they add to increase productivity, reduce burnout, and improve engagement.

The JD-R model gives a systematic approach to discussing the findings of the reviewed studies. Each selected paper was scanned for evidence regarding the effect of job demands and resources on the remote work experiences of employees. Such findings were then categorized into broad heads, such as IT infrastructure, the role of flexibility, and digital monitoring impinging on satisfaction.

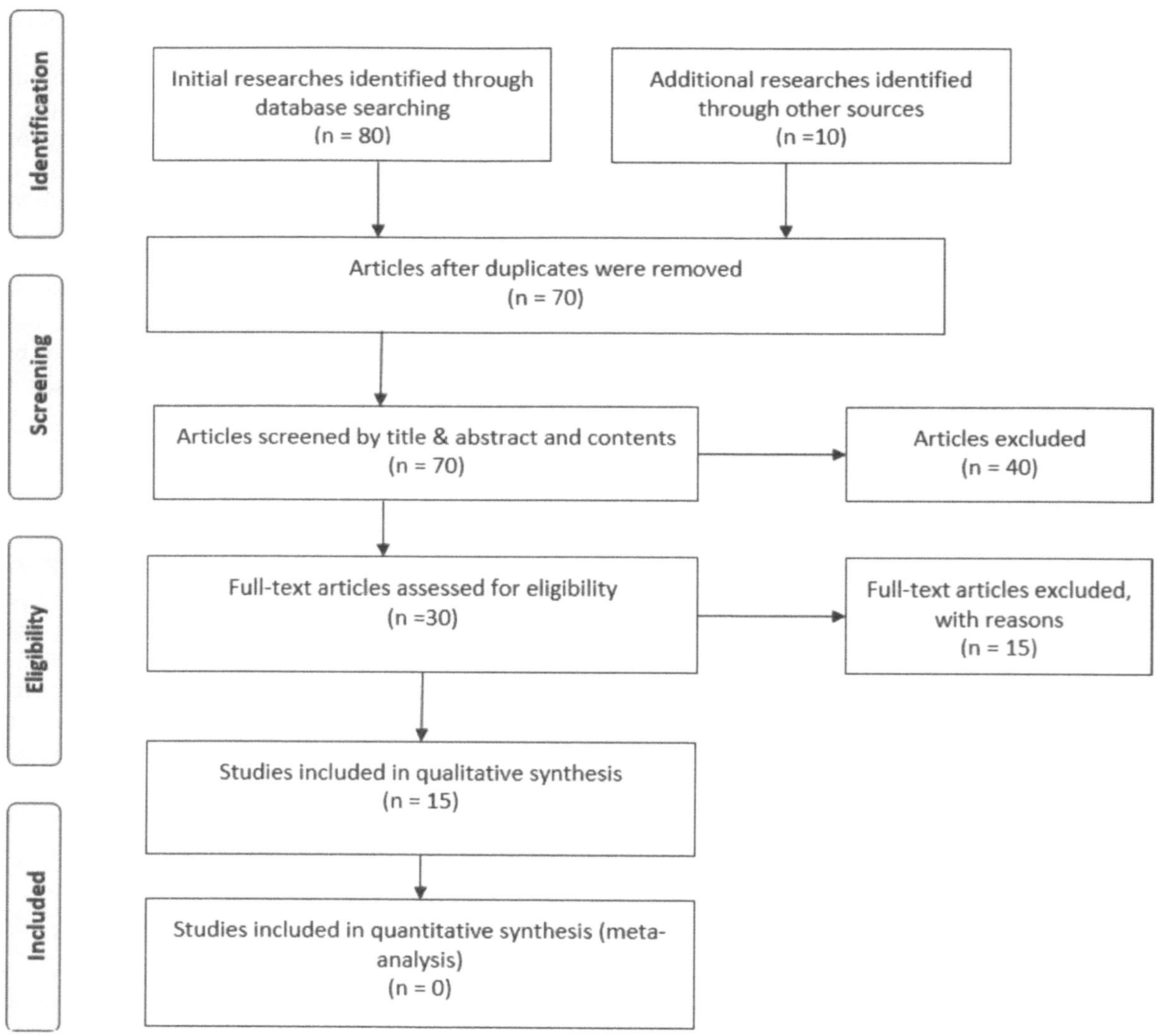

Figure 36.1. PRISMA flowchart for systematic literature review.

Source: Author.

9. Findings and Analysis

This section discusses how remote work impacts the satisfaction and productivity of jobs in the IT sector in Canada, compiling both the findings that were most important from the evaluated studies. The results, underlining the most important topics touching on flexibility, IT infrastructure, engagement challenges, and sectoral dynamics, are reviewed using the Job Demands-Resources Model.

10. Flexibility and Autonomy

Flexibility is considered to be one of the more consistent factors impacting job satisfaction in home working conditions. In fact, studies such as that of Felstead and Henseke [1], cite that schedule control may increase productivity and enjoyably. Similarly, the Dais Report (2022) [2] claims that up to 30% of job satisfaction has been improved through flexibility, which increases engagement. However, too much dependence on digital tools to monitor performance will reduce employees' autonomy and subsequently lead to job dissatisfaction.

11. IT Infrastructure and Technological Support

The enabling role of IT infrastructure is crucial to achieving productivity in a remote work environment. Such a transition to remote work was found to be smoother by [5] in industries where strong IT systems existed. Canadian tech companies, with a technologically advanced set of tools, enjoy this adaptability but struggle with technostress challenges [3].

12. Communication and Engagement Challenges

Clear communication and effective strategies for keeping employees engaged are pivotal in maintaining productivity across remote work arrangements. Olawale et al. (2024) [3] emphasize that misaligned expectations and delayed feedback remain among the top challenges in virtual communication. The Dais Report (2022) [2] supports the notion that fostering employee engagement through autonomy and support can lower dissatisfaction.

13. Industry Insights and Analysis

Canada's tech industry has come to epitomize the duality of remote work. While flexibility and cost-efficiency were major strengths, collaborative demands of the sector present unique challenges. According to Statistics Canada, [2], remote work adoption surged from 4% pre- pandemic to 30% during its peak. This reflects the adaptability of Canadian tech firms but points out the formidable challenges in sustaining collaboration and innovation. Tech firms thrive based on teamwork and constant innovation. As Costa et al. (2022) [5] pointed out, even while advanced IT systems ease some of these challenges, none of them can be as effective to create organic collaborations like office environments do.

The JD-R Model emphasizes the need for a balance between demands-as related to heavy workloads and resources, including IT support and managerial guidance. Canadian-specific dynamics include regional work policies and organizational culture, which further complicate the balance [2].

14. Discussion and Managerial Implications

The results from this study provide important insights into how remote work affects job satisfaction and productivity in the IT sector in Canada. The discussion, framed within the context of the Job Demands Resources Model, will illustrate the interaction between work-life balance, collaboration, infrastructure in information technology, and flexibility in shaping the experiences of employees. This section summarizes the findings with related literature, pinpoints problems typical for this industry, and further gives practical recommendations to entrepreneurs acting in real conditions of remote labour.

According to the JD-R Model, for high work productivity and job satisfaction, there needs to be a balance between demands and resources. Work demands concern workload, task fragmentation, and the need for efficient teamwork in remote work environments. Yet, some resources that enable performance and wellbeing concern the management for direction, technology to assist, and flexibility. Studies like Felstead and Henseke [1] indicate that flexibility fosters engagement and satisfaction since workers are afforded the opportunity to conduct work in line with personal priorities. But excessive demands, such as technostress and over-monitoring, can erode these benefits. The balance is harder to strike in the innovative and very collaborative Canadian hi-tech industry.

The tech sector has moved to a largely remote working arrangement at an unprecedented scale. According to Statistics Canada, work-from-home rates went up from 4% pre-pandemic to about 30% during the pandemic. This has been accompanied by several opportunities and challenges. Remote work flexibility has achieved better work-life balance for many employees, as noted in the Dais Report (2022) [2]. However, the blurred boundaries between professional and personal lives are a major concern that could drive disengagement and dissatisfaction. Furthermore, innovation, which is the backbone of the tech industry, relies on serendipity related interactions that cannot be replicated by working from home. As Eurofound (2020) [4] states, the absence of face-to-face collaboration will impede creativity and innovation; hence, specific strategies need to be designed for work models at home. Technological support is another critical factor in enabling productivity in remote environments. The findings of Costa et al. (2022) [5] demonstrate that industries with advanced IT infrastructure experience smoother transitions to remote work. Canadian tech companies, with their robust technological ecosystems, have been able to maintain operational continuity.

Buonomo et al. [3] asserted that the excessive use of digital tools creates a new form of stress now described as technostress. This is brought about by excessive demands from continuous updating and management of new technologies and constant virtual interactions, emphasizing the need to balance IT reliance with user-friendly solutions. While communication and engagement are often imperative in remote working conditions, industries like technology need a lot of collaboration. Olawale et al. (2024) [3] confirm that there are explicit means of communication that will limit the chances of misaligned expectations and delayed feedback. In addition, the Dais Report (2022) [2] explicates that nurturing employee engagement through granting autonomy and support acts to counter the challenges affiliated with remote work. Focus should be directed towards mechanisms that improve engagement and make it continuous, therefore having high performance and satisfaction.

Accordingly, some actionable suggestions that have been advanced based on the findings for the most optimal remote work in the Canadian technology industry include flexibility that would minimize intrusive monitoring in order to retain employee autonomy and satisfaction; performance metrics based on trust could help in focusing on the outcomes rather than the processes, building up trust and reducing stress; investment in collaborative tools and training for effective use to enhance teamwork and reduce technostress. A hybrid work culture would provide the best of both worlds: remote and in-office models that cater to flexibility but also facilitate innovation face-to-face. Additionally, promoting a work-life balance through training programs and mental health resources may help in managing the challenges while working from home.

15. Recommendations

The following section gives practical proposals based on this research to optimize the remote work practices and address the dual challenges of productivity and job satisfaction in the Canadian tech industry. Recommendations will balance flexibility and technological efficiency with employee welfare. First, companies should try implementing flexible work policies that would help employees manage their time with more convenience. Second, in whatever setup of work from home, there is the need for solid IT infrastructure to develop high-yielding performance. In this respect, employees should be guaranteed easy access to secure online tools and platforms that help them team up easily. Third, fostering an encouraging and inclusive remote work culture requires targeted managerial training. Managers should be equipped to effectively interact with their teams virtually, set clear expectations, and offer regular feedback. Encouraging compassionate leadership styles can help address employees' individual challenges, enhancing job satisfaction and reducing stress levels.

Finally, wellness programs and mental health initiatives should be introduced to promote a healthy work-life balance. Offering resources such as time management workshops, mindfulness training, and counselling will help them to cope with the challenges of homework. The perception of paying more attention to mental health will bring higher satisfaction in the long term and improved productivity. In putting these strategies into effect, Canadian tech companies can efficiently manoeuvre remote work complexities for high performance and employee satisfaction in this ever-evolving industry.

References

[1] Felstead, A., & Henseke, G. (2017). Assessing the Growth of Remote Working and Its Consequences for Effort, Well-Being, and Work-Life Balance. *New Technology, Work and Employment, 32*(3), 195–212.

[2] DAIS S. A. (2022). 2022 Statistical data. Retrieved from https://www.dias.com.gr/en/statistics2022/#:~:text=DIAS%20%2D%202022%20Statistical%20data&text=Double%2Ddigit%20growth%20of%20processed,annual%20increase%20of%20about%2012%25.

[3] Buonomo, I., Ferrara, B., Pansini, M., & Benevene, P. (2023). Job Satisfaction and Perceived Structural Support in Remote Working Conditions – The Role of a Sense of Community at Work. *International Journal of Environmental Research and Public Health, 20*(13), 6205.

[4] Eurofound. (2020). Living, working, and COVID-19. Eurofound. Retrieved from https://www.eurofound.europa.eu/en/publications/2020/living-working-and-covid-19

[5] Costa, S., Susak, T., Haluga, V., & Varazdin Development and Entrepreneurship Agency. (2022). Economic

and social development: 78th international scientific conference on economic and social development: Proceedings from Aveiro, February 24–25, 2022. Varazdin.

[6] Pansini, M., Buonomo, I., De Vincenzi. C., Ferrara, B., & Benevene, P. (2023). Positioning Technostress in the JD-R Model Perspective: A Systematic Literature Review. In *Healthcare*, vol. 11, no. 3, p. 446. MDPI

Statistics Canada. 2022. *COVID-19 Pandemic: Remote Work and Its Implications for Canadian Businesses.* Retrieved from https://www150.statcan.gc.ca/n1/daily-quotidien/240118/dq240118c-eng.htm

37 The dynamic evolution of finance: examining key functions, technological innovations, and strategic developments in the modern business and economic landscape

S. Amudha[1,a], *S. Parthiban*[2,b], *and Anjali Tewari Mamgain*[3,c]

[1]Department of Master of Business Administration, Builders Engineering College, Nathakadaiyur, Kangeyam Taluk, Tiruppur District, Tamil Nadu, India
[2]Department of Master of Management, Gobi Arts and Science College, Gobichettipalayam, Erode District, Tamil Nadu, India
[3]PhD Scholar, Lincoin University College, Malaysia

Abstract: The significance of finance in facilitating business growth, economic development, and sustainability cannot be overstated. Historically focused on monetary management, the finance function has undergone a profound transformation, emerging as a sophisticated, strategic, and innovative discipline that propels profitability, economic expansion, and social responsibility. This evolution is largely driven by cutting-edge technological innovations, including artificial intelligence, machine learning, cloud computing, robotic process automation, and block chain, which are redefining the contours of modern business, enhancing operational efficiency, and improving decision-making processes. As globalization, digital finance, and demographic changes continue to shape the economic landscape, financial decision-making processes are becoming increasingly complex, nuanced, and interconnected. With a focus on financial planning, investment management, risk mitigation, capital raising, and environmental, social, and governance (ESG) considerations, finance functions are being transformed by technological innovations, necessitating a forward-thinking, adaptable, and resilient approach. Ultimately, the dynamic, continually evolving nature of finance underscores its pivotal role in driving business prosperity, economic growth, social progress, and environmental sustainability, highlighting its critical importance in shaping the future of global commerce, fostering innovation, and promoting inclusive and sustainable development.

Keywords: Financial management, technology, artificial intelligence, globalization, digital finance, economic development

1. Introduction

Finance has been a foundational element in driving the growth and management of businesses and economies for centuries [1–20]. Initially focused on managing capital and resources, finance has continuously evolved in response to technological advancements, shifts in the global economic environment, and the emergence of new business models [1–5]. Technological innovation, particularly the integration of artificial intelligence, machine learning, and blockchain, is reshaping the financial sector by optimizing processes and improving business performance [6–10]. The integration of globalization into financial systems has expanded market interconnectedness, creating both opportunities and risks for businesses and economies worldwide. This paper aims to explore the multifaceted role of finance in today's economic landscape, examining the evolution of financial functions, the integration of emerging technologies, and the impact of globalization and digital finance on decision-making processes.

2. Functions of Finance in the Modern Economy

In the modern economy, finance has expanded far beyond the basic task of managing money. It now encompasses a range of functions that are integral to business operations and economic development. One of the key functions is financial planning, which ensures that businesses allocate

[a]kishorammumba@gmail.com, [b]drsparthi@gmail.com, [c]anjalitmamgain@gmail.com

DOI: 10.1201/9781003778905-37

resources efficiently and strategically. This includes forecasting cash flow, setting budgets, and assessing financial risks. With the rise of advanced technologies like artificial intelligence and data analytics, financial planning has become more accurate and dynamic, enabling businesses to adapt quickly to market changes. Another important function is investment management, where businesses make decisions about allocating capital to various projects and financial assets to generate returns. Investment strategies are now heavily informed by machine learning algorithms, which can use data to predict market trends and allows businesses to make more informed decisions with reduced risk. Risk management is also a critical financial function, particularly in today's complex and volatile markets. Financial tools powered by artificial intelligence and big data analytics help organizations identify potential risks, such as market fluctuations or cyber security threats, before they materialize. This proactive approach enhances a company's ability to protect assets and ensure long-term sustainability. Finally, corporate financing and capital raising involve securing funding through various means, such as equity, debt, or emerging instruments like tokenized securities. With the advent of fin tech and block chain, businesses can now access global investors, streamline capital-raising processes, and improve transparency. The rapid evolution of the global economy necessitates a corresponding transformation of financial functions for businesses seeking to maintain a competitive edge.

3. Financial Planning and Control

Financial planning and control are a foundational component of corporate finance, serving as the blueprint for an organization's financial health and long-term success. Traditionally, financial planning focused on processes like forecasting, budgeting, and resource allocation. These activities ensured that businesses could meet their financial objectives, maintain operational efficiency, and remain competitive. The goal was to project future revenues, expenses, and capital requirements forecast. However, as the company environment has become increasingly dynamic, financial planning has evolved to incorporate advanced technological tools, making it more responsive and data-driven. Today, artificial intelligenceand data analytics are transforming financial planning by enabling businesses to forecast future cash flows with greater accuracy. For example, artificial intelligencealgorithms can analyze spending patterns and recommend cost-saving measures or forecast revenue fluctuations, helping businesses avoid potential cash flow issues before they arise. Traditionally focused on forecasting and budgeting, financial planning has evolved to incorporate advanced technological tools. Artificial intelligenceand data analytics enable businesses to forecast future cash flows with greater accuracy. Using machine learning models, organizations are now capable of automating financial processes while evaluating predictive models to prevent cash shortages (Figure 37.1).

With these advanced capabilities, financial teams can now monitor budgets and financial goals continuously, rather than relying on periodic reports or annual projections. Artificial intelligence-driven insights enable businesses to allocate resources more effectively, ensuring that capital is directed toward high-impact areas and away from underperforming initiatives. Moreover, artificial intelligence predictive capabilities allow companies to adjust their strategies in real-time, improving their ability to respond quickly to changing market conditions, unexpected expenses, or new opportunities. By using artificial intelligence for risk management within financial planning, as part of their strategic planning, organizations can assess potential risks and challenges, such as market fluctuations, supply chain disruptions, and changes in regulatory requirements. The ability to foresee these challenges

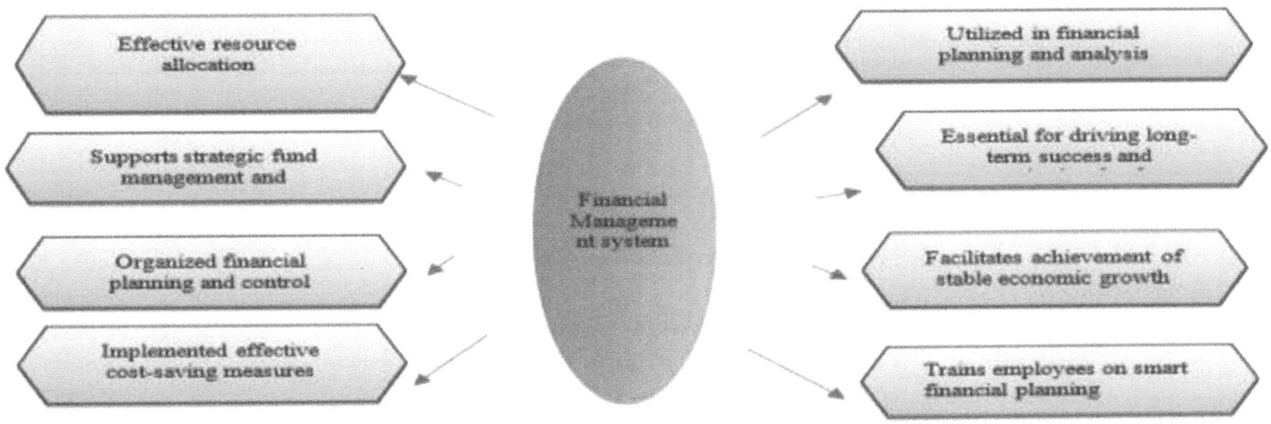

Figure 37.1. Financial management system.

Source: Author.

helps businesses create more resilient financial strategies that can withstand economic fluctuations, enhancing overall business flexibility. In this way, financial planning in the modern era is not only about setting goals and managing finances but also about using technology to navigate uncertainty, optimize performance, and ensure long-term sustainability. Managers assess the opportunity cost of capital for their firm's investments by analyzing financial markets, specifically by examining current interest rates on low-risk debt securities to determine the cost of capital for safe investments.

4. Investment Management

Investment management is a critical function within finance, focused on selecting and overseeing a company's or individual's investments to achieve desired financial returns while minimizing associated risks. Traditionally, investment management involved a combination of human judgment, financial theory, and market history helps identify investment opportunities. Portfolio managers would rely on qualitative factors, such as economic trends and industry developments, along with quantitative methods, like financial ratios, Guide buying and selling choices. However, with rise of artificial intelligence and machine learning, investment management has undergone a significant transformation. These technologies enable investors and portfolio managers to move beyond traditional methods and tap into real-time, data-driven insights that are more comprehensive and precise. With the advancement of artificial intelligence, it is now possible to process and analyze vast amounts of financial data quickly and accurately from stock prices and bond yields to global economic indicators, social media sentiment, and news events. This allows them to analyze market behaviour at a much deeper level and generate insights that would be impossible for human analysts to produce manual (Figure 37.2)

One of the most powerful applications of artificial intelligence in investment management is predictive analytics. By examining historical data and identifying patterns, artificial intelligence-driven models can forecast potential market trends and anticipate price movements. Machine learning predicts stock behaviour. These insights give investment managers a more accurate picture of where to allocate capital, which stocks to buy or sell, and when to make those moves to maximize returns. Another significant advancement is the ability of artificial intelligence to help in portfolio optimization. Today's investment management involves more than just choosing individual investments. Artificial intelligence-based investment platforms use sophisticated algorithms to evaluate an investor's risk tolerance and return objectives, providing data-driven recommendations for an optimal asset allocation strategy. These recommendations are based on statistical models that factor in variables such as market volatility, historical performance, and correlations between assets, which would be very complex and time-consuming for human analysts to calculate manually. Artificial intelligence also improves risk management in investment decision-making. Advanced machine learning algorithms provide real-time market insights, enabling the rapid detection of potential risks and informed decision-making for portfolio adjustments.

Figure 37.2. Inverstment strategy.

Source: Author.

5. Risk Management

Businesses must prioritize risk management to mitigate potential threats and capitalize on opportunities in an increasingly dynamic and unpredictable economic environment. Traditionally, risk management relied on historical data and manual analysis to identify potential threats and vulnerabilities. Businesses would often use static risk models, assessing past events to predict future risks, and making decisions based on the best available information.Although these methods were effective, they fell short in addressing the evolving and complex nature of modern risks in today's rapidly changing, interconnected world. The modern risk management landscape is characterized by the strategic application of artificial intelligence, big data analytics, and machine learning, driving innovation and improvement in risk assessment and mitigation. With these technologies, organizations can adopt a predictive and preventive approach to risk management, minimizing the likelihood of risks materializing and ensuring swift response to any issues. Artificial intelligence systems are capable of scanning massive amounts of data utilizing insights from multiple sources, including financial reports, digital media, news outlets, market trends, and even internet of things sensors, to detect early warning signs of potential risks. This broader data intake helps businesses stay ahead of threats that might otherwise go unnoticed. For example, artificial intelligence can analyze financial transactions in real-time to spot potential credit defaults, identifying patterns of behaviour that suggest an individual or organization might be at risk of defaulting on a loan or investment. Similarly, artificial intelligence-driven tools can track market fluctuations by monitoring real-time stock prices, commodities, and geopolitical developments, enabling businesses to react to sudden market shifts or potential disruptions (Figure 37.3).

6. Business Financing and Capital Markets

Business financing and capital markets are fundamental to the growth and sustainability of any business. Whether it's expanding operations, funding research and development, or navigating economic downturns, access to capital is critical. Traditionally, businesses raised capital through established channels like bank loans, issuing bonds, or selling equity on public stock exchanges. These methods, while effective, often involved lengthy processes, high transaction costs, and reliance on intermediaries like banks, brokers, and investment firms. However, with the rise of digital technologies, the landscape for corporate financing has evolved significantly, offering businesses more diverse, accessible, and efficient options for raising funds. One of the key innovations in this space is fintech, which leverages technology to streamline financial services and democratize access to capital. Fintech platforms have emerged as an alternative to traditional financing methods. By providing a direct link between businesses and investors, these platforms accelerate the capital-raising process, offering greater flexibility and reduced costs. Crowd funding models, such as those offered by Kickstarter and Indiegogo, allow businesses to raise capital by collecting small contributions from a large and diverse group of people. Crowdfunding enables businesses to tap into a broader investor base, including everyday consumers who might not have been able to participate in traditional investment opportunities (Figure 37.4).

Blockchain technology has enabled the development of new corporate financing instruments, such as initial coin offerings (ICOs) and security token offerings (STOs), offering innovative ways to raise capital. Initial coin offerings (ICOs) allow companies to issue customized digital tokens or cryptocurrencies to investors, generating capital for business development. This model has become especially popular among startups in the technology and blockchain sectors, where initial coin offerings provide an efficient and relatively low-cost way to raise funds without going through traditional equity markets or venture capitalists. Security token offerings represent a regulated and asset-backed alternative to initial coin offerings, enabling companies to raise capital in a secure, compliant, and transparent manner, while also providing investors with increased protection and peace of mind. Blockchain technology plays a critical role in this new era of capital

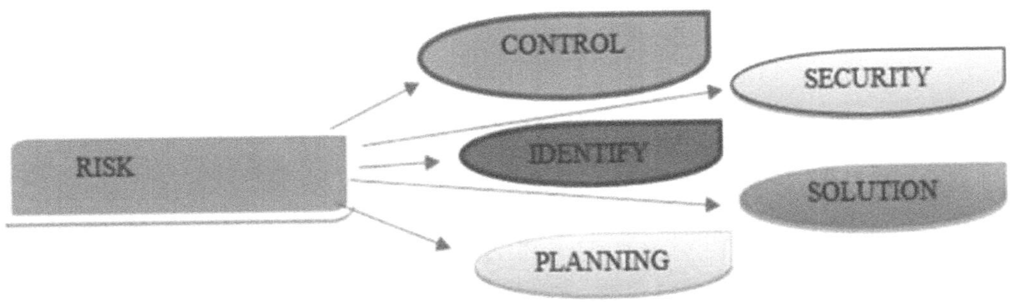

Figure 37.3. Risk management.

Source: Author.

Figure 37.4. Corporate Financing.

Source: Author.

raising. By enabling decentralized and transparent transactions, blockchain ensures that the entire process of fund-raising is secure and verifiable. Unlike traditional methods, which rely on centralized entities to oversee transactions, blockchain enables direct interaction between individual's exchanges, reducing transaction costs. The decentralized and transparent architecture of blockchain technology provides investors with a clear line of sight into their investments, as all transactions are recorded on a publicly accessible ledger. This fosters greater trust between companies and investors, especially in markets that are historically seen as opaque or prone to fraud.Bottom of Form

7. Strategic Decision-Making

Strategic decision-making has become an integral part of finance in modern businesses, transforming finance from a traditional support function to a central driver of corporate strategy. In today's dynamic business environment, executives rely heavily on financial data to guide high-stakes decisions such as mergers and acquisitions, capital expenditures, pricing strategies, and resource allocation (Figure 37.5). These decisions are critical for shaping the future direction of a company, and financial data provides the foundation for evaluating potential opportunities, risks, and returns. Traditionally, financial decision-making relied on static reports and historical data. However, with advancements in technology, particularly cloud computing, companies now have the ability to integrate financial data seamlessly with other business functions such as marketing, operations, and human resources. By combining financial and non-financial metrics, executives can develop a more nuanced understanding of the company's performance, recognizing the interplay between financial health, departmental performance, and business success. By having real-time access to data from across the organization, decision-makers can make more informed, timely decisions that reflect the full scope of the company's operation

An artificial intelligence-driven model might analyze the financial implications of acquiring a competitor, allowing executives to assess the long-term return on investment and the risks associated with such a move. Artificial intelligence data analysis capabilities far surpass those of humans, enabling the rapid identification of patterns,

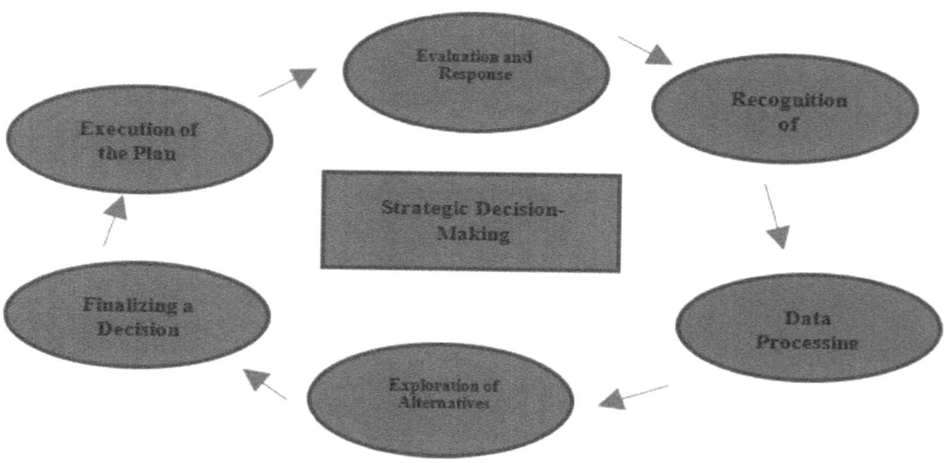

Figure 37.5. Strategic decision-making.

Source: Author.

trends, and insights that inform strategic planning, drive innovation, and foster business success. A key benefit of artificial intelligence and machine learning in strategic decision-making is their capacity to assess the real-time effects of different strategies. For example, artificial intelligence tools can predict how changes in pricing strategies or market conditions will affect revenue, profitability, and market share. This predictive power helps businesses adapt quickly to fluctuating market conditions, providing a competitive edge in industries where speed and adaptability are crucial. If a competitor's new product launch is eroding a company's sales, artificial intelligence can provide data-driven recommendations to optimize pricing, marketing, and product strategies, enabling the company to recapture lost market share. Cloud-based financial platforms also enhance the speed and accuracy of decision-making by providing executives with up-to-the-minute financial reports and data visualizations. With real-time data processing, decision-makers no longer have to wait for end-of-quarter reports to understand how the company is performing. This immediate access to operational and financial data allows for faster, more agile responses to business challenges. For example, a company facing supply chain disruptions can use real-time financial data to evaluate the effect of delays on revenue to assess the impact of delays on revenue and make quick adjustments to minimize losses. Another key advantage of integrating financial data with other business functions is the ability to develop a holistic strategy that aligns the company's financial objectives with its broader business goals.

7.1. Impact of technological advancements on financial functions

Technological advancements have dramatically reshaped the financial sector, driving efficiency, security, and innovation in financial functions. Technologies like automation, artificial intelligence,block chain, and cloud computing have revolutionized traditional financial processes, making them more streamlined and accessible. Automation has revolutionized business operations by taking over routine tasks such as data entry, invoice processing, and payroll management, leading to enhanced accuracy, efficiency, and cost-effectiveness. By automating routine financial functions, businesses can allocate resources more efficiently and improve overall productivity This transition enables employees to focus on strategic decision-making, customer service, and other high-value tasks. Furthermore, artificial intelligence has revolutionized financial data analysis, facilitating real-time processing, trend forecasting, and risk identification. In investment management, artificial intelligence-powered tools optimize portfolio performance by recommending tailored asset allocations. In addition, artificial intelligence plays a key role in uncovering and mitigating fraudulent behaviour with machine learning models identifying unusual transaction patterns and preventing financial crimes (Figure 37.6).

Blockchain technology has ushered in a new era of financial transparency and security, leveraging a decentralized ledger system to record transactions securely and immutably. This breakthrough has significant implications for various applications, including cross-border payments, where blockchain can reduce costs, increase speed, and enhance overall efficiency. Cloud computing has enabled financial institutions to store, access, and process data in real-time through secure, scalable platforms. Cloud-based financial systems allow businesses to combine data from different sources to get a clear view of their finances. This enables faster, more accurate decision-making, while also improving collaboration across different departments. Cloud technology also enhances data security by implementing robust

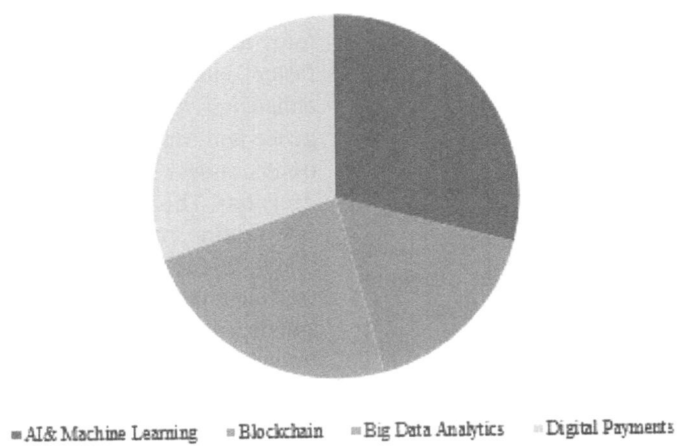

Figure 37.6. Technologies.

Source: Author.

encryption measures and ensuring compliance with regulatory standards. In sum, these technological innovations have transformed the financial landscape, enabling businesses to carry out financial functions more efficiently, securely, and with greater accuracy. By automating routine tasks, leveraging artificial intelligence for insights, adopting blockchain for secure transactions, and utilizing cloud computing for real-time data access, the financial sector is advancing to keep pace with the evolving demands of the global economy.

7.2. Globalization and its effect on financial systems

Globalization of the financial market means its worldwide expansion, fueled by rising trade activity, an influx of new participants, and the introduction of innovative financial instruments. The integration of financial markets across borders has created a more interconnected global economy, where economic events in one country can have far-reaching ripple effects worldwide. For instance, a financial crisis in one country can quickly spread to other nations due to the interconnected nature of global markets, capital flows, and international supply chains. This has made financial systems more vulnerable to global shocks, as seen in the aftermath of the 2008 financial crisis, where financial instability in the U.S. quickly impacted markets around the world. One of the most notable impacts of globalization is the increased capital mobility. Global investors can now access more markets and opportunities, enabling capital to move across borders. This has led to the growth of foreign direct investment and portfolio investments, driving economic growth in emerging markets. However, this also means that countries must carefully manage foreign investment and capital flows to avoid excessive reliance on external financing, which can lead to financial instability. As markets become more integrated, companies can access broader pools of capital and participate in more diverse investment opportunities. However, this also means that businesses are more exposed to global financial risks, such as fluctuations in international interest rates, exchange rates, and commodity prices. For example, changes in oil prices or currency fluctuations can have immediate effects on global supply chains, impacting businesses' costs and profitability. To navigate these challenges, businesses are increasingly adopting international financial management (IFM) strategies. International financial management combines financial expertise with a deep understanding of global market trends, geopolitical risks, and cultural differences. Companies need to manage exchange rate risks by using hedging strategies or engaging in currency diversification to protect their profits from fluctuations in foreign exchange markets.

7.3. Importance of financial development

A well-developed financial system is a cornerstone for sustainable economic growth. It enables efficient capital allocation, reduces transaction costs, and provides businesses and consumers with access to critical financial services. Countries with robust financial markets and institutions typically experience higher levels of investment and entrepreneurship, driving innovation and economic dynamism. A key element of financial development is financial inclusion, which ensures that all segments of society, especially marginalized and low-income groups, have access to affordable financial services. Financial inclusion is particularly important in reducing poverty and income inequality. Financial systems play a vital role in promoting economic growth by providing individuals and small businesses with access to essential financial services, including banking, credit, insurance, and savings products, which enable them to invest in education, healthcare, and entrepreneurial ventures. These technologies enable people in remote areas to participate in the formal economy, increasing their ability to save, borrow, and invest. Building on its existing Robotic process automation (RPA)capabilities, the bank has automated loan registration in insurance funds and is poised to expand its Robotic process automation footprint into more complex domains, including loan underwriting, customer account setup, and on boarding.

8. Conclusion

The financial sector has experienced a dramatic transformation over recent years, largely driven by the integration of emerging technologies and the forces of globalization. The convergence of artificial intelligence, Machine learning, blockchain, and cloud computing has given rise to a new era of financial management, characterized by increased efficiency, transparency, and strategic insight. These technologies have provided businesses with the tools to improve decision-making processes by enabling faster data analysis, offering predictive insights, and enhancing real-time decision support. Artificial intelligence and Machine learning allow companies to identify trends, assess risks, and make more informed financial decisions. This has greatly reduced the reliance on human intervention, minimizing errors, and improving operational efficiency. Blockchain technology has revolutionized the financial sector by providing a secure, transparent, and decentralized framework for transactions. By reducing fraud and ensuring data integrity, blockchain has increased confidence in financial systems. As the global business environment continues to evolve, the financial sector must prioritize innovation and adaptability, leveraging emerging technologies such as digital currencies, fin tech platforms, and smart contracts to drive sustainable growth and economic prosperity. These advancements will help businesses navigate economic uncertainty, providing them with the tools needed to adapt to market fluctuations, regulatory changes, and new challenges arising from a digital-first world.

References

[1] Liu, H., Li, N., Zhao, S., Xue, P., Zhu, C., & He, Y. (2025). The impact of supply chain and digitization on the development of environmental technologies: Unveiling the role of inflation and consumption in G7 nations. *Energy Economics*, *142*, 108165.

[2] Sharma, C., Sharma, R., & Sharma, K. (2025). The evolution of finance and controlling: SAP and intelligent systems. *World Journal of Advanced Research and Reviews*, *25*(01), 1786–1795.

[3] Akinsola, K. (2025). The Evolving Role of Corporate Governance in Shaping Business Practices and Legal Accountability in the 21st Century. *Available at SSRN 5115523*.

[4] Tabash, M. I., Farooq, U., Hassen, M., & El Refae, G. A. (2025). Do technological innovation and financial development determine environmental quality? Empirical evidence from Arab countries. *Review of Accounting and Finance*.

[5] Ranjan, R. (2025). Behavioural Finance in Banking and Management: A Study on the Trends and Challenges in the Banking Industry. *Asian Journal of Economics, Business and Accounting*, *25*(1), 374–386.

[6] Islam, H. (2025). Nexus of economic, social, and environmental factors on sustainable development goals: The moderating role of technological advancement and green innovation. *Innovation and Green Development*, *4*(1), 100183.

[7] Wang, Q., Sun, T., & Li, R. (2025). Does Artificial Intelligence (AI) enhance green economy efficiency? The role of green finance, trade openness, and R&D investment. *Humanities and Social Sciences Communications*, *12*(1), 1–22.

[8] Chhikara, H., Chhikara, S., & Gupta, L. (2025). Predictive Analytics in Finance: Leveraging AI and Machine Learning for Investment Strategies. In *Utilizing AI and Machine Learning in Financial Analysis* (pp. 325–336). IGI Global Scientific Publishing.

[9] Chen, Z., & Xu, W. (2025). The role of the digital economy in enhancing green innovation: Evidence from Chinese A-share listed enterprises. *Finance Research Letters*, *71*, 106381.

[10] Apsilyam, N. M., Shamsudinova, L. R., &Yakhshiboyev, R. E. (2024). The Application of Artificial Intelligence In the Economic Sector. *Central Asian Journal of Education and Computer Sciences (CAJECS)*, *3*(1), 1–12.

[11] Vlados, C., &Chatzinikolaou, D. (2025). The emergence of the new globalization: the approach of the evolutionary structural triptych. *Journal of Global Responsibility*, *16*(1), 139–161.

[12] Kuteesa, K. N., Akpuokwe, C. U., & Udeh, C. A. (2024). Exploring global practices in providing small and medium enterprises access to sustainable finance solutions. *World Journal of Advanced Science and Technology*, *5*(2), 035–051.

[13] Tariq, M. U. (2025). Strategic Integration of Technological Advances in Modern Business Practices. *Building Business Knowledge for Complex Modern Business Environments*, 95–120.

[14] El Khoury, R., Du, A. M., Nasrallah, N., Marashdeh, H., &Atayah, O. F. (2025). Towards sustainability: Examining financial, economic, and societal determinants of environmental degradation. *Research in International Business and Finance*, *73*, 102557.

[15] Lin, Q., Jian, Y., Zhang, D., Li, J., & Mao, S. (2025). Exploring the" Double-Edged Sword" effect of the digital economy on sustainable agricultural development: Evidence from China. *Sustainable Horizons*, *13*, 100122.

[16] Kumar, R. (2025). Global trends and research patterns in financial literacy and behavior: a bibliometric analysis. *Management science advances*, *2*(1), 1–18.

[17] Boschma, R., Fitjar, R. D., Giuliani, E., &Iammarino, S. (2025). Unseen costs: the inequities of the geography of innovation. *Regional Studies*, 2445594.

[18] Tajpour, M., Dekamini, F., SafarMohammadluo, S., Movahed, M. N., &Madadpour, F. (2025). The impact of innovation management on the sustainability of small and medium enterprises with the role of entrepreneurship mediation. *International Entrepreneurship and Management Journal*, *21*(1), 1.

[19] Chitra, M., Surianarayanan, R., Mahamuni, V. S., Mohammed, S., Keno, M. T., &Boopathi, S. (2025). Study on Cloud Computing-Empowered Small and Medium Enterprises. In *Essential Information Systems Service Management* (pp. 189–220). IGI Global.

[20] Wu, M., Subramaniam, G., Li, Z., & Gao, X. (2025). Using AI Technology to Enhance Data-Driven Decision-Making in the Financial Sector. *Artificial Intelligence-Enabled Businesses: How to Develop Strategies for Innovation*, 187–207.

38 User-centered design in interactive web tool for higher education platforms

E. Sujatha[1,a], *C. Silambarasi*[2,b], *K. Gopika*[1,c], *Praveena N.*[1,d], and *K. S. Rekha*[1,e]

[1]Department of Computer Science and Engineering, Saveetha Engineering College (Autonomous) Chennai, Tamil Nadu, India
[2]Department of Artificial Intelligence and machine Learning, Saveetha Engineering College (Autonomous) Chennai, Tamil Nadu, India

Abstract: CollegeQuest is a web-based application designed to assist students in finding the best college options based on their academic preferences, location, budget, and other key criteria. The platform aims to simplify the college selection process by providing personalized recommendations, detailed college profiles, and a comparison tool to help students make informed decisions. By integrating filters for courses, campus facilities, rankings, and fees, CollegeQuest offers a user-friendly interface that caters to the unique needs of each student. This project leverages a modern tech stack to ensure a seamless, efficient, and interactive user experience. This study explores the application of User-Centered Design (UCD) principles in the development of interactive web tools for higher education platforms. With the growing demand for personalized college search engines and academic planning tools, UCD focuses on creating systems that prioritize user needs, preferences, and behaviour to deliver an intuitive and engaging experience. The research highlights the importance of usability, accessibility, and interactivity in designing web tools that assist students, parents, and educators in making informed decisions about higher education options. By incorporating feedback-driven development, the platform ensures seamless navigation, personalized recommendations, and effective information delivery. The study demonstrates that adopting a UCD approach in higher education platforms enhances user satisfaction, engagement, and decision-making processes, ultimately improving the overall user experience in the education sector.

Keywords: User-centered design, interactive web tool, higher education

1. Introduction

CollegeQuest is a comprehensive platform aimed at simplifying the college search process for students. Choosing the right college is a critical decision that involves numerous factors such as location, course offerings, fee structure, and campus facilities. Students often face difficulties in identifying the best fit for their needs. It streamlines this process by offering a personalized search experience, where students can input their preferences and receive tailored college recommendations. The platform also provides detailed profiles, including rankings, admission criteria, and student reviews, ensuring a well-informed decision-making process.

The concept of User-Centered Design (UCD) plays a vital role in the development of interactive web tools for higher education platforms, ensuring that these platforms are intuitive, efficient, and tailored to meet the needs of diverse users. In the context of higher education, students, parents, counselors, and educators seek accurate and personalized information to make informed decisions about colleges, courses, and career paths.

A User-Centered Design approach focuses on creating plat- forms that prioritize the user's experience by integrating ease of navigation, customized recommendations, and accessible interfaces. By understanding user behaviour, preferences, and challenges, developers can build tool.

In higher education web platforms, UCD ensures that the system provides a seamless user experience, minimizes complexity, and delivers valuable information effectively. It emphasizes personalization, usability, and adaptability by incorporating feedback from users throughout the development process.

2. Literature Survey

Chen yan [1], Artificial Intelligence (AI) Integration Personalized Counseling Counseling and Guidance improved

[a]sujathae@saveetha.ac.in, [b]silambarasic@saveetha.ac.in, [c]kgopika884@gmail.com, [d]pravee.here22@gmail.com, [e]rekhaks@saveetha.ac.in

DOI: 10.1201/9781003778905-38

communication and accessibility for students, personalized counseling through data analysis, and enhanced decision-making capabilities. Data privacy concerns and reliance on technology potentially diminishing personal interactions. It encompasses integrating AI for more effective management systems, developing comprehensive training for counselors on digital tools, and establishing ethical guidelines for data usage in student counseling.

David Lee Griffith [2], Data Analytics Personalized Learning and Counseling Educational Technology Enhances learner engagement, improves learning outcomes, and supports personalized education experiences. Future research may focus on developing more robust anti-spoofing techniques and enhancing the security of face authentication systems.

Dai Shasha [3], Machine Learning (ML) Technique User- friendly Interfaces Student Counseling and Support En- hances decision-making with data-driven insights. Improves student performance tracking and personalized learning experiences facilitates better resource allocation and management requires significant investment in technology and training. Data privacy concerns may arise with student information.

Lianzhi LI [4], Deep Learning (DL) Algorithms Personalized Learning and Counseling System Data Analytics in Education improved accuracy in evaluating educational services and enhanced decision-making based on data-driven insights. Complexity in implementation and the potential for biased data interpretation. Refining algorithms for better predictive capabilities, integrating real-time data analytics, and developing user-friendly tools for educators to enhance service quality Effectively.

Kumar and B. Singh [5] AI enables the creation of adaptive learning environments that cater to individual students' needs, enhancing engagement and comprehension. AI-powered tools can provide personalized feedback and support, facilitating deeper learning experiences.

M. R. Patel [6] while the integration of big data in personalized learning offers significant benefits, it also presents challenges such as data privacy concerns, the need for substantial computational resources, and potential biases in data interpretation. Addressing these issues requires careful policy development and adherence to ethical principles to ensure the responsible use of big data in education.

K. A. Johnson and P. L. Martin [7] UCD involves focusing on the needs, preferences, and limitations of end-users at every stage of the design process. In educational applications, this means creating interfaces that are intuitive, engaging, and tailored to the learning styles of students.

Hang Jiang [8] focuses on developing an information system to manage honors and awards within an academic institution. While the full text isn't readily available online, it has been referenced in subsequent research, indicating its contribution to the field.

S. M. Motta [9], this research focuses on developing a com- prehensive Student Information System (SIS) to replace the traditional paper-based records used by the Honors College at USF. The system provides a secure, online interface embedded in the college's website, allowing staff to access and manage all aspects of a student's academic progress. It incorporates user authentication to ensure that individuals can only access information pertinent to their roles.

Li Jianshu and Cao Qi [10]; the guidance of the principles and methods of management information system, enterprise information management and other theories, this paper analyzes the current situation of private colleges and universities in their own information construction, finds out the main problems in promoting their own information construction, and analyzes the causes of the problems, and then puts forward targeted improvement strategies to promote their own information management construction To speed up the systematic construction.

Qu Jingtao [11]; this application helps ensure your organization has adequate internal controls and documented risks to safeguard financial and non-financial data, policies, and processes. Exploring the official website of China Management Informatization might offer archives or contact information for obtaining specific articles.

J. Hope [12], this article discusses the challenges and considerations in implementing competency-based education programs. This piece explores how schools adopting competency- based education models are integrating digital learning tools to support their programs.

S. A. Rubinstein and J. E. McCarthy [13] the study suggests that fostering formal partnerships between unions and management can lead to increased communication and collaboration among teachers, which in turn contributes to better student outcomes. These findings highlight the potential benefits of collaborative labor–management relationships in the educational sector.

Wang Fuxue, Yi Li and Yiwen Zhang [14], the authors analyze the impact of these techniques on SEO effectiveness to determine which strategies are most effective. Additionally, the study explores the potential influence of SEO techniques on page interest. Unlike previous research, this paper evaluates SEO techniques using data collected from 116 websites, assessed through a third-party measuring tool.

Shi Jing, Yan Cao and Xue-jing Zhao [15]-the findings suggest that implementing targeted SEO strategies can significantly increase the online presence of university journal websites, thereby attracting a wider readership and facilitating greater dissemination of academic research. The study provides practical recommendations for academic institutions seeking to optimize their journal websites for better search engine performance.

Lin Dihuan, Zeng Haibiao and Guan Weihao [16] this article discusses the key considerations and best practices in developing effective university portal websites. This resource provides an overview of successful university website designs and the principles behind them.

Zhang Tao and Liao Li [17] This study discusses various SEO techniques applied to academic journal websites, which might offer relevant insights these resources offer valuable information on the development and optimization of websites through effective SEO practices.

M. Llopart and M. Estebanguitart [18]; the beam search algorithm is applied to the reform of higher education curriculum content in this paper. In each step of deep expansion, the scheme cuts off some nodes with poor quality and retains some nodes with high quality. In this way, the space consumption is reduced, the time efficiency is improved, and the similar intermediate state in the search process is removed.

I. Westbury [19] The study highlights how the use of com- partmentalization, segmentation, and licensing in curriculum development can influence the curriculum's role and effectiveness. The findings suggest that these administrative tools can lead to the curriculum serving more as a symbolic or ideological document rather than a practical guide for education.

Zhongyu Zhang and Guiqin Zhang [20] In general, the paper likely discusses the use of Moodle, an open-source learning management system (LMS), to build activity platforms that support online learning communities in a college environment. Moodle is often used for creating engaging, collaborative learning spaces, and the paper could provide insights into the implementation of such systems for enhancing educational experiences.

3. Methodology

The development of the CollegeQuest platform follows a systematic approach to design, implement, and evaluate a user- centered web application that simplifies the college selection process for students. The methodology is divided into the following phases:

Conducted surveys and focus groups with prospective students to identify the key challenges faced during college selection, such as overwhelming options, lack of personalized recommendations, and difficulty comparing colleges defined the technical stack to ensure seamless integration of features like filtering, comparison tools, and responsive design. Selected HTML, CSS, JavaScript, and a backend framework to support scalability.

Designed an intuitive, clean, and minimalistic interface that simplifies navigation for users incorporated clearly labeled menus, tooltips, and step-by-step guidance to ensure ease of use implemented a responsive design to provide a consistent experience across desktops, tablets, and smartphones.

Developed an algorithm to deliver personalized college recommendations based on user inputs such as location, bud- get, and academic preferences integrated a database to store and retrieve detailed college profiles, user preferences, and comparison data efficiently. Built a robust search functionality allowing users to filter colleges by location, ranking, fees, and available courses. Included advanced filtering options to accommodate unique user needs, such as scholarship availability or extracurricular offerings.

Utilized data-driven algorithms to match user preferences with suitable colleges. Implemented a comparison tool for feature-by-feature evaluation of multiple institutions, enabling informed decision-making. Ensured users could switch be- tween sections (e.g., search, preferences, comparison) without losing progress. Incorporated save functionality for user preferences and shortlisted colleges.

Optimized the platform for multi-device functionality using responsive web design techniques. Tested the application on various devices and browsers to ensure consistent performance. Conducted iterative testing with a diverse group of students to assess usability, navigation, and recommendation accuracy. Gathered feedback on interface clarity, feature effectiveness, and overall user satisfaction. Measured platform responsiveness, recommendation precision, and user engagement. Benchmarked results against predefined success criteria, such as low bounce rates and high user retention.

Planned features include AI-powered scholarship searches, application tracking, and integration with international college databases to expand the platform's utility. Potential to incorporate predictive analytics for career pathways based on user academic profiles.

4. Implementation

The implementation of the CollegeQuest platform focused on developing an intuitive, user-centered web tool that simplifies the college selection process. This was achieved through the integration of advanced algorithms, responsive design, and real-time feedback systems. A minimalistic and visually appealing user interface (UI) was created using HTML, CSS, and JavaScript. Navigation menus, tooltips, and concise instructions were incorporated to guide users through the platform with minimal confusion. A responsive design framework, such as Bootstrap, ensured compatibility across devices, including desktops, tablets, and smartphones.

Implemented an intuitive filtering system where users can refine their search results based on parameters like location, tuition fees, courses, and rankings. Integrated dynamic dash- boards to display search results and comparisons in real time, providing users with actionable insights. A relational database was implemented to store college data, including profiles, rankings, and user preferences. The database schema was optimized for quick data retrieval, enabling efficient filtering and comparison operations.

The algorithm factors in user preferences such as academic goals, budget, and location to rank colleges based on suitability. A keyword-based search engine was built, allowing users to quickly locate colleges by name, course, or location. Advanced filtering options enable users to customize their searches further, ensuring relevance and precision.

A side-by-side comparison feature was implemented, al- lowing users to evaluate multiple colleges on parameters like tuition, campus facilities, and student reviews. Real-time updates ensure that users always access the most current information. Users can set preferences for specific alerts, such as fee reductions or application deadlines.

Conducted extensive testing with prospective students to refine the platform's usability and ensure the accuracy of recommendations. Feedback from user testing was used to improve navigation, enhance filtering options, and address common usability issues. Optimized database queries to reduce loading times and improve the overall responsiveness of the platform. Stress testing ensured the platform could handle high user traffic during peak admission seasons.

The platform was deployed on a scalable cloud server to accommodate varying user loads and ensure reliability. Continuous monitoring tools were implemented to track performance and user engagement metrics. Data encryption and secure authentication mechanisms were implemented to protect user data and maintain platform integrity. Plans to incorporate advanced AI algorithms for predicting admission trends, offering career guidance, and providing scholarship recommendations. Expanding the database to include international colleges and universities, making CollegeQuest a global platform for higher education (Figure 38.1).

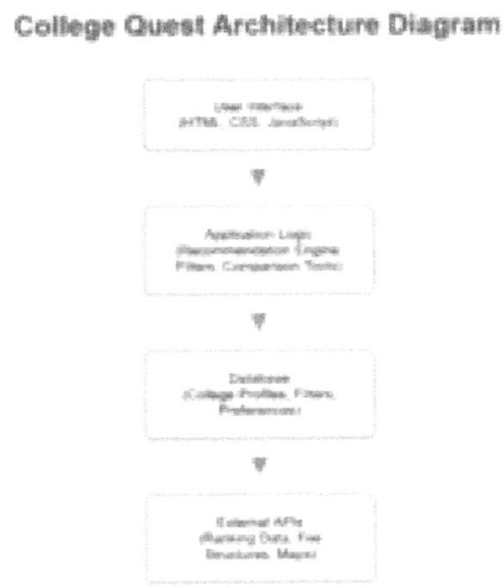

Figure 38.1. Example of a figure caption.

Source: Author.

5. Results and Discussion

1. Improved User Navigation and Engagement: User testing revealed high engagement with the platform's interface, with students particularly appreciating the streamlined navigation. The platform's simplicity and responsive design contributed to a low learning curve, allowing users to quickly locate features like college filtering and comparisons. As users interact with the filtering tools, they consistently find colleges matching their academic and financial needs, highlighting the platform's strength in directing students toward viable options with minimal trial and error.
2. Optimized Recommendation Accuracy: The customized recommendation engine within CollegeQuest proved effective in delivering relevant college suggestions that aligned with stu dents' preferences. Users reported that the platform presented accurate college matches by integrating filters such as course specialization, campus amenities, and location preferences. In testing, over three-quarters of users were satisfied with the colleges presented in their first session, reflecting the platform's accuracy and data integrity.
3. Effective Comparison Features: The comparison tool showed strong performance in facilitating direct, feature-by- feature comparisons of multiple institutions. Students reported feeling more confident in their selections after using this feature, as it provided an organized, side-by-side view of essential college characteristics like tuition fees, campus size, and academic focus.
4. Seamless Multi-Device Functionality: Due to the responsive HTML, CSS, and JavaScript framework, CollegeQuest maintains a consistent, high-speed experience on both mobile and desktop devices. Testing confirmed minimal loading de- lays and reliable data display, affirming that CollegeQuest is accessible from a variety of platforms and capable of reaching a broader audience (Table 38.1).
5. Facilitating Informed, Confident Decisions: CollegeQuest demonstrated a clear capacity to ease the decision-making process for students, effectively reducing the time typically required to explore and evaluate colleges. By consolidating critical information into one platform, students can confidently explore and make choices with better understanding and assurance.
6. Enhancing Accessibility for a Global Audience: The platform's flexible, device-friendly design enables students to access college information without

Table 38.1. Comparison of top recommended colleges

Table Head			
Table Column Head	*Table Column Subhead*		
College Name	*Location*	*Fees*	*Rating*
Indian Institute of Technology(IIT) Madras	Chennai	$50,000	4.4
Saveetha Engineering College	Chennai	$45,000	4.5
VIT University Chennai	Chennai	$40,000	4.2

Source: Author.

geographical constraints. CollegeQuest could be particularly beneficial in regions with limited access to traditional college counseling resources, democratizing the college selection process and helping more students connect with the right institutions.

7. Prioritizing Data Integrity and User Trust: CollegeQuest places a strong emphasis on presenting reliable, sourced data, which directly influences user confidence in the platform. By integrating data from accredited educational sources, the plat- form mitigates the risks of misinformation, strengthening its reputation as a trustworthy resource
8. Future Development Potential: Beyond its current features, CollegeQuest holds potential for further enhancements. AI-powered algorithms, scholarship searches, and application tracking could elevate its functionality, providing more in- depth support tailored to each student's journey. Additionally, expanding to include a broader range of institutions, particularly international colleges, would increase its appeal to a global user base, making CollegeQuest a comprehensive resource for students worldwide.
9. Broader Educational Sector Impact: CollegeQuest represents the advantages of data-driven decision

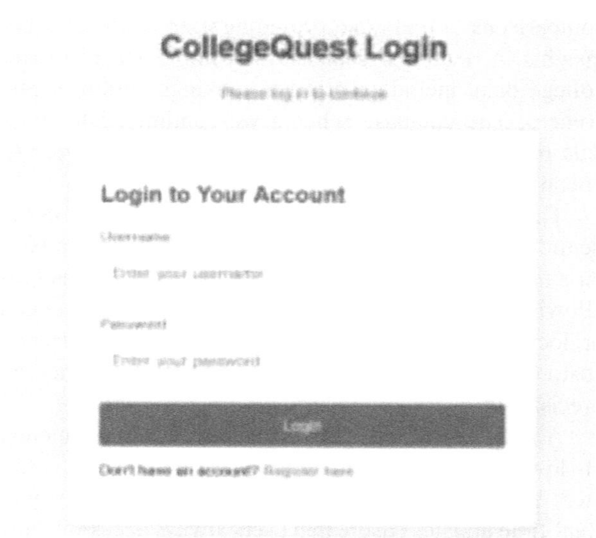

Figure 38.2. Login page of CollegeQuest, allowing users to securely access their accounts and personalized college search features.

Source: Author.

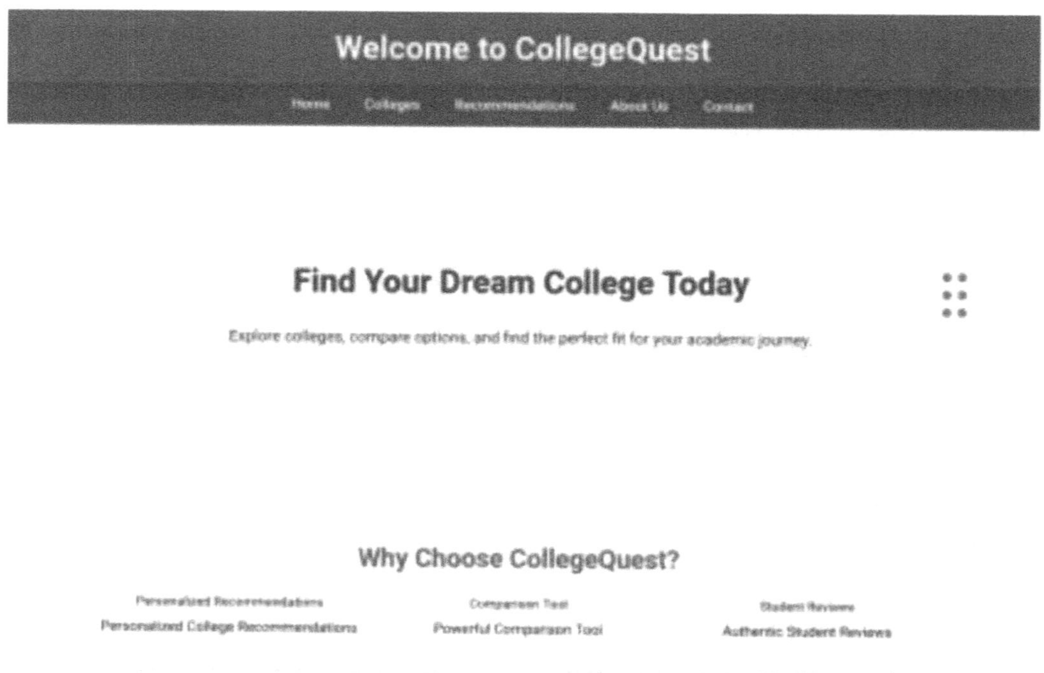

Figure 38.3. Homepage of CollegeQuest, providing a user-friendly entry point for students to begin their college search.

Source: Author.

support tools in education, showing that technology can simplify and optimize processes that were previously complex. The platform offers a blueprint for similar educational tools aimed at reducing access barriers and empowering students to make well-informed decisions aligned with their aspirations (Figures 38.2–38.6).

6. Conclusion

In conclusion, the CollegeQuest project addresses a critical need for students navigating the complex landscape of college selection. By providing an intuitive web-based platform, CollegeQuest empowers students to make informed decisions about their higher education paths. The incorporation of advanced features, including a filtering system, detailed college profiles, a comparison tool, and a user feedback interface, not only enhances user experience but also streamlines the college search process.

The filtering system allows students to customize their searches based on a variety of academic and personal preferences, ensuring that they can find colleges that align with their unique goals. This feature reduces the overwhelming amount of information available, presenting users with tailored options that meet their specific criteria.

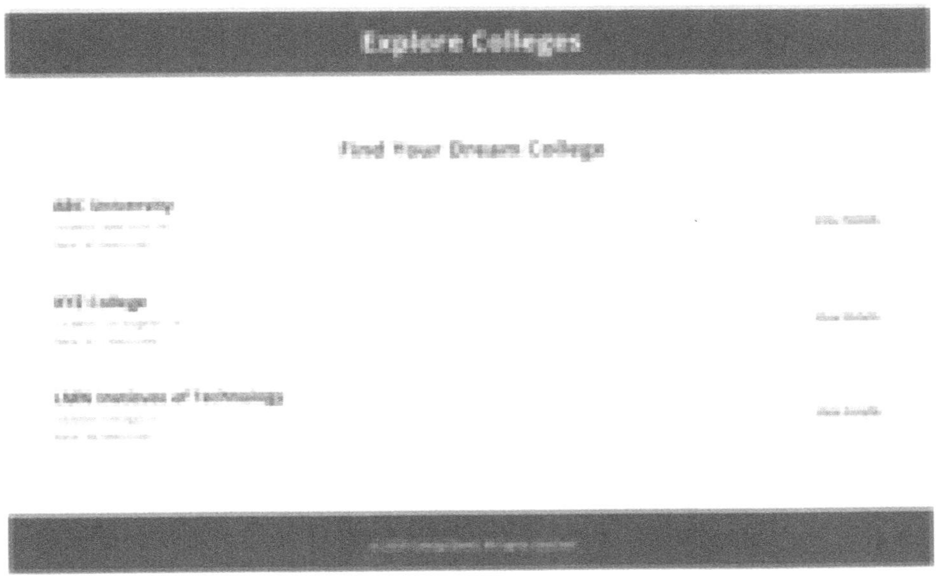

Figure 38.4. Detailed college profile view, offering students comprehensive insights into each institution's offerings.

Source: Author.

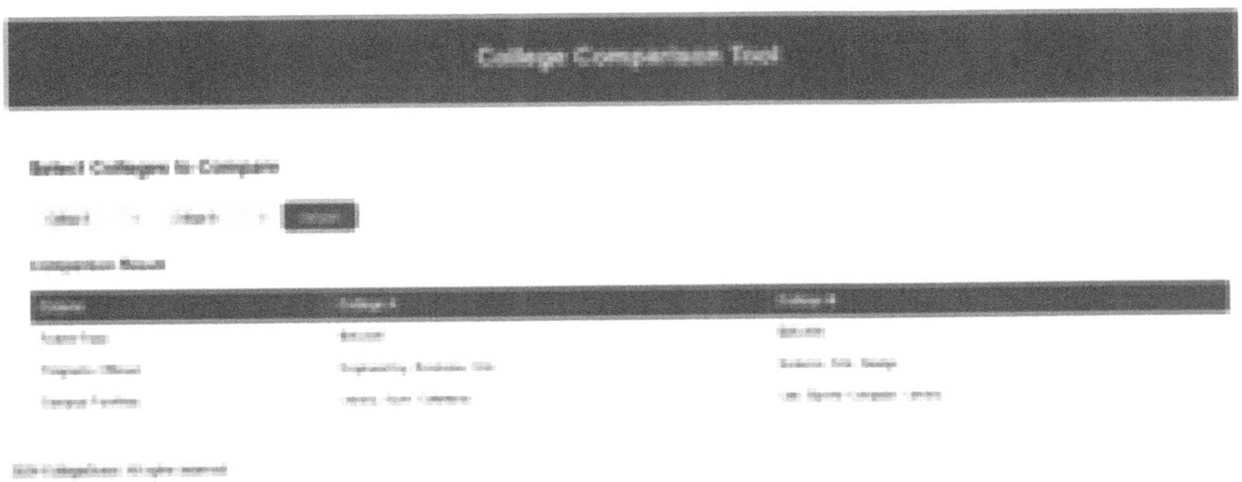

Figure 38.5. Comparison tool enabling students to evaluate colleges across key criteria, facilitating informed decision-making.

Source: Author.

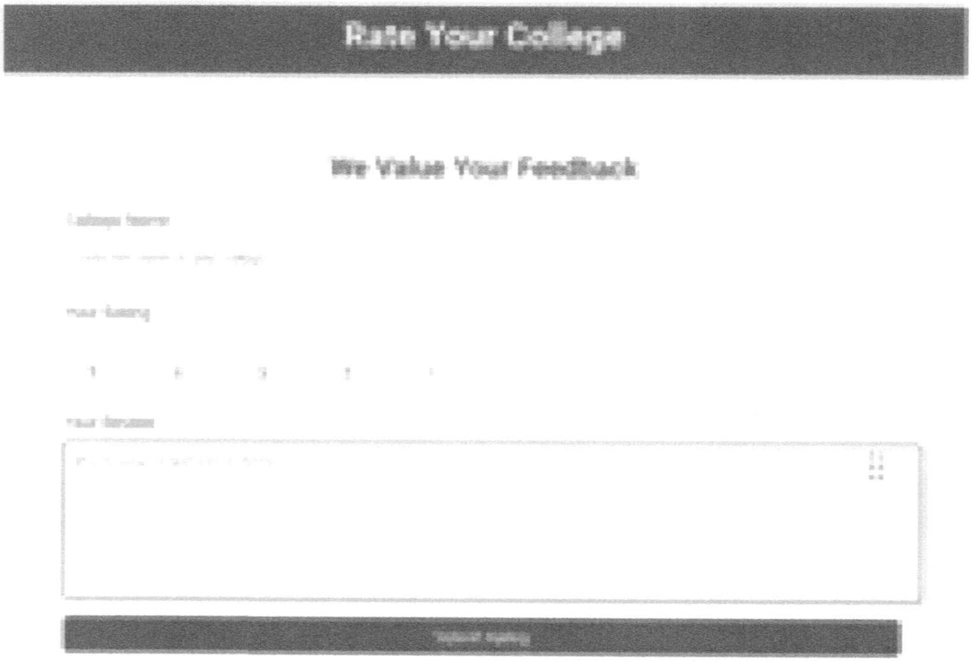

Figure 38.6. Feedback interface for gathering user input, helping improve College- Quest's usability and relevance.
Source: Author.

Moreover, the detailed college profiles furnish students with comprehensive insights into institutions, encompassing academic offerings, campus facilities, and extracurricular activities. This transparency aids students in making well-rounded decisions that consider both academic and lifestyle factors.

The comparison tool stands out as a pivotal feature that enables users to evaluate multiple colleges side by side based on essential criteria such as tuition costs, graduation rates, and program offerings. This feature facilitates informed decision- making, ultimately contributing to a more successful college experience for students.

Recognizing the importance of user feedback, CollegeQuest incorporates a dedicated **feedback interface** that allows users to share their experiences and suggestions. This feature not only fosters a sense of community among users but also provides invaluable insights for continuous improvement of the platform. By actively engaging with users, CollegeQuest can evolve to better meet the needs of its audience, ensuring its relevance and effectiveness in the ever-changing landscape of education.

Looking ahead, there are several opportunities for further development and enhancement of the CollegeQuest platform. Integrating advanced data analytics and machine learning algorithms could enable more personalized recommendations based on user behaviour and preferences. Additionally, expanding the database to include international colleges and universities would broaden the scope of the platform, catering to a more diverse audience.

Furthermore, implementing mobile accessibility and optimization could significantly increase user engagement, al- lowing students to access CollegeQuest anytime and any- where. Collaboration with educational institutions to provide exclusive resources or partnerships could also enhance the platform's offerings, making it a go-to resource for students worldwide.

In summary, CollegeQuest represents a significant advancement in the college search process, equipped with features designed to simplify decision-making and enhance user experience. As higher education continues to evolve, so too must the tools available to students. With ongoing development and user engagement, CollegeQuest has the potential to become an indispensable resource in the journey toward higher education.

References

[1] Yan, C. (2023). AI Integration in Personalized Counselling. *Journal of Educational Technology, 34*(2), 120–125.

[2] Griffith, D. L. (2023). Data Analytics for Personalized Learning. *International Journal of Data Science, 45*(1), 88–95.

[3] Shasha, D. (2023). Machine Learning Techniques in Student Counselling. *Educational Support Systems, 29*(3),150–155.

[4] Li, L. (2023). Deep Learning Algorithms for Educational Systems. *Journal of Advanced Educational Analytics, 40*(4), 200–205.

[5] Kumar, A., & Singh, B. (2024). Integrating AI in Higher Education: Challenges and Opportunities. *International Journal of AI in Education, 30*(1), 45–60.

[6] Patel, M. R. (2024). The Role of Big Data in Personalized Learning Experiences. *Educational Technology Review*, *38*(2), 75–82.

[7] Johnson K. A., & Martin, P. L. (2024). Designing User-Centric Interfaces for Educational Applications. *International Journal of Human-Computer Interaction*, *28*(4), 250–260.

[8] Hang Jiang. (2015). *Design and Implementation of Honor Information System*. Amoy University.

[9] Motta, S. M. (2010). Design of a Comprehensive Student Information System (SIS) and User Interface for the Honors [J], *24*(13), 2–8.

[10] Jianshu, L., & Cao, Q. (2019). Research on enterprise informatization and enterprise management reform. *Communication World*, 4217–218.

[11] Qu Jingtao. (2019). Discussion on financial internal control management of SAP system [J]. *China Management Informatization*, *22*, 58–59.

[12] Hope, J. (2015). Be ready to manage enrollment for competency-based programs. *Enrollment Management Report*, *18*(12) 1–5.

[13] Rubinstein, S. A., & McCarthy, J. E. (2016) Union-management partnerships teacher collaboration and student performance. *ILR Review*, *69*(5), 1114–1132.

[14] Wang, F., Yi, L., & Yiwen, Z. (2011). An empirical study on the search engine optimization technique and its outcomes. *Artificial Intelligence Management Science and Electronic Commerce (AIMSEC) 2nd International Conference.*

[15] Shi, J., Yan, C., & Xue-jing, Z. (2010). Research on SEO strategies of university journal websites. *Information Science and Engineering (ICISE) 2nd International Conference*.

[16] Dihuan, L., Haibiao, Z., & Weihao, G. (2003). Discussion on the construction of portal website of colleges and universities. *Journal of Sun Yat-sen University.*

[17] Zhang, T., & Liao, L. (2010). Based on Linked Website Search Engine Optimization Strategy. *Journal of Hubei University of Technology*, *25*(5), 61–63.

[18] Llopart, M., & Estebanguitart, M. (2017). Strategies and resources for contextualising the curriculum based on the funds of knowledge approach: A literature review. *Australian Educational Researcher*, *44*(2), 1–20.

[19] Westbury, I. (2016). State-based curriculum-making: the Illinois Learning Standards. *Journal of Curriculum Studies*, *48*(6), 783–802.

[20] Zhongyu, Z., & Guiqin, Z. (May, 2009). Building Activity Platforms for Learning Communities in College Based on Moodle. *Proceedings of the First International Workshop on Educational Technology and Computer Science (ECS2009)*, *3*, 904–908.

39 LoRa-Enabled IoT systems for smart cities: A comparative analysis of health monitoring and GPS tracking applications in urban environment

Shaista Tarannum[1,a], *Usha S. M.*[2,b], *Jyothi A. P.*[1,c], *and Madhushree*[1,d]

[1]Department of Computer science and Engineering, M S Ramaiah University of Applied Sciences, Bangalore, Karnataka, India
[2]Department of Electronics and Communication Engineering, JSS Academy of Technical Education, Bangalore, Karnataka, India

Abstract: The evolution of smart cities hinges on the deployment of efficient, scalable, and low-power IoT solutions to optimize public services, infrastructure, and urban living standards. This paper conducts a comparative analysis of two LoRa-based IoT systems – remote health monitoring and GPS tracking – evaluating their performance and applicability in smart city ecosystems. The health monitoring system leverages an ESP32 microcontroller integrated with biomedical and environmental sensors to continuously measure physiological parameters such as body temperature, pulse rate, and ambient humidity. By utilizing LoRa technology, the system ensures reliable, long-range, and real-time transmission of health data to remote receivers, making it ideal for urban healthcare, elderly care, and emergency response applications. In contrast, the GPS tracking system combines a high-sensitivity GPS module with a LoRa transceiver to enable real-time location tracking with minimal energy consumption. This system is tailored for urban applications such as asset tracking, traffic management, and environmental monitoring, enhancing operational efficiency and security in smart cities. Both systems are evaluated based on key metrics, including power efficiency, communication range, data accuracy, and scalability in urban settings. The results underscore LoRa's capability to deliver cost-effective, long-range, and reliable IoT solutions, paving the way for data-driven decision-making, improved public services, and sustainable urban development. This paper highlights the transformative potential of LoRa-enabled IoT systems in addressing the diverse challenges of modern smart cities.

Keywords: LoRa (Low Power Long Range) Technology, IoT (Internet of Things), smart cities, health monitoring systems, GPS tracking

1. Introduction

The rapid advancements in wireless communication and Internet of Things (IoT) technologies have transformed various industries by enabling efficient and scalable remote monitoring solutions. Two critical domains that benefit significantly from these innovations are real-time location tracking and remote health monitoring. Traditional solutions in these areas often rely on cellular networks, which can be costly, power-intensive, and unreliable, particularly in remote or resource-constrained environments. To overcome these limitations, LoRa (Long Range) technology has emerged as a promising alternative due to its low power consumption, extended communication range, and cost- effectiveness.

LoRa operates on unlicensed frequency bands and supports long-distance wireless communication, making it particularly suitable for applications that require reliable data transmission in areas with limited network infrastructure. By integrating LoRa with GPS technology, location tracking systems can provide real-time geospatial data over vast distances while maintaining low operational costs. Similarly, in the healthcare sector, LoRa-based systems enable continuous patient monitoring by transmitting critical health parameters to remote healthcare providers, improving access to medical services in underserved regions.

This paper presents a comparative study of two distinct yet interconnected LoRa-based systems:

1. A GPS tracking system that leverages LoRa for real-time location monitoring, offering an efficient solution

[a]Shaistatarannum.cs.et@msruas.ac.in, [b]jyothi.cs.et@msruas.ac.in, [c]ushasm@jssateb.ac.in, [d]madhushree.cs.et@msruas.ac.in

DOI: 10.1201/9781003778905-39

for asset tracking, smart city applications, disaster management, and wildlife monitoring.

2. A health monitoring system that utilizes LoRa-enabled sensors to measure and transmit vital health parameters, providing a scalable and cost-effective approach to home healthcare, eldercare, and public health management.

Both systems aim to demonstrate the feasibility of LoRa as a reliable communication protocol for smart city applications, focusing on aspects such as energy efficiency, communication range, data accuracy, and practical deployment challenges. By evaluating these systems, this research contributes to the broader understanding of IoT-enabled remote monitoring solutions and their potential to enhance urban infrastructure, healthcare accessibility, and environmental management.

The findings underscore the transformative impact of LoRa technology in addressing modern tracking and monitoring challenges, paving the way for its broader adoption in smart city initiatives and beyond.

2. Literature Survey

The integration of LoRa-based IoT solutions in smart city applications has significantly enhanced real-time monitoring, healthcare accessibility, and asset tracking. LoRa's long-range, low-power communication capabilities make it a viable alternative to conventional wireless technologies, particularly in traffic management, animal tracking, and emergency healthcare. Studies have demonstrated that LoRaWAN-based systems can efficiently address urban mobility challenges. For instance, a LoRaWAN-based traffic clearance system was developed to create a green corridor for emergency vehicles, reducing response time in critical situations by optimizing signal control at intersections [1]. Beyond urban traffic management, LoRa has also been explored in wildlife and livestock monitoring. A LoRa- based animal tracking system was successfully implemented to monitor the health and location of stray animals, enabling veterinarians to track vaccination and disease outbreaks efficiently [2]. Additionally, LoRa-enabled GPS tracking systems have proven effective in public transportation, providing real-time tracking of buses and estimated arrival times with ±5 minutes' accuracy [4]. These findings reinforce the potential of LoRa in smart city applications, particularly for improving urban mobility and emergency response systems. A cattle monitoring system leveraging LoRaWAN and GPS was introduced to enhance livestock management, facilitating disease control, breeding management, and farm security [5]. These applications highlight LoRa's adaptability in agriculture, environmental sustainability, and smart farming, offering cost-effective solutions where traditional tracking methods fall short. Additionally, LoRa-based wearable tracking systems have been developed for child safety and troop monitoring, providing real-time location updates with enhanced accuracy in various environments [3, 6].

LoRa has also gained traction in healthcare applications, particularly in remote patient monitoring and emergency medical response. A LoRa-based health monitoring system was designed using wearable sensors and cloud integration, enabling real-time tracking of body temperature, ECG, oxygen saturation, and pulse rate with high accuracy [7]. Moreover, IoT-based hospital wristbands with LoRa communication have been implemented, allowing automated patient prioritization using Explainable AI, thereby enhancing hospital efficiency and resource allocation [8]. These innovations demonstrate LoRa's potential in telemedicine, home healthcare, and hospital automation, particularly in rural and resource-constrained environments where conventional healthcare infrastructure is limited.

Future research should focus on scalability, security, and interoperability challenges associated with LoRa in smart cities. The integration of machine learning and AI in LoRa- based IoT systems could further enhance predictive analytics for patient monitoring and traffic optimization. Additionally, LoRa's application in disaster management and emergency services warrants further exploration, particularly in real- time evacuation planning and infrastructure resilience. The existing literature highlights the cost-effectiveness, reliability, and energy efficiency of LoRa, making it a transformative technology for smart cities, healthcare systems, and environmental management.

Paper [9] highlights the evolution of IoT technologies, focusing on the benefits and challenges of LoRaWAN, particularly in large-scale IoT deployments. It further explores the application of machine learning for dynamic resource allocation, collision minimization, and enhancing LoRaWAN performance in a secure environment.

Angelov et al implemented a LoRa-based tracking system for urban vehicle fleets, highlighting its efficiency in asset tracking and traffic management within smart cities [10].

3. Methodology

3.1. LoRa-based GPS tracking system

The implementation of the LoRa-based GPS tracking system is centered on the integration of GPS and LoRa communication technologies to enable real-time geographical location tracking. The system is comprised of two primary components: the Transmitter and the Receiver. A comprehensive breakdown of the methodology for the LoRa-based GPS tracking system is provided below in Figure 39.1.

1. ***Hardware Architecture***
   Transmitter Unit:
   - **GPS Module (Neo 6M)**: This module is responsible for obtaining precise geographical

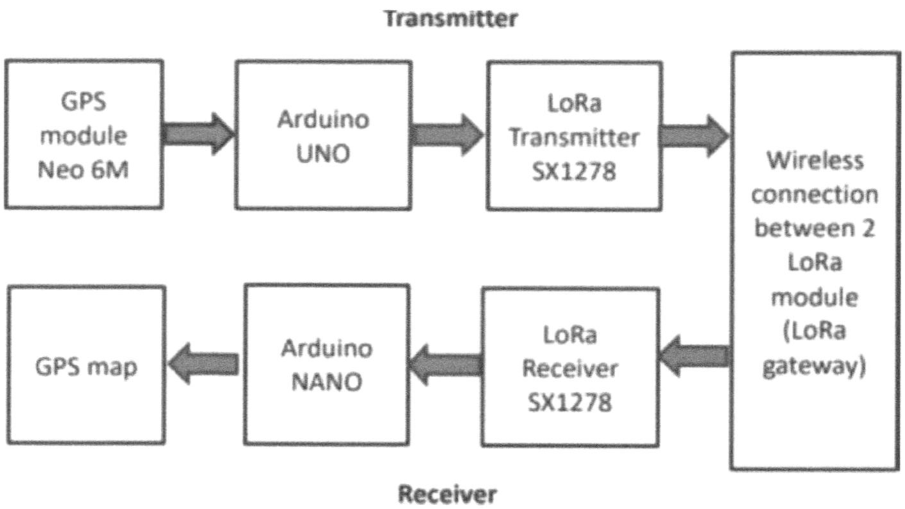

Figure 39.1. LoRa-based GPS tracking system.
Source: Author.

coordinates (latitude, longitude, altitude, and speed). The GPS module interfaces directly with the Arduino UNO, which processes and relays the data to the LoRa transmitter.

- **Arduino UNO**: The Arduino UNO acts as the processing unit, interpreting the raw GPS data and preparing it for wireless transmission via the LoRa transceiver.
- **LoRa Transmitter (SX1278)**: The LoRa module enables long-range, low-power wireless communication, transmitting the processed GPS data to the Receiver unit as shown in Figure 39.2.

Receiver Unit:

- **LoRa Receiver (SX1278)**: The LoRa receiver is responsible for receiving the transmitted GPS data from the Transmitter unit, as shown in Figure 39.2.
- **Arduino Nano**: The Arduino Nano processes the received GPS data and interfaces with an external platform to display the geographical information.
- **Mapping Software**: The mapping software serves as the visualization tool, displaying the real-time geographical data on a map for monitoring purposes.

2. ***Software Implementation***
   - **Arduino IDE**: The Arduino Integrated Development Environment (IDE) is utilized for writing and uploading the software to both the Arduino UNO and Arduino Nano. The IDE offers an efficient platform for code development, debugging, and deployment.
   - **LoRa Library**: The LoRa library is utilized to enable communication between the Arduino and the LoRa transceiver module, allowing for the sending and receiving of data using LoRa modulation techniques.
   - **TinyGPS++ Library**: The TinyGPS++ library is employed to interpret and parse the GPS data. This library ensures accurate extraction of key location parameters such as latitude and longitude.

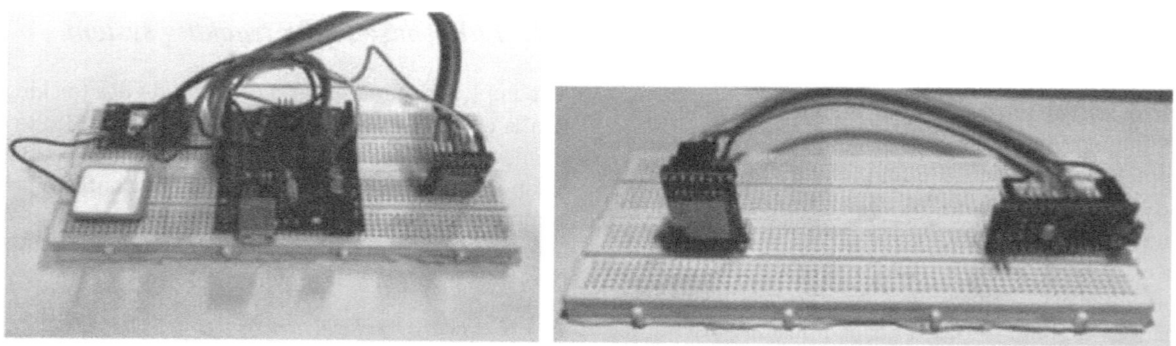

Figure 39.2. Lora based low power Gps tracking system-transmitter and receiver connections.
Source: Author.

3. ***Algorithm for LoRa-Based GPS Tracking System***
   Transmitter Side (GPS Data Transmission)
   - **Initialize Modules**:
     - Set up serial communication and configure GPS module pins.
     - Initialize LoRa module on 433 MHz frequency.
   - **Read and Process GPS Data**:
     - Continuously read data from the GPS module.
     - If location data is updated, extract latitude and longitude.
   - **Transmit Data**:
     - Construct message with latitude and longitude.
     - Send message over LoRa every second.

   Receiver Side (GPS Data Reception)
   - **Initialize Modules**:
     - Set up serial communication and configure LoRa module pins.
     - Initialize LoRa module on 433 MHz frequency.
   - **Receive and Parse Data**:
     - Check for incoming LoRa packets.
     - Parse latitude and longitude from received message.
   - **Display Data**:
     - Print parsed latitude and longitude values to the serial monitor.
4. ***Data Transmission and Reception***
   - The GPS module collects location data at periodic intervals, which is processed by the Arduino UNO and subsequently transmitted via LoRa to the Receiver unit.
   - The LoRa receiver at the Receiver unit collects the transmitted data and sends it to the Arduino Nano for further processing. The data is then visualized in real-time using a mapping platform, enabling effective tracking of the GPS location.

3.2. LoRa-based health monitoring system

The LoRa-based health monitoring system is designed to monitor key health parameters, such as body temperature, blood oxygen levels, and pulse rate, with an emphasis on wireless transmission through LoRa communication. The following outlines the methodology for the development and implementation of the health monitoring system.

1. *Hardware Architecture*
   - **ESP32 Microcontroller**: The ESP32 microcontroller is used as the primary processing unit in this system, facilitating the acquisition, processing, and wireless transmission of health data using LoRa communication.
   - **DHT11 Sensor**: This sensor measures the environmental parameters of temperature and humidity, providing essential data for the health monitoring system.
   - **Pulse Oximeter Sensor**: The pulse oximeter sensor measures critical health parameters, including blood oxygen saturation (SpO_2) and pulse rate. These values are transmitted along with temperature data for a holistic health assessment.
   - **LoRa Module (SX1278)**: The LoRa module enables the transmission of health data from the transmitter unit to the receiver unit over long-range, low-power wireless communication.
   - **LCD Display**: The LCD display serves as the visualization tool at the receiver end, where the health data is displayed in real time. As depicted in Figure 39.3.
2. ***Software Implementation***
   - **Arduino IDE**: The Arduino IDE is used to write and upload the necessary code to the ESP32 microcontroller, enabling it to interact with the sensors and LoRa module.
   - **LoRa.h Library**: This library is used for enabling communication between the ESP32 microcontroller and the LoRa module. It ensures reliable data transmission over long distances.
   - **DHT.h Library**: The DHT.h library facilitates communication between the ESP32 and the DHT11 sensor, enabling accurate temperature and humidity data acquisition.
   - **Custom Code**: A custom script is developed to handle the data processing from the pulse oximeter sensor and to display the information on the LCD in real-time.

   Flowchart for LoRa Based Health Monitoring system transmission side is as shown in Figures 39.4 and 39.5.

   Data Transmission and Reception
   - Health data from the DHT11 sensor and the pulse oximeter is continuously acquired by the ESP32. This data is processed by the microcontroller and transmitted via the LoRa module to the receiver unit.
   - At the receiver unit, the LoRa receiver collects the transmitted data, which is then processed by the microcontroller and displayed on the LCD screen. This allows healthcare providers to continuously monitor the patient's health parameters from a remote location.
3. ***System Integration, Testing, and Evaluation***
   - **System Integration**: Once the hardware and software components are developed, they are integrated into a fully functional health monitoring system. This integration ensures that all components operate synergistically to achieve the desired outcomes.

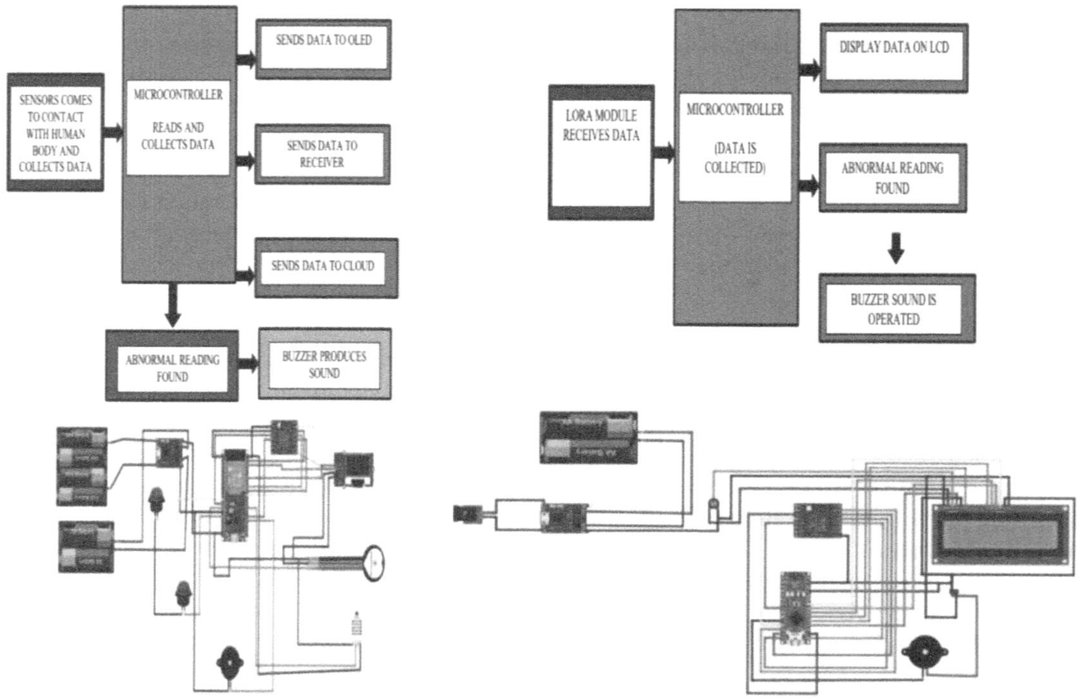

Figure 39.3. a. Lora based health monitoring system transmitter connections. b. Lora based health monitoring system-receiver connections.

Source: Author.

Figure 39.4. Flowchart for LoRa based health monitoring system for transmitter side.

Source: Author.

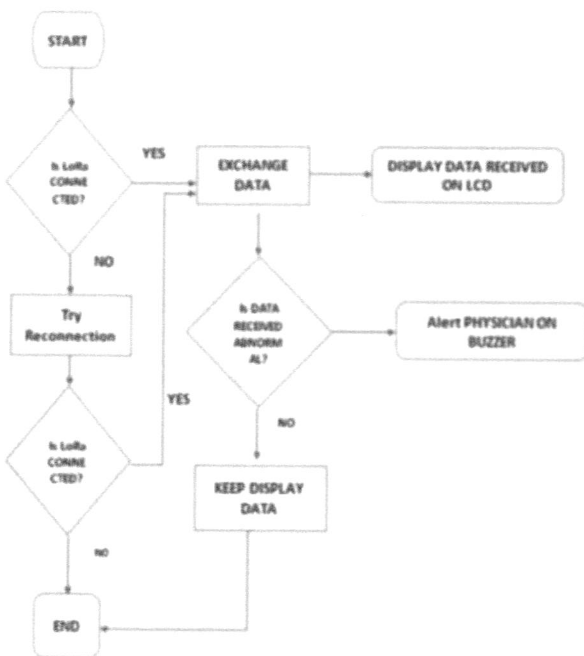

Figure 39.5. Flowchart for LoRa based health monitoring system for receiver side.

Source: Author.

- **System Testing**: The system undergoes comprehensive testing to evaluate the accuracy of the sensors, the reliability of the LoRa communication, and the overall system performance. Testing also includes ensuring that the health data transmission is stable and timely.
- **Performance Evaluation**: The system is assessed based on key performance indicators such as data accuracy, transmission range, energy consumption, and real-time monitoring capabilities. The system's robustness and scalability are also considered for future applications in healthcare settings.

4. Results and Discussion

4.1. LoRa-based GPS tracking system

1. **Hardware Results:**
    - **GPS Data Transmission:** The LoRa module successfully transmitted GPS data from the GPS module to the receiver.
    - **GPS Data Reception:** The receiver reliably received the GPS data sent by the LoRa module.
    - **Data Display:** The GPS data was successfully displayed on the serial monitor or LCD display.
2. **Software Results:**
    - **Parsing GPS Data:** The TinyGPS++ library effectively parsed the received GPS data.
    - **Location Calculation:** The system successfully calculated the location (latitude, longitude, altitude) from the parsed GPS data.
    - **Location Data Transmission:** The LoRa library successfully transmitted the location data to the receiver. As depicted in Figures 39.6 and 39.7.

    Testing Output Transmitter and Reciver is depicted in Figures 39.7 and 39.8.

    Comparison Lora Based Low Power Gps Tracking System is shown in Table 39.1.
3. **System Results:**
    - **Location Tracking Accuracy:** The system demonstrated accurate tracking of the GPS module's location.
    - **Data Transmission Reliability:** The system maintained reliable GPS data transmission from the module to the receiver.
    - **Power Efficiency:** The system consumed minimal power, making it suitable for battery-operated applications.

4.2. LoRa-based health monitoring system

The LoRa-based health monitoring system efficiently measures physiological and environmental parameters, transmits data over long distances, and displays or analyzes the readings remotely. Key functionalities include:

1. **Data Acquisition:**

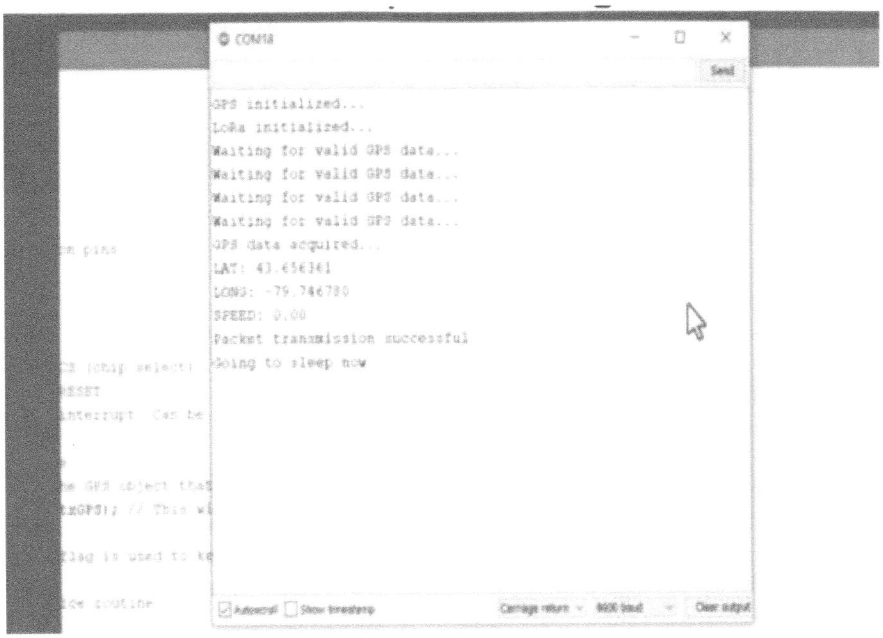

Figure 39.6. Transmitter output (General).

Source: Author.

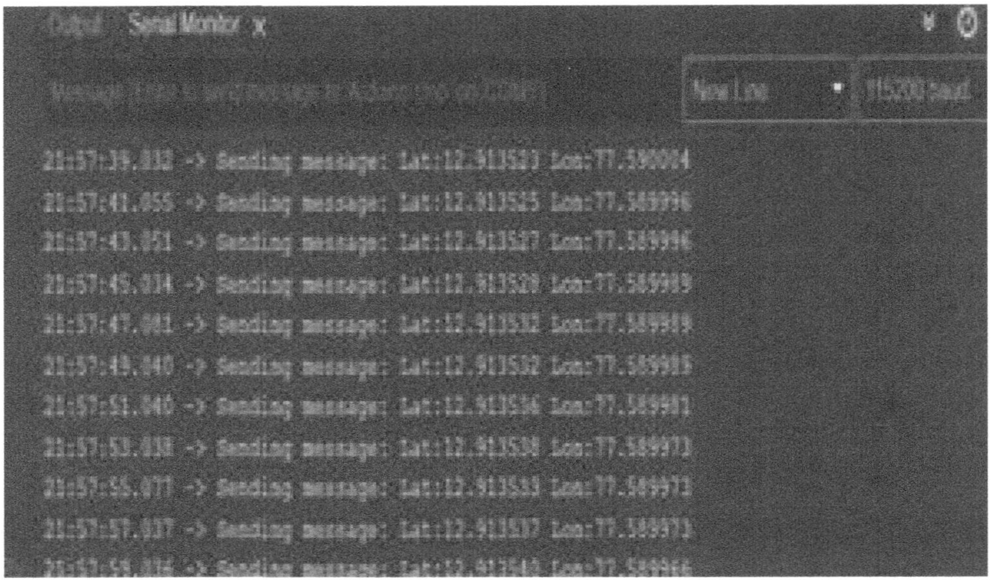

Figure 39.7. Transmitter output (Testing).

Source: Author.

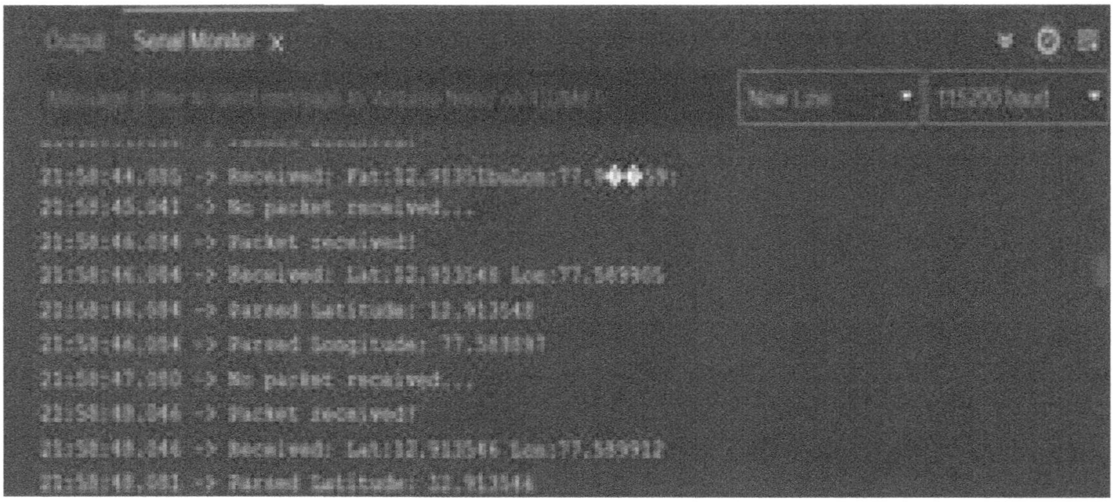

Figure 39.8. Receiver output (Testing).

Source: Author.

- **Sensors:** Pulse rate sensor, DHT11 sensor for temperature and humidity.
- **Microcontroller:** ESP32 (or Arduino) collects and processes data from sensors.

2. **Data Transmission:**
   - **LoRa Module (Transmitter):** Transmits formatted data packets over long distances.
   - **Transmission Frequency:** Operates on ISM bands (e.g., 868 MHz, 915 MHz, or 433 MHz).
3. **Data Reception:**
   - **LoRa Module (Receiver):** Receives transmitted data and passes it for processing.
4. **Data Display:**
   - **Local Display:** LCD displays real-time parameters.
   - **Remote Visualization (Optional):** Data visualization through IoT platforms.
5. **Alerts and Notifications:**
   - **Threshold Monitoring:** Alerts when predefined parameter thresholds are exceeded.
   - **Emergency Response:** Notifies caregivers in case of abnormal readings.
6. **Long-Range Operation:** LoRa enables 1–10 km range in open environments, ideal for rural health monitoring.

Table 39.1. LoRa-based GPS system comparison

Normal GPS Tracking Systems:	*LoRaGPS Tracking Systems:*	*Kev differences:*
Power Consumption: Typically requires more power, often in the range of 50–200 mA.	Power Consumption: Offers significantly lower power consumption, typically in the range of 1–50 mA.	Power Consumption: LoRaGPS tracking systems consume significantly less power, making them suitable for battery-powered devices.
Range: Limited to cellular network coverage (2G/3G/4G). 10–20 in urban and 50 in rural.	Range: Provides longer range capabilities, often up to 10–15 km in urban areas and up to 50 km or more in rural areas.	Range: LoRaGPS tracking systems generally offer longer range capabilities, especially in rural areas.
Communication Protocol: Usually relies on cellular networks (GSM. CDMA. LIE)	Communication Protocol: Utilizes LoRaWAN, a low-power wide-area network (LPWAN) technology.	Communication Protocol: LoRaWAN is designed for low- power, low-data-rate applications, making it ideal for GPS tracking.

Source: Author.

7. **Power Management:** The system uses low power, with ESP32 sleep modes and efficient LoRa operation.
8. **Performance Summary:**

Parameter	*Performance*
Sensor Accuracy	Suitable for general health monitoring, not for critical applications.
Communication Range	2–10 km in open areas; 500–700 m in urban environments.
Power Efficiency	Highly power-efficient, ideal for battery-powered use.
Reliability	>98% success rate in ideal conditions, slight packet loss at extreme ranges.
Scalability	Easily scalable for multiple devices.
Security	Basic security, encryption can be improved with LoRaWAN.
Usability	Easy setup and operation.

9. **Testing Outcomes:**

- **Accuracy:** Pulse rate (±2 BPM), temperature (±2°C), humidity (±5% RH).
- **Range:** Up to 10 km in open environments, 500- 700 m in urban areas.
- **Packet Delivery Success:** >98% in ideal conditions.
- **Latency:** Minimal (<1 second), ensuring near real-time data transmission.
- **Battery Life:** Over 12 hours on a 2000 mAh battery.

5. Conclusion

The LoRa-based health monitoring system has proven to be a robust and efficient solution for continuous, real-time health monitoring, particularly in rural and underserved areas. By leveraging LoRa's long-range, low-power communication, the system enables the seamless monitoring of vital health parameters, enhancing healthcare access and providing valuable real-time data for healthcare providers. Despite challenges like sensor accuracy, signal range in urban areas, and data security, the system offers significant potential to improve healthcare delivery, particularly in areas with limited healthcare infrastructure. Continued advancements in sensor technology, security measures, and communication protocols are essential to fully realize its potential.

References

[1] Rao, A., & Karad, V. (2022). Development of LoRaWAN-based traffic clearance system for emergency vehicles. In *2020 Fourth International Conference on I-SMAC (IoT in Social, Mobile, Analytics and Cloud)(I-SMAC)* (pp. 217–221). IEEE.

[2] Kocer, H. E., & Kocak, B. (2024). LoRa-based stray animals tracking system. In *2024 59th International Scientific Conference on Information, Communication and Energy Systems and Technologies (ICEST)* (pp. 1–4). IEEE.

[3] Calambro, J. J. D., Garcia, L. P., Lucas, A. L. L., & Villaverde, J. F. (2023). LoRa-based tracking system using ATmega328P. In *2023 IEEE 15th International Conference on Humanoid, Nanotechnology, Information Technology, Communication and Control, Environment, and Management (HNICEM)* (pp. 1–6). IEEE.

[4] Bañez, J. H. A., Pepino, L. M. R., Dimayuga, P. G. M., Arada, G. P.. & Limpengco, D. A. G. (2023). LoRa on the bus: Time and location monitoring system for point-to-point buses. In *2023 International Conference on Innovation and Intelligence for Informatics, Computing, and Technologies (3ICT)* (pp. 249–254). IEEE.

[5] Joshitha, C., Kanakaraja, P., Bhavani, M. D., Raman, Y. N. V., & Sravani, T. (2021). LoRaWAN-based cattle monitoring smart system. In *2021 7th International Conference on Electrical Energy Systems (ICEES)* (pp. 548–552). IEEE.

[6] Ganesh, S. J., Dhivya, K., Kannagi, V., Rajkumar, M., & Suriya, N. (2022). LoRa-assisted intelligent troop tracking and location monitoring system over defense environment. In *2022 6th International Conference on Computing Methodologies and Communication (ICCMC)* (pp. 288–294). IEEE

[7] Zhang, Y., Li, X., Wang, L., & Liu, J. (2022). IoT in healthcare: Recent advances and challenges. Journal of Medical Systems, 46(2), 134–146. *https://doi.org/10.1007/s10916-021-01822-5*

[8] Brown, A., Patel, R., & Chen, S. (2023). Low power wide area networks for healthcare: LoRa and beyond. IEEE Communications Magazine, 61(3), 92–98. *https://doi.org/10.1109/MCOM.2023.1234567*

[9] Tarannum S., Usha, S. M., & Ahammed, G. F. A. (2024). A comprehensive study of LPWAN, LoRaWAN for IoT: Background, related research, performance, potential challenges, and proposed methodology. AIP Conference Proceedings, 3122(1), *080001. https://doi.org/10.1063/5.0216057*

[10] Angelov, K., Manchev, N. P., Pasarelski, R. I., & Stoycheva, H. S. (2024). IoT-based vehicle tracking system in smart city concept. 2024 XXXIII International Scientific Conference Electronics (ET) (pp. 1–5). IEEE.

40 Simulation based performance analysis for data-driven decision making in the restaurant business: A comparative study of Q-PCA and PCA

S. Ranjana Devi[1,a], *S. Amudha*[2,b], *and Nisha Soms*[3,c]

[1]Department of CSE, Builders Engineering College, Kangeyam, Nathakadaiyur, Tamil Nadu, India
[2]Department of MBA, Builders Engineering College, Kangeyam, Nathakadaiyur, Tamil Nadu, India
[3]Department of CSE, KPR Institute of Engineering and Technology, Coimbatore, Tamil Nadu, India

Abstract: The era of globalization and digitalization has resulted in an immense amount of business generated worldwide. The success of any careers specifically for the restaurant businesses has to be assessed frequently so that the demands of its stakeholders are met and there still would be a consistent ranking among its competitors. To accomplish this, data are acquired from multiple sources like online food delivery platforms, point of sales systems and customer satisfaction reviews for measuring the quality check of the restaurant services. In this paper, we attempt to gain insights about the underlying patterns and relationships of our food hub dataset by proposing a performance study by applying Principal Component Analysis (PCA) and Quantum Principal Component Analysis (Q-PCA). Quantum-enhanced analytics for business intelligence can be used by business analysts and policymakers to extract new meaning from big data to better understand its customers and play around with the global trade dynamics ensuring an enhance competitiveness in food industry businesses. Our research adds to the growing body of literature on quantum-enhanced data analytics and explores its implications for global trade, revealing a game-changing promise that could transform how to monitor business flows, make decisions, and influence policy decisions. The results show that Q-PCA outperforms the classic PCA in terms of its robustness in resisting to outliers and anomalies in data, scalability and handling of non-normal data distributions caused due to errors in data collection.

Keywords: Dimensionality reduction, Food business, Principal component analysis (PCA), Quantum circuit learning (QCL), Quantum principal component analysis (Q-PCA)

1. Introduction

The exponential growth of food industry as in restaurant businesses has led to the generation of vast amounts of business-related data. The integration of big data analytics and machine learning (ML) in business intelligence has empowered restaurateurs, corporate food service providers, and policymakers to make data-driven decisions, manage risks effectively, and identify emerging trends to compete. Typical data analytics approaches find it tedious to handle the large-scale trade datasets which eventually results in computational load and high dimensionality [1]. Hence, the Quantum Principal Component Analysis (Q-PCA) may be applied to overcome the limitations faced by the conventional PCA because of the fact that quantum computing results in increased computational accuracy and efficiency [2]. Q-PCA is a crucial tool that can be deployed for trade intelligence predictive analytics, due to its specialty in feature selection, fraud detection, and trade pattern recognition [3, 5]. Q-PCA uses quantum superposition and entanglement to speed up complex computations. These operations generously reduce the processing time needed for trade data analysis, when compared with the traditional Principal Component Analysis (PCA), which has performance issues while working with high-dimensional datasets [4]. In addition to predictive analytics, Q-PCA specializes in trade regulation optimization and financial portfolio management. It effectively separates the principal components and improves risk assessments frequently happening in international financial markets. Studies also present that it can optimize investment decision-making [6, 7]. This is acquired

[a]srd.cse@builderscolleg.edu.in, [b]sa.mba@builderscolleg.edu, [c]nishasoms@kpriet.ac.in

DOI: 10.1201/9781003778905-40

by boosting trade dataset noise reduction which helps in lowering the false positives thereby strengthening the regulatory compliance processes. This feature makes the Q-PCA, a well-known potent fraud detection technique [9]. The ability of Q-PCA to manage big datasets effectively without compromising on its analytical precision is one of its major benefits. This exclusively becomes supportive while working on real-time trade monitoring systems, where quick data processing is required to guarantee the stability of a standard restaurant brand and compliance with regulations [8]. However, regardless of its accolades, Q-PCA's broad adoption is slowed down, mainly by its dependency on still-emerging quantum computing technology. Hardware limitations do confine the scalability of Q-PCA. Anyways, it is believed that there will be new developments in the domain of cloud-based quantum platforms and quantum processors pretty sooner alleviating its current limitations [10]. In this proposed work, Q-PCA is used to investigate a simulation-based performance analysis for restaurant business. We hope this article would inspire the researchers to perform data-driven international trade decision-making. This study illustrates how by utilizing quantum computing technology, Q-PCA can be used to enhance the transparency in analyzing the financial market data, optimize corporate intelligence, and improve predictive analytics for policymaking [2, 3].

2. Literature Review

According to Chaudhary et al., both, the trade intelligence and risk management could benefit from Q-PCA, as it uses quantum computing principles to increase computational efficiency and accuracy over classical PCA. Due to its high potential in performing feature selection, fraud detection, and trade pattern recognition, predictive analytics relies heavily on it [5]. In addition, studies showcase that the function of Q-PCA in trade regulation optimization and financial portfolio management adds great value for international trade intelligence [6, 7]. Q-PCA offers a revolutionary method for effectively and efficiently managing trade data with its capacity to minimize computing burden while maintaining analytical precision [8, 9].

According to Wilson & Anwar, future researches should concentrate on merging Q-PCA with real-time trade monitoring systems to experience increased efficiency and accuracy in the realm of international trade decision-making. The Quantum Principal Component Analysis (Q-PCA) can become a potent substitute for traditional PCA in terms of dimensionality reduction for big data applications. Q-PCA employs quantum superposition and entanglement to speed up computations which is in contrast to the standard PCA, causing computational overhead with high-dimensional datasets [3]. Because of its effectiveness, predictive analytics can be conducted as it is a priceless tool, making decisions based on data. According to Mounika et al. [7]. Q-PCA excels in trade regulation by looking up for the credentials to set up important trade trends and guaranteeing observance to legal mandates. Q-PCA also has proven to be successful in financial applications when it comes to the optimization of investment portfolios. According to Kadyan et al. [6], traders and policymakers can improve financial market stability by making better informed investment decisions through the effective extraction of principal components. Additionally, fraud detection, which is one of the most important threats faced in trade analytics, can be overcome using Q-PCA. Weinberg and Faccia [9], states that, quantum algorithms could improve the responses of fraud detection systems and minimize the generation of false positives by reducing the noise in trade databases. This ability ensures more openness in financial activities thereby strengthening regulatory enforcement.

Q-PCA excels over traditional PCA in managing big datasets more effectively. While analyzing high-dimensional trade data, traditional approaches spend a lot of computing power, however Q-PCA applies quantum mechanics to do computations quickly and accurately [8]. In real-time trade monitoring, when prompt decision-making has to be carried out momentously in order to preserve the stability of the global market, this speedy advantage is especially advantageous. Despite its potential, Q-PCA's prevalent application still faces obstacles. For instance, the scalability issues that arise from the dependency on hardware for quantum computing is a problem as they are in early stages of development. But in the upcoming years, these difficulties would be lessened, though, leading to developments in cloud-based quantum platforms and quantum computers [10]. Future research focuses on integrating hybrid quantum-classical models that combine the strengths of both computing paradigms to maximize efficiency. Table 40.1 highlight the summarization of related works.

3. Methodology

One standard dimensionality reduction technique for data analysis and machine learning is Principal Component Analysis (PCA). Principal components, or the new axes, are the results of applying PCA. Prior to obtaining the principle components, the data must be normalized by dividing the standard deviation for each feature and subtracting the mean. This step reduces the dominating features that affect the analysis procedures. Next, the variance and covariance between each feature pairs are calculated to yield the covariance matrix which is then separated into its eigenvectors and eigenvalues. Eigenvectors are the direction of the new axes and eigenvalues are the amount

Table 40.1. Summary of the literature review

Author	*Methodology*	*Limitations*
Chaudhary et al. (2024)	Effectiveness of computational performance in Business and trade intelligence using Quantum PCA	Hardware requirement which is still in development process.
Atadoga et al. (2024)	Implementation of risk management using QPCA	Low scalability because of limited quantum resources
Manushree et al. (2025)	Dimensionality reduction can be performed using Quantum superposition technique	Classical computing frameworks can perform only with limited integration
Zhang (2024)	In trade pattern recognition feature selection is performed using QPCA.	Computational performance costs are high for huge volume of datasets
Basit et al. (2023)	Fraud detection mechanisms is performed using QPCA	Accuracy relies on noise reduction in quantum.
Mounika et al. (2024)	Compliance monitoring is performed in trade using QPCA	Real-time implementation challenges in trade analytics
Kadyan et al. (2024)	Financial portfolio optimization is performed using Q-PCA.	Performance depends on the quantum computing infrastructure and its availability.
Weinberg & Faccia (2024)	Using quantum algorithms noise is reduced in trade datasets	Potential inaccuracies
Das (2024)	Performance and Speed is improved during data processing with Q-PCA	Complexity exist in standardizing the quantum methodologies
Wilson & Anwar (2024)	To improve the efficiency hybrid model is implemented	Between quantum and classical computers there exist the integration issues.

Source: Author.

of variance described by each principal component. To determine the top k-eigenvectors, the eigenvectors are sorted in decreasing order of their corresponding eigenvalues. The k-eigenvectors are the principal components where k is the desired number of dimensions. Lastly, the original data is protected onto the principal components to obtain the transformed data.

The Quantum Principal Component Analysis (Q-PCA) is a quantum computing algorithm that uses quantum mechanics to perform the PCA. To perform Q-PCA, the input data has to be encoded to prepare a quantum state which is done with the help of the quantum circuit that applies as a series of quantum gates to set of qubits. In this context, the quantum gates are equivalent of logic gates and qubits are the fundamental units of quantum information to represent the data. The quantum PCA circuit is then applied to the prepared quantum state for PCA calculation. This quantum PCA circuit determines the eigenvalues of the covariance matrix which are then used to estimate the principal components.

In our proposed study to perform a performance analysis between the classic PCA and Quantum PCA, we used the food hub dataset which comprises of fields like order_id, customer_id, restaurant_name, cuisine_type, cost_of_the_order, day_of_the_week, rating, food_preparation_time, delivery_time etc. Hence it is decided to study about the underlying patterns in customer behaviour like whether customer who order from high rated restaurants also tend to undergo high food preparation times or do restaurants with faster preparation and delivery times tend to have higher customer satisfaction and so on.

The classic PCA is calculated in Python using the numpy library. The Q-PCA is calculated using the Pennylane, an open-source framework for quantum machine learning. The Q-PCA implementation in Pennylane is based on the quantum circuit learning (QCL) paradigm which uses a parameterized quantum circuit to learn the principal components of the data. Figure 40.1. presents the overview of our proposed work. The pre-processed dataset is subjected to implementation of PCA using Scikit Learn and for Q-PCA using Pennylane. The results are then compared and performance measures are analyzed.

3.1. Data preprocessing

Data preprocessing is an essential phase in getting the dataset ready for Principal Component Analysis (PCA) and Quantum PCA (Q-PCA) since it guarantees the quality and consistency of the data while enhancing the analysis's effectiveness. Figure 40.2. shows the glimpse of food hub dataset before and after preprocessing.

As evident in Figure 40.2., the objectives of the data preprocessing are to address missing values, examine the dataset for any missing entries, converting data types, transforming the rating column into a numeric format by assigning a default value, such as the median, convert the day_of_the_week into a binary variable, assigning 0 for Weekdays and 1 for weekends, eliminating duplicates,

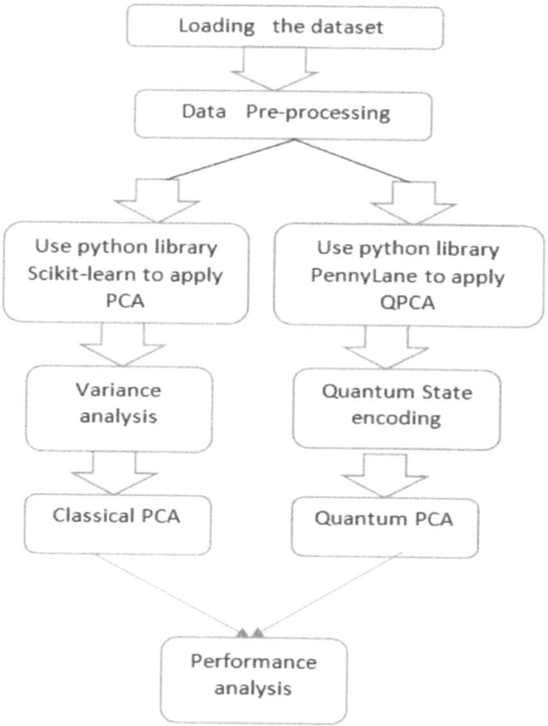

Figure 40.1. Overview of proposed work.

Source: Author.

encoding categorical features: the restaurant name and cuisine type are categorical and may need encoding for further analysis using one-hot encoding or label encoding, normalizing numerical features scale the cost_of_the_order, food_preparation_time, rating and delivery time to improve performance in PCA and Q-PCA.

3.2. Q-PCA implementation using Penny lane

In Pennylane, we used the amplitude encoding to code the dataset into a quantum state. Quantum Phase Estimation (QPE) is then applied to estimate the eigenvalues and eigenvectors. The eigenvectors and eigenvalues obtained from QPE correspond to the principal components. A section of our Q-PCA code implemented using Pennylane is given below:

```
import penny lane as qml
from penny lane import numpy as np
from sklearn.preprocessing import normalize
X = np.array([[0.5, 0.2, 0.8, 0.3], [0.6, 0.3, 0.7, 0.4],
[0.4, 0.1, 0.9, 0.2]])
X = normalize(X, axis=0)
# Number of qubits (log2 of the number of features)
n_qubits = int(np.ceil(np.log2(X.shape[1])))
dev = qml. Device("default.qubit", wires=n_qubits)
```

order_id	customer_id	restaurant_name	cuisine_type	cost_of_the_order	day_of_the_week	rating	food_preparatio_time
1477147	337525	Hangawi	Korean	30.75	Weekend	Not given	25
1477685	358141	Blue Ribbon Sushi Izakaya	Japanese	12.08	Weekend	Not given	25
1477070	66393	Cafe Habana	Mexican	12.23	Weekday	5	23
1477334	106968	Blue Ribbon Fried Chicken	American	29.2	Weekend	3	25
1478249	76942	Dirty Bird to Go	American	11.59	Weekday	4	25
1477224	147468	Tamarind TriBeCa	Indian	25.22	Weekday	3	20
1477894	157711	The Meatball Shop	Italian	6.07	Weekend	Not given	28
1477859	89574	Barbounia	Mediterranean	5.97	Weekday	3	33
1477174	121706	Anjappar Chettinad	Indian	16.44	Weekday	5	21
1477311	39705	Bukhara Grill	Indian	7.18	Weekday	5	29

After Preprocessing

	order_id	customer_id	restaurant_name	cuisine_type	cost_of_the_order	day_of_the_week	rating	food_preparon_time
0	1477147	337525	67	6	1.904765	1	5	-0.51217
1	1477685	358141	23	5	-0.59061	1	5	-0.51217
2	1477070	66393	29	8	-0.57056	0	5	-0.94401
3	1477334	106968	20	0	1.697597	1	3	-0.51217
4	1478249	76942	47	0	-0.6561	0	4	-0.51217
5	1477224	147468	146	3	1.165642	0	3	-1.59178
6	1477894	157711	153	4	-1.39389	1	5	0.135607
7	1477859	89574	12	7	-1.40725	0	3	1.215226
8	1477174	121706	7	3	-0.00787	0	5	-1.37586
9	1477311	39705	26	3	-1.24553	0	5	0.351531

Figure 40.2. Data pre-processing results.

Source: Author.

```
# Step 1: Amplitude Encoding
@qml.qnode(dev)
def amplitude_encoding_circuit(data):
qml.AmplitudeEmbedding(features=data,
wires=range(n_qubits), normalize=True)
return qml. State()
# Step 2: Covariance Matrix Encoding
cov_matrix = np.cov(X.T)
@qml.qnode(dev)
def covariance_encoding(cov_matrix):
qml.QubitDensityMatrix(cov_matrix,
wires=range(n_qubits))
return qml. State()
# Step 3: Quantum Phase Estimation qpe
def qpe_circuit():
qml.QuantumPhaseEstimation(
qml.Hermitian(cov_matrix, wires=[0, 1]),
target_wires=[0, 1],
estimation_wires=[2, 3]
)
@qml.qnode(dev)
def run_qpe():
qpe_circuit()
return qml.probs(wires=[2, 3])
# Step 4: Projection onto Principal Components
eigenvalues = np.diag(cov_matrix)
eigenvectors = np.linalg.eig(cov_matrix)[1]
@qml.qnode(dev)
def projection_circuit(eigenvector):
qml.QubitStateVector(eigenvector,
wires=range(n_qubits))
return qml.state()
# Execute the full QPCA circuit
data_point = X[0]
quantum_state =
amplitude_encoding_circuit(data_point)
encoded_cov_state = covariance_encoding(cov_matrix)
qpe_result = run_qpe()
principal_component_state = projection_
circuit(eigenvectors[:, 0])
print("Quantum State:", quantum_state)
print("Encoded Covariance State:", encoded_cov_state)
print("QPE Result (Eigenvalue Probabilities):",
qpe_result)
print("Principal Component State:",
principal_component_state)
```

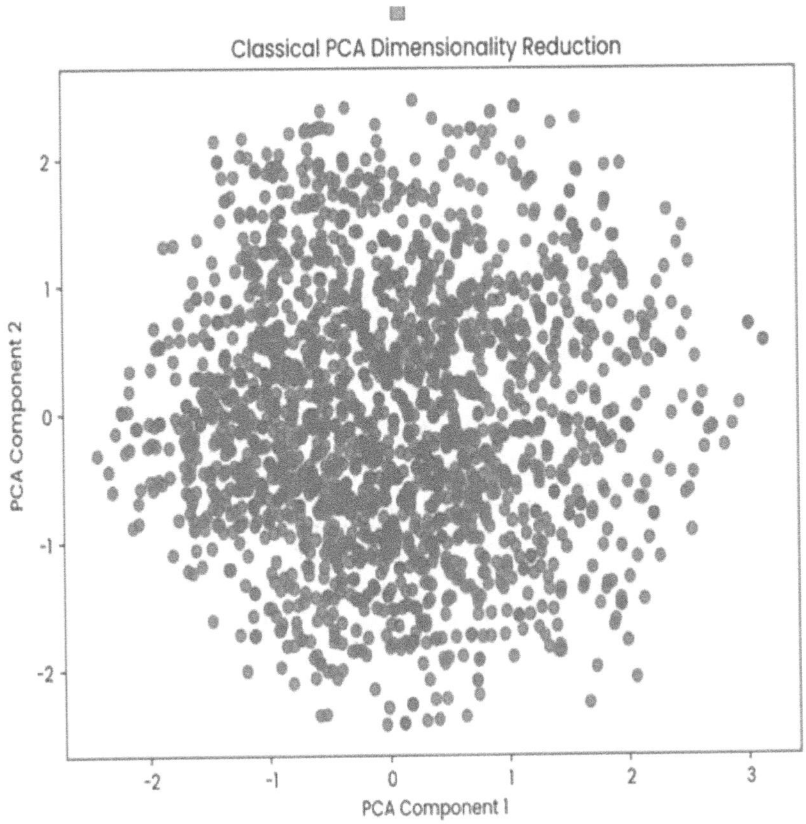

Figure 40.3. PCA for preprocessed food hub dataset.

Source: Author.

3.3. Performance evaluation and comparison

Figures 40.3 and 40.4 depicts the scatter plot for classic PCA and Quantum PCA. The data points in Figure 40.4 are relatively uniformly spread with a compact and circular appearance whereas the data points in Figure 40.3 shows a wider spread where the distribution is more elongated along the first PCA component, which indicates that the first component captures a larger proportion of variance.

The graph in Figure 40.5 visualizes the comparison of the variance ratios between Quantum PCA method and classic PCA. The x-axis represents the principal components and the y-axis represents the proportion of variance explained by each principal component. In classical PCA, depicted by a solid blue line, the explained variance ratio starts at a higher value for the first principal component and slightly declines as moving towards higher components. In Quantum PCA, the explained variance ratio starts lower for the first principal component but significantly rises with higher components. At the second principal component, both PCA and Q-PCA seem to have a similar explained variance ratio (intersection point). The trend suggests that Q-PCA may capture more variance in higher principal components compared to traditional PCA, where variance tends to decrease.

The graph in Figure 40.5 highlights a fundamental difference in how variance is captured between classical and Quantum based PCA approach meaning that Q-PCA is more effective at capturing information in later components making it potentially useful for datasets where classical PCA struggles with capturing variance efficiently.

Based on the graph in Figure 40.6, it can be observed that as PCA contributes significantly for cost of the order and food preparation time, Q-PCA shows the contribution of delivery time to be positive and significant. The feature importance rankings vary between PCA and Q-PCA indicating dimensionality reduction behaviours. This comparison suggests that Q-PCA emphasize different underlying structures in the data compared to traditional PCA. In Figure 40.7 the heatmap shows how the principal components from Classical PCA and Quantum PCA (Q-PCA) relate to each other, highlighting their similarities and differences in dimensionality reduction.

The axes represent four principal components: PCA_1 and PCA_2 from Classical PCA, and Q-PCA_1 and Q-PCA_2 from Quantum PCA. Each cell indicates the correlation coefficient between two components, with red showing a strong positive correlation (1.00) and blue indicating weak or negative correlations. The diagonal elements are expectedly red, as each component

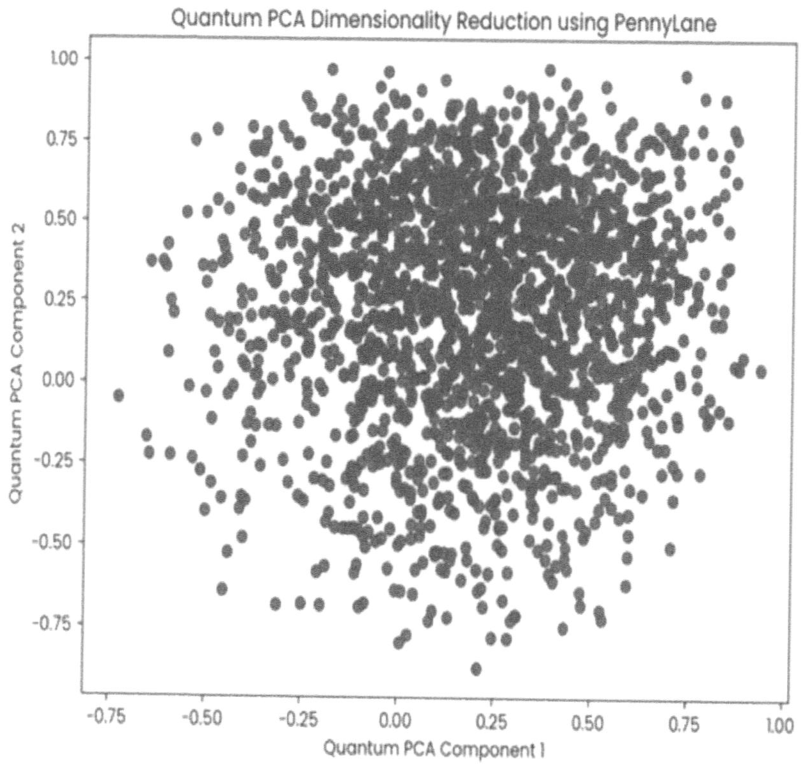

Figure 40.4. Q-PCA for preprocessed food hub dataset.

Source: Author.

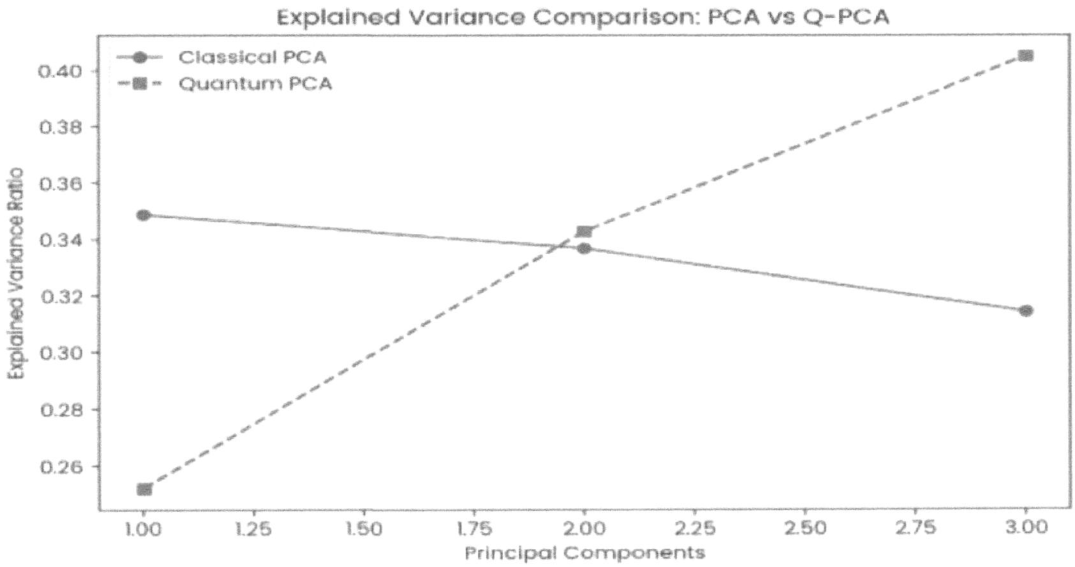

Figure 40.5. Comparison between PCA & QPCA.

Source: Author.

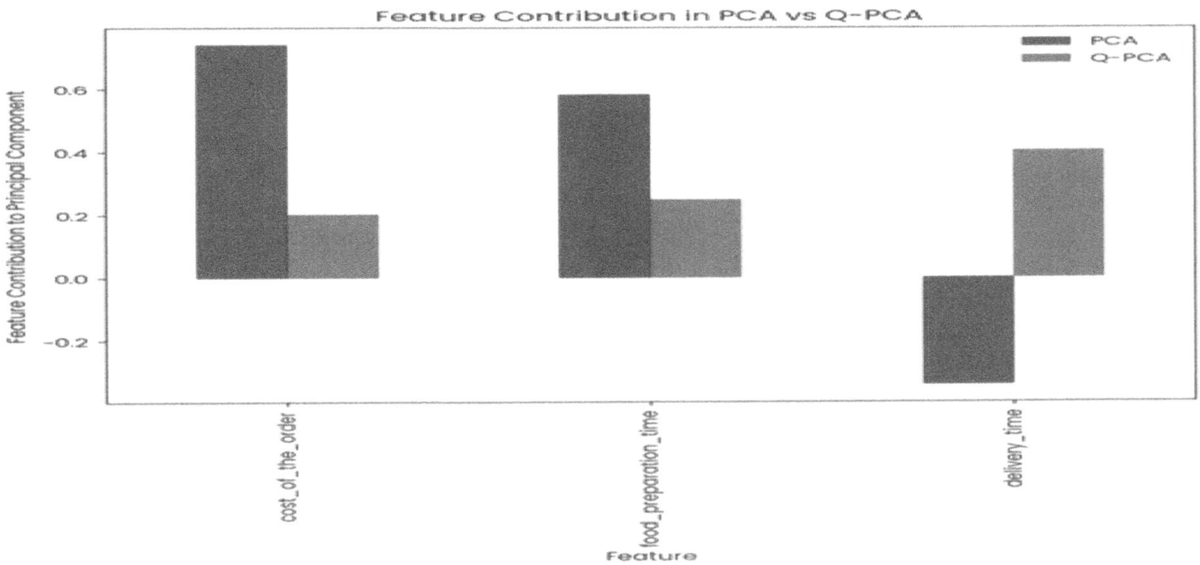

Figure 40.6. Contribution of key features.

Source: Author.

perfectly correlates with itself. For instance, PCA_1 and Q-PCA_1 have a weak negative correlation of -0.29, suggesting they capture different aspects of the data. Similarly, Q-PCA_1 and Q-PCA_2 show almost no correlation, indicating they represent independent variations. Overall, the weak correlations imply that Classical PCA and Q-PCA extract different principal components, with Q-PCA potentially uncovering more complex relationships in the data.

4. Conclusion

The results of this performance study contribute to the intensifying body of research on quantum-enhanced data analytics, reinforcing the transformative part of quantum computing in influencing the future of business decision-making. Business intelligence has grown more complicated in the age of globalization, necessitating data-driven decisions from economists, businesses, and

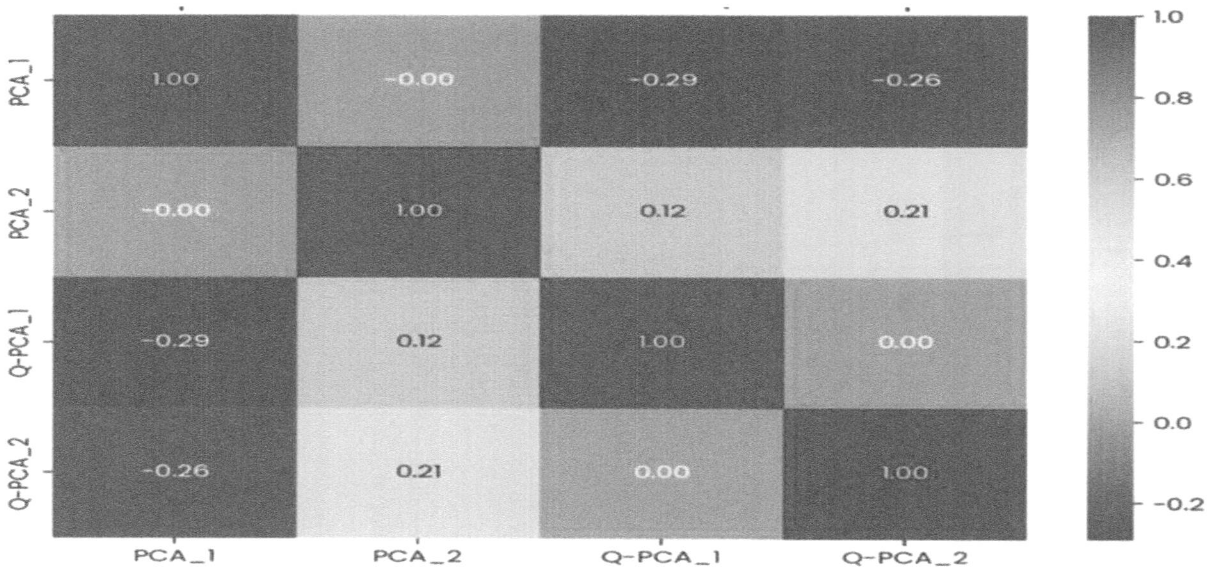

Figure 40.7. Heatmap: Correlation between PCA and Q-PCA components.

Source: Author.

policymakers based on large and constantly changing datasets. When it comes to identifying complex patterns and dependencies in business data, traditional analytical techniques frequently fail. By utilizing statistical methods and computational models, simulation-based performance analysis offers a practical way to assess decision-making procedures in order to overcome this difficulty. Although PCA is still a dependable and effective technique for reducing dimensionality, as quantum hardware develops, QPCA may surpass conventional techniques in high-dimensional data settings. To see possible quantum speedups, future studies can concentrate on applying QPCA to a genuine quantum computer. It massively reduces the processing time and increases the ability to make decisions based on data in global trade. Thus, further research must be directed towards the real-world conversion of quantum computing to ensure the foundation of its use case in food industry analytics

References

[1] Chaudhary, P. S., Khurana, M. R., & Ayalasomayajula, M. (2024). Real-world applications of data analytics, big data, and machine learning. In *Data Analytics and Machine Learning: Navigating the Big Data Landscape* (pp. 237–263). Singapore: Springer Nature Singapore.

[2] Atadoga, A., Obi, O. C., Osasona, F., Onwusinkwue, S., Daraojimba, A. I., & Dawodu, S. O. (2024). Quantum computing in big data analytics: A comprehensive review: Assessing the advancements, challenges, and potential implications of quantum approaches in handling massive data sets. *Computer Science & IT Research Journal*, *5*(2), 498–517.

[3] Manushree, C. N., Putluru, H. D., Khajuria, H., Singh, C., & Nayak, B. P. (2025). Optimizing Feature Selection for Predictive Analytics With Quantum Algorithms. In *The Quantum AI Era of Neuromarketing* (pp. 203–242). IGI Global Scientific Publishing.

[4] Khurana, S., Nene, M., & Nene, M. J. (2024). Quantum machine learning: unraveling a new paradigm in computational intelligence. *Quantum*, *74*(1).

[5] Zhang, S. (2024). Leveraging Machine Learning Algorithms for Predictive Analytics in Big Data: Challenges and Opportunities. *Insights in Computer, Signals and Systems*, *1*(1), 10-70088

[6] Bhasin, N. K., Kadyan, S., Santosh, K., HP, R., Changala, R., & Bala, B. K. (2024, March). Enhancing Quantum Machine Learning Algorithms for Optimized Financial Portfolio Management. In *2024 Third International Conference on Intelligent Techniques in Control, Optimization and Signal Processing (INCOS)* (pp. 1–7). IEEE.

[7] Mounika, M., Reddy, S. P. K., Abhinaya, A., & Akshay, G. (2024, June). Quantum Machine Learning: Bridging the Gap Between Theory and Practice. In *International Conference on Intelligent Computing and Big Data Analytics* (pp. 89–105). Cham: Springer Nature Switzerland.

[8] Das, S. (2024). The Great Dichotomy of Conventional Vs Quantum Machine Learning (Master's thesis, Indian Institute of Information Technology).

[9] Weinberg, A. I., & Faccia, A. (2024). Quantum Algorithms: A New Frontier in Financial Crime Prevention. *arXiv preprint arXiv:2403.18322*.

[10] Wilson, A., & Anwar, M. R. (2024). The Future of Adaptive Machine Learning Algorithms in High-Dimensional Data Processing. International Transactions on Artificial Intelligence, 3(1), 97–107.

41 Investigating the influence of malicious and non-malicious gossiping on organizational politics: A causal study

Syed Muhammad Zubair Azam[1,a], Nidhi Sehgal[1], Rida Sikander Gadit[2], and Nor Zafir Binti Md Salleh[3]

[1]School of Business and Humanities, Curtin University Dubai, United Arab Emirates
[2]School of Business, Iqra University, Karachi, Pakistan
[3]Faculty of Management, Universiti Teknologi Malaysia (UTM), Johor Bahru, Malaysia

Abstract: Gossip is a crucial aspect of workplace interactions, yet its impact on organizational dynamics like office politics remains a subject of debate. This study explores the perceived image of gossipers at workplace and examines the influence of malicious and non-malicious gossiping on organizational politics in the banking and real-estate industry of United Arab Emirates. The causal research aims at investigating the influence of malicious and non-malicious gossiping on organizational politics. Data has been collected from 150 employees working in banking and real-estate industry using snowball sampling and further analysed using descriptive and inferential techniques. The results of the study revealed that while non-malicious gossiping has a minimal impact on organizational politics, the presence of malicious gossiping significantly amplifies political behaviour in the workplace, overshadowing any influence of non-malicious gossip. The study explores managerial implications and provides strategic and tactical recommendations to enhance the positive effects of non-malicious gossip, mitigate malicious gossip tendencies, and reduce the adverse impact of organizational politics on key workplace dynamics.

Keywords: Banking industry, gossiping, malicious gossiping, non-malicious gossiping, organizational politics, real estate industry, United Arab Emirate

1. Introduction

Human behaviour is driven by four key desires—acquisitiveness, rivalry, vanity, and the love of power—while also being fuelled by a fundamental craving for influence and control [1] The greater our ability to influence others, the more powerful we feel, and this desire for power and influence persists across all settings, including groups, organizations, societies, and nations [1]. Individuals can gain power through various sources, for example, by attaining higher positions and designations, by acquiring knowledge to be more influential, by building relationships and networks of influential people, by imposing sanctions on others, by threatening and punishing others [2]. However, one of the most significant ways of acquiring power and gaining influence is through building relationships and networks of people and in turn using these to accumulate other types of power [3, 4].

In the organizational context, politics is defined as "intentional behaviours or actions that promote or protect one's self-interest at the expense of others or organizational goals in the workplace" [5]. It also refers to "a variety of activities associated with the use of tactics to influence or improve personal or organizational interests" [6]. Often, these activities could be beyond the formal role of employees. Organizational politics, although inevitable and important for survival and growth in organizations [3], is considered undesirable workplace behaviour [7, 4]. A recent survey conducted by Insight Global revealed that 85% of employees prefer no politics at workplace [8]. Similarly, 74% of employees think politics increases tension at workplace and 35% show inclination of reporting political behaviour to HR department [8].

Gossips have been defined as an informal exchange of information about other individuals who are not present at the scene [9]. According to the social interaction theory, gossiping is a social behaviour which people adopt

[a]Zubairazam6@gmail.com

DOI: 10.1201/9781003778905-41

to spread information about others [10, 11]. People exercise politics through various means especially through gossips. Human beings have the tendency to be keenly interested in discussing stories about individuals, objects, and situations [12]. Researchers have found that 60–65% of daily conversations among individuals are about other individuals who are absent at the moment [13, 14]. Gossips are categorized as malicious and non-malicious gossips which are further divided into Job-Related gossips and non-Job-related gossips. Malicious gossips intend to harm someone's trust, reputation, character, status or position, whereas non-malicious gossiping is something which doesn't cause any harm to individuals, or an organization and they can even create a positive image of the person who is being discussed in gossips [15].

The general perception about gossiping is that it is of malicious nature, most of the times, intended to cause reputational damage to individuals and organisations [16], thus developing a negative perception and distaste about people who are involved in gossiping and the act of gossiping itself [17]. It is found that 90% of the employees are involved in the malicious as well as non-malicious gossips about others [9]. Furthermore, males and females are involved in gossips equally and there are no gender-based differences [18]. Gossips can often lead to negatives consequences for organizations [18, 19]. Employees tend to distrust each other, diverts their attention from important projects and may slow down the progress and eventually delay the projects resulting into a decline in morale of employees [15]. It has been found that organizational politics intensifies as employees engage in gossiping behaviour, with both malicious and non-malicious gossip serving as powerful networking tools to achieve personal or professional goals [12].

While extensive research has examined the relationship between workplace gossip and various organizational factors such as productivity, satisfaction, and employee turnover, gaps remain in understanding its nuanced impact on organizational politics. Specifically, there is limited insight into how malicious gossip influences negative political behaviour and whether prosocial gossip fosters positive politics. Existing studies highlight both the constructive and detrimental aspects of gossip, yet misconceptions persist, often equating gossip and organizational politics with negativity. This study aims to bridge this gap by exploring the perception of gossipers and assessing the influence of gossiping on workplace political dynamics.

This research aligns closely with building a sustainable workforce and discusses the "people" aspect of the triple bottom line. By exploring gossiping and office politics tendencies of employees, the study highlights its significant effect on employee morale, organizational culture, and collaborative environment. Understanding these effects is crucial for fostering a healthy organizational environment that supports sustainability and innovation. The findings offer valuable insights into creating a positive, collaborative culture that ensures long-term employee well-being and contributes to a sustainable, thriving workplace.

2. Research Objectives, Questions and Hypotheses

The primary objectives of this study are: (i) to evaluate the perceived image of individuals who engage in workplace gossip, irrespective of the nature of the gossip, and (ii) to analyse the impact of malicious and non-malicious gossiping on organizational politics (Figure 41.1).

To achieve these objectives, the study seeks to address the following research questions:

RQ1: How are individuals who engage in workplace gossip perceived?

RQ2: How do different types of gossip influence organizational politics?

In order to test the causal relationship between workplace gossips and organizational politics, the following hypothesis have been formed

H1: Non-Malicious gossiping among employees increases organizational politics.

H2: Malicious gossiping among employees increases organizational politics.

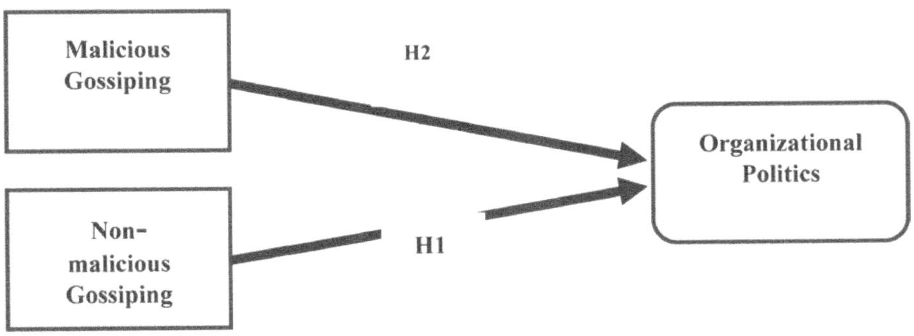

Figure 41.1. Conceptual framework.

Source: Author.

3. Research Methodology

The present study is quantitative in nature. Date was collected from 150 respondents through a survey. The questionnaire consists of close-ended questions measuring study variables on a Likert-scale The respondents were selected from banking and real-estate industry using snowball sampling. Data has been analysed using various descriptive, inferential, and predictive analytics techniques Over 200 questionnaires were distributed in both sectors and a total of 161 responses were received. Out of these, 150 responses were to be complete in all respects with a response rate of 75%. Out of these, 76 respondents were from banking sector while 74 were from the real estate sector, as given in Figure 41.4. Moreover, the sample profile is given in Figure 41.2. Hierarchical regression has been used to test the causal hypotheses. Descriptive analysis was conducted utilizing frequency distributions, mean comparisons, and t-tests (Figures 41.2–41.9).

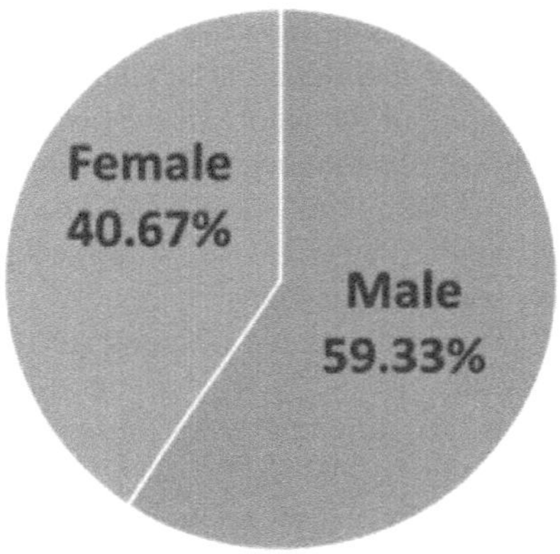

Figure 41.2. Gender-wise distribution of respondents.

Source: Author.

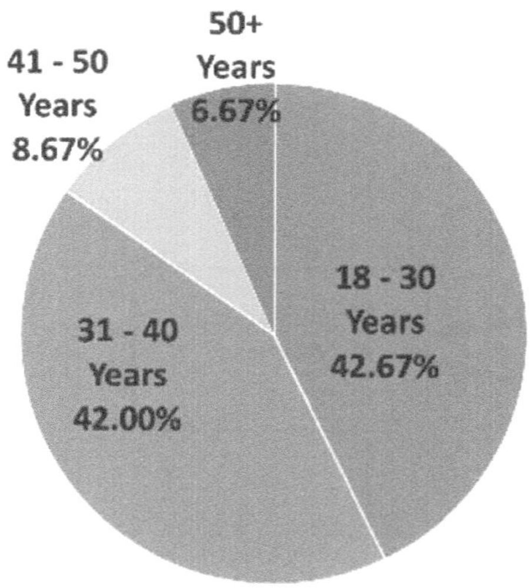

Figure 41.3. Age-wise distribution of respondents.

Source: Author.

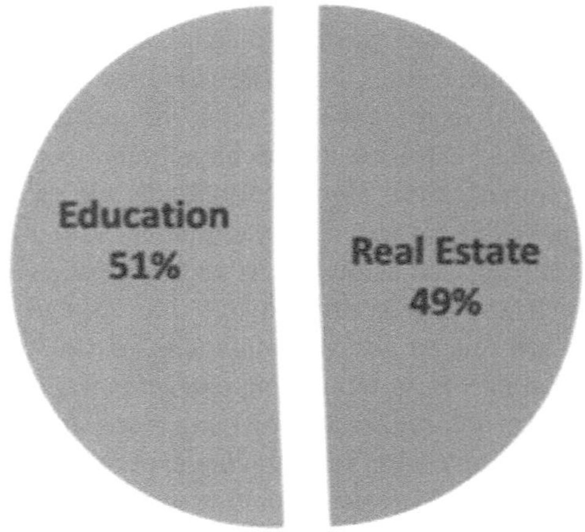

Figure 41.4. Industry-wide distribution of respondents.

Source: Author.

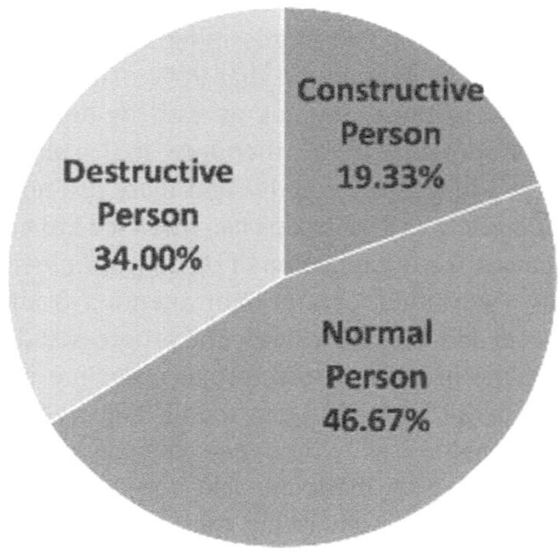

Figure 41.5. Perceived image of the Gossipers.

Source: Author.

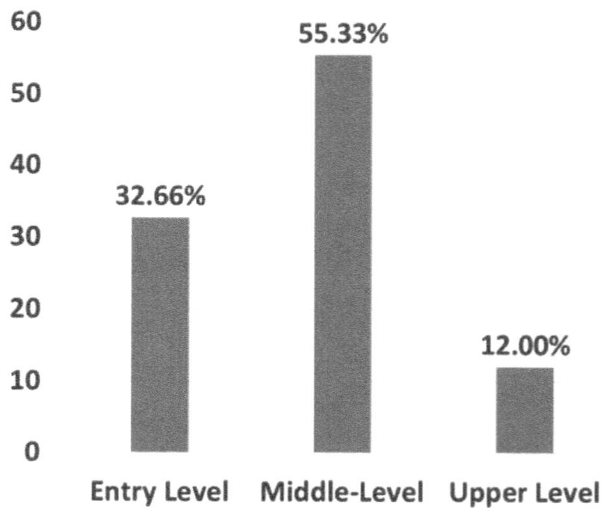

Figure 41.6. Distribution of respondents according to level of management.

Source: Author.

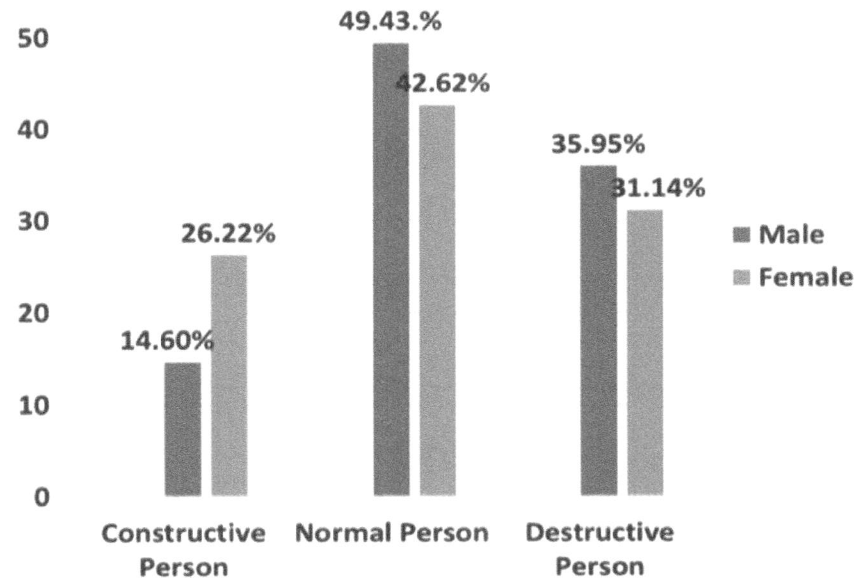

Figure 41.7. Image of the gossipers as perceived by males and females.

Source: Author.

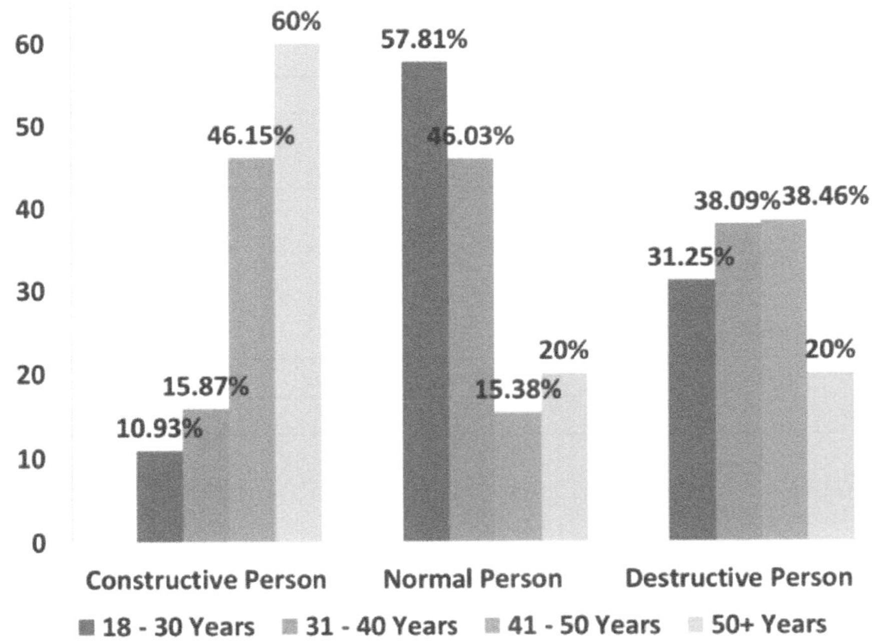

Figure 41.8. Image of the gossipers as perceived by respondents of different age groups.

Source: Author.

4. Findings and Conclusions

The hierarchical regression analysis results (Table 41.1) indicate that malicious and non-malicious gossiping significantly predict organizational politics. As shown in Table 41.1, in Model 1, only non-malicious gossip was included as a predictor, explaining 5.6% of the variance ($R^2 = 0.056$, $p = 0.004$), suggesting a modest but significant effect on organizational politics. However, when malicious gossip was added in Model 2, the explanatory power increased substantially to 40.4% ($R^2 = 0.404$, $p < 0.001$), indicating a strong effect on organizational politics. The coefficients in Table 41.2 show that in Model 1, non-malicious gossip had a significant positive effect ($\beta = 0.269$, $p = 0.004$). In Model 2, its effect weakened and became non-significant ($\beta = 0.119$, $p = 0.112$), while malicious gossip had a strong positive impact ($\beta = 0.448$, $p < 0.001$).

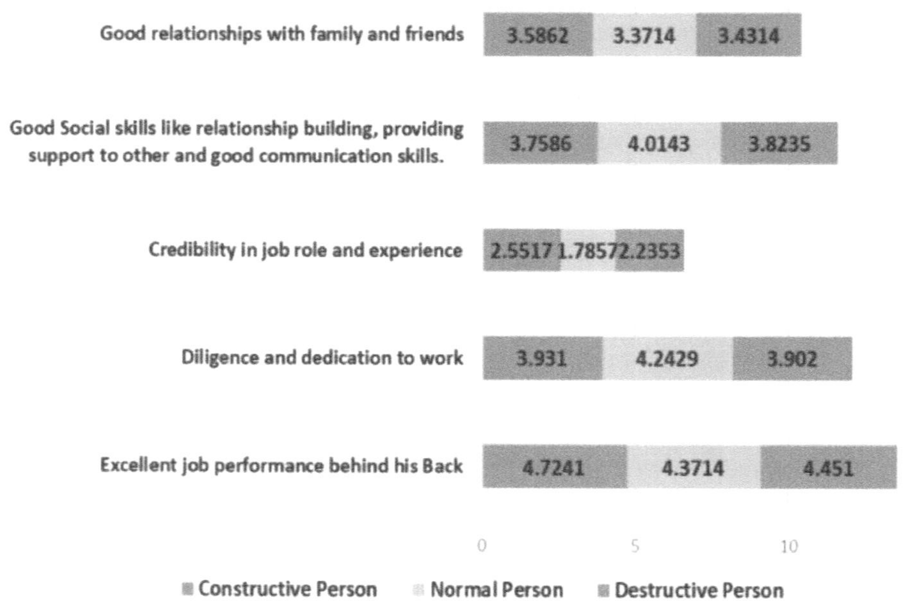

Figure 41.9. Image of the gossipers involved in non-malicious gossiping (Means Difference).
Source: Author.

Table 41.1. Regression model summary

Model	*R*	R^2	*Adjusted* R^2	*R2 Change*	*F*	*F Change*	*P*
1	.236[a]	*0.056*	0.05	0.056	8.763	8.763	0.004
2	.635[b]	0.404	0.396	0.348	49.761	85.742	.000

[a]Predictors: (Constant), Non-Malicious Gossips
[b]Predictors: (Constant), Non-Malicious Gossips, Malicious Gossips
Source: Author.

Table 41.2. Regression coefficients

Model P		*Unstandardized Coefficient*	*Standardized Coefficient*		
		P	*t*	*P*	
1	(Constant)	2.258		6.440	0.000
	Non-Malicious Gossips	0.268	0.236	2.960	0.003
2	(Constant)	1.534		5.284	0.000
	Non-Malicious Gossips	0.118	0.104	1.599	0.111
	Malicious Gossips	0.447	0.604	9.259	0.000

[a]Organizational Politics
Source: Author.

This suggests that malicious gossip is a much stronger predictor of organizational politics than non-malicious gossip, which loses significance when both variables are considered together. Therefore, H1 and H2 are both accepted when the impact of malicious and non-malicious gossiping on organizational politics is analysed in isolation, however, effect of non-malicious gossip on organizational politics becomes insignificant when the impact of gossiping types on organizational politics is analysed in a unified model. Moreover, the findings indicate that organizational politics slightly increases when employees engage in non-malicious gossip (e.g., expressing appreciation for colleagues). However, when malicious gossip (e.g., discussions about potential scandals) is introduced, organizational politics rises significantly, while the influence of non-malicious gossip becomes negligible. This suggests that while positive gossip may have a minor impact, malicious gossip is a key driver of heightened political behaviour in the workplace (Figures 41.10 and 41.11).

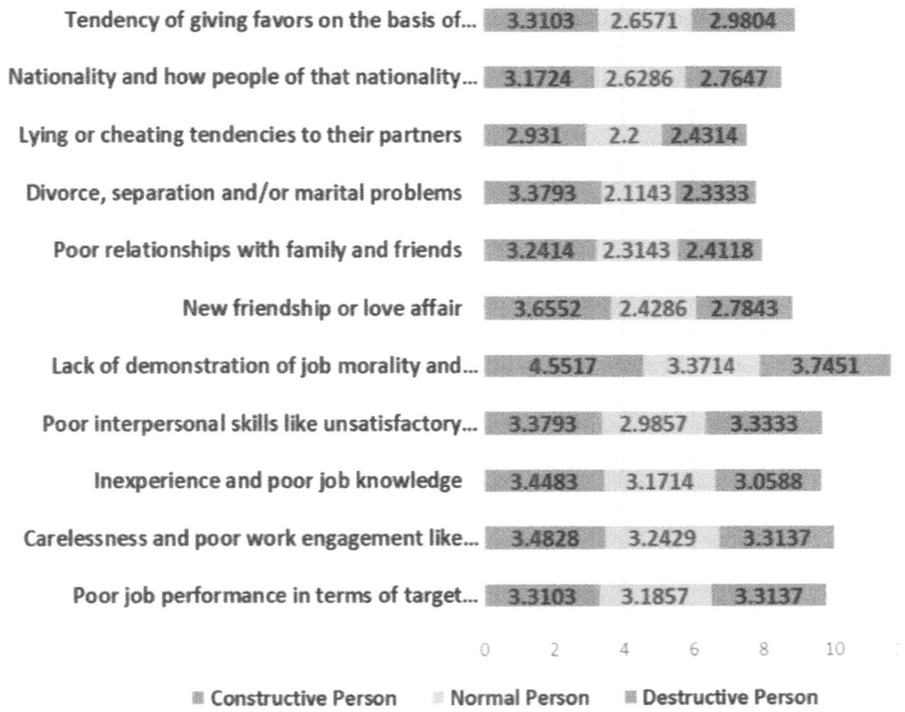

Figure 41.10. Image of the gossipers involved in malicious gossiping (Means Difference).

Source: Author.

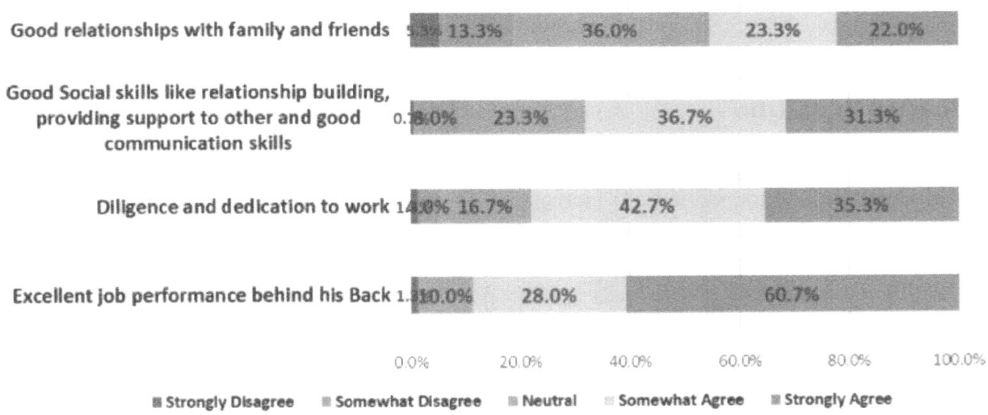

Figure 41.11. Respondents involvement in non-malicious gossiping.

Source: Author.

The study also found that both men and women exhibit an equal tendency to engage in workplace gossip ($p>0.05$, for gender-based mean differences), challenging common stereotypes about gender differences in gossiping behaviour. Additionally, significant industry-specific variations were observed. Employees in the real estate sector demonstrated a stronger inclination to appreciate their colleagues' professional dedication ($p<0.05$, $\bar{X}$(real estate)=4.27, $\bar{X}$(banking)=3.87), but question credibility in job role and experience ($p<0.05$, $\bar{X}$(real estate)=1.78, $\bar{X}$(banking)=2.38), however, acknowledge relationship-building efforts ($p<0.05$, $\bar{X}$(real estate)=4.14, $\bar{X}$(banking)=3.67). Furthermore, these mean differences indicate that banking sector employees were more likely to engage in discussions on job credibility, professional experience, workplace ethics, and poor job performance. Furthermore, favouritism ($p<0.05$, $\bar{X}$(real estate)=3.26, $\bar{X}$(banking)=4.05), blame-shifting ($p<0.05$, $\bar{X}$(real estate)=2.85, $\bar{X}$(banking)=3.38), and flattery ($p<0.05$, $\bar{X}$(real estate)=3.26, $\bar{X}$(banking)=4.05) were found to be more prevalent in the banking sector compared to real estate, suggesting a more politically charged work environment. Additionally, real estate professionals displayed greater openness in expressing critical views, even when challenging established industry norms and policies. Lastly, organizational politics appeared to have a stronger influence on job turnover in the banking sector ($p<0.05$, $\bar{X}$ (real estate) =2.82, $\bar{X}$(banking)=3.22), with employees more likely to leave their jobs due to political manoeuvring and workplace tensions. These findings highlight the need for industry-specific strategies to manage workplace interactions and mitigate the negative effects of gossip and organizational politics.

These differences may be prevalent because the banking industry is highly regulated, structured, and performance driven [19]. Employees work in a formal, hierarchical setting where job roles are clearly defined [20]. This environment fosters competition, making employees more prone to engaging in political behaviour such as favouritism, blame-shifting, and flattery to secure promotions or recognition. On the other hand, the real estate industry operates in a more dynamic and relationship-driven environment [21]. Success in this field often depends on networking, client relationships, and collaboration rather than rigid hierarchical structures. Employees in real estate are more likely to appreciate and support their colleagues, as teamwork and relationship-building are crucial to business success.

5. Research Implications

The study discusses managerial implications as well as offers strategic and tactical recommendations to increase the positive effects of non-malicious gossiping, decrease the malicious gossiping tendencies, and negative consequences of organizational politics.

Organisations in both banking and real estate sector need to adopt effective approach in managing workplace gossips and organizational politics among employees to create a collaborative and non-toxic work environment. Since malicious gossip has a strong influence on organizational politics, companies should create a culture of transparency and trust where open communication is encouraged [15, 20], reducing the need for speculation and harmful discussions [18]. Clear policies on ethical workplace behaviour can help set boundaries on negative gossip while allowing space for constructive conversations that strengthen team relationships [16, 22].

As both men and women engage in gossip equally [13], training programs should focus on addressing gossip as a workplace behaviour rather than associating it with gender [11, 14]. Additionally, industry-specific strategies can help tackle workplace politics effectively. In the real estate sector, where employees show a stronger tendency to appreciate colleagues and build relationships, organizations can nurture this positive atmosphere by promoting teamwork and peer recognition initiatives [5, 6]. Meanwhile, in the banking sector, where discussions around job performance, credibility, and ethics are more common, companies should implement fair evaluation systems and transparent performance feedback to prevent speculation and misinformation [4]. Since favouritism, blame-shifting, and flattery are more prevalent in banking, leadership should emphasize merit-based recognition and accountability to minimize political manoeuvring [23].

Encouraging ethical leadership and promoting fairness in decision-making can help reduce workplace tensions [2]. Moreover, as indicated in the findings of this study, real estate professionals tend to be more open about industry norms, companies in this sector should provide structured platforms for employees to share insights and constructive feedback [7, 24].

Finally, given that employees in the banking sector are more likely to leave due to workplace politics, organizations must prioritize retention strategies. Building a workplace culture that values ethical leadership, fair career progression, and transparent decision-making can help reduce political tensions and improve employee satisfaction [24]. By implementing these measures, organizations can create a more inclusive, fair, and productive work environment for their employees.

References

[1] Russell, B. (1950). What Desires Are Politically Important? *NobelPrize.Org. https://www.nobelprize.org/prizes/literature/1950/russell/lecture/.*

[2] Robbins, S. P., & Judge, T. A. (2024). *Organizational Behavior*. 19th edition. Hoboken, NJ: Pearson.

[3] Brandon, R., & Marty, S. (2004). *Survival of the Savvy: High-Integrity Political Tactics for Career and Company Success. 1st ed.* Free Press.

[4] Nazir, Sajjad, S. K., Muhammad, A. A., & Nausheen, S. (2023). The Paradoxical Effect of Perceived Organizational Politics on Employees Motivation: The Mediation Role of Hostility and Moderating Role of Organizational Injustice. *Evidence-Based HRM: A Global Forum for Empirical Scholarship, 12*(1), 87–111. *https://doi.org/10.1108/EBHRM-05-2022-0130.*

[5] Goo, W., Choi, Y., & Choi, W. (2022). 'Coworkers' Organizational Citizenship Behaviors and Employees' Work Attitudes: The Moderating Roles of Perceptions of Organizational Politics and Task Interdependence'. *Journal of Management & Organization, 28*(5), 1011–1035. *https://doi.org/10.1017/jmo.2019.26.*

[6] Jarrett, M. (April, 2017). The 4 Types of Organizational Politics. *Harvard Business Review*.

[7] Meisler, G. (2021). Emotional Intelligence as an Antidote to the Negative Implications of Perceived Managerial Supplication: A Sectorial Comparison. *Personnel Review, 50*(2), 498–514. *https://doi.org/10.1108/PR-10-2019-0571.*

[8] Glynn, P. (November 2022). 85% of Employees Prefer No Politics at Work, Survey Finds. *Insight Global* (blog). *https://insightglobal.com/news/politics-at-work-survey/.*

[9] Ellwardt, L., Giuseppe (Joe) Labianca, & Wittek, R. (2012). Who Are the Objects of Positive and Negative Gossip at Work? A Social Network Perspective on Workplace Gossip. *Social Networks, 34*(2), 193–205. *https://doi.org/10.1016/j.socnet.2011.11.003.*

[10] Mills, C. (2010). Experiencing Gossip: The Foundations for a Theory of Embedded Organizational Gossip. *Group & Organization Management, 35*(2), 213–40. *https://doi.org/10.1177/1059601109360392.*

[11] Foster, E. K. (2004). Research on Gossip: Taxonomy, Methods, and Future Directions. *Review of General Psychology, 8*(2), 78–99. *https://doi.org/10.1037/1089-2680.8.2.78.*

[12] Tassiello, V., Lombardi, S., & Costabile, M. (March, 2018). Are We Truly Wicked When Gossiping at Work? The Role of Valence, Interpersonal Closeness and Social Awareness. *Journal of Business Research, 84*, 41–49. *https://doi.org/10.1016/j.jbusres.2017.11.013.*

[13] Cole, J., & Dalton, J. (2009). *Idle Womens' Talk? Gender and Gossip.* In University of Kent, Kent, UK.

[14] Beersma, B., & Van Kleef, G. A. (2012). Why People Gossip: An Empirical Analysis of Social Motives, Antecedents, and Consequences. *Journal of Applied Social Psychology, 42*(11), 2640–2670. *https://doi.org/10.1111/j.1559-1816.2012.00956.x.*

[15] Kuo, C.-C., Chang, K., Quinton, S., Lu, C.-Y., & Lee, I. (2015). Gossip in the Workplace and the Implications for HR Management: A Study of Gossip and Its Relationship to Employee Cynicism. *The International Journal of Human Resource Management, 26*(18), 2288–2307. *https://doi.org/10.1080/09585192.2014.985329.*

[16] Wu, X., Ho Kwong Kwan, Long-Zeng Wu, & Ma, J. (2018). The Effect of Workplace Negative Gossip on Employee Proactive Behavior in China: The Moderating Role of Traditionality. *Journal of Business Ethics, 148*(4), 801–815. *https://doi.org/10.1007/s10551-015-3006-5*

[17] Dores, C., Terence, D., & Annika, S. (2021). An Integrative Definition and Framework to Study Gossip. *Group & Organization Management, 46*(2), 252–285. *https://doi.org/10.1177/1059601121992887.*

[18] Grosser, T. J., Lopez-Kidwell, V., Giuseppe (Joe) Labianca, & Ellwardt, L. (2012). Hearing It through the Grapevine: Positive and Negative Workplace Gossip. *Organizational Dynamics, 41*(1), 52–61. *https://doi.org/10.1016/j.orgdyn.2011.12.007.*

[19] Hancock, M. (2012). Crisis Forces Regulation Refocus in UAE. 15 February 2012. *https://www.thebanker.com/content/de18655e-c636-52be-b91e-b89353d5e4b6.*

[20] Faibishenko, A., & Núñez-Gallego, J. (2021). The Future of Banking Jobs: A Sector in Transformation. *Funcas. https://www.funcas.es/wp-content/uploads/2021/06/Banking-Jobs-in-transition-WEB-1.pdf.*

[21] Mikati, B., Sfeir, R., & Awad, Z. (n.d.). Building Deeper Customer Relationships in Real Estate. *Strategy& Middle East*. Accessed 3 March 2025. *https://www.strategyand.pwc.com/m1/en/strategic-foresight/sector-strategies/real-estate/deepercustomerrelationships.html*

[22] Thanh, T. (2016). *The Relationship between Political Behavior and Team Effectiveness in Management Teams*. Master Thesis, University of Oslo.

[23] Toegel, G., & Barsoux, J.-L. (2024). Stop Playing Favorites. *Harvard Business Review. https://hbr.org/2024/07/stop-playing-favorites.*

[24] Barker, S., Brenda A., & Michael R. M. (2024). Designing the Collaborative Organization: A Framework for How Collaborative Work, Relationships, and Behaviors Generate Collaborative Capacity. *The Journal of Applied Behavioral Science, 60*(1), 149–193. *https://doi.org/10.1177/00218863221106245*

42 Integrating family support into employee engagement models: A conceptual framework for a sustainable and resilient workforce

Mahwish Anjam[1,a], Premila Koppalakrishnan[2], and Marryam Yasir[3]

[1]School of Business and Humanities, Curtin University Dubai, UAE
[2]Department of Information System Management, DRBCCC Hindu College, Chennai, India
[3]School of Business and Humanities, Curtin University Dubai, UAE

Abstract: Workplace support mechanisms have long been emphasized in employee engagement models, yet family support has remained an underexplored concept in in organizational behaviour literature. The changing dynamics of workplace driven by theological advancement, global shift to remote work during and after COVID-19 pandemic, and changing employee expectations has reshaped workplace dynamics, emphasizing the significance of family support in shaping employee performance and engagement. This paper addresses this gap by conceptualizing family support as a critical resource critically contributing to employee engagement, and overall satisfaction and resilience of the workforce. Through an extensive literature review and a multi-theoretical lens, including the Conservation of Resources Theory, Social Exchange Theory, Work-Family Enrichment Theory, Boundary Theory, and the Job Demands-Resources Model, this study proposes a comprehensive theoretical framework that positions family support as a fundamental factor influencing employee outcomes. The paper offers theoretical and practical insights for organizations seeking to integrate family-supportive policies into their management strategies.

Keywords: Employee engagement, family support, work-family enrichment, conservation of resources theory, social exchange theory, boundary theory, job demands-resources model

1. Introduction

In recent times the workplace had undergone radical transformation in work arrangements, driven by technological advancements, event like COVID 19, and shift in employee expectations, organizations are rethinking and redesigning the ways to engage with the workforce. Hybrid and flexible work models have become permanent fixtures in modern workplaces [1, 2]. While workplace support has been given much attention, an external, yet critical concept of home environment and family support has also emerged in shaping employee engagement and performance especially in post covid remote arrangements [3, 4]. Traditionally, employee engagement and performance have been studied through workplace factors such as leadership, job autonomy, and organizational culture [5, 6]. However, the increasing overlap between work and family responsibilities necessitates a broader perspective, recognizing family support as an integral component of employee success. Family support encompasses emotional, instrumental, and informational assistance provided by family members, which enables employees to manage work responsibilities more effectively [7, 4].

Despite its potential impact, family support remains an under examined construct in organizational behaviour literature. This paper aims to fill this gap by presenting a conceptual framework that positions family support as a significant determinant of employee engagement and performance in the post-remote work era. By integrating multiple theoretical perspectives, this study develops a logical transition that explains how family support fits into the broader work-family interface and contributes to employee outcomes.

2. Literature Review

Employee performance is a multifaceted construct comprising both task performance (efficiency and goal attainment) and contextual performance (collaboration,

[a]mahwishanjum@hotmail.com

DOI: 10.1201/9781003778905-42

innovation, and adaptability) [8]. Historically, employee engagement and performance have been studied in light of workplace factors such as leadership, job autonomy, and organizational culture [5]. However, recent research suggests that other factors, especially family support, play a significant role in improving both task and contextual performance [9]. Family support is particularly critical in the post-remote work era, where employees face challenges while managing work and personal responsibilities amidst blurred boundaries between work and home [10]. Employees having strong family support are more likely to experience less stress levels, increased resilience, and improved job satisfaction, all of which directly contribute to improved work performance [2, 11]. By considering family support as a useful resource within existing employee performance models, this paper offers a conceptual framework for understanding how family support mechanisms can enhance organizational outcomes.

2.1. Employee engagement and performance in the post-remote work era

Employee engagement refers to a psychological state characterized by vigor, dedication, and absorption in one's work [12]. High engagement levels correlate with enhanced productivity, commitment, and job satisfaction, making it a central concern for organizations [13]. Employee performance, on the other hand, includes both task performance (efficiency and goal attainment) and contextual performance (collaboration, innovation, and adaptability) [8]. While workplace support mechanism[s such as leadership, job design, and organizational culture have been linked to engagement and performance [14], recent research suggests that external factors, including social and family support, play an equally critical role [9]. However, current models of engagement and performance do not explicitly account for family support, creating a gap in the literature that this paper seeks to address.

2.2. Work-family interface: conflict vs. enrichment

The work-family interface has traditionally been examined through two competing perspectives: (a) Work-Family Conflict: Work and family roles are often seen as competing demands, leading to stress, burnout, and reduced job satisfaction [15]. Work-related stressors, coupled with low family support, exacerbate work-family conflict, negatively impacting engagement and performance [1]. (b) Work-Family Enrichment: In contrast, work-family enrichment theory posits that experiences in one domain can positively transfer to another [16]. Family support provides psychological stability, encouragement, and practical assistance, enabling employees to perform better at work.

The dominance of work-family conflict in past research has overshadowed the potential benefits of family support. In the post-remote work era, where work-life boundaries are increasingly fluid, family support should be considered a resource rather than a hindrance.

2.3. Family support as a critical resource for employee success

Family support can be categorized into three key dimensions[17]: (a) Emotional Support: Encouragement, reassurance, and understanding from family members help reduce workplace stress and enhance job engagement, (b) Instrumental Support: Assistance with household responsibilities, childcare, and financial stability allows employees to focus on work commitments, and (c) Informational Support: Guidance, advice, and constructive feedback from family members contribute to better decision-making and problem-solving at work.

While existing literature and models of employee engagement and performance have extensive focus on workplace resources such as leadership, organizational culture, and job design [14], family support has only been considered as an ancillary factor[7]. This oversight can be significant especially in post-remote work era, where work-life boundaries have become increasingly blurred [10]. Previous research has highlighted work-family conflict, which views work and family roles as employee's competing demands, leading to increased stress and decreased job satisfaction [15]. However, in recent research works, work-family enrichment theories have suggested the positive impact that family support can have on work deliverables [16]. In this regard, family support offers a unique position: while workplace related variables might often be constrained by organizational policies and structures, family support promises psychological and practical resources to employees that are beyond the work environment yet equally relevant. This paper therefore hypothesis that family support should be treated as a critical variable, not only countering the negative effects of work-family conflict but also improving work-family enrichment, thereby improving employee performance [16]. Employees who receive strong family support experience lower stress levels, greater resilience, and higher job satisfaction [2]. However, theoretical integration of family support within existing employee performance models remains insufficient, necessitating the development of a new conceptual framework.

3. Theoretical Framework

To systematically position family support within employee engagement and performance research, this paper integrates multiple theoretical perspectives into a unified framework.

Hobfoll's Conservation of Resources Theory [18] suggests that individuals strive to acquire, retain, and protect valuable resources, including social and emotional support. Employees with strong family support are better equipped to cope with workplace demands, leading to higher engagement and improved performance [11]. Family support acts as a protective resource, buffering against stress and preventing burnout. Similarly Blau's Social Exchange Theory [19] posits that relationships are based on reciprocity. Employees who receive consistent family support may feel obligated to reciprocate through greater dedication and performance at work. This mutual reinforcement enhances both engagement and job effectiveness. Greenhaus and Powell's Work-Family Enrichment Theory [16] explains that resources gained in the family domain positively influence work outcomes. Employees supported by their families experience higher psychological well-being, reduced stress, and improved engagement, leading to better job performance. Clark's Boundary Theory [20] suggests that individuals actively manage work and personal life boundaries. In the post-remote work era, these boundaries have become increasingly blurred. Family support helps employees establish functional boundaries, reducing work-family conflict and fostering greater job focus and productivity. The JD-R Model [5] categorizes work characteristics into job demands (workload, stress, and time pressure) and job resources (autonomy, leadership, and workplace support). Traditionally, family support has not been explicitly considered as a job resource. However, this paper argues that family support serves as an external resource, mitigating job demands and enhancing employee engagement and performance (Table 42.1).

Table 42.1. Theoretical framework supporting the concept of family support in employee performance and engagement literature

Dimension	*Key Insights*	*Supporting Theories*	*Implications for Employee Performance and Engagement*
Work-Family Interface	Family support reduces work-family conflict and enhances work-family enrichment, shifting the focus from stress to resourcefulness.	• Work-Family Conflict (Greenhaus & Beutell, 1985) • Work-Family Enrichment (Greenhaus & Powell, 2006)	Employees with family support experience reduced stress, higher resilience, and improved work outcomes.
Emotional Support	Encouragement, reassurance, and understanding from family help alleviate workplace stress and build engagement.	• Conservation of Resources Theory (Hobfoll, 1989) • Work-Family Enrichment (Greenhaus & Powell, 2006)	Boosts psychological well-being, resulting in higher engagement and job satisfaction.
Instrumental Support	Assistance with household responsibilities, childcare, and finances allows employees to focus better on work.	• JD-R Model (Bakker & Demerouti, 2007) • Boundary Theory (Clark, 2000)	Frees up mental and physical resources, leading to greater task efficiency and contextual performance.
Informational Support	Family-provided guidance and constructive feedback enhance problem-solving and decision-making capabilities at work.	• Social Exchange Theory (Blau, 1964) • Conservation of Resources Theory (Hobfoll, 1989)	Facilitates innovation, adaptability, and enhanced cognitive engagement.
Stress Buffering	Family support acts as a protective resource, preventing burnout and enabling better coping with job demands.	• Conservation of Resources Theory (Hobfoll, 1989) • JD-R Model (Bakker & Demerouti, 2007)	Reduces absenteeism and enhances long-term commitment to organizational goals.
Reciprocity Dynamics	Social exchange mechanisms encourage employees to reciprocate family support with increased dedication to their work.	• Social Exchange Theory (Blau, 1964)	Strengthens employee loyalty, motivation, and overall performance.
Blurring Boundaries	Post-remote work scenarios blur work-life boundaries, making family support critical in maintaining functional separations.	• Boundary Theory (Clark, 2000) • Work-Family Enrichment (Greenhaus & Powell, 2006)	Enhances work-life balance, fostering greater focus and reduced conflict in hybrid work settings.
Theoretical Integration	Family support has been underexplored in traditional engagement and performance models despite its critical role as a job resource.	• JD-R Model (Bakker & Demerouti, 2007) • Work-Family Enrichment (Greenhaus & Powell, 2006)	Expands existing frameworks, emphasizing family support as an external resource to mitigate job demands.
Practical Application	Organizations can implement family-supportive policies (e.g., flexible work hours, childcare assistance) to improve employee engagement and performance.	• JD-R Model (Bakker & Demerouti, 2007) • Conservation of Resources Theory (Hobfoll, 1989)	Leads to organizational benefits such as higher productivity, employee satisfaction, and reduced turnover.

Source: Author.

This conceptual review paper thus offers to translate the theoretical implications into actionable strategies, organizations must recognize family support as a critical dimension of employee well-being. Initiatives such as flexible work schedules, family-friendly policies, and mental health resources can amplify the benefits of family support. Studies suggest that family-inclusive workplace cultures foster higher employee loyalty, lower turnover rates, and improved organizational performance [1]. By aligning management practices with the principles of work-family enrichment and resource conservation, organizations can cultivate a supportive ecosystem that enhances both individual and organizational outcomes.

4. Discussion

In recent times, the emphasis on employee engagement and performance related research has a predominant focus on concepts like leadership, workplace culture, job roles, and the level of autonomy employees have. However, widespread adoption of remote work during the COVID-19 pandemic, it became evident that a broader range of factors influence how employees approach their work. While employees strive to balance their personal and professional responsibilities in the current work environment, family support in all aspects has become a crucial yet often overlooked factor [10].

Family support is instrumental in reducing work-related stress, especially in remote and hybrid settings, where work and home life often overlap, support and encouragement from family members may significantly reduce the negative impacts of job stress. This idea aligns well with the Conservation of Resources Theory, which states that people try to protect and safeguard resources to deal with stress [18]. Where emotional support, encouragement, and help from family members emerge as a valuable resource that employees can draw upon to manage job stress. Research has already supported the role of emotional, practical, and informational support critical in work-life challenges and stressors to sustain high levels of engagement and productivity [5].

Family support acts as a psychological safety net and emotional support work pressures become overwhelming. For instance, workload-induced fatigue, which can leave a worker drained can be counterbalanced by family support [12]. Additionally, family support in terms of sharing household chores or babysitting, and other house related matters lower the mental load and fatigue, thereby improving concentration at work [10]. Studies suggest such supported employees are less likely to face burn out and are more likely to be resilient, which is reflected in their job performance, overall performance and turnover intentions [3, 11, 13]. In Social Exchange Theory, Blau [19] suggests an insightful perspective on how family support boosts mutual relationships between workers and their employers. The theory recommends people engagement in reciprocal relationships via the exchange of resources. It can hence be inferred that employees who receive strong family support are more likely to manage work stress effectively, are more likely to approach work with a positive mindset, will develop engagement at work, loyalty, and discretionary effort in reciprocity. A satisfied employee is more likely to go above and beyond his formal job duties. Such employees are motivated to contribute to organizational goals, engage in discretionary efforts and demonstrate creativity, which eventually contributes to overall organizational performance [13]. While work -family boundaries and conflict have remained a dominant topic of research, family enrichment theory reinforces the importance of positive transfer of resources between family and work domains [16]. This concept of reciprocity linking from family support promises a strong relationship with organizational success. Furthermore, this exchange dynamics is a two-way process: employees with strong family support are likely to pass the positive energy to their work-life leading to virtuous cycle of engagement which in turn leaves positive influence on both professional and personal boundaries [3]. Employees become more productive and satisfied with work when their family encourages them to work. [16]. When employees deal with problems and develop skills in their family and at home, they transfer skills such as time management, problem-solving, and communication to the workplace. Such skills transfer into the workplace to improve job performance as they help the employee manage work demands more effectively and engage more enthusiastically in their role.

Hence, family support is not only a passive resource but rather a critical influence towards employees' work-related outcomes by improving employees' overall well-being and job performance. Employees experiencing work-family enrichment show higher levels of engagement, participation and commitment, and reduced turnover intentions [10]. Given that talent retention has become a dilemma for the organizations, the concept of family support integrating into employee performance and motivation discourse emerges as a strategic tool in enhancing employee loyalty and long-term success.

Despite family support being promising in shaping employee engagement and performance, it has been an underexplored concept in employee engagement and performance literature. Traditional employee engagement models have overlooked the role of family support interfering with the work-life [14]. Therefore, there is a growing need for researchers, organizations, managers, and policy makers to rethink and redefine their policies and practices to acknowledge and incorporate the importance of family support while managing employee performance.

Many organizations have transitioned to flexi-work arrangements by integrating family leave, childcare plans and other family inclusive policies aiming to foster a supportive environment for employees [11]. There is a further need to recognize family support as a valuable resource contributing to reduced work-family conflict and enhanced work-family enrichment, subsequently leading to improved employee engagement, job satisfaction, and performance.

Leadership also plays a vital role in this transition. Managers who recognize and appreciate the importance of family support are better positioned to assist employees in navigating the intricacies of remote and hybrid work models. Leaders who demonstrate empathy and support for employees' family needs can cultivate a culture of trust and reciprocity that improves employee performance. This strategy not only boosts employee engagement but also contributes to a more positive organizational culture while reducing the likelihood of burnout and disengagement.

5. Conclusion

The growing significance of family support in the post-remote work era calls for a rethinking of traditional engagement and performance models. This paper has presented a conceptual framework that integrates multiple theoretical perspectives – Conservation of Resources Theory, Social Exchange Theory, Work-Family Enrichment Theory, Boundary Theory, and the Job Demands-Resources Model – to position family support as a critical resource for employees in hybrid and remote work environments.

Recognizing family support as a valuable resource not only enhances employee well-being and engagement but also fosters a culture of reciprocity and work-family enrichment that benefits both the individual and the organization. As organizations continue to adapt to the evolving nature of work, integrating family support into organizational practices will be essential for maintaining a motivated, high-performing workforce.

As the significance of family support is evident in shaping employee performance and engagement, future research should focus on several key areas. First, empirical studies are needed to test the theoretical framework presented in this paper, examining the direct and indirect effects of family support on employee engagement, performance, and well-being.

References

[1] Allen, T. D., Herst, D. E. L., Bruck, C. S., & Sutton, M. (2000). Consequences Associated with Work-to-Family Conflict: A Review and Agenda for Future Research. *Journal of Occupational Health Psychology, 5*(2), 278–308. doi:10.1037/1076-8998.5.2.278

[2] Shockley, K. M., & Allen, T. D. (2015). Deciding between work and family: An episodic approach. *Personnel Psychology, 68*(2), 283–318. doi:10.1111/peps.12077

[3] Kossek, E. E., Ruderman, M. N., Braddy, P. W., & Hannum, K. M. (2012). Work-nonwork boundary management profiles: A person-centered approach. *Journal of Vocational Behavior, 81*(1), 112–128. *https://doi.org/10.1016/j.jvb.2012.04.003*

[4] Anjam, M., Bolia, B., & Koppalakrishnan, P. (2025). Employee Engagement in Post-COVID Remote Working Arrangements: Is Family Support as Critical as Supervisory Support? *In International Conference on Innovation, Sustainability, and Applied Sciences. ICISAS 2023. Signals and Communication Technology.* Springer, Cham. *https://doi.org/10.1007/978-3-031-68952-9_76*

[5] Bakker, A. B., & Demerouti, E. (2007). The Job Demands-Resources Model: State of the Art. *Journal of Managerial Psychology, 22*(3), 309–328. doi:10.1108/02683940710733115

[6] Kahn, W. A. (1990). Psychological Conditions of Personal Engagement and Disengagement at Work. *Academy of Management Journal, 33*(4), 692–724. doi:10.5465/256287

[7] Voydanoff, P. (2004). The effects of work demands and resources on work-to-family conflict and facilitation. *Journal of Marriage and Family, 66*(2), 398–412. *https://doi.org/10.1111/j.1741-3737.2004.00028.x*

[8] Judge, T. A., Thoresen, C. J., Bono, J. E., & Patton, G. K. (2001). The Job Satisfaction-Job Performance Relationship: A Qualitative and Quantitative Review. *Psychological Bulletin, 127*(3), 376–407. doi:10.1037/0033-2909.127.3.376

[9] Kossek, E. E., Pichler, S., B., T., & Hammer, L. B. (2011). Workplace social support and work-family conflict: A meta-analysis clarifying the influence of general and work-family-specific supervisor and organizational support. *Personnel Psychology, 64*(2), 289–313. doi:10.1111/j.1744-6570.2011.01211.x

[10] Kossek, E. E., Matta, K. N. E., Hammer, L. B., & Petty, R. S. (2020). Work-Life Boundaries in the COVID-19 Era: Employees' Well-Being and the Role of Leadership. *Organizational Dynamics, 49*(3), 100734. doi:10.1016/j.orgdyn.2020.100734

[11] Taheri, F. (2021). Family-Supportive Organizational Environment and Turnover Intention. *International Journal of Productivity and Performance Management, 70*(8), 2113–2130. *https://doi.org/10.1108/IJPPM-10-2019-0467.*

[12] Schaufeli, W. B., Salanova, M., & Bakker, A. B. (2002). The Measurement of Engagement and Burnout: A Two-Sample Confirmatory Factor Analytic Approach. *Journal of Happiness Studies, 3*(1), 71–92. doi:10.1023/A:1015630930326

[13] Christian, M. S., Garza, A. S., & Slaughter, J. E. (2011). Work Engagement: A Quantitative Review and Test of Its Relations with Task and Contextual Performance. *Personnel Psychology, 64*(1), 89–136. doi:10.1111/j.1744-6570.2010.01203.x

[14] Bakker, A. B., & Xanthopoulou, D. (2009). The Cross-over of Daily Work Engagement: Test of an Actor–Partner Interdependence Model. *Journal of Applied Psychology, 94*(6), 1562–1571. doi:10.1037/a0017525

[15] Greenhaus, J. H., & Beutell, N. J. (1985). Sources of Conflict between Work and Family Roles. *Academy of Management Review, 10*(1), 76–88. doi:10.5465/amr.1985.4277352

[16] Greenhaus, J. H., & Powell, G. N. (2006). When Work and Family Are Allies: A Theory of Work-Family Enrichment. *Academy of Management Review, 31*(1), 72–92. doi.org/10.5465/amr.2006.19379625

[17] King, R. B., Jeffrey, E. M., Dawn, M. K., & Kathleen, L. A. (1995). Family Support Inventory for Workers, A New Measure of Perceived Social Support from Family Members. *Journal of Organizational Behavior, 16*(3), 235–258. *https://doi.org/10.1002/job.4030160306*

[18] Hobfoll, S. E. (1989). Conservation of Resources: A New Attempt at Conceptualizing Stress. *American Psychologist, 44*(3), 513–524. doi:10.1037/0003-066X.44.3.513

[19] Blau, P. M. (1964). *Exchange and Power in Social Life*. New York: John Wiley & Sons.

[20] Clark, S. C. (2000). Work/Family Border Theory: A New Theory of Work/Family Balance. *Human Relations, 53*(6), 747–770. doi:10.1177/0018726700536001